Face Recognition in Adverse Conditions

Maria De Marsico
Sapienza University of Rome, Italy

Michele Nappi
University of Salerno, Italy

Massimo Tistarelli
University of Sassari, Italy

A volume in the Advances in
Computational Intelligence and Robotics
(ACIR) Book Series

Managing Director:	Lindsay Johnston
Production Editor:	Jennifer Yoder
Development Editor:	Austin DeMarco
Acquisitions Editor:	Kayla Wolfe
Typesetter:	John Crodian
Cover Design:	Jason Mull

Published in the United States of America by
Information Science Reference (an imprint of IGI Global)
701 E. Chocolate Avenue
Hershey PA 17033
Tel: 717-533-8845
Fax: 717-533-8661
E-mail: cust@igi-global.com
Web site: http://www.igi-global.com

Library of Congress Cataloging-in-Publication Data

Face recognition in adverse conditions / Maria De Marsico, Michele Nappi, Massimo Tistarelli, editors.
    pages cm
 Includes bibliographical references and index. ISBN 978-1-4666-5966-7 (hardcover) -- ISBN 978-1-4666-5967-4 (ebook) -- ISBN 978-1-4666-5969-8 (print & perpetual access) 1. Face perception. I. De Marsico, Maria, editor of compilation.
  BF242.F33 2014
  153.7'58--dc23
                    2014003260

This book is published in the IGI Global book series Advances in Computational Intelligence and Robotics (ACIR) (ISSN: 2327-0411; eISSN: 2327-042X)

British Cataloguing in Publication Data
A Cataloguing in Publication record for this book is available from the British Library.

For electronic access to this publication, please contact: eresources@igi-global.com.

Advances in Computational Intelligence and Robotics (ACIR) Book Series

ISSN: 2327-0411
EISSN: 2327-042X

MISSION

While intelligence is traditionally a term applied to humans and human cognition, technology has progressed in such a way to allow for the development of intelligent systems able to simulate many human traits. With this new era of simulated and artificial intelligence, much research is needed in order to continue to advance the field and also to evaluate the ethical and societal concerns of the existence of artificial life and machine learning.

The **Advances in Computational Intelligence and Robotics (ACIR) Book Series** encourages scholarly discourse on all topics pertaining to evolutionary computing, artificial life, computational intelligence, machine learning, and robotics. ACIR presents the latest research being conducted on diverse topics in intelligence technologies with the goal of advancing knowledge and applications in this rapidly evolving field.

COVERAGE

- Adaptive & Complex Systems
- Agent Technologies
- Artificial Intelligence
- Cognitive Informatics
- Computational Intelligence
- Natural Language Processing
- Neural Networks
- Pattern Recognition
- Robotics
- Synthetic Emotions

IGI Global is currently accepting manuscripts for publication within this series. To submit a proposal for a volume in this series, please contact our Acquisition Editors at Acquisitions@igi-global.com or visit: http://www.igi-global.com/publish/.

The Advances in Computational Intelligence and Robotics (ACIR) Book Series (ISSN 2327-0411) is published by IGI Global, 701 E. Chocolate Avenue, Hershey, PA 17033-1240, USA, www.igi-global.com. This series is composed of titles available for purchase individually; each title is edited to be contextually exclusive from any other title within the series. For pricing and ordering information please visit http://www.igi-global.com/book-series/advances-computational-intelligence-robotics/73674. Postmaster: Send all address changes to above address. Copyright © 2014 IGI Global. All rights, including translation in other languages reserved by the publisher. No part of this series may be reproduced or used in any form or by any means – graphics, electronic, or mechanical, including photocopying, recording, taping, or information and retrieval systems – without written permission from the publisher, except for non commercial, educational use, including classroom teaching purposes. The views expressed in this series are those of the authors, but not necessarily of IGI Global.

Titles in this Series

For a list of additional titles in this series, please visit: www.igi-global.com

Face Recognition in Adverse Conditions
Maria De Marsico (Sapienza University of Rome, Italy) Michele Nappi (University of Salerno, Italy) and Massimo Tistarelli (University of Sassari, Italy)
Information Science Reference • copyright 2014 • 325pp • H/C (ISBN: 9781466659667) • US $235.00 (our price)

Mathematics of Uncertainty Modeling in the Analysis of Engineering and Science Problems
S. Chakraverty (National Institute of Technology - Rourkela, India)
Information Science Reference • copyright 2014 • 441pp • H/C (ISBN: 9781466649910) • US $225.00 (our price)

Global Trends in Intelligent Computing Research and Development
B.K. Tripathy (VIT University, India) and D.P. Acharjya (VIT University, India)
Information Science Reference • copyright 2014 • 601pp • H/C (ISBN: 9781466649361) • US $235.00 (our price)

Exploring Innovative and Successful Applications of Soft Computing
Antonio D. Masegosa (Universidad de Granada, Spain) Pablo J. Villacorta (Universidad de Granada, Spain) Carlos Cruz-Corona (Universidad de Granada, Spain) M. Socorro García-Cascales (Universidad Politécnica de Cartagena, Spain) María T. Lamata (Universidad de Granada, Spain) and José L. Verdegay (Universidad de Granada, Spain)
Information Science Reference • copyright 2014 • 375pp • H/C (ISBN: 9781466647855) • US $190.00 (our price)

Research Developments in Computer Vision and Image Processing Methodologies and Applications
Rajeev Srivastava (Indian Institute of Technology (BHU), India) S. K. Singh (Indian Institute of Technology (BHU), India) and K. K. Shukla (Indian Institute of Technology (BHU), India)
Information Science Reference • copyright 2014 • 451pp • H/C (ISBN: 9781466645585) • US $195.00 (our price)

Handbook of Research on Novel Soft Computing Intelligent Algorithms Theory and Practical Applications
Pandian M. Vasant (Petronas University of Technology, Malaysia)
Information Science Reference • copyright 2014 • 1018pp • H/C (ISBN: 9781466644502) • US $495.00 (our price)

Intelligent Technologies and Techniques for Pervasive Computing
Kostas Kolomvatsos (University of Athens, Greece) Christos Anagnostopoulos (Ionian University, Greece) and Stathes Hadjiefthymiades (University of Athens, Greece)
Information Science Reference • copyright 2013 • 351pp • H/C (ISBN: 9781466640382) • US $195.00 (our price)

Mobile Ad Hoc Robots and Wireless Robotic Systems Design and Implementation
Raul Aquino Santos (University of Colima, Mexico) Omar Lengerke (Universidad Autónoma de Bucaramanga, Colombia) and Arthur Edwards-Block (University of Colima, Mexico)
Information Science Reference • copyright 2013 • 344pp • H/C (ISBN: 9781466626584) • US $190.00 (our price)

www.igi-global.com

701 E. Chocolate Ave., Hershey, PA 17033
Order online at www.igi-global.com or call 717-533-8845 x100
To place a standing order for titles released in this series, contact: cust@igi-global.com
Mon-Fri 8:00 am - 5:00 pm (est) or fax 24 hours a day 717-533-8661

Table of Contents

Section 1
Preliminaries and Reviews

Section 2
Face Recognition under Real World PIE Variations

Section 3
Example Applications

Section 4
Future Research Directions

Detailed Table of Contents

Section 1
Preliminaries and Reviews

This section will first provide a review of present applications of face recognition. The critical overview of open problems will then introduce possible approaches and solutions. These will be discussed in more detail in the rest of the book.

Chapter 1

> *Massimo Tistarelli, University of Sassari, Italy*
> *Stan Z. Li, Chinese Academy of Science, China*

The first chapter of the book provides a bird's-eye view over of the recent application of face recognition in present real-world scenarios. The first and most popular applications of face recognition have been related to security and access control. Nowadays, the analysis of human faces can further effectively support law enforcement, improve man-machine interaction, and be used in an even wider set of applications. Many of these aim at improving interaction rather than achieving high security, so that they require higher flexibility than accuracy and capability to deal with minimally constrained environments.

Chapter 2

> *Stefanos Zafeiriou, Imperial College London, UK*
> *Irene Kotsia, Middlesex University London, UK & Imperial College London, UK*
> *Maja Pantic, Imperial College London, UK*

The problem of face recognition using images captured in uncontrolled environments still remains an open issue. In this chapter, the authors provide an overview of the existing fully automatic face recognition technologies for these scenarios. They present the existing databases appropriate for such a problem and summarize the challenges that arise. The authors conclude by presenting the opportunities that exist in the field.

Chapter 3

Harry Wechsler, George Mason University, USA

The overall coverage of the chapter is about moving face recognition. We can assume that it is possible to dramatically improve the current performance of existing biometric tools by fusing the rich spatial, temporal, and contextual information available from the multiple views made available by video (rather than still images) in the wild and operational real-world problems. Instead of relying on a "single best frame approach," one must confront uncontrolled settings by exploiting all available imagery to allow the addition of new evidence, graceful degradation, and re-identification.

Section 2
Face Recognition under Real World PIE Variations

This section discusses in more detail the present face recognition issues related to Pose, Illumination, and Expression (PIE) variations. Besides these classical problems, more recent research lines are focused on demographics and different kinds of disguise (e.g. plastic surgery), which may hinder recognition. 3D-based methods seem to provide better performance than 2D-based ones, but they are generally computationally expensive and may not be feasible in real-world settings. A further comparison is among global and local methods. The latter seem more robust to partial distortions, which are caused by PIE. Multimodal fusion offers further support to the problem of recognition in adverse conditions.

Chapter 4

Dat Chu, University of Houston, USA

Shishir Shah, University of Houston, USA

Ioannis A. Kakadiaris, University of Houston, USA

Performing face recognition under extreme poses and lighting conditions is still a challenging task for current state-of-the-art biometric algorithms. This task is even more challenging when there is insufficient training data available in the gallery, or when the gallery dataset originates from one side of the face while the probe dataset originates from the other. The chapter presents a new method for computing the distance between two biometric signatures acquired under such challenging conditions.

Chapter 5

Stefano Berretti, University of Florence, Italy

Alberto del Bimbo, University of Florence, Italy

Pietro Pala, University of Florence, Italy

Identity recognition using 3D scans of the face has been recently proposed as an alternative or complementary solution to conventional 2D face recognition approaches. Based on these premises, this chapter first introduces the general and main methodologies for 3D face recognition, shortly reviewing the related literature by distinguishing between global and local approaches. Then it presents and discusses two 3D face recognition approaches that are robust to facial expression variations and share the common idea of accounting for the spatial relations between local facial features.

Occlusion is a common problem in uncooperative scenarios. The focus of this chapter is to illustrate the problems caused by 3D occlusion, and to go over solutions. It reviews 3D face identification approaches, with focus on occlusion scenarios, introduces 3D databases containing occlusions, and presents a prototype system with solutions for occlusion at landmarking, registration, feature extraction, and matching stages.

Illumination variation is one of the well-known problems in face recognition, especially in uncontrolled environments. This chapter presents an extensive and up-to-date survey of the existing techniques to address this problem. This survey covers the conventional passive techniques that attempt to solve the illumination problem by studying the visible light images, in which face appearance has been altered by varying illumination, as well as the active techniques that aim to obtain images of face modalities invariant to environmental illumination.

Facial Expression Analysis systems have come a long way since the earliest approaches in the early 1970s. We are now at a point where the first systems are commercially applied, most notably smile detectors included in digital cameras. As one of the most comprehensive and objective ways to describe facial expressions, the Facial Action Coding System (FACS) has received significant and sustained attention within the field. In this chapter, the authors give an overview of 2D and 3D FACS recognition and summarise current challenges and opportunities.

Early proposed algorithms for face recognition were generally holistic, in the sense they consider the face object as a whole. Recently, challenging benchmarks demonstrated that they are not adequate in unconstrained environments. Therefore, the researchers' attention is now turning on local features that demonstrated to be more robust to a large set of non-monotonic distortions. However, they are opening new questions (e.g. Which criteria are being used to select the most representative features?). Hybrid approaches show a high potential in terms of recognition accuracy when applied in uncontrolled settings, as they integrate complementary information from both local and global features.

Norman Poh, University of Surrey, UK
Chi Ho Chan, University of Surrey, UK
Josef Kittler, University of Surrey, UK

Sensory data quality information can be used with advantage to combat the effect of the degradation phenomena. This can be achieved by using the auxiliary quality information as features in the fusion stage of a multiple classifier system, which uses the discriminant function values from the first stage as inputs. Data quality can be measured directly from the sensory data. Different architectures have been suggested for decision-making using quality information. Examples of these architectures are presented, and their relative merits discussed. The problems and benefits associated with the use of auxiliary information in sensory data analysis are illustrated on the problem of personal identity verification using in biometrics.

Neslihan Kose, EURECOM, France
Jean-Luc Dugelay, EURECOM, France
Richa Singh, IIIT – Delhi, India
Mayank Vatsa, IIIT – Delhi, India

Challenges in automatic face recognition can be classified in several categories such as illumination, image quality, expression, pose, aging, and disguise. In this chapter, the focus is on recognizing face images with disguise variations. Even though face recognition with disguise variations is a major challenge, the research studies on this topic are still quite limited. Here the authors define disguise variations first, and then provide an overview of the existing databases used for disguise analysis. Next, the studies that are dedicated to the impact of disguise variations on existing face recognition techniques are introduced, followed by a collection of several proposed robust state-of-the-art techniques.

Hugo Proença, University of Beira Interior, Portugal
Gil Santos, University of Beira Interior, Portugal
João C. Neves, University of Beira Interior, Portugal

In several real scenarios, a full facial picture cannot be obtained nor the iris properly imaged. Some useful biometric information can be extracted from the periocular area (i.e. the vicinity of the eyes). This is a relatively new idea and is regarded as a good trade-off between using the whole face or the iris alone. The periocular area can be particularly useful on less constrained conditions. This chapter provides a comprehensive summary of the most relevant research conducted in the scope of ocular (periocular) recognition methods.

Section 3
Example Applications

Chapter 13

Andrea F. Abate, University of Salerno, Italy
Stefano Ricciardi, University of Salerno, Italy
Genoveffa Tortora, University of Salerno, Italy

One of the new research lines emerging in the field of face recognition is face-based people re-identification. This is the task of recognizing new occurrences of an individual's face once it has been detected and its initial position determined. Re-identification may span different times and also different locations, if supported by a network of non-overlapping cameras. This chapter presents the main issues and challenges specifically related to face-based people re-identification, as well as the most promising techniques and results.

Chapter 14

Vittoria Bruni, Sapienza University of Rome, Italy & National Research Council, Italy
Domenico Vitulano, National Research Council, Italy

This chapter analyzes the role of human early vision in image and video processing, with particular reference to face perception, recognition, and tracking. The main topics covered are some important neurological results that have been successfully used in face detection and recognition, as well as those that seem to be promising in giving new and powerful tools for face tracking, which remains a less investigated topic from this new standpoint.

Chapter 15

Anastasios Doulamis, Technical University of Crete, Greece
Athanasios Voulodimos, National Technical University of Athens, Greece
Theodora Varvarigou, National Technical University of Athens, Greece

Automatic recognition of human actions from video is probably one of the most challenging research topics of computer vision. This chapter introduces a new descriptor, the Human Constrained Pixel Change History (HC-PCH), which is based on PCH but focuses on human body movements over time. The modification of the conventional PCH entails the calculation of two probabilistic maps, based on human face and body detection, respectively. These HC-PCH features are used as input to an HMM-based classification framework, which exploits redundant information from multiple streams through sophisticated fusion methods, resulting in enhanced activity recognition rates.

This chapter presents some issues related to automatic face image tagging techniques. Their main purpose is to support the organization (indexing) and retrieval (or easy browsing) of images or videos in large collections. The involved techniques include algorithms and strategies for handling very large face databases, mostly acquired in real conditions.

This chapter discusses different possibilities to use face recognition on smart mobile devices. Online authentication is a critical problem: here it is shown how three-factor authentication can address many pressing issues. The chapter also discusses how such a system could be attacked and focuses on replay attacks, which have yet to be seriously addressed in the literature.

Section 4
Future Research Directions

The concluding chapter is devoted to a bird's-eye survey of the main achievements in the field of face recognition and on sketching the most promising research lines.

This chapter discusses the main outcomes from both the most recent literature and the research activities summarized in this book. Of course, a complete review is not possible. It is evident that each issue related to face recognition in adverse conditions can be considered as a research topic in itself and would deserve a dedicated book. However, it is interesting to provide a compass to orient one in the presently achieved results in order to identify open problems and promising research lines.

Foreword

Over the last 13 years, recognition processes involving the use of biometric technology have received increasing interest from both the scientific community and ICT industrial companies. One of the reasons is because, with the increased integration of computers and Internet into our everyday lives, it is necessary to protect sensitive and personal data as well as access to critical services. The main factor spurring the adoption of biometric identification is that it offers several advantages over traditional methods using ID cards (tokens) or PIN numbers (passwords). Indeed, unlike biometric traits, PINs or passwords may be forgotten or suffer sniffing as well as cracking attacks, while passports and drivers' licenses may be forged, stolen, or lost. The combination of biometrics and PINs can potentially prevent unauthorized physical or logical access in a more robust way.

The selection of a particular biometrics for use in a specific application involves a weighting of several factors, and usually no single biometric trait will meet all the requirements of every possible application. As a result, biometric systems, deployed to enhance security and reduce fraud in real-time recognition, can handle various traits, separately or in multimodal architectures, as for example face, iris, and fingerprint. Among those biometrics, face seems to be the weaker one even if it is the easiest to collect.

Face is a dynamic biometrics whose anatomic elements can change both rapidly, on the time scale of seconds during modification of expression and/or pose and/or illumination, and more slowly over time due to ageing. Despite this, identification frameworks involving the use of face recognition technology are expanding rapidly worldwide. Some respond to specific needs, such as in forensics for criminal identification. However, the recent progresses in both biometric sensors and detection/recognition algorithms have led to the deployment of several systems based on face recognition in a large number of civilian and government applications. Those include computer log-in/log-off, financial transactions, international border crossing, national ID cards, physical access control, and welfare disbursement, just to cite a few. The above considerations have inspired this book.

Although a lot of books, monographs, journal special issues, surveys, and papers on face recognition have been and continue to be published, demonstrating an ever-growing interest of the scientific community from one side, and the continuous advancements and new achievements on the other side, this book provides an innovative perspective that analyzes the theoretical and practical aspects of the problem. In this scenario, the interest of the research has focused on the new frontier of face recognition, where degraded data are acquired in the visible wavelength and uncontrolled setups, with subjects moving and with possibly widely varying capture distance, expression, pose, illumination, and resolution.

Recently, several progresses have been achieved in face recognition, and the chapters of this book demonstrate this. In practice, as you can read in the book, modern deployed face recognition systems have proven their effectiveness and robustness in relatively uncontrolled scenarios, exploiting interoperability among different capture devices operating with different resolution and sometimes combining 2D and 3D modalities.

The editors' efforts were therefore focused on selecting a collection of contributions from leading researchers in the context of face recognition in order to cover all the topics that I believe are the most challenging. Therefore, in my opinion, the theoretical and practical results reported here form the basis for current and future research on face-based identification, so they can serve as a point of reference for both young researchers, who approach biometrics for the first time, as well as for experts.

Mislav Grgic
University of Zagreb, Croatia

Mislav Grgic *received B.Sc., M.Sc., and Ph.D. degrees in electrical engineering from the University of Zagreb, Faculty of Electrical Engineering and Computing (FER), Zagreb, Croatia, in 1997, 1998, and 2000, respectively. Since July 1997, he has worked at the Department of Wireless Communications at FER. He was a visiting researcher at the University of Essex, Colchester, United Kingdom (1999-2000). In June 2010, he was promoted to Full Professor. Since October 2010, he has served as a Vice Dean for Research at FER. He has participated in several scientific projects and published more than 180 papers in books, journals, and conference proceedings in the area of image and video compression, content-based image retrieval, face recognition, and digital mammography (computer-aided detection and diagnosis of breast cancer). Prof. Grgic is a full member of the Croatian Academy of Engineering (HATZ).*

Preface

Face recognition has always been one of the most intriguing research topics in the area of pattern recognition. The final goal of approaches tackling this problem is to equal the ability of human beings of recognizing their counterparts, though in variable conditions. Early prototypes soon achieved very encouraging results, but the recognition conditions were strictly controlled: frontal pose, controlled illumination, neutral expression, uniform background, same devices used for enrolling and testing. As the technology advances and new user needs arise, laboratory settings become more and more obsolete and related techniques useless. The new frontier is recognition in less and less controlled and often adverse conditions, and interoperability among different capture devices (e.g. with different resolution). In practice, the searched outcome is robustness to both subject and environment conditions. The possible uses range from security and forensics to mobile applications and social indexing and sharing of large collections of photo resources. The challenges to deal with are both traditional ones, namely Pose, Illumination, and Expression (PIE) variations, and novel ones, such as the influence of demographics and of voluntary or involuntary disguise (e.g. the effects of makeup or plastic surgery). An essential support in this challenge may come from the continuous technological advances. Capture sensors of increasing accuracy and decreasing cost make new performance achievable. This opens new possibilities for software design (e.g. the use of GPU for computing intensive and parallelizable activities). On the other hand, for the same reason, new results soon become obsolete. This spurs an ongoing need for new literature updates. Even if many books about face recognition can be found, one can easily verify that their contents are constantly changing. As a matter of fact, this is also testified by the published new editions.

The aim of the present book is to overview ways to approach to the "hardest" settings in face recognition. We will present possible solutions to specific problems, as well as propose a comparison between 2D and 3D techniques and between global and local strategies. It is interesting to underline that, in most cases, the best solutions are hybrid ones. This can be expected since limits of a line may be often compensated by strengths of the competing one. Accuracy vs. high computational complexity, high computational times vs. requirements for real-time processing, interoperability vs. advantages from special-purpose equipment are further issues to be addressed.

We asked well-known and esteemed experts to contribute with their research perspective on the most relevant aspects related to the above topics. We hope that this will be of interest to both novice researchers in the field and to those aiming at having a deeper insight into the recent approaches and available literature about specific aspects of the general problem.

To help the reader orient in the provided contents, we overview the topics addressed by each chapter.

The first chapter of the book "Real World Applications: A Literature Survey" by Tistarelli and Lin provides a bird's-eye view over of the recent application of face recognition in present real world scenarios. Due to space constraints, this overview will not be exhaustive, yet will provide a good starting point for those who are approaching this challenging and fascinating research field. Moreover, it will highlight that, even though the first and most popular applications of face recognition have addressed problems related to security and access control, the analysis of human faces can effectively underlie law enforcement, man-machine interaction, robotics, and the aid to disabled people, to mention a few. Many emerging applications require a biometric system to facilitate a better interaction with a generally limited population. Therefore, a very high recognition accuracy may not be required and sacrificed to achieve a higher flexibility and capability to deal with minimally constrained environments.

Despite achieved results, face recognition, when images are acquired in uncontrolled environments (e.g., outdoors with variable pose and illumination) still remains a challenging issue, even if a lot of research has been conducted, enabling the field to reach a certain level of maturity. The chapter "Unconstrained Face Recognition" by Zafeiriou et al. presents an overview of the existing fully automatic face recognition technologies for uncontrolled scenarios, including also a description of the existing databases for such topic which are available at present to provide a common evaluation ground for new techniques addressing such topics. In particular, the authors investigate fully automatic unconstrained face recognition methodologies avoiding any manual interaction, usually containing the following modules: (1) face detection, (2) face landmark localization or face alignment, and (3) face recognition. They focus on a number of approaches, some proposed during 1990s and others more recently. The first group of techniques includes: 1) Elastic Graph Matching, which is a simplification of the so-called Dynamic Link Architecture (DLA) and the Active Appearance Models (AAM); 2) 3D morphable models introduced as a generalization of AAMs using a dense 3D shape model. The second group includes: 1) parametric motion models combined with decomposition/component analysis techniques to perform joint alignment and decomposition, and 2) facial landmark localization algorithms. A complete review of the databases that can be used for face recognition in an uncontrolled acquisition scenario is also provided.

In the chapter titled "Face Recognition Methods for Uncontrolled Settings," H. Wechsler discusses face recognition methods operating in relatively uncontrolled multiple views scenario, with subjects moving, at widely varying distances, in the visible wavelength, or in the near infrared spectrum. Deployed face recognition systems that process heavily degraded data, usually work on a single best frame approach achieving modest results in term of accuracy. To improve the current performances an effective strategy is the fusion of the rich spatial, temporal, and contextual information available from the multiple views. In this extremely challenging context, the most complex problems to tackle are persistence for biometric data, adversarial biometrics, open rather than closed set recognition, covariate shift, cross-dataset generalization, alignment and registration, interoperability, scalability, and finally, the design of full-fledged biometrics including segmentation/detection, recognition, and tracking. The chapter faces in exhaustive way the strategies for the design of a unified framework that involves multi-task and transfer learning, using metric learning and side information.

Among the most challenging tasks related to face identification under extreme poses and illumination, we can surely mention recognition with insufficient training data available or with gallery images originating from one side of the face while the probe images originates from the other one. The chapter "3D Face Recognition in the Presence of Partial Data: A Semi-Coupled Dictionary Learning Approach" by Chu et al. deals with a new technique for computing the distance between two biometric signatures acquired under such challenging conditions. The proposed method computes a jointly optimized solution that incorporates the reconstruction cost, the discrimination cost, and the semi-coupling cost. It is focused on the use of dictionary learning to address the problem of partial face recognition. The authors also extend the achieved results to 2D signatures under varying pose and illumination changes, by using 3D signatures as a coupling term. Their strategy improves significantly the performances with respect to previous approaches. In fact, the experimental results, performed on UHDB11 database, demonstrate the robustness and accuracy of the proposed technique compared with the current state-of-the-art.

Recently, 3D face recognition has been demonstrated to be an effective alternative or complementary solution to traditional 2D face recognition-based systems. PIE distortions can be addressed along this line. An interesting chapter in this sense, titled "3D Face Recognition using Spatial Relations," by Berretti et al. discusses two 3D face recognition methods exploiting 3D spatial information in order to improve the accuracy in the presence of non-neutral facial expressions. Initially, the authors provide a wide description of the most recent 3D face recognition techniques starting from a standard classification of methods that can be distinguished as *holistic, region-based, hybrid,* and *multimodal.* Then they focus on region-based solutions using spatial relations. The second part of the chapter introduces the first face recognition technique, which detects characterizing features of the face by measuring the spatial displacement between iso-geodesic stripes. Experimental results, tested on the FRGC v2.0 and SHREC08 data sets, demonstrate the robustness of the proposed method in the presence of strong facial expressions, also achieving a low computational complexity thanks to an appropriate index structure. The second proposed scheme is based on relational spatial information between face detected keypoints and exploits facial curves transformation. This technique is tested on the UND/FRGC v2.0 and Gavab datasets and demonstrates a higher effectiveness in comparison with other approaches proposed in the literature.

In uncontrolled acquisition scenarios, the problem of 3D occlusions is one of the most interesting challenges in face recognition. The focus of the chapter "Robust 3D Face Identification in the Presence of Occlusions" by Alyuz et al. is to describe the problems caused by 3D occlusions and to provide some solutions. The first part of the chapter presents face recognition concepts and a wide survey on 3D face recognition techniques from the perspective of occlusion handling. In a detailed way, the authors underline the faults of traditional 3D face recognizers working in the presence of occlusions and summarize the approaches proposed in the 3D face recognition literature related to robustness to occlusion. Furthermore, several 3D databases are suggested to evaluate occlusion robustness. A possible solution to deal with occlusions is a novel recognition framework merging different techniques singularly proposed by the authors for different stages of a face recognizer: (1) registration, combining a nose detection approach and the adaptive model based alignment technique; (2) occlusion detection; (3) feature extraction and classification using the masked projection approach.

In uncontrolled scenarios, illumination changes degrade the performances of face recognition systems. The chapter "Illumination Invariant Face Recognition: A Survey" by Chan et al. provides an extensive description on existing techniques attempting to solve the illumination problem. The authors present several techniques that can be distinguished as *passive,* analyzing the visible spectrum images where face appearance is changed by illumination variations, and *active,* using active imaging techniques to obtain face images captured in consistent illumination condition, or images of illumination invariant modalities. Passive methods can be subsequently grouped in four classes: illumination variation modelling, illumination invariant features, photometric normalisation, and 3D morphable model. Usually in the application of active methods, additional devices, such as optical filters, active illumination sources, or specific sensors, have to be involved to provide different modalities of face images, possibly invariant to illumination changes. Several modalities can be adopted, but the most promising are 3D images, thermal infrared images, and near-infrared hyper-spectral images. Finally, the chapter discusses experimental results achieved on Yale B, Harvard, and FRGC datasets, from which the difficulty in comparing the performances between active and passive methods emerges. A future suggested strategy could be the design of hybrid frameworks fusing active and passive techniques.

Over the past 30 years, several papers on facial expression recognition methods have been proposed, demonstrating the interest of the scientific community towards this topic. A comprehensive survey on 2D/3D Facial Action Coding System (FACS) is presented in the chapter "Facial Action Recognition in 2D and 3D" by Valstar et al. The first part of the chapter is devoted to an in-depth description of the state of the art including both psychologists/neuroscientists researches and automatic facial expression analysis, with an emphasis on facial Action Units (AU) recognition in intensity video sequences. A review of the existing free publicly available datasets is then introduced, grouping them into four classes: 2D posed expression, 2D spontaneous expression, 3D static analysis, and 3D dynamic analysis. Finally, the authors propose a section about the facial expression recognition methods, where several 2D and 3D AU detection techniques are discussed and compared. The comparative analysis of the mentioned approaches suggests that recognition of AUs is more accurate if 3D information is available, and that the recognition of spontaneous 3D AUs is more challenging than that of posed ones.

Still in the context of face recognition in uncontrolled acquisition scenarios, the chapter "Local vs. Global: Intelligent Local Face Recognition" by Riccio et al. discusses about the comparison between local and global features involved in face identification process. The authors provide a complete analysis of local approaches for face recognition, which are grouped in three main classes, namely local appearance based methods, local derivative patterns, and Scale Invariant Feature Transform (SIFT)-based approaches. They demonstrate that some drawbacks encountered by global techniques can be overcome. As a matter of fact, a number of local techniques achieve a good robustness to pose and illumination variations, or occlusions, even if the most used local operators, such as Local Binary Pattern and Gabor Features and SIFT, are not fully invariant to non-monotonic variations. As holistic and local methods generally provide complementary information, the final suggestion is to design hybrid schemes combining features to further improve the recognition accuracy.

All the chapters of this book discuss, under different points of view, how recognising faces under adverse conditions is still the most important challenge in the design of face recognition systems for real-world applications. The factors causing distortions in face appearance over time, either a few seconds or a longer period, may have a significant negative impact on the accuracy of recognition algorithms. These factors can be related to changes in the camera characteristics (e.g. for visible, infrared, or thermal camera), to environmental conditions (illumination, background noise, etc.), and / or the behaviour/evolution of the subject (e.g. pose, motion, aging). Recent approaches use sensory data quality information to determine and tackle the effects of the degradation phenomena. Different architectures have been suggested for decision making using quality information. The chapter "Fusion of Face Recognition Classifiers under Adverse Conditions" by Poh et al. presents examples of these architectures and discusses their relative merits. The authors show that the information about the data quality can significantly enhance the effectiveness of the multiple expert approach. In the normalization approach discussed, they attempt to reverse the changes to the signal which are caused by distortions through the application of preprocessing algorithms that try to stabilize the data to be classified. In the multiple classifier approach, they express signal changes in the form of quality measures, which are used as auxiliary features during fusion. In this way, the final decision is influenced by both the expert opinions and by measures of the signal quality.

Among the factors possibly hindering automatic face recognition, we also have to mention disguise variations, which may result as challenging as PIE variations. Kose et al., in their chapter, "Recognizing Face Images with Disguise Variations," discuss this problem, focusing on its impact on existing face recognition techniques. The disguise variations can be classified in several categories such as minimal variations (two face images captured at different time instances), variations in hairstyle, variations due to make-up, variations due to beard and moustache, variations due to facial accessories (occlusion), variations due to aging and wrinkles, variations due to plastic surgery, and multiple variations. In order to assess the performances in terms of accuracy of face recognition algorithms, the authors present a complete list of databases for disguise analysis, underlining the characteristics for each one. The second part of the chapter provides an exhaustive study demonstrating that most face recognition systems are not robust against disguise variations, except for a limited group of techniques. The authors conclude that the current state-of-the-art is not satisfactory and more robust approaches have to be designed for occlusion detection and face recognition with disguise variations. Finally, the chapter points out some future research direction in this area.

Recent works in literature have examined the use of ocular region-based recognition, which appears to be a good trade-off between the whole face and the iris alone in unconstrained biometric recognition. In this scenario, the chapter "Using Ocular Data for Unconstrained Biometric Recognition" by Proença et al. presents a wide description of the most relevant techniques for ocular (periocular) recognition, since such biometric feature demonstrated to be highly different between individuals and relatively stable over lifetime. Several developed methods exploit texture analysis and key-point extraction, using heterogeneous types of information in this region such as shapes of eyelids, texture of the skin and iris, distribution of eyelashes, and skin key points. The authors also discuss about the main features of several datasets available for related experiments and compare the performance of the most recent algorithms in terms of recognition accuracy.

Another interesting field for face recognition research is related to video analysis. Deployed face recognition systems from video source are mainly focused on recognition and re-identication, where the second one is a recent research line emerging in the last years. The chapter titled "Face in Person Re-Identification" by Abate et al. deeply describes the main issues and challenges related to face-based people re-identification, underlining the most promising existing techniques. The authors discuss the present flaws in the accuracy of the re-identification process, which are related to limitations of both hardware (surveillance camera sensor size, image resolution, frame rate, etc.) and software (robustness of algorithms to PIE wide variations, low resolution and occlusions, sub real-time or offline computing time, lower performance in unsupervised operation, etc.). However, the chapter suggests that the recent improvements in surveillance cameras, as the increase of frame rate and resolution, could easily improve the performance of re-identification systems. Re-identification algorithms supported by a more robust acquisition will be able to exploit a deeper integration level of recognition and tracking, temporal reasoning, and spatial layout of the different cameras for pruning the set of candidate matches, brightness transfer function between different cameras to track individuals over multiple non-overlapping cameras, and smart controlled pan/tilt/zoom cameras to overcome poor capturing quality.

Continuing along the line of tracking, in recent years, the role of human early vision system in image and video processing aiming at face perception, recognition, and tracking, received an increasing interest from the international community. In this scenario, the chapter "Methods and Perspectives in Face

Tracking Based on Human Perception" by Bruni and Vitulano regards the role of human perception in the face tracking task. The authors introduce the main approaches to face detection and tracking problems, showing that the Human Visual System can solve some important image processing problems. The second part of the chapter focuses on visual concepts used in the face detection and representation processes, underlining some features useful for human tracking in subsequent frames. Furthermore, this chapter discusses existing results, their advantages and limits, and finally presents some future perspectives and potential applications of novel theoretical results based on Kolmogorov complexity for efficiently coding information, Minimum Description Length, and Normalized Information Distance.

Doulamis et al., in their chapter "Human Face Region Detection Driving Activity Recognition in Video," focus on Human Constrained Pixel Change History (HC-PCH)-based descriptor for human activity identification, using face and body detection from video sequences. First, a face detector algorithm, based on two chrominance colour components probabilistic theory, performs in real-time the identification of facial regions. Then, a body detector exploiting location beneath the facial region extracts biometric measures of human body. From the probabilistic map obtained by face and body detections HC-PCH descriptor is derived, becoming the input for an HMM-based classification framework, to support multiple camera streams in order to solve occlusions through the use of fusion methods. The experimental results demonstrate the accuracy of the HC-PCH-based descriptor validated on a real world surveillance dataset.

The storing and indexing, as well as the quick retrieval, of images or videos in large collections is an open problem. Face tagging is an increasingly important step in this process. The continuous growth of social applications and the spreading very-large scale diffusion of available capture devices, from digital cameras to smart phones, have shifted the problem from contexts like institutions, publishing companies, etc. to personal settings. In general, the task is lighter when it pertains to personal collections (e.g. the photos of participants in a social network) due to the limited amount of images as well as of relevant subjects. When this operation can be performed in a totally automatic way, we speak of automatic face tagging. The chapter "Automatic Face Image Tagging in Large Collections" by Barra et al. presents an overview of face recognition techniques used in related applications. It also presents a number of approaches to handle large-scale face datasets as well as some automatic face image tagging techniques. Many approaches still provide only a semi-automatic solution for this problem.

The rapid development of mobile devices has determined the birth of a new generation of software designed and developed for smartphones and tablets. Many tasks usually performed by desktops are migrating to these devices. The chapter "Secure Face Recognition for Mobile Applications" by Lowell and Smith examines the use of commodity smart mobile devices, such as the video camera, to support face recognition. The authors focus on a couple of challenging topics, namely the choice of the application driver that will ensure the widespread adoption of such a biometric system and the security issues that must still be resolved before smart mobile devices can successfully act as biometric sensors. They first introduce biometrics on mobile devices and subsequently draw the current strategy to resolve spoofing and replay attacks in face recognition context. Spoofing attacks, but above all replay attacks, still remain a serious threat; the authors suggest that a successful research is the only way to create opportunities for using face recognition on mobile devices.

The final chapter of the book, "Face Recognition in Adverse Conditions: A Look at Achieved Advancements" by De Marsico and Nappi, attempts to discuss the main outcomes from both the most recent literature and the research activities summarized in this book. Of course, a complete review is not possible, since each issue related to face recognition in adverse conditions can be considered as a research topic in itself. However, it is interesting to provide an overview of achieved results, in order to identify open problems and to spur the emergence of new promising research lines.

Maria De Marsico
Sapienza University of Rome, Italy

Michele Nappi
University of Salerno, Italy

Massimo Tistarelli
University of Sassari, Italy

Section 1
Preliminaries and Reviews

This section will first provide a review of present applications of face recognition. The critical overview of open problems will then introduce possible approaches and solutions. These will be discussed in more detail in the rest of the book.

Chapter 1
Real World Applications:
A Literature Survey

Massimo Tistarelli
University of Sassari, Italy

Stan Z. Li
Chinese Academy of Science, China

ABSTRACT

The analysis of face images has been extensively applied for the recognition of individuals in several application domains. Most notably, faces not only convey information about the identity of the subject, but also a number of ancillary information, which may be equally useful to anonymously determine the characteristics of an individual. Even though the first applications of face recognition have been related to security and access control, nowadays the analysis of human faces is related to several applications including law enforcement, man-machine interaction, and robotics, just to mention a few. This chapter explores the analysis of face images.

INTRODUCTION

Visual perception is probably the most important sensing ability for humans to enable social interactions and general communication. As a consequence, face recognition is a fundamental skill that humans acquire early in life and which remains an integral part of our perceptual and social abilities throughout our life span (Allison, Puce, & McCarthy, 2000;Bruce & Young, 1986). Not only faces provide information about the identity of people, but also about their membership in broad demographic categories of humans (including sex, race, and age), and about their current emotional state (Hornak, Rolls, & Wade,

1996;) (Tranel, Damasio, & Damasio, 1988; Calder, Young, Rowland, Perrett, Hodges, & Etcoff, 1996; Humphreys, Donnell, & Riddoch, 1993;Calder & Young, 2005). Humans "sense" these information effortlessly and apply it to the ever-changing demands of cognitive and social interactions.

This chapter aims to provide an overview of the most interesting applications of human face analysis and recognition. Due to space constraints this overview can not be exhaustive, yet it provides a good starting point for those who are willing to approach this challenging and fascinating technology and research field.

DOI: 10.4018/978-1-4666-5966-7.ch001

Human Face Analysis in "The Real World"

The difficulties often encountered in the analysis of human faces stems from the high variability of the face as an object. This is due to both intrinsic and extrinsic factors. The former include the plasticity of the face itself, the motion of the facial mussels producing different facial expressions, the feeding conditions changing the fat mass, the skin hydration, the presence of aesthetic products such as facial lotion and make-up, and the pose of the head. The latter include the illumination conditions, the background and the general environment, the imaging sensor and camera, the distance of the subject from the camera.

APPLICATIONS RELATED TO SECURITY

Security is possibly the application domain where face recognition systems have been most often deployed. Yet, these not always have been translated in a direct success.

Access Control

From this view point, real applications can be divided into categories: cooperative and non-cooperative in terms of subject's cooperation; controlled and non-controlled in terms of setting operational environment. Cooperation of subjects is often related to the head pose issue. Cooperative face recognition applications are often designed to operate in a near distance between camera and face. The user is required to look straight to the camera with neutral expression and eyes open in order to be granted a permission or authorization, such as entering to a restricted area, withdrawing money from ATM.

In a controlled operational environment, illumination could be purposely designed and set in such a way that the face is captured with front lighting, the most favorable way for the system to perform well. The control may be designed to also constrain the head pose to be frontal. The worst case is non-cooperative user in an un-controlled setting, in which paramount difficulties and challenges present to face recognition applications systems.

Access control and in a similar operational manner, time attendance, is a near distance type of cooperative and controlled applications of face recognition. Such a system is placed in a convenient location and designed easy to use, and the illumination is set the best way as possible. The user is required to face to the camera and he or she is willing to do so. Technically the least challenging, this is therefore the basic of all types. Such an application can be in either one-to-one verification or one-to-many identification.

Figure 1 illustrates the applications of face verification at the 2008 Beijing Olympic Games. This system verifies the identity of a ticket holder (spectator) at entrances to the National Stadium (Bird's Nest). Each ticket is associated with a unique ID number, and the ticket holder is required to submit his registration form with a two-inch ID/passport photo attached. The face photo is scanned into the system. At the entrance, the ticket is read in by an RFID reader, and the face image is captured using a video camera, which is compared with the enrollment photo scan, and the verification result is produced (Figure 2).

Even in a purposely controlled condition, illumination is still a problem in many cases, especially for one-to-many identification, because the environment is hardly designed for face recognition. One solution could use a camera flash to light in frontal direction, but this is generally not acceptable by the user. To solve this problem, Li invented a near-infrared (NIR) face recognition system to overcome the problem encountered in to the conventional visible light (VIS) based methods (Li, Zhang, Liao, Zhu, Chu, Ao, & He, 2006; Li, Chu, Ao, Zhang, & He, 2006; Li, Chu, Liao, & Zhang, 2007). The NIR face recognition technology has effectively solved the problem incurring

Figure 1. Face verification used at the 2008 Beijing Olympic Games

Figure 2. Immigration control at China-Hong Kong, China-Macau borders and Beijing International Airport

in cooperative and controlled applications. It has also been used at the China-Hong Kong border control (Figure 3).

APPLICATIONS RELATED TO FORENSIC SCIENCE

Forensic Science is possibly the first application scenario where biometrics has been successfully exploited. Since the multi-modal identification system introduced by Alphonse Bertillon in the late 19th century, much progress has been made. Most probably, the best known success story in the application of biometric technologies in forensics is the automated fingerprint identification system (AFIS), which is now being used by the majority of police forces throughout the world. However, much progress has been made also concerning other biometric modalities and face analysis as well.

Nowadays, Forensic biometrics can be defined as the scientific discipline that makes use of the biometric technologies for the demonstration of the existence and the investigation of infringements, the individualization of perpetrators and the description of modus operandi. These tasks are embedded in several forensic processes, including: forensic investigation, forensic evaluation, forensic intelligence and automated surveillance.

Law Enforcement

Human face analysis has been always crucial in law enforcement. One example is the identification of criminals from artist sketches. In many police station the eyewitness or a victim of a crime, can provide a description of suspect to a police artist who generates a forensic sketch. Law enforcement agencies disseminate the sketch to media and citizens can provide tips about suspect's identity. This is often a slow and tedious process which may require a long time before the perpetrator of the crime can be identified. A proposed solution is to directly and automatically match the face sketch to a mugshot database of known criminals.

This is a very difficult problem as it requires to compare quite different images, where facial features may be depicted in different ways. In fact, while a sketch drawn by an artist basically depicts the main shape features of a face, a picture contains much more textural information. The challenge is then to produce a common representation which makes the two samples directly comparable in some feature space. As such, several approach have been proposed to perform the direct matching of mugshots with face sketches (Figure 4).

In (Wang & Tang, 2009), Tang et al. proposed a face photo retrieval system using viewed sketch drawings. By transforming a photo image into a sketch, the difference between photo and sketch is significantly reduced, thus allowing effective matching between the two. The transformation is

Figure 3. Dual camera (an NIR and a visual) and NIR illumination for face recognition and positioning relative to the face

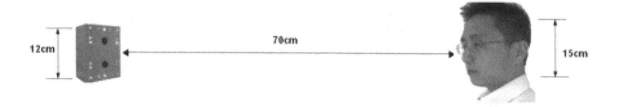

Figure 4. Sample face image and sketch drawn from a police artist

Reproduced from The New York Times August 19th 2013

performed by applying a PCA transformation to the shape and texture components of the mugshots dataset. To improve the synthesis performance, shape and texture information are separately extracted and analyzed from a face photo. Finally, a Bayesian classifier is used to recognize the probing sketch from the synthesized pseudo-sketches. Experiments on a data set containing 606 people reached a top accuracy of 97% at rank 10.

Both forensic sketches (i.e. sketches drawn from the description of a eyewitness) and viewed sketches (i.e. sketches drawn by an artist while viewing the picture of the subject) pose challenges to face recognition due to the fact that probe sketch images contain different textures compared to the gallery photographs they are being matched against. However, forensic sketches pose additional challenges due to the inability of a witness to exactly remember the appearance of a suspect and her subjective account of the description, which often results in inaccurate and incomplete forensic sketches.

Klare and Jain proposed both an holistic (Klare, Li, & Jain, 2011) and a part-based (Han, Klare, Bonnen, & Jain, 2013) approach for genuine forensic sketch identification. In the holistic matching, the sketch is first scaled and rotated based on the eye position on the mugshot. The aligned sketch and the mugshot are filtered to extract the same textural features both along the image points located by extracting the SIFT and on a regular square grid. A subspace projection is learnt for each bag of patches obtained from the extracted feature sets. The final representation is a concatenation of all learnt representations. This system was tested on a dataset provided by a local police authority reaching a recognition rate of about 25% on rank 10 and 45% on rank 50. Even though these rates may seem very poor if compared with the performance of automated identification from mugshots, the proposed matching suspects need to be further checked and validated by a human operator anyway.

Supporting Evidence in Court Cases

The acceptance of digital information as a source of evidence in court cases has been increasing over the past decades. The main limitation so far has been the lack of a proper integration of face recognition algorithms within the standard procedures adopted by forensic experts.

The task of a forensic examiner is simply to compare a latent trace, left on the crime scene, with a live sample from a suspect or persecuted person. This could be easily assimilated to the one-to-one face matching performed by any face recognition system. However, there is a crucial difference between the requirements for the forensic support in court cases and any other application of face recognition. For any application, a high recognition accuracy is generally required. On the contrary, in forensic applications, it is of the utmost importance to ensure an innocent is not misclassified as the perpetrator of a criminal offense. This can be better understood considering the shape of a general ROC curve, as in Figure 2. The threshold to be adopted by the system depends on the operating point to be chosen along the curve. In security-related applications, the operating point in the ROC curve will be chosen on the far right, along the curve. In forensic applications, the operating point will be chosen on the far left, minimizing the probability of a false match i.e. the conviction of an innocent.

For this reason, when called for a court case, forensic examiners provide to the judge a well documented report of their analysis. The report is aimed to define an objective probability that a given trace found on the crime scene has been left by a given suspect. The trace can be from any source, such as an image taken from a surveillance camera and containing the face of the person who committed the criminal action.

Over the last decades several tools for the analysis of faces, in support of forensic examiners, have been produced. Most, if not all, of them do not allow to provide a definitive decision whether the two face samples match. Rather, they provide several tools to reveal and highlight the main differences and similarities among two face images. These tools generally also provide a support to edit the report to be produced. The aim of the analysis is to provide a proof of evidence, with a given probability, that two given face images belong to the same person. As the final decision about the accusation for a crime will be taken by the court itself, the forensic examiner will never report that a given face image belongs to the perpetrator of a crime. The examiner will always state the probability of a match between two pictures, as well as the supporting evidence for the conclusion reported. This mode of operation automatically excludes, in every country, the feasibility of a "black box" or "eyes closed" operation, where the forensic examiner is completely substituted by an automatic system. Every legal system requires the human intervention, not only in the decision process, but also in the production of the proof of evidence for the court. The reliability of an automatic face recognition system can not be considered, at present, as an evidential proof of correct matching between two forensic samples.

Scherier et al. (2011) propose a Bayesian approach to combine descriptive attributes related to the face of an individual. The proposed algorithm is capable of combining incomplete observations to enhance the match probability. The potential of the proposed system is the capability to combine several kind of attributes, including both "soft biometrics" traits and descriptive attributes, i.e. labels given to an image to describe any aspect of its appearance. The paper also provides direct evidence for the feasibility of the noisy-OR function as an approximation of the conditional probability table.

Most often, forensic examiners perform the face analysis on the basis of peculiar features such as scars, moles and freckles in the face. The aim of this analysis is to provide a bunch of robust features which are peculiar to the face being examined. In (Park & Jain, 2010) Park and Jain proposed a system to incorporate traditional facial features as well facial marks to provide a robust description of the subject's face. Bicego et al. (2008) proposed a method to automatically extract facial marks, or any peculiar features of a given face image. The method is based on the computation of the degree of similarity or dissimilarity of corresponding facial regions, picked at random, between two subjects. The distinctiveness of individual facial features between subjects is given by their mutual distance in the feature space. This approach to facial feature selection may allow to facilitate a pairwise matching between a sample image related to a crime scene and the picture of a suspect.

Face Surveillance

Face surveillance refers to face identification, such as of watch-list, in surveillance videos (Barr, Bowyer, Flynn, & Biswas, 2012). Surveillance camera is used to capture images in a surveillance area and identifies faces in the video. Such a system operates at a distance of greater than 3 meters between the camera and subjects. In face surveillance, however, user cooperation with respect to the biometric sensor, i.e. video camera, may not be imposable, and is impossible for applications of watch-list surveillance. Non-frontal face images can result, causing further problems. When the view of the camera covers a wide enough area and the proportion of the face in the image can be small. This can lead to low resolution of the face portion, which degrades both the performances of face detection and the recognition engines. Choosing a long focal length lens can increase the proportion of the face in the image, but also narrows down the view. When a subject is moving, the face image captured at a distance can be blurred. This may be solved by using a high speed camera and a small aperture lens (for large depth of view).

For these reasons, face surveillance is one of most challenging face recognition applications. Control methods need to be done. Given current technologies, it is recommended that face surveillance be deployed in semi-controlled applications, such as at a security check point or a passage, as illustrated in the following figure, with a high resolution camera and designed lighting for obtaining high resolution, front-lighted frontal face images.

Applications of such a system can be extended to identify VIP customers. Technical issues are similar to watch-list surveillance. Differences are more in the deployment. Cameras need not be so hidden and the VIPs may not mind being serviced with the help of the system. Extra features may be added for customer analysis. This includes demographic identification such as gender, age, profession, race, etc, in addition to person identification (Figure 5).

Figure 5. CCTV surveillance camera and people walking through a passage for semi-controlled face recognition

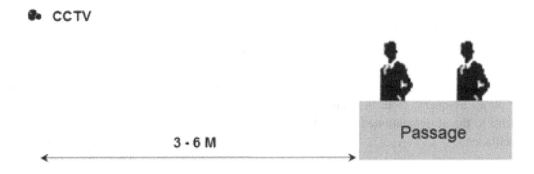

Criminal Investigations

This application mainly involves to search over a database of face images for those most similar to a given a query face image of suspect. Such a system may involve large databases and a technical requirement is search speed.

- **Face database search:** Given a photo of a suspect, criminal investigation department wishes to find candidates from databases of criminal records with face photos, residence registrations, and others. The search should be automatic, fast and hopefully accurate enough. The search can treat different databases with different priority. For example, that of criminal records is searched first to find most likely candidates. If not satisfactory, citizen databases could be searched. When a database is large, for example, millions, conditions can be imposed by location, gender, age group. Candidates found by computer search are further examined by forensic experts to narrow down and make conclusion.
- **Surveillance video search:** Surveillance video cameras (CCTV) are nowadays deployed widely in many cities. Recorded surveillance videos can provide useful evidences for criminal investigation. Surveillance video search works in a similar way to face database search, except for that the face database is built from recorded videos. The construction of such a database involves detection of faces from video, followed by facial feature extraction from each detected face to represent the face. Both face crops and features are then stored into the database. The face database search techniques can then reply, given a face photo as query. Note that this is in contrast to the aforementioned online face surveillance.

APPLICATIONS RELATED TO SERVICES

In the last decade a number of applications have been proposed designed to facilitate the fruition of services from fidelized customers. Such applications can be broadly divided into two sets: customer services and customer analysis.

- **Customer service:** Clubs, shops, hotels and restaurants want to improve their services to their VIP customers. The techniques are similar to watch-list face surveillance. A surveillance video camera or a USB camera is used to capture the face image, and face features are then extracted and compared against the VIP face database.
- **Customer analysis:** Commercial agents wish to analyze customers' behavior and make inference from user statistics. This could be assisted by automatic demographic identification of gender, age, race and body features, facial wear, clothing, etc. and by analysis of their attentions and stay to certain goods.

APPLICATION-ORIENTED DATABASES

New challenges often require the collection of new data which better depict the application scenario. For this reason, a number of face databases have been collected over time to allow researcher to investigate new ideas and approaches to the most common applications. A good list of the currently available face databases can be found on the "Face recognition" Web page maintained by Mislav Grgic, from the University of Zagreb, and Kresimir Delac, from b4b Ltd.

Even though security and access control are the most common scenarios considered, there is an increasing number of datasets considering quite interesting problems in matching visual patterns in faces. Given the abundance of face image and video datasets it is beyond the scope of this chapter to perform an exhaustive list of all available face databases. However, a few representative and more recent examples, to give the flavor of the research areas deserving further attention, are listed here.

SCface: Surveillance Cameras Face Database

SCface is a database of static images of human faces. Images were taken in uncontrolled indoor environment using five video surveillance cameras of various qualities. Database contains 4160 static images (in visible and infrared spectrum) of 130 subjects. Images from different quality cameras mimic the real-world conditions and enable robust face recognition algorithms testing, emphasizing different law enforcement and surveillance use case scenarios (Grgic, Delac, & Grgic, 2011). The SCface database was designed mainly as a mean of testing face recognition algorithms in real-world conditions. In such a setup, one can easily imagine a scenario where an individual should be recognized comparing one frontal mug shot image to a low quality video surveillance still image.

NIST Mugshot Identification Database

The NIST Special Database 18, contains 8-bit gray scale images of mugshot photographs. This database is being distributed for use in developing and testing of mugshot identification systems. The database contains images of 1573 individuals (cases) with a total of 3248 images stored in NIST's IHead raster data format. The mugshots are mainly of male cases, with the database containing 1495 male cases and 78 female cases. The database images consist of both front views and side views (profiles), although not every case has both a front and profile.

Japanese Female Facial Expression (JAFFE) Database

This is an example of posed facial expressions mugshots database. The database contains 213 images of 7 facial expressions (6 basic facial expressions + 1 neutral) posed by 10 Japanese female models. Each image has been rated on 6 emotion adjectives by 60 Japanese subjects. Even though the current trend in facial expression and emotion recognition is to perform testing on elicited natural expressions, this is a valuable dataset to study individual facial action units (Lyons, Budynek, & Akamatsu, 1999).

Face Video Database of the Max Planck Institute for Biological Cybernetics

This database contains short video sequences of facial Action Units recorded simultaneously from six different viewpoints, recorded in 2003 at the Max Planck Institute for Biological Cybernetics. The video cameras were arranged at 18 degrees intervals in a semi-circle around the subject at a distance of roughly 1.3m. The cameras recorded 25 frames/sec at 786x576 video resolution, non-interlaced. In order to facilitate the recovery of rigid head motion, the subject wore a head-plate with 6 green markers. The Website contains a total of 246 video sequences in MPEG1 format.

Labeled Faces in the Wild

Labeled Faces in the Wild is a database of face photographs designed for studying the problem of unconstrained face recognition. The data set contains more than 13,000 images of faces collected from the Web. Each face has been labeled with the name of the person pictured. 1680 of the people pictured have two or more distinct photos in the data set. The only constraint on these faces is that they were detected by the Viola-Jones face detector. More details can be found in (Huang, Ramesh, Berg, & Learned-Miller, 2007).

There are now four different sets of LFW images including the original and three different types of "aligned" images. The aligned images include "funneled images" (Huang & Learned-Miller, 2007), LFW-a, which uses an unpublished method of alignment, and "deep funneled" images (Huang, Mattar, Lee, & Learned-Miller, 2012). Among these, LFW-a and the deep funneled images produce superior results for most face verification algorithms over the original images and over the funneled images.

Plastic Surgery Face Database

The plastic surgery face database is a real world database that contains 1800 pre and post surgery images pertaining to 900 subjects. For each individual, there are two frontal face images with proper illumination and neutral expression: the first is taken before surgery and the second is taken after surgery. The database contains 519 image pairs corresponding to local surgeries and 381 cases of global surgery (e.g., skin peeling and face lift). The details of the database and performance evaluation of several well known face recognition algorithms is available in (Singh, Vatsa, Bhatt, Bharadwaj, Noore, & Nooreyezdan, 2010).

MOBIO: Mobile Biometry Face and Speech Database

The MOBIO database consists of bi-modal (audio and video) data taken from 152 people (McCool, Marcel, Hadid, Pietikäinen, Matějka, Černocký, Poh, Kittler, Larcher, Lévy, Matrouf, Bonastre, Tresadern, & Cootes, 2012). The database has a female-male ratio or nearly 1:2 (100 males and 52 females) and was collected from August 2008 until July 2010 in six different sites from five different countries. This led to a diverse bi-modal database with both native and non-native English speakers.

In total 12 sessions were captured for each client: 6 sessions for Phase I and 6 sessions for Phase II. The Phase I data consists of 21 questions with the question types ranging from: Short Response Questions, Short Response Free Speech, Set Speech, and Free Speech. The Phase II data consists of 11 questions with the question types ranging from: Short Response Questions, Set Speech, and Free Speech. A more detailed description of the questions asked of the clients is provided below.

The database was recorded using two mobile devices: a mobile phone and a laptop computer. The mobile phone used to capture the database was a NOKIA N93i mobile while the laptop computer was a standard 2008 MacBook. The laptop was only used to capture part of the first session, this first session consists of data captured on both the laptop and the mobile phone.

ChokePoint

The ChokePoint dataset was designed for experiments in person identification/verification under real-world surveillance conditions using existing technologies (Wong, Chen, Mau, Sanderson & Lovell, 2011). An array of three cameras was placed above several portals (natural choke points in terms of pedestrian traffic) to capture subjects walking through each portal in a natural way. While a person is walking through a portal, a sequence of face images (i.e. a face set) can be captured. Faces in such sets have variations in terms of illumination conditions, pose, sharpness, as well as misalignment due to automatic face localization/detection. Due to the three cameras configuration, one of the cameras is likely to capture a face set where a subset of the faces is near-frontal.

The dataset consists of 25 subjects (19 male and 6 female) in portal 1 and 29 subjects (23 male and 6 female) in portal 2. The recording of portal 1 and portal 2 are one month apart. The dataset has frame rate of 30 fps and the image resolution is 800X600 pixels. In total, the dataset consists of 54 video sequences and 64,204 labeled face images. In all sequences, only one subject is presented in the image at a time. The first 100 frames of each sequence are for background modeling where no foreground objects were presented.

VADANA: Vims Appearance Dataset for facial ANAlysis

The VADANA dataset has been collected from face pictures of several subjects across age progression (Somanath, Rohith, & Kambhamettu, 2011). The main characteristics of VADANA, which distinguish it from current benchmarks, is the large number of intra-personal pairs (order of 168 thousand); natural variations in pose, expression and illumination; and the rich set of additional meta-data provided along with standard partitions for direct comparison and bench-marking efforts.

MORPH Database (Craniofacial Longitudinal Morphological Face Database)

MORPH is the largest publicly available longitudinal face database (Ricanek & Tesafaye, 2006). It is actively being used in over 30 countries. The MORPH data corpus embraces thousands of facial images of individuals across time, collected in real-world conditions (not a controlled collection). Moreover, these images are available to the public for continued research, and we encourage studies of forensic science relevance and utility. MORPH is comprised of two datasets, or "albums," Album1 and Album2. Album 1 contains digital scans of 515 photographs of individuals taken between October 26, 1962 and April 7, 1998 which we refer to as acquisition dates. The acquisition dates correspond to increasing ages for individuals in the database; these dates range anywhere from 46 days to 29 years after the earliest photograph. A stats sheet for Album1 is available. Album 2 contains longitudinal digital photographs collected over several years. Album2 is still evolving

and images are acquired quarterly. Both albums include meta data for race, gender, date of birth, and date of acquisition.

Long Distance Heterogeneous Face Database (LDHF-DB)

The LDHF database contains both visible (VIS) and near-infrared (NIR) face images at distances of 60m, 100m, and 150m outdoors and at a 1m distance indoors. Face images of 100 subjects (70 males and 30 females) were captured; for each subject one image was captured at each distance in daytime and nighttime. All the images of individual subjects are frontal faces without glasses, and collected in a single sitting. Short distance (1m) visible light images were collected under a fluorescent light by using a DSLR camera with Canon F1.8 lens, and NIR images were collected using the modified DSLR camera and NIR illuminator of 24 IR LEDs without visible light. Long distance (over 60m) VIS images were collected during the daytime using a telephoto lens coupled with a DSLR camera, and NIR images were collected using the DSLR camera with NIR light provided by RayMax300 illuminator (Maeng, Liao, Kang, Lee, & Jain, 2012).

YouTube Faces Database

The data set contains 3,425 videos of 1,595 different people. All the videos were downloaded from YouTube. An average of about 2 videos are available for each subject.

In designing this video data set and benchmarks the example of the 'Labeled Faces in the Wild' LFW image collection has been followed. Specifically, the goal was to produce a large scale collection of videos along with labels indicating the identities of people appearing in each video stream. The data was collected by using the 5,749 names of subjects included in the LFW data set to search YouTube for videos of these same individuals. The top six results for each query were downloaded and assembled into the dataset (Wolf, Hassner, & Maoz, 2011).

Female Makeup Datasets

Three datasets of female face images were assembled for studying the impact of makeup on face recognition (Chen, Dantcheva, & Ross, 2013).

- **YMU (YouTube Makeup):** Face images of 151 subjects were obtained from YouTube video makeup tutorials. The images of the subjects were captured before and after the application of makeup. There are four shots per subject: two shots before the application of makeup and two shots after the application of makeup. This dataset includes some variations in expression and pose.
- **VMU (Virtual Makeup):** Face images of 51 caucasian female subjects in the FRGC repository (http://www.nist.gov/itl/iad/ig/frgc.cfm) were synthetically modified to simulate the application of makeup. A publicly available software (www.taaz.com) was used to perform this alteration.
- **MIW (Makeup in the "wild"):** Face images of subjects with and without makeup were downloaded from the Internet.

3D Mask Attack Database (3DMAD)

The 3D Mask Attack Database (3DMAD) is a biometric (face) spoofing database. It currently contains 76500 frames of 17 persons, recorded using Kinect for both real-access and spoofing attacks. Each frame consists of: a depth image (640x480 pixels – 1x11 bits); the corresponding RGB image (640x480 pixels – 3x8 bits); manually annotated eye positions (with respect to the RGB image).

The data was collected in 3 different sessions for all subjects and for each session 5 videos of 300 frames are captured. The recordings are done under controlled conditions, with frontal-view and neutral expression. The first two sessions are dedicated to the real access samples, in which subjects are recorded with a time delay of ~2 weeks between the acquisitions. In the third session, 3D mask attacks are captured by a single operator (attacker) (Erdogmus & Marcel, 2013).

FUTURE RESEARCH DIRECTIONS

Research in application-oriented biometrics can not be disjoint from the basic research in biometrics. As far as new algorithms are designed and new challenges are overcome, also new applications can be envisaged. Along this direction, new applications related to the everyday use of technologies can be designed. As such, biometrics can be adopted as a general "enabling technology" which allows users to better receive goods and services. On the other hand, there is an emerging need for more flexible systems which can cope with more relaxed constraints concerning the acquisition setup and environmental conditions. While traditional security applications often allow to constrain or structure the environment to limit the variability of the biometric data to be processed, the larger deployment of biometric technologies can be only achieved by devising flexible systems which allow a better usability. This includes to facilitate the use by elderly as well as untrained or very young people. Along this line, it is not always the capability to identify one subject among billions which makes a system better applicable. Rather, the flexibility of the system to take advantage of a number of redundant information and of interacting with the user, may open a variety of potential applications related to everyday life.

CONCLUSION

This chapter attempted an overview of some of the most prominent applications of face recognition. Even though it could not provide an exhaustive list of all successful face biometric systems, it defined a panorama of the current state of the art.

New biometric applications are the result of new algorithms. However, recognition performances are not the ultimate paradigm of a successful application of face recognition. As faces convey an abundance of information. Including the age, gender, mood, ethnicity, these information can be also exploited to devise better applicable systems. On the other hand, many emerging applications, including robotics and the aid to disabled people, primarily require a biometric system to facilitate a better interaction with a, generally small, population of subjects. As such, a very low False Acceptance Rate or, conversely, a very high recognition accuracy, may not be required. While, a higher flexibility and the capability to deal with minimally constrained environments, would greatly improve the applicability of future face biometric systems in the real world.

REFERENCES

Allison, T., Puce, A., & McCarthy, G. (2000). Social perception from visual cues: role of the STS region. *Trends in Cognitive Sciences*, *4*, 267–278. doi:10.1016/S1364-6613(00)01501-1 PMID:10859571

Barr, J. R., Bowyer, K. W., Flynn, P. J., & Biswas, S. (2012). Face Recognition From Video: A Review. *International Journal of Pattern Recognition and Artificial Intelligence*, *26*(5). doi:10.1142/S0218001412660024

Bicego, M., Brelstaff, G., Brodo, L., Grosso, E., Lagorio, A., & Tistarelli, M. (2008). Distinctiveness of faces: a computational approach. *ACM Transactions on Applied Perception*, *5*(2), 1–18. doi:10.1145/1279920.1279925

Bruce, V., & Young, A. W. (1986). Understanding face recognition. *The British Journal of Psychology*, *77*(3), 305–327. doi:10.1111/j.2044-8295.1986.tb02199.x PMID:3756376

Calder, A., & Young, A. (2005). Understanding the recognition of facial identity and facial expression. *Nature Reviews. Neuroscience*, *6*, 641–651. doi:10.1038/nrn1724 PMID:16062171

Calder, A., Young, A., Rowland, D., Perrett, D., Hodges, J., & Etcoff, H. (1996). Facial emotion recognition after bilateral amygdala damage: Differentially severe impairment of fear. *Cognitive Neuropsychology*, *13*, 699–745. doi:10.1080/026432996381890

Chen, C., Dantcheva, A., & Ross, A. (2013). Automatic Facial Makeup Detection with Application in Face Recognition. In *Proc. of 6th IAPR International Conference on Biometrics* (ICB). IAPR.

Erdogmus, N., & Marcel, S. (2013). Spoofing in 2D Face Recognition with 3D Masks and Anti-spoofing with Kinect. In *Proc. of IEEE Conf. on Biometrics: Theory, Applications and Systems*. IEEE.

Grgic, M., Delac, K., & Grgic, S. (2011). *SCface - Surveillance cameras face database*.

Han, H., Klare, B., Bonnen, K., & Jain, A. K. (2013). Matching composite sketches to face photos: A component based approach. *IEEE Trans. IFS*, *8*(1), 191–204.

Hornak, J., Rolls, E., & Wade, D. (1996). Face and voice expression identification in patients with emotional and behavioral changes following ventral frontal lobe damage. *Neuropsychologia, 34*, 173–181. doi:10.1016/0028-3932(95)00106-9

Huang, G. B., & Learned-Miller, E. (2007). Unsupervised joint alignment of complex images. In *Proc. of IEEE International Conference on Computer Vision* (ICCV). IEEE.

Huang, G. B., Mattar, M., Lee, H., & Learned-Miller, E. (2012). Learning to Align from Scratch. In Proceedings of Advances in Neural Information Processing Systems (NIPS). NIPS.

Huang, G. B., Ramesh, M., Berg, T., & Learned-Miller, E. (2007). *Labeled Faces in the Wild: A Database for Studying Face Recognition in Unconstrained Environments*. University of Massachusetts at Amherst, Technical Report 07-49.

Humphreys, G., Donnelly, N., & Riddoch, M. (1993). Expression is computed separately from facial identity, and it is computed separately for moving and static faces: Neuropsychological evidence. *Neuropsychologia, 31*, 173–181. doi:10.1016/0028-3932(93)90045-2 PMID:8455786

Klare, B., Li, Z., & Jain, A. K. (2011). Matching forensic sketches to mug shot photos. *IEEE Transactions on Pattern Analysis and Machine Intelligence, 33*(3), 639–646. doi:10.1109/TPAMI.2010.180 PMID:20921585

Li, S. Z., Chu, R., Liao, S., & Zhang, L. (2007). Illumination invariant face recognition using near-infrared images. *IEEE Transactions on Pattern Analysis and Machine Intelligence, 29*(4), 627–639. doi:10.1109/TPAMI.2007.1014 PMID:17299220

Li, S. Z., Chu, R. F., Ao, M., Zhang, L., & He, R. (2006). Highly accurate and fast face recognition using near infrared images. In *Proc. of IAPR International Conference on Biometrics* (ICB-2006), (pp. 151-158). IAPR.

Li, S. Z., Zhang, L., Liao, S. C., Zhu, X. X., Chu, R. F., Ao, M., & He, R. (2006). A near-infrared image based face recognition system. In *Proc. of 7th IEEE International Conference Automatic Face and Gesture Recognition* (FG-2006), (pp. 455-460). IEEE.

Lyons, M. J., Budynek, J., & Akamatsu, S. (1999). Automatic Classification of Single Facial Images. *IEEE Transactions on Pattern Analysis and Machine Intelligence, 21*(12), 1357–1362. doi:10.1109/34.817413

Maeng, H., Liao, S., Kang, D., Lee, S. W., & Jain, A. K. (2012). Nighttime Face Recognition at Long Distance: Cross-distance and Cross-spectral Matching. In *Proc. of 11th Asian Conference on Computer Vision*. ACCV.

McCool, C., Marcel, S., Hadid, A., Pietikäinen, M., Matějka, P., & Černocký, J. … Cootes, T. (2012). Bi-Modal Person Recognition on a Mobile Phone: using mobile phone data. In *Proc. IEEE ICME Workshop on Hot Topics in Mobile Mutlimedia*. IEEE.

Park, U., & Jain, A. K. (2010). Face Matching and Retrieval Using Soft Biometrics. *IEEE Trans. Information Forensics and Security, 5*(3), 406–415. doi:10.1109/TIFS.2010.2049842

Ricanek, K., & Tesafaye, T. (2006). MORPH: A Longitudinal Image Database of Normal Adult Age-Progression. In *Proc. IEEE 7th International Conference on Automatic Face and Gesture Recognition*, (pp. 341-345). IEEE.

Scheirer, W. J., Kumar, N., Ricanek, K., Belhumeur, P. N., & Boult, T. E. (2011). Fusing with Context: a Bayesian Approach to Combining Descriptive Attributes. In *Proc. of 1ˢᵗ IEEE Int.l Joint Conference on Biometrics*, (pp. 1-8). IEEE.

Singh, R., Vatsa, M., Bhatt, H. S., Bharadwaj, S., Noore, A., & Nooreyezdan, S. S. (2010). Plastic Surgery: A New Dimension to Face Recognition. *IEEE Transaction on Information Forensics and Security, 5*(3), 441–448. doi:10.1109/TIFS.2010.2054083

Somanath, G., Rohith, M. V., & Kambhamettu, C. (2011). VADANA: A dense dataset for facial image analysis. In *Proc. BeFIT 2011 – First IEEE International Workshop on Benchmarking Facial Image Analysis Technologies (held in conjunction with ICCV 2011)*. IEEE.

Tranel, D., Damasio, A., & Damasio, H. (1988). Intact Recognition of Facial Expression, Gender, and Age in Patients with Impaired Recognition of Face Identity. *Neurology, 38*, 690–696. doi:10.1212/WNL.38.5.690 PMID:3362363

Wang, X., & Tang, X. (2009). Face Photo-Sketch Synthesis and Recognition. *IEEE Transactions on Pattern Analysis and Machine Intelligence, 31*(11), 1955–1967. doi:10.1109/TPAMI.2008.222 PMID:19762924

Wolf, L., Hassner, T., & Maoz, I. (2011). Face Recognition in Unconstrained Videos with Matched Background Similarity. In *Proc. of IEEE Conf. on Computer Vision and Pattern Recognition (CVPR)*. IEEE.

Wong, Y., Chen, S., Mau, S., Sanderson, C., & Lovell, B. C. (2011). Patch-based probabilistic image quality assessment for face selection and improved video-based face recognition. In *Proc. of IEEE Computer Vision and Pattern Recognition Workshops (CVPRW)*, (pp. 74-81). IEEE.

KEY TERMS AND DEFINITIONS

Biometric Security: Controlled access to logical or physical facilities achieved through biometric authentication; as an alternative definition, all countermeasures able to assure robustness of templates and spoofing avoidance.

Face Databases: Databases of face images in controlled/uncontrolled conditions, used to assess algorithms and applications.

Face Recognition: Recognition (verification or identification) of a subject from an image of her face; in verification, the subject claims an identity which is matched with the current image (1:1); in identification there is no identity claim, so that the comparison entails the whole gallery of enrolled subjects (1:N).

Face Recognition Applications: Any kind of application where recognition of a subject from her face can be useful, from authentication, to forensics, to ambient intelligence.

Face Recognition Challenges: Face recognition in uncontrolled or even adverse conditions is still very hard to achieve; moreover, pose, illumination, and expression (PIE) challenges which have been traditionally addressed in this field are nowadays integrated with the investigation of problems related to demographics, especially gender, ethnicity and age.

Face Surveillance: Video-surveillance activity based of detection, tracking and possibly recognition of subjects within a controlled environment.

Forensic Biometrics: Use of biometric for forensic applications, like latent fingerprints recognition or recognition of a suspect from a sketched identikit.

Real World Application: In laboratory settings, acquisition conditions for face images, or for any other biometric trait, are usually quite controlled; however, recognition at a distance as well as in further adverse conditions is typical of real world applications.

Chapter 2
Unconstrained Face Recognition

Stefanos Zafeiriou
Imperial College London, UK

Irene Kotsia
Middlesex University London, UK & Imperial College London, UK

Maja Pantic
Imperial College London, UK

ABSTRACT

The human face is the most well-researched object in computer vision, mainly because (1) it is a highly deformable object whose appearance changes dramatically under different poses, expressions, and, illuminations, etc., (2) the applications of face recognition are numerous and span several fields, (3) it is widely known that humans possess the ability to perform, extremely efficiently and accurately, facial analysis, especially identity recognition. Although a lot of research has been conducted in the past years, the problem of face recognition using images captured in uncontrolled environments including several illumination and/or pose variations still remains open. This is also attributed to the existence of outliers (such as partial occlusion, cosmetics, eyeglasses, etc.) or changes due to age. In this chapter, the authors provide an overview of the existing fully automatic face recognition technologies for uncontrolled scenarios. They present the existing databases and summarize the challenges that arise in such scenarios and conclude by presenting the opportunities that exist in the field.

INTRODUCTION

Unveiling the way humans perceive identities has been of great interest to psychologists for at least five decades (Bruner & Tagiuri, 1954). It nowadays constitutes one of the most popular research areas in experimental psychology (Bruce & Young, 1986; Sinha, Balas, Ostrovsky, & Russell, 2006). The interested reader can find a nice summary of research findings regarding human perception of identities in (Sinha, Balas, Ostrovsky, & Russell, 2006).

Automatic face recognition was first attempted in the 1960s (Bledsoe, 1964) and 1970s (Kelly, 1970). A pioneer in the field was Takeo Kanade (1973), who first attempted facial features localization in order to match them for face recognition. Since then, face recognition became one of

DOI: 10.4018/978-1-4666-5966-7.ch002

the mainstream applications of image analysis and computer vision, creating a wealth of scientific research (the interested reader may refer to Chellappa, Charles, and Saad (1995) and Zhao, Chellappa, Phillips, and Rosenfeld (2003) to see the progress of face recognition during the past 30 years and until 2003).

The collection of face databases, among the first large object databases that were created, made face recognition the main application for certain domains of statistical machine learning and pattern recognition and particular for the domain of component analysis (CA). CA includes methods such as Principal Component Analysis (Turk & Pentland, 1991; Kirby & Sirovich, 1990), Linear Discriminant Analysis (Belhumeur, Hespanha, & Kriegman, 1997), Independent Component Analysis (Bartlett, Movellan, & Sejnowski, 2002) and Nonnegative Matrix Factorization (Zafeiriou, Tefas, Buciu, & Pitas, 2006).

Face recognition can be further distinguished into a set of sub-problems, each of which dealing with the different challenges met by using different problem formulations according to the machine learning and matching algorithms it employs:

1. Closed-set Face Identification (CFI) (Chellappa, Charles, & Saad, 1995; Zhao, Chellappa, Phillips, & Rosenfeld, 2003). In CFI all testing identities are known at training. That is, the system always assigns an identity to the testing images and the identity will be of a subject from the training set. CFI falls under the general category of multiclass classification problems and can be easily formulated within the current statistical machine learning frameworks. The measure that is usually used in CFI is the classification accuracy (i.e., number of correctly classified samples over the number of total samples in the dataset).

2. Open-set Face Identification (OFI), also known as Watch List (Li & Wechsler, 2005; Scheirer, Boult, de Rezende Rocha, & Sapkota, 2013). In OFI incomplete knowledge of the world is given by the training data and images of unknown persons can be submitted to the system during testing. The system should be able to not only assign one of the identities in the Watch List but also to assign the identity "Other" if the submitted face does not belong to one of the subjects in the list (Scheirer, Boult, de Rezende Rocha, & Sapkota, 2013). It is obvious that OFI can be applied to considerably more problems than CFI. However using a huge class "Other" introduces considerable challenges in formulating proper statistical machine learning frameworks.

3. Face Identity Verification (Zafeiriou, Tefas, & Pitas, 2007) (also referred to as Face Authentication (Duc, Fischer, & Bigun, 1999; Kotropoulos, Tefas, & Pitas, 2000)). A FIV system should be able to automatically decide, given a test facial template and a reference one, whether they correspond to the same subject. FIV has numerous applications including identity control in airports, identity verification in biometric systems etc. Usually, FIV is formulated as a two class problem, i.e client (or genuine) faces vs impostor faces. That way, given enough samples per person, powerful person-specific models can be built (Zafeiriou, Tefas, & Pitas, 2007). The performance of face verification systems is measured in terms of the False Rejection Rate (FRR) achieved at a fixed False Acceptance Rate (FAR). There is a trade off between FAR and FRR. That is, it is possible to reduce either of them with the risk of increasing the other one. This trade off between the FAR and FRR can create

a curve, where FRR is plotted as a function of FAR. This curve is called Receiver Operating Characteristic (ROC) curve. The performance of a verification system is often quoted by a particular operating point of the ROC curve where FAR=FRR. This operating point is called Equal Error Rate (EER).

4. Face matching (also recently referred to as Face Similarity Problem (FSP), as introduced with the Labeled Faces 'in-the-Wild' (LFW) database (Huang, Mattar, Berg, & Learned-Miller, 2008). The FSP problem can be formulated as follows: given two facial images or videos determine whether they correspond to the same person. The FSP problem is closely related to FIV and this is the reason why many researchers use FIV to refer to FSP. Nevertheless, FSP and FIV have crucial differences. In FIV the identity being claimed is known, while in FPS, as formulated in (Huang, Mattar, Berg, & Learned-Miller, 2008; Wolf, Hassner, & Taigman, 2011), the claimed identity is not known, a feature that makes is more general. Also, the training procedure of FPS is different than that of FIV (Zafeiriou, Tefas, & Pitas, 2007; Huang, Mattar, Berg, & Learned-Miller, 2008). That is, in FSP, the training set contains only matching pairs of images (i.e., a pairs of images of the same person) and non-matching pairs (i.e., a pairs of facial images of different persons). No identity information is explored (also referred to as "restricted protocol" of LFW). Hence, the general goal is to learn what two matching pairs should like rather than train persons-specific models, as in FIV. Furthermore, the idea of face similarity has been applied to other problems such as action similarity (Kliper-Gross, Hassner, & Wolf, 2012) and face matching from videos (Wolf, Hassner, & Maoz, 2011).

The majority of the face recognition literature deals concerns FIV and CFI. Nevertheless, lately FSP has received much attention due to the fact that it was introduced with the first facial database collected in totally unconstrained conditions (Huang, Mattar, Berg, & Learned-Miller, 2008).

The majority of the research in the first three problems was concentrated on datasets captured in well-controlled laboratory conditions. Initially small scale databases were collected, like ORL (Samaria & Harter, 1994) and M2VTS (Pigeon & Vandendorpe, 1997) databases. After some years medium/large scale databases were introduced, like FERET (Messer, Matas, Kittler, Luettin, & Maitre, 1999; Phillips, Wechsler, Huang, & Rauss, 1998) and XM2VTS (Phillips, Moon, Rizvi, & Rauss, 2000). In XM2VTS EER as low as 0.42% has been reported for faces manually aligned (Tzimiropoulos, Zafeiriou, & Pantic, 2012; Zafeiriou, Tzimiropoulos, Petrou, & Stathaki, 2012), and around 1% for automatically aligned faces (Zafeiriou, 2012). In FERET database accuracy as high as 100% has been reported for certain experimental setups, using manually aligned faces. However, it has been recently shown that this is by far the case when considering fully automatic face recognition. In particular, in fully automatic face recognition scenarios, even quite recent methodologies report as low 21% in FERET DUP-II experimental setup (Deng, Hu, Lu, & Guo, 2013; Wagner, Wright, Ganesh, Zhou, & Ma, 2009). FERET DUPI and DUPII experimental setups are considered quite challenging in fully automatic face recognition (Deng, Hu, Lu, & Guo, 2013; Wagner, Wright, Ganesh, Zhou, & Ma, 2009).

In this chapter we investigate on fully automatic unconstrained face recognition methodologies. With fully automatic face recognition we refer to the problem of face recognition without any manual intervention. It usually contains the following steps: (1) face detection, (2) face landmark localization or face alignment and (3) face recognition. Arguably, correct face detection and alignment plays the most crucial rule in robust face recognition (something that has been stressed by many pioneers in the field such as Takeo Kanade (Matthews, Xiao, & Baker, 2007). With unconstrained we refer to the problem of performing face recognition using images collected in unconstrained conditions. This includes face recognition across different poses and illumination conditions, under partial occlusion, under extreme expressions, under facial changes such as aging and cosmetic/plastic surgeries etc. It also includes face recognition using mobile devices, face recognition in surveillance scenarios and in extremely challenging scenarios such as one sample face recognition.

FULLY AUTOMATIC FACE RECOGNITION

The vast majority of the first approaches in face recognition assumed that a set of manually aligned and cropped images were available. Hence, the main goal was to try to identify the person in the image or verify his/her identity given a set of the perfectly aligned images. This was indeed the prevalent paradigm, since the application of Principal Component Analysis (PCA) (Turk & Pentland, 1991), with the so-called eigenfaces. With the introduction of PCA the problem of face recognition was reformulated as a Component Analysis (CA) problem (other researchers refer to this problem as subspace learning problem (Shakhnarovich & Moghaddam, 2011), in which given a set of well-aligned images, one should find a small set of components, much smaller than the image dimensionality, which can provide a low-dimensional subspace in which the faces can be well-separated. To that end, many CA techniques were proposed and applied, such as Linear

Discriminant Analysis (LDA) with the so-called Fisherfaces (Belhumeur, Hespanha, & Kriegman, 1997), Nonnegative Matrix Factorization (NMF) with the so-called NMFfaces (Zafeiriou, Tefas, Buciu, & Pitas, 2006), Locality Preserving Projections with the so-called Laplacianfaces (He, Yan, Hu, Niyogi, & Zhang, 2005) etc. and tensor component analysis with the so called Tensorfaces (Vasilescu & Terzopoulos, 2002). Since CA techniques try to capture pixel-wise correlations, careful manual alignment is imperative (otherwise the correlations that are modelled refer to different parts of the face). Furthermore, the fact that the majority of CA techniques find components by optimizing a cost function (which is defined using an least squares based cost function on the pixel domain), makes them very sensitive to outliers (Wright, Yang, Ganesh, Sastry, & Ma, 2009; De La Torre & Black, 2003).

A limited number of approaches that dealt with the problem of fully automatic face recognition were proposed during that period (90s). The most prominent paradigms being the so-called Elastic Graph Matching (Lades, Vorbruggen, Buhmann, Lange, Von der Malsburg, Wurtz, & Konen, 1993; Wiskott, Fellous, Kuiger, & Von Der Malsburg, 1997), which is a simplification of the so-called Dynamic Link Architecture (DLA) and the Active Appearance Models (AAM) (Edwards, Cootes, & Taylor, 1998; Cootes, Edwards, & Taylor, 2001). Later the 3D morphable models (Blanz & Vetter, 2003, 1999), were introduced, as a generalization of AAMs using a dense 3D shape model. Recently we witnessed the development of highly accurate and real time face alignment methodologies (Cao, Wei, Wen, & Sun, 2012; Xiong & De la Torre, 2013; Tzimiropoulos, Alabort-i-Medina, Zafeiriou, & Pantic, 2013; Asthana, Zafeiriou, Cheng, & Pantic, 2013). These methodologies make the development of highly robust fully face recognition systems feasible (Chen, Cao, Wen, & Sun, 2013).

ELASTIC GRAPH MATCHING

A widely used technique for face recognition is the Elastic Graph Matching (EGM) algorithm (Lades, Vorbruggen, Buhmann, Lange, Von der Malsburg, Wurtz, & Konen, 1993; Wiskott, Fellous, Kuiger, & Von Der Malsburg, 1997). EGM is a simplification of the so-called Dynamic Link Architecture (DLA) (Lades, Vorbruggen, Buhmann, Lange, Von der Malsburg, Wurtz, & Konen, 1993; Wiskott, Fellous, Kuiger, & Von Der Malsburg, 1997). In EGM, the subject's deformable model (a reference face graph) is created by overlaying an elastic sparse graph on the object image and then calculating a multi-scale filter bank response at each graph node. This way, a feature vector is assigned to every node, the so-called jet. Both linear, e.g. Gabor wavelets (Lades, Vorbruggen, Buhmann, Lange, Von der Malsburg, Wurtz, & Konen, 1993; Wiskott, Fellous, Kuiger, & Von Der Malsburg, 1997; Duc, Fischer, & Bigun, 1999), and non-linear, e.g. morphological filters (Kotropoulos, Tefas, & Pitas, 2000; Tefas, Kotropoulos, & Pitas, 2002), have been applied to fill the jets. The graph matching process is implemented by a stochastic optimization of a cost function which takes into account both jet similarities and grid deformations. Coarse-to-fine procedures based on sampling (Wiskott, Fellous, Kuiger, & Von Der Malsburg, 1997; Duc, Fischer, & Bigun, 1999; Kotropoulos, Tefas, & Pitas, 2000; Tefas, Kotropoulos, & Pitas, 2002) are usually applied to perform graph matching.

A lot of research has been conducted in order to boost the performance of EGM for face recognition and verification (Zhang, Yan, & Lades, 1997; Wiskott, 1997; Wurtz, 1997; Kotropoulos, Tefas, & Pitas, 2000; Zafeiriou, Tefas, & Pitas, 2005; Shin, Park, & Kim, 2007; Shin, Kim, & Choi, 2007; Krüger, 1997). For example, in (Wiskott, Fellous, Kuiger, & Von Der Malsburg, 1997), the graph structure has been enhanced by introducing a stack like structure, the so-called bunch graph, and has been tested for face recognition. For every node in the bunch graph structure, a set of jets has been measured for different instances of a face (e.g., with open or closed mouth, open or shut eyes). This way, the bunch graph representation can cover a variety of possible changes in the appearance of a face.

Discriminant techniques have been also employed in order to enhance the classification performance of EGM. The use of linear discriminant techniques at the feature vectors for the extraction of the most discriminating features has been proposed in (Duc, Fischer, & Bigun, 1999; Kotropoulos, Tefas, & Pitas, 2000). Several schemes that aim at weighting the graph nodes according to their discriminatory power have also been proposed in (Kotropoulos, Tefas, & Pitas, 2000), (Wolf, Hassner, & Taigman, 2011), (Krüger, 1997), and (Tefas, Kotropoulos, & Pitas, 2001). A combined discriminant scheme has been proposed in (Zafeiriou, Tefas, & Pitas, 2005, Zafeiriou, Tefas, & Pitas, 2007), in which discriminant analysis has been employed in every step of the elastic graph matching procedure for face verification. In (Lyons, Budynek, & Akamatsu, 1999; Lyons, Budynek, Plante, & Akamatsu, 2000), LDA has been applied in a graph-wise manner (i.e., the feature vectors that have been used in LDA were used as graph jets), contrary to the methods in (Kotropoulos, Tefas, & Pitas, 2000), and (Zafeiriou, Tefas, & Pitas, 2007) in which node-specific discriminant transforms have been calculated. Moreover, a series of discriminant techniques in graph-based representations with Gabor features have been proposed in (Guo, & Dyer, 2005). The methods in (Guo, & Dyer, 2005) have some resemblance with EGM but have not implemented an elastic graph matching procedure since landmark selection and matching has been manually performed. In (Shin, Park, & Kim, 2007) and (Shin, Kim, & Choi, 2007), robust Gabor-based features have been proposed and novel wrapping elastic graph matching procedure has been introduced, being robust against rotation and scaling. Moreover, in

(Shin, Park, & Kim, 2007) a novel kernel-based method for feature extraction has been proposed and used for face recognition. Finally, in (Zafeiriou, Tefas, & Pitas, 2007) a methodology that automatically constructs person-specific graphs placed on his\her discriminant facial features was presented. These graphs could substitute the rectangular evenly distributed graphs (Kotropoulos, Tefas, & Pitas, 2000; Tefas, Kotropoulos, & Pitas, 2002) and the graphs having their nodes manually located at predefined facial fiducial points.

EGM methodologies were the first to be applied in fully automatic face recognition scenarios. Nevertheless, the majority of EGM architectures have been applied only in CFI and FIV scenarios. The drawbacks of EGM based approaches are threefold:

1. Apart from the bunch graph methodologies (Wiskott, Fellous, Kuiger, & Von Der Malsburg, 1997), that just stuck jets measured for different instances of faces, no generative statistical methodology has been applied for statistical representation of the graphs (contrary, for example, to AAMs that use a powerful statistical representation for the face).

2. In majority of cases the features used for building the jets, such as Gabor and morphological features, encode weak neighbourhood relationships. It is expected that the use of Histogram of Oriented Gradients (HoG) (Albiol, Monzo, Martin, Sastre, & Albiol, 2008; Dalal & Triggs, 2005), Scale Invariant Feature Transform (SIFT) (Lowe, 2004) or Local Binary Patterns (LBP) (Ahonen, Hadid, & Pietikäinen, 2004), that can encode pixel neighbourhood relationships in a robust manner, could lead to substantial performance increase in unconstrained conditions.

3. Graph matching has been implemented as a heuristic sampling procedure over the image space (Kotropoulos, Tefas, & Pitas, 2000; Tefas, Kotropoulos, & Pitas, 2002) and there is no guarantee of convergence to a local minimum (contrary to AAMs for which convergence is guaranteed).

Finally, it is worth noticing that EGM procedure bears certain similarities with the so-called pictorial structures, which represent an object by a collection of parts arranged in a deformable configuration (Felzenszwalb & Huttenlocher, 2005; Fischler & Elschlager, 1973). In pictorial structures the appearance of each facial part is modelled separately, and the deformable configuration is represented by spring-like connections between pairs of parts. Similarly to EGM, pictorial structures optimize a cost function that takes into account independently the local texture similarity and structure (graph) configuration. The further exploration of the relationship between EGM and pictorial structures constitutes an interesting topic of further research. Also pictorial structures, even though were applied for general object detection and recognition, their power to face recognition has not been fully explored.

ACTIVE APPEARANCE MODELS

Active Appearance Models (AAMs) are one of the most well-studied technique for building and fitting facial deformable models (Cootes, Edwards, & Taylor, 2001; Matthews & Baker, 2004). They are also among the first methods applied for fully automatic face recognition (Edwards, Cootes, & Taylor,. 1998). AAMs use statistical models to describe shape and texture variation. In particular, a statistical model of shape is built from a set of (manually) annotated fiducial facial points describing the shape of the object of interest. In order to approximately retain only the variability that is attributed to non-rigid deformations, the shape points are put in correspondence (usually by removing global similarity transforms using Generalized Procrustes Analysis (Matthews, & Baker, 2004). Similarly, a statistical model of the texture is built using images of the object that have been normalized with respect to the shape points (so-called shape-free textures). This requires a pre-defined reference frame (usually defined in terms of the mean shape) and a global motion model or the warp (e.g. Piece-Wise Affine (Matthews & Baker, 2004) or Thin Plate Spline (TPS) (Cootes, Edwards, & Taylor, 2001; Papandreou & Maragos, 2008). The two main assumptions behind AAMs are that (1) for every test (unseen) image there exists a test shape and set of texture weights for which the test shape can be warped onto the reference frame and expressed as a linear combination of the shape-free training textures and (2) the test shape can be written as a linear combination of the training shapes. Under the previous assumptions the both the shape parameters and texture parameters are retrieved by minimizing the sum of squared errors between the shape-free texture and its reconstruction by the statistical texture model. The solution of such an optimization problem is referred to as model fitting.

Several works have been proposed to solve the AAM fitting optimization problem (Cootes, Edwards, & Taylor, 2001; Gross, Matthews, & Baker, 2005; Papandreou & Maragos, 2008; Amberg, Blake, & Vetter, 2009). Most notable methodologies include the regression-based method (Scheirer, Boult, de Rezende Rocha, & Sapkota, 2013), the very fast project-out inverse compositional algorithm (PIC) (Matthews & Baker, 2004) (which has been heavily criticized for its inability to perform well under generic fitting scenarios, i.e., fit images of unseen identities), the simultaneous inverse compositional

algorithm (Gross, Matthews, & Baker, 2005), and a variation of the simultaneous inverse compositional algorithm that operates in a projected space (Papandreou & Maragos, 2008). A complete project-out compositional framework for fitting AAMs was proposed in (Amberg, Blake, & Vetter, 2009). Due to the popularity of the PIC algorithm (Matthews & Baker, 2004), attributed mainly to its extremely low computational complexity, methodologies such as (Papandreou & Maragos, 2008; Amberg, Blake, & Vetter, 2009), which can provide near real-time fitting, have not received much attention.

AAMs are often criticized for a variety of reasons. The most common is that defining a linear statistical model of texture that explains variations in identity, expressions, pose and illumination, is a very challenging task, especially in the intensity domain. Furthermore, the large variation in facial appearance makes it very difficult to perform regression from texture differences to shape parameters. Additionally, occlusion cannot be easily handled, and, in general, requires the application of robust estimators on the least squares loss function. Finally, joint optimization with respect to shape and texture parameters may create numerous local minima in the cost function thus making it difficult for the algorithms to reach optimal solutions. Hence, for many years it was widely believed that AAMs are suitable only for person-specific settings (i.e. FIV) rather than generic face alignment. Recently, it was shown that by using a robust statistical space and a robust kernel AAMs can be employed for generic face alignment (Tzimiropoulos, Alabort-i-Medina, Zafeiriou, & Pantic, 2013) and hence can be used for fully automatic face recognition. Finally, recently it was also shown that AAMs can be used for fully automatic face recognition in unconstrained conditions in the LFW database (Asthana, Marks, Jones, Tieu, & Rohith, 2011).

3D MORPHABLE MODELS

The 3D Morphable Model (3DMM) (Blanz & Vetter, 2003; Blanz & Vetter, 1999; Romdhani & Vetter, 2003; Romdhani, Blanz, & Vetter, 2002; Romdhani, 2005; Amberg, 2011) can be considered a generalization of AAMs. That is, a 3DMM is a generative face model consisting of linear models of shape and texture. As AAMs, 3DMMs are learned from data. The training data consist of registered examples of the 3D shape and texture of faces. The faces are parameterized as triangulated meshes. In this context, registered means that every face is in the same parameterization, i.e. shares the same triangulation, and that semantically all corresponding points, such as the corners of the eye, are at the same position, having the same number of vertices. The main differences between AAMs and 3DMM are threefold: (1) the shape is not any more a sparse set of landmarks but a dense tessellated 3D surface (Blanz & Vetter, 2003; Blanz & Vetter, 1999; Romdhani & Vetter, 2003; Romdhani, Blanz, & Vetter, 2002); (2) the associated texture model is usually considered as albedo (i.e, the reflecting power of a surface), and hence not depending on the illumination and (3) 3DMMs are associated with a 3D motion model. 3DMM are powerful models that can be used for fully automatic face recognition under different illumination and poses. To the best of our knowledge, the 3DMM presented in (Blanz & Vetter, 2003), was one of the first methods to show that fully automatic pose invariant face recognition is feasible.

Some of the difficulties regarding building and fitting 3DMMs include:

1. In order to build a 3DMM dense correspondences between 3D dense facial shapes are required. As the problem is not straightforward, many methodologies have been proposed to find dense correspondences between dense 3D shapes, including optical flow (Blanz & Vetter, 2003, 1999) and application of TPS to the 2D unfolding of the 3D faces (Cosker, Krumhuber, & Hilton, 2011).

2. Incorporating additional parameters, such as illumination direction, camera parameters etc, increases the dimensionality of the problem. This is turn makes the optimization problem more prone to get stuck to undesirable local optima.

3. The 3D motion model of 3DMM does not adhere an effective inverse compositional framework (Matthews, Xiao, & Baker, 2007). Hence, in general, the optimization procedure is based on additive rules, that do not allow for real or near-real time implementations. Even the recent inverse compositional approximations for 3DMM fitting (Romdhani & Vetter, 2003; Romdhani, Blanz, & Vetter, 2002) are quite computational expensive.

RECENT FACE ALIGNMENT AND FACE RECOGNITION

Lately, there exist two main trends regarding fully automatic face recognition. The first one involves incorporating parametric motion models into decomposition/component analysis techniques and performing joint alignment and decomposition. Prominent examples include (Deng, Hu, Lu, & Guo, 2013) and (Wagner, Wright, Ganesh, Zhou, & Ma, 2009; Huang, Huang, & Metaxas, 2008; Wagner, Wright, Ganesh, Zhou, Mobahi, & Ma, 2012). In Wagner, Wright, Ganesh, Zhou, Mobahi, and Ma (2012) parametric face registration was solved using a series of linear programs that iteratively minimize the sparsity of the registration error. This lead to an efficient and effective alignment algorithm for face images that works for a large range of variation in translation, rotation, and scale, even when the face is only partially visible due to eyeglasses, closed eyes and open mouth, sensor saturation, etc. However, the drawback of this line of research is that it requires many images per person to exist in the database. For example in the challenging one-sample face recognition experiments of FERET DUP II the authors reported results around 20% face recognition (Wagner, Wright, Ganesh, Zhou, Mobahi, & Ma, 2012). Towards a similar direction, the very recent methodology (Deng, Hu, Lu, & Guo, 2013) proposes a method for the simultaneous image alignment and extraction of principal components. A parametric affine motion model is incorporated and an alternating optimization approach is applied, by first applying a Lukas-Kanade alignment using linear variations (i.e., the components) to the images and then PCA to the aligned images.

The second line of research applies recent state-of-the-art facial landmark localization algorithms (Chen, Cao, Wen, & Sun, 2013; Asthana, Marks, Jones, Tieu, & Rohith, 2011) and subsequently either performs 3D face alignment followed by face recognition (Asthana, Marks, Jones, Tieu, & Rohith, 2011), or extracts many different features in many different resolutions around the facial landmarks, and then performs dimensionality reduction followed by recognition (Chen, Cao, Wen, & Sun, 2013). An excellent representative of this line of research is the recently proposed methodology in (Chen, Cao, Wen, & Sun, 2013). In this paper, the authors exploit the excellent landmark localization accuracy of their methodology proposed in (Cao, Wei, Wen, & Sun, 2012). Then, at each of the landmarks and for several scales they extract dense features (the final concatenated feature vector can be as big as a 100K dimensional vector). A sparse regression approach is also proposed to perform dimensionality reduction. Superior performance is reported in the LFW under the unrestricted protocol (known identity information).

FACE RECOGNITION IN UNCONSTRAINED CONDITIONS

In this Section we will review the publicly available databases that can be used to assess the performance of face recognition algorithms in real-world settings. Even though some have been collected in controlled conditions, they can still be used to evaluate the performance of certain real-world unconstrained settings. For example, the standard databases used to test algorithms under different illuminations include the extended YALE (Georghiades, Belhumeur, & Kriegman, 2001; Lee, Ho, & Kriegman, 2005) and the combined pose, illumination and extreme expression Multi-PIE (Gross, Matthews, Cohn, Kanade, & Baker, 2010). Furthermore, the AR (Martinez, 1998) database is the standard test-bed for testing algorithms when partial occlusion is present. Recently, it was shown that image gradient orientations are particularly robust to face recognition under occlusion reporting results as high as 95% for a challenging one-sample training scenario (i.e., training with one un-occluded facial sample and testing in all occluded samples) (Tzimiropoulos, Zafeiriou, & Pantic, 2012).

In the following, we will review the databases that can be used for face recognition under: (1) age variations; (2) pose and illumination variations; and (3) cosmetic surgery. Furthermore, we will review the databases collected for particular real-world unconstrained face recognition scenarios such as: (1) face recognition using mobile devices; (2) face recognition using surveillance cameras; and (3) face recognition from images collected from the Web (also referred to as 'in-the-wild'). For a survey of face databases before 2005 the interested ready may refer to (Gross, 2005). Table 1 summarizes the described databases.

FACE RECOGNITION UNDER AGE VARIATIONS

Lately, age invariant face recognition has attracted the scientific community's attention (Park, Tong, & Jain, 2010; Li, Park, & Jain, 2011). Even though some of the first collected databases, such as FERET (Phillips, Wechsler, Huang, & Rauss, 1998; Phillips, Moon, Rizvi, & Rauss, 2000) include some mild aging (i.e., images captured after one or two years), the only publicly avail-

Table 1. Publicly available databases that cover some of the challenges that systems, dealing with unconstrained recognition scenario, face

Condition	Reference	Reference	Subjects
Age	FGNET MORPH	(Lanitis, Taylor & Cootes, 2002) (Ricanek & Tesafaye, 2006)	82 4,664
Pose	PIE MULTI-PIE	(Sim, Baker & Bsat, 2003) (Gross, Matthews, Cohn, Kanade, & Baker, 2010)	68 337
Illuminations	YALE YALE B MULTI-PIE	(Georghiades, Belhumeur, & Kriegman, 2001) (Georghiades, Belhumeur, & Kriegman, 2001) (Gross, Matthews, Cohn, Kanade, & Baker, 2010)	15 28 337
Cosmetic Surgery	Plastic Surgery	(Singh, Vatsa, Bhatt, Bharadwaj, Noore & Nooreyezdan, 2010, Bhatt, Bharadwaj, Singh & Vatsa, 2013)	900
Mobile	MOBIO	(McCool, Marcel, Hadid, Pietikäinen, Matějka, Černocký, Poh, Kittler, Larcher, Lévy, Matrouf, Bonastre, Tresadern & Cootes, 2012)	152
Surveillance	SCface FOCS MBGC	(Grgic, Delac & Grgic, 2011) (O'Toole, Harms, Snow, Hurst, Pappas, Ayyad & Abdi, 2005) (Phillips, Flynn, Beveridge, Scruggs, O'Toole, Bolme, et.al, 2009)	130 295 146
Face Recognition from Web collected images (in the wild)	LFW Youtube PubFig	(Huang, Mattar, Berg & Learned-Miller, 2008) (Wolf, Hassner & Maoz, 2011) (Kumar, Berg, Belhumeur & Nayar, 2009)	10 1,595 5,749

able databases for age invariant face recognition with a large aging interval between images, are FG-NET (Lanitis, Taylor, & Cootes, 2002) and MORPH (Ricanek & Tesafaye, 2006).

The FG-NET database contains 1,002 face images of 82 subjects (12 images/subject) at different ages, with the minimum and maximum age being 0 (<12 months) and 69 years, respectively. The MORPH database contains two albums, namely: Album1 and Album2. MORPH Album1 contains 1,690 images from 625 different subjects (2-7 images/subject), while MORPH-Album 2 contains 15,204 images from 4,039 different subjects (3-8 images/subject). There are no standardized protocols accompanying the databases (Lanitis, Taylor, & Cootes 2002; Ricanek & Tesafaye, 2006). The best results reported so far are around 48% and 84% recognition rate in FG-NET and MORPH, respectively.

POSE INVARIANT FACE RECOGNITION

One of the first databases collected to test face recognition algorithms under different poses was the so-called UMIST database(Graham & Allinson, 1998). The standard set of databases used for pose invariant face recognition include PIE (Sim, Baker, & Bsat, 2003), FERET (Phillips, Wechsler, Huang, & Rauss, 1998; Phillips, Moon, Rizvi, & Rauss, 2000) and the recently introduced Multi-PIE (Gross, Matthews, Cohn, Kanade, & Baker, 2010).

In more detail, the most recent CMU PIE database consists of 41,368 face images of 68 subjects. The face images were captured by 13 synchronized cameras and 21 flashes, under varying pose, illumination, and expression. Its extension, the CMU Multi-PIE face database contains more than 750,000 images of 337 people recorded in up to four sessions over the span of five months. Subjects were imaged under 15 view points and 19 illumination conditions while displaying a range of facial expressions. In addition, high resolution frontal images were acquired as well.

One of the first techniques to show that pose invariant face recognition is feasible was the 3DMM (Blanz & Vetter, 2003). Since, then other techniques have been proposed, some inspired from matching algorithms in stereo (Castillo & Jacobs, 2009) and others using a Markov Random Field (MRF) approach to match images across pose (Ho & Chellappa, 2013). Recently, dense image descriptors around landmarks have been used for this task (Chen, Cao, Wen, & Sun, 2013). The most promising approach appears to be the application of a 3DMM model, but since fitting an 3DMM (Blanz & Vetter, 2003) is a quite computationally expensive procedure new methodologies following the paradigm of (Chen, Cao, Wen, & Sun, 2013) need to be proposed.

FACE RECOGNITION UNDER ILLUMINATION CHANGES

The most widely used databases for testing face recognition algorithms under illumination changes are the YALE and the Extended YALE B (Georghiades, Belhumeur, & Kriegman, 2001; Lee, Ho, & Kriegman, 2005) The MULTI-PIE dataset (Gross, Matthews, Cohn, Kanade, & Baker, 2010) can also be used for this task.

More precisely, the Yale face database contains 165 gray-scale images of 15 individuals. There are 11 images per subject, one per different facial expression or configuration: center-light, w/ glasses, happy, left-light, w/no glasses, normal, right-light, sad, sleepy, surprised, and wink. The extended Yale B database contains 16128 images of 28 subjects under 9 poses and 64 illumination conditions.

A wealth of research has been proposed regarding illumination invariant face recognition mainly concerning either normalization of image intensities (Shashua & Riklin-Raviv, 2001) or extraction of features that are robust again illumination changes (Tzimiropoulos, Zafeiriou, & Pantic, 2012; Zhang, Tang, Fang, Shang, & Liu, 2009, Chan, Tahir, Kittler, & Pietikäinen, 2013) (a recent survey can be found in (Zou, Kittler, & Messer, 2007).

FACE RECOGNITION IN COSMETIC SURGERY

In (Singh, Vatsa, Bhatt, Bharadwaj, Noore, & Nooreyezdan, 2010; Bhatt, Bharadwaj, Singh, & Vatsa, 2013) the first database consisting of facial samples before and after plastic surgery was proposed. The authors downloaded real world pre and post surgery images mainly from some plastic surgery Websites. These Websites contain images of faces as well as non-faces plastic surgery procedures. From these images, the authors manually filtered non-face images along with occluded or partial face images. In total, the plastic surgery database consists of 1800 full frontal face images pertaining to 900 subjects. The database contains a wide variety of cases such as Rhinoplasty (nose surgery), Blepharoplasty (eyelid surgery), brow lift, skin peeling, and Rhytidectomy (face lift). The database contains 519 image pairs corresponding to local surgeries and 381 cases of global surgery (e.g., skin peeling and face lift).

FACE RECOGNITION IN MOBILE DEVICES

To the best of our knowledge the only database containing samples from mobile devices in MO-BIO database. MOBIO database (McCool, Marcel, Hadid, Pietikäinen, Matějka, Černocký, Poh, Kittler, Larcher, Lévy, Matrouf, Bonastre, Tresadern, & Cootes, 2012) was captured using two mobile devices: one being a Nokia N93i mobile phone and the other being a standard 2008 MacBook laptop. The first session was a joint session with two separate recordings, one on the laptop computer and a second recording on the mobile phone captured on the same day at approximately the same time. Capturing the database on a mobile phone meant that the database acquisition was inherently uncontrolled as the mobile phone was given to the user. This means that the recording device was no longer in a fixed position.

The MOBIO database consists of bi-modal (audio and video) data taken from 152 people. The database has a female-male ratio or nearly 1:2 (100 males and 52 females) and was collected from August 2008 until July 2010 in six different sites from five different countries. This led to a diverse bi-modal database with both native and non-native English speakers. In total 12 sessions were captured for each client: 6 sessions for Phase I and 6 sessions for Phase II. The Phase I data consists of 21 questions with the question types ranging from: Short Response Questions, Short Response Free Speech, Set Speech, and Free Speech. The Phase II data consists of 11 questions with the question types ranging from: Short Response Questions, Set Speech, and Free Speech

Recently a face recognition competition was run in MOBIO exploring the case of only manually aligned images (Günther, Costa-Pazo, Ding, Boutellaa, Chiachia, Zhang et. al., 2013). Fully automatic face recognition in MOBIO is left for a future study.

FACE RECOGNITION FOR SURVEILLANCE

The main datasets collected for face recognition in a surveillance setting is (Grgic, Delac, & Grgic, 2011), the Video Challenge Problem of the Mul-

tiple Biometric Grand Challenge Database (Phillips, Flynn, Beveridge, Scruggs, O'Toole, Bolme et. al., 2009) and the Face and Ocular Challenge Series (FOCS) (O'Toole, Harms, Snow, Hurst, Pappas, Ayyad, & Abdi, 2005).

In (Grgic, Delac, & Grgic, 2011) the SCface database of static images of human faces has been presented. Images were taken in uncontrolled indoor environment using five video surveillance cameras of various qualities. The database contains 4,160 static images (in visible and infrared spectrum) of 130 subjects. Images from different quality cameras mimic real-world conditions and enable robust face recognition algorithms testing, emphasizing different law enforcement and surveillance use case scenarios.

The Multiple Biometric Grand Challenge (MBGC) problems consist of data collected for three challenge problems: the Video Challenge Problem (surveillance scenario), the Portal Challenge Problem and the Still Face Challenge Problem. The data for the Video Challenge Problem were collected with HD and Standard Definition (SD) video cameras. The data were collected in hallways, atria, and outdoors with unconstrained pose and illumination. In the Video Challenge Problem version 1, the data consisted of: 1) two types of video sequences: walking and activity. In the walking sequences, the subjects walked towards the camera. In the activity sequences, the subjects performed an action that required subjects to look away from the camera. An example action is picking up or looking at a book. 2) two types of video sequences: walking and conversation. In the walking sequences the subjects walked towards the camera. In the conversation sequences, a camera is looking down on a conversation between two subjects. One subject's back is to the camera and this subject is to be ignored in the experiments. The MBGC Video version 1 dataset contains 399 walking (frontal-face) and 371 activity (profile-face) video sequences recorded of 146 subjects. Both types of sequences were collected in standard definition (SD) format (720x480 pixels) and high definition (HD) format (1440x1080 pixels). The 399 walking sequences consist of 201 sequences in SD and 198 in HD. For the 371 walking video sequences, 185 are in SD and 186 are in HD. There exist several challenging conditions in these videos, including frontal and profile faces in shadow, and profile faces sometimes being heavily covered by one's hair.

The video challenge of Face and Ocular Challenge Series (FOCS) (O'Toole, Harms, Snow, Hurst, Pappas, Ayyad, & Abdi, 2005) was designed to match frontal v.s. frontal, frontal v.s. non-frontal, and non-frontal v.s. non-frontal video sequences. The FOCS UT Dallas dataset used in the challenge contains 510 walking (frontal face) and 506 activity (non-frontal face) video sequences recorded from 295 subjects with frame size 720x480 pixels. The sequences were acquired on different days. In the walking sequences, the subject is originally positioned far away from the video camera, walks towards it with a frontal pose, and finally turns away from the video camera showing the profile face. The subject stands and talks with another person with a non-frontal face view to the video camera. The sequences contain normal head motions that occur during a conversation; e.g., the head turning up to 90 degrees, hand raising and/ or pointing somewhere.

Face images captured by surveillance cameras usually have poor resolution in addition to uncontrolled poses and illumination conditions, all of which adversely affect the performance of face matching algorithms. Recent works such as (Biswas, Aggarwal, Flynn, & Bowyer, 2013) and (Biswas, Bowyer, & Flynn, 2012) tackle the problem of fully automatic matching of surveillance quality facial images to high-resolution images in frontal pose, which are often available during enrolment.

FACE RECOGNITION IN THE WILD

Labeled Faces in the Wild (Mattar, Berg, & Learned-Miller, 2008), is a database of face photographs designed for studying the problem of unconstrained face recognition. The data set contains more than 13,000 images of faces collected from the Web. Each face has been labelled with the name of the person pictured. 1680 of the people pictured have two or more distinct photos in the data set. The only constraint on these faces is that they were detected by the Viola-Jones face detector.

The YouTube Faces Database (Wolf, Hassner, & Maoz, 2011) is a database of face videos designed for studying the problem of unconstrained face recognition in videos.

The data set contains 3,425 videos of 1,595 different people. All the videos were downloaded from YouTube. An average of 2.15 videos are available for each subject. The shortest clip duration is 48 frames, the longest clip is 6,070 frames, and the average length of a video clip is 181.3 frames.

In (Kumar, Berg, Belhumeur, & Nayar, 2009) criticised LFW database due to the fact it contains strong contextual cues (i.e., the background can be effectively used to measure the similarity between images) and a new database, so-called PubFig, which does not suffer from this problem was introduced. PubFig data consists of 60,000 images of 200 people. The larger number of images per person (as compared to LFW) allows the construction of subsets of data across different poses, lighting conditions, and expressions, while still maintaining a sufficiently large number of images within each set. Images in the data set were downloaded from the Internet using the person's name as the search query on a variety of image search engines, such as Google Images and flickr. This data set is well-suited for recognition experiments.

CONCLUSION AND DISCUSSION

For the past 20 years, the dominant paradigm of face recognition consisted of classical holistic subspace-based methods. Even though it was recently shown that, given a precise face alignment, robust subspace methods that exhibit an excellent performance in real-world settings (including recordings under various illuminations and partial occlusions) do exist, the problem of fully automatic face recognition still remains open. Even though recently, methods that combine subspace estimation and image alignment to tackle the problem of fully automatic face recognition were proposed, face recognition in totally unconstrained conditions (including not only illumination changes and partial occlusions, but also changes due to pose, aging and even cosmetic surgery) imposes extra challenges which are far from being addressed by the current technology (even though considerable steps have been made the past 10 years). One way to address these challenges is to develop huge annotated databases and learn from them. For example in (Taigman & Wolf, 2011) the authors showed very good performance by leveraging billions of facial images of over 100,000,000 individuals. Unfortunately, such databases are not publicly available. Even if they were, it is very difficult to be used by researchers in academia without access to very powerful serves. Very recently in (Chen, Cao, Wen, & Sun, 2013) it was shown that similar to (Taigman & Wolf, 2011) performance can be achieved without the need to learn from this volume of data, but by exploiting high dimensional features and formulating proper learning algorithms.

REFERENCES

Ahonen, T., Hadid, A., & Pietikäinen, M. (2004). Face recognition with local binary patterns. In *Proceedings of Computer Vision-ECCV* (pp. 469–481). ECCV.

Albiol, A., Monzo, D., Martin, A., Sastre, J., & Albiol, A. (2008). Face recognition using HOG–EBGM. *Pattern Recognition Letters*, *29*(10), 1537–1543. doi:10.1016/j.patrec.2008.03.017

Amberg, B. (2011). *Editing Faces in Videos*. (PhD Thesis).

Amberg, B., Blake, A., & Vetter, T. (2009). On compositional image alignment, with an application to active appearance models. In *Proceedings of IEEE Conference on Computer Vision and Pattern Recognition* (CVPR). IEEE.

Asthana, A., Marks, T. K., Jones, M. J., Tieu, K. H., & Rohith, M. (2011). Fully automatic pose-invariant face recognition via 3D pose normalization. In *Proceedings of IEEE International Conference on Computer Vision* (ICCV), (pp. 937-944). IEEE.

Asthana, A., Zafeiriou, S., Cheng, S., & Pantic, M. (2013). Robust discriminative response map fitting with constrained local models. In *Proceedings of IEEE Conference on Computer Vision and Pattern Recognition* (CVPR), (pp. 3444-3451). IEEE.

Bartlett, M. S., Movellan, J. R., & Sejnowski, T. J. (2002). Face recognition by independent component analysis. *IEEE Transactions on Neural Networks*, *13*(6), 1450–1464. doi:10.1109/TNN.2002.804287 PMID:18244540

Belhumeur, P. N., Hespanha, J. P., & Kriegman, D. J. (1997). Eigenfaces vs. fisherfaces: Recognition using class specific linear projection. *IEEE Transactions on Pattern Analysis and Machine Intelligence*, *19*(7), 711–720. doi:10.1109/34.598228

Bhatt, H. S., Bharadwaj, S., Singh, R., & Vatsa, M. (2013). Recognizing Surgically Altered Face Images using Multi-objective Evolutionary Algorithm. *IEEE Transactions on Information Forensics and Security*, *8*(1), 89–100. doi:10.1109/TIFS.2012.2223684

Biswas, S., Aggarwal, G., Flynn, P. J., & Bowyer, K. W. (2013). Pose-Robust Recognition of Low-Resolution Face Images. *IEEE Transactions on Pattern Analysis and Machine Intelligence*. doi:10.1109/TPAMI.2013.68

Biswas, S., Bowyer, K. W., & Flynn, P. J. (2012). Multidimensional scaling for matching low-resolution face images. *IEEE Transactions on Pattern Analysis and Machine Intelligence, 34*(10), 2019–2030. doi:10.1109/TPAMI.2011.278 PMID:22201067

Blanz, V., & Vetter, T. (1999). A morphable model for the synthesis of 3D faces. In *Proceedings of the 26th annual conference on Computer graphics and interactive techniques*. ACM Press/Addison-Wesley Publishing Co.

Blanz, V., & Vetter, T. (2003). Face recognition based on fitting a 3D morphable model. *IEEE Transactions on Pattern Analysis and Machine Intelligence, 25*(9), 1063–1074. doi:10.1109/TPAMI.2003.1227983

Bledsoe, W. W. (1964). The model method in facial recognition (Tech. rep. PRI:15). Palo Alto, CA: Panoramic research Inc.

Bruce, V., & Young, A. (1986). Understanding face recognition. *The British Journal of Psychology, 77*(3), 305–327. doi:10.1111/j.2044-8295.1986.tb02199.x PMID:3756376

Bruner, I. S., & Tagiuri, R. (1954). The perception of people. In *Handbook of Social Psychology* (Vol. 2, pp. 634–654). Reading, MA: Addison-Wesley.

Cao, X., Wei, Y., Wen, F., & Sun, J. (2012). Face alignment by explicit shape regression. In *Proceedings of IEEE Conference on Computer Vision and Pattern Recognition* (CVPR), (pp. 2887-2894). IEEE.

Castillo, C. D., & Jacobs, D. (2009). Using Stereo Matching with General Epipolar Geometry for 2-D Face Recognition Across Pose. *IEEE Transactions on Pattern Analysis and Machine Intelligence, 31*(12), 2298–2304. doi:10.1109/TPAMI.2009.123 PMID:19834149

Chan, C. H., Tahir, M., Kittler, J., & Pietikäinen, M. (2013). Multiscale local phase quantisation for robust component-based face recognition using kernel fusion of multiple descriptors. *IEEE Transactions on Pattern Analysis and Machine Intelligence, 35*(5), 1164–1177. doi:10.1109/TPAMI.2012.199 PMID:23520257

Chellappa, R., Charles, L. W., & Saad, S. (1995). Human and machine recognition of faces: A survey. *Proceedings of the IEEE, 83*(5), 705–741. doi:10.1109/5.381842

Chen, D., Cao, X., Wen, F., & Sun, J. (2013). Blessing of Dimensionality: High-dimensional Feature and Its Efficient Compression for Face Verification. *In Proceedings of IEEE Conference on Computer Vision and Pattern Recognition (CVPR)*. IEEE.

Cootes, T. F., Edwards, G. J., & Taylor, C. J. (2001). Active appearance models. *IEEE Transactions on Pattern Analysis and Machine Intelligence, 23*(6), 681–685. doi:10.1109/34.927467

Cosker, D., Krumhuber, E., & Hilton, A. (2011). A FACS valid 3D dynamic action unit database with applications to 3D dynamic morphable facial modelling. *In Proceedings of International Conference on Computer Vision (ICCV)*. ICCV.

Dalal, N., & Triggs, B. (2005). Histograms of oriented gradients for human detection. In *Proceedings of IEEE Conference on Computer Vision and Pattern Recognition* (CVPR), (pp. 886-893). IEEE.

De La Torre, F., & Black, M. J. (2003). A framework for robust subspace learning. *International Journal of Computer Vision, 54*(1-3), 117–142. doi:10.1023/A:1023709501986

Deng, W., Hu, J., Lu, J., & Guo, J. (2013). Transform-Invariant PCA: A Unified Approach to Fully Automatic Face Alignment, Representation, and Recognition. *IEEE Transactions on Pattern Analysis and Machine Intelligence.* doi:10.1109/TPAMI.2013.194 PMID:24101334

Duc, B., Fischer, S., & Bigun, J. (1999). Face authentication with Gabor information on deformable graphs. *IEEE Transactions on Image Processing, 8*(4), 504–516. doi:10.1109/83.753738 PMID:18262894

Edwards, G. J., Cootes, T. F., & Taylor, C. J. (1998). Face recognition using active appearance models. In *Proceedings of Computer Vision (ECCV)*. Springer.

Felzenszwalb, P. F., & Huttenlocher, D. P. (2005). Pictorial structures for object recognition. *International Journal of Computer Vision, 61*(1), 55–79. doi:10.1023/B:VISI.0000042934.15159.49

Fischler, M. A., & Elschlager, R. A. (1973). The representation and matching of pictorial structures. *IEEE Transactions on Computers, 100*(1), 67–92. doi:10.1109/T-C.1973.223602

Georghiades, A. S., Belhumeur, P. N., & Kriegman, D. J. (2001). From few to many: Illumination cone models for face recognition under variable lighting and pose. *IEEE Transactions on Pattern Analysis and Machine Intelligence, 23*(6), 643–660. doi:10.1109/34.927464

Graham, D. B., & Allinson, N. M. (1998). Characterizing virtual eigensignatures for general purpose face recognition. *Face Recognition: From Theory to Applications, 163*, 446–456. doi:10.1007/978-3-642-72201-1_25

Grgic, M., Delac, K., & Grgic, S. (2011). SCface–surveillance cameras face database. *Multimedia Tools and Applications, 51*(3), 863–879. doi:10.1007/s11042-009-0417-2

Gross, R. (2005). Face databases. In *Handbook of Face Recognition* (pp. 301–327). Academic Press. doi:10.1007/0-387-27257-7_14

Gross, R., Matthews, I., & Baker, S. (2005). Generic vs. person specific active appearance models. *Image and Vision Computing.* doi:10.1016/j.imavis.2005.07.009

Gross, R., Matthews, I., Cohn, J., Kanade, T., & Baker, S. (2010). Multi-pie. *Image and Vision Computing, 28*(5), 807–813. doi:10.1016/j.imavis.2009.08.002

Günther, M., Costa-Pazo, A., Ding, C., Boutellaa, E., Chiachia, G., Zhang, H., et al. (2013). The 2013 Face Recognition Evaluation in Mobile Environment. In *Proceedings of 6th IAPR International Conference on Biometrics*. IAPR.

Guo, G. D., & Dyer, C. R. (2005). Learning from examples in the small sample case: Face expression recognition. *IEEE Transactions on Systems, Man, and Cybernetics. Part B, Cybernetics, 35*(3), 479–488. doi:10.1109/TSMCB.2005.846658

He, X., Yan, S., Hu, Y., Niyogi, P., & Zhang, H. J. (2005). Face recognition using laplacianfaces. *IEEE Transactions on Pattern Analysis and Machine Intelligence, 27*(3), 328–340. doi:10.1109/TPAMI.2005.55 PMID:15747789

Ho, H. T., & Chellappa, R. (2013). Pose-Invariant Face Recognition Using Markov Random Fields. *IEEE Transactions on Image Processing, 22*, 1573–1584. doi:10.1109/TIP.2012.2233489 PMID:23247858

Huang, G. B., Mattar, M., Berg, T., & Learned-Miller, E. (2008). Labeled faces in the wild: A database for studying face recognition in unconstrained environments. In *Proceedings of Workshop on Faces in 'Real-Life 'Images: Detection, Alignment, and Recognition*. Academic Press.

Huang, J., Huang, X., & Metaxas, D. (2008). Simultaneous image transformation and sparse representation recovery. In *Proceedings of IEEE Conference on Computer Vision and Pattern Recognition*. IEEE.

Kanade, T. (1973). *Computer recognition of human faces*. Basel, Switzerland: Birkhauser.

Kelly, M. D. (1970). *Visual identification of people by computer* (Tech. rep. AI-130). Stanford AI Project.

Kirby, M., & Sirovich, L. (1990). Application of the Karhunen-Loeve procedure for the characterization of human faces. *IEEE Transactions on Pattern Analysis and Machine Intelligence, 12*(1), 103–108. doi:10.1109/34.41390

Kliper-Gross, O., Hassner, T., & Wolf, L. (2012). The action similarity labeling challenge. *IEEE Transactions on Pattern Analysis and Machine Intelligence, 34*(3), 615–621. doi:10.1109/TPAMI.2011.209 PMID:22262724

Kotropoulos, C., Tefas, A., & Pitas, I. (2000). Frontal face authentication using morphological elastic graph matching. *IEEE Transactions on Image Processing, 9*(4), 555–560. doi:10.1109/83.841933 PMID:18255429

Kotropoulos, C., Tefas, A., & Pitas, I. (2000). Morphological elastic graph matching applied to frontal face authentication under well-controlled and real conditions. *Pattern Recognition, 33*(12), 31–43. doi:10.1016/S0031-3203(99)00185-5

Krüger, N. (1997). An algorithm for the learning of weights in discrimination functions using A priori constraints. *IEEE Transactions on Pattern Analysis and Machine Intelligence, 19*(7), 764–768. doi:10.1109/34.598233

Kumar, N., Berg, A. C., Belhumeur, P. N., & Nayar, S. K. (2009). *Attribute and simile classifiers for face verification*. Computer Vision. doi:10.1109/ICCV.2009.5459250

Lades, M., Vorbruggen, J. C., Buhmann, J., Lange, J., Von der Malsburg, C., Wurtz, R. P., & Konen, W. (1993). Distortion invariant object recognition in the dynamic link architecture. *IEEE Transactions on Computers, 42*(3), 300–311. doi:10.1109/12.210173

Lanitis, A., Taylor, C. J., & Cootes, T. F. (2002). Toward automatic simulation of aging effects on face images. *IEEE Transactions on Pattern Analysis and Machine Intelligence, 24*(4), 442–455. doi:10.1109/34.993553

Lee, K. C., Ho, J., & Kriegman, D. J. (2005). Acquiring linear subspaces for face recognition under variable lighting. *IEEE Transactions on Pattern Analysis and Machine Intelligence, 27*(5), 684–698. doi:10.1109/TPAMI.2005.92 PMID:15875791

Li, F., & Wechsler, H. (2005). Open set face recognition using transduction. *IEEE Transactions on Pattern Analysis and Machine Intelligence, 27*(11), 1686–1697. doi:10.1109/TPAMI.2005.224 PMID:16285369

Li, Z., Park, U., & Jain, A. K. (2011). A discriminative model for age invariant face recognition. *IEEE Transactions on Information Forensics and Security, 6*(3), 1028–1037. doi:10.1109/TIFS.2011.2156787

Lowe, D. G. (2004). Distinctive image features from scale-invariant keypoints. *International Journal of Computer Vision, 60*(2), 91–110. doi:10.1023/B:VISI.0000029664.99615.94

Lyons, M. J., Budynek, J., & Akamatsu, S. (1999). Automatic classification of single facial images. *IEEE Transactions on Pattern Analysis and Machine Intelligence*, *21*(12), 1357–1362. doi:10.1109/34.817413

Lyons, M. J., Budynek, J., Plante, A., & Akamatsu, S. (2000). Classifying facial attributes using a 2-d gabor wavelet representation and discriminant analysis. In *Proceedings of International Conference on Automatic Face and Gesture Recognition*, (pp. 202–207). Academic Press.

Martinez, A. M. (1998). *The AR face database*. CVC Technical Report, 24.

Matthews, I., & Baker, S. (2004). Active appearance models revisited. *International Journal of Computer Vision*, *60*(2), 135–164. doi:10.1023/B:VISI.0000029666.37597.d3

Matthews, I., Xiao, J., & Baker, S. (2007). 2d vs. 3d deformable face models: Representational power, construction, and real-time fitting. *International Journal of Computer Vision*, *75*(1), 93–113. doi:10.1007/s11263-007-0043-2

McCool, C., Marcel, S., Hadid, A., Pietikäinen, M., Matějka, P., Černocký, J., et al. (2012). Bi-Modal Person Recognition on a Mobile Phone: using mobile phone data. In *Proceedings of IEEE ICME Workshop on Hot Topics in Mobile Mutlimedia*. IEEE.

Messer, K., Matas, J., Kittler, J., Luettin, J., & Maitre, G. (1999). XM2VTSDB: The extended M2VTS database. In *Proceedings of Second international conference on audio and video-based biometric person authentication*, (pp. 964-966). Academic Press.

O'Toole, A. J., Harms, J., Snow, S. L., Hurst, D. R., Pappas, M. R., Ayyad, J. H., & Abdi, H. (2005). Recognizing people from dynamic and static faces and bodies: Dissecting identity with a fusion approach. *Vision Research*, *51*(1), 74–83. doi:10.1016/j.visres.2010.09.035 PMID:20969886

Papandreou, G., & Maragos, P. (2008). Adaptive and constrained algorithms for inverse compositional active appearance model fitting. In *Proceedings of IEEE Conference on Computer Vision and Pattern Recognition* (CVPR). IEEE.

Park, U., & Tong, Y., & Jain, Anil K. (2010). Age-invariant face recognition. *IEEE Transactions on Pattern Analysis and Machine Intelligence*, *32*(5), 947–954. doi:10.1109/TPAMI.2010.14 PMID:20299717

Phillips, P. J., Flynn, P. J., Beveridge, J. R., Scruggs, W. T., O'Toole, A. J., & Bolme, D. et al. (2009). Overview of the multiple biometrics grand challenge. In *Proceedings of Advances in Biometrics* (pp. 705–714). Academic Press. doi:10.1007/978-3-642-01793-3_72

Phillips, P. J., Moon, H., Rizvi, S. A., & Rauss, P. J. (2000). The FERET evaluation methodology for face-recognition algorithms. *IEEE Transactions on Pattern Analysis and Machine Intelligence*, *22*(10), 1090–1104. doi:10.1109/34.879790

Phillips, P. J., Wechsler, H., Huang, J., & Rauss, P. J. (1998). The FERET database and evaluation procedure for face-recognition algorithms. *Image and Vision Computing*, *16*(5), 295–306. doi:10.1016/S0262-8856(97)00070-X

Pigeon, S., & Vandendorpe, L. (1997). The M2VTS multimodal face database (release 1.00). In *Proceedings of Audio-and Video-Based Biometric Person Authentication*. Springer. doi:10.1007/BFb0016021

Ricanek, K., & Tesafaye, T. (2006). Morph: A longitudinal image database of normal adult age-progression. In Proceedings of Automatic Face and Gesture Recognition, (pp. 341-345). Academic Press.

Romdhani, S. (2005). *Face Image Analysis using a Multiple Feature Fitting Strategy.* (PhD Thesis).

Romdhani, S., Blanz, V., & Vetter, T. (2002). Face identification by fitting a 3D morphable model using linear shape and texture error functions. In *Proceedings of ECCV.* ECCV.

Romdhani, S., & Vetter, T. (2003). Efficient, robust and accurate fitting of a 3D morphable model. In *Proceedings of IEEE International Conference on Computer Vision* (ICCV), (pp. 59-66). IEEE.

Samaria, F. S., & Harter, A. C. (1994). Parameterization of a stochastic model for human face identification. In *Proceedings of the 2nd IEEE workshop on Applications of Computer Vision.* IEEE.

Scheirer, W. J., Boult, T. E., de Rezende Rocha, A., & Sapkota, A. (2013). Toward Open Set Recognition. *IEEE Transactions on Pattern Analysis and Machine Intelligence, 35*(7), 1757–1772. doi:10.1109/TPAMI.2012.256 PMID:23682001

Shakhnarovich, G., & Moghaddam, B. (2011). Face recognition in subspaces. In *Handbook of Face Recognition.* Springer. doi:10.1007/978-0-85729-932-1_2

Shashua, A., & Riklin-Raviv, T. (2001). The quotient image: Class-based re-rendering and recognition with varying illuminations. *IEEE Transactions on Pattern Analysis and Machine Intelligence, 23*(2), 129–139. doi:10.1109/34.908964

Shin, H.-C., Kim, S.-D., & Choi, H.-C. (2007). Generalized elastic graph matching for face recognition. *Pattern Recognition Letters, 28*(9), 1077–1082. doi:10.1016/j.patrec.2007.01.003

Shin, H.-C., Park, J. H., & Kim, S.-D. (2007). Combination of warping robust elastic graph matching and kernel-based projection discriminant analysis for face recognition. *IEEE Transactions on Multimedia, 9*(6), 1125–1136. doi:10.1109/TMM.2007.898933

Sim, T., Baker, S., & Bsat, M. (2003). The CMU pose, illumination, and expression database. *IEEE Transactions on Pattern Analysis and Machine Intelligence, 25*(12), 1615–1618. doi:10.1109/TPAMI.2003.1251154

Singh, R., Vatsa, M., Bhatt, H. S., Bharadwaj, S., Noore, A., & Nooreyezdan, S. S. (2010). Plastic surgery: A new dimension to face recognition. *IEEE Transactions on Information Forensics and Security, 5*(3), 441–448. doi:10.1109/TIFS.2010.2054083

Sinha, P., Balas, B., Ostrovsky, Y., & Russell, R. (2006). Face recognition by humans: Nineteen results all computer vision researchers should know about. *Proceedings of the IEEE, 94*(11), 1948–1962. doi:10.1109/JPROC.2006.884093

Taigman, Y., & Wolf, L. (2011). *Leveraging billions of faces to overcome performance barriers in unconstrained face recognition.* arXiv preprint arXiv:1108.1122.

Tefas, A., Kotropoulos, C., & Pitas, I. (2001). Using support vector machines to enhance the performance of elastic graph matching for frontal face authentication. *IEEE Transactions on Pattern Analysis and Machine Intelligence, 23*(7), 735–746. doi:10.1109/34.935847

Tefas, A., Kotropoulos, C., & Pitas, I. (2002). Face verification using elastic graph matching based on morphological signal decomposition. *Signal Processing, 82*(6), 833–851. doi:10.1016/S0165-1684(02)00157-3

Turk, M., & Pentland, A. (1991). Eigenfaces for recognition. *Journal of Cognitive Neuroscience*, *3*(1), 71–86. doi:10.1162/jocn.1991.3.1.71 PMID:23964806

Tzimiropoulos, G., Alabort-i-Medina, J., Zafeiriou, S., & Pantic, M. (2013). Generic active appearance models revisited. In *Proceedings of Computer Vision–ACCV*. Springer.

Tzimiropoulos, G., Zafeiriou, S., & Pantic, M. (2012). Subspace learning from image gradient orientations. *IEEE Transactions on Pattern Analysis and Machine Intelligence*, *34*(12), 2454–2466. doi:10.1109/TPAMI.2012.40 PMID:22271825

Vasilescu, M. A. O., & Terzopoulos, D. (2002). Multilinear analysis of image ensembles: Tensorfaces. In *Proceedings of Computer Vision*. Springer.

Wagner, A., Wright, J., Ganesh, A., Zhou, Z., & Ma, Y. (2009). Towards a practical face recognition system: Robust registration and illumination by sparse representation. In *Proceedings of IEEE Conference on Computer Vision and Pattern Recognition* (CVPR), (pp. 597-604). IEEE.

Wagner, A., Wright, J., Ganesh, A., Zhou, Z., Mobahi, H., & Ma, Y. (2012). Toward a practical face recognition system: Robust alignment and illumination by sparse representation. *IEEE Transactions on Pattern Analysis and Machine Intelligence*, *34*(2), 372–386. doi:10.1109/TPAMI.2011.112 PMID:21646680

Wiskott, L. (1997). Phantom faces for face analysis. *Pattern Recognition*, *30*(6), 837–846. doi:10.1016/S0031-3203(96)00132-X

Wiskott, L., Fellous, J. M., Kuiger, N., & Von Der Malsburg, C. (1997). Face recognition by elastic bunch graph matching. *IEEE Transactions on Pattern Analysis and Machine Intelligence*, *19*(7), 775–779. doi:10.1109/34.598235

Wolf, L., Hassner, T., & Maoz, I. (2011). Face recognition in unconstrained videos with matched background similarity. In *Proceedings of IEEE Conference on Computer Vision and Pattern Recognition* (CVPR), (pp. 529-534). IEEE.

Wolf, L., Hassner, T., & Taigman, Y. (2011). Effective unconstrained face recognition by combining multiple descriptors and learned background statistics. *IEEE Transactions on Pattern Analysis and Machine Intelligence*, *33*(10), 1978–1990. doi:10.1109/TPAMI.2010.230 PMID:21173442

Wright, J., Yang, A. Y., Ganesh, A., Sastry, S. S., & Ma, Y. (2009). Robust face recognition via sparse representation. *IEEE Transactions on Pattern Analysis and Machine Intelligence*, *31*(2), 210–227. doi:10.1109/TPAMI.2008.79 PMID:19110489

Wurtz, R. P. (1997). Object recognition robust under translations, deformations, and changes in background. *IEEE Transactions on Pattern Analysis and Machine Intelligence*, *19*(7), 769–775. doi:10.1109/34.598234

Xiong, X., & De la Torre, F. (2013). Supervised Descent Method and its Applications to Face Alignment. In *Proceedings of IEEE Conference on Computer Vision and Pattern Recognition* (CVPR). IEEE.

Zafeiriou, S. (2012). Subspace learning in Krein spaces: complete kernel fisher discriminant analysis with indefinite kernels. In *Proceedings of Computer Vision*. Springer. doi:10.1007/978-3-642-33765-9_35

Zafeiriou, S., Tefas, A., Buciu, I., & Pitas, I. (2006). Exploiting discriminant information in nonnegative matrix factorization with application to frontal face verification. *IEEE Transactions on Neural Networks*, *17*(3), 683–695. doi:10.1109/TNN.2006.873291 PMID:16722172

Zafeiriou, S., Tefas, A., & Pitas, I. (2005). Exploiting discriminant information in elastic graph matching. *In Proceedings of IEEE International Conference on Image Processing* (ICIP). IEEE.

Zafeiriou, S., Tefas, A., & Pitas, I. (2007a). The discriminant elastic graph matching algorithm applied to frontal face verification. *Pattern Recognition*, *40*(10), 2798–2810. doi:10.1016/j. patcog.2007.01.026

Zafeiriou, S., Tefas, A., & Pitas, I. (2007b). Learning discriminant person-specific facial models using expandable graphs. *IEEE Transactions on Information Forensics and Security*, *2*(1), 55–68. doi:10.1109/TIFS.2006.890308

Zafeiriou, S., Tzimiropoulos, G., Petrou, M., & Stathaki, T. (2012). Regularized kernel discriminant analysis with a robust kernel for face recognition and verification. *IEEE Transactions on Neural Networks and Learning Systems*, *23*(3), 526–534. doi:10.1109/TNNLS.2011.2182058

Zhang, J., Yan, Y., & Lades, M. (1997). Face recognition: Eigenface, elastic matching, and neural nets. *Proceedings of the IEEE*, *85*(9), 1423–1435. doi:10.1109/5.628712

Zhang, T., Tang, Y. Y., Fang, B., Shang, Z., & Liu, X. (2009). Face recognition under varying illumination using gradientfaces. *IEEE Transactions on Image Processing*, *18*(11), 2599–2606. doi:10.1109/TIP.2009.2028255 PMID:19635700

Zhao, W., Chellappa, R., Phillips, P. J., & Rosenfeld, A. (2003). Face recognition: A literature survey. [CSUR]. *ACM Computing Surveys*, *35*(4), 399–458. doi:10.1145/954339.954342

Zou, X., Kittler, J., & Messer, K. (2007). Illumination invariant face recognition: A survey. In *Proceedings of Biometrics: Theory, Applications, and Systems*. Academic Press.

KEY TERMS AND DEFINITIONS

3DMM: 3D Morphable Model.

Active Appearance Model (AAM): A computer vision algorithm for matching a statistical model of object shape and appearance to a new image.

CFI: Closed-set Face Identification.

DLA: Dynamic Link Architecture.

Elastic Graph Matching (EGM): Elastic Graph Matching is one of the pattern recognition techniques in computer science. It can be defined as an optimization problem of two-dimensional warping specifying corresponding pixels between subjected images.

Face Identity Verification (FIV): Face Identity Verification is the problem of verifying a person's identity claim.

Face Similarity Problem (FSP): Face Similarity Problem is the problem according to which the similarity of two facial images is found (whether they belong to the same person or not).

Histogram of Oriented Gradients (HOG): Histogram of Oriented Gradients are feature descriptors used in computer vision and image processing for the purpose of object detection. The technique counts occurrences of gradient orientation in localized portions of an image.

Local Binary Patterns (LBP): Local Binary Patterns is a very popular texture descriptor that summarizes in a single value the relationship between each pixel and its surroundings, in terms of relative intensity. Histograms of these values are generally built and used as feature descriptors.

Linear Discriminant Analysis (LDA): Linear discriminant analysis is a method used in statistics, pattern recognition and machine learning to find a linear combination of features which characterizes or separates two or more classes of objects or events.

Labeled Faces in-the-Wild (LFW): Labeled Faces 'in-the-Wild' is a database of labeled, face images intended for studying Face Recognition in unconstrained images.

Non-Negative Matrix Factorization (NMF): Non-negative Matrix Factorization is a group of algorithms in multivariate analysis and linear algebra where a matrix V is factorized into (usually) two matrices W and H, with the property that all three matrices have no negative elements.

OFI: Open-set Face Identification.

Principal Component Analysis (PCA): Principal component analysis is a statistical procedure that uses orthogonal transformation to convert a set of observations of possibly correlated variables into a set of values of linearly uncorrelated variables called principal components.

Scale-Invariant Feature Transform (SIFT): Scale-Invariant Feature Transform attempts to find particular regions (keypoints) in the image that are singular in terms of their statistical properties. The related matching strategy tries to find correspondences among keypoints in different images.

Chapter 3
Face Recognition Methods for Uncontrolled Settings

Harry Wechsler
George Mason University, USA

ABSTRACT

The overall coverage of the chapter is about moving face recognition out of the comfort zone and dramatically improving the current performance of existing biometric tools by fusing the rich spatial, temporal, and contextual information available from the multiple views made available by video (rather than still images) in the wild and operational real-world problems. Instead of relying on a "single best frame approach," one must confront uncontrolled settings by exploiting all available imagery to allow the addition of new evidence, graceful degradation, and re-identification. Uncontrolled settings are all-encompassing and include Aging-Pose, Illumination, and Expression (A-PIE), denial and deception characteristic of incomplete and uncertain information, uncooperative users, and unconstrained data collection, scenarios, and sensors. The challenges are many: most important among them lack of persistence for biometric data, adversarial biometrics, open rather than closed set recognition, covariate shift, cross-dataset generalization, alignment and registration, interoperability, scalability, and last but not least, the deployment of full-fledged biometrics that include detection, authentication, informative sampling, and tracking. The overall recommendations are synergetic and should consider for implementation and processing purposes the regularization, statistical learning, and boosting triad complemented by sparsity and grouping (feature sharing) to deal with high-dimensional data and enhanced generalization. The recurring theme is that of a unified framework that involves multi-task and transfer learning using metric learning and side information.

INTRODUCTION

This chapter discusses face recognition methods for the intertwined objectives of interoperability and enhanced generalization for the joint purposes of biometric authentication and identity management applications as encountered during real-world security operations confounded by uncontrolled settings. Current and emerging biometric protocols for both identity management and performance evaluation are critically assessed. Protocols are needed to enforce regulations, track the use and

DOI: 10.4018/978-1-4666-5966-7.ch003

misuse of biometric systems, e.g., functional creep where data collected for one purpose is used for a different one, and safeguard overall security, integrity, and privacy. Performance and validation, which should be metered using uncontrolled-settings and interoperability, determine the robustness and reliability of the authentication decisions made and their side-effects, if any. Robustness is about high sensitivity and high specificity when coping with adversarial information, e.g., biometric variability including but not limited to data capture during image formation, and incomplete ("occlusion") and corrupt ("disguise") biometric footprints. Reliability is about consistency (in the limit) and stability of the predictions made during authentication. Both robustness and reliability are mostly a function of information uncertainty and variability, with learning and adaptation the methods of choice to enhance them. Uncontrolled-settings are characteristics of real life scenarios, which go beyond mass screening to include surveillance using smart camera networks, tagging driven by social networks and/or Internet, and biometric management of crowds. Performance for uncontrolled settings is hard to come by, is usually anecdotal, and is definitely significantly less than the performance advertised for large scale but tightly controlled FRVT biometric evaluations. Furthermore, ground truth is not available, false positives are not disclosed, and false negatives are not available. Policymakers should insist on adequate and enforceable performance metrics that can be independently corroborated and don't casually take "an unbiased look at data sets bias" (Torralba, 2011). Interoperability and validation are further paramount for the effective and ethical use of biometrics.

Biometric identity, for all practical purposes, is about information rather than data. Data are confined to qualitative or quantitative attributes of a variable or set of variables. Data, typically the results of measurements, are often viewed as the lowest level of abstraction from which information

and then knowledge are derived. Raw biometric data, i.e. unprocessed identity data, refers to a mere collection of images. Information, however, stands for data together with their implicit or explicit reference assuming the status of evidence. The etymology and semiotics of the word "information" are clear on this aspect. They involve communication and meaning, and their hallmarks are those of entropy and uncertainty. Last but not least "information" has value and establishes context to inform and instruct, and ultimately to control behavior using meta-planning and meta-recognition. Knowledge is the next stage of abstraction, with information management operating at a higher level of categorization, where generalization and predictions can now be made, e.g., demographics and stratification including gender, race, age, disabilities, mobility, and employment status. Public policy can be ultimately influenced by such demographics and their perceived dynamics. Towards that end, the problem of identification bears not only on criminology but also on civil identification (Gates, 2011).

The Quo Vadis for this chapter is about how to move forward on face recognition under uncontrolled settings. It is about making the case for leveraging similarity, sparsity, and statistical learning for the joint purposes of encoding, interoperability, learning, and ultimate validation. The case is made throughout that multiple-views and multiple cues need to be integrated in order to accrue evidence that overcomes the inherent uncertainty and adversarial conditions encountered during enrollment and querying. The objectives are many and go beyond traditional still-frame authentication. They also include new and all encompassing biometric models for representation, training, and matching; open set recognition; protocols; and re-identification. Three roadmaps cover our discussion: biometrics challenges, current authentication methods built around regularization, and solutions and venues for future research built around multi-task learning.

- **Biometric challenges:**
  - Age-Pose, Illumination, and Expression (A-PIE) and Image Quality
  - Covariance Shift
  - Alignment, Correspondence, and Registration
  - Open Set Authentication and Clustering
  - Interoperability
  - High-Dimensional Data and Scalability
  - Biometric Data Sets, Metrics, and Performance Evaluation
  - Contents-Based Image Retrieval (CBIR) and Photo Tagging
  - Video Processing
  - Face in a Crowd and Re-Identification
  - Identity Management
  - Security and Privacy
- **Regularization:**
  - Face Representation
  - Association and Similarity
  - Compressive Sensing and Sparsity
  - Expectation-Maximization (EM) and Stochastic Relaxation
  - Deep Learning
  - Complexity and Generalization
  - Statistical Learning
  - Competitive Learning and Self-Organization
  - Link Analysis
- **Multi-task learning:**
  - Face Space and Chorus of Prototypes
  - Order and Ranking
  - Local Estimation and Collective Classification
  - Semi-Supervised Learning and Transduction
  - Recognition-by-Parts
  - Data Fusion and Ensemble Methods
  - Active Learning, Sampling, and Tracking

- Domain Knowledge and Learning with Side Information
- Transfer Learning
- Indexing and Local Sensitivity Hash (LSH)
- Change, Drift and Imposter Detection

BACKGROUND

Biometrics is all encompassing with face recognition playing the major role. The reasons are many and go beyond tradition and habitude. The subject usually is mostly passive during data capture, which makes identification relatively simple to handle. There has been, however, much realization that current face recognition methodology is still lacking regarding both scope and reach. The recent call for papers (CFP) for a Special Issue on *Real-World Face Recognition* issued in March 2010 by *IEEE Transactions on Pattern Analysis and Machine Intelligence* (Hua et al., 2011), includes as a matter-of-fact the statement "Face recognition in well-controlled environments is relatively mature and has been heavily studied, but face recognition in uncontrolled or moderately controlled environments is still in its early stages." There is also the covert use of biometrics, e.g., human identification from distance (HID), again a big challenge due to varying multi-view geometry and varying dynamics. Significant efforts have been undertaken over the last several years to alleviate the concerns expressed above and to advance the state-of-the art for biometric authentication.

The face processing space for biometrics purposes can be conceptualized as an n-D space with its axes indexing variability along dimensions that are related to the data acquisition conditions encountered first during enrollment and later on during authentication. The axes describe among others the geometry used during image acquisition, e.g., A-PIE, motion and/or temporal change, and last but not least the impact of un-cooperative subjects, e.g., imposters. Image variability and correspondence using precise alignment required for matching during authentication are still major challenges for still face recognition. Characteristic of un-cooperative subjects are occlusion and disguise or equivalently denial and deception. Disguise can be deliberate and used by imposters for nefarious purposes. Deception is most effective in cluttered environments when it becomes easier to hide, thanks to many distracters. Occlusion and disguise, however, are not always deliberate. Examples for accidental occlusion occur for crowded environments processed by CCTV, when only parts of faces are visible from time to time and not necessarily in the right 3D morphing sequence. Normal phenomena with deceptive impact include bags under the eyes, which affect eye location and thus face detection and normalization, wrinkles from aging, medical conditions (allergies, injuries, and moles), fatigue, and facial hair.

Biometrics cannot continue to assume that the personal signatures used for face authentication are complete, constant, and time-invariant. Most clients are indeed legitimate and honest. They have nothing to hide, and have all the incentives to cooperate. The very purpose of biometrics, however, is to provide security from imposters seeking to breach security and/or from un-cooperative subjects. The challenge for biometrics is therefore to expand the scope and utility of biometric authentication engines by gradually removing unwarranted assumptions on the completeness and quality of the biometric data captured. Note that even during mass screenings enrollment and authentication take place at multiple locations, physically and temporally separated, with different human operators whose performance varies due to training and fatigue. The capture devices used vary too in terms of their working condition. Proper validation of protocols and performance, including the cumulative effect of such varying conditions, is thus hard to estimate and predict.

The scope and reach for biometrics are all encompassing. They consider appearance, behavior, and cognitive state or intent for the purpose of digital identification. Forensics, complementary to biometrics (Dessimoz & Champod, 2008), address data collection and decision-making for legal purposes. Identity management mediates between biometrics and forensics. In particular, identity management stands for the application of management principles to the acquisition, organization, control, dissemination, and strategic use of biometric information for security and privacy purposes. It is responsible with authentication, e.g., (ATM) verification, identification ("recognition"), and large scale screening and surveillance. Information management is also involved with change detection, de-duplication, retention, and/or revision of biometric information as people age and/or experience illness. This informs our discussion on moving biometrics from the current comfort zone where one is confined to still imagery acquired under controlled settings to an expanded framework where incomplete information and uncertainty, characteristic of multiple-view (video) frames and uncontrolled settings, become the norm. Gonzales-Rodriguez et al. (2007) provide strong motivation from forensic sciences for the evidential and discriminative use of the likelihood ratio and this informs our discussion below.

Discriminative methods support practical intelligence, in general, and biometric inference and prediction, in particular. Progressive processing, evidence accumulation, and fast decisions are their hallmarks. There is no time and opportunity for expensive density estimation and marginalization characteristic of generative methods. Such methods link the Bayesian framework, forensics, and likelihood ratios (odds), on one side, and complexity, randomness, and statistical learning, on the other side. Additional philosophical and linguistic arguments that support the discriminative approach have to do with practical reasoning and epistemology, when recalling from Hume, that "all kinds of reasoning consist in nothing but a comparison and a discovery of those relations, either constant or inconstant, which two or more objects bear to each other." This is similar to non-accidental coincidences and sparse but discriminative codes for association" (Barlow, 1989). This illuminates the possibility of framing the problem of representation in terms of similarity (to a chorus of prototypes) and statistical learning for the purpose of robust and reliable non-parametric authentication, e.g., support vectors (SV) [for kernel SVM] that correspond to active constraints that identify the critical training examples needed to maximize the separation margin. Formally, "the goal of pattern classification can be approached from two points of view: informative [generative] - where the classifier learns the class densities or discriminative – where the focus is on learning the class boundaries without regard to the underlying class densities (Rubinstein and Hastie, 1997). Discriminative methods avoid estimating how the data has been generated and instead focus on estimating their posteriors similar to the use of likelihood ratios and odds.

The biometric terminology used throughout is standard (Wechsler, 2007). The tasks are those of face verification (1-1), identification (1-N), and surveillance (N-M with N>>M) using closed and open set matching protocols, and overall multi-layer categorization including face detection, face authentication, and demographics / binning (age, gender, ethnicity). Biometric operation involves training and learning the face space, encoding and enrollment (image quality check and signature / template generation), matching, decision-making and identity management. Training and encoding can use the same methods or not (see also emerging trends). Security, integrity, and privacy for biometric data are expected throughout. Human faces have to be represented before recognition can take place. The role played by representation is most important, and it probably exceeds that played by recognition, known also as classification or identification. Kant described the problem of

how anything in the mind can be a "representation" of anything outside the mind as the most difficult riddle in philosophy. We can recognize transformed and dimensionally-reduced as well as original human faces in their "raw" form. The representations, learned and/or evolved through visual experience, are directly related to the context they operate within and the tasks they have to accomplish. The non-accidental properties of human faces are the particular dimensions the human face representations become tuned for. Such properties eventually induce the features extracted to represent human faces.

The repertoire of features chosen corresponds to coordinate axes and they define the face space. The basic repertoire includes holistic representations, e.g., Principal Component Analysis (PCA), Fisherfaces, and Independent Component Analysis (ICA), local representations, e.g., Gabor wavelets, SIFT and bag-of-features (BOF), SURF, Local Binary Patterns (LBP), HOG, global / holistic GIST descriptors (Oliva & Torralba, 2001), and spatial Gaussian and Laplacian pyramids. The GIST descriptors do not require any form of segmentation and are global in nature. GIST descriptors (Douze et al., 2009), referred to as some spatial envelope to serve as counterpart to earlier geons, are compact summaries suitable for large image collections on tasks related to image search and indexing, finding parts of the relevant image in large data sets, and re-identification, e.g., copy detection and image completion. The perceptual dimensions encoded are those of naturalness, openness, roughness, expansion, and ruggedness. Cox and Pinto (2011) have recently suggested "a large-scale feature search approach to generating new, more powerful feature representations in which a multitude of complex, nonlinear, multilayer neuromorphic feature representations are randomly generated and screened to find those best suited for the task at hand." The representation, biologically inspired by V1 and Neocognitron, was used to advantage on LWF.

There has been renewed interest in the combined use of different recognition cues and their possible use for face recognition, e.g., shape and texture. The human face is characterized by both face contents, e.g., texture, and the overall head configuration (see below) including context (neck and shoulders), landmarks, and face outline. One example for such an encoding and recognition scheme is the enhanced Fisher classifier (EFC), which employs the enhanced Fisher linear discriminant model (EFM) on integrated shape and texture ('shape-free image') features (Liu & Wechsler, 2001). Shape encodes the geometry of a face, while texture provides a normalized shape-free image by warping the original face image to the mean shape, i.e., the average of aligned shapes. The dimensionalities of the shape and the texture spaces are first reduced using PCA. The corresponding but reduced shape and texture features are then integrated through a normalization procedure to form augmented / concatenated features. The dimensionality reduction procedure, constrained by EFM for enhanced generalization, maintains a proper balance between the spectral energy needs of PCA for adequate representation, and the Fisher linear discriminant (FLD) discrimination requirements, which stipulate that the eigenvalues of the within-class scatter matrix should not include small trailing values after the dimensionality reduction procedure as they appear in the FLD denominator. Experiments, using face images subject to varying illumination and/ or expression, show that 1) the integrated shape and texture features carry the most discriminating information followed in order by texture, masked images, and shape images; and 2) the combined encoding and face recognition method, EFC, performs the best among the eigenfaces methods using L_1 and L_2 distances, and the Mahalanobis distance using a common covariance matrix for all classes or a pooled within-class covariance matrix.

One needs to augment the standard face representations in use today. This includes both hybrid encoding schemes and context. Another novel representation expands on the use of appearance and geometry to model the face using the combined face (F), head (H), neck (N), and shoulders (S) structure (Ramanathan & Wechsler, 2010). The proposed representation combines appearance-based recognition (PCA or Fisherfaces) and holistic anthropometric-based recognition, with the latter including linear and non-linear geometrical measurements across the extent of F, H, N, and S. The first processing stage considers feature extraction and selection with PCA and PCA + LDA employing an energy based cut-off criteria to select the eigenfaces basis, while the anthropometric features are chosen using a correlation based feature selection. The extracted geometric features include horizontal and vertical distances, linear and non-linear (curves) measurements, and overall head, face, neck and shoulder measurements. The anthropometric feature set also includes several non-linear measurements, namely, curve (arc) lengths. The linear measurements include inter-eye distance, inter-shoulder distance, mid point of mouth to mid point of nose, etc. The feature set also includes curves related to the eyes, mouth, shoulder, neck, etc. The best appearance-based and anthropometric-based features found are then optimally combined in a second stage using neural networks or boosting, with the distance between chin and neck, length of nose, and length of eyebrow found the best among anthropometric measurements. Experiments for both occluded and disguised images show that the hybrid (appearance-based and holistic anthropometric) boosting method outperforms both (i) stand alone PCA and Fisherfaces; and (ii) PCA or PCA + LDA augmented by only anthropometric face features.

SIMILARITY, SPARSITY, AND STATISTICAL LEARNING

Perception for Helmholtz is merely inference. It is through immersion in our surrounding world and through development that people gradually learn to see and recognize objects, and in particular human faces. Nature alone is not enough and rich nurturing, i.e., learning, is crucial. Learning is mostly about model selection and prediction. Learning denotes adaptive changes to enable some system to do the same tasks drawn from the same population more efficiently the next time. In particular, learning models associations that are then used to infer some output given its inputs, i.e., ID authentication from a given face representation. Face appearance varies while its identity remains constant. Eminent for reliable face recognition is the ability to both specialize and generalize, while maintaining a separation margin that withstands input variability. Towards that end, the "only solution is to incorporate learning capabilities within the vision system." Learning balances between internal representations and external regularities. We note here that the inferences made are merely predictions because learning can only approximate ground truth. Similarity and sparsity are the medium that interfaces between the face representation discussed earlier and statistical learning (theory) methods (Vapnik, 2000). The methods discussed range from semi-supervised learning and transduction to structured methods characteristic of multi-task and transfer learning. The structures alluded to are all encompassing and are modeled using regularization and optimization for trading off approximation (empirical) error (data fitting) with complexity vis-à-vis shared groups and features, for the purpose of sparsity and generalization. The starting point is the (mathematical) regularization framework that leads to statistical learning, support vector machines (SVM), kernels, and link analysis (Laplacian) networks. This is discussed next.

Regularization is critical for successful statistical modeling of "modern" data, which is high-dimensional usually noisy. Regularization — implicitly or explicitly — is the core of most successful learning methods. In particular, (Tikhonov) regularization trades off fitting the data and lowering the solution norm using cross-validation, e.g., grid search. As an example, ridge regression and Lasso use the same square loss function but different norms on the solution sought after, e.g., L_2 and L_1, respectively. When the loss function is the hinge loss and the penalty is the L_2 norm for coefficients SVM emerges. Technical implementations of Structural Risk Minimization (SRM) leading to non-linear / binary SVM expansions / classifiers $g(\mathbf{x})$ (best using the hinge loss) show illuminating relations between SVM using sparse "support vectors" (SV) prototype similarity representations and radial basis functions (RBF), neural networks (NN), Parzen expansions [except that $g(\mathbf{x})$ are not pdf and only the support vectors found participate in expansions] and regularization using Lagrange optimization (Theodoridis and Koutroumbas, 2009). In particular, the inner product of the features vectors mapped (using Φ) to a new (higher dimensional) space can be expressed (in Reproducing kernel Hilbert space H) using the "kernel trick" K as $<\Phi(\mathbf{x}), \Phi(\mathbf{z})> = K(x, z)$ [Mercer's Theorem]. Generalization is related to reducing the number of prototype SVs compared to the original number of training examples. Sparsity comes from including the margin, a regularizer term ("priors") to solve an ill-posed problem and avoid over-fitting, in the cost function $J(\mathbf{w}, \xi)$ that is subject to minimization,

$$J(w, \xi) = \frac{1}{2} \|w\|^2 + C \sum_{i=1}^{N} I(\xi_i).$$

The resulting classifiers / regressors are

$$g(\mathbf{x}) = \sum_{j=1}^{N} a_j \mathbf{K}(\mathbf{x}, \mathbf{x_j})$$

using the *Representer Theorem* for the regularized cost

$$\sum_{i=1}^{N} \text{LOSS}(g(\mathbf{x}_i), y_i) + \Omega\|g\|$$

for some loss function LOSS and kernels (Gram matrix) *K* placed at the training points. Similar rationale as above and use of *link analysis* methods (including the Laplacian matrix *L* of the graph) allows regularization to expand the scope of classifiers / regressors g(**x**) and cover for spatial ("context") and temporal ("frames") trajectories. This leads to the following optimization problem (Belkin et al., 2006).

$$\arg \min_{g \in H} \frac{1}{N_l} \sum_{i=1}^{N_l} L(g(\text{xi}), \text{yi}) + \gamma H \left\|g\right\|_H^2 +$$

$$\frac{\gamma_l}{N^2} \sum_{i,j=}^{N_l + N_j} (g(\text{xi}) - g(\text{xj}))2 \, W(i, j)$$

where $N^2 = (N_l + N_u)^2$, both labeled "*l*" and unlabeled "*u*" examples are used, and semi-supervised learning (SSL) proximity constraints (that near by examples carry similar labels / values) are used. This eventually leads to a new optimization problem for Laplacian L = D − W.

$$\arg \min_{g \in H} \frac{1}{N_l} \sum_{i=1}^{N_l} L(g(\mathbf{x}_i), y_i) + \gamma_H \left\|g\right\|_H^2 + \frac{\gamma_l}{N^2} g^T L g$$

with the Representer Theorem summation going now over both labeled and unlabeled examples, and the solution referred to as the Laplacian regularized kernel least squares (LRKLS) (Theodoridis & Koutroumbas, 2009). The interpretation of the mapping *g* says that it is synthesized by a weighted superposition of Gaussian blobs, each centered at the location x_i of one of the training samples. The approximation *g* is similar to radial basis functions (RBF) and hybrid learning when the number of Gaussian blobs is narrowed down using (unsupervised) clustering, e.g., K - means or EM, before actual (supervised) regularization takes place. Last but not least the regularization framework can also assume a Bayesian interpretation (Poggio & Smale, 2003). The data term (for fidelity) using a quadratic loss function is optimal in response to additive Gaussian noise, while the penalty term or stabilizer Ω corresponds to priors given on the hypothesis space of admissible models. The mapping *g* learned by regularization corresponds then to the MAP estimate.

ISSUES, CONTROVERSIES, PROBLEMS

The face representations discussed earlier are fed to matching classifiers for authentication purposes. The classifiers' core function is that of measuring similarity between unknown probes (test images) and enrolled (gallery) identities. Under the Bayesian framework this is done using generative methods using density estimation, priors, and MAP confined to closed set recognition. This requires parametrization and marginalization, which are complex and cumbersome processes to be carried out on large scale and in a high-dimensional space. The alternative shown here using statistical learning seeks instead for non-parametric and discriminative recognition methods that enable open set recognition with the negative class of unknown imposters "hallucinated." In addition to open set recognition, statistical learning, e.g., transduction, and boosting, are shown to facilitate recognition-by-parts and are suitable to deal with uncertainty coming from noisy, occluded, and/or disguised biometric imagery.

Compressive sensing "has become one of the standard methods of face recognition. [However,] the sparsity assumption, which underpins much of this work is not supported by data" (Shi et al., 2011). We first recall here reports on the use of sparse representations for robust face recognition using L_1 minimization (Wright et al., 2009) that presume "perfect registration, no self-shadowing, occlusion, or specularities," and that face recognition is a typical small-size problem. Shi et al. go further to note that the lack of sparsity [assumed but not proven] in the data "means that compressive sensing cannot be guaranteed to recover the exact signal, and therefore that sparse approximations may not deliver the robustness or performance desired." The authors proceed to show that a simpler L_2 approach to face recognition is not only significantly more accurate, but also more robust and much faster than compressive sensing. Formally, in order to exploit the presumed sparsity for $A = [x_1, ..., x_n] \in R^{mxn}$, assuming that any test image lies in the subspace spanned by the training images belonging to the same person, one should generate a random matrix $\Phi \in R^{dxm}$ (where d ≪ m) and seek for a sparse vector α that minimizes the L_1 minimization problem

$$min_{\alpha \in R^n} \left\|\alpha\right\|1 \text{ s.t. } \Phi x = \Phi A\alpha \text{ or equivalently}$$
$$\left\|\phi x - \phi A\alpha\right\|2 \leq \mu$$

In contrast to the L_1 case, Shi et al. argue for and show better results for estimating α using the L_2 norm and solving instead

$$argmin_{\alpha \in R^n} \left|\left|x - A\alpha\right|\right|_2^{2}$$

They suggest that even when the system is over determined, the optimal solution (in the sense of the smallest reconstruction error) can be recovered by $\alpha = (A^T A)^{-1} A^T x$ (similar to regularized least-squares and ridge regression using the pseudo-inverse matrix solution). Rigamonti et al.

(2011) have also shown that enforcing the sparsity constraints actually does not improve recognition performance. Last but not least, Xu et al. (2012) indicate that sparsity and stability (both important for generalization ability) are fundamentally at odds with each other, and therefore L_1-regularized regression (Lasso) cannot be stable, while L_2-regularized regression, known to have strong stability, is not sparse. Much motivation for the use of sparsity comes from the analysis of the primate visual cortex and the belief that increasing the sparsity of the basis functions (i.e., the dimensionality of the face space) does reduce the capacity of the classifier and increases its generalization (see below).

Convolutional (using alternating local filters, non-linearities, and max-pool layers) realized as distributed (connectionist / belief) networks (LeNet) (Jarrett et al., 2009), *deep learning* (Bengio, 2009), and feed-forward hierarchical architectures are all related. Inspiration and motivation for such learning models comes from the visual cortex hyper-columnar architecture of simple and complex (receptive field) cells enunciated by Hubel and Wiesel, the Neocognitron (Fukushima, 1980), self-organization (Kohonen, 1982), sparse coding with an over complete basis set (Olhausen & Field, 1997), hierarchical cortex models (Serre et al., 2007), and last but not least the need for multi-level abstraction and automatically generated rather than hand crafted features for representation. Deep learning mediates between image analysis and machine learning as it implements a hierarchical (multi-level) architecture that learns / consists of fine ("low-level") to coarse ("high-level") internal feature representation of the world. Beyond object and face recognition, deep learning has been shown to facilitate transfer learning and domain adaptation using shared network (including lateral inhibition) structure. Learning for *LeNet* is unsupervised and requires very few labeled examples. Jarrett et al. have further shown that the use of non-linearities that include rectification and local contrast normalization is the single most important ingredient for good accuracy. The Google Brain team led by Ng and Dean has created a neural network that learned to recognize / detect higher-level concepts, e.g., faces only from watching (without having to label images as containing a face or not) unlabeled images taken from YouTube videos (Le et al., 2012). Deep learning, characteristic of unsupervised learning, learns to build features that span increasing receptive fields, one layer at a time, eventually culminates in the emergence of an analogue for specific grandmother cells that are sensitive to detecting high level concepts, e.g., cat and/or face. Huang et al. (2012) have recently use deep learning for face verification. While deep learning is appealing for its class specific feature detectors and straight-forward learning paradigms, questions remain about the validity and use of such methods for recognition tasks, in general, and face biometrics, in particular. As inputs alternate and/or change over time, one would assume that the concepts the grandmother cells are sensitive to change too. Another perennial problem about the very existence of biological grandmother cells questions the identity of their ultimate reader.

SOLUTIONS AND RECOMMENDATIONS

Transduction is different from inductive inference. It is *local estimation* ("inference") that moves from particular(s) to particular(s). In contrast to inductive inference, where one uses empirical data to approximate a functional dependency (the inductive step [that moves from particular to general] and then uses the dependency learned to evaluate the values of the function at points of interest (the deductive step [that moves from general to particular]), one now directly infers (using transduction) the values of the function only at the points of interest from the training data (Vapnik, 2000). Inference now takes place using both labeled and unlabeled data, which are complementary to each other. Transduction incorporates unlabeled data, characteristic of test samples, in the decision-making process responsible for their labeling ("prediction"), and seeks for a consistent and stable labeling across both (near-by) training ("labeled data") and test data, something referred to as *collective classification*. Towards that end, transduction seeks to authenticate unknown faces in a fashion that is most consistent with the given identities of known but similar faces (from an enrolled gallery / data base of raw images and/or face templates). The search for putative labels (for unlabeled samples) seeks to make the labels for both training and test data compatible or equivalently to make the training and test error consistent.

Kolmogorov complexity and randomness using minimum description length (MDL) are closely related. Transduction chooses from all the possible labeling ("identities") for test data the one that yields the largest randomness deficiency, i.e., the most probable labeling. Towards that end, similarity, *order and rankings* are driven by strangeness and p-values. The strangeness measures the lack of typicality (for a face or face component) with respect to its true or putative (assumed) identity label and the labels for all the other faces or parts thereof. Formally, the strangeness measure α_i is the (likelihood) ratio of the sum of the k nearest neighbor (KNN) distances d from the same class y divided by the sum of the KNN distances from all the other classes $(\neg y)$. The smaller the strangeness, the larger its typicality and the more probable its (putative) label y is. The strangeness facilitates both feature selection (similar to Markov blankets) and variable selection (dimensionality reduction). One finds empirically that the strangeness, classification margin, sample and hypothesis margin, posteriors, and odds, are all related via a monotonically non-decreasing function with a small strangeness amounting to a large margin (Li & Wechsler, 2005).

The likelihood-like definitions for strangeness are intimately related to discriminative methods. The p-values compare ("rank") the strangeness values to determine the credibility and confidence in the putative classifications ("labeling") made. The p-values bear resemblance to their counterparts from statistics but are not the same. They are determined according to the relative rankings of putative authentications against each one of the identity classes known to the enrolled gallery using the strangeness. The p-value construction, where l is the cardinality of the training set T, constitutes a valid randomness (deficiency) test approximation for some putative label y assigned to a *new* example e, $p_y(e) = \#$ (i: $\alpha_i \geq \alpha_{new}^y$)/($l +$ 1) (Ho & Wechsler, 2008). p-values assess the extent to which the biometric data supports or discredits the null hypothesis H0 (for some specific authentication). When the null hypothesis is rejected for each identity class known, one finds that the test image lacks mates in the gallery and answers for the query with "none of the above." This corresponds to forensic exclusion with rejection, characteristic of open set recognition (lack of familiarity) with authentication implemented using *Open Set Transduction Confidence Machine (TCM) – KNN* (Li & Wechsler, 2005). TCM facilitates *outlier detection*, in general, and *imposter detection*, in particular.

Semi-supervised learning (SSL) (Chapelle et al., 2006), similar to transduction, learns from both labeled and unlabeled data to eventually label test data. Similar examples are expected to carry the same label and cluster together in a lower-dimensional manifold. Face identification iteratively compares face images against some gallery and returns an ordered list of candidate identities in terms of their similarity to the query. Scoring, ranking and inference are done using the strangeness and p – values, respectively. Changing ("label flipping") the given class assignments (characteristic of imposter behavior) provides the bias needed to determine ("infer") the rejection

threshold required to recognize familiarity and make an authentication, or alternatively, to reject the probe as unknown. Towards that end, one relabels the training examples, one at a time, with all the ("imposter") putative labels except the one originally assigned to it. The PSR (peak-to-side) ratio, $PSR = (p_{max} - p_{min}) / p_{stdev}$, traces the characteristics of the resulting p-value distribution and determines, using cross validation, the [a priori] threshold used to identify ("infer") imposters. The PSR values found for impostors are low because imposters do not mate and their relative strangeness is high (and p-value low). Outliers are deemed as imposters and are thus rejected (Li & Wechsler, 2005). The same cross-validation is used for similar purposes during boosting for the purpose of *data fusion*, in general, and *recognition-by-parts*, in particular.

Uncertainty and decision-making are closely intertwined and their resolution depends on context and goals. No single model exists for all pattern recognition problems and no single method is applicable for all problems. Rather what we have is a bag of tools and a bag of problems. This is exactly what data fusion is tasked to do with biometrics that need to be authenticated. The principled combination rule for data fusion proposed here is grounded in statistical learning using transduction and boosting. Authentication takes place using sequential ("cascade") aggregation of different components ("parts"), which are referred to in the boosting framework as weak learners. This corresponds to an ensemble of method ("mixtures of experts"). The discussion on data fusion is relevant to both generic multi-level and multi-layer fusion in terms of functionality and granularity. Multi-level fusion involves feature / parts, score ("match"), and detection ("decision"), while multi-layer fusion involves modality, quality, and method (algorithm). The components are realized as weak learners whose relative performance is driven by transduction using strangeness and p-value, while their aggregation is achieved using boosting. Recognition-by-Parts using transduction and boosting (Li & Wechsler, 2009) is most suitable to overcome uncontrolled settings due to occlusion and disguise.

Standard boosting bears a close relation to L_1-regularized optimization. The exponential loss (AdaBoost), logistic loss (LogitBoost), and hinge loss (LP-Boost) are usually employed for loss functions. AdaBoost, LogitBoost, and boosting with generalized hinge loss can all be seen as entropy maximization in the dual (Shen et al., 2012). Ada-Boost (Freund & Shapire, 1996) minimizes using greedy optimization a functional whose minimum defines logistic regression (Friedman, Hastie, & Tibshirani, 2000). It is functionally similar to an ensemble of SVM (Vapnik, 2000). [Note also that logistic regression supports discriminative methods, e.g., label y = 1 if $P\{y = 1 | x\} / P\{y = 0 | x\} > 1$.] The basic assumption behind boosting is that "weak" learners are combined to learn any target ("class") concept with probability $1 - \eta$. Weak learners, usually built around simple features, learn to classify at better than chance (with probability $1/2 + \eta$ for $\eta > 0$). AdaBoost works by adaptively and iteratively re-sampling the data to focus learning on examples that the previous weak (learner) classifier could not master, with the relative weights of misclassified examples increased ("refocused") after each iteration. Ada-Boost involves choosing T effective components h_t to serve as weak (learners) classifiers and using them to construct the separating hyper-planes or alternatively the strong H classifier. AdaBoost converges to the posterior distribution of y conditioned on x, and the strong but greedy classifier H in the limit becomes the log-likelihood ratio test. The multi-class extensions for AdaBoost are AdaBoost.M1 and .M2, the latter one used to learn strong classifiers with the focus now on both difficult examples to recognize and labels hard to discriminate. Different but specific alternatives can be used to minimize Type II error or equivalently to maximize the power $(1 - \beta)$ of the weak learner (Duda, Hart, & Stork, 2000). During cascade learning each weak learner ("classifier")

is trained to achieve (minimum acceptable) hit rate $(1 - \beta)$ and (maximum acceptable) false alarm rate α. Upon completion, boosting yields the strong classifier $H(\mathbf{x})$, which is a collection of discriminative biometric components playing the role of weak learners. The hit rate after T iterations is $(1 - \beta)^T$ and the false alarm α^T.

The strangeness is the thread to implement both representation and boosting (learning, inference, and prediction for the purpose of authentication). The strangeness, which implements the interface between the biometric representation (including attributes and/or parts) and boosting, combines the merits of filter and wrapper classification methods. The coefficients and thresholds for the weak learners, including the thresholds needed for open set recognition and rejection are learned using validation images, which are described in terms of components ("parts") similar to those found during enrollment. The best feature correspondence for each component is sought between a validation and a training biometric face image over the component ("parts" or "attributes") defining that component. The strangeness of the best component found during training is computed for each validation biometric image under all its putative class labels c (c = 1,..., C). Assuming M validation biometric images from each class, one derives M positive strangeness values for each class c, and M(C – 1) negative strangeness values. The positive and negative strangeness values correspond to the case when the putative label of the validation and training image are the same. or not, respectively.

The strangeness values are *ranked* for all the components available, and the best weak learner h_i is the one that maximizes the recognition rate over the whole set of validation biometric images V for some component i and threshold θ_i. A component ("part") is chosen as a weak learner during each iteration. The level of significance α determines the scope for the null hypothesis H0. Experimental results (Li and Wechsler, 2009) illustrate the feasibility and utility of model-free and non-parametric recognition-by-parts using boosting and transduction for categorical face recognition including both face detection and open set face identification. The results show that the combined boosting and transduction realization of face detection confirms psychophysical findings reported by Balas and Sinha (2006), among them Result 5 "that of the different facial features, eyebrows were indeed found most important for face detection" (Layer 1 categorization: face vs. background). The best weak learner found corresponds to the part that yields the largest coefficient when boosting starts. The explanation for this finding is straightforward. The eyebrows are highly "discriminative" due to their emotive contents, stability, location above a convexity that makes them less susceptible to shadow, illumination changes, and displacement due to movement.

Another example that illustrates the role of parts and local region analysis comes from their use for face recognition after and despite plastic surgery (De Marsico et al., 2011). The proposed methods implement the region-based approach in different ways. FARO (FAce Recognition against Occlusions and Expression Variations) divides the face into relevant regions (left eye, right eye, nose and mouth) and then codes them independently using Partitioned Iterated Function System (PIFS) processing, while FACE (Face Analysis for Commercial Entities) applies a localized version of image correlation index. Finally, the Split Face Architecture (SFA), adaptive and integrative in nature, would leverage any known recognition methods, from PCA to most recent ones (including FARO and FACE), assuming it is possible to divide the face into regions. The experimental results reported show that local region analysis yields much better performance than state-of-the art methods applied to the whole face.

Sampling, during learning and/or data streaming, and *tracking*, are concerned with data collection and evidence accumulation in order to choose the most (functionally) relevant image frames. This helps with improving the classification margin for generalization purposes, stability in learning, and consistency in predictions. The solution described here, characteristic of *active learning*, is driven by transduction and realized using the strangeness and p-values (Ho & Wechsler, 2008). The p-values measure diversity and disagreement in opinion regarding the true label of an unlabeled example when it is iteratively assigned all the possible putative labels. Let p_i be the p-values obtained for a particular example x_{n+1} using all possible labels i = 1, . . ., M. Sort the sequence of p-values in descending order such that the first two p-values, say, p_j and p_k are the two highest p-values found with corresponding labels j and k, respectively. The label assigned to the unknown example is therefore j while its p-value is p_j. This value defines the *credibility* of the classification. If the credibility for p_j is not high enough (using a priori thresholds found using cross-validation) the prediction is rejected. The difference between the top two p-values can be further used as a *confidence* value for the prediction made. Note that, the smaller the confidence, the larger the ambiguity regarding the proposed label. Predictions are therefore not bare but associated with specific reliability measures, those of credibility and confidence. This assists both decision-making and data fusion. Data collection and evidence accumulation along considerations as those listed above and using query by transduction (QBT) (Ho & Wechsler, 2008) are briefly described next.

Assume $p_j > p_k$, and consider three possible cases of p-values, p_j and p_k: Case 1: p_j is "high" and p_k is "low." Prediction "j" has high credibility and high-confidence value; Case 2: both p_j and p_k are "high." Prediction "j" has high credibility but low-confidence value; and Case 3: both p_j and p_k are "low." Prediction "j" has low credibility and low-confidence. High uncertainty in prediction occurs for both Case 2 and Case 3, when $p_j \approx p_k$. Define as information "closeness" the quantity $I(x_{n+1}) = p_j - p_k$, which indicates the information contents possessed by example x_{n+1}. As $I(x_{n+1})$ approaches 0, the more uncertain one is about classifying the example x_{n+1}, and the larger the information gain when one is told about its label. One should therefore add this example, with its (true) label, to the training set because it provides new information about the learning map for classification. Performance evaluation includes the temporal dimension with learning curves graphed over time. Learning stability implies that after some initialization period, the error rate for the learning curve, error (t), is relatively small, its slope is also relatively small, and its overall appearance is that of a smooth curve (Vovk et al., 2005). One can expand on QBT and employ all the p-values rather than the top two. This leads to generalized query by transduction (GQBT) (Balasubramanian, 2009), where one considers the disagreement between the p-values from all the classes. Towards that end, one constructs a matrix Q using pair wise differences of p-values and defines $I(x_{n+1})$ as the largest eigenvalue for Q^{-1}. Note that GQBT reduces to QBT when only the top two p-values are considered.

One venue for future research would expand the scope of biometric space regarding information contents and processes vis-à-vis both recognition-by-parts and the binary and relative features discussed earlier on. Regarding the biometric space, Balas and Sinha (2006) have argued that "it may be useful to also employ region-based strategies that can compare noncontiguous image regions." They further showed that "under certain circumstances, comparisons [using dissociated dipole operators] between spatially disjoint image regions are, on average, more valuable for recognition than features that measure local contrast." This is consistent with the expectation that recognition-by-parts architectures should learn [using boosting and transduction] "optimal" sets of regions' comparisons for biometric authentication across varying data capture conditions and contexts. The choices made on such combinations for both multi-level and multi-layer ("hierarchical") similarity driven fusion amount to "rewiring" operators and processes. Rewiring corresponds to an additional

processing and competitive biometric stage. As a result, the repertoire of information available to biometric inference should now range over local, global, and non-local (disjoint) data characteristics, while adding the temporal dimension (rather than frame-based bag-of-words) a distinct possibility. Ordinal rather than absolute codes become then feasible for gaining invariance to small changes in inter-region and temporal contrast. Disjoint and "rewired" patches of information contain more diagnostic information and are expected to perform best for "expression," self-occlusion, and varying image capture conditions, e.g., A-PIE. The multi-feature and rewired based biometric image representations and processes together with example-based biometric ("prototype") representations enable all encompassing flexible matching and compares favorably against feed-forward architectures modeled around *Neocognitron* inspired rigid convolutional networks trained using deep learning.

FUTURE RESEARCH DIRECTIONS

We discuss here emerging trends and challenges at the interface between face space training and encoding using regularization, similarity, and sparsity, for enhanced interoperability and meta-planning, subject to uncontrolled settings. The emerging trends addressed are those of compressive sensing, multi-task and transfer learning, re-identification, and scalability.

Coates and Ng (2011) discussed recently the importance of *encoding versus training* using sparse coding and vector quantization. One can carry over the same discussion to face recognition as we do here. Recall that training takes place while learning the dictionary D for face space, and encoding corresponds to enrollment using D for the purpose of deriving biometric signatures and templates. The interesting questions that need to be addressed and resolved are as follows. One should question first to what extent choosing a good encoder is more important than spending resources on training. Early experiments have shown that training is less important than the quality and quantity of the data used for encoding and subsequent enrollment, and that (a) training to learn the face space is less important than the quality of images during enrollment and testing, (b) the size of the subject gallery affects performance, and (c) it does not make much difference if the face space is derived from biometric data coming from the same dataset source as that used for enrollment and testing (El Khiyari et al., 2012). The "surprising" findings as reported by Coates and Ng suggest that "1. When using sparse coding as the encoder, virtually any training algorithm can be used to create a suitable dictionary. We can use [vector quantization] VQ, or even randomly chosen [patch] examples [similar to the use of prototypes] to achieve very high performance [and even random weights for subsequent projections]. 2 Regarding the choice of dictionary, a very simple encoder (a soft threshold function) can often be competitive with sparse coding." It appears then that the choice of basis functions "may not be as critical as one might imagine." The dictionary D can be learned using L_1-penalized sparse coding "regularization"

$$min_{D,\alpha(i)} \sum_i \left\| D\alpha^{(i)} - \mathbf{x}^{(i)} \right\|_2^2 + \lambda \left\| \alpha^{(i)} \right\|_1$$

The above minimization, subject to $\left\| D^{(j)} \right\|_2^2 = 1$, $\forall$ j, employs alternative minimization cycles over the sparse code $\alpha^{(i)}$ and the dictionary D. The results reported indicate that "the main value of the dictionary is to provide a highly over-complete basis on which to project the data before applying an encoder." Also interesting to note is the fact that VQ "is quite capable of competing with more complex algorithms; it simply ensures that there is at least one dictionary entry near any

densely populated areas in the input space [and span the space of inputs equitably]." While it is now well established that sparse signal models are well suited to restoration tasks and can effectively be learned from image and video data, recent research (Mairal et al., 2008) has been aimed at learning discriminative sparse models instead of purely reconstructive ones. Towards that end, the authors propose a new step in that direction, with a novel sparse representation for signals belonging to different classes in terms of a shared dictionary and multiple class-decision functions g_i $(\mathbf{x}, \boldsymbol{\alpha}, \boldsymbol{\theta})$. Given some input signal x and fixed (but iteratively changing as explained above) dictionary D and parameters $\boldsymbol{\theta}$, the supervised sparse coding problem for the class c can be augmented using some softmax discriminative cost function. The linear variant of the proposed model admits a simple probabilistic interpretation, while its most general variant admits an interpretation in terms of kernels.

Binary and relative visual attributes are recent developments in face representation for the purpose of face verification and image search, e.g., CBIR. One can use such attributes, similar in concept to a GIST envelope for the human face, to compose and/or generate face descriptions at different levels of specificity, suitable for face authentication, image search, zero-shot (transfer) learning, and HCI. "Attribute" classifiers use binary classifiers trained to recognize the presence or absence of describable aspects of visual appearance (e.g., gender, race, and age), while "simile" classifiers remove manual labeling required for attribute classification and instead learn the similarity of faces, or region of faces, to specific reference people (Kumar et al., 2011). Note that neither method requires challenging alignment between image pairs. Relative attributes are more intuitive in use and enable richer textual descriptions for new face images (Parikh & Grauman, 2011). Given training data and (both ordered and unordered) relative attributes relations, SVM learns ranking functions, which can predict the relative strength of each visual cue in novel ("unseen") images. Similar to "simile" classifiers, zero-shot (transfer) learning for unseen categories leverages their list of attributes (relative to known "seen" images) and assignment takes place for highest likelihood, e.g., MAP. The parameters of the generative model for unseen categories are selected under the maximum likelihood (ML) guidance of the relative descriptions from the known "seen" images. Such transfer corresponds to importing priors from the knowledge of the models of seen categories. The *associate-predict* model for face recognition is yet another realization for relative visual attributes (Yin et al., 2011).Here "each identity contains multiple images with large intra-personal variation. When considering two faces under significantly different settings (e.g., frontal and non-frontal) one first associates one input face with alike identities from the generic identity data set. Using the associated faces, one can then "predict" the appearance of one input face under the setting of another input face, or discriminatively "predict" the likelihood whether two input faces are from the person or not." The challenges for such models are scalability beyond just a few subjects, and availability of enough data to train and build-up the gallery for real-world face recognition scenarios.

Object recognition, in general, and face recognition, in particular, are by definition inverse problems and ill posed problems. Uncontrolled settings and lack of adequate training data compound the ill-posed aspect. *Learning with side information* is gaining increased attention and appeal to make such ill-posed problems well-posed, such that in the limit they admit a solution, the solution is unique, and there is stability in the solution's behavior when conditions, say image capture, slightly change. Side information plays the role of constraints that facilitate the search for admissible solutions and conceptually can be thought of as one way to enhance the generic regularization approach, which we find again and again behind most methods for both representa-

tion and classification. Much of learning with side information has to do with redefining the face space, i.e., choosing and deriving better face representation in a fashion sometime similar to using the faces themselves as reference (basis) images, i.e., a chorus of prototypes that span the individual or generic / abstract face space, and similarity kernels to derive the representation of faces ("features") of interest, on one side, and hierarchical (two-level) (same-vs.-different classifiers (for face verification, on the other side. Recall again that the prototypes are conceptually similar to support vectors and are therefore responsible for generalization ability. The overall theme underlying learning with side information is to "learn the relevant structures in the data by reducing irrelevant variability while amplifying relevant variability; learn relevant structures by maximizing the mutual information with relevant data and minimizing mutual information with irrelevant data; integrate meta-features and latent information" (Wolf & Levy, 2013).

The specific methods proposed for learning with side information are characteristic of **n**-shot learning, e.g., *zero and one shot learning*. Zero-shot learning helps with testing on unknown test categories, while one-shot learning helps with cases where only very limited training data is available, in the limit just one example. Further compounding the ill-posed aspect is sometimes also the lack of data for testing beyond some high level semantic description using binary and/or relative attributes, which corresponds to zero-shot learning. We note here for completeness the functional similarity between learning with side information for dealing with uncontrolled settings, and the use of side information and helper biometric data for encryption purposes. One big challenge in biometric cryptosystems is to align a query with the template that is available only in the transformed domain without revealing any information about the stored template. The alignment must be done therefore in the transformed domain where the transformed version of the template does not carry sufficient information for alignment. Therefore, auxiliary (helper) data, e.g., orientation field (similar to fingerprints), is needed and used to assist in alignment. The secret is revealed using the helper data ("side information") only when the query Q is sufficiently similar to the template T. Similar arguments hold during Iterative Closest Point (ICP) alignment using fuzzy vault with helper data (Uludag & Jain, 2006).

The side information for face verification corresponds to domain specific knowledge and facilitates transfer knowledge. Note that side information can carry similar or different information from that made available for training data, e.g., labels and/or variability. Examples for two level classifiers include manual annotation for binary and/or relative features (to some fixed set of face references) and 2nd stage simile classifiers (Kumar et al., 2011); one-shot and two-shot classifiers (characteristic of one-shot learning) using one or both test images as positive examples and some additional but fixed data set of (background) references images as negative examples (for 1st stage) and LDA (for 2nd stage) (Wolf et al., 2011) (with background examples supplying "contradictions" for *universum* learning) ; Tom-vs.-Pete Classifiers, which learn to discriminate among different subjects with their binary outputs used as features in a second stage same-or-different verification classifier on face pairs (Berg & Belhumeuer, 2012). The side information for face verification amounts to domain specific knowledge and facilitates knowledge transfer. Similar to semi-supervised learning (but not to multidimensional scaling), some distances and/or equivalence (same, different, and ordered) relations are provided and/or sampled to learn a discriminative metric that generalize to unseen examples. Such type of learning is known as metric learning (Xing et al., 2003) and is discussed next.

Metric learning helps to realize the similarity and cluster assumptions behind semi-supervised learning and transduction. Both semi-supervised learning and transduction learn from annotated ("labeled") and unlabeled (side – information) data, semi-supervised learning to classify (via implied generalization and induction) across "all" domain, while transduction is limited to classify only the unlabeled data used to learn the classifier. We first recall the very definition of strangeness ("typicality") using KNN distances to samples coming from the same or different classes. Typicality, which mediates between similarity and dissimilarity, is related to margin and odds. It further ranks and order examples under putative label assignment using p-values and facilitates metric learning. This is useful for information retrieval settings, in general, and face verification, in particular, where similarity and ordering constraints become available from click-through feedback. Yet another advantage comes from its straightforward use to multi-class rather than binary classification as it is the case with SVM. One representative example for distance metric learning is the Large Margin Nearest Neighbor (LMNN) classifier (Weinberger et al., 2006), which was used for face recognition. In the absence of prior domain knowledge, most KNN use the Euclidean distance for similarity. One can do better than that when domain knowledge becomes available and the Mahalanobis distance rather than the Euclidean distance is sought for and used. Towards that end, regularization "penalizes large distances between each input and its KNN and small distances between each input and all other inputs that do not share the same label." Information-Theoretic Metric Learning (ITML) (Davis et al., 2007) is another representative example for distance metric learning. The search for the Mahalanobis distance seeks to minimize the differential relative (KL) entropy between two multivariate Gaussians. ITML is fast and scalable because no eigenvalue computation or semi-definite programming is required."

Transfer learning leverages different settings using either knowledge (feature, group, and/or structure) sharing or zero-shot learning when no training data is available for unseen categories ("classes"). Knowledge sharing employs regularization (see below), while zero-shot learning employs hierarchy-based knowledge transfer using similar and global context while augmenting training using hyponyms for positive examples, attribute-based knowledge transfer using direct attribute prediction (DAP) and cross-modal transfer (Klare & Jain, 2013), direct similarity-based knowledge transfer (Rohrbach et al., 2012), domain adaption using discriminative learning and covariate shift, and deep learning of low-level image features possibly using auto-encoding. The situation where the training input points and test input points follow different distributions, while the conditional distribution of output values given input points is unchanged, encountered during aging, has been referred to as *covariate shift*. Under *covariate shift*, standard model selection techniques such as cross validation do not work since its unbiasedness is no longer maintained (Sugiyama et al., 2007). The same authors address the problem using importance weighted cross validation (IWCV). Bickel et al. (2009) follow-up on IWCV for the purpose of discriminative learning under covariate shift by bypassing the intermediate step —intrinsically model-based— step of estimating training and test distributions. Towards that end, one estimates first the bias of the training sample, and then learns the classifier on a weighted version of the training sample using importance sampling. This leads to kernel logistic regression and an exponential model classifier.

Statistical Learning Theory (SLT) (Vapnik, 2006) provides several cases of learning with side information referred to as learning with structured data or alternatively as data-dependent regularization. Learning with contradictions or Universum SVM (Weston et al., 2006) incorporates additional examples into the original (binary) classification problem, i.e., virtual ("hallucination") samples, for the purpose of "boosting" the generalization performance. The virtual samples do not belong to either class, and the model chosen to explain the training data is the one that allows the largest number of contradictions within the margin. Relatively few and very small scale applications to biometrics have been tried so far, e.g., gender classification using Universum-Boost (U-Boost) on a population consisting of only 32 males and 20 females (Shen et al., 2012) compared to about 3,000 subjects used by others in earlier experiments (Gutta et al., 2000). The challenge for Universum learning goes beyond scale. It has to do mostly with judicious choice of universum ("contradiction") samples, something still waiting for a principled solution.

Another SLT variant for learning with side information is Learning Using Privileged Information (LUPI) where the additional ("side") information is available only for training data, e.g., group membership. Two LUPI algorithmic realizations are available, SVM+ (Pechyony et al., 2010) and SVM- (Wolf and Levy, 2013). Group membership is treated later on as regularization using the unifying theme of multi - source fusion for visual analytics. Processing unconstrained video goes much beyond that required for still face images. Towards that end SVM $\ominus$ (reads SVM-minus to indicate the elimination of a factor that is irrelevant to the task at hand) leverages the temporal dimension to overcome the fact that "confounding factors change state during the video sequence" while taking advantage of the "opportunity to eliminate spurious similarities" and the coherence that distinguishes between subjects based on overall and timely behavior that is not available in frozen still frames. Rather than augmenting training data with privileged information as SVM+ does, SVM $\ominus$ discards irrelevant 3D pose induced similarities. In particular, SVM $\ominus$ "learns to discriminate between positive and negative examples in a way that is uncorrelated with the discriminative function learned on an additional feature set. The appearance descriptors are the main features, and the additional information is based on estimated 3D head pose." Matched

Background Similarity Scores (MBGS) expand on one-shot similarity (OSS) scores introduced earlier using multiple one-sided OSS scores (ultimately fed to SVM for final discrimination) for matching two sets X_1 and X_2 using some set B for background samples that would induce a subset B_1 of nearest neighbors for X_1, which are selected to best represent misleading sources of variation, e.g., pose (and other viewing conditions). Learning with side information can benefit additional biometrics functionalities and is briefly addressed next.

Transfer learning and one-shot learning are intimately related. It is about the ability to synthesize and learn new object classes from existing information about different, previously learned classes using one or just a few examples rather than larger training data sets. Transfer learning supports learning new objects using their similarity or alternatively shared features / structure ("priors") to familiar objects. Structure informs among others transformations and it is this aspect that guides our discussion on face *alignment*. *Vectorization* denotes the process of aligning (bringing into *correspondence*) an image with a reference image or model. Congealing (Miller et al., 2000) expands on vectorization to define "the simultaneous vectorization of each of a set of images to each other." For a set of training images of a certain category, congealing iteratively transforms each image to minimize the images' joint pixel wise entropies E. One starts with a set of images I_i and corresponding transform matrices U_i, which upon convergence will encode and map the transformation of I_i into latent images I_i^L, which minimizes the joint pixel-wise entropies. For each image I_i one iterates through affine transformations A and tests if AU_i decreases the joint pixel-wise entropy. If it does, one then sets $U_i = AU_i$. Upon convergence, $U_i(I) = I_i^L$, and $T = U_i^{-1}$ transforms the latent image back to the original image. One can then "develop a probability density over the set of transforms that arose from the congealing process. This density over transforms may be shared by many [other classes], and demonstrates how using this density as "prior knowledge" can be used to develop a classifier based on only a single training example for each class." By maintaining the congealing sequence of distribution fields, one can align a new image by transforming it, step wise, according to the saved distribution field from the corresponding iteration of the original congealing. One should note that identity preserving alignment that avoids over-alignment should be preferred. It bypasses mean shape using parts-based correspondence and alignment and makes "use of the reference dataset to distinguish geometry differences due to pose and expression (that need to be normalized) from those pertaining to identity, e.g., thicker lips or wider nose" (Berg & Belhumeuer, 2012), similar in functionality to SVM $\ominus$.

Another functionality met by transfer learning is that of *cross-modal biometric recognition* for heterogeneous face recognition (HFR), e.g., matching two face images from alternate imaging modalities, such as an infrared image to a photograph, or a sketch to a photograph. HFR systems are needed when the gallery databases are populated with photographs (e.g. mug shots or passport photographs) but the probe images are often limited to some alternate modality. Towards that end, Klare and Jain (2013) employ subspace methods with non-linear kernel similarities used to locate any image within a coordinate system defined by a collection of prototype face images. "The prototype subjects (i.e., the training set) have an image in each modality (probe and gallery), and the coordinates of an image are located using prototype images from the corresponding modality. Random sampling is introduced into the HFR framework to better handle challenges arising from the small sample size problem. The merits of the proposed approach, called Prototype Random Subspace (P-RS), are demonstrated on four different heterogeneous scenarios: (i) near infrared to photograph, (ii) thermal to photograph, (iii) viewed sketch to photograph, and (iv) forensic sketch to photograph." The local representation concatenates the Cartesian product of filters (DOG, CSDN, and Gaussian) and descriptors (MLBP and SIFT). There is affinity between coupling such multiple functional representations with kernel similarity and *multiple kernels learning* (MKL) (Bach et al., 2004) seen as a concatenation of features maps. MKL employs $\mathbf{K} = \sum_{j=1}^{m}$ $\eta_j K_j$ with the kernel summation equivalent to concatenating feature spaces given as *m* "feature maps" $\Phi j : \mathbf{X} \rightarrow F_j$. Minimization takes place with respect to $f_j \in F_j$, the predictor is f (**x**) =

$$\sum_{j=1}^{m} f_j^T \Phi_j (\mathbf{x}),$$

regularization by

$$\sum_{j=1}^{m} \left\| \mathbf{f}_j \right\|^2$$

is equivalent to using

$$\mathbf{K} = \sum_{j=1}^{m} K_j,$$

and regularization by

$$\sum_{j=1}^{m} \left\| \mathbf{f}_j \right\|$$

imposes sparsity similar to (non-parametric) group Lasso. MKL amounts here to data fusion of several feature maps ("channels") and is shown later on to be a particular case of multi-source feature learning where one can choose from feature and/or source.

Fast indexing and search addresses storage and retrieval, and is data-driven. It involves dimensionality reduction using *random projections and locality-sensitive hashing (LSH)*. A random projection reduces the dimensionality of a high dimensional input space in order to make learning the prediction model more efficient. It employs a matrix of random numbers to project input vec-

tors to a new and lower-dimensional feature space. The Gaussian distribution is often used to generate such random numbers, and the columns of the transform matrix are normalized to yield column vectors of length 1. The input vectors are projected by multiplying each row of the input matrix by a column in the transformation random matrix. This is equivalent to performing feature selection based on linear combinations of input features. The number of columns in the transformation matrix determines the dimensionality of the new feature space. According to the Johnson - Lindenstrauss Lemma (Dasgupta & Gupta, 2002), if there are "n" rows and "d" columns in the input feature matrix and "k" columns in the transformation matrix, where $k >$

$$\frac{4 \log n}{\varepsilon^2 / 2 - \varepsilon^3 / 3}$$

with $\varepsilon \in (0,1)$, then, with high probability, the squared distance between a pair of transformed vectors will be close to the squared distance between the original input vectors, with the distance scaled by k / d.

As we have seen so far, the challenge in most of face recognition and statistical learning is that of searching for nearest neighbors (in similarity) and gracefully scale up to high – dimensions. To make large scale image search practical, approximate similarity search methods have been recently proposed. Here a predictable loss in accuracy for high-dimensional queries is traded for fast sublinear scalable search. In particular, LSH provides probabilistic guarantees for retrieving $(1 + \varepsilon)$–near neighbors bounded by O ($n^{1/(1+\varepsilon)}$) (Kulis et al., 2009). The fundamental idea behind LSH is to first build a family of hash functions H such that for each function, the probability of collision is much higher for the high-dimensional points which are close to each other than it is for those which are far apart; next, given a query point, find the near neighbors using the same hashing functions and retrieving elements stored in any buckets indexed by the query point (Slaney & Casey, 2008). KNN search is easily accommodated by using the list of collisions (due to hashing) and sorting them by their similarity to the query of interest.

Re-Identification authenticates and matches objects across multiple but possibly disjoint fields of view and video frames for the purpose of sequential authentication over space and time. Detection and seeding for initialization do not presume known identity and allow for re-identification of objects and/or faces whose identity might remain unknown. Specific functionalities involved in re-identification include clustering and selection, recognition-by-parts, anomaly and change detection, sampling and tracking, fast indexing and search, sensitivity analysis, and their integration for the purpose of identity management (Nappi and Wechsler, 2012). The overall architecture proposed is data-driven and modular, on one side, and discriminative and progressive, on the other side. The architecture is built around autonomic computing (Ganek & Corbi, 2003), which provides for closed-loop control. The challenge addressed throughout are those of evidence-based management and meta-planning, to progressively collect and add value to biometric data in order to generate knowledge that leads to purposeful and gainful action including active learning for the overall purpose of re-identification. A venue for future research includes adversarial learning when re-identification can become possibly "distracted" due to deliberate and corrupt information.

Multi-Task Learning (MTL) (Evgeniou and Pontil, 2004), and *Multi-Source Learning (MSL)* complete the discussion on regularization. Given a matrix **W** (d, m) and a pair of norms $\|\cdot\|_p$ and $\|\cdot\|_q$ one denotes the mixed norm $L_{p,q}$ as $\| W \|_{p,q} = (\sum_i ((\sum_j x_{ij}^q)^{1/q})^p)^{1/p}$ that is, apply the q-norm on the columns of **W** and the p-norm on the resulting d-dimensional vector. Given some weight matrix **W** such that W = P + Q where P

captures shared features and Q discovers outlier tasks, regularization exploits relationships among tasks and is formulated as

$$min_{W,P,Q} \sum_{i=1}^{m} \| X_i^T w_i - y_i \|^2 + \lambda_1 \| P \|_{1,2} + \lambda_2 \| Q^T \|_{1,2} \text{ such that } W = P + Q$$

The interpretation for the above MTL minimization problems is as follows (Gong et al., 2012). The first regularization terms is based on group Lasso penalty on row groups of P and seeks that all related tasks should select a common set of features. Similarly, the columns of Q consist of all zero or non-zero elements, with the non-zero columns corresponding to outlier tasks. MSL handles both feature level analysis (and pruning) and source (modality / kernel) level analysis. MSL facilitates data fusion, similar to MKL, and multi-view learning. Formally, given a collection of m samples from a number S of data sources X = {X1, .., XS} ϵ $R^{m \times n}$, y$\in R^m$, Xiang et al. (2013) seek a linear model

$$y = \sum_{i=1}^{s} X_i \beta_i + \varepsilon = X \beta + \varepsilon$$

that minimizes $LOSS(\beta) + \Omega(\beta)$ or equivalently

$$min_{\alpha,\gamma} \frac{1}{2} \| y - \sum_{i=1}^{s} \gamma_i X_i \alpha_i \|_2^2 + \sum_{i=1}^{s} \frac{\lambda_i}{p} \| \alpha_i \|_p^p + \sum_{i=1}^{s} \frac{\eta_i}{pq} \| \gamma_i \|^q$$

where γ are the mixing coefficients for data sources and α denotes the feature model. Assigning different values to p and q leads to different regularization and feature models (p, q) = (1, ∞) corresponds to l_1 – norm / regularization (Lasso) and sparse solution / feature selection, (p, q) = (2, 1) corresponds to $l_{2,1}$ – norm / regularization and group Lasso for source selection (and MKL), (p, q) = (∞,1) leads to group Lasso and source selection, and (p, q) = (1, 2) leads to sparse group Lasso for both source and feature selection. Non-linear predictors using boosting is one alternative to regularization using mixed norms. One recent realization of boosting is ShareBoost (Shalev-Shwartz, 2011), which considers multiclass prediction using forward greedy selection to both minimize training loss and overcome NP-hardness (with column sparsity bounded by some value s). Towards that end, one seeks to use only few features such that their number increases only sub-linearly with the number of possible classes. This implies that features should be shared by several classes. ShareBoost is shown to best mixed-norm regularization in terms of evaluation time, sparsity, and training time.

Interoperability and Uncontrolled Settings apply to both *Datasets and Protocols*. There has been some confusion about the correct and standard terminology introduced earlier regarding biometric use with much reference being now made to pair matching rather than verification vis-à-vis the Labeled Faces in the Wild (LFW) face database, and even worse with some referring to verification as face identification. There is also lack of appreciation to basic results owed to Daugman regarding the infeasibility of identification (as repeated verification) on very large databases or to the improper use of score normalization using side (cohort) information, which one should not expect to be possible during testing (Wechsler, 2007). Score normalization has been used for some FRVT evaluations but not for NIST speech evaluations. Uncontrolled (also referred to as "unconstrained") settings (vis-à-vis image capture and image quality conditions) are intertwined with both the datasets and protocols used for the purpose of performance evaluation. There should be much interest in experiments that report results on mixing diverse and heterogeneous datasets rather than individual datasets, on *cross-dataset generalization*, where one trains on one data set,

while testing on another, and even better to report on results for sequestered data and/or full-fledged deployed systems rather than mere algorithmic implementations tuned on the same dataset time after time. Towards that end, Beveridge et al. (2011) argue that "it is much more common to find relationships in which two images that are hard to match to each other can be easily matched with other images of the same person. In other words, these images are simultaneously both high and low quality. The existence of such "contrary" images represents a fundamental challenge for approaches to biometric *image quality* that cast quality as an intrinsic property of a single image. Instead it indicates that quality should be associated with pairs of images. In exploring these contrary images, we find a surprising dependence on whether elements of an image pair are acquired at the same location, even in circumstances where one would be tempted to think of locations as interchangeable. The results presented have important implications for anyone designing face recognition evaluations as well as those developing new algorithms."

Cox and Pinto (2011) comment further that there are "concerns that the [much in vogue] LFW set does not necessarily accurately reflect the "full" problem of unconstrained face recognition remain. LFW includes only a handful of examples per individual, and these photographs were often taken in the same setting and at the same event. Furthermore, Kumar et al. (2011) showed that human observers were able to perform at greater-than-90% correct [rate] even when the faces themselves wee masked out of the test images, indicating that the LFW background is more than sufficient for solving the task at a level higher than the current state of the art." The authors make additional important observations that "remarkably similar sets of face pairs are failed, and that LFW is biased toward frontal views because faces must be first detected by a Viola-Jones face detector, which is biased for frontal detection. Worth to note that much face authentication still takes place on masked images, which discard context information, and is not consonant with the way people perceive and recognize faces. Worth to note too are the comments made by Torralba and Efros (2011) on an *"unbiased look at dataset bias,"* in particular the realization that "one major issue for many popular dataset competitions is *"creeping overfitting*," as algorithms over time become too adapted to the dataset, essentially memorizing all its idiosyncrasies, and losing ability to generalize," and that computer vision datasets, which are [merely] supposed to be a representation of the world, "instead of helping us to train models that work in the real open world, have become closed worlds unto themselves." Last but not least, one has also to contend with the negative set bias, both size and contents, while learning with side information; statistical significance when attesting overall performance among competing algorithms; and assessing the degree of manual processing involved. Methods should not become over-engineered for nuances of a data set, with modest performance gains indicative of over-fitting.

Meta-Planning sequences among processing modules while making strategic choices among modalities, methods, algorithms, and parameters. Biometric architecture should be modular and integrated, on one side, and discriminative and progressive in nature, on the other side. At its core are autonomic computing (Ganek & Corbi, 2003) and W5+. Autonomic computing, also referred to as self-management provides basic functionalities, e.g., self-configuration (for planning and organization), self-optimization (for efficacy), self-protection (for security purposes), and self-healing (to repair malfunctions). W5+ answers questions related to *What* data to consider, *When* to get / capture the data and from *Where*, and *How* to best process the data. The *Who* (is) question about identity is most relevant to biometrics and identity management. Directed evidence accumulation would also consider and document the explanation *Why* dimension. The *Why* dimension links observations and hypotheses (models) duly ascribed (abducted possibly using analogy reason-

ing, Bayesian (belief) networks, and/or causality) and expectations to be met. The Bayesian networks (for inference and validation purposes) assist with optimal and incremental / progressive smart data collection, e.g., multi-view integration. In a fashion similar to signal processing and transmission, the "progressive" aspect signifies incremental access and/or display of crucial evidence, which at some point is enough to solve the biometric "puzzle" and/or make re-identification apparent. The challenge is to enable Evidence-Based Management (EBM) to progressively add value to Data as it is morphed into Knowledge and leads to purposeful and gainful Action (DKA).

Meta-Recognition (Scheirer et al., 2012), complementary to Meta-Planning and different from meta-analysis (because it does not draw broad conclusions over multiple studies), is a post-recognition score analysis that considers the underlying nature of the score distribution and predicts when a recognition algorithm is succeeding or failing, and if necessary adjusts the recognition decisions and mediates control information, perhaps signaling for a specific response action, e.g., operator intervention, further acquisition of data, and so on. Three basic but different methods can address the interplay between non-match and matching distributions: score normalization using cohort analysis, statistical extreme value theory (EVT) (without requiring training data), and machine learning. As discussed earlier, score normalization effectively performs identification in the verification mode using varying cohorts, which are not available during real-world operation (Wechsler, 2007). The key insight for EVT (Scheirer et al., 2012) is that "if the best score is a match, then it should be an outlier with respect to the non-match (tail distribution) model. [Towards that end] use a hypothesis test to determine if the top score is an outlier by considering the amount of the cumulative distribution function (CDF) that is to the right of the top score, or determine the probability of failure directly from the inverse CDF of that score." While EVT assumes i.i.d. samples, it can be generalized to weaker assumptions of exchangeability, and similar considerations follow from outlier / imposter detection using strangeness / typicality and p-values (Ho & Wechsler, 2008), e.g., QBT and GQBT, and change detection using martingale (Ho & Wechsler, 2010). Machine learning using SVM found to performs best (Scheirer et al., 2012), takes for features the separation between the top score and second best score (similar to the confidence defined earlier using p-values to assess ambiguity of the response score) or feature vectors consisting of different length sequences of score differences using the tail of the score distribution and starting at consecutive ranked scores. The vectors are tagged with binary (correct + 1 or incorrect -1) labels and a corresponding binary SVM is derived. Note that the feature vectors used would be more informative if they carry the credibility value we derived earlier on using transaction (in the context of active learning). Questions linger regarding the sensitivity of the three Meta-Recognition methods listed above vis-à-vis cross-data set generalization, Pattern Specific Error Inhomogeneities (PSEI) characteristic of biometric menagerie / zoo (Yager & Dunstone, 2010), covariate shift, on one side, and comparative assessment against order and rankings using transduction, on the other side, with rankings more robust than mere matching scores and further intertwined with exchangeability and martingale for change and drift detection.

CONCLUSION

The overall coverage of the chapter is about moving face recognition out of the comfort zone and dramatically improve the current performance of existing biometric tools by fusing the rich spatial, temporal, and contextual information available from the multiple views made available by media (rather than still) in the wild and operational real-world problems. Instead of relying on a "single best frame approach," one must confront uncontrolled settings by exploiting all available imagery to allow addition of new evidence, graceful degradation, and re-identification. Uncontrolled settings are all encompassing and include A-PIE, denial and deception characteristic of incomplete and uncertain information, uncooperative users, and unconstrained data collection, scenarios, and sensors. The challenges are many, most important among them lack of persistence for biometric data, adversarial biometrics, open rather than closed set recognition, covariate shift, cross-dataset generalization, alignment and registration, scalability, and last but not least the deployment of full-fledged biometrics that include detection, authentication, informative sampling, and tracking. Scalability refers to both large sets of subjects and large sets of (possibly multi-modal) images for each subject. The overall recommendations are synergetic and should consider for implementation and processing purposes the regularization, statistical learning, and boosting triad complemented by sparsity and grouping (feature sharing) to deal with high-dimensional data and enhanced generalization. The recurring theme is that of a unified framework that involves multi-task and transfer learning using metric learning and learning with side information. The next and probably ultimate frontier is that of a digital footprint that is multi-modal and holistic in nature and consists of (full-fledged appearance <head, face, trunk, and body>, behavior, and intent) biometrics, context, domain (soft biometrics) knowledge and history, 3D morphable heads, merging novel views for same identity, and GPS location. Similar to Big

Data, search for sub-linear process time for massive amounts of biometric data should consider cloud and distributed computing, LSH, Map Reduce, and Hadoop. Randomness, essential to LSH, is all encompassing. As an example, Random Forests (RF) leverage the combined use of re-sampling and bootstrap ("bagging"), on one side, and ensemble learning ("boosting"), on the other side. RF usually best competing classification methods, e.g., Support Vector Machines (SVM). Security, data integrity, and privacy are important too with de-identification, de-duplication, cancellable biometrics, trustworthy components, and functional creep avoidance topping the list.

Heraclitus of Ephesus (c. 500 B.C.) claimed that all things are in flux and that everything is constantly changing. One can not step into the same river twice since the river is never the same. Hence the variability of biometrics and the "permanent" challenge to handle in a reliable fashion the ever changing human faces. Parmenides of Elea (c. 515 – 450 B.C.) thought quite differently from Heraclitus. He sought what is permanent and never changing, and proposed a duality of appearance and reality. The changing world registered by our senses is merely an illusion. There are alternatives or hypotheses about illusory appearances and they have to be searched to ferret out the reality behind them. Parmenides claimed that it is only through reason that one can indirectly learn about "real" existence, which by itself is permanent, i.e., unchanging and unmoving. How to navigate between those seemingly Scylla and Charybdis rocks of beliefs? It was Democritus (c. 460 – 370 B.C.) who, while trying to reconcile between Heraclitus and Parmenides, came to claim that there is place for both permanence and change. One should therefore search through the continuous change for some fixed reality. *What is permanent and unique is the change itself.* Permanence is found in the essence of things, while change comes from motion. According to David Hume there appear to be only three principles of connection among

ideas, namely resemblance, contiguity (in time or place), and cause or effect. This corresponds to similarity across the face space, spatial-temporal coherence, and learning and inference. There is a growing realization that tracking and recognition, i.e., change and permanence, are complementary to each other. What is indeed unique to objects, in general, and faces, in particular, and constitutes their essence, is the particular way each human face changes or morphs across multiple views and time. The spatial – temporal trajectories traced by faces are unique to each individual and should serve for their reliable identification and authentication notwithstanding uncontrolled settings.

REFERENCES

Bach, F., Thibaux, R., & Jordan, M. I. (2004). Computing regularization paths for learning multiple kernels. Advances in Neural Information Processing Systems (NIPS), 17.

Balas, B. J., & Sinha, P. (2006). Region-based representations for face recognition. *ACM Transactions on Applied Perception*, *3*(4), 354–375. doi:10.1145/1190036.1190038

Balasubramanian, V., Chakraborty, S., & Panchanathan, S. (2009). Generalized query by transduction for online active learning. In *Proceedings of Computer Vision Workshop (CVW) (12th Int. Conf. on Computer Vision)*. Kyoto, Japan: CVW.

Barlow, H. B. (1989). Unsupervised learning. *Neural Computation*, *1*, 295–311. doi:10.1162/neco.1989.1.3.295

Belkin, V., Niyogi, P., & Sindhwani, V. (2006). Manifold regularization: A geometric framework for learning from examples. *Journal of Machine Learning Research*, *7*, 2399–2434.

Bengio, Y. (2009). Learning deep architectures for AI. *Foundations and Trends in Machine Learning, 2*(1), 1–127. doi:10.1561/2200000006

Berg, T., & Belhumeur, P. (2012). Tom-vs-Pete classifiers and identity-preserving alignment for face verification. In *Proc. British Machine Vision Conference (BMVC)*. Guildford, UK: BMVC.

Beveridge, J. R., et al. (2011). When high-quality face images match poorly. In *Proc. 9th Int'l Conf. Automatic Face and Gesture Recognition (AFGR)*, (pp. 572- 578). Santa Barbara, CA: AFGR.

Bickel, S., Bruckner, M., & Scheffer, T. (2009). Discriminative learning under covariate shift. *Journal of Machine Learning Research, 10*, 2137–2155.

Chapelle, O., Scholkopf, B., & Zie, A. (Eds.). (2006). *Semi – Supervised Learning*. Cambridge, MA: MIT Press. doi:10.7551/mitpress/9780262033589.001.0001

Coates, A., & Ng, A. Y. (2011). The importance of encoding versus training with sparse coding and vector quantization. In *Proc. 25th Int. Conf. on Machine Learning*. Bellevue, WA: Academic Press.

Cox, D., & Pinto, N. (2011). Beyond simple features: A large-scale feature search approach to unconstrained face recognition. In *Proc. IEEE Automatic Face and Gesture Recognition (AFGR)*. Santa Barbara, CA: IEEE.

Dasgupta, S., & Gupta, A. (2002). An elementary proof of a theorem of Johnson and Lindenstrauss. *Random Structures and Algorithms, 22*(1), 60–65. doi:10.1002/rsa.10073

Davis, J. V., Kulis, B., Jain, P., Sra, S., & Dhillon, I. S. (2007). Information theoretic metric learning. In *Proc. 24th Int. Conf. on Machine Learning (ICML)*. Corvallis, OR: ICML.

De Marsico, M., Nappi, M., Ricci, D., & Wechsler, H. (2011). Robust face recognition after plastic surgery using local region analysis. In *Proc. Int. Conf. on Image Analysis and Recognition (ICIAR)*. Burnaby, Canada: ICIAR.

Douze, M., Jegou, H., Sandhawalia, H., Amsaleg, L., & Schmid, C. (2009). Evaluation of GIST descriptors for Web-scale image search. In *Proc. 8th ACM Int. Conf. on Image and Video Retrieval (CIVR)*. Santorini Island, Greece: ACM.

Duda, R. O., Hart, P. E., & Stork, D. G. (2000). *Pattern Classification* (2nd ed.). Wiley.

Evgeniou, T., & Pontil, M. (2004). Regularized multi-task learning. In *Proc. 17th ACM SIGKDD Int. Conf. Knowledge Discovery Data Mining*, (pp. 109–117). ACM.

Freund, Y., & Shapire, R. E. (1996). Experiments with a new boosting algorithm. In *Proc. 13th Int. Conf. on Machine Learning (ICML)*. Bari, Italy: ICML.

Friedman, F. H., Hastie, T., & Tibshirani, R. (2000). Additive logistic regression: A statistical view of boosting. *Annals of Statistics, 28*, 337–407. doi:10.1214/aos/1016218223

Fukushima, K. (1980). Neocognitron: A self-organizing neural network model for a mechanism of pattern recognition unaffected by shift in position. *Biological Cybernetics, 36*(4), 193–202. doi:10.1007/BF00344251 PMID:7370364

Ganek, A., & Corbi, T. (2003). The dawning of the autonomic computing era. *IBM Systems Journal, 42*(1), 5–18. doi:10.1147/sj.421.0005

Gates, K. A. (2011). *Our Biometric Future: Facial Recognition Technology and the Culture of Surveillance*. New York University Press.

Gong, P., Yr, J., & Zhang, C. (2012). Robust multi-task feature learning. In *Proc. 18th Conf. on Knowledge Discovery and Data Mining (KDD)*. Beijing, China: ACM.

Gonzalez-Rodriguez, J., Rose, P., Ramos, D., Toledano, D. T., & Ortega-Garcia, J. (2007). Emulating DNA: Rigorous quantification of evidential weight in transparent and testable forensic speaker recognition. *IEEE Trans. on Audio. Speech and Language Processing*, *15*(7), 2104–2115. doi:10.1109/TASL.2007.902747

Gutta, S., Huang, J., Phillip, P. J., & Wechsler, H. (2000). Mixtures of experts for categorization of human faces based on gender and ethnic origin and pose discrimination. *IEEE Transactions on Neural Networks*, *11*(4), 948–960. doi:10.1109/72.857774 PMID:18249821

Ho, S. S., & Wechsler, H. (2008). Query by transduction. *IEEE Transactions on Pattern Analysis and Machine Intelligence*, *30*(9), 1557–1571. doi:10.1109/TPAMI.2007.70811 PMID:18617715

Ho, S. S., & Wechsler, H. (2010). A Martingale framework for detecting changes in the data generating model in data streams. *IEEE Transactions on Pattern Analysis and Machine Intelligence*, *32*(12), 2113–2127. doi:10.1109/TPAMI.2010.48 PMID:20975112

Hua, G., Yang, M. H., Learned-Miller, E., Ma, Y., Turk, M., Kriegman, D. J., & Huang, T. S. (2011). Introduction to the special section on real-world face recognition. [PAMI]. *IEEE Transactions on Pattern Analysis and Machine Intelligence*, *33*(10), 1921–1924. doi:10.1109/TPAMI.2011.182

Huang, G. B., Lee, H., & Learned-Miller, E. (2012). Learning hierarchical representations for face verification with convolutional deep belief networks. In *Proc. of Computer Vision and Pattern Recognition (CVPR)*. Providence, RI: CVPR. doi:10.1109/CVPR.2012.6247968

Jarrett, K., Kavukcuoglu, K., Ranzato, M., & LeCun, Y. (2009). What is the best multi-stage architecture for object recognition? In *Proc. 12th Int. Conf. on Computer Vision (ICCV)*. Kyoto, Japan: ICCV.

Khiyari, H., DeMarsico, M., Abate, A., & Wechsler, H. (2012). Biometric interoperability across training, enrollment, and testing for the purpose of face identification. In *Proc. IEEE Workshop on Biometric Measurements and Systems for Security and Medical Applications*. Salerno, Italy: IEEE.

Klare, B., & Jain, A. (2013). Heterogeneous face recognition using kernel prototype similarities. *IEEE Transactions on Pattern Analysis and Machine Intelligence*, *35*(6), 1410–1422. doi:10.1109/TPAMI.2012.229 PMID:23599055

Kohonen, T. (1982). Self-organized formation of topologically correct feature maps. *Biological Cybernetics*, *43*(1), 59–69. doi:10.1007/BF00337288

Kulis, B., Jain, P., & Grauman, K. (2009). Fast similarity search for learned metrics. *IEEE Transactions on Pattern Analysis and Machine Intelligence*, *31*(12), 2143–2157. doi:10.1109/TPAMI.2009.151 PMID:19834137

Kumar, N., Berg, A. C., Belhumeur, P. N., & Nayar, S. K. (2011). Describable visual attributes for face verification and image search. *IEEE Transactions on Pattern Analysis and Machine Intelligence*, *33*(10), 1962–1977. doi:10.1109/TPAMI.2011.48 PMID:21383395

Le, Q. V., et al. (2012). Building high-level features using scale unsupervised learning. In *Proc. 29th Int. Conf. on Machine Learning (ICML)*. Edinburgh, UK: ICML.

Li, F., & Wechsler, H. (2005). Open set face recognition using transduction. *IEEE Transactions on Pattern Analysis and Machine Intelligence*, *27*(11), 1686–1698. doi:10.1109/TPAMI.2005.224 PMID:16285369

Li, F., & Wechsler, H. (2009). Face authentication using recognition-by-parts, boosting and transduction. *Int.* [IJPRAI]. *Journal of Artificial Intelligence and Pattern Recognition*, *23*(3), 545–573. doi:10.1142/S0218001409007193

Liu, C., & Wechsler, H. (2001). Shape-and-texture based enhanced Fisher classifier for face recognition. *IEEE Transactions on Image Processing*, *10*(4), 598–608. doi:10.1109/83.913594 PMID:18249649

Mairal, J., Bach, F., Ponce, J., & Sapiro, G. (2008). *Supervised dictionary learning*. INRIA, Report de Recherche #6652.

Miller, E. G., Matsakis, N. E., & Viola, P. A. (2000). Learning from one example through shared densities on transforms. In *Proc. Computer Vision and Pattern Recognition (CVPR)*. Hilton Head, SC: CVPR. doi:10.1109/CVPR.2000.855856

Nappi, M., & Wechsler, H. (2012). Robust re-identification using randomness and statistical learning: Quo Vadis. *Pattern Recognition Letters*, *33*(14), 1820–1827. doi:10.1016/j.patrec.2012.02.005

Nowak, E., & Jurie, F. (2007). Learning visual similarity measures for comparing never seen objects. In *Proc. Computer Vision and Pattern Recognition (CVPR)*. Minneapolis, MN: CVPR. doi:10.1109/CVPR.2007.382969

Oliva, A., & Torralba, A. (2001). Modeling the shape of the scene: A holistic representation of the spatial envelope. *International Journal of Computer Vision*, *42*(3), 145–175. doi:10.1023/A:1011139631724

Olshausen, B. A., & Field, D. A. (1996). Emergence of simple-cell receptive field properties by learning a sparse code for natural images. *Nature*, *381*, 607–609. doi:10.1038/381607a0 PMID:8637596

Parikh, D., & Grauman, K. (2011). Relative attributes. In *Proc. 13th Int. Conf. on Computer Vision (ICCV)*. Barcelona, Spain: ICCV.

Pechyony, D., Izmailov, R., Vashist, A., & Vapnik, V. (2010). SMO-style algorithms for learning using privileged information. In Proc. Data Mining (DMIN), (pp. 235 - 241). CMIN.

Poggio, T., & Smale, S. (2003). The mathematics of learning: Dealing with data. *Notices of ASM*, 537– 544.

Ramanathan, V., & Wechsler, H. (2010). Robust face recognition for occlusion and disguise using holistic anthropometric and appearance-based features and boosting. *Pattern Recognition Letters*, *30*, 2425–2435. doi:10.1016/j.patrec.2010.07.011

Rigamonti, R., Brown, M. A., & Lepetit, V. (2010). Are sparse representations really relevant for image classification? In *Proc. Computer Vision and Pattern Recognition (CVPR)*. Colorado Springs, CO: CVPR.

Rohrbach, M., Stark, M., & Schiele, B. (2011). Evaluating knowledge transfer and zero-shot learning in a large scale setting. In *Proc. Computer Vision and Pattern Recognition (CVPR)*. Colorado Springs, CO: CVPR. doi:10.1109/CVPR.2011.5995627

Rubinstein, Y. D., & Hastie, T. (1997). Discriminative vs. informative learning. In Proceedings of Knowledge and Data Discovery (KDD), (pp. 49–53). ACM.

Scheirer, W. J., Rocha, A., Parris, J., & Boult, T. E. (2012). Learning for meta-recognition. *IEEE Transactions on Information Forensics and Security*, 7(4), 1214–1224. doi:10.1109/TIFS.2012.2192430

Serre, T., Wolf, L., Bileschi, S., Riesenhuber, M., & Poggio, T. (2007). Robust object recognition with cortex-like mechanisms. *IEEE Transactions on Pattern Analysis and Machine Intelligence*, 29(3), 411–426. doi:10.1109/TPAMI.2007.56 PMID:17224612

Shale-Schwartz, S., Wexler, Y., & Shashua, A. (2011). ShareBoost: Efficient multiclass learning with feature sharing. In *Proceedings of Advances in Neural Information Processing Systems (NIPS)*. Granada, Spain: NIPS.

Shen, C., Wang, P., & Wang, H. (2012). UBoost: Boosting with the Universum. *IEEE Transactions on Pattern Analysis and Machine Intelligence*, 34(4), 825–832. doi:10.1109/TPAMI.2011.240 PMID:22156096

Shi, Q., Erikkson, A., Van den Hengel, A., & Shen, C. (2011). Is face recognition really a compressive sensing problem? In *Proc. Computer Vision and Pattern Recognition (CVPR)*. Colorado Springs, CO: CVPR. doi:10.1109/CVPR.2011.5995556

Slaney, M., & Casey, M. (2008). Locality-sensitive hashing for finding nearest neighbors. *IEEE Signal Processing Magazine*, 128–131. doi:10.1109/MSP.2007.914237

Sugiyama, M., Krauledat, M., & Muller, K. R. (2007). Covariate shift adaptation by importance weighted cross validation. *Journal of Machine Learning Research*, 8, 985–1005.

Torralba, A., & Efros, A. A. (2011). Unbiased look at dataset bias. In *Proc. Computer Vision and Pattern Recognition (CVPR)*. Colorado Springs, CO: CVPR.

Uludag, U., & Jain, A. (2006). Securing fingerprint template: Fuzzy vault with helper data. In *Proc. IEEE Workshop on Privacy Research in Vision*. New York: IEEE.

Vapnik, V. (2000). *The Nature of Statistical Learning Theory* (2nd ed.). Springer. doi:10.1007/978-1-4757-3264-1

Vapnik, V. N. (2006). *Estimation of Dependencies Based on Empirical Data: Empirical Inference Science: Afterword of 2006*. Springer.

Vovk, V., Gammerman, A., & Shafer, G. (2005). *Algorithmic Learning in a Random World*. Springer.

Wechsler, H. (2007). *Reliable Face Recognition Methods*. Springer. doi:10.1007/978-0-387-38464-1

Weinberger, K. O., Blitzer, J., & Saul, L. K. (2006). Distance metric learning for large margin nearest neighbor classifier. In *Proceedings of Advances in Neural Information Processing Systems (NIPS)*. Vancouver, Canada: NIPS.

Weston, J., Collobert, R., Sinz, F., Bottou, L., & Vapnik, V. (2006). Inference with the Universum. In *Proc. 23rd Int. Conf. Machine Learning*, (pp. 1009–1016). Academic Press.

Wolf, L., Hassner, T., & Taigman, Y. (2011). Effective unconstrained face recognition by combining multiple descriptors and learned background statistics. *IEEE Transactions on Pattern Analysis and Machine Intelligence*, 33(10), 1978–1990. doi:10.1109/TPAMI.2010.230 PMID:21173442

Wolf, L., & Levy, N. (2013). The SVM-minus similarity score for video face recognition. In *Proc. Computer Vision and Pattern Recognition (CVPR)*. Portland, OR: CVPR. doi:10.1109/CVPR.2013.452

Wright, J., Yang, A. Y., Ganesh, A., Sastry, S. S., & Ma, Y. (2009). Robust face recognition via sparse representation. *IEEE Transactions on Pattern Analysis and Machine Intelligence, 31*(2), 210–227. doi:10.1109/TPAMI.2008.79 PMID:19110489

Xiang, S., Yuan, L., Fan, W., Wang, Y., Thompson, P. M., & Ye, J. (2013). Multi-source learning with block-wise missing data for Alzheimer's disease prediction. In *Proc. 19th Conf. on Knowledge Discovery and Data Mining (KDD)*. Chicago, IL: ACM.

Xing, E., Ng, A., Jordan, S., & Russell, S. (2003). Distance metric learning with applications to clustering with side-information. In *Proceedings of Advances in Neural Information Processing Systems (NIPS)*. Vancouver, Canada: NIPS.

Xu, W., Caramanis, C., & Mannor, S. (2012). Sparse algorithms are not stable: A no free-lunch theorem. *IEEE Transactions on Pattern Analysis and Machine Intelligence, 34*(1), 187–193. doi:10.1109/TPAMI.2011.177 PMID:21844627

Yager, N., & Dunstone, T. (2010). The biometric menagerie. *IEEE Transactions on Pattern Analysis and Machine Intelligence, 32*(2), 220–230. doi:10.1109/TPAMI.2008.291 PMID:20075454

Yin, Q., Tang, X., & Sun, J. (2011). An associate-predict model for face recognition. In *Proc. Computer Vision and Pattern Recognition (CVPR)*. Colorado Springs, CO: CVPR.

KEY TERMS AND DEFINITIONS

Active Learning: Choosing what can benefit biometric learning / training most and when.

Chorus of Prototypes: Type of face space when the coordinate axes correspond to particular faces, e.g., celebrities, or face luster driven by diversity, e.g., demographics. Similar to dictionaries used in sparse coding.

Collective Classification: Ensemble classification where similar faces cluster and are labeled in a similar fashion. Similarity can include events and relationships, e.g., photo tagging.

Covariance Shift: Difference in data distribution between training and test data sets.

Data Fusion and Ensemble Methods: Multi-sensory and/or multi-functional combination of methods and/or features for the purpose of authentication. Multi-sensory suites of interest include iris, fingerprints, and face biometrics. Methods can combine PCA and LDA, e.g., Fisherfaces, while simple stump features are most suitable for cascade face detection, similar to boosting.

Deep Learning: Automatic learning of feature / image (face) representations substitute for handcraft features using hierarchical and distributed networks trained with stochastic gradient descent (SGD).

Face Space: Forensic basis to represent faces. The repertoire of features chosen corresponds to coordinate axes. It is relevant to change, drift, and imposter detection, on one side, and to face aging, in particular.

Interoperability: Operational ability across diverse and heterogeneous biometric data sets rather than on individual data sets, for the purpose of cross-data set generalization, where one trains on one data set, while still able to query / test on another, possibly leveraging transfer learning.

Local Estimation / Classification: Estimation and classification should be performed on filtered / binned data, with the filter, e.g., "gender," discarding candidates whose characteristics are different from those of the query. As an example, male queries should not search the female gallery.

Local Sensitivity Hash (LSH): LSH makes large scale image search practical using approximate similarity search methods, with a predictable loss in accuracy for high-dimensional queries traded for fast sub-linear scalable search. The fundamental idea behind LSH is to first build a family of hash functions H such that for each function, the probability of collision is much higher for the high-dimensional points which are close to each other than it is for those which are far apart.

Open Set Recognition: Allow for reject option when match is not enrolled.

Ranking: Matching any face biometric for identification purposes returns candidate faces that are ordered / ranked in terms of their similarity to the query. The particular order of candidates and particular ranking of ground truth match generates the Cumulative Matching Curve (CMC).

Recognition-by-Parts: Face recognition driven by face components and their configuration rather than by the whole face.

Re-Identification: Matching objects and/or their parts across multiple but possibly disjoint fields of view and video frames for the purpose of sequential authentication over space and time. Detection and seeding for initialization do not presume known identity and allow for re-identification of objects and/or faces whose identity might remain unknown.

Semi-Supervised Learning and Transduction: Semi-supervised learning and transduction, complementary to each other, learn from both annotated ("labeled") and unlabeled (side – information) data, with semi-supervised learning to classify (via implied generalization and induction) across "all" domains, while transduction limited to classify only the unlabeled data used to learn the classifier.

Statistical Learning: Learning driven by complexity control, e.g., support vector machines (SVM), which seeks to avoid over-fitting and under-fitting. It suggests sensitivity and stability analysis for both authentication and generalization ability.

Transfer Learning: Learning from one domain and transferring the knowledge gained to similar tasks, e.g., learning about face representation from one data set and using that knowledge for another data set, similar to deep learning.

Section 2
Face Recognition under Real World PIE Variations

This section discusses in more detail the present face recognition issues related to Pose, Illumination, and Expression (PIE) variations. Besides these classical problems, more recent research lines are focused on demographics and different kinds of disguise (e.g. plastic surgery), which may hinder recognition. 3D-based methods seem to provide better performance than 2D-based ones, but they are generally computationally expensive and may not be feasible in real-world settings. A further comparison is among global and local methods. The latter seem more robust to partial distortions, which are caused by PIE. Multimodal fusion offers further support to the problem of recognition in adverse conditions.

Chapter 4

3D Face Recognition in the Presence of Partial Data:
A Semi-Coupled Dictionary Learning Approach

Dat Chu
University of Houston, USA

Shishir Shah
University of Houston, USA

Ioannis A. Kakadiaris
University of Houston, USA

ABSTRACT

Performing face recognition under extreme poses and lighting conditions remains a challenging task for current state-of-the-art biometric algorithms. The recognition task is even more challenging when there is insufficient training data available in the gallery, or when the gallery dataset originates from one side of the face while the probe dataset originates from the other. The authors present a new method for computing the distance between two biometric signatures acquired under such challenging conditions. This method improves upon an existing Semi-Coupled Dictionary Learning method by computing a jointly-optimized solution that incorporates the reconstruction cost, the discrimination cost, and the semi-coupling cost. The use of a semi-coupling term allows the method to handle partial 3D face meshes where, for example, only the left side of the face is available for gallery and the right side of the face is available for probe. The method also extends to 2D signatures under varying poses and lighting changes by using 3D signatures as a coupling term. The experiments show that this method can improve recognition performance of existing state-of-the-art wavelet signatures used in 3D face recognition and provide excellent recognition results in the 3D-2D face recognition application.

DOI: 10.4018/978-1-4666-5966-7.ch004

1. INTRODUCTION

With the proliferation of newer sensors capable of capturing higher quality data, the problem of face recognition remains ever interesting for its wide applicability to numerous real life applications (e.g., law enforcement, aid distribution, health care administration, personnel management, video game augmentation, virtual personal assistance). While the problem of face recognition from a frontal view without occlusions under various lighting conditions has been extensively investigated, few have addressed the problem by using a bridging three-dimensional (3D) representation of the data.

Three dimensional data of the face is an empowering medium. The Face Recognition Vendor Test (FRVT) 2006 (Phillips et al., 2007) demonstrated the usefulness of 3D data in the task of recognition. In this large-scale test, algorithms using 3D data performed equally well against algorithms that use very high resolution 2D data in the task of face recognition. However, algorithms using 3D shape data have an inherent advantage at dealing with variations in pose and illumination. Although the cost of 3D sensors is still high, the success of household entertainment devices capable of producing depth information (e.g., Microsoft Kinect) suggests that 3D sensors will be widely available in the near future. Thus, it is especially beneficial to take advantage of 3D data in addressing current recognition challenges involving either 3D or 2D data.

One of these challenges is incomplete or partial 3D data due to occlusion. For example, when the subject in front of the camera looks sideways, the sensor can only capture part of the face due to the face's convexity. Because there is significant visual difference between a partial face and a complete face, the ability to recognize subjects with only a partial face is particularly desirable.

Existing methods address this challenge by taking advantage of the intrinsic symmetry of the face (Passalis & Perakis, 2011), splitting the face into multiple parts (Li, Imai, & Kaneko, 2010), or learning the variation of the face through robust descriptors (Liao & Jain, 2011). These methods, however, suffer from specific limitations ranging from an exhaustive weight search step to reduce the size of the signature (Passalis & Perakis, 2011), being limited to use with frontal faces (Li et al., 2010), or the dictionary for the descriptors being neither optimized for the task of recognition nor for reconstruction of the original descriptors (Liao & Jain, 2011).

Another of these challenges is to handle 2D face recognition under both strong pose and lighting condition changes. These variables result in great variations in the observed data (Figure 13) and make the recognition task particularly challenging. Previous works have addressed this problem by fitting appearance models, using pose-robust and light-robust descriptors or by hallucinating 3D views of the 2D subject.

Contrary to existing methods, our approach tackles the problem of face recognition using 3D partial data and the problem of 2D face recognition under pose and lighting variations by learning a dictionary that jointly optimizes for reconstruction cost, discrimination cost, and semi-coupling cost. The semi-coupling cost favors dictionaries learned for different partial and 2D faces to be linearly mappable to the encoding of 3D frontal faces. Our contributions include the following:

1. Developed a new face recognition method that uses 3D data when only part of the 3D facial data are available or when only 2D facial data are available in gallery and probe.
2. Developed a jointly-optimized solution to the problem of semi-coupling dictionary learning for face recognition using partial data.
3. Provided semantically sound error terms with intuitive parameters in the dictionary learning objective function.

Our method uses the Haar wavelet signatures proposed by Kakadiaris et al. (2007). In order to effectively use this robust signature for the task of recognition, an exhaustive weight search is required to find the best sub-signature of the full wavelet set. Our method has the advantage of removing this computationally expensive step. Furthermore, it is also extensible to other types of signatures (e.g., signatures of low resolution faces, signatures of face sketches) and does not explicitly require reconstruction/hallucination for the task of recognition. The method also works when there is only a single capture per subject in the gallery.

The rest of the chapter is organized as follows. Section 2 covers the current state-of-the-art methods in partial/2D face recognition and dictionary learning. Section 3 describes our approach to the problem of face recognition by using a bridging 3D representation. Section 4 describes the dataset used and the experiments. Finally, Section 5 finalizes this work and offers concluding remarks.

2. BACKGROUND

2.1 Face Recognition Overview

This section briefly summarizes the accomplishments and ongoing work of the UH biometrics group in the area of image and video-based face recognition.

Face recognition (FR) is an attractive biometric since it can be done passively and unobtrusively at a comfortable distance. The performance of most existing FR systems is broadly affected by varying illumination conditions, changes in pose, and poor image quality (e.g., blurry images, low resolution). Although 3D FR does not suffer from inherent problems of pose and illumination variations, it is not feasible to limit FR to using 3D data. *Our approach is to leverage a generic annotated 3D face model to address variations related to pose, illumination, and resolution to improve FR*

from unconstrained images and videos. In the following, we briefly describe our progress in the development of methods for (i) super-resolution and image enhancement to tackle distance, sensor and resolution inefficiencies; (ii) methods for 3D model generation by fitting a generic 3D model to one or multiple images for pose normalization; and (iii) outdoor illumination normalization methods.

Super-Resolution and Enhancement: We have developed and continue to improve methods to obtain super-resolution (SR) facial images from low-resolution, noisy, and blurred facial images. Our approach is motivated by the observation that high-frequency information in facial images plays a significant role in the performance of FR systems. Therefore, we propose to recover an SR image of a given low-resolution image by adding high-frequency components from an *a priori* learned model (Bilgazyev & Efros, 2011). The high-frequency components of SR are computed as the weighted sum of high-frequency components of facial images from a training database. The weights are determined through manifold learning via sparse representation techniques. Specifically, a single dictionary is learned from the coupled high frequency components of high- and low-resolution image patches. The patches overlap to impose local consistency in reconstruction. During reconstruction, the dictionaries are decoupled and the sparse representation of the low resolution patches is directly used to recover the sparse representation of the high-resolution patches. For the case of blurred images, even after applying state-of-the-art deblurring methods, the performance of the FR systems does not improve considerably. This can be attributed to the fact that a linear blur model cannot account for the non-linear outliers often existing in real imaging systems. These outliers generally fall in the category of saturated pixels, non-Gaussian noise, nonlinear response curve of the cameras, and/or the residual artifacts after denoising. We have developed an Application Specific Image Enhancement method (ASIE) for facial images

(Bilgazyev & Kurkure, 2013). We first perform denoising and deblurring and then apply a novel residual artifact removal step to obtain an enhanced image using sparse encoding methods (Figure 1). We formulate it as an example-based super resolution problem where prior knowledge is obtained offline from the training examples using sparse representation techniques.

Experience with Geometric Models of the Face: Our group has developed a 3D-3D FR software (UR3D) (Kakadiaris & Passalis, 2007) that achieved a verification rate of 97.1% at 10^{-3} false acceptance rate and ranked first in the 3D-shape section of the 2007 FR Vendor Test organized by NIST. Currently, our system has broken the bar-

rier of 99% verification rate (Ocegueda & Fang, 2013) and gave the best results for the recognition of identical twins when compared with other five state-of-the-art methods (Vijayan & Bowyer, 2011). Recently, we have developed a 3D-2D FR system (UH2D) (Toderici & Passalis, 2010) that handles large pose and illumination variations. The principle of UR2D is the explicit use of a 3D deformable face model that allows for the registration of 3D and 2D data and facilitates face alignment, pose and illumination normalization and local facial signature extraction. We have proposed and built upon a 3D-2D FR scenario where the gallery (or target) set consists of raw 3D shape and 2D texture data and the probe (or query) in-

Figure 1. Depiction of the (a) low-resolution image captured using a tracking surveillance camera and (b) its enhancement using our method. (c) Magnification of the regions in (a), and visual output of (d) denoising, (e) deblurring, and (f) artifact removal steps of ASIE. FR results from FaceIt after using the spatial resolution enhancement methods. Note that when ASIE is used, the recognition rates are higher than using two other existing methods.

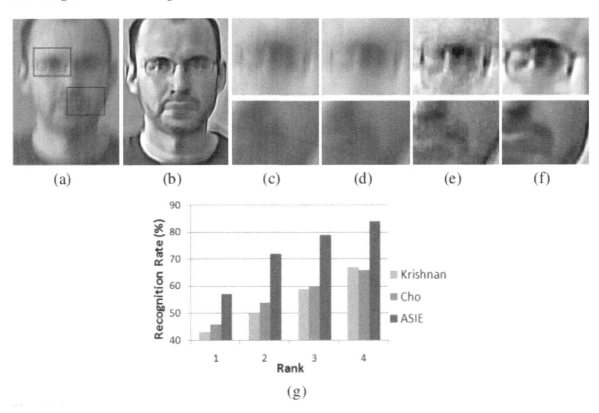

volves a collection of 2D facial images. During enrollment or gallery processing, subject-specific 3D annotated models are built by using the available raw 3D data and 2D texture. During recognition, the probe 2D images are projected onto a normalized image space using the subject-specific 3D models in the gallery and landmark-based 3D-2D projection estimation. This allows for the construction of personalized, pose-normalized signatures on a one-to-one basis for verification or one-to-many for identification purposes. A bidirectional relighting algorithm, using an analytical skin reflectance model, is ap-

plied for non-linear, local illumination normalization of the registered face texture images and a global similarity metric based on local edge-orientation correlations provides a similarity score for a single gallery-probe comparison. Statistically significant results were obtained outperforming existing methods (Figure 2).

Pose Normalization using a generic 3D model: Our framework for FR extracts an appearance-based facial signature through model-based registration and alignment. A generic 3D annotated face model is fit to the data and pose normalization is accomplished by lifting texture from images

Figure 2. (a) Overview of UH2D; (b) comparison with the LIRIS-3Da 3D-2D system and with the results of a 2D FR commercial system using multi-pose, 3D-generated galleries

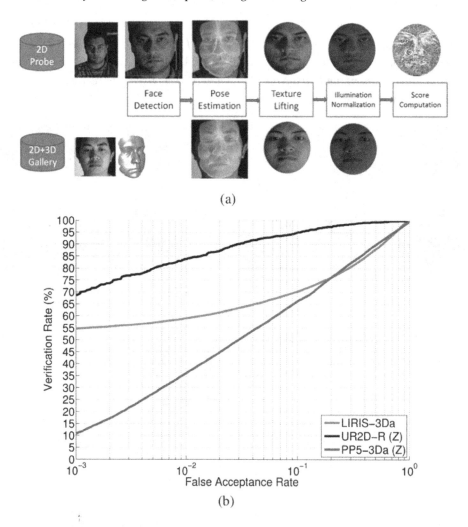

(a)

(b)

and video. In doing so, we formulate a 2D-driven method for 2D pose estimation and 3D-2D fitting of a point 3D face model (3D facial landmarks), map the resulting 2D fitted point model to clusters of dense 3D models, and learn the representation and 3D-2D correspondence for selecting a dense (surface) 3D model.

Illumination Normalization: Outdoor illumination conditions are quite different from indoor illumination in several aspects. First, the illumination intensity and color vary with the weather and time of the day. Second, high dynamic range can be generated on the faces, with the shadow being the low end and the specular reflection being the high end. Third, reflection of sky or sunlight from surfaces, such as water, can create extra lighting sources with low incident angles. All these variations add a level of difficulty that has rarely been taken into account in the relevant literature. Based on our experience with illumination normalization (Zhao & Chu, 2013; Zhao & Shah, 2012, 2013) we are developing methods to normalize the outdoor illumination on the face texture and estimate the face albedo.

2.2 Partial Data

Passalis (Passalis & Perakis, 2011) addressed the problem of partial faces by mirroring the external forces used in their fitting step while maintaining the internal force (i.e., spring-like force amongst the data points). The resulting fitted data thus retains both the intrisic facial shape of the annotated face model (AFM) while fitting to the available data from one side of the face. This approach allows the wavelet method used by Kakadiaris (Kakadiaris & Passalis, 2007) to be applied on the final fitted data. This approach suffers from the same problem as Kakadiaris and Passalis, (2007) since it requires the same exhaustive weight search to determine which subset of the signature performs best in the task of recognition. It also works best on data that can be mirrored along the vertical axis.

Liao (Liao & Jain, 2011) addresses the facial occlusion without prior alignment of the images by utilizing SIFT (Lowe, 1999) image descriptors. This method learns a dictionary for the SIFT descriptors per class. Recognition is performed by selecting the class with dictionary atoms that best reconstruct the probe signal. However, this method does not optimize for a better set of dictionary atoms. Instead, it directly uses the gallery descriptors as dictionary atoms. Zhang and Li (2010) have shown that a trained dictionary reduces the sparse encoding complexity and guarantees a better performance in the task of recognition. This is why the authors had to use an approximation method to solve the multi-class sparse encoding problem.

Recently, Gan and Xiao (2011) improved upon Nagesh and Li's B-JSM algorithm (Nagesh & Li, 2009) to handle occlusion in 2D face recognition. The algorithm modifies the classification function following the observation that "inter-class energy difference of training images corresponding to the test image occluded region is smaller than non-occluded region." This algorithm, however, still requires multiple training images per class, and only handles artificial occlusions on frontal images.

Jiang proposed the LC-KSVD algorithm (Jiang, Lin, & Davis, 2011) which improves upon Zhang and Li 's Discriminative KSVD algorithm (Zhang & Li, 2010). Jiang's method claims improvement over Zhang and Li's dictionary learning scheme by incorporating an extra constraint called label consistency. However, this extra constraint generates an extra variable (called L in Jiang et al. (2011)) in the optimization which has unclear semantics, especially with respect to the L_2 loss which was used in the chapter.

Wang, Zhang, Liang, and Pan (2012) solved the problem of synthesizing from a sketch image to a real photo by learning two separate dictionaries and iteratively optimizing for a linear matrix that connects the encodings generated by each dictionary. Their approach improved upon Yang (Yang & Wright, 2010) by removing the restriction that encodings of both dictionaries be exactly the same. Their method performed well in the task of image synthesis. However, since the optimization is iterative, the resulting dictionary atoms were not guaranteed to be jointly optimized.

Rara (Rara, Farag, & Davis, 2011) attempted to solve the problem of 3D shape reconstruction using an approach similar to ours. Their method finds a mapping from the 2D feature point PCA coefficients to the 3D shape PCA coefficients using the Ordinary Least Square method. In comparison, our method finds a mapping between the sparse encodings by solving with ridge regression as part of our optimization. Thus, our method not only finds a more representative dictionary, it also jointly solves the coupling problem presented in (Rara et al., 2011).

3. METHODS

We propose a method to perform face matching and face identification that (i) can cope with partial data in gallery and probe even when there is only one single dataset per subject, and (ii) can work even when these datasets are from different configurations (i.e., the gallery dataset contains 2D facial data under lighting and pose variations while the probe dataset contains 3D data from the right side of the face). Our method (i) requires a training dataset to learn the variation and mapping of each configuration, and (ii) assumes that the type of configuration is known for each dataset (i.e., given a dataset, we know to which of the available configurations it belongs: frontal 3D, left-face 3D, 2D, ...).

Our method has a training module and a deployment module. In training, we learn a set of dictionaries, classifiers and mapping for the different configurations. An overview of the training pipeline is depicted in Figure 3. In deployment, our method classifies the input probe by how

similar their configurations' classifiers responses are compared to those of the gallery (Section 3.2). The recognition pipeline is depicted in Figure 10.

3.1 Training

We perform training using a training cohort. This training cohort needs to have at least one dataset per configuration per subject. This cohort should contain the subject label and the configuration label for each dataset. These configurations can be a frontal face configuration (F), a left face configuration (L) or a right face configuration (R). Extension to 2D data is straightforward. We simply denote another configuration (2D) and apply the same steps below. For purposes of clarity, we omit the 2D configuration in our algorithm section. However, the L configuration and the R configuration should be taken as any configuration observable of the given data.

If the training cohort contains data for all the subjects in the gallery and probe, it can be used directly. If there are only two datasets per subject (one for gallery, one for probe), a training cohort from an external database can be used as long as the training cohort contains at least one dataset per configuration per subject. These subjects need not appear in the gallery and probe.

Algorithm 1 summarizes the steps involved in training. The symbols D, W, T, X and A will be defined in the upcoming sections.

3.1.1 Step 1: Extracting Signatures

To normalize the effects of pose, expression, and lighting, we fit an Annotated Face Model (AFM) developed by Kakadiaris and Passalis (2007) to the input mesh (Figure 4). The AFM is an annotated model constructed from the mean of a set of aligned 3D meshes. The AFM has the advantage of having an injective mapping between its 3D points to points on a 2D surface. In computer graphics, this is referred to as having a *UV mapping*. Such mapping allows data that exist per 3D mesh point

Figure 3. Overview of the discriminative semi-coupled dictionary learning algorithm

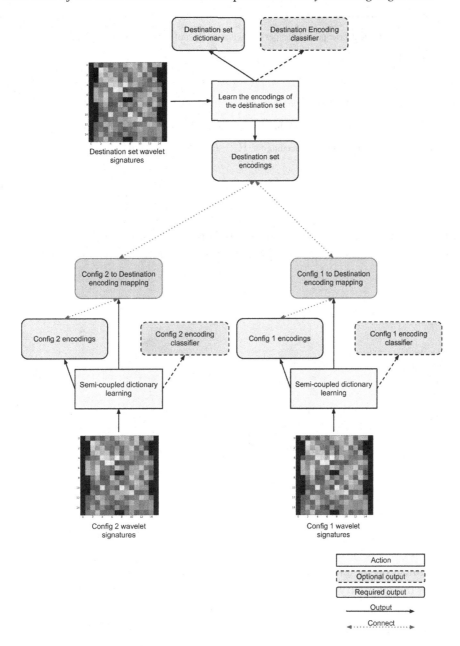

be represented on a 2D image called a geometry image (Gu, Gortler, & Hoppe, 2002).

The AFM provides a frame of reference similar to that of the mean shape in Active Shape Model (ASM) (Cootes, Taylor, Cooper, & Graham, 1995). However, unlike ASM, one does not have to retrain the AFM on a new dataset. The AFM is also annotated with semantic information (e.g., which region is the nose, which region is the mouth, etc.) which can, in turn, carry extra information for each part (e.g., different weights can be attached to different regions). Given an AFM, for every input mesh we can normalize its position and scale. Then, by using the AFM's UV mapping, we can

Algorithm 1. Training

Input: Training cohort that contains one dataset per subject per configuration. List of configurations $= \left\{ F, L, R \right\}$.

Output: D_F, D_L, D_R, W_F, W_L, W_R, $T_{L \to F}$, $T_{R \to F}$.

1. Extract signatures: X_F, X_L, X_R.

2. Obtain a dictionary, a classifier, and the encoding for the destination configuration $\mathrm{F}: D_F, W_F, A_F$ using Equation 2.

3. Obtain a dictionary, a classifier, a mapping and the encoding for $\mathrm{L}: D_L, W_L, T_{L \to F}, A_L$ using Equation 3.

4. Obtain a dictionary, a classifier, a mapping and the encoding for $\mathrm{R}: D_R, W_R, T_{R \to F}, A_R$ using Equation 3.

Figure 4. Fitting an AFM to an input mesh. (a) The AFM (color) in the same coordinate system as the input mesh; (b) the AFM is aligned with the input mesh; (c) the AFM is fitted to the input mesh; (d) the fitted mesh output.

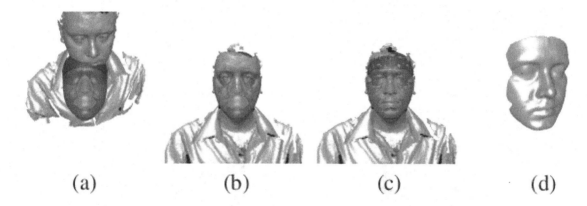

(a) (b) (c) (d)

generate the geometry image representation of these fitted meshes for further processing while retaining their alignment on the grid.

Figure 5 depicts the geometry image representation of the fitted mesh in Figure 4(d). Each pixel in the geometry image contains the (x, y, z) coordinate triplet of a mesh point. Once mapped to a regular grid, the geometry image can be used by algorithms that take as input a 2D array. We can, then, extract the Haar wavelet packets (Stoll-nitz, DeRose, & Salesin, 1996) from such a geometry image. This wavelet has been shown to perform very well in the task of recognition (Ka-kadiaris & Passalis, 2007).

The AFM allows not only geometry information to be converted to a 2D image but also any piece of information that exists per vertex of the mesh (e.g., normal information, texture information, depth information, lighting condition). In Figure 6, the normal image of the same subject is depicted. Each pixel in the normal image contains the (N_x, N_y, N_z) vector triplet of a normal vector at the corresponding point. That is, if G is the geometry image of size $k \times k$, and N is the normal image of size $k \times k$, the value at $G(i, j)$ is the (x, y, z) coordinate of the point whose normal vector information is stored at $N(i, j) \forall i, j \in [1, k]$.

Figure 5. The geometry image representation of a fitted mesh. (a) The geometry with channels (x, y, z) mapped to (r, g, b) for visualization; (b) only the x-channel of the geometry image; (c) only the y-channel of the geometry image; (d) only the z-channel of the geometry image.

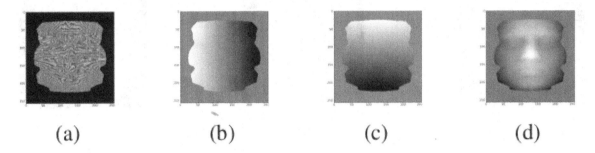

(a)   (b)   (c)   (d)

Figure 6. The normal image representation of a fitted mesh. (a) The normal with channels (N_x, N_y, N_z) mapped to (r, g, b) for visualization; (b) only the N_x-channel of the normal image; (c) only the N_y-channel of the normal image; (d) only the N_z-channel of the normal image.

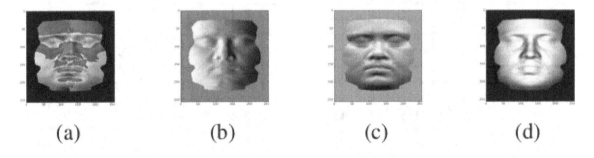

(a)   (b)   (c)   (d)

Once fitted to the AFM and converted to the geometry image, the input meshes remain aligned to each other at each pixel of the geometry image. This means that the wavelet packets extracted for each mesh are aligned to each other (i.e., wavelet packets of the same location represent each subject information at the same scale and orientation). This is important because it allows us to learn the information contained in each packet independently. This greatly speeds up the processing time. The full four-level Walsh wavelet packets are extracted from the geometry image and normal image of each input mesh. These wavelet packets contain the gradient information at multiple scales and levels of the respective geometry image and normal image.

Since the wavelet packets of geometry and normal correspond to each other, one can splice two corresponding wavelet packets (one from geometry, one from normal) together to increase the pixel utilization in each wavelet image. Figure 7 depicts an example of extracting the wavelet signatures from the geometry image and normal image. Figure 8 depicts the first packet from the geometry wavelet and from the normal wavelet spliced together to conserve space. Once spliced, the packet data is organized into $16 \times 16 = 256$ packets each of size $16 \times 16 \times 3$ pixels (Figure 9). This splicing operation allows us to perform one learning step for both the geometry and normal information. It also focuses on the upper part

Figure 7. The geometry packet (a) is spliced into the top half of the output packet (b), while the normal packet (c) is spliced into the bottom half of the output packet (b).

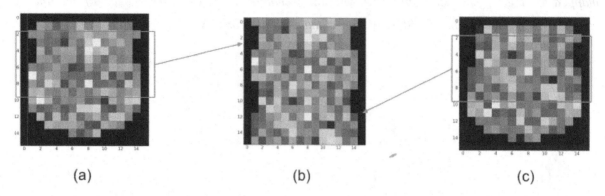

(a)　　　　　　　　　　(b)　　　　　　　　　　(c)

Figure 8. The wavelets as extracted from the geometry image (a) and normal image (b).

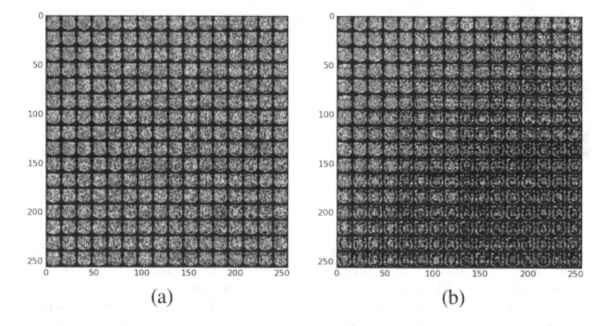

(a)　　　　　　　　　　　　(b)

of the face which is more rigid in the presence of facial expression.

While these packets have good performance in the task of full face recognition, they do not perform well in the task of partial face recognition. A complete packet set also uses up valuable storage space. Thus, to increase the performance and decrease the storage requirement, Kakadiaris performed a combinatorial search for a set of 40 out of 256 packets that perform best for a training dataset. These 40 wavelet packets were selected using Simulated Annealing (Siarry, Berthiau, Durbin, & Haussy, 1997). To forego such an expensive search, we propose a variation of LC-KSVD that learns a set of dictionary atoms which perform well in recognition for the training set. Such a dictionary, once trained, will also reduce the storage requirement of all signatures since only the encoding coefficients need to be stored. However, such training is only possible

Figure 9. Four-level Walsh wavelets extracted from geometry and normal image of a fitted mesh. (a) 16 × 16 wavelet packets; (b) X-channel of the wavelet packets; (c) Y-channel of the wavelet packets; (d) Z-channel of the wavelet packets.

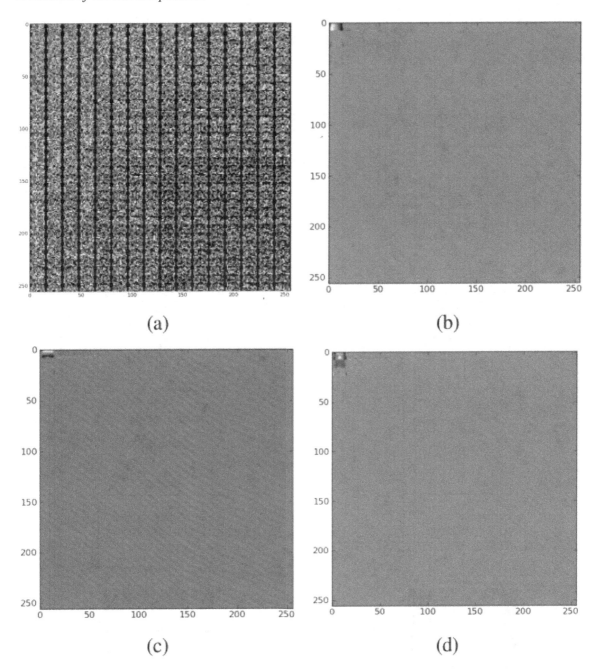

(a)

(b)

(c)

(d)

when there exist enough data in the gallery. In the case of partial face recognition, we need a set of dictionary atoms capable of reconstructing the original signal while performing well in discriminating the subjects. Hence, we propose the Semi-Coupled Dictionary Learning with KSVD method (SCD-KSVD) that ties together these different representations while simultaneously optimizing for both the reconstruction and the discrimination error (Section 3.1.3).

Figure 10. Overview of the matching steps for the discriminative semi-coupled dictionary learning algorithm

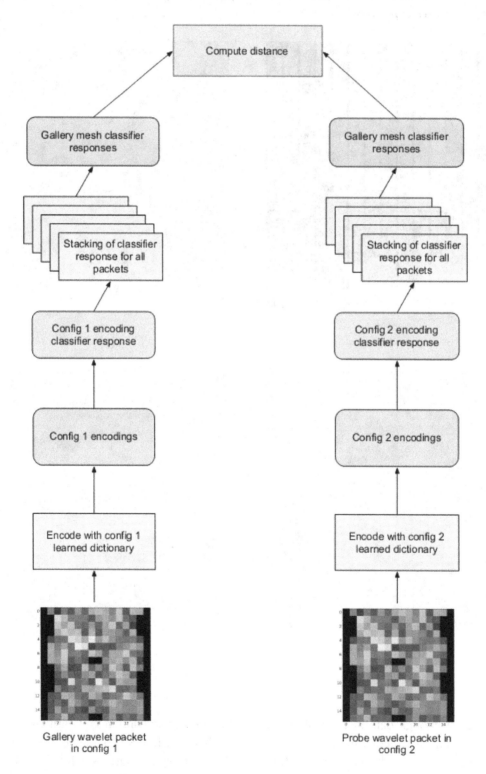

3.1.2 Step 2: Learn the Dictionary, Classifier and Encoding for the Destination Configuration F

Since the training cohort contains at least one training sample per configuration per subject, we elect to choose one of these configurations (F) as the *destination configuration*. Features extracted from data in the F configuration will be referred to as *destination features*. The destination feature should be the feature that has previously performed well in the face recognition task.

Let X be the wavelet signature extracted from all training meshes for a single packet. We need to learn a dictionary D that represents this packet across all training data for our subjects. If we are only interested in the reconstruction of the destination signature (e.g., frontal high resolution full face) from a partial signature (e.g., side face signature), a dictionary learning method that solves for the reconstruction cost (Equation 1) should suffice:

$$\arg\min_{(D,A)} \frac{1}{2} \| X - DA \|_2^2 + \alpha \| A \|_0 \qquad (1)$$

where A is the encoding matrix. Each column of A is a vector of coefficients describing how much each atom in D contributes to the reconstruction of the signal in the corresponding column in X, and α is the weighting parameter determining the relative importance between reconstruction and sparsity. This formulation is the typical l_1 norm relaxation to the l_0 norm sparse dictionary learning. It can be solved using either Mairal's method (Mairal, Bach, Ponce, & Sapiro, 2010) or Aharon's method (Aharon, Elad, & Bruckstein, 2005) by solving for the l_0 directly.

If we want to also perform recognition on the destination encodings, it is beneficial to optimize for the extended formulation proposed by Zhang's (Zhang & Li, 2010) DSVD method:

$$\arg\min_{D,W,A} \| X - DA \|_2^2 + \alpha \| H - WA \|_2^2$$
$$s.t. \| A \|_0 < \varepsilon \qquad (2)$$

where H is the label matrix and ε is the parameter which controls how many non-zero elements are allowed per encoding vector. The label matrix H's columns contain the label for the corresponding columns in X. A label column in H has all zero elements except at the row whose index corresponds to the class encoded. For example, a label column for a signature of the 5th subject has the 5th row with the value of one, and zero in all other rows.

If we choose to use this method, we will obtain a matrix W aside from D and A. Each column of the matrix W is a linear classifier that measures how likely an encoding encoded with D is to belong to a specific class provided in H. In other words, given an encoding vector a, the index of the maximum value in the vector $W * a$ corresponds to the predicted class of x.

3.1.3 Steps 3 and 4: Discriminative Semi-Coupled Dictionary Learning with K-SVD (DSC-KSVD)

To differentiate the dictionary and encoding of the other configurations' signatures from the dictionary and encoding of the destination signature, we shall refer to the dictionary trained for destination signature as D_F and the encodings obtained with such dictionary for our training data as A_F. These values can be obtained by solving either Equation 1 or Equation 2.

As described in Step 1 of Algorithm 1, we extract the signatures from the training set for the L and R configurations. The method of Kakadiaris (Kakadiaris & Passalis, 2007) provides a multitude of options that can be configured to work with different signatures. For example, we can fit only the left side of the AFM (or only the right side of the AFM) to learn the relationship between signatures obtained with such fitting versus the normal frontal fitting. Let X_L and X_R be the signatures obtained from data in configuration L and configuration R, respectively. Our task is then, for each configuration, to learn a dictionary (D_i) that represents its data, a classification matrix (W_i) that classifies its encodings, and a linear mapping ($T_{i \to F}$) that maps such encodings to the corresponding destination encoding A_F.

$$\arg \min_{D_i, W_i, T_i, A_i} \\ \| Y_i - D_i A_i \|_2^2 + \alpha \| H_i - W_i A_i \|_2^2 + \beta \| A_F - T_{i \to F} A_i \|_2^2 \tag{3}$$

$$s.t. \| A_i \|_0 < \varepsilon_p, \forall i \in \left\{ L, R \right\}$$

The formulation solves the semi-coupling problem posed by (Wang, et al., 2012) in the same framework used by (Jiang, et al., 2011) while overcoming Jiang's inability to provide a semantic for the term L used in the optimization. This formulation is thus simple as it only requires one single optimization with KSVD. The formulation is also semantically sound: $T_{i \to F}, i \in \left\{ L, R \right\}$ can be used to map between encodings. Furthermore, it guarantees a jointly optimized solution, and thus it addresses the drawback of Wang et al. (2012).

3.2 Face Matching

Once we have performed training, for each non-destination configuration $i \in \left\{ L, R \right\}$ we have the following information.

- A dictionary D_i for encoding a signal in this configuration.
- A classifier W_i that gives the class of an encoding encoded with D_i.

- A transformation $T_{i \to F}$ that takes an encoding in this configuration to the destination configuration.

First, sparse coding is applied on the gallery signatures X_i^G, and the probe signatures X_j^P to obtain their respective encoding A_i^G and A_j^P

$$\arg \min_{A_j} \| X_j - D_{config(j)} A_j \|_2^2 + \alpha \| a \|_1 \tag{4}$$

where j is the index of the dataset. $config()$ is a lookup function that gives us the configuration of a specific gallery or probe.

Then, these encodings are projected into a subspace that measures how similar they are with respect to the subjects in the training cohort. The cosine distance between these two projections provides us the similarity of two datasets:

$$d\left(X_i^G, X_j^P \right) = d\left(W_{config\left(X_i^G \right)} A_i^G, W_{config\left(X_j^P \right)} A_j^P \right) \tag{5}$$

wherein

$$d(x, y) = \frac{xy}{\| x \|_2 \| y \|_2},$$

X_i^G is the ith gallery signature and X_j^P is the jth probe signature. Such information is available during matching either as part of the data or via detection. For example, we typically know which side of the face the data is from by knowing from which camera the capture was acquired. In cases where such information is not available (e.g., UND side face dataset), we can use techniques such as landmark detection.

The method is summarized in Algorithm 2.

Algorithm 2. Matching one probe dataset versus one gallery dataset

---

Input: D_F, D_L, D_R, W_F, W_L, W_R, $T_{L \to F}$, $T_{R \to F}$, $config\left(G_i\right)$, $config\left(P_j\right)$.

Output: distance score.

1. Extract the signature for G_i: X_i^G.

2. Extract the signature for P_j: X_j^P.

3. Solve Equation 4 for A_i^G.

4. Solve Equation 4 for A_j^P.

5. Compute score using Equation 5.

---

4. EXPERIMENTS

4.1 Databases

4.1.1 Face Recognition Grand Challenge (FRGC2) Database

The FRGC2 database (Phillips et al., 2005) was created by the University of Notre Dame in the years 2003 to 2004. The 3D meshes were captured in both controlled (i.e., indoor, full frontal under studio lights) and uncontrolled conditions (i.e., hallways, atria, outdoors). The images were acquired with a Minolta Vivid 900/910 sensor positioned approximately 1.5*m* from the subject. The still images of the subject were taken with a Canon Powershot G2 camera at the resolution of either 1704x2272 or 1200x1600 pixels. The database consists of 466 subjects in 4007 captures. An example of a capture for subject id 04584 is depicted in Figure 11. It is worth noting that for our experiments, we only use the 3D information of these meshes.

4.1.2 University of Notre Dame Side Face Database (UND)

The University of Notre Dame Side Face Database (University of Notre Dame, 2008) consists of two sets of partial face captures: UND45LR and UND60LR. The UND45LR set consists of 236 scans

Figure 11. Sample data from the FRGC2 database: (a) the mesh of the subject; (b) the mesh of the subject with texture

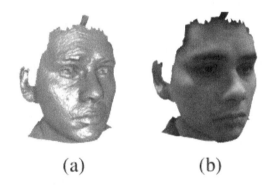

(a)   **(b)**

captured with the sensor at approximately $45°$ and $-45°$ azimuth. The UND60LR set consists of 174 scans captured with the sensor at approximately $60°$ and $-60°$ azimuth. Each subject within one of the sets appears exactly twice: once in the left scan and once in the right scan. Thus, this database is especially challenging not only because of the inherent characteristic of the data (i.e., left side of the face vs. right side of the face) but also because of the lack of training data. Methods that require training data will not work in this dataset without a previously learned model. Figure 12 depicts one subject available in both the UND45LR set and the UND60LR set. Note that not all subjects have data available in both sets.

Figure 12. A sample dataset from the UND data-base for the same subject: (a) left side from the UND45LR; (b) right side from the UND45LR; (c) left side from the UND60LR; and (d) right side from the UND60LR.

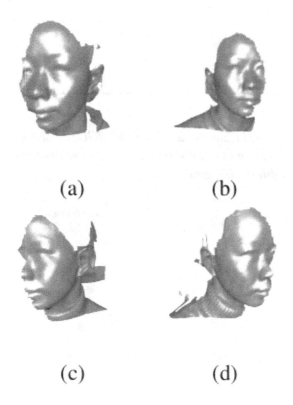

(a)   (b)

(c)   (d)

4.1.3 University of Houston Face Database 11 (UHDB11)

The University of Houston Face Database 11 (Computational Biomedicine Lab of University of Houston, 2009) consists of 23 subjects captured in 12 different poses (3 pitch variations and 4 yaw variations). Each capture includes 3D information acquired from 3dMD Two-Pod system (*3dmd: 3D imaging systems and Software*, 2012) and 2D information acquired from a Canon DSLR camera. Subjects were asked to look at 4 preset markers on the background in order to adjust their yaw variation. For pitch variations, the subjects were asked to tilt their heads up, not to tilt their heads,

and to tilt their heads down. The lighting variations are from 6 diffuse directional lights positioned in the front hemisphere of the subject face. The lights are grouped into two columns, each with three lights approximately at $45°$, $0°$, and $-45°$ zenith. The two columns are approximately at $35°$ and $-35°$ azimuth. Thus, each subject will have $3 \times 4 \times 6 = 72$ variations. A sample set of captures available for subject ID 94008 is available in Figure 13.

This database contains a good variation in both lighting conditions and poses of the subjects. However, since the subjects were asked to position their faces with preset markers, their poses are not similarly aligned with respect to the camera. Thus, this database presents a rather challenging dataset for the task of recognition under variation of pose and lighting conditions.

4.2 Face Identification

To assess the performance of our method on a challenging dataset wherein training data for our specific subjects are not available, we opt to use the UND side face dataset (see Section 4.1.2).

Table 1 describes the parameter choices for our methods. Methods which only optimize for the reconstruction cost in the Destination Signature Dictionary Learning step (shown as "R") solve for the basic dictionary learning task in Equation 1. The expansion (Equation 2) which improves the dictionary atoms to take into account discriminality is shown as "R + D." For comparison, method $UR3D$ uses the 40 packets Passalis found to perform best in the task of partial face recognition on the UND dataset. To compare the improvement of Passalis et al.'s packet choice, we also include the performance of $UR3DRaw$ method where the full 256-packet signature is used. To show a head-to-head comparison, we do not perform score normalization on these results.

Figure 13. Data available per subject in UHDB11. Each column is one lighting condition. Each row is one subject's pose.

Table 1. Parameter choices for different methods of DSC-KSVD (R: Reconstruction. D: Discrimination. S: Semi-coupling)

Method Name	Destination Signature Dictionary Learning	Partial Signature Dictionary Learning	Signature for Distance
$DSC - KSVD - PS - A_1$	R	R + S	Cosine distance of classifier decision
$DSC - KSVD - PS - A_2$	R	R + S + D	Cosine distance of classifier decision
$DSC - KSVD - PS - A_3$	R + D	R + S	Cosine distance of classifier decision
$DSC - KSVD - PS - A_4$	R + D	R + S + D	Cosine distance of classifier decision
$DSC - KSVD - PS - A_5$	R + D	R + S + D	Cosine distance of classifier decision on destination encodings
$UR3DRaw$			L_1 distance between 256 packet data
$UR3D$			L_1 distance between 40 packet data with trained weight applied per packet

The current state-of-the-art performance on this dataset is provided by the authors of Passalis (Passalis & Perakis, 2011). This method uses a set of 40 wavelet packets which were pre-learned and provided to us by the authors. Figures 14 and 15 depict a comparison of the recognition performance of our method in comparison to Passalis (Passalis & Perakis, 2011). Figures 16 and 17 depict identification performance compared to Passalis (Passalis & Perakis, 2011). Passalis et al.'s (2011) method appears as UR3D on these figures. Also, according to the authors, the final scores used in their paper were obtained after performing score normalization. To make the comparison fair, the above figures do not include score normalization.

We can observe that training a partial dictionary with discriminative error terms can improve the performance of face matching. The performances of

$$DSC - KSVD - PS - A_2$$

and

$$DSC - KSVD - PS - A_4$$

are strictly better than

$$DSC - KSVD - PS - A_1$$

and

$$DSC - KSVD - PS - A_3.$$

The same cannot be said for training the destination dictionary, however. The relative performance difference between

$$DSC - KSVD - PS - A_2$$

Figure 14. Identification performance on UND45LR side face dataset

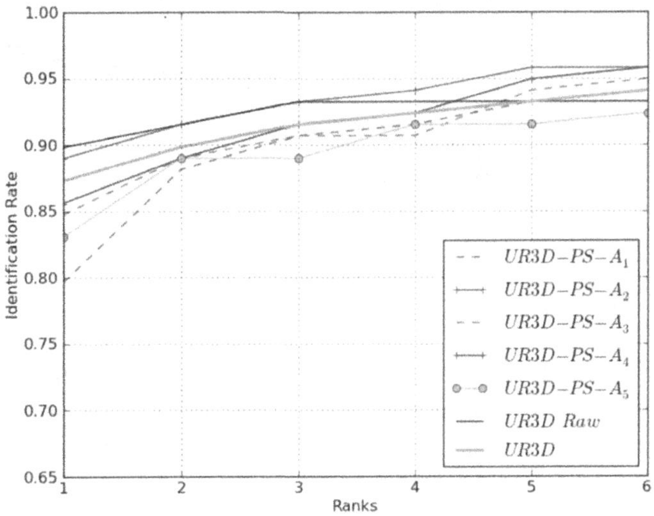

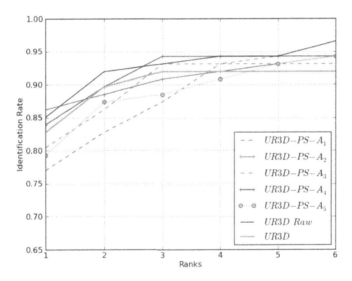

Figure 15. Identification performance on UND60LR side face dataset

and

$$DSC - KSVD - PS - A_4$$

changes in different experiments. We attribute this performance drop to the inability of the learned linear coupling matrix $T_{i \to F}$ to correctly predict the distribution of the encoding when the destination dictionary was trained with discriminative

error cost. Our methods remain consistently comparable, and in most cases better than, $UR3D$. This indicates that our semantically clear objective function that includes a term for the task at hand (face identification) will result in better performance. It also indicates the applicability of our method to the task of partial face recognition. Our performance remains on-par with the current

Figure 16. Recognition performance on UND45LR side face dataset

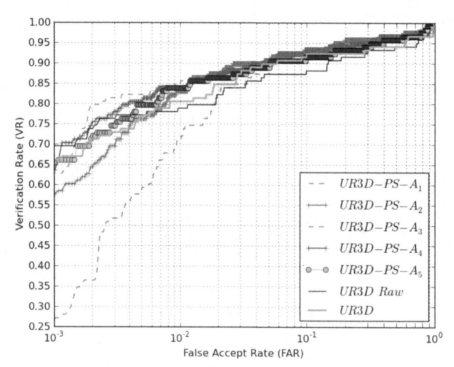

Figure 17. Recognition performance on UND60LR side face dataset

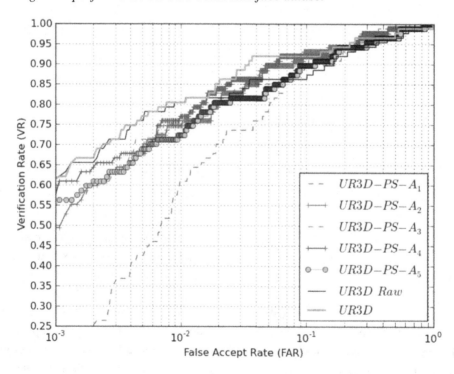

state-of-the-art without resorting to an exhaustive subset search.

It is worth noting that under none of the datasets did the packet signature optimization of Passalis result in an improvement on the performance in comparison to using the raw wavelet signature directly. Our $DSC - KSVD - PS - A_4$ method always produces a lesser performance drop (better) in the task of identification. Our $DSC - KSVD - PS - A_2$ method, on the other hand, always produces a lesser performance drop (better) in the task of recognition.

4.3 3D-2D Identification Experiment

To assess our proposed approach extensibility to other types of signatures, we tackle the interesting but challenging problem of 3D-2D face recognition. Unlike a 2D face recognition scenario, the 3D-2D face recognition scenario assumes that there exists a 3D dataset for each sample in a gallery. For this experiment, we use the UHDB11 database (see Section 4.1.3) since it is the only database we are aware of that has both the 3D mesh and the 2D capture for each dataset.

To normalize the location and orientation of the 2D face within an image, we utilize Kakadiaris' (Kakadiaris & Toderici, 2012) texture lifting method. Using this method, if the corresponding 3D model of the 2D image is known, the texture of the subject capture can be generated from a 2D image. The process is depicted in Figure 18. By performing this step, we bring the 2D image into the geometry image frame of reference. This allows us to extract geometry images and apply our DSC-KSVD approach on 2D images.

However, given a 2D image during testing, its subject ID and corresponding 3D mesh are not known. One can tackle this problem by either utilizing a generic 3D face model or by enumerating over all possible combinations of 2D-image and 3D-mesh pairs. We choose to do the latter because: (i) the solution is simple, and (ii) we will be able to demonstrate our method's ability to learn even the variation in the lifted texture due to an incorrect 3D mesh. Such variation is not subtle. Figure 19 depicts the results of texture lifting for all permutations of three gallery meshes and three probe images. The lifted textures from the first and second subjects can be observed to

Figure 18. Texture lifting process for a 2D gallery image against a known gallery 3D mesh. (a) A cropped 2D image of subject 94011 in the UHDB11 database; (b) the 2D image of the subject with an estimated position of the projected 3D mesh superimposed in white; (c) the lifted texture generated from the 2D image for the 3D mesh. The green pixel indicates location on the texture image where data is not available.

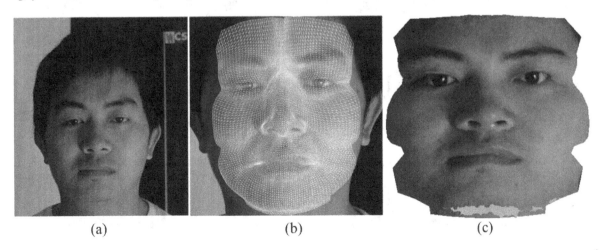

(a)   (b)   (c)

have suffered visible aberrations in the chin, nose and eye areas.

4.3.1 Training with DSC-KSVD

We split the UHDB11 dataset 2D images randomly into 5 parts and picked one part as the gallery while the rest is used for probe. We use the pose-light combination numbered 35 for the 3D mesh of our gallery used in texture lifting. Figure 20 depicts a sample of the randomly selected gallery images. A good variation in lighting conditions and poses is observed for the set. It is worth noting that we deliberately did not select images with good lighting condition or frontal poses to be in the gallery. We want to convincingly show through this experiment that our method will work

with captures of subjects in very challenging head pose configurations and harsh lighting conditions.

We assume that the set of subjects in the database is fixed. Further, we assume that the gallery includes data of subjects who have not been seen previously. For 2D images both in gallery and probe, we perform Kakadiaris's texture lifting approach to obtain $\left(N_g + N_p \right) * N_s$ lifted texture in geometry image space. N_g and N_p are the number of 2D images for gallery and probe respectively. N_s is the number of subjects in our gallery (23 for the case of the UHDB11 database). We extract the same set of wavelet signatures from these lifted texture images (see Section 3.1.1).

Since we know the identity and thus the correct 3D mesh of all gallery images, we perform DSC-KSVD to learn a mapping from the 2D

Figure 19. Texture lifting of three different 2D probe images against three possible gallery 3D meshes. From left to right: 3D mesh of subjects in gallery; fitted 3D mesh of subjects in gallery; column 3, 5, 7: super-imposed fitted 3D mesh of subjects on 2D images; column 4, 6, 8: lifted texture from 2D images in geometry image frame of reference. The green pixels on the lifted texture indicate whether the data is visible at that location.

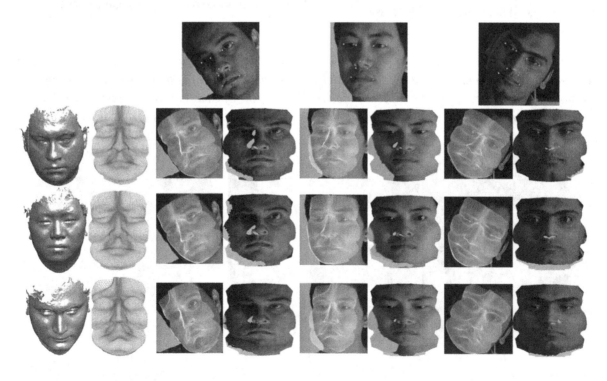

Figure 20. Sample of the 2D images randomly selected as the gallery set for the UHDB11 dataset.

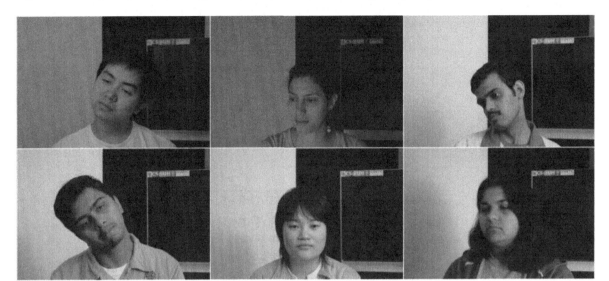

wavelet signatures of each lifted texture to the corresponding 3D wavelet signature of the capture. For example, for 23 lifted texture images of the gallery acquisition 94011d23:

$$94011d23\_940id35.png, \forall i \in \{01, 23\},$$

we learn a transform that maps them to a single fitted 3D mesh of 94011d23. In other words, using the 2D lifted texture as a partial configuration, and the 3D fitted mesh as the destination configuration, our approach learns a dictionary that bridges the error-prone 2D representation with the known well-behaving 3D representation of the data while maintaining good recognition results.

For computing distance and score, we perform the same steps as in the previous experiments. Figures 21 and 22 depict the results of our method on the extension to handle 2D signatures. On its own, the method performs excellently in the task of identification. Its results are on par with the state-of-the-art results on these datasets by Kakadiaris et al. (2012). In contrast, our method is simpler and does not involve a time-consuming relighting step. By using our method, the performance on this very challenging dataset improves by several orders of magnitude (0.6 to 0.87 for Rank-1 identification, 0.02 to 0.55 at FAR 0.001 recognition).

5. CONCLUSION

In this chapter, we demonstrated how to use dictionary learning to address the problem of partial face recognition. Our formulation addresses the previous methods' shortcomings by simultaneously optimizing for our semantically clear objective terms (reconstruction, discrimination, and semi-coupling). Our approach is better than previous approaches because (i) our optimization is jointly optimized instead of piece-wise optimized, (ii) our optimization takes into account the task at hand: discriminating input signatures, and (iii) our optimization outputs a semantically clear mapping function that can be used to bridge signatures of different configurations. We demonstrated that our method can perform well even when training data is from an external dataset and not from the testing dataset. We demonstrated that our methods perform on par with the current state-of-the-art on publicly available databases.

Figure 21. 3D-2D Identification performance on UHDB11 dataset

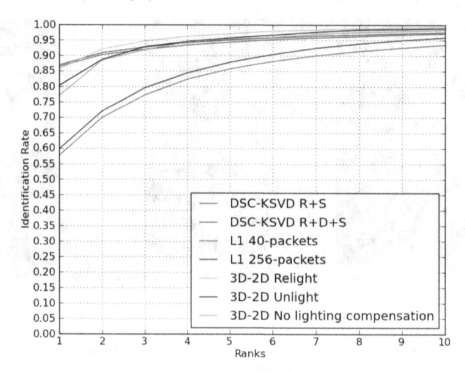

Figure 22. 3D-2D Recognition performance on UHDB11 dataset

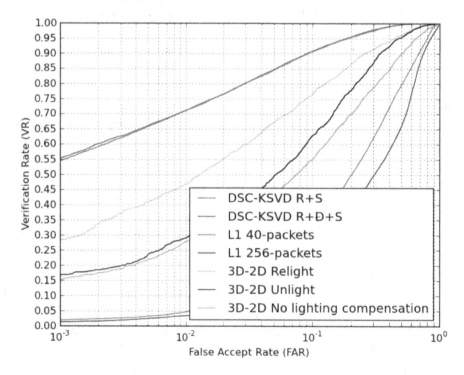

REFERENCES

Aharon, M., Elad, M., & Bruckstein, A. M. (2005). *K-SVD And Its Non-Negative Variant For Dictionary Design*. Paper Presented At The Proc. SPIE Wavelets Xi. New York, NY.

Bilgazyev, E., & Efros. (2011). *Sparse Representation-Based Super-Resolution For Face Recognition At A Distance*. Paper Presented At The British Machine Vision Conference. Dundee, UK.

Bilgazyev, E., & Kurkure. (2013). *ASIE: Application-Specific Image Enhancement For Face Recognition*. Paper Presented At The SPIE Biometric And Surveillance Technology For Human And Activity Identification X. Baltimore, MD.

Computational Biomedicine Lab Of University Of Houston. (2009). *UHDB11 Face Database*. Author.

Cootes, T. F., Taylor, C. J., Cooper, D. H., & Graham, J. (1995). Active Shape Models-Their Training And Application. *Computer Vision and Image Understanding, 61*(1), 38–59.

3. *DMD: 3d Imaging Systems and Software*. (2012). Author.

Gan, J., & Xiao, J. (2011). *An Over-Complete Sparse Representation Approach For Face Recognition Under Partial Occlusion*. Paper Presented At The International Conference On System Science And Engineering. Macau, China.

Gu, X., Gortler, S., & Hoppe, H. (2002). *Geometry Images*. Paper Presented At The 29th International Conference On Computer Graphics And Interactive Techniques (SIGGRAPH). San Antonio, TX.

Jiang, Z., Lin, Z., & Davis, L. S. (2011). *Learning A Discriminative Dictionary For Sparse Coding Via Label Consistent K-SVD*. Paper Presented At The IEEE Conference On Computer Vision And Pattern Recognition. San Francisco, CA.

Kakadiaris, I.A., & Passalis. (2007). Three-Dimensional Face Recognition In The Presence Of Facial Expressions: An Annotated Deformable Model Approach. *IEEE Transactions on Pattern Analysis and Machine Intelligence, 29*(4), 640–649.

Kakadiaris, I.A., & Toderici. (2012). *3D-2D Face Recognition With Pose-Illumination Normalization Using A 3D Deformable Model And Bidirectional Relighting*. Academic Press.

Li, Z., Imai, J., & Kaneko, M. (2010). *Robust Face Recognition Using Block-Based Bag Of Words*. Paper Presented At The International Conference On Pattern Recognition. Istanbul, Turkey.

Liao, S., & Jain, A. K. (2011). *Partial Face Recognition: An Alignment Free Approach*. Paper Presented At The International Joint Conference On Biometrics. Washington, DC.

Lowe, D. (1999). *Object Recognition From Local Scale-Invariant Features*. Paper Presented At The IEEE International Conference On Computer Vision. Kerkyra, Greece.

Mairal, J., Bach, F., Ponce, J., & Sapiro, G. (2010). Online Learning For Matrix Factorization And Sparse Coding. *Journal of Machine Learning Research, 11*, 19–60.

Nagesh, P., & Li, B. (2009). *A Compressive Sensing Approach For Expression-Invariant Face Recognition*. Paper Presented At The IEEE Conference On Computer Vision And Pattern Recognition. Miami, FL.

Ocegueda, O., & Fang. (2013). 3D-Face Discriminant Analysis Using Gauss-Markov Posterior Marginals. *IEEE Transactions On Pattern Analysis And Machine Intelligence, 35*(3), 728-739.

Passalis, G., & Perakis. (2011). Using Facial Symmetry To Handle Pose Variations In Real-World 3D Face Recognition. *IEEE Transactions on Pattern Analysis and Machine Intelligence, 33*(10), 1938–1951.

Phillips, J. P., Scruggs, T. W., O'toole, A. J., Flynn, P. J., Bowyer, K. W., Schott, C. L., & Sharpe, M. (2007). *FRVT 2006 And ICE 2006 Large-Scale Results*. Gaithersburg, MD: National Institute Of Standards And Technology.

Phillips, P. J., Flynn, P. J., Scruggs, T., Bowyer, K. W., Chang, J., Hoffman, K., & Worek, W. (2005). *Overview Of The Face Recognition Grand Challenge*. Paper Presented At The IEEE Computer Society Conference On Computer Vision And Pattern Recognition. San Diego, CA.

Rara, H. M., Farag, A. A., & Davis, T. (2011). *Model-Based 3D Shape Recovery From Single Images Of Unknown Pose And Illumination Using A Small Number Of Feature Points*. Paper Presented At The International Joint Conference On Biometrics. Washington, DC.

Siarry, P., Berthiau, G., Durbin, F., & Haussy, J. (1997). Enhanced Simulated Annealing For Globally Minimizing Functions Of Many-Continuous Variables. *ACM Transactions on Mathematical Software*, *23*(2), 209–228.

Stollnitz, E., Derose, T., & Salesin, D. (1996). *Wavelets For Computer Graphics: Theory And Applications*. Morgan Kaufmann Publishers, Inc.

Toderici, G., & Passalis. (2010). *Bidirectional Relighting For 3D-Aided 2D Face Recognition*. Paper Presented At The IEEE Computer Conference On Computer Vision And Pattern Recognition. San Francisco, CA.

University Of Notre Dame. (2008). *University Of Notre Dame Biometrics Database*. Author.

Vijayan, V., Bowyer, K. W., & Flynn, P. J. Di Huang; Liming Chen; Hansen, M.; Ocegueda, O.; Shah, S.K.; Kakadiaris, I.A., "Twins 3D face recognition challenge," 2011 International Joint Conference on Biometrics (IJCB), pp.1,7,11-13 Oct. 2011

Wang, S., Zhang, L., Liang, Y., & Pan, Q. (2012). *Semi-Coupled Dictionary Learning With Applications To Image Super-Resolution And Photo-Sketch Synthesis*. Paper Presented At The IEEE Conference On Computer Vision And Pattern Recognition. Providence, RI.

Yang, J., & Wright. (2010). Image Super-Resolution Via Sparse Representation. *IEEE Transactions on Image Processing*, *19*, 2861–2873.

Zhang, Q., & Li, B. (2010). *Discriminative K-SVD For Dictionary Learning In Face Recognition*. Paper Presented At The IEEE Conference On Computer Vision And Pattern Recognition. San Francisco, CA.

Zhao, X., & Shah. (2012). *Illumination Normalization Using Self-Lighting Ratios For 3D-2D Face Recognition*. Paper Presented At The European Conference On Computer Vision Workshop: What's In A Face. Firenze, Italy.

Zhao, X., & Chu. (2013). *Uhae: Minimizing Illumination Difference In 3D-2D Face Recognition Using Lighting Maps*. IEEE.

Zhao, X., & Shah. (2013). *Illumination Alignment Using Lighting Ratio: Application To 3D-2D Face Recognition*. Paper Presented At The 10th International Conference On Automatic Face And Gesture Recognition. Shanghai, China.

KEY TERMS AND DEFINITIONS

Albedo: Albedo is the diffuse relflectivity or the reflecting power of a surface. It is defined as the ratio of reflected radiation from a surface to the incident radition upon it.

Descriptors: In the context of images, descriptors are defined as descriptions of the visual features of the contents present in the images. They are meant to describe characteristics of images such as color, texture, geometry, etc.

Face Hallucination: Face hallucination is the clarifying of details or recovery of missing details from an input face image.

Manifold: Manifold is a topology wherein the local neighborhood of each point is homeomorphic to the Euclidean space.

Super-Resolution: This refers to a class of techniques that enhance the resolution of an image.

Sparse Representation: Sparse representations are representations that account for most or all information of a signal with a linear combination of a small number of elementary signals called atoms.

Chapter 5
3D Face Recognition Using Spatial Relations

Stefano Berretti
University of Florence, Italy

Alberto del Bimbo
University of Florence, Italy

Pietro Pala
University of Florence, Italy

ABSTRACT

Identity recognition using 3D scans of the face has been recently proposed as an alternative or complementary solution to conventional 2D face recognition approaches based on still images or videos. In fact, face representations based on 3D data are expected to be more robust to pose changes and illumination variations than 2D images, thus allowing accurate face recognition in real-world applications with unconstrained acquisition. Based on these premises, in this chapter, the authors first introduce the general and main methodologies for 3D face recognition, shortly reviewing the related literature by distinguishing between global and local approaches. Then, the authors present and discuss two 3D face recognition approaches that are robust to facial expression variations and share the common idea of accounting for the spatial relations between local facial features. In the first approach, the face is partitioned into iso-geodesic stripes and spatial relations are computed by integral measures that capture the relative displacement between the sets of 3D points in each pair of stripes. In the second solution, the face is described by detecting keypoints in the depth map of the face and locally describing them. Then, facial curves on the surface are considered between each pair of keypoints, so as to capture the shape of the face along the curve as well as the relational information between keypoints. Future research directions and conclusions are drawn at the end of the chapter.

DOI: 10.4018/978-1-4666-5966-7.ch005

INTRODUCTION

Human target recognition has been an active research area in recent years, with several biometric techniques developed for measuring unique physical and behavioral characteristics of human subjects for the purpose of recognizing their identity. In particular, two different modalities are considered to recognize the identity of a person: *verification* (authentication) and *identification* (recognition). Verification ("Am I who I claim I am?") involves confirming or denying a person's claimed identity. Instead, identification ("Who am I?") requires the system to recognize a person from a list of users in the template database. Due to this, identification is a more challenging problem because it involves one-to-many matching compared to the one-to-one matching required for verification. The idea of automatically recognizing or authenticating users' identity is based on the possibility to extract unique physical features from the anatomical traits that univocally characterize each individual. The features that are most used for this goal can be summarized as follows:

- **Fingerprints and hand geometry**: The most common biometric authentication solution. Provides high accuracy, it is easy to implement (though contact with the sensor is required), showing a low cost. Can be also performed via the Internet (BioWeb);
- **Voice recognition**: Relies on the voice pattern to authenticate individuals, thus resulting very user friendly. However, changing the voice due to sinus congestion, cold or anxiety can produce false negatives results;
- **Eye scans**: Retinal and iris scans are used for authentication. They provide accuracy where physical contact to the scanner is required. The user must focus in particular point of the scanner and hold this position. Low-intensity light might affect the results;

- **Facial recognition**: Looks for the different parts of the face such as the location and shape of the eyes and the nose, cheekbones and the side of the mouth;
- **Signature dynamics and typing patterns**: Looks for patterns in writing pressures at different points in the signature, and the writing speed;
- **Heartbeat biometric authentication**: Identifies the individually unique information of the subject heartbeats;
- **Infrared hand vein pattern biometric**: Uses the shape of the finger vein and infrared is used to make the skin tissue transparent, and highly visible to recognize the veins in the finger.

Depending on the particular application, one or a combination of the diverse biometric modalities listed above can be more appropriate. This is evidenced by the different diffusion and impact that different biometric technologies have on the global market, where fingerprints is the most largely used biometric technique, mainly because of its very high accuracy and simplicity, with face recognition following in third position (2010 data). While biometric technologies are being widely used in *forensics* for criminal identification, recent advancements in biometric sensors and matching algorithms have led to the deployment of biometric authentication in a large number of civilian and government applications, such as *physical access control*, *computer log-in*, *welfare disbursement*, *international border crossing* and *national ID cards*, and so on.

Among the biometric techniques listed above, identity recognition based on facial traits is widely used for its social acceptance, applicability in a range of different contexts and the good balance between risks and benefits associated to its implementation. In fact, face recognition has its main prerogative in not requiring contact or closeness between the acquisition sensor and the captured subject, thus permitting its deployment in a variety of different situations, which span from indoor applications with constrained pose and illumination conditions (for example in capturing face images used for personal identification documents) to the surveillance of vast outdoor areas with unconstrained conditions (as can be the case of a sporting event) using pan-tilt-zoom (PTZ) active cameras.

In fact, automatic human target identification by detecting and matching human faces in 2D still images and videos has been an active research area in pattern recognition since '90s (Zhao et al., 2003). Performance of 2D face matching systems depends on their capability of being insensitive to critical factors such as facial expressions, makeup and aging, but mainly hinges upon extrinsic factors, such as illumination differences, camera viewpoint and scene geometry. The Face Recognition Vendor Test (FRVT, http://face.nist.gov/) is an independent evaluation contest of face recognition algorithms carried out every two/three years by the National Institute of Standards and Technologies (NIST). The FRVT 2002 (Phillips et al., 2003) showed that performance in the presence of illumination variations decreases up to 46 percent, and similar and higher decreases occur for rotations of the face with respect to the frontal case. Great progress was documented in the 2006 FRVT (Phillips et al., 2007). The best performer showed a False Rejection Rate (FRR) inter-quartile range between 0.6 and 1.5 percent at 0.001 False Acceptance Rate (FAR) under controlled illumination, and between 10.3 and 13 percent at 0.001 FAR across illumination. A performance decrease of about one order of magnitude was observed at lower resolution. The inherent limitations of 2D face matching have supported the belief that effective recognition of identity should be obtained through multi-biometric technologies. In particular, the exploitation of the geometry of the anatomical structure of the face rather than its appearance with definition of algorithms and

systems for 3D face matching has been a growing field of research in very recent years.

Three dimensional data have the potential to improve existing face recognition solutions through full 3D solutions or combined 2D+3D approaches. However, 3D data are a more complex source of information than 2D still images, thus requiring the development of specific techniques for several different tasks. First, 3D face acquisition and preprocessing operations precede any 3D face analysis task performed in real contexts. The outcomes of these operations are of paramount importance in that, depending on their quality, the accuracy achievable by any subsequent 3D face analysis can largely vary. Then, a substantial difference exists between approaches that operate in *cooperative* or *non-cooperative* contexts. In the former case, subjects are aware and collaborate to the acquisition process. For example, it can be the case of an access control performed via 3D face acquisition and recognition: in this case the user is asked to assume a predefined position in front of the scanner and the acquisition environment is also set up (for example in terms of background and lighting conditions) in a way that can maximize the quality of the acquisition. Differently, in the latter case, authors cooperate to the acquisition only partially or not at all, in that they can change their pose or even move. In the most challenging cases, the environment can be constituted by outdoor areas with changing illumination conditions, varying background and crowding, thus making extremely challenging the acquisition of face scans of sufficient quality for recognition purposes. In summary, the conversion of 3D scans to efficient and meaningful descriptors of the face is therefore crucial to performing fast processing and particularly to permitting indexing over large data sets for identification. On the other hand, the effectiveness of 3D face recognition is principally concerned with the capability of achieving invariance to face expressions, missing parts and occlusions. In fact, while 3D face models are almost insensitive to lighting conditions, they are affected by pose changes and occlusions, and are even more sensitive than 2D images to face expressions.

The above considerations evidence the richness and potential impact of face recognition applications based on 3D scans. In this Chapter, we present and discuss two recently proposed 3D face recognition solutions that are robust to facial expression variations and share the common idea of accounting for the *spatial relations* between local facial features. The remaining of the Chapter is organized into four main sections as follows:

- In the "Background" Section, we will give more insights on the state of the art solutions for 3D face recognition, distinguishing in particular between global and local recognition approaches;
- In the "3D Face Recognition" Section, we will first motivate the need for accounting spatial relations in 3D face recognition, then two solutions that exploit spatial features of the face are presented: one based on point-wise spatial relations of *iso-geodesic stripes* of the face; the other relying on *keypoints* of depth maps of the face and *facial curves* among them;
- The "Future Research Directions" Section discusses future and emerging trends in 3D face recognition;
- Finally, in the "Conclusions" Section we summarize the overall content of the Chapter also providing concluding remarks.

BACKGROUND

Following an agreed classification (Zhao et al., 2003), the approaches for 3D face recognition can be distinguished as: *holistic*, that perform face matching based on the whole face; *region-based*, that partition the face surface into regions and extract appropriate descriptors for each of them;

hybrid, and *multimodal*, that combine different approaches such as holistic and region-based, or perform both 2D and 3D matching separately and fuse the two matchings together to achieve better recognition accuracy.

Generally speaking, holistic methods are sensitive to face alignment. Moreover, since they take global face measures, they tend to treat face differences that are due to different facial traits and non-neutral expressions in the same way. The performance with these methods can also be very much impaired if the 3D face includes elements like hair, ears, and neck. Region-based approaches promise much higher effectiveness in that, at least in principle they can apply different processing to distinct face regions and therefore filter out those regions that are mostly affected by expression changes or spurious elements. Nevertheless, they are also sensitive to face alignment and useful face regions are hard to detect automatically. Their performance depends on local features and differences in resolution. Hybrid and multimodal approaches provide the highest accuracy, but at the expense of a greater architectural complexity. They are especially suited for verification, less for identification in that do not permit easy indexing.

Among the first 3D face recognition solutions that appeared in the literature, several tried to exploit holistic properties of the face. In this context, several authors have attempted to find the main distinguishing elements of the faces from the direct analysis of face depth images, after realignment to a reference face model. Principal Component Analysis (PCA) was applied to depth images in (Hesher et al., 2002) and to both depth and color image channels in (Tsalakanidou et al., 2003). Conformal transformations have been used in Pan et al. (2005), Wang et al. (2005), and Wang et al., (2006) among others. Since conformal mapping is a one-to-one angle preserving transformation, 3D surface matching is reduced to a simpler 2D image-matching problem. In particular, in (Pan et al., 2005), a region of interest of the face, defined as the intersection between a sphere centered on the nose tip and the 3D face was mapped onto an isomorphic planar circle and eigenface analysis was used to compare faces. In (Samir et al., 2006), 3D faces were instead represented through iso-depth lines projected onto the base plane. Then, shapes of the iso-depth lines were compared, exploiting differential geometry for 2D planar-closed curves. Since face expressions may induce strong alterations of the iso-depth lines, this approach is likely to be very sensitive to expression changes. A similar approach was followed in (ter Haar & Veltkamp, 2008), where the authors used sample points taken at the intersection between contour curves and radial profiles originated from the nose tip, and calculated the Euclidean distances between corresponding points of different faces. As a different approach, some authors have proposed representing 3D faces as points in low-dimensional feature spaces. The 3D coordinates of face points were therefore encoded through transformations, and dimensionality reduction was applied in the feature space. In (Wang & Chua, 2005), 3D spherical Gabor filters were used to extract a view invariant representation of 3D facial models. The authors used a modified version of the Hausdorff distance in order to improve the robustness of matching in the presence of self-occlusions. However, tests were performed on a too small dataset to assess the effectiveness of the approach. In Bronstein et al. (2005), face models were represented with the geometric moments up to the fifth order computed for the 3D face canonical surface. Canonical surfaces were obtained from face surfaces by warping according to a topology preserving transformation so that the Euclidean distance between two canonical surface points is equivalent to the geodesic distance between the corresponding points of the face surface. However, while the effect of expressions is attenuated, a similar attenuation also occurs for discriminating features such as eye sockets and nose. Some limitations of the method were indeed removed in (Bronstein et al., 2006).

Other authors have proposed exploiting the full 3D geometrical information of the face model and performed matching according to point-wise registration, avoiding calculation of features and the consequent loss of information. In Lu & Jain (2006), rules of transformation from neutral to generic expressions were learned from a training set so as to create synthetic 3D models for any expression. Iterative Closest Point (ICP) was then used to align the synthesized models to an input model, handling adaptation to both pose and expression simultaneously. Elastic registration with morphable models was used in Kakadiaris et al. (2007), Passalis et al. (2005), and Amberg et al. (2008). In particular, in Kakadiaris et al. (2007) and Passalis et al. (2005), the points of an annotated 3D face reference model were shifted according to elastic constraints, so as to match the corresponding points of 3D target models in a gallery. Similar morphing was performed for each query face. Then, face matching was performed by comparing the wavelet coefficients of the deformation images obtained from morphing. In Amberg et al. (2008), a 3D morphable model was learned from face models with neutral expression and adapted to gallery and query faces using a variant of the non-rigid ICP algorithm. Distances between the deformation coefficients were used to assess matching. Although registration-based methods support accurate face matching, they perform matching iteratively and are extremely expensive from the computational viewpoint. Attempts to reduce the computational complexity have been proposed in Lu et al. (2006) and Yan & Bowyer (2007).

Region-based approaches can be distinguished by the way in which region segmentation is obtained. In Cook et al. (2006), Log-Gabor templates were used to break a single-range image into a predefined number of overlapping spatial regions at three different frequency scales. These observations were each classified individually, and then combined at the score level. PCA was applied to the responses of the Log-Gabor filters in each sub-region used to reduce the dimensionality. Regions in the proximity of face landmarks were used instead in Husken et al. (2005). Features were extracted at the landmark regions and face matching was performed according to Hierarchical Graph Matching, with graph nodes positioned at the landmarks. In Xu et al. (2008), multiple face regions are originated by intersecting 3D face scans with spheres of increasing radius centered on the middle point between the nose tip and the nasion. In Chang et al. (2006), multiple overlapping regions around the nose are segmented and the scores of ICP matching on these regions are combined together. This idea is extended in Faltemier et al. (2008) by using a set of 38 regions that densely cover the face and selecting the best-performing subset of 28 regions to perform matching using the ICP algorithm. A further improvement of the approach is proposed in Faltemier et al. (2008b) by considering a multi-instance enrollment of gallery scans with multiple expressions (experiments are provided using up to five scans per individual). Accordingly, up to 140 ICP region matches are required to compute the similarity between a probe scan and the scans representing an enrolled individual. Robustness to non-neutral facial expressions is improved at the cost of a greater computational complexity, thus making these approaches more suited to face verification than identification. Other methods have performed segmentation of the 3D face into distinct regions according to the values of the curvature function calculated from the face surface (Lee & Milios, 1990; Gordon, 1992; Moreno et al., 2003). A crucial limitation of curvature-based approaches is the extreme sensibility of curvature values to perturbations of surface points that may occur due to noise, fallacious acquisition, or changes of expressions. In most of the cases, face comparison has been restricted to the comparison of only a few regions, where the effects of expressions are small or null. In particular, in Lee and Milios, (1990), Extended Gaussian Images—that provide a one-to-one mapping between curvature normals and the unit sphere—were created for each convex region and compared by graph matching with relational constraints.

Hybrid and multimodal methods have shown the best recognition results so far, trying to combine multiple processing paths into a coherent architecture, to solve critical aspects of individual methods. Among the multimodal methods, in Chang et al. (2005), the authors proposed applying PCA to face depth images and 2D face images separately and then fusing the results together. In Lu and Jain (2006), ICP registration of the 3D face models was combined with Linear Discriminant Analysis applied to 2D face images, to improve the robustness of 2D face matching in the presence of pose and illumination variations. In Beumier and Acheroy (2001), central and lateral profiles of the face were extracted and compared in both 3D and 2D. In Husken et al. (2005), landmark positions used to define the face regions were also detected on 2D texture images obtained with the 3D face scan. Very high recognition accuracy on the FRGC v2.0 was obtained with the solution reported in Mian et al. (2007) that is both hybrid and multimodal. The authors assembled a fully automated system performing: pose correction (of both the 3D model and the corresponding 2D color image provided by the scanner); automatic region segmentation to account for local variations of the face geometry (by detecting the inflection points around the nose tip); quick filtering of distant faces using SIFTs and 3D Spherical Face Representation (a quantization of the face point cloud into spherical bins centered at the nose tip); and matching of the remaining faces applying a modified ICP to a few regions of the face (eyes, forehead, and nose) that are less sensitive to face expressions.

TWO 3D FACE RECOGNITION SOLUTIONS USING SPATIAL RELATIONS

Region based solutions are potentially more powerful than holistic one, especially in the case of varying facial expressions in that they permit to separate and manage differently the parts of the face that are more affected by facial expressions. However, existing local solutions have processed each region of the face independently from the others, posing little or no attention to the *spatial relations* between regions. Actually, spatial relations between deformable regions of the face and between deformable and rigid regions can be relevant to perform recognition in the presence of facial expressions, since they can provide additional information useful to discriminate between different subjects. Starting from these considerations, in the following we present two 3D face recognition methods that are effective also in the presence of facial expression variations and that account for the spatial relations between local regions of the face in 3D scans. In particular:

- The first approach has been first proposed in Berretti et al. (2006) and later extended in (Berretti et al., 2010) and also applied for ethnicity based face recognition in Berretti et al. (2012). In this approach, all of the 3D points of the face are taken into account and organized into *iso-geodesic stripes* according to their distance from the nose tip, so that the complete geometrical information of the 3D face model is exploited. Then, the relevant information is encoded into a compact representation in the form of a graph that accounts for intra-stripes shape information and inter-stripe spatial relations between each pair of stripes. Face recognition is finally reduced to matching the graphs;

- The second approach is based on the work proposed in Berretti et al. (2011) for 3D face recognition from partial face scans, and subsequently extended in Berretti et al. (2013) for performing face recognition also in the case of scans with expression variations. The idea of this solution is to detect SIFT keypoints from the depth map of pose normalized face scans and then compute SIFT descriptors at these keypoints. Correspondence between keypoints of different scans is established using RANSAC to impose a coherent geometric transformation between matching keypoints. *Facial curves* that connect matching keypoints on the depth map are then used to account for the spatial relations between keypoints.

These approaches can support both face identification (one vs. many comparison) and face verification (one vs. one comparison). However, in the following we will focus mainly on face identification presenting results for this biometric modality.

Accounting Spatial Displacement of Surface Points

In this approach, all of the points of the face are taken into account so that the complete geometrical information of the 3D face model is exploited, but differently from registration methods where matching is obtained by iterative point-wise alignment; here, the relevant information is encoded into a compact representation in the form of a graph and face recognition is finally reduced to matching the graphs. Face graphs have a fixed number of nodes that, respectively, represent iso-geodesic facial stripes of equal width and increasing distance from the nose tip. Arcs between pairs of nodes are annotated with descriptors referred to as 3D Weighted Walkthroughs (3DWWs) that capture the mutual spatial displacement between all the pairs of points of the corresponding stripes and show smooth changes of their values as the positions of face points change. Due to the fixed partitioning into iso-geodesic stripes, 3DWWs between stripes are approximately calculated over the same portions of the face for all individuals, thus permitting discrimination between structural differences in face morphology. Besides, according to the property that iso-geodesic distances do not vary too much under facial expressions, 3DWWs are principally calculated over the same set of points of the stripes under any expressions, with limitations to the range of the possible local modifications, and therefore to the effects of point shifting. This smoothes the differences due to different expressions of the same individual. This representation has the great advantage of a very efficient computation of face descriptors and a very efficient matching operation for face recognition. Moreover, the approach appears very well suited for the task of face identification in very large data sets. In fact, face graphs can be arranged in an appropriate index structure so that the efficiency of search is even improved. In the following, details of the approach are given.

Iso-Geodesic Stripes of the Face

In this approach, the structural information of a face scan is captured through the 3D shape and relative arrangement of iso-geodesic stripes identified on the 3D surface. Iso-geodesic stripes are defined by computing, for every surface point, the normalized geodesic distance between the point and a reference point located at the nose tip of the face. Normalized values of the geodesic distance are obtained by dividing the geodesic distance by the Euclidean eye-to-nose distance, that is, the sum of the distances between the nose tip and the two points located at the inner commissure of the left and right eye fissure, and the distance between the two points at the inner eyes. The algorithm reported in Mian et al. (2007) is used

for the identification of the nose tip and of the two inner eye points. This normalization guarantees invariance of the distance values with respect to scaling of the face scan. Furthermore, since the Euclidean eye-to-nose distance is invariant to face expressions, this normalization factor does not bias values of the distance under expression changes.

Computation of the geodesic distance on the piecewise planar mesh is accomplished through Dijkstra's algorithm and approximates the actual geodesic distance between two surface points with the length of the shortest piecewise linear path on mesh edges. Once values of the normalized geodesic distance are computed for every surface point, iso-geodesic stripes can be identified. For this purpose, the range of the normalized geodesic distance values is quantized into n intervals $c_1, ..., c_n$. Accordingly, n stripes concentric with respect to the nose tip are identified on the 3D surface with the i-*th* stripe corresponding to the set of surface points for which the value of the normalized geodesic distance falls within the limits of interval c_i.

Figure 1(b) shows the projection on the XY plane of the pairs of iso-geodesic stripes of the three subjects in Figure 1(a), thus evidencing the shape variations of the stripes. As an example, Figure 2 shows the first nine iso-geodesic stripes identified on the face scans of two individuals.

Results of the analysis of the deformation that non-neutral facial expressions induce in the shape of the iso-geodesic stripes, as is detailed in Berretti et al. (2010), motivate the decomposition of the facial stripes into three parts: upper-left (UL), upper-right (UR), and lower (L), with respect to the coordinates of the nose tip (see Figure 1(b)). In general, under the effect of non-neutral facial expressions, the region around the mouth undergoes to larger deformations than the other regions of the face. Furthermore, decomposition of the upper part into upper-left and upper-right allows the face representation model to better deal with slight asymmetries of the face that constitute a characterizing trait of some individuals. This subdivision resulted necessary in improving the

Figure 1. (a) Sample face models, with the 4th and 7th iso-geodesic stripes in evidence. The 3DWW relationship descriptors are computed for the UL, UR, and L parts of the stripes pair. (b) Projection of the pairs of iso-geodesic stripes in (a) on the XY plane, with the partitioning of the iso-geodesic stripes into three parts. (Adapted from Berretti et al. (2012)).

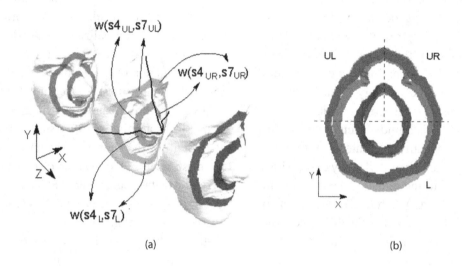

(a)   (b)

Figure 2. The first nine iso-geodesic stripes of two sample face scans. The graphs constructed on a part of the stripes and their matching are also shown. (Adapted from Berretti et al. (2012)).

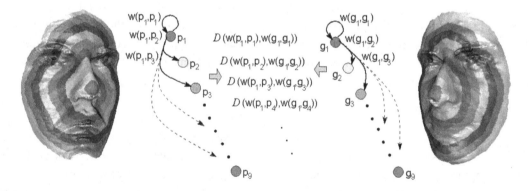

performance of the approach in the case of faces with expression variations (results of the iso-geodesic stripes approach without face partitioning were first reported in Berretti et al. (2006).

Once facial stripes are extracted, distinctive structural features of 3D face scans are captured by describing the point-wise 3D spatial relationships between homologous parts of pairs of iso-geodesic stripes. To this end, the 3D Weighted Walkthroughs (3DWWs) descriptor has been used.

The 3DWW have been first introduced in Berretti et al. (2006), and their use and properties in the context of 3D face recognition have been extensively discussed in Berretti et al. (2010). 3DWW define a set of integral measures over the points of two regions A and B in the 3D domain. These measures are captured through weights $w_{i,j,k}(A,B)$ that encode the number of pairs of points belonging respectively to A and B, whose displacement is captured by the walkthrough $< i, j, k>$ (with i, j, k taking values in $\{-1, 0, +1\}$):

$$w_{i,j,k}(A, B) =$$
$$\frac{1}{K_{i,j,k}} \int_A \int_B C_i(x_b - x_a)C_j(x_b - x_a)C_k(x_b - x_a) \, d\vec{b} \, d\vec{a} \tag{1}$$

where $d\vec{b} = dx_b \, dy_b \, dz_b$ and $d\vec{a} = dx_a \, dy_a \, dz_a$; $K_{i,j,k}$ acts as a normalization factor to guarantee that $w_{i,j,k}$ takes value in $[0,1]$; $C_{\pm 1}(.)$ are the *characteristic functions* of the positive and negative real semi-axis $(0,+\infty)$ and $(-\infty,0)$, respectively; and $C_0(\cdot)$ denotes the *Dirac*'s function that is used to reduce the dimensionality of the integration domain to enable a finite non-null measure.

3DWWs are capable of quantitatively measuring the relative spatial arrangement of two extended sets of 3D points by computing 27 weights and organizing them in a $3 \times 3 \times 3$ matrix. As a particular case, the 3DWWs computed between an extended 3D entity and itself also account for intrinsic shape information. The properties of 3DWW, joined by the geodesic distance computation and face partitioning, provide the method with robustness to expression variations. In fact, geodesic distances between two facial points remain sufficiently stable under expression changes resulting in the fact that the large majority of the points of each stripe still remain within the same stripe, even under facial expression changes. In addition, due to the constrained elasticity of the skin tissue, neighbor points can be assumed to feature very similar motion for moderate facial expressions in most parts of the face.

For all these points, the mutual displacement between the two points is mainly determined by the geometry of the neutral face. This property is preserved by 3DWWs that provide an integral measure of displacements between pairs of points.

Face Representation and Matching

A generic face model F is represented through a set of N_F stripes. In that 3DWWs are computed for every pair of iso-geodesic stripes (including the pair composed by a stripe and itself), a face is represented by a set of $N_F \cdot (N_F + 1)/2$ relationship matrixes. According to the proposed representation, iso-geodesic stripes and 3DWWs computed between pairs of stripes (inter-stripe 3DWW) and between each stripe and itself (intra-stripe 3DWW) have been cast to a graph representation, where intra-stripe 3DWWs are used to label the graph nodes and inter-stripe 3DWWs to label the graph edges (see Figure 2). In order to compare graph representations, distance measures for node labels and for edge labels have been defined. Both of them rely on the L_1 distance measure D defined between 3DWWs (Berretti et al., 2006). The similarity measure between two face models represented through the graphs P and G with nodes p_k and g_k, is then derived as:

$$\mu(P, G) =$$
$$\frac{\alpha}{N_P} \cdot \sum_{k=1}^{N_P} D(w(p_k, p_k), w(g_k, g_k)) +$$
$$\frac{2}{N_P(N_P - 1)} \cdot \sum_{k=1}^{N_P} \sum_{h=1}^{k-1} D(w(p_k, p_h), w(g_k, g_h)) \tag{2}$$

where the first summation in Equation (2) accounts for the intra-stripe 3DWWs' similarity measure, and the second summation evaluates the inter-stripe 3DWWs' similarity measure. The α parameter permits for weighting differently the two distance components, and its value is set to 0.3 in the experiments. This value has been tuned in a preliminary set of experiments on the FRGC v1.0 database and shows that in order to support face recognition, inter-stripe spatial relationships are more discriminant than intra-stripe spatial relationships. Implicitly, Equation (2) assumes that the number of nodes N_P in graph P is not greater than the number of nodes N_G of graph G. This can be assumed with no loss of generality in that if $N_P > N_G$, graphs P and G can be exchanged.

Following these considerations, distances between faces of two individuals are measured by computing the 3DWW for each pair of iso-geodesic stripes separately in the three face parts and then comparing the 3DWWs of homologous pairs in the two faces. The final dissimilarity measure is obtained by averaging the distances in the three parts. According to Equation (2), the overall run-time complexity can be estimated as $O(N^2_P T_D)$; T_D being the complexity in computing D, which is estimated to be a constant value (Berretti et al., 2010). This permits efficient implementation for face identification in large datasets and also with the use of appropriate index structures, with great savings in performance. More details on the index structure supporting graph indexing and its performance are discussed in Berretti et al. (2001).

The method, participated in the SHREC 2008 3D face recognition contest, and has been further evaluated on the FRGC v2.0 benchmark dataset, which is the de facto standard for comparing 3D face recognition methods. The main characteristics of these datasets and the face identification rate scored by the method are summarized below.

Face Identification Results: SHREC 2008

The SHREC 2008 dataset (Doudi et al., 2008) is characterized by facial scans with very large pose and expression variations and noisy acquisition. It includes 3D face scans of 61 adult Caucasian individuals (45 males and 16 females). For each individual, nine scans are taken that differ in the acquisition viewpoint and facial expressions, resulting in a total of 549 facial scans. In particular, for each individual, there are two frontal face scans with *neutral* expression, two face scans where the

subject is acquired with a *rotated* posture of the face (around $\pm 35°$ looking up or looking down) and neutral facial expression, and three frontal scans in which the person *laughs*, *smiles*, or shows a *random* expression. Finally, there are also a right side and a left side scans nominally acquired with a rotation of $\pm 90°$ left and right. This results in about 67% of the scans having a neutral expression, but just 22% having neutral expression and frontal pose. This dataset has been used to test face recognition accuracy in several other works addressing 3D face recognition in the presence of facial expressions and in the case parts of the face scans are missing.

Using this dataset, the iso-geodesic stripes approach obtained the best ranking at the SHREC 2008 contest scoring rank-1 Recognition Rate of 99.53%. In this experiment, the first frontal neutral scan of each subject is included in the gallery (*neutral*), whereas all the remaining *neutral* and *non-neutral* scans are used as probes. The *Cumulative Matching Characteristics* (CMC) curves are reported in Figure 3(a) separately, for the *neutral* vs. *neutral*, *non-neutral* vs. *neutral*, and *all* vs. *neutral* cases.

Face Identification Results: FRGC v2.0

The FRGC data set (Phillips et al., 2005) includes 3D face scans partitioned into three subsets, namely, the *Spring2003* subset, also known as FRGC v1.0 (943 scans of 275 individuals), and the *Fall2003* and *Spring2004* subsets (4,007 scans of 466 subjects in total) that are commonly identified as the FRGC v2.0 dataset. Face scans are acquired with a Konica-Minolta Vivid 910 laser scanner and given as matrices of 3D points of size 480 x 640, with a binary mask indicating the valid points of the face. Due to different distances of the subjects from the sensor during acquisition, the actual number of points representing a face can vary. Individuals have been acquired with frontal view from the shoulder level, with very small pose variations. Considering the FRGC

Figure 3. CMC of the iso-geodesic stripes approach scored on: (a) SHREC2008; (b) FRGC v2.0. (Adapted from (Berretti et al., 2010)).

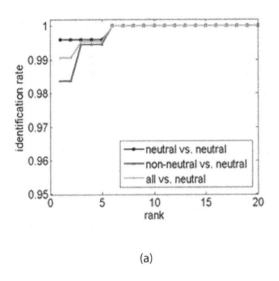

(a)

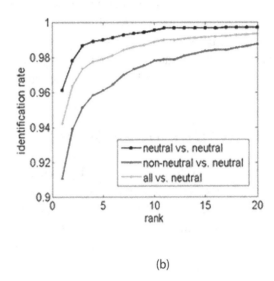

(b)

v2.0, about 59% of the faces have neutral expression, and the others show moderate non-neutral expressions of *disgust*, *happiness*, *sadness*, and *surprise*. Some scans include small occlusions due to hair. FRGC guidelines suggest using the *Spring2003* for training and the remaining two sets for validation.

The CMC curves obtained using this dataset are reported in Figure 3(b). In this case, the experiments have been performed by including the first neutral scan of each subject in the gallery and using all the remaining as probes. Also in this case, separated curves are reported for *neutral* and *non-neutral* probes.

Accounting Spatial Relations of Surface Keypoints

The approach relies on the detection of keypoints on the 3D face surface and the description of the surface in correspondence to these keypoints as well as along facial curves connecting pairs of keypoints. In contrast to solutions where keypoints correspond to meaningful face landmarks, such as the eyebrows, eyes, nose, cheek and mouth

(Gupta et al., 2010), in this approach there is not any particular assumption about the position of the keypoints on the face surface. Rather, the position of keypoints is expected to be influenced by the specific morphological traits of the face of each subject. In particular, an assumption of within subject keypoints repeatability is exploited: the positions of the most stable keypoints—detected at the coarsest scales—do not change substantially across facial scans of the same subject. To further reduce the effect of surface noise and enhance the robustness of the position of keypoints, a spatial clustering approach is adopted so as to replace aggregated keypoints with their cluster centers. According to this, the combination of SIFT detection and spatial clustering is used to identify relevant and stable keypoints on the depth image of the face. Furthermore, *facial curves* are used to model the depth of face scans along the surface lines connecting pairs of keypoints. In doing so, distinguishing traits of a face scan are captured by the SIFT descriptors of detected keypoints, by the spatial arrangement of keypoints and by the set of facial curves identified by each pair of keypoints. In the comparison of two faces, SIFT descriptors are matched to measure the similarity between pairs of keypoints identified on two depth images. Spatial constraints are imposed to avoid outlier matches using RANSAC algorithm. Then, the distance between the two faces is derived by composing the individual distances between facial curves. In the following, details of the approach are given.

Keypoints of Depth Facial Images

Detection of relevant keypoints from depth images of the face is the first step of the proposed approach. Prior to the detection of keypoints, the 3D scans undergo to a rigid 3D transformation (rotation and translation) so as to normalize their pose to a common reference frame. This is a nontrivial problem by itself, and several approaches have been recently reported for the specific domain of 3D faces (Mian et al., 2007), (Wang et al., 2010). Therefore, we rely on existing methods to derive a few landmarks of the face that are detectable with a good accuracy also in acquisitions with large pose variations, and use them to perform face alignment. This is accomplished by computing the 3-D rotation and translation transform that minimizes the mean Euclidean distance of corresponding landmarks. Once the landmarks are detected and used for initializing the alignment process, the pose of the 3D faces is then refined according to a rigid transformation using the ICP algorithm (Besl & Mc Kay, 1992). In this way, 3D points are registered with respect to a reference model obtained by averaging a selected set of FRGC v1.0 scans with neutral expression and frontal pose. As a result, the acquired scans are normalized to a common pose and depth images of the face are extracted.

The resulting depth images are used to extract face keypoints by running the SIFT keypoints detector (Vedaldi & Fulkerson, 2008). When applied to depth images, SIFT keypoints detect blobs of depth values, corresponding to scale-space extrema of the scale normalized difference

of Gaussians operator. Since blobs in depth scans correspond to regions whose depth values differ compared to the surrounding, detected keypoints correspond to local protrusions/intrusions of the face surface.

For each keypoint, the corresponding SIFT descriptor is computed using a 16×16 pixel support. This small support size, gives to the approach robustness to missing parts, resulting, at the same time, sufficient to establish consistent correspondences between keypoint descriptors. The properties of the SIFT descriptor make it capable of providing a compact yet powerful local representation of the depth image and, as a consequence, of the face surface. As an example, Figure 3 shows the depth images derived from the 3D face scans of five different subjects. The 3D face scans are arranged into four columns, each column showing two scans of the same subject: the gallery scan, and one frontal neutral probe scan. In all the cases, the keypoints detected on the depth image are evidenced with a "+" red sign. Figure 4 demonstrates the main advantage of using keypoints over landmarks: the higher number of detected keypoints compared to the number of typical face landmarks increases the number of facial curves that are considered for matching, and this improves the robustness of matching.

Facial Curves

The information that is captured by SIFT descriptors of the keypoints is not discriminant enough to support accurate recognition of the identity of the subject. In the proposed approach, additional information necessary to discriminate the identity of each subject is captured by considering facial curves extracted from pairs of keypoints. For the clarity of notation, we assume that after the preprocessing, each facial scan is aligned to a common reference system, so that the X axis is aligned to the face left/right direction, the Y axis to the face top/bottom direction and the Z axis to the face normal direction. Thus, the facial scan

Figure 4. Detected keypoints on the facial scans of three different individuals from the FRGC v2.0 dataset. Each column shows the gallery scan and one frontal probe scan of the same individual. A large part of the keypoints are repeatably identified at the same neighborhoods for the same individual. (Adapted from Berretti et al. (2013)).

Gallery scans
FRGC v2.0
dataset

Probe scans
FRGC v2.0
datasett

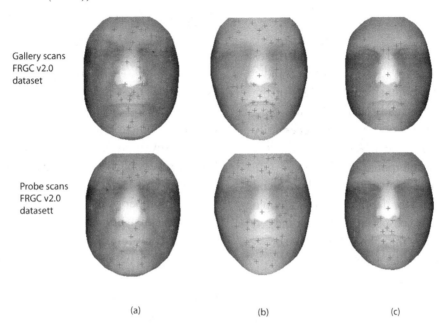

(a) (b) (c)

can be regarded as the result of sampling a scalar function $I(x)$: $\Omega \rightarrow R$ on a discrete 2D grid of points $\Omega \subset R^2$.

A generic point on the facial surface is identified through the notation $(x, I(x))$. One pair of keypoints $(x_1, I(x_1))$ and $(x_2, I(x_2))$ on the facial surface I identifies one facial curve corresponding to the curve segment (delimited by $(x_1, I(x_1))$ and $(x_2, I(x_2))$) where the facial surface I intersects the plane Π orthogonal to the plane XY and passing through the two keypoints $(x_1, I(x_1))$ and $(x_2, I(x_2))$ (see Figure 5).

Accordingly, in the continuous domain, the facial curve identified by the pair $(x_1, I(x_1))$ and $(x_2, I(x_2))$ can be expressed, given $T = \| \mathbf{x_1} - \mathbf{x_2} \|$, as a parametric curve $C^I_{x1,x2}(t)$: $[0,T] \rightarrow R^3$, defined as follows:

Figure 5. Two keypoints $(x_1, I(x_1))$ and $(x_2, I(x_2))$ on the facial surface identify a facial curve. The curve is given by the intersection of the facial surface with the plane orthogonal to the plane XY and passing through the two keypoints. (Adapted from Berretti et al. (2013)).

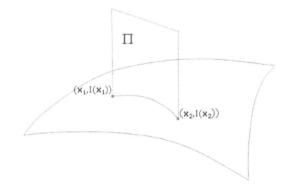

$$C^I_{x_1,x_2}(t) = (x(t), I(x(t))),$$
with (3)

$$x(t) = \left(1 - \frac{t}{T}\right)x_1 + \frac{t}{T}x_2 \quad t \in [0, T]$$

In the discretized domain, the parameter t takes values on a discrete set $t_0, ..., t_n$ with $t_0 = 0$ and $t_n = T$. Furthermore, since the values of the facial surface are actually available only on a discrete grid and values of $x(t_i)$ do not necessarily fit these grid points, values of $I(x(t_i))$ are estimated through a bilinear interpolation scheme.

As an example, Figure 6(a) shows three facial curves derived from the depth image of a sample individual. It can be observed in (b) that the red facial curve captures the shape of the face across a path that evidences the nose protrusion.

Comparison of the identity of two face representations is accomplished by matching their corresponding facial curves. Given the facial curve $C_1(t)$, $t \in [0, T_1]$ identified by the keypoint pair (x_1, x_2) of the face scan I_1, and the facial curve $C_2(t)$, $t \in [0, T_2]$, identified by the keypoint pair (x_3, x_4) of the face scan I_2, assuming the keypoints (x_1, x_2) match with the keypoints (x_3, x_4), the distance between the two facial curves is measured as:

$$D(C_1(t), C_2(t)) = \int_0^{\min\{T_1, T_2\}} \left|C_1(t) - C_2(t)dt\right| \quad (4)$$

being $|C_1(t) - C_2(t)|$ the absolute distance between depth values of the curves. In doing so, it should be noted that looking to the matching keypoints as nodes, a complete graph of facial curves is derived between keypoints (i.e., a facial curve is considered between every pair of matching keypoint), so that the number of facial curves grows quadratically with the number of matching keypoints.

We note that, unlike other solutions using keypoints that only rely on local descriptors computed in the keypoint neighborhood (Claes et al., 2011), this approach is characterized by the use of the relational information between keypoints, creating a sort of graph of curves on the face that changes across different subjects based on the position of extracted keypoints.

Figure 6. (a) A 3D face scan with three facial curves between keypoints evidenced in different colors. (b) 2-D plot of the facial curve between the left inner eye and the right cheek (i.e., the intersection of the facial surface with the orthogonal plane as illustrated in Figure 5). In the plot, the horizontal axis reports the number of pixels (measured in the depth image projection of the 3D scan) between the two keypoints which define the facial curve; the vertical axis represents the depth along the facial curve, normalized in the [0,1] interval. (Adapted from Berretti et al. (2013)).

(a)

(b)

Matching Face Representations

Given two face scans, the decision about whether they represent the same person or not relies on the comparison of the facial curves detected on the two scans. However, in order to support accurate recognition, comparison of facial curves should also take into account some geometric constraints about the position of facial curves on the face.

Given two face models, their comparison is performed by jointly matching the keypoints and the facial curves under the constraint of consistent spatial arrangement of corresponding keypoints on the two face models. First, SIFT descriptors of the keypoints detected in the probe and the gallery are compared, so that for each keypoint in the probe, a candidate corresponding keypoint in the gallery is identified. In particular, a keypoint k_p in the probe scan is assigned to a keypoint k_g in the gallery scan, if k_p and k_g match each other among all keypoints, that is if and only if k_p is closer to k_g than to any other keypoint in the gallery, and k_g is closer to k_p than to any other keypoint in the probe. For this purpose, proximity of keypoints is measured through the Euclidean distance between 128-dimensional SIFT descriptors associated with the keypoints. As an example, Figure 7(a) shows all the keypoints detected on scans of a same subject, whereas in Figure 7(b) only the matching keypoints are retained and plotted.

This analysis of proximity of keypoint descriptors results in the identification of a candidate set of keypoint correspondences. Identification of the actual set of keypoint correspondences must pass a final constraint targeting the consistent spatial arrangement of corresponding keypoints in the probe and the gallery. The RANSAC algorithm (Fischler & Bolles, 1981) is used to identify outliers in the candidate set of keypoint correspondences. This involves generating transformation hypotheses using a minimal number of correspondences and then evaluating each hypothesis based on the number of inliers among all features under that hypothesis. In our case, we modeled the problem of establishing correspondences between sets of keypoints detected on the depth maps of two matching scans as that of identifying points that are related via a rotation, scaling and translation. In this way, corresponding keypoints whose spatial arrangement is an outlier are removed from the match. An example of the application of RANSAC is reported in Figure 7(b), where some keypoints are left unassigned in the match between two faces due to their low spatial coherence with respect to the others (i.e., the keypoints not connected by green lines in the figure). In Figure 7(c), the facial curves between a pair of matching keypoints are shown for the gallery and probe of a same subject.

Given a probe (p) and a gallery (g) scan, the correspondences between probe and gallery facial

Figure 7. Example of matching scans of a same subject: (a) All keypoints; (b) Matching keypoints and their correspondence after outliers removal with RANSAC; (c) Facial curves between a pair of matching keypoints whose distance contributes to the measure of face similarity. (Adapted from Berretti et al. (2013)).

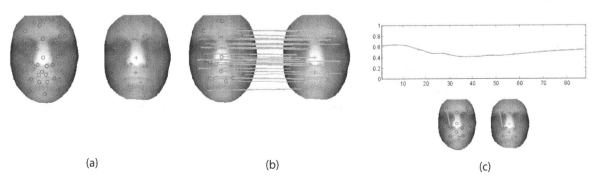

(a)   (b)   (c)

curves identified by the RANSAC algorithm are computed and the top (lowest valued) normalized distances are averaged to measure the distance between the probe and the gallery scans.

This method has been tested on the UND dataset that also includes scans with side views of the face, so as to test the robustness with respect to missing parts of the face. The main features of the UND dataset and the obtained results are summarized below.

Face Identification Results: UND/FRGC Dataset

The Ear database from *University of Notre Dame* (UND, 2008), collections F and G was created for ear recognition purposes and contains side scans with a yaw rotation (around the vertical axis) of 45°, 60° and 90°. Similarly to Perakis et al. (2009), we did not use the 90° side scans in that the large part of the face is occluded from the sensor, so that it does not contain enough useful information for face recognition purposes. We used the 45° side scans (119 subjects, with 119 left and 119 right scans) and the 60° side scans (88 subjects, with 88 left and 88 rights scans). As noted in Perakis et al. (2009), it should be considered that even though these side scans are marked as 45° and 60° by the creators of the database, the measured average yaw angle of rotation is 65° and 80°, respectively. As an example, Figure 8 shows the gallery scan and the 60° side scans after pose normalization for a sample subject.

In any case, we refer to the side scans with the naming used in the UND database (45° and 60°). The institution collecting the UND database is the same that defined the FRGC v2.0 database. So, there is a partial overlap between subjects in the two datasets. However, not all subjects exist in both the UND and FRGC v2.0 databases. In fact, the number of common subjects between the gallery scans (i.e., frontal scans in the FRGC

Figure 8. Examples from the UND dataset: Three scans of the same subject are shown. In (a) the frontal gallery scan is given. In (b) and (c) the scans acquired with the subject rotated of 60° on the left and on the right side are shown, respectively (Please note that the side scans have been rotated in frontal pose for better visualization). (Adapted from Berretti et al. (2013)).

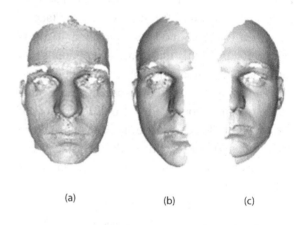

(a)   (b)   (c)

v2.0) and the 45° side scans is 39, and between the gallery scans and the 60° side scans is 33. According to this and following Perakis et al. (2009), in our experiments we considered the following test datasets:

- **DB45F:** Gallery set has one frontal scan for each of the 466 subjects of the FRGC v2.0. Probe set has two 45° side scans (left and right) for each of the 39 subjects;
- **DB60F:** Gallery set has one frontal scan for each of the 466 subjects of the FRGC v2.0. Probe set has two 60° side scans (left and right) for each of the 33 subjects.

In both cases, there is only one gallery scan per subject (466 scans in total), and the gallery coincides with that of the FRGC v2.0 dataset. In addition, all the subjects included in the probe set are also present in the gallery set (the opposite is not always true). In the following, we will also use UND45 left/right and UND60 left/right to refer to the probe sets constituted by the 45° side scans (left and right) and by the 60° side scans (left and right), respectively. Results are reported in Figure 9(a) and (b) for the case of 45° and 60° side scans, respectively.

Comparative Evaluation

In Table 1, we summarize the most effective 3D face recognition methods appeared in the last few years (methods are sorted in the Table according to their publication year). The comparison is performed based on the following indicators:

- **Fully 3D:** This column indicates if the method uses just the 3D data of each scan or also exploits the 2D data (texture) of the face;
- **Registration:** This column indicates if the method requires a preliminary alignment of the scans with respect to a reference system or a reference (template) model. In almost all the cases, this relies on the detection of some facial landmarks (also called fiducial points) as well as on the applica-

tion of some rigid or deformable registration (that can be a time consuming operation). Where possible, some details on the used landmarks and the registration technique (*rigid* or *deformable*) are reported;

- **Scalability / Indexing:** This point expresses the capability of individual approach to scale up to real world applications. This accounts for the sustainability of the overall processing pipeline on large datasets in terms of the computational cost required for preprocessing, registration, feature extraction and comparison of face description. *Indexing* more properly accounts for the possibility of the approach to be combined with efficient indexing structures that can speed up the face identification process;
- **Occlusions / Missing parts:** This column reports about the capability of the approach to support face identification also in the case in which parts of the face are occluded (for example by hands, glasses, scarf, etc) or missing (due for example to pose variations);

Figure 9. CMC curves for the method based on keypoints and facial-curves approach scored on: (a) UND45; (b) UND60. (Adapted from Berretti et al. (2013)).

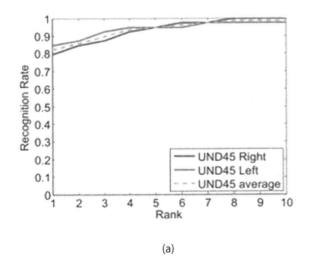

(a)

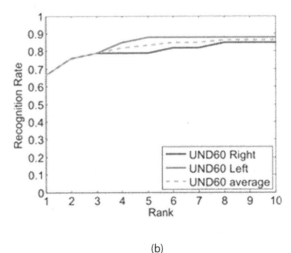

(b)

Table 1. Comparison of state of the art 3D face recognition approaches. Recognition rates are compared on the FRGC v2.0 dataset: values reported in the Table are those appearing in the respective works.

Method	Fully 3D	Registration	Scalability / Indexing	Occlusions / Missing Parts	RR @rank-1 (FRGC v2.0)
Kakadiaris et al. (2007)	Y	Rigid + Deformable	Medium / N	N / N	97.0%
Mian et al. (2007)	Y	Rigid (nose side and tip)	High / N	N / N	93.5%
Faltemier et al. (2008a)	Y	Rigid (nose tip)	Low / N	N / N	97.2%
Wang et al. (2010)	N (face detection in 2D)	Rigid (nose tip + symmetry plane)	Medium / N	N / N	98.3%
Queirolo et al. (2010)	Y	Rigid (nose base, side and tip, inner eyes corner)	Low / N	N / N	98.4%
Alyuz et al. (2010)	Y	Rigid (nose tip and leftmost/ rightmost points of the lower nose border region, inner eye corner)	Medium / N	Y / Y	97.5%
Spreeuwers (2011)	Y	Rigid (nose tip + symmetry plane)	High / N	N / N	99.0%
Drira et al. (2013)	Y	Rigid (nose tip)	Low / N	Y / Y	97.0%
Smeets et al. (2013)	Y	N	Low / N	Y / Y	89.6%
Iso-geodesic stripes (2010)	*Y*	*Rigid (nose tip, inner eyes corner)*	*High / Y*	*N / N*	*94.1%*
Keypoints + facial curves (2013)	*Y*	*Rigid (nose tip, inner eyes corner)*	*Medium / N*	*Y / Y*	*95.6%*

- **RR @rank-1:** The last column in the Table reports, as quantitative measure of comparison, the recognition rate (RR) at rank-1 for the identification experiment performed on the FRGC v2.0 dataset. This is possible since all the reported methods have been tested on the FRGC v2.0, following the same protocol for the identification experiment. In particular, in this experiment the first neutral scan of each subject is included in the gallery (466 scans in total), whereas all the remaining scans are used as probes (3541 in total).

All these methods are designed to support a certain degree of facial expression variation, without substantial decrease of the recognition accuracy. So, all these solutions can be considered robust to facial expressions (at least for the level of expression variations included in the FRGC v2.0 dataset).

From the Table, it can be observed as almost all the methods are fully 3D and require some form of registration. In most of the cases this is obtained by detecting some fiducial points and using the ICP algorithm. For the current methods, the most challenging aspects are represented by the robustness to occlusions and missing parts and by the scalability (indexing). Actually, robustness of the identification in the case of missing parts and occlusions is supported by a few methods. Though some of them can be extended to address these additional issues, some other are based on more rigid assumptions (as face symmetry) that are not compatible with occluded or missed parts of the face.

Scalability and indexing are still distant goals. One motivation for this is the small size of the datasets that are available for testing (the FRGC v2.0 is the largest one in terms of included subjects, but it is still limited to 466 individuals). Overall the recognition rates of all the methods are quite good, ranging from 89.6% to 99.5%. This is an indication of the effectiveness of the methods developed so far, though an alert should be posed for the risk of over fitting on the FRGC 2.0 data. In other words, our claim is that concentrating the evaluation of new methods on this dataset is important for comparison purposes but, at the same time can result in some bias of the methods, if they are mainly targeted to improve the performance on this dataset rather than to provide solutions with general features and applicability.

About the two methods summarized in this Chapter, we can emphasize some of their distinguishing traits. As emerges from the Table, the iso-geodesic stripes solution is one of the few solutions that permits high scalability and also easy combination with indexing structures. As for the solution based on SIFT keypoints and facial curves, it is positively distinguished by the capability to support face recognition also in the case of occlusions and missing parts.

FUTURE RESEARCH DIRECTIONS

Human identity recognition based on 3D scans of the face is an active area of research with many new

solutions appeared in the last years. Though very high recognition accuracies have been reached on several benchmark datasets, like the FRGC v2.0, the *Bosphorus* and the *Binghamton* University 3D facial expression database, solutions for 3D face recognition and facial expression recognition are still preliminary. In fact, there are several topics related to 3D faces that require much more investigation and which are attracting an increasing interest as current and future research directions:

- 3D face *acquisition* and *preprocessing*;
- 3D face *datasets* with challenging scans for recognition and facial expression recognition;
- In *cooperative* contexts
  - 3D to 3D face recognition on (*large*) *databases*;
  - 3D to 3D face recognition with *aging*;
  - 3D to 3D *face ethnicity / gender* recognition;
  - 3D to 3D *static facial expressions* recognition;
- In *semi-cooperative* or *non-cooperative* contexts
  - 3D to 3D face recognition in presence of *pose variations* and *occlusions*;
  - 4D (3D + time) *dynamic facial expression* recognition;
  - 3D *low-resolution* to 3D *high-resolution* face recognition;
  - 2D to 3D face recognition *hybrid / multimodal*.

In this scenario, the presented 3D face recognition approaches can be regarded as innovative solutions capable to enhance the robustness to facial expression variations (approach based on *iso-geodesic stripes*) and also to missing parts of the face (approach based on *keypoints* and *facial curves*).

CONCLUSION

In this Chapter, we have presented two approaches to 3D face recognition that are characterized by the use of spatial information of the 3D face in order to improve the recognition accuracy in the presence of facial expressions.

The first approach captures characterizing features of the face by measuring the spatial displacement between iso-geodesic stripes. The method has several distinguishing features that make it suited for face identification in large data sets. In particular, it does not use iterative point-wise adaptation; instead, facial information is captured into a graph-like compact face descriptor that has good invariance to facial expressions and, at the same time, good discrimination capability between face structural differences. Descriptors can be obtained with low computational complexity and matched efficiently using appropriate index structures, with great savings in the performance for identification in large data set. Experiments that have been performed on the FRGC v2.0 and SHREC08 data sets have also shown very high effectiveness in the presence of strong facial expressions with the performance in the top ranked ones.

The second approach captures relational spatial information between detected keypoints of the face using facial curves. First, the SIFT keypoints detector and descriptor are used to identify and characterize keypoints on depth images of the face. Detected keypoints are used to identify a set of facial curves, each curve representing the variation of the face surface along a path that connects a pair of keypoints. The approach makes no assumption about the correspondence of detected keypoints to specific landmarks on the face. Therefore, it can support the comparison of the curves extracted from probe and gallery scans even if the probe scan represents just a part of the face. To improve the accuracy of recognition, the RANSAC algorithm is used to remove outlier keypoints matching so as to retain just the matching pairs that show a consistent geometric transformation. Experiments carried out on the UND/FRGC v2.0 dataset show the viability of the approach, which favorably compares with other approaches proposed in the literature.

REFERENCES

Alyüz, N., Gökberk, B., & Akarun, L. (2010). Regional registration for expression resistant 3-D face recognition. *IEEE Transactions on Information Forensics and Security*, 5(3), 425–440. doi:10.1109/TIFS.2010.2054081

Amberg, B., Knothe, R., & Vetter, T. (2008). SHREC'08 Entry: Shape Based Face Recognition with a Morphable Model. In *Proceedings of IEEE International Conference on Shape Modeling and Applications*, (pp. 253-254). IEEE.

Berretti, S., del Bimbo, A., & Pala, P. (2006). Description and Retrieval of 3D Face Models using iso-Geodesic Stripes. In *Proceedings of ACM SIGMM International Workshop on Multimedia Information Retrieval* (MIR'06), (pp. 13-22). ACM.

Berretti, S., del Bimbo, A., & Pala, P. (2010). 3D Face Recognition using iso-Geodesic Stripes. *IEEE Transactions on Pattern Analysis and Machine Intelligence*, 32(12), 2162–2177. doi:10.1109/TPAMI.2010.43 PMID:20975115

Berretti, S., del Bimbo, A., & Pala, P. (2011). Facial Curves between Keypoints for Recognition of 3D Faces with Missing Parts. In *Proceedings of IEEE Computer Vision and Pattern Recognition Workshop on Multi Modal Biometrics*, (pp. 49-54). IEEE.

Berretti, S., del Bimbo, A., & Pala, P. (2012). Distinguishing Facial Features for Ethnicity based 3D Face Recognition. *ACM Transactions on Intelligent Systems and Technology*, 3(3), 1–20. doi:10.1145/2168752.2168759

Berretti, S., del Bimbo, A., & Pala, P. (2013). Sparse Matching of Salient Facial Curves for Recognition of 3D Faces with Missing Parts. *IEEE Transactions on Information Forensics and Security, 8*(2), 374–389. doi:10.1109/TIFS.2012.2235833

Berretti, S., del Bimbo, A., & Vicario, E. (2001). Efficient matching and indexing of graph models in content-based retrieval. *IEEE Transactions on Pattern Analysis and Machine Intelligence, 23*(10), 1089–1105. doi:10.1109/34.954600

Besl, P. J., & Mc Kay, N. D. (1992). A method for registration of 3-D shapes. *IEEE Transactions on Pattern Analysis and Machine Intelligence, 14*(2), 239–256. doi:10.1109/34.121791

Beumier, C., & Acheroy, M. (2001). Face Verification from 3D and Grey Level Clues. *Pattern Recognition Letters, 22*(12), 1321–1329. doi:10.1016/S0167-8655(01)00077-0

Bronstein, A. M., Bronstein, M. M., & Kimmel, R. (2005). Three Dimensional Face Recognition. *International Journal of Computer Vision, 64*(1), 5–30. doi:10.1007/s11263-005-1085-y

Bronstein, A. M., Bronstein, M. M., & Kimmel, R. (2006). Robust Expression Invariant Face Recognition from Partially Missing Data. In *Proceedings of European Conference on Computer Vision*, (pp. 396-408). Academic Press.

Chang, K. I., Bowyer, K. W., & Flynn, P. J. (2005). An Evaluation of Multimodal 2D + 3D Face Biometrics. *IEEE Transactions on Pattern Analysis and Machine Intelligence, 27*(4), 619–624. doi:10.1109/TPAMI.2005.70 PMID:15794165

Chang, K. I., Bowyer, K. W., & Flynn, P. J. (2006). Multiple Nose Region Matching for 3D Face Recognition under Varying Facial Expression. *IEEE Transactions on Pattern Analysis and Machine Intelligence, 28*(6), 1695–1700. doi:10.1109/TPAMI.2006.210 PMID:16986549

Claes, P., Smeets, D., Hermans, J., Vandermeulen, D., & Suetens, P. (2011). SHREC'11 track: Robust fitting of statistical model. In *Proceedings of Eurographics Workshop on 3D Object Retrieval*, (pp. 89–95). Academic Press.

Cook, J., Chandran, V., & Fookes, C. (2006). 3D Face Recognition Using Log-Gabor Templates. *British Machine Vision Conference, 2*, 769-778.

Daoudi, M., ter Haar, F., & Veltkamp, R. (2008). *SHREC contest session on retrieval of 3D face scans*. Shape Modeling International.

Drira, H., Ben Amor, B., Srivastava, A., Daoudi, M., & Slama, R. (2013). 3D Face Recognition Under Expressions, Occlusions and Pose Variations. *IEEE Transactions on Pattern Analysis and Machine Intelligence, 35*(9), 2270–2283. doi:10.1109/TPAMI.2013.48 PMID:23868784

Faltemier, T. C., Bowyer, K. W., & Flynn, P. J. (2008). A Region Ensemble for 3D Face Recognition. *IEEE Transactions on Information Forensics and Security, 3*(1), 62–73. doi:10.1109/TIFS.2007.916287

Faltemier, T. C., Bowyer, K. W., & Flynn, P. J. (2008b). Using Multi Instance Enrollment to Improve Performance of 3D Face Recognition. *Computer Vision and Image Understanding, 112*(2), 114–125. doi:10.1016/j.cviu.2008.01.004

Fischler, M. A., & Bolles, R. C. (1981). Random sample consensus. *Communications of the ACM, 24*(6), 381–395. doi:10.1145/358669.358692

Gordon, G. (1992). Face Recognition Based on Depth and Curvature Features. In *Proceedings of IEEE Conference on Computer Vision and Pattern Recognition*, (pp. 808-810). IEEE.

Gupta, S., Markey, M. K., & Bovik, A. C. (2010). Anthropometric 3D face recognition. *International Journal of Computer Vision, 90*(3), 331–349. doi:10.1007/s11263-010-0360-8

Hesher, C., Srivastava, A., & Erlebacher, G. (2002). Principal Component Analysis of Range Images for Facial Recognition. In *Proceedings of International Conference on Imaging Science, Systems, and Technology*. Academic Press.

Husken, M., Brauckmann, M., Gehlen, S., & Malsburg, C. (2005). Strategies and Benefits of Fusion of 2D and 3D Face Recognition. In *Proceedings of IEEE Workshop Face Recognition Grand Challenge*. IEEE.

Kakadiaris, I. A., Passalis, G., Toderici, G., Murtuza, N., Lu, Y., Karampatziakis, N., & Theoharis, T. (2007). Three-Dimensional Face Recognition in the Presence of Facial Expressions: An Annotated Deformable Approach. *IEEE Transactions on Pattern Analysis and Machine Intelligence*, *29*(4), 640–649. doi:10.1109/TPAMI.2007.1017 PMID:17299221

Lee, J. C., & Milios, E. (1990). Matching Range Images of Human Faces. In *Proceedings of IEEE International Conference on Computer Vision*, (pp. 722-726). IEEE.

Lu, X., & Jain, A. K. (2006). Deformation Modeling for Robust 3D Face Matching. In *Proceedings of IEEE Conference on Computer Vision and Pattern Recognition*, (pp. 1377-1383). IEEE.

Lu, X., Jain, A. K., & Colbry, D. (2006). Matching 2.5d Face Scans to 3D Models. *IEEE Transactions on Pattern Analysis and Machine Intelligence*, *28*(1), 31–43. doi:10.1109/TPAMI.2006.15 PMID:16402617

Mian, A. S., Bennamoun, M., & Owens, R. (2007). An Efficient Multi-modal 2D-3D Hybrid Approach to Automatic Face Recognition. *IEEE Transactions on Pattern Analysis and Machine Intelligence*, *29*(11), 1927–1943. doi:10.1109/TPAMI.2007.1105 PMID:17848775

Moreno, A. B., Sànchez, A., Vélez, J. F., & Dìaz, F. J. (2003). Face Recognition Using 3D Surface-Extracted Descriptors. In *Proceedings of Irish Machine Vision and Image Processing Conference*. Academic Press.

Pan, G., Han, S., Wu, Z., & Wang, Y. (2005). 3D Face Recognition Using Mapped Depth Images. In *Proceedings of IEEE Conference on Computer Vision and Pattern Recognition*, (Vol. 3, pp. 175-18). IEEE.

Passalis, G., Kakadiaris, I. A., Theoharis, T., Toderici, G., & Murtuza, N. (2005). Evaluation of 3D Face Recognition in the Presence of Facial Expressions: An Annotated Deformable Model Approach. In *Proceedings of IEEE Workshop Face Recognition Grand Challenge Experiments*, (Vol. 3, pp. 171-179). IEEE.

Perakis, P., Passalis, G., Theoharis, T., Toderici, G., & Kakadiaris, I. A. (2009). Partial matching of interpose 3D facial data for face recognition. In *Proceedings of IEEE International Conference on Biometrics: Theory, Applications, and Systems*, (pp. 1–8). IEEE.

Phillips, P. J., Flynn, P. J., Scruggs, T., Bowyer, K. W., Chang, J., Hoffman, K., et al. (2005). Overview of the face recognition grand challenge. In *Proceedings of IEEE Workshop on Face Recognition Grand Challenge Experiments*, (pp. 947–954). IEEE.

Phillips, P. J., Grother, P., Micheals, R. J., Blackburn, D., Tabassi, E., & Bone, M. (2003). *FRVT 2002: Evaluation report. National Institute of Standards and Technology*. NIST.

Phillips, P. J., Scruggs, W. T., O'Toole, A. J., Flynn, P. J., Bowyer, K. W., Schott, C. L., & Sharpe, M. (2007). *FRVT 2006 and ICE 2006 large-scale results. National Institute of Standards and Technology*. NIST.

Queirolo, C. C., Silva, L., Bellon, O. R. P., & Pamplona Segundo, M. (2010). 3D Face Recognition Using Simulated Annealing and the Surface Interpenetration Measure. *IEEE Transactions on Pattern Analysis and Machine Intelligence*, *32*(2), 206–219. doi:10.1109/TPAMI.2009.14 PMID:20075453

Samir, C., Srivastava, A., & Daoudi, M. (2006). Three-Dimensional Face Recognition Using Shapes of Facial Curves. *IEEE Transactions on Pattern Analysis and Machine Intelligence*, *28*(11), 1853–1863. doi:10.1109/TPAMI.2006.235 PMID:17063689

Smeets, D., Keustermans, J., Vandermeulen, D., & Suetens, P. (2013). meshSIFT: Local surface features for 3D face recognition under expression variations and partial data. *Computer Vision and Image Understanding*, *117*(2), 158–169.

Spreeuwers, L. (2011). Fast and Accurate 3D Face Recognition. *International Journal of Computer Vision*, *93*(3), 389–414. doi:10.1007/s11263-011-0426-2

ter Haar, F., & Veltkamp, R. (2008). A 3D Face Matching Framework. In *Proceedings of IEEE International Conference on Shape Modeling and Applications* (pp. 103-110). IEEE.

Tsalakanidou, F., Tzovaras, D., & Strintzis, M. (2003). Use of Depth and Colour Eigenfaces for Face Recognition. *Pattern Recognition Letters*, *24*(9/10), 1427–1435. doi:10.1016/S0167-8655(02)00383-5

University of Notre Dame Biometrics Database. (2008). Retrieved from http://www.nd.edu/@cvrl/UNDBiometricsDatabase.html

Vedaldi, A., & Fulkerson, B. (2008). *VLFeat: An Open and Portable Library of Computer Vision Algorithms*. Retrieved from http://www.vlfeat.org/

Wang, S., Wang, Y., Jin, M., Gu, X., & Samaras, D. (2006). 3D Surface Matching and Recognition Using Conformal Geometry. In *Proceedings of IEEE Conference on Computer Vision and Pattern Recognition*, (Vol. 2, pp. 2453-2460). IEEE.

Wang, Y., Chiang, M.-C., & Thompson, P. M. (2005). Mutual Information-Based 3D Surface Matching with Applications to Face Recognition and Brain Mapping. In *Proceedings of IEEE International Conference on Computer Vision* (pp. 527-534). IEEE.

Wang, Y., & Chua, C.-S. (2005). Face Recognition from 2D and 3D Images Using 3D Gabor Filters. *Image and Vision Computing*, *11*(23), 1018–1028. doi:10.1016/j.imavis.2005.07.005

Wang, Y., Liu, J., & Tang, X. (2010). Robust 3D face recognition by local shape difference boosting. *IEEE Transactions on Pattern Analysis and Machine Intelligence*, *32*(10), 1858–1870. doi:10.1109/TPAMI.2009.200 PMID:20724762

Xu, D., Hu, P., Cao, W., & Li, H. (2008). Shrec'08 Entry: 3D Face Recognition Using Moment Invariants. In *Proceedings of IEEE International Conference on Shape Modeling and Applications*, (pp. 261-262). IEEE.

Yan, P., & Bowyer, K. W. (2007). A Fast Algorithm for ICP-Based 3D Shape Biometrics. *Computer Vision and Image Understanding*, *107*(3), 195–202. doi:10.1016/j.cviu.2006.11.001

Zhao, W., Chellappa, R., Phillips, P. J., & Rosenfeld, A. (2003). Face recognition: A literature survey. *ACM Computing Surveys*, *35*(4), 399–458. doi:10.1145/954339.954342

ADDITIONAL READING

Alyüz, N., Gökberk, B., & Akarun, L. (2008). 3D face recognition system for expression and occlusion invariance. *IEEE International Conference on Biometrics: Theory, Applications, and Systems*, pp. 1–7.

Bagdanov, A. D., del Bimbo, A., & Masi, I. (2011). The Florence 2D/3D hybrid face dataset. ACM workshop on Human Gesture and Behavior Understanding, pp.79–80.

Ballihi, L., Ben Amor, B., Daoudi, M., Srivastava, A., & Aboutajdine, D. (2012). Boosting 3D-geometric features for efficient face recognition and gender classification. *IEEE Transactions on Information Forensics and Security*, 7(6), 1766–1779. doi:10.1109/TIFS.2012.2209876

Berretti, S., del Bimbo, A., & Pala, P. (2012). Superfaces: A super-resolution model for 3D faces. *Workshop on Non-Rigid Shape Analysis and Deformable Image Alignment*, pp.73-82.

Berretti, S., Werghi, N., Del Bimbo, A., & Pala, P. (2013). Matching 3D Face Scans using Interest Points and Local Histogram Descriptors. *Computer Graphics*, 37(5), 509–525. doi:10.1016/j.cag.2013.04.001

Colombo, A., Cusano, C., & Schettini, R. (2009). Gappy PCA classification for occlusion tolerant 3D face detection. *Journal of Mathematical Image and Vision*, 35(3), 193–207. doi:10.1007/s10851-009-0165-y

Drira, H., Ben Amor, B., Daoudi, M., & Srivastava, A. (2010). Pose and expression-invariant 3D face recognition using elastic radial curves. *British Machine Vision Conference*, pp. 1–11.

Drira, H., Ben Amor, B., Srivastava, A., Daoudi, M., & Slama, R. (2013). 3D Face Recognition under Expressions, Occlusions, and Pose Variations. *IEEE Transactions on Pattern Analysis and Machine Intelligence*, 35(9), 2270–2283. doi:10.1109/TPAMI.2013.48 PMID:23868784

Farkas, L. G., & Munro, I. R. (1987). *Anthropometric Facial Proportions in Medicine*. Thomas Books.

Huang, D., Ardabilian, M., Wang, Y., & Chen, L. (2012). 3D face recognition using eLBP-based facial representation and local feature hybrid matching. *IEEE Transactions on Information Forensics and Security*, 7(5), 1551–1564. doi:10.1109/TIFS.2012.2206807

Lowe, D. (2004). Distinctive image features from scale-invariant key points. *International Journal of Computer Vision*, 60(2), 91–110. doi:10.1023/B:VISI.0000029664.99615.94

Mian, A. S., Bennamoun, M., & Owens, R. (2008). Keypoint detection and local feature matching for textured 3D face recognition. *International Journal of Computer Vision*, 79(1), 1–12. doi:10.1007/s11263-007-0085-5

Mian, A. S., Bennamoun, M., & Owens, R. (2010). On the repeatability and quality of keypoints for local feature-based 3D object retrieval from cluttered scenes. *International Journal of Computer Vision*, 89(2–3), 348–361. doi:10.1007/s11263-009-0296-z

Moreno, A. B., & Sánchez, Á. (2004). Gavabdb: A 3D face database. *Workshop on Biometrics on the Internet*, pp.75–80.

Mpiperis, I., Malassiotis, S., & Strintzis, M. (2008). Bilinear models for 3-D face and facial expression recognition. *IEEE Transactions on Information Forensics and Security*, 3(3), 498–511. doi:10.1109/TIFS.2008.924598

Passalis, G., Perakis, P., Theoharis, T., & Kakadiaris, I. A. (2011). Using facial symmetry to handle pose variations in real-world 3D face recognition. *IEEE Transactions on Pattern Analysis and Machine Intelligence*, 33(10), 1938–1951. doi:10.1109/TPAMI.2011.49 PMID:21383396

Peyre, G. (2009). Toolbox graph. In MATLAB central file exchange select.

Salti, S., Tombari, F., & Di Stefano, L. (2013). Performance evaluation of 3D keypoint detectors. *International Journal of Computer Vision, 102*(2–3), 198–220.

Savran, A., Alyüz, N., Dibeklioğlu, H., Çeliktutan, O., Gökberk, B., Sankur, B., & Akarun, L. (2008). Bosphorus database for 3D face analysis. *COST 2101 Workshop on Biometrics and Identity Management*, pp.47–56.

University of Notre Dame Biometrics Database. (2008). Available: http://www.nd.edu/@cvrl/UNDBiometricsDatabase.html

Veltkamp, R., van Jole, S., Drira, H., Ben Amor, B., Daoudi, M., Li, H., et al. (2011). SHREC'11 track: 3D face models retrieval. *Eurographics Workshop on 3D Object Retrieval*, pp.89–95.

Xu, C., Tan, T., Wang, Y., & Quan, L. (2006). Combining local features for robust nose location in 3D facial data. *Pattern Recognition Letters, 27*(13), 1487–1494. doi:10.1016/j.patrec.2006.02.015

Yin, L., Wei, X., Sun, Y., Wang, J., & Rosato, M. (2006). A 3D facial expression database for facial behavior research. *IEEE International Conference on Automatic Face and Gesture Recognition*, pp.211–216.

Zaharescu, A., Boyer, E., & Horaud, R. (2012). Keypoints and local descriptors of scalar functions on 2D manifolds. *International Journal of Computer Vision, 100*(1), 78–98. doi:10.1007/s11263-012-0528-5

KEY TERMS AND DEFINITIONS

3D Face Recognition: Face recognition based on the comparison of the full 3D geometry of scans of the face acquired with 3D scanners. Expected to be more robust against illumination changes than face recognition based on 2D still images.

3D Geometric Transformation Using RANSAC: RANSAC involves generating transformation hypotheses using a minimal number of correspondences and then evaluating each hypothesis based on the number of inliers among all features under that hypothesis. The problem of establishing correspondences between sets of keypoints detected on the depth maps of two matching scans is modeled as that of identifying points that are related via a *rotation*, *scaling* and *translation* (RST transformation).

3D Spatial Relations: Account for the mutual positions of 3D points in the 3D space.

3D Weighted Walkthrough: Integral measure that captures the relative displacement of two sets of 3D points, considering the mutual spatial relationships between any pairs of points in the two sets.

Face Recognition System: A computer application for automatically identifying or verifying a person from a 2D still image / video / 3D scan / 3D video source. A common approach to do this is comparing selected facial features from the unknown test face and a facial database of known faces.

Facial Curves: Two keypoints on the facial surface identify a facial curve. The curve is given by the intersection of the facial surface with the plane orthogonal to the plane XY of the projection depth image and passing through the two keypoints.

Geodesic Distance on 3D Surface: Shortest path between two points on the surface.

Iso-Geodesic Stripes: Regions of the 3D face that include points that are in a certain range of geodesic distances from a source point of the face (e.g., the nose tip).

SIFT Keypoints of Depth Maps: SIFT keypoints on depth images detect blobs of depth values, corresponding to scale-space extrema of the scale normalized difference of Gaussians operator. Since blobs in depth scans correspond to regions whose depth values differ compared to the surrounding, detected keypoints correspond to local protrusions/intrusions of the face surface.

Chapter 6
Robust 3D Face Identification in the Presence of Occlusions

Nese Alyuz
Bogazici University, Turkey

Berk Gokberk
University of Twente, The Netherlands

Lale Akarun
Bogazici University, Turkey

ABSTRACT

The face is one of the most natural biometrics, and as such, its acceptance by users is high. While biometrics such as fingerprint and iris can only be acquired with active cooperation of the user, the face can be acquired from a distance. This makes it an attractive modality for uncooperative scenarios. However, in such scenarios, occlusion is a common problem. The focus of this chapter is to illustrate the problems caused by 3D occlusion, and to go over solutions. The authors review 3D face identification approaches with focus on occlusion scenarios, introduce 3D databases containing occlusions, and present a prototype system with solutions for occlusion at landmarking, registration, feature extraction, and matching stages.

INTRODUCTION

The term *biometrics* refers to automated systems where physiological or behavioral characteristics of an individual are used for identification purposes. Face, fingerprint, iris, retinal image, vein, or voice can be listed among the physiological features used in biometric systems. Among others, face is the most familiar-to-human modality, since our cognitive system often utilizes facial data

to recognize people. Moreover, face modality is highly preferred for automated systems, since the biometric data can be acquired in a contactless manner and it can be employed for non-cooperative scenarios. Due to these advantages, face recognition has a wide application domain, including surveillance, access control and human-computer interaction practices. Hence, it has been a popular research topic for the last three decades. Further research in the last decade showed that, face

DOI: 10.4018/978-1-4666-5966-7.ch006

recognition in constrained acquisition scenarios can reach the performance levels of high security modalities such as fingerprint and iris (Phillips, 2007).

Initially, the face recognition studies focused on identifying people from their two dimensional (2D) facial images (Zhao, 2003). However, when non-cooperative and uncontrolled scenarios are considered, recognizing individuals from their 2D face scans remains as a challenging task. The main challenges including illumination differences, pose variations, and presence of facial expressions; triggered the shift of face representation from 2D modality to 3D. In the 3D domain, illumination differences, pose and expression variations can be better handled since the true geometric information residing in the 3D data is utilized. This shift was supported by the emerging sensor technology allowing acquisition of the 3D facial geometry. With the advances in sensing technology, large evaluation 3D face datasets became publicly available. In 2006, the Face Recognition Grand Challenge (FRGC) (Phillips, 2005) was presented as the first large evaluation set.

The interest in 3D face recognition systems caused an enormous growth in research studies focusing on the 3D modality. A thorough survey of previously proposed 3D face recognizers can be found in (Bowyer, 2006; Scheenstra, 2005; Abate, 2007a) and details of some fundamental concepts can be overviewed in (Gokberk, 2008; Abate, 2007b; Papatheodorou, 2007). Besides the problem of expression handling, which has been extensively studied in recent years (Mian, 2008; Faltemier, 2008; Kakadiaris, 2007; Alyuz, 2010; Queirolo, 2010; Wang, 2010; Spreeuwers, 2011), occlusion variations remains as a challenging task. Although occlusions appear as a practical problem for realistic scenarios, they are not investigated well in the literature. Mainly, there are two types of occlusions. First of all, pose variations can cause self-occlusions during acquisition, where a part of the facial surface hinders acquisition of another region shadowed with respect to the sensor.

These occlusions appear as missing data in the facial surface. The other type of occlusions can be caused by external objects such as hand, hair, scarf, eyeglasses and other objects. The second class of occlusions is more complex to handle, since the occluding objects alter the 3D facial geometry. In this chapter, we mainly focus on the second class of occlusions, where exterior objects partially cover the facial surface. Hereafter, the term "occlusion" will refer to occlusions caused by exterior objects. In the literature review section, we summarize the approaches handling exterior occlusions. Moreover, we briefly mention the classification approaches used for the first type of occlusions, since these classification approaches can be useful after the occlusions are detected and removed.

The recognition problem includes two different scenarios: (1) verification, and (2) identification. In verification, the probe face is presented with a claimed identity, and the system checks if the claimed identity is correct. In identification, the probe face is compared against a set of gallery images, and the identity is searched among the gallery subjects. In this paper, we mainly focus on the identification problem, using identification and classification terms interchangeably to refer to this scenario. In the literature, the term "recognition" is sometimes used to refer to identification, which we omitted here to avoid any confusion when identification is considered.

BACKGROUND

Face Identification Concepts and the Occlusion Challenge

In the presence of occlusions over the facial surface, alterations of the geometry complicate the identification process, affecting different stages of face identification systems. The main steps of a face identifier can be listed as: face detection, landmark localization, coarse and fine registration, feature extraction, and classification. An overall diagram for a traditional face identifier is given in Figure 1. Face detection is the process of localizing the facial surface and determining its coverage. After the facial surface is detected, it is often necessary to detect some fiducial points, referred to as landmarks, such as nose tip, eye or mouth corners. In contrast, some landmark points can be detected beforehand, serving as a guide for the face detector. The landmark points can be beneficial in the initial alignment of surfaces. The process of registration is the process of aligning two surfaces, so that they can be compared for classification purposes. Registration can be divided into two stages, where an initial registration can be used to coarsely align two surfaces, and it can then be followed by a fine alignment to obtain a dense correspondence. After the facial surfaces are registered, facial features can be extracted to represent the discriminative information inherent in the surfaces. In some studies, the registration step is discarded and feature extraction is obtained using transformation independent descriptors. Some of these methods include systems based on keypoints. Keypoints are points with some specific geometrical properties, but are not necessarily at meaningful locations as landmarks. Keypoints are then used to extract transformation invariant features from a region of interest around these locations and the extracted information can be directly utilized to identify faces. The extracted features, either directly obtained without any alignment or right after the registration process, are incorporated into the classification approach to reveal the most probable identity of the scan in question.

When the facial surface is occluded, all of these stages will be affected to some extent. Therefore, when a standard face identifier is employed on occluded faces, probable errors occurring at each step will accumulate and result in an enormous degradation in the identification performance. A robust face identifier should handle the occlusion problem at different stages: (1) the registration stage, which can cover face detection, landmark or keypoint localization, determination of region of interest (ROI), and coarse or fine alignment of surfaces; (2) detection and handling of occlusions, where removal or restoration can be employed; (3) classification, where either restored or partial faces are used. Here, we focused on the problem of occlusion handling, considering these three stages. The main problems at each step are detailed, and the probable solutions proposed in the literature are summarized in the literature review section.

3D Databases used to Evaluate Robustness to Occlusion

Before giving the literature review of face identification systems considering occluded facial surfaces, we briefly introduce the publicly available 3D face databases including occlusion variations. Sorted according to the level of challenge, the

Figure 1. Overall diagram of a traditional face identifier

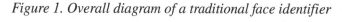

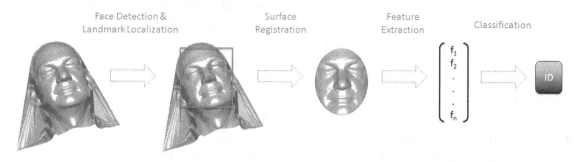

mostly referred databases can be listed as follows: (1) University of Milano Bicocca 3D Face Database (UMB-DB); (2) Bosphorus Database; (3) Face Recognition Grand Challenge Version 2 (FRGC v.2). Although the FRGC v.2 database includes only small occlusions (caused by hair over the forehead region or caused by facial hair such as mustache or beard), some systems report results on it.

The UMB-DB database (Colombo, 2011a) is collected to evaluate 3D face recognition systems, mainly focusing on the occlusion scenario. It is acquired from a total of 142 subjects, and there are a total of 1473 scans. The non-occluded scans (a total of 883 scans) include neutral and expressive scans. The other 590 scans include occlusions caused by scarves, hats, hands, eyeglasses, and other realistic exterior objects. In the literature, recognition results are reported using the available experimental protocol of (Colombo, 2011a). The gallery set contains the first neutral scan of each subject, and the probe set consists of the occlusion subset. The gallery and probe sets contain 142 neutral and 590 occluded scans, respectively. The occlusions in this database are more challenging and the location and amount of occlusion vary greatly. The occlusion percentage histogram given in Table 1 for UMB-DB occlusions, clearly shows that this set includes challenging occlusions. Some occlusion examples from the UMB-DB database are given in Figure 2, illustrating how challenging the occlusions can be.

The Bosphorus database (Savran, 2008) is acquired to enable evaluation of three main challenging scenarios of a realistic 3D face recognizer. The database includes scans of (1) pose variations, including both realistic and extreme poses; (2) expression variations, including an extensive set

Table 1. The coverage histogram table of the occlusions over the facial surface for Bosphorus and UMB-DB databases.

Database	Scans	Occlusion Coverage (up to)								
		10%	20%	30%	40%	50%	60%	70%	80%	90%
UMB-DB	590	128	75	118	76	75	81	23	11	3
Bosphorus	381	57	165	103	29	13	3	1	0	0

Figure 2. Sample images from the UMB-DB (upper row) and Bosphorus (bottom row) occlusion subsets

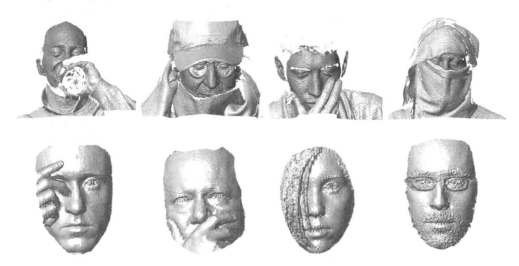

of action units in addition to a set of universally accepted expressions; (3) typical oclusions, that are probable to occur in real life. For a total of 105 subjects, there are 4666 scans. The total number of neutral and occluded scans are 299 and 381, respectively. There are four different types of occlusions as shown in Figure 2, bottom row: (1) Occlusion of the eye area by eyeglasses; (2) occlusion of the eye area by a hand, (3) occlusion of the mouth area by a hand, (4) occlusion caused by hair. Table 1 includes the occlusion percentage histogram for the occluded images of the Bosphorus database. It is clear that most of the occlusions cover 30% or less of the facial surface.

The FRGC v.2 (Phillips, 2005) is a database widely used in the literature of 3D face recognition, since it contains a large number of scans collected from a large number of subjects. In total, there are 4007 frontal images of 466 subjects. The neutral subset of 2365 images contains non-occluded images with neutral expression. The remaining faces include expression variations such as happiness, sadness, surprise, anger, disgust, and cheek puffing. Although no occlusion-specific acquisition scenario is considered for occlusion variations, there are several scans, which can be considered to include occlusions. Some scans have hair occlusion in small portions of the forehead region, and some others include facial hair. In (Ming, 2012), it is stated that more than 40% of the images include hair occlusions. For most of the studies reporting

results on FRGC v.2, the experimental protocol given in (Phillips, 2005) is used. The gallery set contains the first scan of each subject (a total of 466 scans), and the probe set contains all the remaining 3541 images. Details about three of the databases are summarized in Table 2.

LITERATURE REVIEW: OCCLUSION HANDLING AT DIFFERENT STAGES OF A 3D FACE IDENTIFIER

Handling expression and pose variations in 3D faces, has attracted wide interest in the literature. Occlusion variations, on the other hand, have only recently been studied by a few groups. In this section we summarize the literature related to occlusion handling in 3D face identification. We group the studies into three partitions. First, papers considering only partial occlusions over the forehead region (caused by hair) are summarized. Then, details about the studies experimenting on the occlusion datasets (Bosphorus and UMB-DB databases) are given. Lastly, we mention some important studies considering missing data handling, mostly due to self-occlusions. Although self occlusions are outside the scope of this chapter we include these studies here, since if it is possible to detect and remove occluded areas, classification techniques applicable to incomplete data will be beneficial. All of the approaches reviewed in

Table 2. 3D face databases that contain occlusions

Database	Subjects	Occluded Images	Occlusion Types	Occlusion Difficulty	Pose/ Expression Variations in Occluded Images	Presence of Non-Facial Body Parts (Shoulder, Torso etc)	Average 3D Points
UMB-DB (Colombo, 2011a)	142	590	Hand, hair, scarf, objects	Extreme	Both	Yes	100-150K
Bosphorus (Savran, 2008)	105	381	Hand, hair, eyeglasses	Moderate	Slight pose variations	No	50K
FRGC v.2 (Phillips, 2005)	466	~1400 (Ming, 2012)	Hair in forehead region	Low	Only expressions	Yes	100-150K

this section are summarized in Table 3 to give a quick overview.

Handling of Partial Hair Occlusions: Evaluations on the FRGC v.2 Database

Some studies in the 3D face identification literature focus on performance improvement obtained by partial hair occlusions over the forehead region. In (Li, 2012), the facial surfaces are smoothed to remove spikes using Gaussian filtering, and small holes are filled using interpolation. For face detection and ROI extraction, the nose tip is detected and it is used to center and crop the facial area. For

nose tip detection, shape index map is utilized to find nose tip candidates. Nose tip template is fitted to nose candidates, and the best fit is labeled as the nose tip. A predefined radius value is employed to crop the facial surface. For initial alignment, Principal Component Analysis (PCA) is used to normalize facial pose. Here, Y and Z axes appear as the largest and smallest eigenvalued vectors, respectively. Fine alignment is carried out by the Iterative Closest Point (ICP) algorithm. After normalization, the most dissimilar faces in the gallery are rejected using the central profile curve. After narrowing the search space, six facial regions are segmented and curves extracted in these regions are used to map deformations. Once again, ICP is

Table 3. Summary of 3D face identification methods dealing with the occlusion problem

Reference	Database	Detection and Alignment Methods	Occlusion Handling	Holistic (H) vs. Regional (R)	Matching	Identification Accuracy
(Li, 2012)	FRGC	Nose detection, PCA, ICP	Region selection	R	ICP based curve matching	97.50%
(Ming, 2012)	FRGC	ASM, nose tip detection, axis-angle representation	Group sparse representation	H	Spectral analysis of graph embedding	93.59%
(Liu, 2012)	Bosphorus	Coarse Reg.: SDM for nose tip, Fine Reg.: ICP	Rejection strategy in ICP	H	ICP distance	97.90%
(Berretti, 2013)	Bosphorus	Keypoint detection meshDoG	Keypoint matching	H	Curve matching	93.20%
(Li, 2011)	Bosphorus	Keypoint detection, HoG, HoS, HoGS	Keypoint matching	H	Matched salient point count	99.21%
(Drira, 2013)	Bosphorus	Nose tip, radial curves	Recursive ICP for occ. detection	H	Elastic shape analysis	78.63% (occ. removed), 87.06% (restored curves)
(Colombo, 2011b)	UMB-DB	Nose tip & inner eye coordinates, ICP	Detection and restoration by Gappy PCA	H	Fisherfaces	Bosphorus: 91.18% (eye), 74.75% (mouth), 94.23% (eyeglasses), 90.47% (hair) UMB-DB: 56.50%
(Alyuz, 2013)	Bosphorus, UMB-DB	Nose detection, adaptive model selection, ICP	Adaptive model based ICP, detection by distance to average face	R	Fisherfaces with masked projection	Bosphorus: 93.70% UMB-DB: 74.75%

used for partial curve matching. The deformations will result in smaller similarity scores. Hence, they will probably be rejected in the classification process, where curves with high similarity scores are fused to obtain a final identification. The results reported on the FRGC v.2 database (97.5%) make this method a probable solution for small occlusions.

In (Ming, 2012), large pose and expression variations are considered, where results for hair occlusions of FRGC v.2 are reported. First, the facial area is localized using the 2D texture and range images. For localization, the Active Shape Model is utilized over the texture image, and the profile image is extracted. Normalization is handled using the symmetry plane. Next, the nose tip is detected and the facial area is extracted by cropping with a predefined radius value around the nose tip. Fine alignment of the facial surface is achieved using the axis-angle representation and then transforming the point cloud to align it with the reference model. Afterwards, bounding sphere representation is utilized to represent surfaces, where robustness to large expression and pose variations is achieved. After the representation, robust group sparse regression model based on sparse representation (Peng, 2011) is proposed for feature extraction, where the effect of occlusions and corruptions is minimized. The classification is handled by a spectral analysis of graph embedding.

Handling of Complex Occlusions: Evaluations on Bosphorus and UMB-DB Databases

A few studies attack the occlusion challenge and evaluate their system on the occlusion datasets. In (Liu, 2012), the facial surfaces are represented by Spherical Depth Map (SDM), where a sphere is fitted to the facial point cloud, allowing pose normalization and alignment. For pose normalization, convexities of the facial surface are extracted using an algorithm called Emerging from Sphere.

The convexity maxima serve as nose tip candidates. From the candidates, the most probable nose tip and its orientation is extracted using Histogram of Gradient features and Support Vector Machine classifier. The registration is handled by using the nose tip and its orientation, and rotating the face around the center of the fitted sphere. The SDM representation is further utilized for down-sampling and cropping purposes. Fine surface registration is handled by the ICP algorithm, where a rejection strategy is embedded into the original ICP. At each iteration, a predefined percentage of the most distant point pairs are discarded and the remaining point sets are utilized for transformation calculations. This rejection strategy enables the elimination of occluded surface points from the registration process. The overall system is evaluated on the Bosphorus database, where an identification rate of 97.9% is achieved at a rejection rate of 40%. The performances reported for different occlusion types can be found in Table 3. This is the best performance reported on the Bosphorus occlusion subset. However, it assumes visibility of nose tip, and only a small portion of the facial surface is occluded.

In Smeets (2013), Berretti (2013), and Li (2011), the main challenge considered is the handling of expression variations or incomplete facial data. However, they have additionally reported results on the Bosphorus occlusion subset. All of these systems are based on keypoint extraction in order to obtain a pair of corresponding salient features to be considered later in the classification process. In (Smeets, 2013), meshSIFT is employed to obtain local shape description. In Berretti (2013), meshDoG is used as the local shape descriptor to describe the local neighborhood around the extracted keypoints. Similarly in (Li, 2011), various local descriptors are employed around the keypoints. Histogram of gradients, histogram of shape index, and histogram of gradient of shape index are the utilized local descriptors to describe the surface locally. Face similarity is then measured by comparing inlier pairs of matching keypoints.

The main assumption is that most stable keypoints will be repeatedly extracted for the scans of an individual. Moreover, the RANSAC algorithm is shown to be beneficial when eliminating outlier matches, especially caused by occluded facial regions. The identification result reported on the Bosphorus occlusion subset is 93.2% for Berretti (2013). In Li (2011), fusing different types of descriptors, an identification rate of 99.21% is achieved on the Bosphorus occlusion subset. As the results of Berretti (2013) and Li (2011) set forth, employment of keypoints can be considered as a possible solution for occlusion handling.

In Drira (2013), a facial surface representation employing radial curves propagating from the nose tip is proposed to handle different types of challenges. Unfortunately, details about nose tip extraction are not sufficient; and in the experiments including occluded surfaces, manually located nose tip locations are used. Prior to extraction of the facial curves, the occlusion detection and removal are handled in corporation with the registration process, namely the recursive ICP algorithm. At each iteration, the surface points that are more distant to the model than a predefined threshold are removed. Therefore, after registration, an occlusion-free facial surface is obtained. Afterwards, using the nose tip, a reference curve vertically passing through the symmetry plane is extracted. Then, several radial curves slicing the facial surface by planes passing through the nose tip are obtained. Using a total of 40 curves, quality filtering is applied to remove curves containing insufficient information and elastic shape analysis is applied for classification purpose. For the Bosphorus occlusion subset, an identification rate of 78.63% is obtained over the occlusion removed surfaces. They have also reported an identification rate of 87.06%, where incomplete facial curves are restored using a statistical modeling of radial curves.

Alyuz (2012a) proposes to detect nose area based on curvature information. The detected nose area center is then used for initial registration. In Alyuz (2012b), an occlusion-robust registration approach is proposed based on the area localization idea of the previously proposed nose detector. Several regions, such as nose, eyes, and mouth, are detected and checked for validity. Based on the validity of regions, an adaptive model is selected for the fine registration step. Using an adaptive model for registration enables to discard occluded parts and to employ only the non-occluded facial regions. In Alyuz (2013), masked projection is proposed to further improve the robustness of the face identifier to occlusions. In masked projection, the occlusion masks are incorporated into the subspace analysis techniques to extract features only from the available surface information. As the results obtained on the Bosphorus and UMB-DB databases, nose area can be detected with sufficient accuracy, whereas the adaptive-model based registration improves the registration results. Moreover, masked projection, enabling the use of incomplete data, yields high classification performance.

Handling of Incomplete Data at the Classification Stage

In this section, we summarize studies considering incomplete data from the view of classification. If the occluded areas are localized accurately, removal of detected occlusions will result in incomplete facial surfaces. Therefore, classification approaches proposed for incomplete data handling can be applied to surfaces after occlusion detection and removal.

In Passalis (2011), an extended version of the Annotated Face Model (AFM) (Kakadiaris, 2007), is utilized for fitting the model to the incomplete surface in a non-rigid manner. Here, the problem of missing data is handled by incorporating the facial symmetry property. Therefore, the missing surfaces are filled prior to classification. When high pose variations are present, the faces can be left- or right-half scans. Therefore, in addition to the whole face representation, they have obtained left and right-half representations, resulting in multiple representations for each facial image. On these representations, wavelet analysis is carried out to obtain the classification features. If the facial surfaces are known to have specific types of occlusions (such as occlusions covering left/ right or top/bottom halves), and the occlusions are detected and removed accurately, this idea can be applied to extract features prior to classification.

(Berretti, 2013) extract keypoints as a first step. Then, the curves connecting pairs of keypoints are used to define the relative change in the corresponding surface regions. This way, the spatial relations between the keypoints are introduced. SIFT features are used to find inlier keypoint pairs between two different surfaces, whereas the facial curves within each surface are used for classification purposes. Handling of incomplete surfaces is automatically handled, since no keypoints will be extracted from these regions, and keypoint pairs from regions missing in at least one of the surfaces will not be chosen. As stated in the previous section, utilizing keypoints for incomplete or occluded surfaces can be beneficial for face identification purposes. These methods should be evaluated on datasets with challenging occlusions, such as the UMB-DB dataset.

In Colombo (2009), a face detection and registration method is proposed which is robust to occlusion variations. The facial surface is extracted by detecting nose tip and inner eye corners, assuming that at least two landmarks are available. The detection of landmark candidates is based on curvature analysis. From the candidates, possible encapsulated regions are selected and used together with ICP for alignment. The correct alignment is chosen by the Gappy PCA method (Everson, 1995). Then a final registration by ICP is performed, which discards any surface point not representing the facial surface well at each iteration. In Colombo (2011b), using this registra-

tion strategy, they have focused on an occlusion detection and restoration strategy, so that any standard classification approach can be utilized afterwards. The registered surfaces are projected onto a shape space, which is constructed using a training set of non-occluded and pre-aligned faces. After the back projection to the original face space, the distance between reconstructed and occluded surface is used to find a preliminary occlusion mask. This initial mask is further refined by excluding the detected surface points from the computation of the reconstruction error. After the refinement of the occlusion mask, back projection to the original face space is obtained by the Gappy PCA algorithm, giving a restored version of the originally occluded face. On the Bosphorus occlusion subset, they have obtained an identification performance of 91.18%, 74.75%, 94.23%, and 90.47% respectively for the eye, mouth, eyeglasses, and hair occlusion types.

CASE STUDY: DESIGNING AN OCCLUSION ROBUST FACE IDENTIFIER

In this section, we summarize a 3D face identification system to deal with occlusion variations. Here, the occlusion challenge is handled at three different stages of a face identifier: (1) registration, which merges the nose detection approach of Alyuz (2012a) and the adaptive model based alignment technique of (Alyuz, 2012b); (2) occlusion detection, which is used in the works of Alyuz (2012a, 2012b); (3) feature extraction and classification, where the masked projection approach of Alyuz (2013) is employed. At each step, we try to point out possible problems with specific examples. Then we briefly mention the employed approaches and summarize the results.

Registration of Occluded Surfaces

As stated before, we examine the registration process, which is composed of the following stages: Face localization, ROI extraction, coarse and fine surface alignment. For face detection, nose tip localization is one of the mostly preferred approaches, since the nose region has a prominent surface structure and it can be accurately labeled. However, for occluded surfaces, detection of the nose tip as a single surface point becomes a complicated process. To incorporate the spatial facial information, several nose tip candidates can be detected and the final nose tip can be determined using a matching criterion to a nose template, as proposed in Liu (2012). Similarly, it is possible to tackle the face detection problem by localizing the nose area, as initially proposed in Alyuz (2012a). Instead of estimating the nose tip locations, the nose region is searched using a nose template, and the best fit gives the detected nose area. The center of the detected nose area is utilized for initial alignment that is necessary for ICP to converge to a final fine registration. Here, we start by evaluating the nose detection performance, since the accuracy of the nose detector will directly affect the subsequent stages.

The nose detection algorithm of Alyuz (2012a) employs the surface curvature information, which is advantageous due to its rotation and translation invariance. Two curvature maps, namely shape index and curvedness, are computed for the facial surface. The shape index map provides a smooth transition between concave (values between 0 and 0.5) and convex (values between 0.5 and 1) shapes.

On the other hand, the curvedness measures the rate of curvature at the given point. Since nose area has a convex structure, first of all, the shape index is thresholded (by a threshold of 0.5) to eliminate concave parts. Afterwards, the convex shape index is weighted with the curvedness map to integrate the measure of the curvature:

$$WSI(i) = SI(i) * C(i)$$

where $WSI(i)$ is the curvedness-weighted shape index value at point i. To localize the nose on this final map, template matching is utilized. For template construction, the average nose model is obtained by manually cropping an average face model and the nose template is constructed by computing the WSI map. Given a test image, normalized cross-correlation is computed for template matching, and the region mostly resembling the nose structure is located as the nose region.

The nose detector is evaluated on two challenging databases, Bosphorus and UMB-DB, where the results are given in Table 4. The first and the third rows show that the nose detection approach can accurately locate the nose area for non-occluded neutral facial scans, where a detection rate of 100% is obtained both for the neutral subsets of the Bosphorus and the UMB-DB databases. For the occluded scans, this approach still appears as a viable approach. For the Bosphorus and the UMB-DB occlusions, acceptable results are given in second and fourth rows, respectively. Here, it should be noted that the detection accuracies for

Table 4. Nose detection results for the Bosphorus and UMB-DB databases

Database	Scan Type	Scan Count	Detection Rate (%)
Bosphorus	Neutral	299	100.00
	Occlusion	381	98.69
UMB-DB	Neutral	441	100.00
	Occlusion	590	93.90

the first three rows are obtained by comparing the center of the detected nose area and the manually labeled nose tip. If the distance between these two points is shorter than a predefined threshold, then the located nose area is accepted as correct. The threshold (*11 mm*) is set empirically using the manual nose tip locations and the detected nose area centers for the FRGC v.2 database. For the fourth row, the quantitative evaluation was not possible. For most of the UMB-DB occlusions, the nose tip is covered and the manual nose tip location is not present. Therefore, for the UMB-DB occlusions, the detected nose areas are inspected visually. Although the UMB-DB occlusions are challenging with the nose area covered for many of the scans, the obtained detection rate is quite high.

After the facial surface is detected by locating the nose area, registration should be handled. To decrease the computational cost of the ICP method, employment of an average face model (Gokberk, 2006) can be beneficial. For initial registration, the nose area center for the probe face and the average face model can be used to translate the whole probe surface to the average face. This initialization will be sufficient for scans with limited pose variations. However, the occlusions over the facial surface will complicate the subsequent fine registration step. Since the occlusions alter the surface information, the ICP algorithm considering the whole facial surface will fail. In Alyuz (2012b), we proposed a model-based registration approach to cope with occlusion variations. For an occluded face, the non-occluded patches are determined and a model with the corresponding average patches is selected. Therefore, only the non-occluded parts are considered in correspondence matching, while still benefiting from the use of a model for alignment. Next, some further details about the adaptive model selection are given.

To determine the non-occluded patches, first, the fiducial patch locations are estimated using the detected nose area center and the spatial information. On the average model, the displacement vectors between the nose and other patch centers

are computed. Then, using the detected nose center of the probe face, the probable patch centers are estimated. Around the probable patch centers, the patches are sought in pre-defined bounding box using template matching. The main patches considered are the eyes and mouth, whereas an additional set of half patches are also utilized: left-right nose halves, upper-lower nose halves, and left-right eyes. These additional half patches will be beneficial for different kinds of occlusions. Patch templates are constructed by computing the *WSI* maps of the patch models, which are manually cropped from the whole face model. Since some patches will not be visible due to occlusions, the template matching scores should be evaluated for validity. To determine the validity of each patch, thresholding is applied on template matching scores. The thresholds used for patch validity are calculated from the scores of a separate non-occluded and neutral database. The probe patches that have dissimilarity scores below the threshold define the valid parts. The patch validity values are then used for the model selection. The respective valid patches are selected from the average face model, and these average patches constitute *the adaptive alignment model*. In the experiments, we have used 17 different adaptive registration models, which are given in Figure 6 (a). The selected model is used when registering the probe face using the ICP algorithm. Since the model employed in the fine alignment step is chosen according to the occlusion, the ICP algorithm automatically selects the respective non-occluded parts as corresponding surface point sets and estimates the alignment parameters using only the non-occluded regions. Hence, the overall registration approach becomes robust to occlusions. To visualize the effect of model selection when occlusions are present, an example face is given in Figure 3. Here, the facial surface registered with face, nose, and adaptive model are given in (a), (b), and (c), respectively. As this example illustrates, when the facial surface is partially occluded, registering to a holistic face

Figure 3. An occluded face registered with (a) the face model, (b) the nose model, and (c) the adaptive model. In (c), automatically selected adaptive model is shown in red

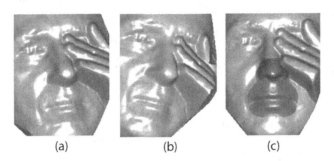

(a)   (b)   (c)

model is problematic. Employing a nose model can be beneficial if the nose region is not occluded. However, including other non-occluded parts into the model is beneficial, where a greater part of the surface is utilized.

For a quantitative evaluation of the registration strategy, we compare the performance of the model-based registration using different models, namely the face model, the nose model, and the adaptively selected model. After the surfaces are aligned, occlusion masks are used to discard the occluded parts, both from the gallery and the probe surfaces. Then, a depth-based classifier is employed. After registration, regular resampling is employed and the surfaces are represented as a vector of depth-values. By occlusion masking, the respective parts of the vectors are discarded. When two surfaces are to be compared, the total distance between the corresponding valid depth values is computed and divided by the count of the valid points. For classification, 1-NN classifier is employed, where the distance values

serve as dissimilarity measures. In Table 5, the classification performances on the Bosphorus and the UMB-DB databases using three different registration models are given. As these results indicate, using a bigger model is beneficial for non-occluded scans. However, when the occluded subsets are considered, it is clear that aligning with the whole face model is not applicable, and using an adaptive model instead of using only a nose model is advantageous.

Occlusion Detection and Handling

In a typical face identification system, the registration step is often followed by feature extraction and classification processes. However, in the presence of occlusions, extraction of features will be affected by the surface alteration. Therefore, prior to feature extraction, occluded parts can be detected, so that the facial surface can be better represented knowing which regions belong to the face. The most straight forward approach for

Table 5. Relative standing of the registration approaches considering different models

Database	Acquisition Type	Probe Count	Identification Rates (%)		
			Face Model	**Nose Model**	**Adaptive Model**
Bosphorus	Neutral	194	100.00	97.94	100.00
	Occlusion	381	60.63	79.00	83.99
UMB-DB	Neutral	299	98.66	85.28	97.32
	Occlusion	590	47.29	46.27	65.25

occlusion detection includes the analysis of the difference between the input face and an average face, as used in Colombo (2009). The main assumption with this approach is if there is an exterior object causing occlusion over a facial part, the distance to the average model for this specific region will be large. Therefore, the occluded areas can be detected by thresholding the absolute difference between the occluded input face and an average face model. Since the facial surfaces are regularly resampled after registration, occlusion detection considers only the depth values for comparison. The final occlusion mask is obtained after post-processing operations of morphological dilation and connected component analysis.

To evaluate the accuracy of the occlusion detection and to determine a threshold value for further experiments, manually labeled occlusion masks are used. Here, we have utilized *precision* and *recall* values to compute *F-measure* (Powers, 2011), which serves as the evaluation measure of the occlusion detection module. In a classification scenario, precision is the ratio of the number of true positives to the total number of elements that are labeled as positives, whereas recall is the ratio of the number of true positives to the total number of elements that are actually positives. Therefore, precision gives the fraction of the retrieved examples that are relevant, and recall gives the fraction of the relevant instances that are retrieved. In the context of occlusion detection, precision defines the percentage of the correct ones among all the detected pixels, whereas recall is the percentage of the detected ones among all the occlusion pixels. In occlusion detection, it is important to detect most of the occluded pixels. In addition, it is not desirable to label non-occluded pixels as occlusion. Therefore, neither precision nor recall is enough to evaluate the detection accuracy. Therefore, we have utilized the *F-measure*, which is a measure combining precision and recall. In general, the *F-measure* can be computed as:

$$F_\beta = \left(1 + \beta^2\right) \frac{precision * recall}{\beta^2 \, precision + recall}$$

Here, β defines the weight given to precision versus recall. In our experiments, F_1 measure is employed. F_1 gives the harmonic mean of precision and recall, and it is referred to as the *balanced* F-score. For face recognition, it is important to exclude almost all of the occluded parts, whereas the discarded facial parts should be minimal.

To evaluate the occlusion detection performance for different threshold values and to determine a threshold to be used in further experiments, we have constructed a subset of occluded images from the Bosphorus database. We have selected a set of 70 images, including different types and amounts of occlusions, for which the ground truth occlusion masks are precisely labeled. The precision-recall vs. threshold and F-measure vs. threshold plots are given Figure 4. The plot given in (a) shows the trade-off between the precision and recall of the detector with varying threshold values, whereas in (b) it is shown how the F-measure changes for different thresholds. Using the F-measure vs. threshold plot, an appropriate threshold value can be selected to estimate occluded surface regions.

After the occluded areas are detected, they should be removed prior to feature extraction. However, the obtained incomplete data cannot be directly used with traditional feature extractors and classifiers. If traditional methods are to be employed, the missing parts should be estimated using the available facial information. As an estimation method, we have analyzed the partial Gappy PCA approach of Alyuz (2012a). Gappy PCA (Everson, 1995) was proposed as a PCA variant to handle data with missing components. With Gappy PCA, it is possible to reconstruct original signal up to a certain degree when the signal contains missing values. Prior to estimation, Gappy PCA method constructs a general model of facial data using a training set of non-occluded

Figure 4. Performance evaluation plots of the occlusion detection method: (a) precision-recall vs. threshold, and (b) F_1 vs. threshold plots

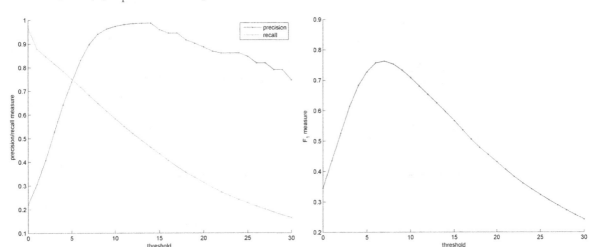

(a)　　　　　　　　　　　　　　(b)

images. The basis vectors are determined using a training set of non-occluded face images. A face image can then be estimated using a subset of these basis vectors. The difference between PCA and Gappy PCA is that in Gappy PCA, the incomplete data is approximated using only the available parts by incorporating the occlusion mask into the computation of the reconstruction error. Additionally in partial Gappy PCA, the reconstructed facial data is only used to fill the missing parts, while the non-occluded facial regions are left unaltered. Further algebraic details about Gappy PCA and partial Gappy PCA can be found in Alyuz (2012a).

In Figure 5, a reconstruction example obtained by Gappy PCA is given for a challenging UMB-DB occlusion scan. As visualized in second row, the quality of the restored face depends on the subspace dimensionality of the Gappy PCA. As the dimensionality increases, the restored facial surface gets more similar to the original surface. Here, it should be noted that although the restored face appears as an appropriate resemblance, it is only an approximation and the discriminative information needed for classification can be lost. Partial GPCA can be an alternative to reduce the

negative effect of restoration, where the restored surface information is utilized only for missing parts. In Table 6, we have included the face identification experiments, where a global depth-based classifier is utilized. For comparative purposes, we have included the depth-based classifier results obtained using the original occluded surfaces and the occlusion-removed surfaces. The results are given in fourth and fifth rows, where the same test database (Bosphorus or UMB-DB) or the FRGC v.2 is utilized for training. As these results indicate, occlusion handling is necessary, either by removal or restoration. For restoration, using the test set for training, which includes a non-occluded scan of the probe face, performs better. However, even when the test set is utilized for training, restoration is not as good as occlusion removal for a classification scenario.

Feature Extraction and Classification

Although restoring occluded parts result in complete approximation of a facial image, the restored faces may not always be optimal for classification purposes. Since restoration only provides an approximation of the missing parts, restored parts

Figure 5. Restoration of a registered occlusion-free face using Gappy PCA method. Restored faces with different Gappy PCA dimensionalities (D) are provided as examples.

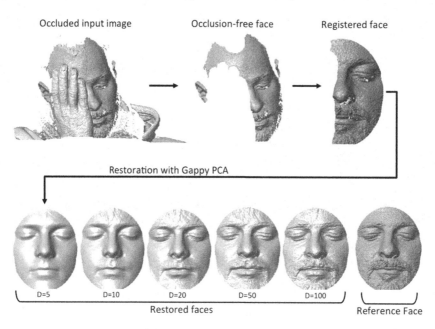

Table 6. Global depth-based classifier results for original, occlusion-removed, and restored facial surfaces of the Bosphorus database

Data Type	Training Set	Identification Rate (%)	
		Bosphorus	**UMB-DB**
Original	N/A	69.29	47.46
Occlusion-Removed	N/A	84.51	65.08
Occlusion-Restored	Self Gallery(Bosphorus/UMB-DB)	77.69	55.59
Occlusion-Restored	FRGC v.2	77.17	52.03

may not add extra discriminative information. Therefore, instead of incorporating restoration into traditional 3D face identification scenarios, it is worthwhile to modify classification approaches so that they are applicable to incomplete data. In this section, we experiment with the masked projection technique proposed in Alyuz (2013), and the algorithmic details are briefly mentioned below.

Model-based registration technique yields ordered and same-sized vectors as the resulting face images, enabling use of subspace analysis techniques. By using subspace techniques like

PCA or Fisherfaces, the redundancy is removed from the data and the most important information is represented in a much smaller feature space. However, when the surfaces are incomplete due to occlusion removal, subspace approaches cannot be directly applied. The first idea to deal with incomplete data, would be to remove the pixels that are not present in the probe image from all of the training and gallery images, as in Tarres (2005). Using the masked training images, the subspace representing the partial surfaces can be learned by the Fisherfaces approach (Belhumeur,

1997). However, this approach is not feasible, since each probe face will have different pixels missing and a separate training phase is required. In Alyuz (2013), a projection masking approach is proposed to obtain the adaptive subspace. The general projection matrix is learned using a set of non-occluded complete training images. Then, the adaptive projection matrix is obtained by masking, without the need for mask-specific training. The masked probe and gallery images are projected onto the subspace, and classification is performed. Below, we briefly summarize the algebraic details.

Let's assume that a projection matrix W is learned from a set of non-occluded training faces. For a probe face, after the occlusion detection and removal stages, we have an incomplete feature vector $\hat{x}$. The completed version $\tilde{x}$ can be computed using the projection matrix and a coefficient vector:

$$\tilde{x} = W\tilde{y}$$

Here, neither the coefficient vector nor the completed version is known. Therefore, the above equation cannot be used and the occlusion mask should be incorporated to employ only the information at hand. The coefficient vector $\tilde{y}$ can be computed by minimizing the *masked* error term, where the information about the missing components are discarded using the masked norm (Everson, 1995). By minimizing the masked error term with respect to $\tilde{y}$, we see that the completed version can be found by:

$$\hat{x}_m = W_m \tilde{y}$$

To calculate the coefficient vector, the inverse of W_m is needed. Since W_m is constructed from W by setting occluded regions to zero, it is no longer orthogonal and its inverse is not equal to its transpose. Therefore, we first orthogonalize W_m:

$$W_\perp = W_m \left(W_m^{'} W_m \right)^{-1/2}.$$

Then, the coefficient vector can be computed as:

$$\tilde{y} = W_\perp^{'} \hat{x}_m.$$

The masked projection matrix is applied both to the probe and to the gallery image using the corresponding mask of the probe face. The most important trick is that the gallery images are projected to the adaptive subspace using the *masked* projection matrix, rather than the original projection matrix W, since these two matrices define different subspaces. The subspace of W is trained using a subset of complete facial surfaces. When W_m is constructed, parts corresponding to occlusions are eliminated from the original matrix. Therefore, the orthogonal vector sets defining the subspaces are different for W and W_m (hence for W and $W_\perp$). The idea of projecting the gallery images with masked projection, in addition to the probe images, is the main difference between the proposed approach and the Gappy PCA method of (Everson, 1995). After the projection to the adaptive subspace, the dissimilarity between the probe and gallery coefficients can be computed by the angular cosine distance measure. To obtain the final identification rates, the regional dissimilarity measures are fused by the product rule and 1-NN classification is employed.

In Table 7, we compare four different classification strategies based on the subspace analysis technique: (1) The standard Fisherfaces (Belhumeur, 1997) on original data, where no occlusion removal or restoration is applied; (2) the standard Fisherfaces on restored data, where the missing parts are restored by partial Gappy PCA of (Alyuz, 2012a); (3) the standard Fisherfaces applied on the masked probe features obtained by Gappy PCA (Everson, 1995); and (4) the proposed

Table 7. Global identificaiton accuracies with the standard and the masked Fisherfaces approaches

Method	Fisherfaces Approach	Gallery Data	Probe Data	Bosphorus	UMB-DB
Fisherfaces (Belhumeur, 1997)	Standard	Original	Original	53.28	43.56
Fisherfaces with Restoration (Alyuz, 2012a)	Standard	Original	Restored	83.46	60.34
Fisherfaces with Gappy PCA (Everson, 1995)	Masked	Original	Masked	85.83	66.10
Masked Fisherfaces (Alyuz, 2013)	Masked	Masked	Masked	87.40	69.15

masked Fisherfaces, where the globally learned projection matrices are masked to obtain projections of both the gallery and the probe images. For the training of the Fisherfaces method, the FRGC v.2 neutral subset is employed. As the results in Table 7 indicate, restoring occluded parts offers an improvement over original surfaces. For the Bosphorus database, the performance is improved by 30%; for the more challenging UMB-DB database, the improvement is 17%. However, we see that it is beneficial to remove the occluded parts, instead of restoring them. For the last two rows, the occlusions of the probe images are removed, whereas for the third row, restoration is employed. For the Bosphorus, 2-4% further increase is obtained; whereas for the UMB-DB, a more significant performance improvement (about 6-9%) is achieved. Furthermore, Masked Fisherfaces approach (last row) yields better results than of Gappy PCA. For a fair comparison, the parameters used for the compared dimensionality reduction techniques are identically chosen (the dimensions used for PCA and Fisherfaces are 150 and 100, respectively). As these results indicate, instead of restoring occluded areas, it is beneficial to employ the masked projection, which incorporates only the non-occluded surface regions. Moreover, the masked projection should be used to project both the gallery and the probe images.

For occluded scans, the facial surfaces will be partially available. If the facial surfaces are considered as a combination of local regions instead of a single whole surface, the regional classifiers corresponding to non-occluded parts will not be affected. Therefore, further improvement can be obtained by using multiple regional classifiers. Here, we study the benefits of using multiple regional classifiers in the masked projection framework.

For our experiments, 40 different regions are utilized, which are visualized in Figure 6 (b). For regional experiments, we have incorporated both the occlusion and the regional masks into the masked projection. Furthermore, we have experimented with both the ground truth and the automatically detected occlusion masks. The identification rates, where the regional classifiers are fused by the product rule, are given in Table 8. The global classification results are included in the first row for comparative purposes. As these results indicate, considering the facial surface as a collection of local regions is beneficial to handle occluded area, whereas automatic occlusion detection approach is open for improvement.

As proposed in Tarres (2005), a possible approach to deal with missing data in subspace analysis, is to remove the corresponding missing pixels from the training data and to learn the projection matrix from the masked training samples. Although this approach is not practical in occluded faces since each occlusion is unique, for comparative purposes, we have obtained identification rates on the Bosphorus database using this masked training idea of Tarres (2005). The occlusion mask of the probe is used to discard corresponding locations from the training images, and training specific to the probe's mask is obtained on the partial images. The regional

Figure 6. Facial regions used for (a) registration and (b) classification

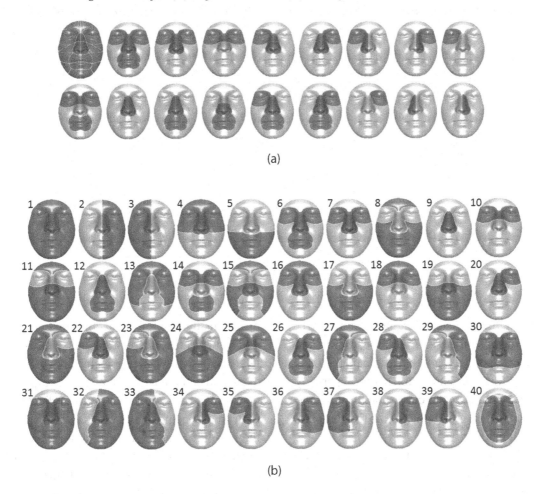

(a)

(b)

Table 8. Regional identification accuracies with the masked projection approach

Method	Occlusion Mask	Bosphorus	UMB-DB
Global Masked Projection	Manual	87.40	69.15
Regional Masked Projection	Manual	93.18	73.56
Regional Masked Projection	Automatic	92.91	68.47

results of masked training and masked projection approaches are compared in Figure 7, where manually labeled occlusion masks are utilized. In contrast to our expectations, the newly proposed masked projection strategy performs even better for all of the 40 different regions. Since in the masked projection approach, the regional projection matrix is learned from the complete training regions, the relation between the original face space and the lower-dimensional subspace is represented better. Therefore, instead of training the projection matrices separately for each probe face, it is beneficial to obtain a complete regional projection matrix in an offline manner and then

Figure 7. Regional identification rates obtained for the Bosphorus database using manual occlusion masks are given for the masked training (blue) and masked projection (green) approaches

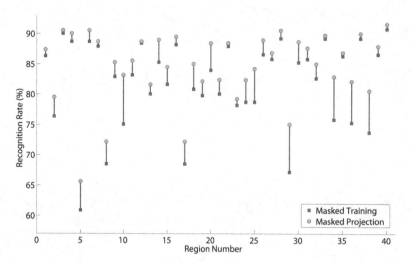

to compute the corresponding projection matrix using the occlusion mask. In addition, the masked projection strategy is a more feasible method. Instead of re-training a projection matrix separately for each probe face, the corresponding masked projection matrix is computed from the complete projection matrix

For evaluating the impact of occlusion on the identification performance, we have analyzed the correctly and incorrectly identified samples for varying sizes of occluded areas. In Figure 8, the histograms of occlusion percentages are given for (a) the Bosphorus, and (b) the UMB-DB databases, where correctly and incorrectly classified sample counts are shown respectively in green and red. As these figures indicate, faces with small occlusions are easy to deal with. For the highly occluded scans, a higher percentage of the examples are misclassified. However, in overall, the experimented face identifier can be applicable to occluded scans, especially if they are known to have a limited coverage of occlusions.

Figure 8. Occluded area histogram for (a) the Bosphorus, and (b) the UMB-DB database. Correctly (green) and incorrectly (red) classified sample counts are shown for different occlusion percentage ranges.

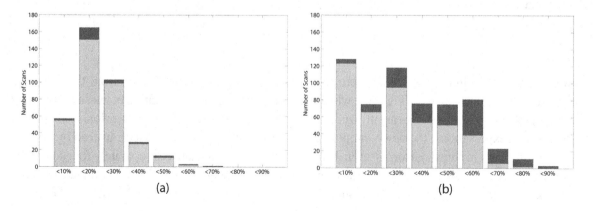

CONCLUSION AND FUTURE RESEARCH DIRECTIONS

In this chapter, we have reviewed 3D face identification techniques from the perspective of occlusion handling. In unconstrained 3D face identification scenarios, acquisition will be handled in a noncooperative way and the facial surfaces can be partially occluded. Here, we have briefly mentioned how a traditional 3D face identifier will be affected by the presence of occlusions and we have summarized the approaches proposed in the 3D face identification literature for robustness to occlusion. As a case study, we have merged different techniques proposed for different stages of a face identifier to deal with occlusions. The nose detection of Alyuz (2012a), the adaptive model based registration of (Alyuz, 2012b), the occlusion detection method used in the experiments of Alyuz (2012a,2012b), and the masked projection classification technique of Alyuz (2013) are briefly summarized and the results are analyzed. As these results indicate, nose area detection to serve as the face detector appears as a viable approach, even for the occluded scans. Registering surfaces with an adaptive model has the advantage of a model-based technique, and is advantageous over using only a small region such as the nose. Furthermore, if the occluded parts can be accurately labeled, the masked projection technique is a good subspace alternative to extract facial features for classification. The performance can be further improved by considering the facial surface as a collection of local patches.

Although the face identifier investigated here for robustness to occlusion appears as a probable solution, there is still room for improvement. The weakest link in the identifier is definitely the occlusion detector. A more complex technique can improve the detection performance, yielding an overall performance increase. For example, the surfaces can be compared against a more complex average face representation. Besides the occlusion detection step, the registration stage can also be improved. If the occlusions can be detected accurately prior to registration, these areas can be discarded to find a better surface correspondence with a variant of the ICP method. However, it is a very complicated task to find occluded regions over an unregistered surface. Registering faces and detecting occlusions can be handled in an iterative manner, where the initial registration and the occlusion mask can be improved at each iteration.

REFERENCES

Abate, A. F., Nappi, M., Riccio, D., & Sabatino, G. (2007). 2D and 3D face recognition: A survey. *Pattern Recognition Letters*, *28*(14), 1885–1906. doi:10.1016/j.patrec.2006.12.018

Abate, A. F., Ricciardi, S., & Sabatino, G. (2007). 3D face recognition in a ambient intelligence environment scenario. In K. Delac, & M. Grgic (Eds.), *Face recognition*. I-Tech.

Alyuz, N., Gokberk, B., & Akarun, L. (2010). Regional registration for expression resistant 3-D face recognition. *IEEE Trans. on Information Forensics and Security*, *5*(3), 425–440.

Alyuz, N., Gokberk, B., Spreeuwers, L., Veldhuis, R., & Akarun, L. (2012). Robust 3D face recognition in the presence of realistic occlusions. In *Proceedings of International Conference on Biometrics*. Academic Press.

Alyuz, N., Gokberk, B., & Akarun, L. (2012). Adaptive model based 3D face registration for occlusion invariance. In *Proceedings of European Conference on Computer Vision - Workshops - Benchmarking Facial Image Analysis Technologies*.

Alyuz, N., Gokberk, B., & Akarun, L. (2013). 3D Face Recognition under Occlusion using Masked Projection. *IEEE Trans. on Information Forensics and Security*, *8*(5), 789–802. doi:10.1109/TIFS.2013.2256130

Belhumeur, P., Hespanha, J., & Kriegman, D. (1997). Eigenfaces vs. fisherfaces: Recognition using class specific linear projection. *Transactions on Pattern Analysis and Machine Intelligence, 19*(7), 711–720. doi:10.1109/34.598228

Berretti, S., del Bimbo, A., & Pala, P. (2013). Sparse matching of salient facial curves for recognition of 3-D faces with missing parts. *Transactions on Information Forensics and Security, 8*(2), 374–389. doi:10.1109/TIFS.2012.2235833

Bowyer, K., Chang, K., & Flynn, P. (2006). A survey of approaches and challenges in 3D and multi-modal 3D+2D face recognition. *Computer Vision and Image Understanding, 101*(1), 1–15. doi:10.1016/j.cviu.2005.05.005

Colombo, A., Cusano, C., & Schettini, R. (2009). Gappy PCA classification for occlusion tolerant 3D face detection. *Journal of Mathematical Imaging and Vision, 35*(3), 193–207. doi:10.1007/s10851-009-0165-y

Colombo, A., Cusano, C., & Schettini, R. (2011). UMB-DB: A database of partially occluded 3D faces. In *Proceedings of International Conference on Computer Vision – Workshops* (pp. 2113–2119). Academic Press.

Colombo, A., Cusano, C., & Schettini, R. (2011). Three-dimensional occlusion detection and restoration of partially occluded faces. *Journal of Mathematical Imaging and Vision, 40*(1), 105–119. doi:10.1007/s10851-010-0252-0

Drira, H., Ben Amor, B., Srivastava, A., Daoudi, M., & Slama, R. (2013). 3D face recognition under expressions, occlusions and pose variations. *Transactions on Pattern Analysis and Machine Intelligence, 35*(9), 2270–2283. doi:10.1109/TPAMI.2013.48 PMID:23868784

Everson, R., & Sirovich, L. (1995). Karhunen–Loeve procedure for gappy data. *Journal of the Optical Society of America. A, Optics, Image Science, and Vision, 12*(8), 1657–1664. doi:10.1364/JOSAA.12.001657

Faltemier, T. C., Bowyer, K. W., & Flynn, P. J. (2008). A region ensemble for 3-D face recognition. *Transactions on Information Forensics and Security, 3*(1), 62–73.

Gokberk, B., Irfanoglu, M. O., & Akarun, L. (2006). 3D shape-based face representation and feature extraction for face recognition. *Image and Vision Computing, 24*(8), 857–869. doi:10.1016/j.imavis.2006.02.009

Gokberk, B., Salah, A. A., Akarun, L., Etheve, R., Riccio, D., & Dugelay, J. L. (2008). 3D face recognition. In D. Petrovska-Delacretaz, G. Chollet, & B. Dorizzi (Eds.), *Guide to Biometric Reference Systems and Performance Evaluation* (pp. 1–33). Springer Verlag.

Kakadiaris, I. A., Passalis, G., Toderici, G., Murtuza, N., Lu, Y., Karampatziakis, N., & Theoharis, T. (2007). Three-dimensional face recognition in the presence of facial expressions: An annotated deformable model approach. *Transactions on Pattern Analysis and Machine Intelligence, 29*(4), 640–649. doi:10.1109/TPAMI.2007.1017 PMID:17299221

Li, H., Huang, D., Lemaire, P., Morvan, J.-M., & Chen, L. (2011). Expression robust 3D face recognition via mesh-based histograms of multiple order surface differential quantities. In *Proceedings of International Conference on Image Processing* (pp. 3053–3056). Academic Press.

Li, X., & Da, F. (2012). Efficient 3D face recognition handling facial expression and hair occlusion. *Image and Vision Computing, 30*(9), 668–679. doi:10.1016/j.imavis.2012.07.011

Liu, P., Wang, Y., Huang, D., & Zhang, Z. (2012). Recognizing occluded 3D faces using an efficient ICP variant. In *Proceedings of International Conference on Multimedia and Expo* (pp. 350–355). Academic Press.

Mian, A. S., Bennamoun, M., & Owens, R. (2008). An efficient multimodal 2D-3D hybrid approach to automatic face recognition. *Transactions on Pattern Analysis and Machine Intelligence, 29*(11), 1927–1943. doi:10.1109/TPAMI.2007.1105 PMID:17848775

Ming, Y., & Ruan, Q. (2012). Robust sparse bounding sphere for 3D face recognition. *Image and Vision Computing, 30*(8), 524–534. doi:10.1016/j.imavis.2012.05.001

Papatheodorou, T., & Rueckert, D. (2007). 3D face recognition. In K. Delac, & M. Grgic (Eds.), *Face Recognition*. I-Tech. doi:10.5772/4848

Passalis, G., Perakis, P., Theoharis, T., & Kakadiaris, I. A. (2011). Using facial symmetry to handle pose variations in Real-World 3D face recognition. *Transactions on Pattern Analysis and Machine Intelligence, 33*(10), 1938–1951. doi:10.1109/TPAMI.2011.49

Peng, Y., Ganesh, A., Wright, J., Xu, W., & Ma, Y. (2011). RASL: robust alignment by sparse and low-rank decomposition for linearly correlated images. *Transactions on Pattern Analysis and Machine Intelligence, 18*, 315–322.

Phillips, P., Scruggs, W., O´Toole, A., Flynn, P., Bowyer, K., Schott, C., & Sharpe, M. (2007). FRVT 2006 and ICE 2006 large-scale results. National Institute of Standards and Technology, 7408.

Phillips, P. J., Flynn, P., Scruggs, T., Bowyer, K., Chang, J., Hoffman, K., et al. (2005). Overview of the face recognition grand challenge. In *Proceedings of Computer Society Conference on Computer Vision and Pattern Recognition*. Academic Press.

Powers, D. M. W. (2011). Evaluation: From precision, recall and f-measure to roc, informedness, markedness & correlation. *Journal of Machine Learning Technologies, 2*(1), 37–63.

Queirolo, C. C., Silva, L., Bellon, O., & Segundo, M. P. (2010). 3D face recognition using simulated annealing and the surface interpenetration measure. *Transactions on Pattern Analysis and Machine Intelligence, 32*(2), 206–219. doi:10.1109/TPAMI.2009.14 PMID:20075453

Savran, A., Alyuz, N., Dibeklioglu, H., Celiktutan, O., Gokberk, B., Sankur, B., & Akarun, L. (2008). Bosphorus database for 3D face analysis. In *Biometrics and Identity Management* (pp. 47–56). Academic Press. doi:10.1007/978-3-540-89991-4_6

Scheenstra, A., Ruifrok, A., & Veltkamp, R. C. (2005). A survey of 3D face recognition methods. *Lecture Notes in Computer Science, 3546*, 891–899. doi:10.1007/11527923_93

Smeets, D., Keustermans, J., Vandermeulen, D., & Suetens, P. (2013). meshSIFT: Local surface features for 3D face recognition under expression variations and partial data. *Computer Vision and Image Understanding, 117*(2), 158–169.

Spreeuwers, L. (2011). Fast and accurate 3D face recognition. *International Journal of Computer Vision, 93*(3), 389–414. doi:10.1007/s11263-011-0426-2

Tarres, F., Rama, A., & Torres, L. (2005). A novel method for face recognition under partial occlusion or facial expression variations. In *Proceedings of ELMAR International Symposium* (pp. 163–166). ELMAR.

Wang, Y., Liu, J., & Tang, X. (2010). Robust 3D face recognition by local shape difference boosting. *Transactions on Pattern Analysis and Machine Intelligence, 32*(10), 1858–1870. doi:10.1109/TPAMI.2009.200 PMID:20724762

Zhao, W., Chellappa, R., & Rosenfeld, A. (2003). Face recognition: a literature survey. *Computing Surveys*, *35*, 399–458. doi:10.1145/954339.954342

KEY TERMS AND DEFINITIONS

Adaptive Model Based Registration: Model-based fine alignment approach, where the alignment model is selected according to the non-occluded facial regions.

Curvedness: Measure to describe the rate of curvature at a given surface point.

Curvedness-Weighted Shape Index: Measure which integrates the curvedness and convexity thresholded shape index values.

Fisherfaces: Dimensionality reduction technique often used in face analysis, where an initial reduction with Principal Component Analysis is followed by a second phase of supervised reduction performed by Linear Discriminant Analysis.

Gappy Principal Component Analysis: A variant of the Principal Component Analysis that can handle data with missing components.

Global Masked Projection: Technique that enables the use of subspace analysis techniques on incomplete data. The missing parts are denoted via an occlusion mask, and this mask is utilized to construct the mask-specific projection matrix from a globally trained matrix.

Regional Masked Projection: A variant of the masked projection technique, where region masks are incorporated instead of the occlusion mask to construct the regional projection matrices from the global one, without the need for separate regional training phases.

Shape Index: Curvature measure to describe the local surface topology, giving a smooth transition between concave and convex regions.

Chapter 7
Illumination Invariant Face Recognition:
A Survey

Chi Ho Chan
University of Surrey, UK

Xuan Zou
University of Surrey, UK

Norman Poh
University of Surrey, UK

Josef Kittler
University of Surrey, UK

ABSTRACT

Illumination variation is one of the well-known problems in face recognition, especially in uncontrolled environments. This chapter presents an extensive and up-to-date survey of the existing techniques to address this problem. This survey covers the conventional passive techniques that attempt to solve the illumination problem by studying the visible light images, in which face appearance has been altered by varying illumination, as well as the active techniques that aim to obtain images of face modalities invariant to environmental illumination.

1. INTRODUCTION

For many applications, the performance of face recognition systems in controlled environments has now reached a satisfactory level; however, there are still many challenges posed by uncontrolled environments. Some of these challenges are posed by the problems caused by variations in illumination, face pose, expression, and etc. The effect of variation in the illumination conditions in particular, which causes dramatic changes in the face appearance, is one of those challenging problems (Zhao, Chellappa, Phillips, & Rosenfeld, 2003) that a practical face recognition system needs to face. To be more specific, the varying

DOI: 10.4018/978-1-4666-5966-7.ch007

direction and energy distribution of the ambient illumination, together with the 3D structure of the human face, can lead to major differences in the shading and shadows on the face. Such variations in the face appearance can be much larger than the variation caused by personal identity (Moses, Adini, & Ullman, 1994). The variations of both global face appearance and local facial features also cause problems for automatic face detection/localisation, which is the prerequisite for the subsequent face recognition stage. Therefore the situation is even worse for a fully automatic face recognition system. Moreover, in a practical application environment, the illumination variation is always coupled with other problems such as pose variation and expression variation, which increase the complexity of the automatic face recognition problem.

A number of illumination invariant face recognition approaches have been proposed in the past years. Existing approaches addressing the illumination variation problem fall into two main categories. We call the approaches in the first category "passive" approaches, since they attempt to overcome this problem by studying the visible spectrum images in which face appearance has been altered by illumination variations.

The other category contains "active" approaches, in which the illumination variation problem is overcome by employing active imaging techniques to obtain face images captured in consistent illumination condition, or images of illumination invariant modalities. Existing reviews related to illumination invariant face recognition can be found in (Chen, Er, & Wu, 2006; Li, Chu, Liao, & Zhang, 2007; Liu, Lam, & Shen, 2005; Zhao et al., 2003). However, these reviews focused either only on passive approaches or only on active approaches. The review presented in this chapter is more extensive than previous reviews and covers more recent techniques in both groups, such as Generalized Photometric Stereo (Zhou, Aggarwal, Chellappa, & Jacobs, 2007), Total-Variance Quotient Image(Chen, Yin, Zhou, Comaniciu, &

Huang, 2005), and Active Differential Imaging (Zou, Kittler, & Messer, 2005). These techniques have been shown to be successful in dealing with illumination variations.

2. PASSIVE APPROACHES

Passive approaches can be divided into four groups: illumination variation modelling, illumination invariant features, photometric normalisation, and 3D morphable model. The performance of typical passive approaches is presented in Table 1.

2.1 Illumination Variation Modelling

The modelling of face images under varying illumination can be based on a statistical model or physical model. For statistical modelling, no assumption concerning the surface property is needed. Statistical analysis techniques, such as PCA (Eigenface) and LDA (Fisherface), are applied to the training set which contains faces under different illuminations to achieve a subspace which covers the variation of possible illumination. In physical modelling, the model of the process of image formation is based on the assumption of certain object surface reflectance properties, such as Lambertian reflectance.

2.1.1 Linear Subspaces

Hallinan (1994) showed that five eigenfaces were sufficient to represent the face images under a wide range of lighting condition. Shashua proposed *Photometric Alignment* approach to find the algebraic connection between all images of an object taken under varying illumination conditions (Amnon Shashua, 1997). An order k Linear Reflectance Model for any surface point p is defined as the scalar product $x \cdot a$, where x is a vector in the k-dimensional Euclidean space of invariant surface properties (such as surface normal, albedo, and so forth), and a is an arbitrary

Table 1. Identification error rates of passive illumination invariant approaches (%)

Category	Method	Yale B					Harvard				PIE
		2	3	4	5	overall	2	3	4	5	
Illumination Variation Modelling	Eigenface (Belhumeur, Hespanha, & Kriegman, 1997)	0	25.8	75.7	-	-	0	4.4	41.5	-	-
	Eigenface w/o 1st3 (Belhumeur, et al., 1997)	0	19.2	66.4	-	-	0	4.4	27.7	-	-
	Fisherface (Belhumeur, et al., 1997)	-	-	-	-	-	0	0	4.6	-	-
	3D Linear Subspace (Belhumeur, et al., 1997)	0	0	15.0	-	-	0	4.4	9.2	-	-
	Cone-Attached (Georghiades, Belhumeur, & Kriegman, 2001)	0	0	8.6	-	-	-	-	-	-	-
	Cone-Casted (Georghiades, et al., 2001)	0	0	0	-	-	-	-	-	-	-
	Segment Linear Subspace (Batur & Hayes, 2001)	0	0	0	-	-	-	-			-
	Generic Intrinsic Illum. Sub.(C. P. Chen & Chen, 2005)	0	0	11	-	-	-	-	-	-	3.0
	Spherical Harmonics(Lei Zhang & Samaras, 2006)	0	0	2.8	-	-	-	-	-	-	-
	9 point lights (Lee, Ho, & Kriegman, 2001)	0	0	2.8	-	-	-	-	-	-	1.9
	Generalized Photo. Stereo (Zhou, et al., 2007)	-	-	-	-	-	-	-	-	-	0.9
Illumination Insensitive Features	Gradient Angle (H. F. Chen, Belhumeur, & Jacobs, 2000)	0	0	1.4	-	-	-	-	-	-	-
	Gabor Phase (Laiyun, Shiguang, Xilin, & Wen, 2006)	0	0	2.8	4.7	-	-	-	-	-	-
	Quotient Image (A. Shashua & Riklin-Raviv, 2001)	1.7	38.1	65.9	76.7	-	-	-	-	-	-
	Quotient Image Relighting (Shan, Gao, Cao, & Zhao, 2003)	0	0	9.4	17.6	-	0	16.2	42.9	71.6	-
	Self Quotient Image (Haitao, Li, & Yangsheng, 2004)	2.0	1.0	3.0	-	-	-	-	-	-	-
	Morphological Quotient Img (Y. Zhang, Tian, He, & Yang, 2007)	0	0	0	0.5	-	-	-	-	-	-
	Total-Variation Quotient Img (T. Chen, et al., 2005)	0	0	0	-	-	-	-	-	-	-
	Antisotropic Smoothing (Gross & Brajovic, 2003)	1.0	1.0	6.0	-	-	-	-	-	-	-
Photometric Normalisation	Histogram Equalization (Shan, et al., 2003)	0	11.0	44.9	55.6	-	1.1	47.9	70.0	87.6	-
	Gamma Intensity Correc. (Shan, et al., 2003)	0	11.9	60.1	72.5	-	5.6	54.6	77.1	84.6	-
	DCT in Log domain (W. Chen, et al., 2006)	0	0	0.18	1.71	-	-	-	-	-	0.36
	Wavelet Reconstruction (Du & Ward, 2005)	0	0	5.24	9.17	-	-	-	-	-	-
	Local Normalisation (Xie & Lam, 2006)	-	-	-	-	0.5	-	-	-	-	0
	DoG(L.-H. Chen, Yang, Chen, & Cheng, 2011)	0	6.39	1.75	0.97						0
	NDFs(L.-H. Chen, et al., 2011)	0	0	0	0						0
3D Morphable Model(Blanz & Vetter, 2003)		-	-	-	-	-	-	-	-	-	0.2

vector. The image intensity $I\left(p\right)$, at location p, of an object with an order k reflection model can be represented by a linear combination of a set of k images of the object. For Lambertian surface under distant point sources and in the absence of shadows, all the images lie in a 3D linear subspace of the high dimensional image space, which means that they can be represented by a set of 3 images, each from a linearly independent source. Given three images of this surface under three known and linearly independent light sources, the surface normal and the albedo can be recovered. This is known as *Photometric Stereo*. Shashua claimed the *attached shadows*, which are caused by points where the angle between surface normal n_p and the direction of light source s is obtuse $\left(n_p \cdot s < 0, \text{ therefore } I\left(p\right) = 0\right)$, do not have a significant adverse effect on the photometric alignment scheme. However, the *cast shadows* caused by occlusion cannot be modelled using the above framework.

Belhumeur et al. (1997) presented the so-called *3D linear subspace* method for illumination invariant face recognition, which is a variant of the photometric alignment method. In this linear subspace method, three or more images of the same face taken under different lighting are used to construct a 3D basis for the linear subspace. The recognition proceeds by comparing the distance between the test image and each linear subspace of the faces belonging to each identity. The Fisher Linear Discriminant(also called FisherFace) method is also proposed in Belhumeur et al. (1997) in order to maximise the ratio of the between-class scatter and the within-class scatter of the face image set to achieve better recognition performance.

Batur and Hayes (2001) proposed a segmented linear subspace model to generalize the 3D linear subspace model so that it is robust to shadows. Each image in the training set is segmented into regions that have similar surface normal by k-Mean clustering, then for each region a linear subspace is estimated. Each estimation only relies on a specific region, so it is not influenced by the regions in shadow.

2.2.2 Illumination Cone

Belhumeur and Kriegman (1998) proved that all images of a convex object with Lambertian surface from the same viewpoint but illuminated by an arbitrary number of distant point sources form a convex *Illumination Cone*. The dimension of this illumination cone is the same as the number of distinct surface normals. This illumination cone can be constructed from as few as three images of the surface, each under illumination from an unknown point source. The illumination cone is a convex combination of extreme rays given by $x_{i,j} = \max\left(Bs_{i,j}, 0\right)$, where $s_{i,j} = b_i \times b_j$, and b_i, b_j are two different rows of a matrix B where each row is the product of albedo with surface normal vector. Kriegman and Belhumeur (2001) showed that for any finite set of point sources illuminating an object viewed under either orthographic or perspective projection, there is an equivalence class of object shapes having the same set of shadows. These observations are exploited by Georghiades et al. (2001) for face recognition under variable lighting.

2.2.3 Spherical Harmonics

Spherical Harmonics method is proposed by Basri and Jacobs (2001), and contemporarily by Ramamoorthi and Hanrahan (2001). Assuming arbitrary light sources (point sources or diffuse sources) distant from an object of Lambertian reflectance property, Basri and Jacobs (2003)show that ignoring cast shadow the intensity of object surface can be approximated by a 9-dimensional linear subspace based on a Spherical Harmonic representation.

Lei & Samaras (2006) proposed two methods for face recognition under arbitrary unknown lighting by using the spherical harmonics representation, which requires only one training image per subject and no 3D shape information. In the first method (Zhang & Samaras, 2003) the statistical model of harmonic basis images are built based on a collection of 2D basis images. For a given training face image, the basis images for this face can be estimated based on Maximum A Posterior estimation. In the second method (Lei, Sen, & Samaras, 2005) a 3D morphable model and the harmonic representation are combined to perform face recognition with both illumination and pose variation.

2.2.4 Nine Point Lights

Lee et al. (Lee, et al., 2001) showed that there exists a configuration of nine point source directions such that a subspace resulting from nine images of each individual under these nine lighting sources is effective at recognition under a wide range of illumination conditions. The advantage of this method is that there is no need to obtain a 3D model of surface as in the spherical harmonics approach (Basri & Jacobs, 2003), or to collect a large number of training images as in the statistical modelling approaches.

2.2.5 Generalized Photometric Stereo

Recently, Zhou et al. (2007) analyzed images of the face class with both the Lambertian reflectance model and the linear subspace approach. The human face is claimed to be an example of a so-called Linear Lambertian Object, which is not only an object with Lambertian surface, but also a linear combination of basis objects with Lambertian surfaces. The albedo and surface normal vectors of each basis object for the face class form a matrix called class-specific albedo/shape matrix, which can be recovered by a Generalized Photometric Stereo process from the bootstrap set. The model is trained using Vetter's 3D face database

(Blanz & Vetter, 2003). Excellent performance was reported. The work was further extended for multiple light sources.

2.3 Illumination Invariant Features

Adini et al. (1997) presented an empirical study that evaluates the sensitivity of insensitive image representations with respect to changes in illumination. These representations include edge map, image intensity derivatives, and image convolved with a 2D Gabor-like filter. All of the above representations were also followed by a log function to generate additional representations. However, the recognition experiment on a face database with lighting variation indicated that none of these representations is sufficient by itself to overcome the image variation due to the change of illumination direction.

2.3.1 Features Derived from Image Derivatives

Line edge map (Gao & Leung, 2002) is proposed for face recognition by Gao and Leung. The edge pixels are grouped into line segments, and a revised Hausdorff Distance is designed to measure the similarity between two line segments. Chen et al. (2000) showed that for any image, there are no discriminative functions that are invariant to illumination, even for objects with Lambertian surface. However, they showed that the probability distribution of the image gradient is a function of the surface geometry and reflectance, which are the intrinsic properties of the face. The *direction of image gradient* is revealed to be insensitive to illumination change. The recognition performance using gradient direction is close to the illumination cone approach. *Relative Image Gradient* feature is applied by Wei and Lai (2004) and Yang et al. (2002) for robust face recognition under lighting variation. The relative image gradient $\bar{G}(x, y)$ is defined as

$$\bar{G}\left(x,y\right) = \frac{\left|\nabla I\left(x,y\right)\right|}{\max_{(u,v)\in W(x,y)}\left|\nabla I\left(u,v\right)+c\right|},$$

where $I\left(x,y\right)$ is the image intensity, ∇ is the gradient operator, $W\left(x,y\right)$ is a local window cantered at *(x,y)*, and *c* is a constant value to avoid dividing by zero.

Zhao and Chellappa (2000) presented a method based on *Symmetric Shape from Shading* for illumination insensitive face recognition. The symmetry of every face and the shape similarity among all faces are utilized. A prototype image with normalized illumination can be obtained from a single training image under unknown illumination. Their experiments showed that using the prototype image significantly improved the face recognition based on PCA and LDA.

Sim and Kanade (2001) developed a statistical shape from shading model to recover face shape from a single image and to synthesize the same face under new illumination. The surface radiance $i(x)$ for location x is modelled as $i\left(x\right) = n\left(x\right)^{T} \times s + e$, where *n(x)* is the surface normal with albedo, *s* is the light source vector, *e* is an error term which models shadows and specular reflections. A bootstrap set of faces with labelled varying illuminations is needed to train the statistical model for *n(x)* and *e*. The illumination for an input image can be estimated using kernel regression based on the bootstrap set, then *n(x)* can be obtained by Maximum A Posterior estimation and the input face under a new illumination can be synthesized.

2.3.2 Quotient Image

Shashua and Riklin-Raviv (2001) treat face as an *Ideal Class of Objects*, i.e. the objects that have the same shape but differ in the surface albedo. The *Quotient Image* $Q_y\left(u,v\right)$ of object *y* against object *a* is defined by

$$Q_y\left(u,v\right) = \frac{\rho_y\left(u,v\right)}{\rho_a\left(u,v\right)},$$

where $\rho_y(u,v)$, $\rho_a(u,v)$ are albedo of the two objects. The image Q_y depends only on the relative surface texture information, and is independent of illumination. A bootstrap set containing *N* faces under three unknown independent illumination directions is employed. Q_y of a probe image $Y(u,v)$ can be calculated as

$$Q_y\left(u,v\right) = \frac{Y\left(u,v\right)}{\sum_j A_j\left(u,v\right)x_j},$$

where $\bar{A}_j\left(u,v\right)$ is the average of images under illumination *j* in the bootstrap set, and coefficients, x_j, can be determined from all the images in bootstrap set and $Y(u,v)$. Then the recognition is performed based on the quotient image.

Based on the assumption that faces are an Ideal Class of objects, Shan et al. (Shan, et al., 2003) proposed *Quotient Illumination Relighting*. When the illumination in the probe image and the pre-defined canonical illumination condition are both known and exist in the bootstrap set, the rendering can be performed by a transformation learnt from the bootstrap set.

Chen and Chen (C. P. Chen & Chen, 2005) proposed a *Generic Intrinsic Illumination Subspace* approach. Given the Ideal Class assumption, all objects of the same ideal class share the same Generic Intrinsic Illumination Subspace. Considering attached shadows, the appearance image of object *i* in this class under a combination of *k* illumination sources $\left\{l_i\right\}_{i=1}^{k}$ is represented by

$$I_i\left(x,y\right) = \rho_i\left(x,y\right)\sum_{j=1}^{k}\max\left(n\left(x,y\right)l_j,0\right),$$

where $\rho_i\left(x,y\right)$ is the albedo, and $n(x,y)$ is the surface normal vector of all objects in the class. The illumination image is defined as $L\left(x,y\right) = \sum_{j=1}^{k}\max\left(n\left(x,y\right)l_j,0\right)$. The illumination images of a specific Ideal Class form a subspace called Generic Intrinsic Illumination Subspace, which can be obtained from a bootstrap set. For a given image the illumination image can be estimated by $L=Bl$, where $l = \arg\min\left\|Bl - L^*\right\|$.

Here B is the basis matrix of the intrinsic illumination subspace, and L^* is an initial estimation of illumination image based on smoothed input image. Finally $\rho\left(x,y\right)$ can be obtained by

$$\rho\left(x,y\right) = \frac{I\left(x,y\right)}{L\left(x,y\right)}.$$

The method was evaluated on CMU-PIE and Yale B face databases and showed significantly better results than the Quotient Image method. It is also shown that enforcing non-negative light constraint will further improve the results.

2.3.3 Retinex Approach

In *Retinex* approaches the luminance is estimated by the smoothed image. The image can then be divided by the luminance to obtain the reflectance, which is an invariant feature to illumination. A single Gaussian function is applied to smooth the image in the single scale retinex approach (Jobson, Rahman, & Woodell, 1997b), and the sum of several Gaussian functions with different scales is applied in the multi-scale retinex approach (Jobson, Rahman, & Woodell, 1997a). Logarithm transform is employed to compress the dynamic range in (Jobson, et al., 1997a, 1997b).

Wang et al. (2004) defined *Self-Quotient Image*, which is essentially a multi-scale retinex approach, however instead of using isotropic smoothing as in Jobson et al. (1997a), anisotropic

smoothing functions with different scales are applied. Each anisotropic smoothing function is a Gaussian weighted by a thresholding function. Zhang et al. (2007) proposed a Morphological Quotient Image(MQI) method in which mathematical morphology operation is employed to smooth the original image to obtain a luminance estimate.

Gross and Brajovic (2003) solve luminance L for the retinex approach by minimizing an anisotropic function over the image region

$$\Omega : J\left(L\right) =$$
$$\iint_\Omega \rho\left(x,y\right)\left(L - I\right)^2 dxdy + ,$$
$$\lambda \iint_\Omega \left(L_x^2 + L_y^2\right)dxdy$$

where $\rho\left(x,y\right)$ is space varying permeability weight which controls the anisotropic nature of the smoothing. L_x and L_y are the spatial derivatives of L, and I is the intensity image. The parameter λ controls the relative importance of two terms. The isotropic version of function $J(L)$ can be obtained by discarding $\rho\left(x,y\right)$.

In the Total-Variation based Quotient Image(TVQI) approach (T. Chen, et al., 2005), the luminance $u(x)$ is obtained by minimizing $\iint_\Omega \left|\nabla u\left(x\right)\right| + \lambda\left|I\left(x\right) - u\left(x\right)\right| dx$ over all points x in image $I(x)$.

2.3.4 Transformation Domain Features

Recently methods based on the frequency domain representation have received attention. Savvides et al. (2004b) performed PCA in the phase domain and achieved impressive results on the CMU-PIE database (Sim, Baker, & Bsat, 2002). This so-called *Eigenphase* approach improved the performance dramatically compared to Eigenface, Fisherface and 3D linear subspace approach. Meanwhile, they further showed that even with partial face images the performance of the Eigenphase approach remains excellent and the advantages over other approaches are even more significant. Heo et al. (2005) showed that applying Support Vector Machines directly on phase can lead to even better performance than the Eigenphase approach mentioned above.

In Chunyan, Savvides, & Kumar (2005) a quaternion correlation method in a wavelet domain is proposed and good performance is achieved on the CMU-PIE database with only one training sample per subject. The subband images after discrete wavelet decomposition are encoded into a 2-D quaternion image. Quaternion Fourier Transform is then performed to transfer the quaternion image to quaternion frequency domain, where a quaternion correlation filter is applied. Qing et al. (2006) showed that the Gabor phase is tolerant to illumination change and has more discriminative information than phase in the Fourier spectrum.

Savvides et al. proposed a series of works based on advance correlation filters (Savvides et al., 2006; Savvides, Kumar, & Khosla, 2004a). A pre-whitening spectrum stage is usually adopted to emphasize higher frequency components followed by phase matching.

Llano et al. (2006) examined the sensitivity of several frequency domain representations of face image to illumination change. Those representations are the magnitude, phase, real part and imaginary part of the Fourier spectrum of original face image, and those of gradient image. The gradient image is defined as an image where each pixel has a complex value with the horizontal gradient of the original image as the real part, and the vertical gradient as imaginary part. The experimental results on the normal illumination set and the darken set of the XM2VTS face database showed that the real part of the Fourier spectrum of the gradient image is less sensitive to illumination change than other representations.

2.3.5 Local Binary Pattern

Local Binary Pattern (LBP) (Maenpaa & Pietikainen, 2003) is a non-parametric transform which maps the ordinal contrast measures between B neighbours and the centre pixel to a B-bit string. This non-parametric transform is invariant to any monotonic transformation of the grey scale. Ahonen et al. (2004) are the first group to implement the LBP descriptor for face recognition.

The drawback of LBP is that random noise could result in a situation where the reference value, i.e., the centre pixel of the LBP operator, changes by a single unit, thereby altering all eight neighbouring ordinal contrast measurements. This results in LBP misrepresenting local structure. Various methods have been proposed to enhance the robustness of the LBP operator to counteract such an effect. The authors in Tan and Triggs (2007) have proposed local ternary patterns (LTP), which extend LBP by increasing the feature dimensionality depending on the sign of the centre bit. However, LTP is sensitive to monotonic transformations.

The authors in Jin, Liu, Lu, & Tong (2004) and Zabih and Woodfill (1994) proposed a variant LBP operator which performs ordinal contrast measurement with respect to the average or median of the pixel neighbourhood instead of the centre pixel to reduce the effect of a single noisy reference.

A more effective solution is LBP's extension to provide a multiresolution operator which can be accomplished either by increasing the radius of the operator (Chan, Kittler, & Messer, 2007; Maenpaa & Pietikainen, 2003), or alternatively by down-sampling the original image after low-pass filtering and then applying an LBP operator of fixed radius. Multi-block LBP (MBLBP) (Liao, Zhu, Lei, Zhang, & Li, 2007) is an example of the latter category which replaces intensity values in the computation of LBP with the mean intensity value of image blocks. Wolf et al. (n.d.) pointed out that MBLBP is effective in face detection but it does not perform well for face recognition in their experiment. The difference between these two categories of multiresolution LBP operators is that in the case of the one using low-pass filtering it is difficult to extract the contrast energy in small blocks across large distances because a differential operator, large enough to span the required distance, must trade resolution for the block size (Balas & Sinha, 2003). This kind of property (Sinha, 2002) has been proven to be important for face detection under different illumination conditions. In summary, the shortcoming of the conventional differential operators, such as Gabor and MBLBP, is the correlation of the size of an operator's block and the distance spanned by that operator. Therefore, Wolf et al. (n.d.) propose a patch based LBP (PLBP) in which the block size and inter-block distance parameters are decoupled. In fact, the former category of multiresolution operators aims to decouple the distance between block and block size in which the bock is denoted as an impulse function. LBP values in each region are generally statistically summarised in the form of a histogram in order to gain robustness to image rotation and translation often caused by automatic face detection and/or localisation.

2.4 Photometric Normalization

Histogram Equalisation (Gonzalez & Woods, 1992) is the most commonly used approach. By performing histogram equalisation, the histogram of the pixel intensities in the resulting image is flat. It is interesting that even for images with controlled illumination (such as face images in the XM2VTS database), applying histogram equalisation still offers performance gain in face recognition (Short, 2006).

Shan et al. (2003) proposed *Gamma Intensity Correction* for illumination normalisation. The corrected image $G(x,y)$ can be obtained by performing an intensity mapping: $G\left(x,y\right) = cI\left(x,y\right)^{\frac{1}{\gamma}}$, where c is a gray stretch parameter, and γ is the Gamma coefficient.

In Homomorphic filtering approach (Gonzalez & Woods, 1992) the logarithm of the equation of the reflectance model is taken to separate the reflectance and luminance. The reflectance model often adopted is described by $I\left(x,y\right) = R\left(x,y\right) * L\left(x,y\right)$, where $I(x,y)$ is the intensity of the image, $R(x,y)$ is the reflectance function, which is the intrinsic property of the face, and $L(x,y)$ is the luminance function. Based on the assumption that the illumination varies slowly across different locations of the image and the local reflectance changes quickly across different locations, a high-pass filtering can be performed on the logarithm of the image $I(x,y)$ to reduce the luminance part, which is the low frequency component of the image, and amplify the reflectance part, which corresponds to the high frequency component.

Du and Ward (2005) performed illumination normalization in the wavelet domain. Histogram equalisation is applied to low-low subband image of the wavelet decomposition, and simple amplification is performed for each element in the other 3 subband images to accentuate high frequency components. Uneven illumination is removed in the reconstructed image obtained by employing inverse wavelet transform on the modified 4 subband images.

Xie and Lam (2006) proposed an illumination normalization method which is called *Local Normalization*. They split the face region into a set of triangular facets, the area of which is small enough to be considered as planar patch. The main idea of this approach is to normalize the intensity values within each facet to be of zero mean and unit variance.

Short et al. (2004) compared five photometric normalization methods, namely illumination insensitive Eigenspaces, Multiscale Retinex method, Homomorphic filtering, a method using isotropic smoothing to estimate luminance, and one using anisotropic smoothing (Gross & Brajovic, 2003). Each method is tested with/without histogram equalisation performed in advance. Interestingly it was found that histogram equalisation helped in every case. It is shown that using anisotropic smoothing method as photometric normalisation led to the most consistent verification performance for experiments across the Yale B, BANCA (Bailly-Bailli, et al., 2003; Messer, Matas, Kittler, Luettin, & Maître, 1999) and XM2VTS (Messer et al., 1999) databases.

Chen et al. (2006) employed DCT to compensate for illumination variation in the logarithm domain. The uneven illumination is removed in the image reconstructed by inverse DCT after a number of DCT coefficients corresponding to low frequency are discarded.

Recently, a difference of Gaussian (DoG) filter has been proposed by the authors in (Gang & Akbarzadeh, 2009; Tan & Triggs, 2007) to improve face recognition in the presence of varying illumination. Chen et al. (2011) derived a Wiener filter approach based on the natural delighting filters (NDFs) to achieve the illumination-invariant image.

2.5 3D Morphable Model

Blanz and Vetter (2003) proposed face recognition based on fitting a 3D morphable model. The 3D morphable model describes the shape and texture of face separately based on the PCA analysis of the shape and texture obtained from a database of 3D scans. To fit a face image under unknown pose and illumination to the model, an optimisation process is needed to optimize shape coefficients, texture coefficients along with 22 rendering parameters to minimise the difference of the input image and the rendered image based on those coefficients. The rendering parameters include pose angles, 3D translation, ambient light intensities, directed light intensities and angles, and other parameters of the camera and colour channels. The illumination model of Phong is adopted in the rendering process to describe the

diffuse and specular reflection of the surface. After fitting both the gallery images and the probe images to the model, the recognition can be performed based on the model coefficients for shape and texture. Good recognition performance across pose and illumination is achieved in experiments on CMU-PIE and FERET face database.

3. ACTIVE APPROACHES

In active approaches additional devices (optical filters, active illumination sources or specific sensors) usually need to be involved to actively obtain different modalities of face images that are insensitive to or independent of illumination change. Those modalities include 3D face information (Bowyer, Chang, & Flynn, 2004) and face images in those spectra other than visible spectra, such as thermal infrared image (Kong, Heo, Abidi, Paik, & Abidi, 2005) and near-infrared hyper-spectral image (Pan, Healey, Prasad, & Tromberg, 2003).

3.1 3D Information

3D information is one of the intrinsic properties of a face, which is invariant to illumination change. The surface normal information is also used in some passive approaches described in the previous section, however, they are recovered from the intensity images captured by the visible light camera. In this section we talk about the 3D information acquired by active sensing devices like 3D laser scanners or stereo vision systems.

3D information can be represented in different ways. The most commonly used representations are range image, profile, surface curvature, Extended Gaussian Image (EGI), Point Signature, and etc. Surveys on 3D face recognition approaches can be found in Bowyer et al. (2004), Bowyer, Chang, and Flynn (2006) and Scheenstra, Ruifrok, and Veltkamp (2005). The 3D modality can be fused with 2D modality, i.e. texture, to achieve better performance (Bowyer et al., 2006; Chang, Bowyer, & Flynn, 2005). Nevertheless, it should be noted that the 2D face images which are combined with 3D face information as reported in Bowyer et al. (2006) and Chang et al. (2005) are captured in a controlled environment. It is still not clear how much the fusion will help in the case of uncontrolled environment due to the impact of uncontrolled illumination on the 2D face intensity images.

Kittler et al. (2005) reviewed the full spectrum of 3D face processing, from sensing to recognition. The review covers the currently available 3D face sensing technologies, various 3D face representation models and the different ways to use 3D model for face recognition. In addition to the discussion on separate 2D and 3D based recognition and the fusion of different modalities, the approach involving 3D assisted 2D recognition is also addressed.

3.2 Infrared

Visible light spectrum ranges from $0.4\mu m$-$0.7\mu m$ in the electromagnetic spectrum. The infrared spectrum ranges from $0.7\mu m$ -10mm. It can be divided into 5 bands, namely: Near-Infrared(Near-IR) $(0.7$-$0.9\mu m)$, the Short-Wave Infrared (SWIR) $(0.9$-$2.4\mu m)$, the Mid-Wave Infrared(MWIR) $(3.0$-$8.0\mu m)$, the Long-Wave Infrared(LWIR) $(8.0$-$14.0\mu m)$, and Far-Infrared(FIR) $(14.0\mu m$-10mm$)$. Near-IR and SWIR belong to reflected infrared $(0.7$-$2.4\mu m)$, while MWIR and LWIR belong to thermal infrared $(2.4\mu m$-14mm$)$. Similar to the visible spectrum, the reflected infrared contains the information about the reflected energy from the object surface, which is related to the illumination power and the surface reflectance property. Thermal Infrared directly relates to the thermal radiation from object, which depends on the temperature of the object and emissivity of the material (Kong et al., 2005).

3.2.1 Thermal Infrared

A survey on visual and infrared face recognition is presented in Kong et al. (2005). Wilder at al. (1996) showed that with minor illumination changes and for subjects without eyeglasses, applying thermal image for face recognition does not lead to significant difference compared to visible images. However, for scenarios with huge illumination changes and facial expressions, superior performance was achieved based on radiometrically calibrated thermal face images than that based on visible image (Socolinsky & Selinger, 2002; Socolinsky, Selinger, & Neuheisel, 2003). The experiments in Chen, Flynn, & Bowyer (2003) show that the face recognition based on thermal images degrades more significantly than visible images when there is a substantial passage of time between the acquisition of gallery images and probe images. This result was proved to be reproducible by Socolinsky and Selinger (2004b), however it is shown that with a more sophisticated recognition algorithm the difference of recognition performance across time based on thermal face and visible face is small.

Despite the independence of visible light, the thermal imagery has its own disadvantages. The temperature of the environment, physical conditions and psychological conditions will affect the heat pattern of the face (Bebis, Gyaourova, Singh, & Pavlidis, 2006). Meanwhile, the infrared is opaque to eyeglasses. All the above motivate the fusion of thermal infrared image with visible images for face recognition. Various fusion schemes have been proposed (Bebis et al., 2006; Chen et al., 2003; Kong et al., 2005; Socolinsky & Selinger, 2004a) and shown to lead to better performance than the recognition based on either modality alone. The thermal face recognition experiments are usually conducted on the face database from the University of Notre Dame (Chen et al., 2003) or the Equinox face database (Equinox). The former contains the visible spectrum images and LWIR images of 240 subjects without glasses, but with different lighting and facial expressions. The latter was collected by Equinox Corp. and contains the visible images and LWIR images of a total of 115 subjects.

In Socolinsky and Selinger (2004a), thermal face recognition is performed in an operational scenario, where both indoor and outdoor face data of 385 subjects is captured. When the system is trained on indoor sessions and tested on outdoor sessions, the performance degrades no matter whether one is using thermal imagery or visible imagery. However, the thermal imagery substantially outperformed visible imagery. With the fusion of both modalities, the outdoor performance can be close to indoor face recognition.

3.2.2 Active Near-IR Illumination

The Near-IR band falls into the reflective portion of the infrared spectrum, between the visible light band and the thermal infrared band. It has advantages over both visible light and thermal infrared. Firstly, since it can be reflected by objects, it can serve as an active illumination source, in contrast to thermal infrared. Secondly, it is invisible, making active Near-IR illumination unobtrusive. Thirdly, unlike thermal infrared, Near-IR can easily penetrate glasses.

Pan et al. (2003) performed face recognition in hyperspectral images. A CCD camera with a liquid crystal tunable filter was used to collect images with 31 bands over near-infrared range. It was shown the hyperspectral signatures of the skin from different persons are significantly different, while those belonging to the same person are stable.

Most recently, Li et al. (2007) proposed a face recognition system based on active Near-IR lighting provided by Near-IR Light-Emitting Diodes (LEDs). The Near-IR face image captured by this device is subject to a monotonic transform in the gray tone, LBP feature is then extracted to compensate for this monotonic transform to obtain an illumination invariant face representation. Zhao and Grigat (Zhao & Grigat, 2005) performed face recognition in Near-IR images based on Discrete Cosine Transform(DCT) feature and SVM classifier.

Although infrared image is invariant to visible illumination, it is not independent of the environmental illumination. This is because environmental illumination contains energy in a wide range of spectra, including infrared. The variation of the infrared component in the environmental illumination will impose variation in the captured image.

One solution to maximize the ratio between the active source and the environmental source is to apply synchronized flashing imaging by Hizem et al. (2006). A powerful active illumination source is desirable. Illuminants such as LEDs can provide very powerful flash but only for very short time to avoid the internal thermal effects which might destroy the LEDs. The idea in Hizem et al. (2006) is to synchronize the sensor exposure time with the powerful flash. The sensor is exposed to the environmental illumination only for the same short exposure time as the flash. Since the power of the flash is usually much stronger than the environmental illumination, the contribution of the environmental illumination to the captured image will be minimized.

Nevertheless, the illumination variation problem can only be alleviated but not completely solved by the above mentioned approach. For indoor environment, the infrared energy in environmental illumination is low and will not cause much problem, while in outdoor environment, the infrared energy can be very strong.

3.2.3 Active Differential Imaging

Active Differential Imaging can be applied to solve the illumination variation problem even for the outdoor application. In active differential imaging, an image is obtained by the pixel-to-pixel differentiation between two successive frames: one with an active illuminant on and one with the illuminant off. Assuming a still scene, a linear response of the camera to the scene radiation and no saturation, the difference image of these two frames contains only the scene under the active illuminant, and is completely independent of the environmental illumination. Due to its invisibility, Near-IR illumination usually serves as the active illumination for the active differential imaging system. Face recognition experiments carried out on the face images captured by active Near-IR differential imaging system achieved very low error rates even in the scenario with dramatic ambient illumination changes (Hizem et al., 2006; Ni, Krichen, Hizem, Garcia-Salicetti, & Dorizzi, 2006; Zou et al., 2005; Zou, Kittler, & Messer, 2007). It is further shown in Zou (2007) that this active Near-IR differential imaging technique significantly outperformed some typical passive approaches for illumination problem. Specific sensors which can perform differential imaging have been proposed in Miura et al. (1999), Yang Ni and Xie-Long (2002), and Teuner (1999).

In a practical scenario there can be possible violation of the assumptions that active differential imaging relies on. Firstly the subject may move during the capture. The solution to this problem would be employing a fast capture system or a motion compensation technique as in Zou (2007). Secondly, to avoid saturation under strong sunshine, the dynamic intensity range of the image illuminated by active illumination source has to be sacrificed. A sensor with large dynamic intensity range (e.g. 16 bit) can serve as a solution to this problem.

4. DISSCUSSIONS

The performance of typical passive approaches is shown in Table 1. The first subset of Yale B or Harvard is used as training/gallery set for the tests on the rest subsets. There are some passive approaches which are not included in this table, this is because either their performance was less significant, or the experiment was not done on a standard database or using a standard protocol, therefore it is not fair to compare their performance with those listed in the table.

It can be seen that some passive approaches achieved excellent performance. However, it can not be concluded that the illumination problem is well solved. Although good performance is usually reported for most techniques, each technique has its own drawbacks. The illumination modelling methods require training samples from controlled illumination. The physical modelling of the image formation generally requires the assumption that the surface of the object is Lambertian, which is violated for real human faces.

The statistic modelling methods require training samples from as many as possible different illumination conditions to ensure a better performance. The performance of many photometric normalisation methods severely depends on the choice of parameters (James Short, Kittler, & Messer, 2005).

In addition to the individual drawbacks for each approach, there are some common issues. Firstly, it should be noticed that all the experiments are conducted on manually marked data. The sensitivity to localisation error still needs to be investigated for all approaches. Secondly, the databases to evaluate techniques are of very small size. For instance, Yale B contains images of only 10 subjects. The performance of illumination invariant approaches on large scale face dataset is still unknown. How much discriminative information has been lost after the suppression of the illumination effect?

As for active approaches, it should be investigated how much the active sensing process will be influenced by the environmental illumination. For example, a number of 3D acquisition techniques make use of intensity/infrared image pairs for 3D reconstruction. The variation in the environmental illumination might cause a problem for the accuracy of 3D reconstruction in those systems.

Usually it is difficult to compare the performance between passive approaches and active approaches because the datasets to test passive approaches are captured under different illumination conditions with the databases captured by active approaches. There is only one exception: in Zou et al. (2005), faces under ambient illumination were collected simultaneously when collecting a database with the active differential imaging system. Based on experiments on this face database the active differential imaging technique is shown to be significantly superior to the conventional passive approaches.

Moreover, it would be interesting to see whether the active approaches and passive approaches can be combined to better solve the illumination problem in a practical scenario.

Face Recognition Grand Challenge (FRGC) experiment 4 was designed for uncontrolled illumination problem. For more information about the performance of those algorithms submitted for evaluation please refer to Phillips, Flynn, Scruggs, Bowyer, and Worek (2006) and Phillips et al. (2007).

5. CONCLUSION

An extensive survey of passive and active approaches to address the illumination problem has been presented in this chapter. The performance, advantages and drawbacks of passive and active approaches have been summarized. Future directions for the research on illumination invariant face recognition have also been suggested.

3D acquisition is computationally expensive and the cost of the 3D devices is usually high. The cooperation from the client is required. Meanwhile, it is worthwhile investigating the performance of 3D acquisition in an uncontrolled environment. A number of 3D acquisition techniques make use of intensity/infrared image pairs for 3D reconstruction. The variation in the environmental illumination might cause problem for the accuracy of 3D reconstruction in those systems.

The outdoor environment contains illumination across a wide range of spectrum, so the simple idea to apply filter to obtain images in those spectra other than visible band will not lead to an image which is independent of environmental illumination.

REFERENCES

Adini, Y., Moses, Y., & Ullman, S. (1997). Face recognition: The problem of compensating for changes in illumination direction. *IEEE Transactions on Pattern Analysis and Machine Intelligence, 19*(7), 721–732. doi:10.1109/34.598229

Ahonen, T., Hadid, A., & Pietikainen, M. (2004). Face recognition with local binary patterns. *Computer Vision - Eccv 2004, Pt 1, 3021,* 469-481.

Bailly-Bailli, E., Bengio, S., Bimbot, R., et al. (2003). *The BANCA database and evaluation protocol.* Paper presented at the 4th international conference on Audio- and video-based biometric person authentication. New York, NY.

Balas, B. J., & Sinha, P. (2003). *Dissociated Dipoles: Image representation via non-local comparisons.* Paper presented at the CBCL Paper #229/AI Memo #2003-018. Cambridge, MA.

Basri, R., & Jacobs, D. (2001). Lambertian reflectance and linear subspaces. In *Proceedings of Eighth IEEE International Conference on Computer Vision,* (pp. 383-390). IEEE.

Basri, R., & Jacobs, D. W. (2003). Lambertian reflectance and linear subspaces. *IEEE Transactions on Pattern Analysis and Machine Intelligence, 25*(2), 218–233. doi:10.1109/TPAMI.2003.1177153

Batur, A. U., & Hayes, M. H. (2001). Linear subspaces for illumination robust face recognition. In *Proceedings of IEEE Computer Society Conference on Computer Vision and Pattern Recognition*, (vol. 2, pp. 296-301). IEEE.

Bebis, G., Gyaourova, A., Singh, S., & Pavlidis, I. (2006). Face recognition by fusing thermal infrared and visible imagery. *Image and Vision Computing*, 24(7), 727–742. doi:10.1016/j.imavis.2006.01.017

Belhumeur, P. N., Hespanha, J. P., & Kriegman, D. J. (1997). Eigenfaces vs. Fisherfaces: Recognition using class specific linear projection. *IEEE Transactions on Pattern Analysis and Machine Intelligence*, 19(7), 711–720. doi:10.1109/34.598228

Belhumeur, P. N., & Kriegman, D. J. (1998). What is the set of images of an object under all possible illumination conditions? *International Journal of Computer Vision*, 28(3), 245–260. doi:10.1023/A:1008005721484

Blanz, V., & Vetter, T. (2003). Face recognition based on fitting a 3D morphable model. *IEEE Transactions on Pattern Analysis and Machine Intelligence*, 25(9), 1063–1074. doi:10.1109/TPAMI.2003.1227983

Bowyer, K. W., Chang, K., & Flynn, P. (2004). A survey of approaches to three-dimensional face recognition. In *Proceedings of the 17th International Conference on Pattern Recognition*, (vol. 1, pp. 358-361). Academic Press.

Bowyer, K. W., Chang, K., & Flynn, P. (2006). A survey of approaches and challenges in 3D and multi-modal 3D+2D face recognition. *Computer Vision and Image Understanding*, 101(1), 1–15. doi:10.1016/j.cviu.2005.05.005

Chan, C. H., Kittler, J., & Messer, K. (2007). Multi-scale local binary pattern histograms for face recognition. *Advances in Bioethics*, 4642, 809–818.

Chang, K. I., Bowyer, K. W., & Flynn, P. J. (2005). An evaluation of multimodal 2D+3D face biometrics. *IEEE Transactions on Pattern Analysis and Machine Intelligence*, 27(4), 619–624. doi:10.1109/TPAMI.2005.70 PMID:15794165

Chen, C. P., & Chen, C. S. (2005). Lighting normalization with generic intrinsic illumination subspace for face recognition. In *Proceedings of Tenth IEEE International Conference on Computer Vision*, (pp. 1089-1096). IEEE.

Chen, H. F., Belhumeur, P. N., & Jacobs, D. W. (2000). In search of illumination invariants. In *Proceedings of IEEE Conference on Computer Vision and Pattern Recognition, Proceedings*, (pp. 254-261). IEEE.

Chen, L.-H., Yang, Y.-H., Chen, C.-S., & Cheng, M.-Y. (2011). *Illumination invariant feature extraction based on natural images statistics -- Taking face images as an example.* Paper presented at the 2011 IEEE Conference on Computer Vision and Pattern Recognition. New York, NY.

Chen, T., Yin, W. T., Zhou, X. S., Comaniciu, D., & Huang, T. S. (2005). Illumination normalization for face recognition and uneven background correction using total variation based image models. In *Proceedings of 2005 IEEE Computer Society Conference on Computer Vision and Pattern Recognition*, (vol. 2, pp. 532-539). IEEE.

Chen, W., Er, M. J., & Wu, S. (2006). Illumination compensation and normalization for robust face recognition using discrete cosine transform in logarithm domain. *Trans. Sys. Man Cyber. Part B*, 36(2), 458–466. doi:10.1109/TSMCB.2005.857353

Chen, X., Flynn, P. J., & Bowyer, K. W. (2003). *Visible-light and infrared face recognition.* Paper presented at the Proc. Workshop on Multimodal User Authentication. New York, NY.

Chunyan, X., Savvides, M., & Kumar, B. V. K. V. (2005). *Quaternion Correlation Filters for Face Recognition in Wavelet Domain.* Paper presented at the Acoustics, Speech, and Signal Processing, 2005 (ICASSP '05). New York, NY.

Chyuan-Huei, T., Shang-Hong, L., & Long-Wen, C. (2002). *Robust face matching under different lighting conditions.* Paper presented at the Multimedia and Expo, 2002. ICME '02. New York, NY.

Du, S., & Ward, R. (2005). Wavelet-based illumination normalization for face recognition. In *Proceedings of 2005 International Conference on Image Processing (ICIP),* (pp. 2129-2132). ICIP.

Equinox. (n.d.). Retrieved from http://www.equinoxsensors.com/product/hid.html

Gang, H., & Akbarzadeh, A. (2009). *A robust elastic and partial matching metric for face recognition.* Paper presented at the Computer Vision, 2009 IEEE 12th International Conference on. New York, NY.

Gao, Y. S., & Leung, M. K. H. (2002). Face recognition using line edge map. *IEEE Transactions on Pattern Analysis and Machine Intelligence,* 24(6), 764–779. doi:10.1109/TPAMI.2002.1008383

Georghiades, A. S., Belhumeur, P. N., & Kriegman, D. J. (2001). From few to many: Illumination cone models for face recognition under variable lighting and pose. *IEEE Transactions on Pattern Analysis and Machine Intelligence,* 23(6), 643–660. doi:10.1109/34.927464

Gonzalez, R. C., & Woods, R. E. (1992). *Digital image processing.* Reading, MA: Addison-Wesley.

Gross, R., & Brajovic, V. (2003). *An image preprocessing algorithm for illumination invariant face recognition.* Paper presented at the 4th international conference on Audio- and video-based biometric person authentication. New York, NY.

Haitao, W., Li, S. Z., & Yangsheng, W. (2004). *Face recognition under varying lighting conditions using self quotient image.* Paper presented at the Automatic Face and Gesture Recognition. New York, NY.

Hallinan, P. W. (1994). A Low-Dimensional Representation of Human Faces for Arbitrary Lighting Conditions. In *Proceedings of 1994 IEEE Computer Society Conference on Computer Vision and Pattern Recognition,* (pp. 995-999). IEEE.

Heo, J. G., Savvides, M., & Vijayakumar, B. V. K. (2005). Illumination tolerant face recognition using phase-only support vector machines in the frequency domain. *Pattern Recognition and Image Analysis,* 3687, 66–73.

Hizem, W., Krichen, E., Ni, Y., Dorizzi, B., & Garcia-Salicetti, S. (2006). Specific sensors for face recognition. *Advances in Bioethics,* 3832, 47–54.

Jin, H., Liu, Q., Lu, H., & Tong, X. (2004). *Face Detection Using Improved LBP under Bayesian Framework.* Paper presented at the Third International Conference on Image and Graphics. New York, NY.

Jobson, D. J., Rahman, Z. U., & Woodell, G. A. (1997a). A multiscale retinex for bridging the gap between color images and the human observation of scenes. *IEEE Transactions on Image Processing,* 6(7), 965–976. doi:10.1109/83.597272 PMID:18282987

Jobson, D. J., Rahman, Z. U., & Woodell, G. A. (1997b). Properties and performance of a center/surround retinex. *IEEE Transactions on Image Processing,* 6(3), 451–462. doi:10.1109/83.557356 PMID:18282940

Kittler, J., Hilton, A., Hamouz, M., & Illingworth, J. (2005). *3D Assisted Face Recognition: A Survey of 3D Imaging, Modelling and Recognition Approachest*. Paper presented at the 2005 IEEE Computer Society Conference on Computer Vision and Pattern Recognition (CVPR'05). New York, NY.

Kong, S. G., Heo, J., Abidi, B. R., Paik, J., & Abidi, M. A. (2005). Recent advances in visual and infrared face recognition: a review. *Computer Vision and Image Understanding, 97*(1), 103–135. doi:10.1016/j.cviu.2004.04.001

Kriegman, D. J., & Belhumeur, P. N. (2001). What shadows reveal about object structure. *Journal of the Optical Society of America. A, Optics, Image Science, and Vision, 18*(8), 1804–1813. doi:10.1364/JOSAA.18.001804 PMID:11488484

Laiyun, Q., Shiguang, S., Xilin, C., & Wen, G. (2006). *Face Recognition under Varying Lighting Based on the Probabilistic Model of Gabor Phase*. Paper presented at the Pattern Recognition. New York, NY.

Lee, K. C., Ho, J., & Kriegman, D. (2001). Nine points of light: Acquiring subspaces for face recognition under variable lighting. In *Proceedings of 2001 IEEE Computer Society Conference on Computer Vision and Pattern Recognition,* (pp. 519-526). IEEE.

Lei, Z., Sen, W., & Samaras, D. (2005). *Face synthesis and recognition from a single image under arbitrary unknown lighting using a spherical harmonic basis morphable model*. Paper presented at the Computer Vision and Pattern Recognition. New York, NY.

Li, S. Z., Chu, R. F., Liao, S. C., & Zhang, L. (2007). Illumination invariant face recognition using near-infrared images. *IEEE Transactions on Pattern Analysis and Machine Intelligence, 29*(4), 627–639. doi:10.1109/TPAMI.2007.1014 PMID:17299220

Liao, S. C., Zhu, X. X., Lei, Z., Zhang, L., & Li, S. Z. (2007). Learning multi-scale block local binary patterns for face recognition. *Advances in Biometrics. Proceedings, 4642*, 828–837.

Liu, D. H., Lam, K. M., & Shen, L. S. (2005). Illumination invariant face recognition. *Pattern Recognition, 38*(10), 1705–1716. doi:10.1016/j.patcog.2005.03.009

Llano, E. G., Vazquez, H. M., Kittler, J., & Messer, K. (2006). An illumination insensitive representation for face verification in the frequency domain. In *Proceedings of 18th International Conference on Pattern Recognition,* (pp. 215-218). Academic Press.

Maenpaa, T., & Pietikainen, M. (2003). Multi-scale binary patterns for texture analysis. *Image Analysis. Proceedings, 2749*, 885–892.

Messer, K., Matas, J., Kittler, J., Luettin, J., & Maître, G. (1999). *XM2VTSDB: The Extended M2VTS Database*. Paper presented at the Second International Conference on Audio- and Video-based Biometric Person Authentication (AVBPA'99). Retrieved from http://infoscience.epfl.ch/record/82502

Miura, H., Ishiwata, H., Lida, Y., Matunaga, Y., Numazaki, S., Morisita, A., et al. (1999). *A 100 frame/s CMOS active pixel sensor for 3D-gesture recognition system*. Paper presented at the Solid-State Circuits Conference, 1999. New York, NY.

Moses, Y., Adini, Y., & Ullman, S. (1994). Face recognition: The problem of compensating for changes in illumination direction. In J.-O. Eklundh (Ed.), *Computer Vision — ECCV '94* (Vol. 800, pp. 286–296). Springer. doi:10.1007/3-540-57956-7_33

Ni, Y., Krichen, E., Hizem, W., Garcia-Salicetti, S., & Dorizzi, B. (2006). Active differential CMOS imaging device for human face recognition. *IEEE Signal Processing Letters, 13*(4), 220–223. doi:10.1109/LSP.2005.863661

Ni, Y., & Xie-Long, Y. (2002). *CMOS active differential imaging device with single in&amp,#8211,pixel analog memory.* Paper presented at the Solid-State Circuits Conference. New York, NY.

Pan, Z. H., Healey, G., Prasad, M., & Tromberg, B. (2003). Face recognition in hyperspectral images. *IEEE Transactions on Pattern Analysis and Machine Intelligence, 25*(12), 1552–1560. doi:10.1109/TPAMI.2003.1251148

Phillips, P. J., Flynn, P. J., Scruggs, T., Bowyer, K. W., & Worek, W. (2006). *Preliminary Face Recognition Grand Challenge Results.* Paper presented at the Automatic Face and Gesture Recognition. New York, NY.

Phillips, P. J., Scruggs, W. T., O'Toole, A. J., Flynn, P. J., Bowyer, K. W., & Schott, C. L. et al. (2007). *FRVT 2006 and ICE 2006 Large-Scale Results.* Academic Press.

Ramamoorthi, R., & Hanrahan, P. (2001). On the relationship between radiance and irradiance: determining the illumination from images of a convex Lambertian object. *Journal of the Optical Society of America. A, Optics, Image Science, and Vision, 18*(10), 2448–2459. doi:10.1364/JOSAA.18.002448 PMID:11583261

Savvides, M., Abiantun, R., Heo, J., Park, S., Xie, C., & Vijayakumar, B. (2006). *Partial & Holistic Face Recognition on FRGC-II data using Support Vector Machine.* Paper presented at the Computer Vision and Pattern Recognition Workshop, 2006. New York, NY.

Savvides, M., Kumar, B. V. K. V., & Khosla, P. K. (2004a). Corefaces - Robust shift invariant PCA based correlation filter for illumination tolerant face recognition. In *Proceedings of the 2004 IEEE Computer Society Conference on Computer Vision and Pattern Recognition,* (Vol. 2, pp. 834-841). IEEE.

Savvides, M., Kumar, B. V. K. V., & Khosla, P. K. (2004b). Eigenphases vs. Eigenfaces. In *Proceedings of the 17th International Conference on Pattern Recognition,* (vol. 3, pp. 810-813). Academic Press.

Scheenstra, A., Ruifrok, A., & Veltkamp, R. C. (2005). A survey of 3D face recognition methods. *Audio and Video Based Biometric Person Authentication, 3546,* 891–899. doi:10.1007/11527923_93

Shan, S. G., Gao, W., Cao, B., & Zhao, D. B. (2003). Illumination normalization for robust face recognition against varying lighting conditions. In *Proceedings of IEEE International Workshop on Analysis and Modeling of Face and Gestures,* (pp. 157-164). IEEE.

Shashua, A. (1997). On Photometric Issues in 3D Visual Recognition from a Single 2D Image. *International Journal of Computer Vision, 21*(1-2), 99–122. doi:10.1023/A:1007975506780

Shashua, A., & Riklin-Raviv, T. (2001). The quotient image: Class-based re-rendering and recognition with varying illuminations. *IEEE Transactions on Pattern Analysis and Machine Intelligence, 23*(2), 129–139. doi:10.1109/34.908964

Short, J., Kittler, J., & Messer, K. (2004). *A comparison of photometric normalisation algorithms for face verification.* Paper presented at the Automatic Face and Gesture Recognition, 2004. New York, NY.

Short, J., Kittler, J., & Messer, K. (2005). Photometric Normalisation for Face Verification. In T. Kanade, A. Jain, & N. Ratha (Eds.), *Audio- and Video-Based Biometric Person Authentication* (Vol. 3546, pp. 617–626). Springer. doi:10.1007/11527923_64

Short. (2006). Illumination Invariance for Face Verification. University of Surrey.

Sim, T., Baker, S., & Bsat, M. (2002). *The CMU Pose, Illumination, and Expression (PIE) Database.* Paper presented at the Fifth IEEE International Conference on Automatic Face and Gesture Recognition. New York, NY.

Sim, T., & Kanade, T. (2001). *Combining Models and Exemplars for Face Recognition: An Illuminating Example.* Paper presented at the CVPR 2001 Workshop on Models versus Exemplars in Computer Vision. New York, NY.

Sinha, P. (2002). Qualitative representations for recognition. *Biologically Motivated Computer Vision, 2525,* 249–262. doi:10.1007/3-540-36181-2_25

Socolinsky, D. A., & Selinger, A. (2002). *A Comparative Analysis of Face Recognition Performance with Visible and Thermal Infrared Imagery.* Paper presented at the 16th International Conference on Pattern Recognition (ICPR'02). New York, NY.

Socolinsky, D. A., & Selinger, A. (2004a). *Thermal face recognition in an operational scenario.* Paper presented at the Computer Vision and Pattern Recognition, 2004. New York, NY.

Socolinsky, D. A., & Selinger, A. (2004b). *Thermal face recognition over time.* Paper presented at the Pattern Recognition, 2004. New York, NY.

Socolinsky, D. A., Selinger, A., & Neuheisel, J. D. (2003). Face recognition with visible and thermal infrared imagery. *Computer Vision and Image Understanding, 91*(1–2), 72–114. doi:10.1016/S1077-3142(03)00075-4

Tan, X. Y., & Triggs, B. (2007). Enhanced local texture feature sets for face recognition under difficult lighting conditions. *Analysis and Modeling of Faces and Gestures, 4778,* 168–182. doi:10.1007/978-3-540-75690-3_13

Teuner, A. (1999). *Surveillance Sensor Systems Using CMOS Imagers.* Academic Press.

Wei, S. D., & Lai, S. H. (2004). Robust face recognition under lighting variations. In *Proceedings of the 17th International Conference on Pattern Recognition,* (pp. 354-357). Academic Press.

Wenyi, Z., & Chellappa, R. (2000). *Illumination-insensitive face recognition using symmetric shape-from-shading.* Paper presented at the Computer Vision and Pattern Recognition, 2000. New York, NY.

Wilder, J., Phillips, P. J., Cunhong, J., & Wiener, S. (1996). *Comparison of visible and infra-red imagery for face recognition.* Paper presented at the Automatic Face and Gesture Recognition, 1996. New York, NY.

Wolf, L., Hassner, T., & Taigman, Y. (n.d.). *Descriptor Based Methods in the Wild.* Paper presented at the Workshop on Faces in 'Real-Life' Images: Detection, Alignment, and Recognition. Retrieved from http://hal.inria.fr/inria-00326729

Xie, X., & Lam, K.-M. (2006). An efficient illumination normalization method for face recognition. *Pattern Recognition Letters, 27*(6), 609–617. doi:10.1016/j.patrec.2005.09.026

Zabih, R., & Woodfill, J. (1994). Non-parametric local transforms for computing visual correspondence. In J.-O. Eklundh (Ed.), *Computer Vision — ECCV '94* (Vol. 801, pp. 151–158). Springer. doi:10.1007/BFb0028345

Zhang, L., & Samaras, D. (2003). Face recognition under variable lighting using harmonic image exemplars. In *Proceedings of IEEE Computer Society Conference on Computer Vision and Pattern Recognition,* (pp. 19-25). IEEE.

Zhang, L., & Samaras, D. (2006). Face Recognition from a Single Training Image under Arbitrary Unknown Lighting Using Spherical Harmonics. *IEEE Transactions on Pattern Analysis and Machine Intelligence, 28*(3), 351–363. doi:10.1109/TPAMI.2006.53 PMID:16526422

Zhang, Y., Tian, J., He, X., & Yang, X. (2007). MQI Based Face Recognition Under Uneven Illumination. In S.-W. Lee, & S. Li (Eds.), *Advances in Biometrics* (Vol. 4642, pp. 290–298). Springer. doi:10.1007/978-3-540-74549-5_31

Zhao, S., & Grigat, R.-R. (2005). An Automatic Face Recognition System in the Near Infrared Spectrum. In P. Perner, & A. Imiya (Eds.), *Machine Learning and Data Mining in Pattern Recognition* (Vol. 3587, pp. 437–444). Springer. doi:10.1007/11510888_43

Zhao, W., Chellappa, R., Phillips, P. J., & Rosenfeld, A. (2003). Face recognition: A literature survey. *ACM Computing Surveys, 35*(4), 399–459. doi:10.1145/954339.954342

Zhou, S. K., Aggarwal, G., Chellappa, R., & Jacobs, D. W. (2007). Appearance characterization of linear Lambertian objects, generalized photometric stereo, and illumination-invariant face recognition. *IEEE Transactions on Pattern Analysis and Machine Intelligence, 29*(2), 230–245. doi:10.1109/TPAMI.2007.25 PMID:17170477

Zou, X. (2007). *Illumination Invariant Face Recognition based on Active Near-IR Differential Imaging*. University of Surrey.

Zou, X., Kittler, J., & Messer, K. (2005). Ambient Illumination Variation Removal by Active Near-IR Imaging. In D. Zhang, & A. Jain (Eds.), *Advances in Biometrics* (Vol. 3832, pp. 19–25). Springer. doi:10.1007/11608288_3

Zou, X., Kittler, J., & Messer, K. (2007). *Motion compensation for face recognition based on active differential imaging*. Paper presented at the 2007 international conference on Advances in Biometrics. New York, NY.

KEY TERMS AND DEFINITIONS

Active Approach: This approach is employing active imaging techniques to obtain face images captured in consistent illumination condition, or images of illumination invariant modalities.

Active Differential Imaging: An image is obtained by the pixel-to-pixel differentation between two successive frames: one with an active Near-IR illuminant on and one with the illuminant off.

Active Near-IR Illumination: It is a capturing device with Near-IR lighing source. An image captured by this device is then subject to a monotonic transform in the gray tone.

Illumination Invariant Features: Features (image representations) are robust to changes in illumination.

Illumination Variation Modelling: It is a process to model face images under varying illumination based on a statistical model or physical model.

Passive Approach: This approach attempt to overcome the illlumination problem by studying the visible spectrum images.

Photometric Normalization: It is a normalization process to make face images under different illumination to be more canonical.

Chapter 8
Facial Action Recognition in 2D and 3D

Michel Valstar
University of Nottingham, UK

Stefanos Zafeiriou
Imperial College London, UK

Maja Pantic
Imperial College London, UK

ABSTRACT

Automatic Facial Expression Analysis systems have come a long way since the earliest approaches in the early 1970s. We are now at a point where the first systems are commercially applied, most notably smile detectors included in digital cameras. As one of the most comprehensive and objective ways to describe facial expressions, the Facial Action Coding System (FACS) has received significant and sustained attention within the field. Over the past 30 years, psychologists and neuroscientists have conducted extensive research on various aspects of human behaviour using facial expression analysis coded in terms of FACS. Automating FACS coding would make this research faster and more widely applicable, opening up new avenues to understanding how we communicate through facial expressions. Mainly due to the cost effectiveness of existing recording equipment, until recently almost all work conducted in this area involves 2D imagery, despite their inherent problems relating to pose and illumination variations. In order to deal with these problems, 3D recordings are increasingly used in expression analysis research. In this chapter, the authors give an overview of 2D and 3D FACS recognition, and summarise current challenges and opportunities.

DOI: 10.4018/978-1-4666-5966-7.ch008

INTRODUCTION

Scientific work on facial expressions can be traced back to at least 1872 when Charles Darwin (1872) published *The Expression of the Emotions in Man and Animals*. He explored the importance of facial expressions for communication and described variations in facial expressions of emotions. Today, it is widely acknowledged that facial expressions serve as the primary nonverbal means for human beings to regulate interactions with each other (Ekman & Rosenberg, 2005). They communicate emotions, clarify and emphasise what is being said, and signal comprehension, disagreement and intentions (Pantic, 2009).

Two main approaches for facial expression measurement can be distinguished: message and sign judgement (Cohn & Ekman, 2005). Message judgement aims to directly decode the meaning conveyed by a facial display (such as being happy, angry or sad), while sign judgement aims to study the physical signal used to transmit the message (such as raised cheeks or depressed lips). A steadfast of message judgment approaches is the theory of six basic expressions first suggested by Darwin (1872) and later extended by Paul Ekman (2003). They suggested that the six basic emotions, namely anger, fear, disgust, happiness, sadness and surprise, are universally transmitted through prototypical facial expressions. This direct relation underpins all message-judgement approaches. As a consequence, and helped by the simplicity of this discrete representation, prototypic facial expressions of the six basic emotions are the most commonly studied expressions and represent the main message-judgement approach.

There are two major drawbacks of message judgement approaches. Firstly, it cannot explain the full range of facial expressions, as the set of expressions that can be explained is restricted by the set of messages. Secondly, message judgement systems often assume that facial expression and target behaviour (e.g. emotion) have an unambiguous many-to-one correspondence, which is not the case according to studies in psychology (Ambady & Rosenthal, 1992) and in general, relations between messages and their associated displays are not universal, with facial displays and their interpretation varying from person to person or even from one situation to another.

The most commonly used set of descriptors in sign-judgement approaches is that specified by the *Facial Action Coding System* (FACS), (Ekman & Friesen, 1978; Ekman, Friesen, & Hager, 2002). The FACS is a taxonomy of human facial expressions. It was originally developed by Ekman and Friesen in 1978, and revised in 2002. The revision specifies 32 atomic facial muscle actions, named Action Units (AUs), and 14 additional Action Descriptors (ADs) that account for miscellaneous actions, such as jaw thrust, blow and bite. The FACS is comprehensive and objective, as opposed to message-judgement approaches. Since any facial expression results from the activation of a set of facial muscles, every possible facial expression can be comprehensively described as a combination of AUs (as shown in Figure 1). And while it is objective in that it describes the physical appearance of any facial display, it can still be used in turn to infer the subjective emotional state of the subject, which cannot be directly observed and depends instead on personality traits, context and subjective interpretation (Pantic, Nijholt, Pentland, & Huang, 2008).

Over the past 30 years, psychologists and neuroscientists have conducted extensive research using the FACS on various aspects of facial expression analysis. For example, the FACS has been used to demonstrate differences between polite and amused smiles (Ambadar, Cohn, & Reed, 2009) deception detection (Frank & Ekman, 1997), facial signals of suicidal and non-suicidal depressed patients (Heller & Haynal, 1994), as well as voluntary and evoked expressions of pain (Ekman, 2003; Ekman & Rosenberg, 2005). Given the significant role of faces in our emotional and social lives, automating the analysis of facial signals would be very beneficial (Pantic & Bartlett,

Figure 1. Examples of combinations of upper and lower face AUs defined in the FACS, resulting in two prototypical facial expressions

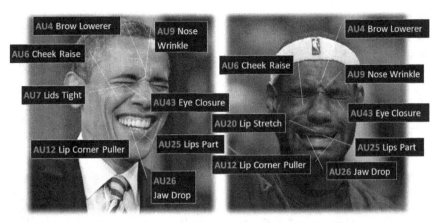

2007). This is especially true for the analysis of AUs. A major impediment to the widespread use of FACS is the time required both to train human experts and to manually score video. It takes over 100 hours of training to achieve minimal competency as a FACS coder, and each minute of video takes approximately one hour to score (Donato, Bartlett, Hager, Ekman, & Sejnowski, 1999; Ekman et al., 2002). It has also been argued that automatic FACS coding can potentially improve the reliability, precision, reproducibility and temporal resolution of facial measurements (Donato et al., 1999).

In spite of these facts, message-judgement approaches have proven to be the most popular. This is to be expected, however, given the complexity of the AU detection problem, for which there are a high number of classes (32 AUs vs. six basic emotions), more subtle patterns, and small inter-class differences. It is also less laborious to collect a dataset of prototypic expressions of the six basic emotions. In fact, automatic message judgement in terms of basic emotions is considered a solved problem nowadays, while machine analysis of AUs is still an open challenge (Valstar, Mehu, Jiang, Pantic, & Scherer, 2012).

Many systems for facial Action Units (AU) recognition in intensity video sequences have been proposed since the early 1990s. However, most of these systems are still highly sensitive to variations in recording conditions such as illumination, occlusions and other changes in facial appearance such as makeup and facial hair. Furthermore, in most cases when 2D facial intensity images are used, it is necessary to maintain a consistent facial pose (preferably a frontal one) in order to achieve a good recognition performance, as even small changes in the facial pose can reduce the system's accuracy. Moreover, single-view 2D analysis is unable to fully exploit the information displayed by the face, as 2D video recordings cannot capture out-of-plane changes of the facial surface, as changes are often not visually perceptible. Hence, many 2D views must be utilised simultaneously if the information in the face is to be fully captured. In order to tackle this problem, 3D data can be acquired and analysed.

When it comes to AU recognition, the subtle changes occurring in the depth of the facial surface are captured in detail when 3D data are used, something that does not happen with 2D data. For example, AU18 (Lip Pucker) is not easily distinguished from AU10+AU17+AU24 (Upper Lip and Chin Raising and Lip Presser) in a 2D frontal view video. On the other hand, in a 3D capture the action is easily identified (see Figure 2). Similarly, AU 31 (Jaw Clencher), can be difficult to detect in a 2D view, but is easily

Figure 2. AU18 (lip pucker) captured in both 2D and 3D. Images (a)-(d) show a nearly frontal view in original 2D and (e)-(h) the reconstructed data from 3D.

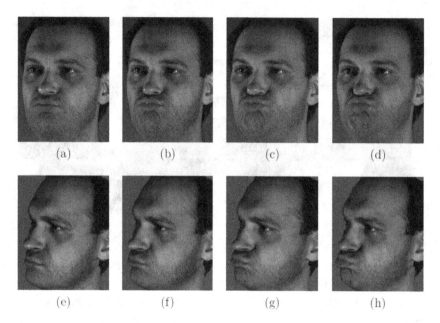

(a)　　　(b)　　　(c)　　　(d)

(e)　　　(f)　　　(g)　　　(h)

captured by the full 3D data (see Figure 3). We will argue in this chapter that recent advances in structured light scanning, stereo photogrammetry and photometric stereo have made the acquisition of 3D facial structure and motion a feasible task.

DATABASES

The need for large, AU labelled, publicly available databases for training, evaluating and benchmarking has been widely acknowledged, and a number of efforts to address this need have been made. In principle, any facial expression database can be extended with AU annotation. However, due to the very time-consuming annotation process, only a limited number of facial expression databases are FACS annotated, and even fewer are publicly available. Here we review the existing datasets in 2D and 3D, surveying only free publicly available databases. Table 1 provides a summary of these FACS-coded databases.

2D Databases

An important distinction between different databases is to what degree the expressions displayed were posed, i.e. produced at will or even on command, and to what extend they were spontaneous, i.e. resulting from natural reaction or interaction. All databases lie somewhere between fully posed and fully spontaneous, but for clarity we will group them here into two discrete classes.

Posed expression databases are usually restricted to convey a single specific emotion/AU per sequence, typically with exaggerated individual features. These expressions are easier to collect, and also easier to classify than spontaneous ones. In the early stages of research into automatic facial expression analysis, most systems were developed and evaluated on posed expressions, collected under homogeneous illumination and frontal head pose, always on a relatively small number of participants of fairly homogeneous demographic make up.

Figure 3. AU31 (jaw clencher) captured in both 2D and 3D. Images (a)-(d) show a nearly frontal view in original 2D and (e)-(h) the reconstructed data from 3D. The area of motion is shown in the circle.

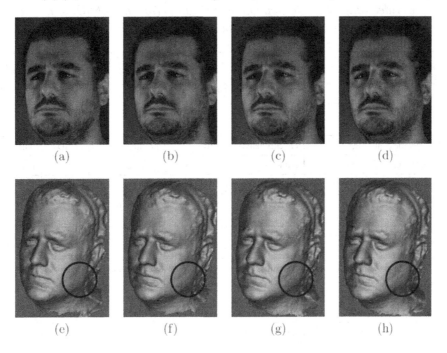

(a)   (b)   (c)   (d)

(e)   (f)   (g)   (h)

The *Cohn-Kanade facial expression database* (CK database, originally CMU-Pittsburgh) is frequently used in studies on the recognition of the six basic emotions and their corresponding AUs (Kanade, Cohn, & Tian, 2000). The database contains over 486 near-frontal-view videos of facial displays produced by 97 participants (18 to 50 years old, 69% female, mostly Caucasian). Participants were instructed to perform a series of 23 facial displays. Each sequence begins with a neutral expression and ends at the apex. The final (apex) frame for each sequence is fully FACS coded and given an emotion label.

The *MMI database* (Parts I-III) includes visual and audio-visual recordings of 69 different participants (44 females, 19 to 62 years old, varied ethnic background) (Pantic, Valstar, Rademaker, & Maat, 2005). Two FACS experts coded the activation and temporal segments of the AUs. There are approximately 780 videos, of which 30 are profile-view and 750 include a dual-view that combines frontal and profile views of the face. The subjects keep a strictly frontal head pose without any head movement.

The *ISL facial expression database* consists of two parts: frontal-view (Tong, Liao, & Ji, 2007) and multi-view (Tong, Chen, & Ji, 2010), containing 42 videos from 10 participants and 40 videos from 8 participants respectively. They were collected under uncontrolled indoor illumination and background. In the multi-view database, the face undergoes large face pose variations (-30 degrees to 30 degrees from left to right) and significant facial expression changes simultaneously.

Spontaneous expression databases involve higher frequency and larger amplitude of out-of-plane head movements, subtler expressions, and subtle transitions to and from the onset and offset phases in comparison to deliberately displayed facial expressions. Taking into account the differences in appearance and timing between spontaneous and posed expressions, it is unsurprising that approaches trained on posed

Table 1. Publicly available FACS-annotated facial expression databases. Elicitation method: On command/Acted/ Induced/Interview. Size: number of subjects. Camera view: frontal/profile/3D. S/D: static (image) or dynamic (video) data. Act: AU activation annotation (number of AUs annotated). oao: onset/ apex/offset annotation. Int: intensity (A/B/C/D/E) annotation.

Database	Reference	Elicitation Method	Subjects	Camera View	S/D	Act	oao	Int
Cohn-Kanade	Kanade et al. (2000)	On command	97	Frontal	D	Full	Y	N
Cohn-Kanade+	Lucey et al. (2010)	Natural	26	Frontal & 15° yaw	D	8	N	N
MMI (Part I-III)	Pantic et al. (2005)	On command	210	Frontal & Profile	SD	Full	Y	N
MMI (Part IV,V)	Valstar & Pantic (2010)	Induced	25	Frontal	D	Full	N	N
ISL Frontal	Tong et al. (2007)	On command	10	Near frontal	D	14	Y	N
ISL Multi-view	Tong et al. (2010)	On command	8	Frontal, 15°, and 30° yaw	D	15	Y	N
SAL	Douglas-Cowie et al. (2008)	Natural	20	Near frontal	D	12	Y	N
SEMAINE	McKeown et al. (2012)	Natural	150	Significant head movement	D	Full	N	N
GEMEP-FERA	Valstar et al. (2011)	Acted	10	Significant head movement	D	12	N	N
UNBC-McMaster	Lucey et al. (2011)	Induced (pain)	129	Frontal	D	10	N	Y
DISFA	Mavadati et al. (2012)	Induced	27	Near-frontal	D	12	N	Y
AM-FED	McDuff et al. (2013)	Induced	N.A.	Various	D	10	N	N
Bosphorus	Savran et al. (2008)	On command	105	3D	S	25	N	Y
ICT-3DRFE	Cosker et al. (2011)	On command	23	3D	S	Full	N	Y
D3DFACS	Stratou et al. (2011)	On command	10	3D	D	Full	N	N

databases fail to generalise to the complexity of real-world scenarios.

The *extended Cohn-Kanade dataset* (CK+ database), (Lucey, Cohn, Kanade, Saragih, & Ambadar, 2010) is the second release of the CK database. It includes an additional 107 sequences of 26 participants. Spontaneous data was included by selecting any naturalistic smile occurring between recording tasks, which added 122 smiles from 66 participants (91% female). Of these, 32% were accompanied by brief utterances. For spontaneous expressions, a set of smile-related action units, AU6, AU12, AU15, AU17, AU23/AU24 and AU25/AU26, were coded for activation (i.e. presence/absence).

The *MMI database (Parts IV-V)* was extended by Valstar and Pantic (2010) to include naturalistic expressions. Audio-visual recordings containing expressions of happiness, disgust and surprise for 25 participants were added. The spontaneous data is collected by showing the participants short clips (e.g. comedy clips or surgery videos), while surprise events occurred naturally without explicit elicitation. This part of the database is coded for smiles, laughter, and basic expression.

The *SEMAINE database* (McKeown, Valstar, Cowie, Pantic, & Schröder, 2011) was designed to engage the participants in a sustained, emotionally coloured conversation with an emotionally stereotyped operator. The expressions were elicited in human-computer and human-human conversations. The database includes high-quality, audio-visual recordings showing a range of related interactions. Video was recorded at 50 fps and at a resolution of 780 x 580 pixels. Participants and operators were recorded frontally by a grey scale camera and a colour camera. In addition, the participants were recorded by a grey scale camera positioned so to capture a profile view. Currently only 11 sequences are sparsely FACS-annotated, although efforts are under way to release full FACS coding of a number of recordings.

The *GEMEP-FERA challenge dataset* (Valstar, Jiang, Mehu, Pantic, & Scherer, 2011) is a subset of the GEMEP database that comprises 158 sequences of 10 participants. All the expressions are acted out by professional actors using *method acting*. Actors were only given instructions of what emotion to portray, not how to portray it. In consequence, the expressions displayed are similar to spontaneous ones. The dataset includes speech-related mouth and face movements, significant amounts of both in- and out-of-plane head rotations, and frequent co-occurrence of AUs. The dataset is split into a training set (including 7 actors), and a test set (including 6 actors, 3 of whom are not present in the training set). For the test set, the labels in terms of frame-based AU activation were not made publicly available. To obtain a performance over the test set, the obtained labels have to be mailed to the challenge organisers, who will return standardised performance measures.

The *UNBC-McMaster Shoulder Pain Expression Archive Database* (Lucey, Cohn, Prkachin, Solomon, & Matthews, 2011) is a publicly available database designed for the purpose of automatic pain analysis. It contains a total of 129 participants (63 male) with shoulder pain. The patients performed a ``range of motion'' test while being recorded. Although the camera is placed in front of the participants, changes in head pose are common. Only pain-related AUs were FACS-annotated (i.e. AUs 4, 6, 7, 9, 10,

12, 20, 25, 26, 27 and 43). With the exception of AU43, each AU was coded on a five level intensity dimension (A-E) on a frame-by-frame basis by one FACS-certified coder. Very precise per-frame facial locations for 66 points are also provided. The UNBC-McMaster pain database is currently the largest publicly available spontaneous expression database for AU analysis.

The *Denver Intensity of Spontaneous Facial Action database* (DISFA) (Mavadati, Mahoor, Bartlett and Trinh, 2012), contains stereo videos of 27 participants (15 males) in a controlled lab environment. Expressions were elicited by showing four minutes long videos to the subjects. Image quality is good (1024x768), and the video is recorded at 20 fps. Frame-based AU activation and intensity labels were manually annotated by two FACS experts for 12 AUs (1, 2, 4, 5, 6, 9, 12, 15, 17, 20, 25 and 26). The database also includes very precise per-frame facial landmark locations for 66 points.

The *Affectiva-MIT Facial Expression Dataset* (AM-FED) (McDuff, Kaliouby, Senechal, Amr, Cohn, & Picard, 2013) consists of 242 facial videos (168,359 frames), which were recorded by the users' Webcams while they were watching one of three intentionally amusing Super Bowl commercials. The videos exhibit non-uniform frame rate and non-uniform lighting. The camera position relative to the viewer varies from video to video and in some cases the screen of the laptop is the only source of illumination. The frame-based AU activation of 10 AUs (AU2, AU4, AU5, AU9, AU12, AU14, AU15, AU17, AU18 and AU26) have been manually coded by at least three FACS trained coders. For AU12 (mouth corner puller) and AU14 (dimpler), the unilateral activation (i.e. left or right side) has also been annotated, together with the location of 22 automatically detected landmark points. This is the first AU-annotated in-the-wild dataset, and the first database with uncontrolled lighting conditions.

3D Databases

A number of databases suitable for 3D facial expression analysis have appeared since 2003, including BU-3DFE (Yin, Wei, Sun, Wang, & Rosato, 2006), BU-4DFE (Yin, Chen, Sun, Worm, & Reale, 2008), Bosphorus (Savran et al., 2008), ICT-3DRFE (Stratou, Ghosh, Debevec, & Morency, 2011), and the recently introduced D3D-FACS (Cosker, Krumhuber and Hilton, 2011). In addition, the first 3D dynamic database containing spontaneous expressions was released, which for simplicity we will abbreviate as BU-4DSP (Zhang, Yin, Cohn, Canavan, Reale, Horowitz, & Liu, 2013). To the best of our knowledge, of these databases only Bosphorus, D3FACS and BU-4DSP contain AU annotations and we will limit our discussion to these three.

The *Bosphorus database* consists of static 3D facial captures. It was recorded using Inspeck Mega Capturor II 3D, which is a commercial structured-light based 3D digitizer device. The database consists of 105 subjects (60 men and 45 women, with the majority of the subjects being Caucasian), 27 of whom were professional actors/ actresses, in various poses, expressions and occlusion conditions. The subjects expressed the 6 six prototypical facial expressions and up to 24 AUs. The database is fully annotated for these 25 AUs. The texture images are of resolution 1600 x 1200 pixels while the 3D faces consist of approximately 35,000 vertices. The database is accompanied by a set of available metadata consisting of 24 manually labelled facial landmarks such as the tip of the nose, inner eye corners, etc.

The *ICT-3DRFE database* is another static database suitable for 3D expression analysis is. It consists of 3D data of very high resolution recorded under varying illumination conditions, in order to test the performance of automatic facial expression recognition systems. The database contains 3D models for 23 subjects (17 male and 6 female) and 15 expressions: the six prototypical expressions, two neutral states (eyes closed and open), two eyebrow expressions, scrunched face expression, and four eye gaze expressions. Each model in the dataset contains up to 1,200,000 vertices with reflectance maps of 1296 x 1944 pixels, a resolution that corresponds to a detail level of sub-millimetre skin pores. The ability to relight the data is ensured by the reflectance information provided with every 3D model. This information allows the faces to be rendered realistically under any given illumination. The database is fully annotated for AU1 (inner brow raise), AU2 (outer brow raise), AU4 (brow lower) and AU5 (upper lid raise). AUs are also assigned an intensity level ranging between 0-1.

The *D3DFACS database* is the first database suitable for dynamic analysis of 3D AUs is. It contains 10 subjects, including 4 FACS experts, performing posed examples of up to 38 AUs and Action Descriptors (ADs). In total, 519 AUs sequences were captured at 60 frames/sec, consisting of approximately 90 frames each. The location of the peak expression in each sequence has been coded by a FACS expert. The database was captured using the 3DMD Face Dynamic System. It is the first database that allowed research into dynamic 3D AU recognition and analysis.

The recently introduced *BU-4DSP database* is the only database that contains annotated spontaneous dynamic 3D AUs is. The database was recorded using the Di3D dynamic face capturing system. Passive stereo photogrammetry was used to create 3D model sequences at the frame rate of 25 frames per second. The geometric face model contains 30,000 to 50,000 vertices. The 2D texture videos are of 1040 x 1392 pixels/ frame. Two experienced FACS-certified coders independently coded all temporal segments (onset, apex and offset) of 27 AUs. For AU 12 and AU 14, intensity was coded as well on a 0-5 ordinal scale using custom software.

FACIAL EXPRESSION RECOGNITION METHODS

A great number of facial expression recognition methods have been proposed thus far, with a recent survey on general affect recognition from audio and video by Zeng, Pantic, Roisman, and Huang (2009) citing 160 works, and a survey by Jiang, Martinez, Valstar, and Pantic (2013) on AU detection alone citing no less than 171 works. Therefore, we will here only discuss the more recent developments, referring the reader to the above-mentioned surveys for further reading.

Methods for Action Unit Detection in 2D

AU activation detection aims to assign, for each AU, a binary label to each frame of an un-segmented sequence indicating whether the AU is active or not. Therefore, *Frame-based AU detection* is typically treated as a multiple binary classification problem, where a specific classifier is trained for each target AU. This reflects the fact that more than one AU can be active at the same time, so AU combinations can be detected by simply detecting the activation of each of the AUs involved. It is also important to take special care when dealing with non-additive AU combinations; such combinations need to be included in the training set for all of the AUs involved. An alternative is to treat non-additive combinations of AUs as independent classes (Tian, Kanade, & Cohn, 2001). That makes the patterns associated with each class more homogeneous, boosting the classifier performance. However, more classifiers have to be trained/evaluated, especially because the number of non-additive AU combinations is large. Finally, the problem can be treated as multi-class classification, where a single multi-class classifier is used per AU. AU combinations (either additive or non-additive) are treated as separate classes, as only one class can be positive per frame, which

makes this approach only practical when a small set of AUs is targeted (Smith & Windeatt, 2011).

AU event detection on the other hand consists of assigning a single label to a pre-segmented sequence of multiple frames. The label should indicate which AUs were active at some point within the sequence. Although obtaining pre-segmented videos is complicated in real scenarios, many early works on automatic AU analysis focus on this type of AU classification. A possible approach is to compute features that depend on the whole sequence, which are then analysed by means of a classifier. Alternatively, all frames of the sequence can be analysed using a per-frame binary classifier, and then a majority vote is used to assign the label to the sequence (Valstar, Patras, & Pantic, 2005). Lien, Kanade, Cohn and Li (2000) proposed to train an HMM to model each specific AU or AU combination targeted. During testing, a maximum likelihood criterion was used, so the assigned label corresponds to the more likely HMM to have generated the sequence of observations. Since the per-frame observations are probabilistic, the final output is obtained by integrating out the per-frame observed labels. More recently, Tax, Hendriks, Valstar and Pantic (2010) used a weakly supervised approach, Multiple Instance Learning. In this framework, examples are defined as sets of frames. A positive example is a set of frames of which at least one frame contains a positive in a classical sense, i.e. an activation of the target AU in this case. This has the advantage of greatly alleviating the burden of manual annotation, and it may be useful for problems where labelling is more subjective than that of AUs.

Features used for detection of AUs traditionally include geometric shape descriptors derived from tracked facial points (e.g. Chu et al., 2013), or static appearance descriptors such as Gabor filters (Bartlett et al., 2006) or Local Binary Patterns (Valstar et al., 2011). A recent trend is the use of dynamic appearance descriptors, which encode both spatial and temporal information. Therefore, dynamic appearance descriptors seem particularly adequate to represent the temporally-structured texture typical of facial actions. LBPs were extended to represent spatio-temporal volumes by Zhao and Pietikainen (2007). To make the approach computationally simple, a spatio-temporal volume is described by computing LBP features only on Three Orthogonal Planes (TOP): XY, XT, and YT, to form the LBP-TOP descriptor. The same extension was proposed for LPQ features by Jiang et al. (2011) and LGBP features by Almaev and Valstar (2013).

In principle, dynamic features, being a generalisation of their static counterparts, result in more powerful representations. This has been shown by Jiang, Valstar, Martinez and Pantic, (2013), who evaluated the performance of LBP, LPQ, LBP-TOP and LPQ-TOP features for automatic AU detection. A significant and consistent performance improvement has been shown when using spatio-temporal features. While the contiguity of pixels in the spatial plane is given by the image structure, temporal contiguity depends on the face registration. Yet interestingly, TOP features were shown to be less sensitive to registration errors than their static counterparts by Almaev and Valstar (2013).

Temporal consistency: AU detection is by nature a temporally structured problem as, for example, the label of the current frame is more likely to be active if the preceding frame is also labelled active. Considering the problem to be structured in the temporal domain is often referred to as enforcing temporal consistency. Graphical models are the most common approach to attain this. For example, Valstar and Pantic (2012) use a modification of the classical Hidden Markov Models. In particular, they substituted the generative model that relates a hidden variable and an observation with a discriminative classifier. Van der Maaten and Hendriks (2012) apply a Conditional Random Field (CRF). This model represents the relations between variables as undirected edges, and the associated potentials are discriminatively trained. In the simplest CRF

formulation, the label assigned to a given frame depends on contiguous labels, i.e., it is conditioned to the immediate future and past observations. Van der Maaten and Hendriks trained one CRF per AU, and each frame was associated to a node within the graph. The state of such nodes is a binary variable indicating AU activation.

Unsupervised detection of facial events: In order to avoid the problem of collecting training data, which impedes development of robust and highly effective approaches to machine analysis of AUs, some recent efforts focus on unsupervised approaches to the target problem. The aim is to segment a previously un-segmented input sequence into relevant "facial events," but without the use of labels during training (De la Torre, Campoy, Ambadar, & Cohn, 2007; Zhou, De la Torre, & Cohn, 2010). The facial events might not be coincident with AUs, although some correlation with them is to be expected, as AUs are distinctive spatiotemporal events. A clustering algorithm is used in these works to group spatiotemporal events of similar characteristics. Furthermore, Zhou et al. (2010) use a dynamic time alignment kernel to normalise the facial events in terms of the speed of the facial action. Despite of its interesting theoretical aspects, unsupervised learning traditionally trails behind in performance to supervised learning, even when small training sets are available. A semi-supervised learning setting might offer much better performance, as it uses all the annotated data together with potentially useful unlabelled data.

Transfer learning: Transfer learning methodologies are applied when there is a significant difference between the distribution of the learning data and the test data. In these situations, the decision boundaries learnt on the training data might be sub-optimal for the test data. Transfer learning encompasses a wide range of techniques designed to deal with these cases (Pan & Yang, 2010). They have only very recently been applied to automatic AU analysis. For example, Chu, De la Torre and Cohn (2013) proposed a new transductive learning method, called a Selective Transfer Machine (STM). Because of its transductive nature, no labels are required for the test subject. At test time, a weight for each training example is computed to maximise the match between the weighted distribution of training examples and the test distribution. Inference is then performed using the weighted distribution. The authors obtained a remarkable performance increase, beating subject-specific models. This can be explained by the reduced availability of subject-specific training examples. However, Chen, Liu, Tu, and Aragones (2013) evaluated standard methodologies for both inductive and transductive transfer learning for AU detection, finding that inductive learning improved the performance significantly while the transductive algorithm led to poor performance.

Transfer learning is a promising approach when it comes to AU analysis, where appearance variations due to identity are often larger than expression-related variations. Therefore, techniques that can capture subject-specific knowledge and transfer it at test time to unseen subjects are very well suited for AU analysis. Similarly, unsupervised learning can be used to capture appearance variations caused by facial expressions without the need for arduous manual labelling of AUs. Both transfer learning and supervised learning thus have a great potential to improve machine analysis of AUs with limited labelled data.

Analysis of AU temporal dynamics: The dynamics of facial actions are crucial for distinguishing between various types of behaviour (e.g. pain and mood). The aim of AU temporal segment detection is to assign a per-frame label belonging to one of four classes: neutral, onset, apex or offset. It constitutes an analysis of the internal dynamics of an AU episode. Temporal segments add important information for the detection of a full AU activation episode, as all labels should occur in a specific order. Furthermore, the AU temporal segments have been shown to carry important semantic information, useful for a later interpreta-

tion of the facial signals (Cohn & Schmidt, 2004; Ambadar et al., 2009).

Temporal segment detection is a multiclass problem, and it is typically addressed by either using a multiclass classifier or by combining the output of several binary classifiers. Probabilistic Graphical Network models can be adapted to this problem to impose temporal label consistency by setting the number of states of the hidden variables to four. The practical difference with respect to the AU activation problem is that the transitions are more informative, as for example an onset frame should be followed by an apex frame and cannot be followed by a neutral frame. Markov Models were applied to this problem by Valstar and Pantic (2012) and Koelstra et al. (2010). An extension of CRF, and in particular a kernelised version of Conditional Ordinal Random Fields, was used instead by Rudovic, Pavlovic and Pantic (2012). In comparison to standard CRF, this model imposes ordinal constraints on the assigned labels. It is important to note that distinguishing an apex frame from the end of an onset frame or beginning of an offset frame by its texture solely is impossible. Apex frames are not characterised by a specific facial appearance or configuration but rather for being the most intense activation within an episode, which is by nature an ordinal relation.

The temporal co-occurrence relations of AUs have been studied in detail by Tong et al. Tong, Liao and Ji (2007) modelled the relationships between different AUs at a given time frame by using a Static Bayesian Network. The temporal modelling is incorporated by a Dynamic Bayesian Network (DBN). They further introduced a unified probabilistic model for the interactions between AUs and other non-verbal cues such as head pose (Tong, Chen, & Ji, 2010). Although traditionally unexploited, this is a natural and useful source of information as it is well known that some AUs co-occur with more frequency due to latent variables such as for example prototypical facial expressions.

AU Intensity estimation: Annotations of intensity are typically quantised into 5 ordinal levels (A, B, C, D, and E) as stipulated in the FACS manual. Some approaches use the confidence of the classification to estimate the AU intensity, under the rationale that the lower the intensity is, the harder the classification will be. For example, Bartlett et al. (2006) estimated the intensity of action units by using the distance of a test example to the SVM separating hyperplane, while Hamm et al. (2011) used the confidence of the decision obtained from AdaBoost. However, the likelihood of an AU being present is not the same as the intensity of an AU and such systems provide a rough indicator of intensity at best.

Multi-class classifiers or regressors are more natural choices for this problem. It is important to note that for this problem the class overlap is large. Therefore, the direct application of a multi-class classifier is unlikely to perform well, and comparably lower than when using a regressor. That is to say, for regression, predicting B instead of A yields a lower error than predicting D, while for a classifier this yields the same error. An attempt of using a multi-class classifier for this task is presented by Mahoor et al. (2009). The authors employed six one-vs.-all binary SVM classifiers, corresponding to either no activation or one of the five intensity levels. The use of a regressor has been a more popular choice. For example, Jeni, Girard, Cohn, and De la Torre (2013) applied Support Vector Regression (SVR) for prediction, while Kaltwang, Rudovic, and Pantic (2012) used Relevance Vector Regression (RVR) instead, resulting in a fully probabilistic output.

AU intensity estimation is a relatively recent problem within the field. It is of particular interest due to the semantic richness of the predictions. However, it is not possible to objectively define rules for the annotation of AU intensities, and even experienced manual coders will have some level of disagreement. Therefore, the large amount of overlap between the classes should be taken into consideration. Regression methodologies are particularly suited, as they penalise a close (but different) prediction less than distant ones. Alternatively, ordinal relations can alleviate this problem by substituting the hard label assignment for softer ones (e.g. grater than).

Methods for Action Unit Detection in 3D

Due to the fact that until recently very few annotated corpora existed that were suitable for 3D AU detection/recognition, the application domain of 3D AU detection/recognition has not been heavily researched.

Tsalakanidou and Malassiotis (2009) used an ASM to track facial landmarks in 3D video streams. Simple geometric facial features such as the 3D Euclidean distance between landmarks and the angle between facial landmarks were used for fully automatic and real time AU recognition from low-resolution 3D streams. Experiments were conducted in a privately collected database, which was not made publicly available. The mean detection rate (correct classification) reported for 11 AUs was about 0.86.

Zhao, Dellandrea, Chen, and Samaras (2010) applied a statistical facial feature model (SFAM) for AU recognition. SFAM is a partial morphable facial model that learns both global variations in 3D landmark configuration and local ones around each landmark in terms of texture and geometry. Experiments were conducted on the Bosphorus database and the mean classification accuracy for 7 AUs was around 0.94. Also positive rates (PR = True Positive (TP)/(TP + False Negative (FN))) and false-alarm rates (FAR = False-Positive (FP)/(TP+FP)) were reported for 16 AUs. The average PR was 0.856 while the average FAR was 0.136.

Savran et al. (2012a) conducted a detailed comparison between 2D and 3D AU recognition on static images. For 3D AU recognition many different features for representation of the 3D facial geometry were applied, including the actual depth image, the mean curvature at each surface point, the Gaussian curvature and the shape index, just to name a few. Many feature extraction methodologies were also applied, including filtering with Gabor wavelets, application of Independent Component Analysis (ICA) and Nonnegative Matrix Factorization (NMF). Finally, many classifiers were applied including AdaBoost, linear and kernel Support Vector Machines (SVMs) etc. Two different experiments were conducted: one on high intensity and one on low intensity AU recognition. In the high intensity AUs the average Area Under the Curve (AUC) was as high as 0.957, while for the low intensity AUs the AUC was as high as 0.836. These were slightly higher than the AUC reported for 2D AUs. Finally, fusion of 3D and 2D slightly but consistently increased performance.

A series of Local Binary Pattern (LBP) based feature extraction methodologies were proposed by Sandbach, Zafeiriou, and Pantic (2012a, 2012b). In particular, they proposed LBP-based methods that use 3D normals, as well as the depth representation of 3D faces. Experiments were conducted in both the Bosphorus and D3DFACS database reporting an average AUC as high as 0.972. In these papers, the first cross-database experiments, with training in Bosphorus and testing in D3DFACS, were reported with an average AUC of 0.894.

Finally, Savran, Sankur, and Bilge (2012b) proposed a method for intensity estimation of AUs. This paper was the extension of (Savran et al. 2012a) for intensity estimation and in a similar fashion many feature representation, extraction and regression techniques were applied. An extensive comparison between 2D and 3D facial representations was also conducted. The average correlation for the lower face AUs and for the 3D modality was 0.52 while for the upper face was 0.68. 2D and 3D modality had similar performance on average and their fusion gave consistently better results.

Experiments in the first spontaneous database were reported by Reale, Zhang, and Yin (2013). Their work extends the idea of a 3D surface primitive feature into 4D space and developed a new feature representation: the so-called "Nebula" features. Given a spatiotemporal volume, the data was voxelised and fit to a cubic polynomial. The principal curvature values, as well as, the directions of least curvature for each of the face region were used to build a histogram-based descriptor for each face region. The concatenated histograms from each of the regions were used to create a final feature vector, which was fed to a Support Vector Machine (SVM) classifier. Experiments were conducted using a leave one out protocol with 16 subjects and 12 AUs. The average recognition AUC was 0.738.

All of the above mentioned approaches confirm the validity of the original hypotheses: that recognition of AUs is more accurate if 3D information is included, and that the problem of recognition of spontaneous 3D AUs is considerably more challenging than that of posed ones.

CONCLUSION

Detection of facial actions has reached a point where it is achieving high accuracy for the simpler scenarios – high intensity actions in frontal view faces under good lighting conditions. Consequently, the focus is shifting in three directions: firstly to address the remaining challenges in ordinary AU activation detection: dealing with non-frontal head pose, more subtle and actions, and less common AU combinations and dynamics. Secondly, researchers are increasingly trying to achieve a more complete analysis of facial actions. Detection of AU intensity, their temporal phases, and the relation between AUs, head actions, and other non-verbal signals is currently actively pursued. The goal of this is ultimately a better inference of underlying latent variables such as emotion or conversational intent. Finally, with facial action detection now proven to be possible in theory, efforts are underway to improve methodologies in terms of real-time computational performance, in order for them to be adopted in various real-world applications.

Promising directions in 2D expression analysis include novel dynamic appearance descriptors, fusion between heterogeneous features, and the resurgent use of geometric features that are receiving renewed attention with the development of robust facial point detectors. On the machine learning side, unsupervised, semi-supervised and transfer learning promise to allow for breakthroughs in natural behaviour understanding as they have the potential to remove the obstacles of the limited availability of annotated data.

Where 3D data is available, it is clear that utilising the depth information in conjunction with appearance and shape information significantly improves AU detection. However, the majority of existing work in the field of 3D AU detection is based on databases of acted, exaggerated expressions of the six basic emotions, even though they rarely occur in our daily life. Yet, increasing evidence suggests that deliberate or acted behaviours differ in appearance and timing from spontaneous ones. In turn, automatic approaches trained in laboratory settings on recordings of acted behaviour fail to generalise to the complexity of expressive behaviours found in real-world settings. We believe that the development of the first database with spontaneous 3D AUs will contribute in the progress of the field. Nevertheless, one database is not enough to perform cross-database experiments that are crucial for testing the generalization abilities of automatic 3D AU recognition systems.

The experiments reported for 3D AU recognition, even in the case of spontaneous expressions, show that average AU recognition performance is good and of course significantly higher than those reported on very challenging 2D videos, such as those in the GEMEP-FERA database. This finding is expected, since the 3D facial modality is neither sensitive to pose nor illumination changes. A major problem in 3D capturing is that each 3D capturing device/software uses its own way for

both creating the 3D mesh, as well as hole filling and smoothing methods for noise reduction in the meshes. This is one of the reasons that there is a significant drop in cross-database experiments.

REFERENCES

Almaev, T., & Valstar, M. F. (2013). Local Gabor binary patterns from three orthogonal planes for automatic facial expression recognition. In *Proceedings of the International Conference on Affective Computing and Intelligent Interaction.* Academic Press.

Ambadar, Z., Cohn, J. F., & Reed, L. I. (2009). All smiles are not created equal: Morphology and timing of smiles perceived as amused, polite, and embarrassed/nervous. *Journal of Nonverbal Behavior*, *33*, 17–34. doi:10.1007/s10919-008-0059-5 PMID:19554208

Ambady, N., & Rosenthal, R. (1992). Thin slices of expressive behavior as predictors of interpersonal consequences: a meta-analysis. *Psychological Bulletin*, *111*(2), 256–274. doi:10.1037/0033-2909.111.2.256

Bartlett, M. S., Littlewort, G., Frank, M., Lainscsek, C., Fasel, I., & Movellan, J. (2006). Automatic recognition of facial actions in spontaneous expressions. *Journal of Multimedia*, *1*(6), 22–35. doi:10.4304/jmm.1.6.22-35

Chen, J., Liu, X., Tu, P., & Aragones, A. (2013). Learning person-specific models for facial expressions and action unit recognition. *Pattern Recognition Letters*, *34*(15), 1964–1970. doi:10.1016/j.patrec.2013.02.002

Chew, S. W., Lucey, P., Saragih, S., Cohn, J. F., & Sridharan, S. (2012). In the pursuit of effective affective computing: The relationship between features and registration. *IEEE Transactions on Systems, Man and Cybernetics. Part B*, *42*(4), 1006–1016.

Chu, W., de la Torre, F., & Cohn, J. F. (2013). Selective transfer machine for personalized facial action unit detection. In *Proceedings of the IEEE Conference on Computer Vision and Pattern Recognition, 2013*. IEEE.

Cohn, J. F., & Ekman, P. (2005). Measuring facial actions. In *The New Handbook of Methods in Nonverbal Behavior Research* (pp. 9–64). Oxford, UK: Oxford University Press.

Cohn, J. F., & Schmidt, K. L. (2004). The timing of facial motion in posed and spontaneous smiles. *International Journal of Wavelets, Multresolution, and Information Processing, 2*(2), 121–132. doi:10.1142/S021969130400041X

Cosker, D., Krumhuber, E., & Hilton, A. (2011). A FACS valid 3D dynamic action unit database with applications to 3D dynamic morphable facial modeling. In *Proceedings of the IEEE International Conference on Computer Vision*, (pp. 2296–2303). IEEE.

Darwin, C. (1872). *The Expression of the Emotions in Man and Animals*. John Murray. doi:10.1037/10001-000

de la Torre, F., Campoy, J., Ambadar, Z., & Cohn, J. F. (2007). Temporal segmentation of facial behavior. In *Proceedings of the IEEE International Conference on Computer Vision*, (pp. 1–8). IEEE.

Donato, G., Bartlett, M. S., Hager, J. C., Ekman, P., & Sejnowski, T. J. (1999). Classifying facial actions. *IEEE Transactions on Pattern Analysis and Machine Intelligence, 21*(10), 974–989. doi:10.1109/34.799905 PMID:21188284

Douglas-Cowie, E., Cowie, R., Cox, C., Amier, N., & Heylen, D. (2008). The sensitive artificial listener: an induction technique for generating emotionally coloured conversation. In *Proceedings of the LREC Workshop on Corpora for Research on Emotion and Affect*. LREC.

Ekman, P. (2003). Darwin, deception, and facial expression. *Annals of the New York Academy of Sciences, 1000*, 205–221. doi:10.1196/annals.1280.010 PMID:14766633

Ekman, P., Friesen, W., & Hager, J.C. (2002). *Facial action coding system*. A Human Face.

Ekman, P., & Friesen, W. V. (1978). *Facial Action Coding System: A technique for the measurement of facial movement*. Consulting Psychologists Press.

Ekman, P., & Rosenberg, L. E. (2005). *What the face reveals: Basic and applied studies of spontaneous expression using the Facial Action Coding System*. Oxford University Press. doi:10.1093/acprof:oso/9780195179644.001.0001

Frank, M. G., & Ekman, P. (1997). The ability to detect deceit generalizes across different types of high-stakes lies. *Journal of Personality and Social Psychology, 72*(6), 1429–1439. doi:10.1037/0022-3514.72.6.1429 PMID:9177024

Hamm, J., Kohler, C. G., Gur, R. C., & Verma, R. (2011). Automated facial action coding system for dynamic analysis of facial expressions in neuropsychiatric disorders. *Journal of Neuroscience Methods, 200*(2), 237–256. doi:10.1016/j.jneumeth.2011.06.023 PMID:21741407

Heller, M., & Haynal, V. (1994). Les visages de la depression de suicide. Kahiers Psychiatriques Genevois (Medecine et Hygiene Editors), 16, 107–117.

Jeni, L. A., Girard, J. M., Cohn, J. F., & de la Torre, F. (2013). Continuous au intensity estimation using localized, sparse facial feature space. In *Proceedings of the IEEE International Conference on Automatic Face and Gesture Recognition*. IEEE.

Jiang, B., Martinez, B., Valstar, M. F., & Pantic, M. (2013). *Automatic Analysis of Facial Actions: A Survey*. Unpublished.

Jiang, B., Valstar, M. F., Martinez, B., & Pantic, M. (2013). *Dynamic appearance descriptor approach to facial actions temporal modelling.* IEEE Transactions of Systems, Man and Cybernetics – Part B.

Jiang, B., Valstar, M. F., & Pantic, M. (2011). Action unit detection using sparse appearance descriptors in space-time video volumes. In *Proceedings of the IEEE International Conf. on Automatic Face and Gesture Recognition*, (pp. 314–321). IEEE.

Kaltwang, S., Rudovic, O., & Pantic, M. (2012). Continuous pain intensity estimation from facial expressions. In *Proceedings of the International Symposium on Visual Computing*, (pp. 368–377). Academic Press.

Kanade, T., Cohn, J. F., & Tian, Y. (2000). Comprehensive database for facial expression analysis. In *Proceedings of the IEEE International Conference on Automatic Face and Gesture Recognition*, (pp. 46–53). IEEE.

Koelstra, S., Pantic, M., & Patras, I. (2010). A dynamic texture based approach to recognition of facial actions and their temporal models. *IEEE Transactions on Pattern Analysis and Machine Intelligence*, *32*(11), 1940–1954. doi:10.1109/TPAMI.2010.50 PMID:20847386

Lien, J. J., Kanade, T., Cohn, J. F., & Li, C. (2000). Detection, tracking, and classification of action units in facial expression. *Robotics and Autonomous Systems*, *31*, 131–146. doi:10.1016/S0921-8890(99)00103-7

Lucey, P., Cohn, J. F., Kanade, T., Saragih, J., & Ambadar, Z. (2010). The extended cohn-kanade dataset (CK+), A complete dataset for action unit and emotion-specified expression. In *Proceedings of the IEEE Conference on Computer Vision and Pattern Recognition*, (pp. 94– 101). IEEE.

Lucey, P., Cohn, J. F., Prkachin, K. M., Solomon, P. E., & Matthews, I. (2011). Painful data: The UNBC-McMaster shoulder pain expression archive database. In *Proceedings of the IEEE International Conference on Automatic Face and Gesture Recognition*, (pp. 57–64). IEEE.

Mahoor, M. H., Zhou, M., Veon, K. L., Mavadati, M., & Cohn, J. F. (2011). Facial action unit recognition with sparse representation. In *Proceedings of the IEEE International Conference on Automatic Face and Gesture Recognition*, (pp. 336– 342). IEEE.

Mavadati, S. M., Mahoor, M. H., Bartlett, K., & Trinh, P. (2012). Automatic detection of non-posed facial action units. In *Proceedings of the International Conference on Image Processing*, (pp. 1817–1820). Academic Press.

McDuff, D., el Kaliouby, R., Senechal, T., Amr, M., Cohn, J. F., & Picard, R. (2013). Affectiva-MIT facial expression dataset (am-fed), Naturalistic and spontaneous facial expressions collected in-the-wild. In *Proceedings of the IEEE conference on Computer Vision and Pattern Recognition*, (pp. 881–888). IEEE.

McKeown, G., Valstar, M. F., Cowie, R., Pantic, M., & Schröder, M. (2012). The SEMAINE database: Annotated multimodal records of emotionally colored conversations between a person and a limited agent. *IEEE Transactions on Affective Computing*, *3*, 5–17. doi:10.1109/T-AFFC.2011.20

Pan, S. J., & Yang, Q. (2010). A Survey on Transfer Learning. *IEEE Transactions on Knowledge and Data Engineering*, *22*(10), 1345–1359. doi:10.1109/TKDE.2009.191

Pantic, M. (2009). Machine analysis of facial behaviour: Naturalistic and dynamic behaviour. *Philosophical Transactions of The Royal Society B: Biological sciences*, *365*(1535), 3505–3513.

Pantic, M., & Bartlett, M. S. (2007). Machine Analysis of Facial Expressions. In *Face Recognition* (pp. 377–416). I-Tech Education and Publishing. doi:10.5772/4847

Pantic, M., Nijholt, A., Pentland, A., & Huang, T. S. (2008). Human-centred intelligent human-computer interaction (hci2), how far are we from attaining it? *International Journal of Autonomous and Adaptive Communications Systems*, *1*(2), 168–187. doi:10.1504/IJAACS.2008.019799

Pantic, M., & Patras, I. (2006). Dynamics of facial expression: Recognition of facial actions and their temporal segments from face profile image sequences. *IEEE Trans. Systems, Man and Cybernetics. Part B*, *36*, 433–449.

Pantic, M., Valstar, M. F., Rademaker, R., & Maat, L. (2005). Web-based database for facial expression analysis. In *Proceedings on the International Conference on Multimedia & Expo*, (pp. 317–321). Academic Press.

Reale, M., Zhang, X., & Yin, L. (2013). Nebula feature: a space-time feature for posed and spontaneous 4D facial behavior analysis. In *Proceedings of the IEEE International Conference on Automatic Face and Gesture Recognition*. IEEE.

Rudovic, O., Pavlovic, V., & Pantic, M. (2012). Kernel conditional ordinal random fields for temporal segmentation of facial action units. In *Proceedings of the European Conference on Computer Vision*. Academic Press.

Sandbach, G., Zafeiriou, S., & Pantic, M. (2012a). Local normal binary patterns for 3D facial action unit detection. In *Proceedings of the IEEE International Conference on Image Processing*, (pp. 1813–1816). IEEE.

Sandbach, G., Zafeiriou, S., & Pantic, M. (2012b). Binary Pattern Analysis for 3D Facial Action Unit Detection. In *Proceedings of the British Machine Vision Conference*. Academic Press.

Savran, A., Alyuz, N., Dibeklioglu, H., Celiktutan, O., Gokberk, B., Sankur, B., & Akarun, L. (2008). Bosphorus database for 3D face analysis. In *Proceedings of the COST workshop on Biometrics and Identity Management*, (pp. 47–56). COST.

Savran, A., Sankur, B., & Bilge, M. T. (2012a). Comparative evaluation of 3D versus 2D modality for automatic detection of facial action units. *Pattern Recognition*, *45*(2), 767–782. doi:10.1016/j.patcog.2011.07.022

Savran, A., Sankur, B., & Bilge, M. T. (2012b). Regression-based intensity estimation of facial Action Units. *Image and Vision Computing*, *30*(10), 774–784. doi:10.1016/j.imavis.2011.11.008

Simon, T., Nguyen, M. H., de la Torre, F., & Cohn, J. F. (2010). Action unit detection with segment-based SVMs. In *Proceedings of the IEEE Conference on Computer Vision and Pattern Recognition*, (pp. 2737–2744). IEEE.

Smith, R. S., & Windeatt, T. (2011). Facial action unit recognition using filtered local binary pattern features with bootstrapped and weighted ECOC classifiers. *Ensembles in Machine Learning Applications*, *373*, 1–20. doi:10.1007/978-3-642-22910-7_1

Stratou, G., Ghosh, A., Debevec, P., & Morency, L.-P. (2011). Effect of illumination on automatic expression recognition: A novel 3D relightable facial database. In *Proceedings of IEEE International Conference on Automatic Face and Gesture Recognition*, (pp. 611–618). IEEE.

Tax, M. J., Hendriks, E., Valstar, M. F., & Pantic, M. (2010). The detection of concept frames using clustering multi-instance learning. In *Proceedings of the International Conference on Pattern Recognition*, (pp. 2917–2920). Academic Press.

Tian, Y., Kanade, T., & Cohn, J. (2001). Recognizing action units for facial expression analysis. *IEEE Transactions on Pattern Analysis and Machine Intelligence*, *23*(2), 97–115. doi:10.1109/34.908962

Tong, Y., Chen, J., & Ji, Q. (2010). A unified probabilistic framework for spontaneous facial action modeling and understanding. *IEEE Transactions on Pattern Analysis and Machine Intelligence, 32*(2), 258–273. doi:10.1109/TPAMI.2008.293 PMID:20075457

Tong, Y., Liao, W., & Ji, Q. (2007). Facial action unit recognition by exploiting their dynamic and semantic relationships. *IEEE Transactions on Pattern Analysis and Machine Intelligence, 29*(10), 1683–1699. doi:10.1109/TPAMI.2007.1094 PMID:17699916

Tsalakanidou, F., & Malassiotis, S. (2009). Robust facial action recognition from real-time 3D streams. In *Proceedings of the IEEE conference on Computer Vision and Pattern Recognition,* (pp. 4–11). IEEE.

Tsochantaridis, I., Joachims, T., Hofmann, T., & Altun, Y. (2005). Large margin methods for structured and interdependent output variables. *Journal of Machine Learning Research, 6,* 1453–1484.

Valstar, M. F., Jiang, B., Mehu, M., Pantic, M., & Scherer, K. (2011). The first facial expression recognition and analysis challenge. In *Proceedings of the IEEE International Conference on Automatic Face and Gesture Recognition.* IEEE.

Valstar, M. F., Mehu, M., Jiang, B., Pantic, M., & Scherer, K. (2012). Meta-analyis of the first facial expression recognition challenge. *IEEE Transactions in Systems, Man and Cybernetics. Part B, 42*(4), 966–979.

Valstar, M. F., & Pantic, M. (2010). Induced disgust, happiness and surprise: an addition to the MMI facial expression database. In *Proceedings of the International Conference on Language Resources and Evaluation,* (pp. 65–70). Academic Press.

Valstar, M. F., & Pantic, M. (2012). Fully automatic recognition of the temporal phases of facial actions. *IEEE Transactions on Systems, Man and Cybernetics. Part B, 1*(99), 28–43.

Valstar, M. F., Patras, I., & Pantic, M. (2005). Facial action unit detection using probabilistic actively learned support vector machines on tracked facial point data. In *Proceedings of the IEEE Conference on Computer Vision and Pattern Recognition,* (pp. 76–84). IEEE.

van der Maaten, L., & Hendriks, E. (2012). Action unit classification using active appearance models and *conditional random fields. Cognitive Processing, 13,* 507–518. doi:10.1007/s10339-011-0419-7 PMID:21989609

Whitehill, J., & Omlin, C. W. (2006). Haar features for FACS AU recognition. In *proceedings of the IEEE International Conference on Automatic Face and Gesture Recognition.* IEEE.

Yin, L., Chen, X., Sun, Y., Worm, T., & Reale, M. (2008). A high-resolution 3D dynamic facial expression database. In *Proceedings of the International Conference on Automatic Face and Gesture Recognition,* (pp. 1–6). Academic Press.

Yin, L., Wei, X., Sun, Y., Wang, J., & Rosato, M. (2006). A 3D facial expression database for facial behavior research. In *Proceedings of the IEEE International Conference on Automatic Face and Gesture Recognition,* (pp. 211–216). IEEE.

Zeng, Z., Pantic, M., Roisman, G. I., & Huang, T. S. (2009). A survey of affect recognition methods: audio, visual, and spontaneous expressions. *IEEE Transactions on Pattern Analysis and Machine Intelligence, 31*(1), 39–58. doi:10.1109/TPAMI.2008.52 PMID:19029545

Zhang, X., Yin, L., Cohn, J. F., Canavan, S., Reale, M., Horowitz, A., & Liu, P. (2013). A high resolution spontaneous 3D dynamic facial expression database. In *Proceedings of the IEEE International conference on Automatic Face and Gesture Recognition*, (pp. 22-26). IEEE.

Zhao, G. Y., & Pietikainen, M. (2007). Dynamic texture recognition using local binary pattern with an application to facial expressions. *IEEE Transactions on Pattern Analysis and Machine Intelligence*, 2(6), 915–928. doi:10.1109/TPA-MI.2007.1110

Zhao, X., Dellandrea, E., Chen, L., & Samaras, D. (2010). AU recognition on 3D faces based on an extended statistical facial feature model. In *Proceedings of the International Conference on Biometrics: Theory Applications and Systems*, (pp. 1–6). Academic Press.

Zhou, F., de la Torre, F., & Cohn, J. F. (2010). Unsupervised discovery of facial events. In *Proceedings of the IEEE Conference on Computer Vision and Pattern Recognition*. IEEE.

Zhu, Y., De la Torre, F., Cohn, J. F., & Zhang, Y. (2011). Dynamic cascades with bidirectional bootstrapping for action unit detection in spontaneous facial behavior. *IEEE Transactions Affective Computing*, 2(2), 79–91. doi:10.1109/T-AFFC.2011.10

KEY TERMS AND DEFINITIONS

2D Face Analysis: Analysis of any aspect of the face from 2-dimensional images, including facial expressions, facial point localisation, demographics estimation, and beauty estimation. Used here in terms of *automatic* analysis of faces from 2-Dimensional images, in particular RGB or monochrome images.

3D Face Analysis: As for 2D Face Analysis, but using depth information instead of 2-dimensional RGB or monochrome images.

Affective Computing: The very broadly defined area of computing that relates to, arises from, or deliberately influences emotion or other affective phenomena. Defined by Rosalind Picard in her book 'Affective Computing' (MIT Press, 1997).

AU (Action Unit): Facial muscle action, used as the atomic unit of a facial expression in FACS. While they are directly related to facial muscles, there is no one-to-one mapping from facial muscles to Action Units. In particular, there are about fifteen muscles located in the face that are primarily involved in the generation of facial expressions. Some AUs involve more than one muscle, and most facial muscles are involved in the activation of multiple AUs.

Automatic Facial Expression Analysis: The use of machines to automatically detect the presence and type of facial expressions, and possibly determine finer-grained aspects of facial expressions such as their intensity, symmetry, or temporal activation pattern.

Automatic Human Behaviour Understanding: Machine interpretation of the meaning underlying the expressive behaviour displayed by humans. Note that expressive behaviour relates to traditional behaviour expressed by the face, body, and voice, and excludes other aspects of more general human behaviour e.g. in the topics of social network analysis, shopping behaviour analysis from loyalty card data etc.

Emotion Recognition: Inference of someone's affective state, used here to mean inference by a machine. Emotions can be described using a number of emotion theories, such as the six basic emotions, Fontaine's Valence-Arousal-Dominance model, or Plutchik's emotion wheel.

FACS (Facial Action Coding System): Extensive and comprehensive manual for human coding of facial expressions in terms of 32 facial muscle actions (Action Units, AUs) and a number of miscellaneous face actions called Action Descriptors (ADs). Originally developed by the psychologists Ekman and Friesen in 1978 based on a system developed by Carl-Herman Hjortsjö. Significantly revised in 2002 by Hager. The revised edition reduced the number of AUs from 45 to 32.

RGBD Face Analysis: As for 2D and 3D Face Analysis, but combining the two modalities for increased performance and mutual disambiguation.

Social Signal Processing: That area of Automatic Human Behaviour Understanding pertaining to interaction between two or more people. In addition, this includes the generation of expressive behaviour.

Chapter 9
Local vs. Global:
Intelligent Local Face Recognition

Daniel Riccio
University of Naples Federico II, Italy

Andrea Casanova
University of Cagliari, Italy

Gianni Fenu
University of Cagliari, Italy

ABSTRACT

Face recognition in real world applications is a very difficult task because of image misalignments, pose and illumination variations, or occlusions. Many researchers in this field have investigated both face representation and classification techniques able to deal with these drawbacks. However, none of them is free from limitations. Early proposed algorithms were generally holistic, in the sense they consider the face object as a whole. Recently, challenging benchmarks demonstrated that they are not adequate to be applied in unconstrained environments, despite of their good performances in more controlled conditions. Therefore, the researchers' attention is now turning on local features that have been demonstrated to be more robust to a large set of non-monotonic distortions. Nevertheless, though local operators partially overcome some drawbacks, they are still opening new questions (e.g., Which criteria should be used to select the most representative features?). This is the reason why, among all the others, hybrid approaches are showing a high potential in terms of recognition accuracy when applied in uncontrolled settings, as they integrate complementary information from both local and global features. This chapter explores local, global, and hybrid approaches.

DOI: 10.4018/978-1-4666-5966-7.ch009

INTRODUCTION

Face recognition represents a very hot research topic and is gaining an increasing attention from both academics and commercial companies due to its potential applications in surveillance, law enforcement, and human-computer interaction. Face authentication systems are very accurate and quite easy to implement under controlled conditions, and literature provides a very wide set of techniques, which are very effective especially with cooperative users. However, recognition performances dramatically drop down when those methods operate in more unrestricted conditions, because of disrupting factors like pose, illumination and expression (PIE) changes, low image resolution, or the presence of structural components like beards, mustaches and glasses. This is principally due to the fact that earlier approaches presented in literature were holistic or global methods, in that they considered the face image as a whole.

Since the presentation of the Principal Component Analysis (PCA) by Turk and Pentland in 1991, holistic approaches have been extensively investigated over the last two decades. PCA finds the principal components of the original face image space and provides an optimal transformation for face representation. PCA based authentication systems project the original face image in a lower dimensional feature space by retaining only coefficients associated with the largest eigenvalues. On the other hand, local distortions such as illumination changes or occlusions on the face image heavily influence the resulting feature vector, causing a significant drop in accuracy that can be ascribed to the fact that the transformation found by the PCA is optimal for representing patterns, but not for recognizing them (Belhumeur *et al.*, 1997), (Duda *et al.*, 2001). Pattern classification requires discriminative features, which is the main motivation for Linear Discriminant Analysis (LDA) (Etemad & Chellappa,1997; Martinez & Kak, 2001) generally outperforming

principal component analysis. LDA minimizes the within-class variance, while maximizing the between-class variance of a given set of images by means of a linear transformation. Both PCA and LDA produce global feature vectors with almost all non-zero coefficients and are very sensitive to local changes on a face image, since each pixel within the image influences almost all dimensions of the subspace projection. On the contrary, the independent component analysis (ICA) (Bartlett *et al.*, 2002) generates spatially localized features, as the vectors it produces are statistically independent. Barlett *et al.* (2002) also shown a different way of applying ICA to a set of face images in order to uniformly spread data samples in the new subspace. In this case, feature vectors exploit fine details to distribute samples in the subspace. PCA, LDA and ICA are all techniques devoted to extract relevant information in a face image as efficiently as possible. Extracted features usually undergo a classification process whose goal is to assign a new face sample submitted to the system to its corresponding class, with different classes representing identities that have been previously enrolled. A different group of approaches involves techniques borrowed from artificial intelligence. Artificial Neural Networks (ANN) (Latha *et al.*, 2009), are largely used for classifying face features because of their ability to learn from training data. Back-propagation neural networks (BPNN) (AL-Allaf *et al.*, 2013) model the way a human being recognizes faces, with the aim of implementing a recognition system that incorporates artificial intelligence. Actually, the work by AL-Allaf *et al.* (2013) is a typical example of the way in which PCA based feature extraction can be combined with BPNN feature classification. Support Vector Machines (SVM) (Vapnik, 1998) have been also largely used in face classification when dealing with local distortions like the occlusions (Hongjun & Martinez, 2009). SVM are a non-probabilistic binary linear classifier and represent a powerful technique for two-class pattern recognition problems. Given a set of training samples, the basic

SVM learns a model from data that assigns new samples into one category or the other with the aim of maximizing the margin between vectors of class 1 and class 2. The authors in (Heisele *et al.*, 2001) investigate on the performances of SVMs when they are applied either on the whole face image or on single face components by concluding that component based classification can significantly outperform the holistic one when dealing with uncontrolled conditions.

While most of the proposed pattern recognition techniques works on two-dimensional images, the face is a 3D object after all. A single view of a 3D real face is strongly influenced by the acquisition conditions (illumination and view angle), thus showing a very high variability in its appearance that causes a dramatic degradation in recognition performances. This led many researchers to focus the attention on techniques that were local rather than global. Component based approaches try to increase the robustness with respect to local distortions by dividing the face into regions of interest and working independently on each part. The most salient aspects of such methods are represented by the face partitioning and the fusion strategy they adopt to collect features or scores produced by each face component. In (Heisele *et al.*, 2003) the authors find that component based approaches can outperform the holistic ones of up to 60% in terms of recognition rate. In their paper, Heisele *et al.* (2003) compare a component-based approach with two global methods with respect to their robustness to pose changes. In all the proposed systems SVM is used as classifier for the feature vectors: in the former case, such vectors are extracted from each component and then combined together, while in the latter case they are built from the gray values of the whole image. The two investigated global methods differ in the way they deal with pose change, as the first one trains a single SVM for each person into the system, while the second one builds a view-specific SVM for each pose. In Zou *et al.* (2007) the authors show that component based methods are more appropriate for machine face authentication than the holistic approaches even when high resolution images are available, by obtaining a recognition rate almost 28% higher than the upper bound provided in FERET experiments. Even if component based approaches significantly improve the recognition accuracy, they are not completely insensitive to face local distortions like PIE and partial occlusions. Performances of both global and component based approaches heavily depend on the alignment and normalization of face images. As an alternative, invariant local features are able to overcome these limitations since they are extracted at precise fiducial points that still remain stable even in presence of local face distortions. Local feature based approaches have been early investigated in visual tasks like texture analysis, because textures are mostly characterized by local features like coarseness, directionality, regularity and roughness. Most local methods that were designed for pattern classification in texture classification pay great attention to the image resolution by implementing a multi-resolution analysis; this makes them particularly suitable for face recognition in surveillance applications, where the low resolution problem degrades the recognition accuracy dramatically. In wider terms, local matching is very robust to a wide set of face distortions like illumination, low resolution, partial occlusions and provides satisfactory results not only for texture analysis (Ullman *et al.*, 2002), but also for face recognition (Ahonen *et al.*, 2004;Zhang *et al.*, 2005). The idea underlying local matching consists in extracting local facial features and comparing local statistics to classify faces. The accuracy of such classification process obviously depends on which distributed features are used for statistical face recognition.

LOCAL APPROACHES FOR FACE RECOGNITION

As discussed in the introduction, face descriptors are generally divided into two main classes, *global* (or *holistic*) and *local,* depending on if they consider the face as a whole object or as a union of regions of interest (Figure 1). Early studies in face recognition had the aim of demonstrating the feasibility of face based recognition systems for granting secure physical access to restricted areas, almost always assuming that the user takes a frontal pose to be recognized. Most proposed approaches were therefore holistic methods that were initially devised for face recognition in controlled conditions. Recently, many commercial entities foreseen the high potential of face recognition in a wider scenario, and shown high interest in integrating face analysis technologies in their commercial products (smart-phone applications, video surveillance, video indexing and retrieval). However, holistic methods are not well suited for real world applications as they encounter serious problems when dealing with local distortions that face images commonly undergoes in unconstrained settings. This can be considered as the real motivation underlying the great interest that local matching arouse in recent years. Local features are largely robust to local distortions like illumination, pose and occlusions, allowing local matching techniques to reach high recognition accuracy even on face images acquired in unconstrained settings. Most local descriptors work on facial regions independently by extracting features from separate regions of interest (ROIs) and gathering them together to form a global face descriptor. Local Binary Pattern (LBP) (Ahonen & Pietikainen, 2006), Gabor features or Local Directional Patterns (LDA) are just some few examples of this category of descriptors. Even if more effective than holistic methods, also local descriptors suffer in presence of non-monotonic illumination variation, age progression and random noise. Indeed, Adini *et al.* (1997) demonstrate that local features are not able by themselves to overcome face illumination variation, that was the reason why the authors in Belhumeur *et al.* (1997) also introduce a technique for modeling these variations. The main goal of this chapter is to provide a quick overview of local intelligent face recognition approaches that have been proposed in literature by grouping them in four main classes, namely appearance based methods, local derivative patterns, local features in transformed domain and Scale Invariant Feature Transform (SIFT) based approaches.

Figure 1. A graphical representation of how different methods process the face image[1] in order to extract salient features: a) holistic methods, b) component based approaches, and c) local operators

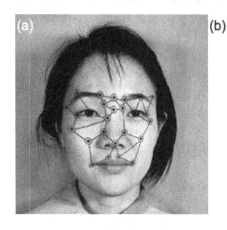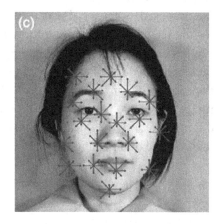

LOCAL APPEARANCE-BASED METHODS

Appearance Based Methods

The appearance based methods are among the most popular approaches that have been used for feature extraction in face recognition. PCA (Turk & Pentland, 1991) and LDA (Belhumeur *et al.*, 1997) are just two examples (Figure 2). Generally LDA outperforms the PCA, as it finds a transformation that is optimal for classification rather than for representation, contrarily to the one provided by PCA.

In 1994 Pentland *et al.* presented one of the first attempts to make appearance model local by presenting a modular eigenspace description technique which did combine salient features extracted from the eyes, nose and mouth in an eigenfeature layer (Pentland *et al.*, 1994). The distance from the feature space is used to detect and code facial features such as eyes, nose and mouth (eigenfeatures). This approach can be thought as an augmented representation of the face, that merges coarse features computed on the whole face with details extracted from independent regions of interest. It comes out from this study that when only eigenfeatures are used to classify faces, the recognition rate still remains comparable with that provided by the global eigenfaces. As one can expect the combination of both eigenfaces and eigenfeatures also produces a slight improvement of the recognition accuracy. Gottumukkal and Asari (2003) further extend this model by considering not only specific face components like eyes, nose and mouth, but dividing the whole face image in *N* generic regular square regions. In the modular PCA a different eigenspace is built for each set of regions. Since PCA weight vectors are computed independently for each of these regions, only those ones corresponding to part of the face image that are affected by illumination distortions or partial occlusions will produce a mismatch with those obtained from a good face sample. Regions that are unaffected by local distortions still closely match with those of the same subject when acquired in normal conditions. The modular PCA outperforms standard PCA in all the proposed experiments, while achieving the best results when N is set to 16 with images of resolution 256×384 pixels.

Fratric and Ribaric (2011) also divide the face image in several overlapping regions, but using LDA to locate and extract optimal discriminant features. A binary feature vector is obtained by retaining only the sign of local features while discarding the magnitude, as high-level measurements are considered more suitable for image reconstruction than for image recognition. Know-

Figure 2. The output of appearance methods for a face image: a) the original image, b) one of its eigenfaces (PCA), c) one of its fisherfaces (LDA)

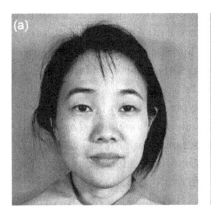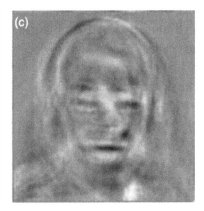

ing that pattern recognition relies on polarity of contrast rather on its absolute value, it is observed that binary feature vectors save enough information to still provide high accuracy in face recognition. On the other hand, binary vectors show a simple structure allowing more efficient ways to compute vector distances. The authors found that overlapping regions provide better results than non overlapping ones in terms of accuracy, while due to the binarization process Local Binary LDA (LBLDA) needs more components than LDA to obtain a better generalization.

The idea of partitioning a face image in small sub-regions is also drawn on by Tahir *et al.* (2011), but Local Phase Quantization histograms (LPQH) (Ahonen *et al.*, 2008) are used in place of discriminant features. LPQH based methods extract a pattern histogram for each face region in order to represent local texture, while a further extension of this concept consists in calculating histograms at different scales, thus obtaining a sort of Multiscale Local Phase Quantization Histogram (MLPQH). Feature classification is then performed by applying Local Linear Regression (LLR) in place of the common LDA. As for LDA, even LLR performances would degrade when face images are affected by illumination changes, since LLR represents a face image as a linear combination of learned class models. Applying LLR on MLPQ histograms allows this method to still retain high performances when local changes occur on face images, as MLPQH features are insensitive to most of these local distortions. The multi-scale histogram descriptor adopted by Tahir *et al.* is also robust to image misalignment between probe and gallery images and provides an improvement of about 50% over the baseline linear regression classifier. De Marsico *et al.* (2010) propose to perform image matching by a localized version of the spatial correlation index. Such index has been adapted to work locally, over single sub-regions r_A and r_B of fixed size in images A and B. For each sub-region r_A identified by the position of its left-upper corner they search, moving in a

limited window around the same position in B, the region r_B which maximizes the correlation $s(r_A, r_B)$. The global correlation S(A,B) is obtained as the sum of the local maxima. In order to improve the accuracy of the method, images undergo a pre-processing step aimed to correct face pose and illumination.

Local Derivative Patterns

Local Binary Pattern (LBP) is among the most commonly used feature extraction techniques in texture analysis and it has been introduced for face recognition in (Ahonen *et al.*, 2004). LBP operator shows two important advantages, namely, it is invariant to monotonic changes in gray pixel values and it is very efficient to compute. Even if face, as a 3D object, can produce non-monotonic transformations of pixels gray level when acquired in 2D, LBP has been largely investigated with great success, since the face image is generally decomposed in a wide set of non overlapping small regions, whose micro-patterns still are well described by this operator. In its basic definition, LBP is a point operator that considers 3×3 square neighborhood for each pixel. The center pixel is used as a threshold the surrounding gray values are compared to, setting the corresponding position to 1 for values greater than the central pixel and 0 otherwise (Figure 3). Doing so, a 8 bit binary label is obtained for each pixel (ranging between 0 and 255), while the histogram of all labels into a given region of interest constitutes the feature vector for that region. After the basic definition has been introduced in Ahonen *et al.* (2004), many variations have been proposed to improve both efficiency and effectiveness of this operator. In Ojala *et al.* (2002), the authors consider different sizes of the pixel neighborhood in order to define a multi-scale LBP operator. The authors generalize the scale and rotation invariant operator in order to detect uniform patterns for any spatial resolution and angular orientation by combining multiple operators in a multi-scale LBP. An LBP

Figure 3. The output of local binary pattern for a face image: a) the original image, b) the corresponding cropped face image, c) the output of LBP

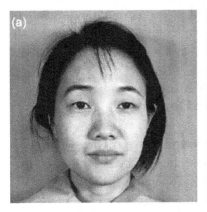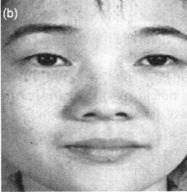

label is considered as a *uniform pattern* only if the number of bitwise changes 0/1 is lower than a fixed threshold. In particular they partitioned the original set of 256 labels in 59 classes, of which the first 58 represent the so called *uniform patterns* and the last one contains all the remaining *non-uniform patterns*. Multi-Scale Block LBP (MB-LBP) further improves the basic LBP operator by considering the average value of a block as a threshold instead of the center pixel (Liao *et al.*, 2007). MB-LBP still can be computed in a efficient manner, by exploiting integral images to compute sub-image means, with the main advantage of encoding both macrostructures and microstructures of image patterns.

Many variations of LBP have been proposed in literature to deal with requirements imposed by specific application contexts (Meena & Suruliandi, 2011). In its basic formulation, LBP only considers uniform patterns that cannot capture high curvature edges, corners or crossing boundaries. Dominant LBP (Liao *et al.*, 2009) does consider those patterns that most frequently occur in a texture. It shows a higher robustness with respect to image noise and is able to capture image textural information in a more effective manner. Multivariate LBP (MLBP) takes into account that natural images are generally multi band (Red, Green and Blue) and is largely used both in image segmentation and

classification (Lucieer *et al.*, 2005). This operator considers neighborhood relations of the central pixel within one band (Red, Green or Blue) and between all bands. Computational efficiency and robustness to illumination changes are the points of strength of the Center Symmetric LBP (CS-LBP) (Heikkila *et al.*, 2009). In CS-LBP, the absolute difference of opposite pixels with respect to the neighborhood center are compared with a fixed threshold t in order to compute bits of the label. Thus LBP and gradient information both contribute to extract salient features, but still maintaining the computational cost very low. Cavalcanti *et al.* (2012) also exploit LBP to make local features robust to illumination changes. However, they apply LBP on gradient faces instead of providing a new variant of the local operator. A gradient face is an image transformation, which is independent on the amount of light incident on each pixel, so resulting in a face representation that is almost invariant to illumination distortions.

Despite its effectiveness in capturing representative local features, LBP suffers from high computational load, since it builds the final feature vector as a concatenation of histograms computed on image sub-regions. This motivates researchers to also investigate on potential solutions to effectively overcome this drawback. Compactness of the resulting feature vector represents the main goal of the LBP Variance (LBPV) operator (Guo *et al.*, 2010), which is mainly used to characterize local contrast information. In this version, each label is proportional to the quantized variance of that label within the current sub-region. The LBPV retains global spatial information while also exploiting local texture information. In Priya and Rajesh (2011), the authors describe a min-max criterion to further reduce the classes of uniform binary patterns from 59 to 36. Doing so, they are able to produce smaller histograms for each sub-region, thus even shortening the final length of the global feature vector.

LBP is a non directional local feature that is computed by means of the first order derivative in images. It is possible to generalize this idea by considering higher order derivatives to capture relationships in a local neighborhood in more detail. As an example, the second order derivative is able to code turning points in a given direction of gray values within the neighborhood. Local Derivative Patterns (LDP) as presented in Zhang *et al.* (2010) can be considered as a generalized form of LBP, as they are able to better describe spatial relationships that characterize local regions. There are studies in literature (Meena & Suruliandi, 2011;Suruliandi *et al.*, 2012), which compare LDP and LBP showing that the former can achieve superior performances than the latter. The idea of integrating directional information into local features produced by derivative operators is further extended by Local Directional Patterns (Jabid *et al.*, 2012), which computes the edge response along all eight directions around the image pixel and generates a binary label according to the relative magnitude value. Features produced by LDP provide a consistent representation even in presence of a significant amount of random noise or non-monotonic illumination changes. In Kabir *et al.* (2012), the authors introduce the LDP variance (LDPv), which further extends the basic local operator by weighting each LDP by its corresponding variance. LDPv is exploited to characterize both contrast and texture information

of local sub-regions at the same time. Generally, LDPv shown better recognition performances than appearance-based methods, even on low resolution images where extracting geometric features can turn in a difficult task.

Local Features in Transformed Domains

Feature extraction is the procedure aimed to generate a representative face descriptor by exploiting either local operators like LBP and LDP, or signal processing methods such as Discrete Cosine Transform (DCT) (Ahmad *et al.*, 1974), Gabor Wavelets (Jones & Palmer, 1987) or Phase Quantization (Rahtu *et al.*, 2012). First attempts to face recognition heavily relied on geometrical features (mouth position, chin shape or nose length), which are dramatically sensitive to changes in head pose and face expression. Researchers turned their attention to more complex signal processing techniques that were able to overcome these limitations by selecting representative features in a transformed domain.

DCT has been deeply investigated in face recognition both in holistic and local approaches. In its simplest formulation (Ekenel & Stiefelhagen, 2005), DCT is applied to all image blocks and the first coefficient is discarded as it represents the average of the gray values. The remaining coefficients are then fused together either at feature level or at decision level. In the first case coefficients of all blocks are concatenated and then passed to the classifier, while in the second fusion scheme, blocks are first classified individually and then responses are fused at decision level. A similar approach is described in Pan and Bolouri (1999), and Scott (2003), where DCT coefficients are directly inputted to a multi-layer perceptron neural network. In some other cases a classifier different from neural network is used like Gaussian Mixture Models in Sanderson and Paliwal (2003), or Hidden Markov Models in Nefian (1999). In Chadha *et al.* (2011), local and global feature are combined together in order to compute the final decision. Global features are computed by applying the DCT to the whole image, while local ones are represented by DCT coefficient of face objects (eyes, nose and mouth). Local and global features are classified independently by a ranking procedure on Euclidean distances computed between test and enrolled faces. Fusion is performed according to an AND policy between responses provided by local and global classification modules.

Given its tolerance to translation, rotation and scaling, 2D Gabor filters also have been studied for local face analysis (Wiskott *et al.*, 1997) (Figure 4). Gabor wavelets show a high selectivity with respect to both spatial frequencies and orientations, thanks to three main parameters, namely, the spatial location, the spatial frequency and the orientation of the kernel. Features produced by Gabor filters generally present a very high dimensionality, thus motivating researchers to spend also a great effort to find optimal strategies to only select best characterizing features, while discarding those one being redundant or meaningless. In (Sang *et al.*, 2007), the Gabor Fisher is made local by applying the Local Feature Analysis (Penev & Atick, 1996), on coefficients produced by Gabor filters. The output of the LFA can be thought as a reconstruction of the original input based on

sphered PCA coefficients, i.e., normalized to have their variance equal to 1. Thus, given an input ensemble, the LFA defines a set of local kernels that optimally match their second-order statistics.

In Zhang *et al.* (2005), the LBP operator is combined with Gabor filters to obtain an LGBP local method. The face image is processed by the LGBP operator in order to obtain local histograms that are concatenated in a single global feature vector. Even if LGBP is robust to partial occlusions, this aspect is not dealt with explicitly. Thus this method is further extended in Zhang *et al.* (2007), where the Kullback–Leibler Divergence is used to take into account the probability of a given region to be occluded, that is used as a weight for the final feature matching process. In Gabor features magnitude and phase carry complementary information; this suggests to fuse them to obtain an enriched feature vector. Chan et al. (2013), observe that accuracy reached by the phase is not quite comparable with that provided by the magnitude, since the former is more sensitive to face misalignment than the latter. The authors encode the phase information with local Gabor XOR patterns and use a block-based Fisher linear discriminant to reduce the dimensionality of the feature vector. Phase quantization has been demonstrated to be robust to uncontrolled illumination and blur (Chan *et al.*, 2013). A multiscale

Figure 4. The output of Gabor filters for a face image: a) the original image, b) the corresponding cropped face image, c) the output of the Gabor filter with 3 scales and 3 orientations

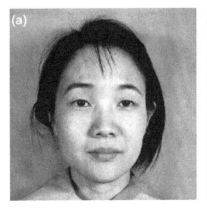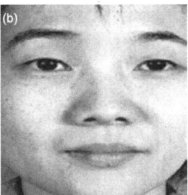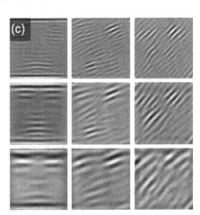

framework is designed to extend LPQ in order to get higher effectiveness. The Multiscale LPQ is computed locally according to a component based schema with the aim of reducing its sensitiveness to misalignments. On the other hand, robustness to illumination variations is obtained by combining MLPQ representation with the MLBP descriptor trough kernel fusion, while the dimensionality of the resulting feature vector is reduced by applying Kernel Discriminant Analysis.

Scale Invariant Feature Transform and Its Variants

Scale Invariant Feature Transform (SIFT) has been proposed by Lowe in Lowe (2004), and is attracting more and more attention from researchers because of many properties making them particularly suitable for matching objects or parts of them. SIFT are invariant to scale and rotation, in addition to being relatively robust to illumination variations and changes in the point of view. The first step performed by SIFT is the detection of a set of points of interest, namely *keypoints*. A local descriptor (generally a gradient based descriptor) is then applied in correspondence of each keypoint in order to extract representative features. Image classification is performed by matching independently all keypoints of the test image with those

of the target image and accounting for the number of hits that are found (Figure 5).

Implementing SIFT for face recognition according to its basic definition can lead to poor recognition accuracy, despite of its robustness and effectiveness in more general object detection and recognition tasks. Indeed, since SIFT is based on a Laplacian local operator, it is too sensitive to noise, which can generate a large amount of meaningless keypoints. With the aim of reducing the number of keypoints by only preserving the useful ones, a pruning criterion is applied to remove low contrast and edge keypoints. Unfortunately, facial keypoints are often located on pixels with very high edge response, thus they are removed even if being quite meaningful for the matching process. The detection of keypoints is also influenced by illumination distortions as the keypoint detector is not completely invariant to changes in illumination. As a consequence, most contributions about SIFT-based face recognition in literature address the two main aspects of keypoint pruning and illumination invariant keypoint detection.

In Majumdar and Ward (2009), SIFT features are ranked according to their discriminative power and only the most discriminating ones are used. Doing so, keypoints that are irrelevant for face recognition are dropped by reducing the computational complexity of about four times,

Figure 5. A graphical example of how the local SIFT works: a) the original image, b) the keypoints detected on two different images of the same subject, c) the matching procedures

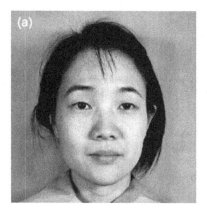
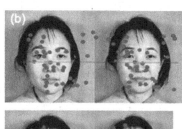
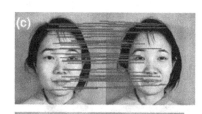
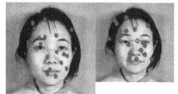

while even increasing the recognition accuracy of 1% on average. Lanzarini *et al.* (2010), propose a keypoint pruning technique based on a binary version of Particle Sworm Optimization (PSO) (Khanesar *et al.*, 2007). Indeed, the original PSO was defined for a space of continuous values, that is not applicable for discrete keypoints produced by the SIFT. In this binary version the position of each particle is defined by a 0/1 value, while the particle speed is represented by the probability of changing its status from 0 to 1 and vice-versa. The improvement in accuracy of such pruning technique over the basic SIFT approach is of about 22%. As already noticed, although SIFT descriptors are partially invariants to illumination changes as they are based on gradient information, the keypoint detector is heavily affected by local illumination variations. Križaj *et al.* (2010) addressed this problem by computing SIFT descriptors at fixed points that are located on a regular grid. In Nowruzi *et al.* (2012) features are extracted under varying illumination conditions and a comprehensive keypoint description file is built to make the method robust to light changes.

CRITICAL ASPECTS AND OPEN QUESTIONS FOR LOCAL APPROACHES

The use of local information partially overcomes some of the typical drawbacks in face recognition (illumination, pose, occlusions), but also opens new questions in turn. Among the critical aspects of local methods, feature selection is the most noteworthy one, as different subjects might have different salient features. Feature selection is of paramount importance as local approaches often generate a feature space with very high dimensionality, which greatly affects the computational complexity of the matching process. Most proposed methods rely on local operators, whose output is generally inputted to a feature selection module or to a dimensionality reduction technique. The

way face patterns are represented heavily affects recognition performance, too. Indeed, holistic and local methods generally provide complementary information suggesting that gathering together features produced by both of them should further improve the recognition accuracy. There are many papers in literature supporting this point of view. Tistarelli et al. (2009), address both feature selection and fusion problems in the SIFT feature space. They divide the face image in small patches and cluster features they produce in order to discard those clusters that are too close in feature space, as they will represent misleading features. The computation and matching of SIFT features is performed independently on face regions as well as on the whole face and then results are fused together at score level by the Dempster-Shafer belief theory. Although most attempts for fusing local and global features deal with SIFTs, there are also some different approaches that integrate features in transformed domains like (Su *et al.*, 2009), which involve both Fourier Transform and Gabor Wavelets. The former is applied to extract a global description of the whole face image by only saving low-frequency coefficients, while the latter is exploited to obtain local features. The Fisher's linear discriminant classifiers are applied to both feature spaces separately and then combined together to form a hierarchical ensemble classifier.

Local Features Selection vs. Fusion

Unlike the Human Visual System, present face recognition algorithms are little adaptable to both local and global distortions. Specific studies (Sinha *et al.*, 2006) pointed out that human perception is less affected by light, pose or expression changes occurring on faces than automatic recognition methods, thank to cognitive processes that rapidly select and fuse salient features. This convinced many research groups in face recognition that robust schemes to prune a large set of original face features and/or to fuse information outputted by different local operators represent a keystone.

However, features extracted from a face image generally differ in structure, dimensionality and saliency, making fusion at the feature level a very complex task. Moreover, important efforts have also been devoted to design rules to combine global and local features . This section provides a short discussion about three cornerstones in this field: i) feature selection, ii) feature combination, iii) boosting, iv) region selection.

The most of present works, which address the feature selection process in face recognition, are devoted to extrapolate a small set of salient information that is inputted to a classifier. Their main goal is the ability of achieving a recognition accuracy, which is comparable to that obtained on the whole set of features, yet with a significantly lower computational cost. In Liang *et al.* (2011) the feature selection problem is treated as a combinatorial approximation problem, where a large penalty term is introduced to characterize the sparsity in the computation of the minimum squared error. In its new formulation, the feature selection problem is then solved by means of either a greedy approach or a convex relaxation method, and its effectiveness has been tested on a large set of Gabor features. The work by Imtiaz and Fattah (2012) also considers 2D wavelet coefficients as features, but it adopts a histogram-based threshold heuristic to retain only the coefficients, whose magnitude is above the threshold (dominant coefficients). This approach shows the desirable property of gathering samples belonging to the same class, while increasing the between-class separability, even if different mother wavelets are used. Almost all works exploiting Gabor coefficients as face features make two main assumptions: i) there is no dependence among feature dimensions (independence), ii) the placement of Gabor kernel over the face is steered by the fact it is applied on a face shape (saliency). In Gökberk *et al (n.d)* the problem of extracting an optimal Gabor basis is casted to a feature selection problem, by relaxing both these assumptions. The author introduce a genetic algorithm to sample the original dense set

of features according to location, frequency and orientation. The dimension of the final subset of features is regulated by introducing a penalty term into the fitness function.

Multi-feature approaches can also be conceived as a special kid of ensemble learning methods, in which salient face regions are considered as features themselves and undergo a pruning process before feature extraction. In this case the feature selection process regards the extraction of a salient set of rectangular regions from the whole set of patches extracted by a face image. There are still few works about this topic and they mainly differ in the criteria they adopt to extrapolate salient patches. In Geng *et al.* (2006) a specific classifier is trained for each region on a given training set of face images; salient regions are then selected according to the responses of the same classifiers on a second set of face images considered as probe. The authors in Imtiaz and Fattah (2012) observed that variations in entropy are strongly correlated with variations in face geometry. They divide the face image in horizontal bands and exploit an entropy based criterion to select the most discriminant regions.

In the last decade, many papers have been proposed to demonstrate that fusion at feature level significantly improves the performance of face recognition systems. On the other hand, recent works on sparse coding provided researchers with a powerful mathematical framework to drop down the computational burden of face recognition methods implementing the information fusion at the feature level. Notwithstanding this, there still remain some open questions: i) noise and redundant information can compromise the recognition performance, ii) the jointly-encoding process still implies a high computational cost, iii) the semantic relationships among features are not taken into account. In Randive and Gonde (2012) the phase of Gabor coefficients is computed by applying a local Gabor XOR pattern operator (LGXP). The phase information is then fused with the coefficient magnitude by means of a block-based Fisher's linear discriminant (BFLD). LDA is also at the base of the method presented in (Tao and Yang, 2012). The face is divided in 4×4 patches according to a predefined grid and for each of them local mean and local texture features are computed. The LDA operator is reformulated as a least square problem and the face classification is performed by solving a multiple optimization problem for combining least square solutions. In Kong *et al.* (2013) the authors extend the supervised dictionary learning (DL) framework to discard noisy information and to include semantic relationships connecting different features. In particular, K dictionaries are computed for all features and represented by means of tensor algebra (Kolda & Bader, 2009; Wang & Kong, 2012), so that the relationships between these dictionaries are used to both improve recognition performance and reduce the computational burden of the system. Boosting classifiers trained on different kinds of local features also seem to represent a promising research line (Zhang *et al.*, 2004; Shen *et al.*, 2004). Indeed, the recognition operation is split into several sub-problems, which are solved separately by exploiting a cascade structure. The cascade framework shows the double advantage of reducing the complexity of the training process and significantly speeding up the testing phase. However, it has the flaw of learning more features than a non cascade structure even for easy problems, resulting in a slower convergence. Some attempts have also been done to merge local and global features. For example, in Wei *et al.* (2010) DCT and 2D Gabor wavelets coefficients are inputted to ICA to only extract independent features to be fused together. The resulting independent features then undergo a classification process performed by a support vector machine (SVM).

CONCLUSION

Face analysis and particularly face recognition is a quite active research area and the number of contributions in this field is even more increasing due to several critical aspects that represent still open questions. Despite the huge number of papers in literature which propose quite different approaches, none of them is able to guarantee recognition performances being comparable with those of the Human Visual System, especially in unconstrained applications. Many of dominant face recognition approaches such as Eigenfaces, Fischerfaces, Neural Networks suffer from local distortions induced on face images by changes in pose, illumination or occlusions. Recent studies propose local features to address non monotonic and local changes. Face region is divided into several regions of interest, from which representative features are extracted by applying a local operator. Features are combined together to form a global vector that usually undergoes a dimensionality reduction process before classification. This chapter has discussed some of the most used local operators like Local Binary Patterns, Gabor Features and SIFT. To select representative features is a critical task in reducing the dimension of the feature vector and is explicitly addressed in many papers. Although being more robust than global descriptors, also local descriptors are not fully invariant to non-monotonic variations. Since holistic and local methods generally provide complementary information, the actual trend is to fuse together features produced by both of them in order to further improve the recognition accuracy.

REFERENCES

Adini, Y., Moses, Y., & Ullman, S. (1997). Face recognition: The problem of compensating for changes in illumination direction. *IEEE Transactions on Pattern Analysis and Machine Intelligence, 19*(7), 721–732. doi:10.1109/34.598229

Ahmad, M., Natarajan, T., & Rao, K. R. (1974). Discrete Cosine Transform. *IEEE Transactions on Computers, 23*(1), 90–94. doi:10.1109/T-C.1974.223784

Ahonen, T., Hadid, A., & Pietikainen, M. (2004). Face recognition with local binary patterns. In *Proceedings of European Conference on Computer Vision*, (pp. 469–481). Academic Press.

Ahonen, T., & Pietikainen, M. (2006). Face Description with Local Binary Patterns: Application to Face Recognition. *IEEE Transactions on Pattern Analysis and Machine Intelligence, 28*(12), 2037–2041. doi:10.1109/TPAMI.2006.244 PMID:17108377

Ahonen, T., Rahtu, E., Ojansivu, V., & Heikkila, J. (2008). Recognition of blurred faces using local phase quantization. In *Proceedings of 19th International Conference on Pattern Recognition*. Academic Press.

Al-Allaf, O. N. A., Tamimi, A. A., & Alia, M. A. (2013). Face Recognition System Based on Different Artificial Neural Networks Models and Training Algorithms. *International Journal of Advanced Computer Science and Applications, 4*(6), 40–47.

Bartlett, M. S., Movellan, J. R., & Sejnowski, T. J. (2002). Face recognition by independent component analysis. *IEEE Transactions on Neural Networks, 13*(6), 1450–1464. doi:10.1109/TNN.2002.804287 PMID:18244540

Belhumeur, P. N., Hespanha, J. P., & Kriegman, D. J. (1997). Eigenfaces vs. Fisherfaces: Recognition using class specific linear projection. *IEEE Transactions on Pattern Analysis and Machine Intelligence, 19*(7), 711–720. doi:10.1109/34.598228

Cavalcanti, G. D. C., Ren, T. I., & Reis, J. R. (2012). Recognition of Partially Occluded Face Using Gradientface and Local Binary Patterns. In *Proceedings of IEEE International Conference on Systems, Man, and Cybernetics*, (pp. 2324-2329). IEEE.

Chadha, A. R., Vaidya, P. P., & Roja, M. M. (2011). Face Recognition Using Discrete Cosine Transform for Global and Local Features. In *Proceedings of International Conference on Recent Advancements in Electrical, Electronics and Control Engineering*, (pp. 502-505). Academic Press.

Chan, C. H., Tahir, M. A., Kittler, J., & Pietikäinen, M. (2013). Multiscale Local Phase Quantization for Robust Component-Based Face Recognition Using Kernel Fusion of Multiple Descriptors. *IEEE Transactions on Pattern Analysis and Machine Intelligence, 35*(5), 1164–1167. doi:10.1109/TPAMI.2012.199 PMID:23520257

De Marsico, M., Nappi, M., & Riccio, D. (2010). Face: face analysis for Commercial Entities. In *Proceedings of IEEE International Conference on Image Processing* (ICIP), (pp. 1597-1600). ICIP.

Duda, R. O., Hart, P. E., & Stork, D. G. (2001). *Pattern Classification* (2nd ed.). New York: Wiley.

Ekenel, H. K., & Stiefelhagen, R. (2005). Local appearance-based face recognition using discrete cosine transform. In *Proceedings of 13th European Signal Processing Conference*, (pp. 1-5). Academic Press.

Etemad, K., & Chellappa, R. (1997). Discriminant analysis for recognition of human face images. *Journal of the Optical Society of America, 14*(8), 1724–1733. doi:10.1364/JOSAA.14.001724

Fratric, I., & Ribaric, S. (2011). Local Binary LDA for Face Recognition. *Biometrics and ID Management*, 144-155.

Geng, X., & Zhi-Hua, Z. (2006). Image Region Selection and Ensemble for Face Recognition. *Journal of Computer Science and Technology*, *21*(1), 116–125. doi:10.1007/s11390-006-0116-7

Gökberk, B., İrfanoğlu, M. O., Akarun, L., & Alpaydın, E. (2007). Learning the best subset of local features for face recognition. *Pattern Recognition*, *40*(5), 1520–1532. doi:10.1016/j.patcog.2006.09.009

Gottumukkal, R., & Asari, V. K. (2003). An improved face recognition technique based on modular PCA approach. *Pattern Recognition Letters*, *25*, 429–436. doi:10.1016/j.patrec.2003.11.005

Guo, Z., Zhang, L., & Zhang, D. (2010). Rotation Invariant texture classification using LBP variance (LBPV) with global matching. *Pattern Recognition*, *43*(3), 706–719. doi:10.1016/j.patcog.2009.08.017

Heikkila, M., Pietikainen, M., & Schmid, C. (2009). Description of interest regions with Local Binary Pattern. *Pattern Recognition*, *42*(3), 425–436. doi:10.1016/j.patcog.2008.08.014

Heisele, B., Ho, P., & Poggio, T. (2001). Face recognition with support vector machines: Global versus component-based approach. In *Proceedings of International Conference on Computer Vision*. Academic Press.

Heisele, B., Ho, P., Wu, J., & Poggio, T. (2003). Face recognition: Component-based versus global approaches. *Computer Vision and Image Understanding*, *91*(1), 6–12. doi:10.1016/S1077-3142(03)00073-0

Hongjun, J., & Martinez, A. M. (2009). Support Vector Machines in face recognition with occlusions. In *Proceedings of IEEE Conference on Computer Vision and Pattern Recognition*. IEEE.

Imtiaz, H., & Fattah, S. A. (2012). A Wavelet-Domain Local Dominant Feature Selection Scheme for Face Recognition. *ISRN Machine Vision*, 1-13.

Jabid, T., Kabir, M. H., & Chae, O. (2012). Local Directional Pattern (LDP) for Face Recognition. *International Journal of Innovative Computing*, *8*(4), 2423–2437.

Jones, J. P., & Palmer, L. A. (1987). An evaluation of the two-dimensional Gabor filter model of simple receptive fields in cat striate cortex. *Journal of Neurophysiology*, *58*(6), 1233–1258. PMID:3437332

Kabir, H., Jabid, T., & Chae, O. (2012). Directional Pattern Variance (LDPv), A Robust Feature Descriptor for Facial Expression Recognition. *International Arab Journal of Information Technology*, *9*(4), 382–391.

Khanesar, M. A., Teshnehlab, M., & Shoorehdeli, M. A. (2007). A novel binary particle swarm optimization. In *Proceedings of Mediterranean Conference on Control & Automation*. Academic Press.

Kolda, T. G., & Bader, B. W. (2009). Tensor decompositions and applications. *SIAM Review*, *51*(3), 455–500. doi:10.1137/07070111X

Kong, S., Wang, X., Wang, D., & Wu, F. (2013). Multiple feature fusion for face recognition. In *Proceedings of 10th IEEE International Conference and Workshops on Automatic Face and Gesture Recognition*, (pp. 1-7). IEEE.

Križaj, J., Štruc, V., & Pavesic, N. (2010). Adaptation of SIFT features for face recognition under varying illumination. In *Proceedings of International Convention on Information and Communication Technology, Electronics and Microelectronics*, (pp. 691-694). Academic Press.

Lanzarini, L., La Battaglia, J., Maulini, J., & Hasperué, W. (2010). Face Recognition Using SIFT and Binary PSO Descriptors. In *Proceedings of International Conference on Information Technology Interfaces*, (pp. 557-562). Academic Press.

Latha, P., Ganesan, L., & Annadurai, S. (2009). Face Recognition Using Neural Networks. *International Journal on Signal Processing*, *3*(5), 153–160.

Liang, Y., Wang, L., Liao, S., & Zou, B. (2011). Feature selection via simultaneous sparse approximation for person specific face verification. In *Proceedings of 18th IEEE International Conference on Image Processing* (ICIP), (pp. 789-792). IEEE.

Liao, S., Law, M. W. K., & Chung, A. C. S. (2009). Dominant Local Binary Patterns for Texture Classification. *IEEE Transactions on Image Processing*, *18*(5), 1107–1118. doi:10.1109/TIP.2009.2015682 PMID:19342342

Liao, S., Zhu, X., Lei, Z., Zhang, L., & Li, S. Z. (2007). Learning Multi-scale Block Local Binary Patterns for Face Recognition. In *Proceedings of International Conference on Biometrics* (LNCS), (vol. 4642, pp. 828–837). Springer.

Lowe, D. G. (2004). Distinctive image features from scale-invariant keypoints. *International Journal of Computer Vision*, *60*(2), 91–110. doi:10.1023/B:VISI.0000029664.99615.94

Lucieer, A., Stein, A., & Fisher, P. (2005). Multivariate Texturebased Segmentation of Remotely Sensed Imagery for Extraction of Objects and Their Uncertainty. *International Journal of Remote Sensing*, *26*(14), 2917–2936. doi:10.1080/01431160500057723

Majumdar, A., & Ward, R. K. (2009). Discriminative SIFT Features for Face Recognition. In *Proceedings of Canadian Conference on Electrical and Computer Engineering*, (pp. 27-30). Academic Press.

Martinez, A. M., & Kak, A. C. (2001). PCA versus LDA. *IEEE Transactions on Pattern Analysis and Machine Intelligence*, *23*(2), 228–233. doi:10.1109/34.908974

Meena, K., & Suruliandi, A. (2011). Local Binary Patterns and its Variants for Face Recognition. In *Proceedings of IEEE-International Conference on Recent Trends in Information Technology*, (pp. 782-786). IEEE.

Nefian, A. (1999). *A Hidden Markov Model-based Approach for Face Detection and Recognition*. (Unpublished doctoral dissertation). Louisiana State University, Georgia Institute of Technology.

Nowruzi, F., Balafar, M. A., & Pashazadeh, S. (2012). Robust Recognition Against Illumination Variations based on SIFT. In *Proceedings of International Conference on Intelligent Robotics and Applications*, (pp. 503-511). Academic Press.

Ojala, T., Pietikäinen, M., & Mäenpää, T. (2002). Multiresolution Gray-Scale and Rotation Invariant Texture Classification with Local Binary Patterns. *IEEE Transactions on Pattern Analysis and Machine Intelligence*, *24*(7), 971–987. doi:10.1109/TPAMI.2002.1017623

Pan, Z., & Bolouri, H. (1999). *High speed face recognition based on discrete cosine transforms and neural networks. (Technical report)*. University of Hertfordshire.

Penev, P., & Atick, J. (1996). Local Feature Analysis: A General Statistical Theory for Object Representation. *Journal of Network Computation in Neural Systems*, *7*(3), 477–500. doi:10.1088/0954-898X/7/3/002

Pentland, A., Moghaddam, B., & Starner, T. (1994). View-based and modular eigenspaces for face recognition. In *Proceedings of International Conference on Computer Vision and Pattern Rectognition*, (pp. 84-91). Academic Press.

Priya, K. J., & Rajesh, R. S. (2011). A Local Min-Max Binary Pattern Based Face Recognition Using Single Sample per Class. *International Journal of Advanced Science and Technology*, *36*(1), 41–50.

Rahtu, E., Heikkilä, J., Ojansivu, V., & Ahonen, T. (2012). Local Phase Quantization for Blur-Insensitive Image Analysis. *Image and Vision Computing*, *30*(8), 501–512. doi:10.1016/j.imavis.2012.04.001

Randive, S., & Gonde, A. (2012). A Novel Approach for Face Recognition Using Fusion of Local Gabor Patterns. [IJECE]. *International Journal of Electrical and Computer Engineering*, *2*(3), 345–352.

Sanderson, C., & Paliwal, K. K. (2003). Features for robust face-based identity verification. *Journal of Signal Processing*, *83*(5), 931–940. doi:10.1016/S0165-1684(02)00497-8

Sang, N., Wu, J., & Yu, K. (2007). Local Gabor Fisher Classifier for Face Recognition. In *Proceedings of Fourth International Conference on Image and Graphics*, (pp. 620-626). Academic Press.

Scott, W. L. (2003). *Block-level Discrete Cosine Transform Coefficients for Autonomic Face Recognition*. (Unpublished doctoral dissertation). Louisiana State University.

Shen, L., Bai, L., Bardsley, D., & Wang, Y. (2005). Gabor Feature Selection for Face Recognition Using Improved AdaBoost Learning. *Advances in Biometric Person Authentication*, *3781*, 39–49. doi:10.1007/11569947_6

Sinha, P., Balas, B., Ostrovsky, Y., & Russell, R. (2006). Face Recognition by Humans: Nineteen Results All Computer Vision Researchers Should Know About. *Proceedings of the IEEE*, *94*(11), 1948–1962. doi:10.1109/JPROC.2006.884093

Su, Y., Shan, S., Chen, X., & Gao, W. (2009). Hierarchical ensemble of global and local classifiers for face recognition. *Transactions on Image Processing*, *18*(8), 1885–1896. doi:10.1109/TIP.2009.2021737 PMID:19556198

Suruliandi, A., Meena, K., & Rose, R. R. (2012). Local binary pattern and its derivatives for face recognition. *IET Computer Vision*, *6*(5), 480–488. doi:10.1049/iet-cvi.2011.0228

Tahir, M. A., Chan, C. H., Kittler, J., & Bouridane, A. (2011). Face Recognition using Multi-Scale Local Phase Quantisation and Linear Regression Classifier. In *Proceedings of IEEE International Conference on Image Processing*, (pp. 765-768). IEEE.

Tao, Y., & Yang, J. (2012). Fusion of Local Features for Face Recognition by Multiple Least Square Solutions. *Lecture Notes in Computer Science*, *7701*, 9–16. doi:10.1007/978-3-642-35136-5_2

Tistarelli, M., Lagorio, A., & Grosso, E. (2009). Face recognition by local and global analysis. In *Proceedings of International Symposium on Image and Signal Processing and Analysis*, (pp. 690-694). Academic Press.

Turk, M., & Pentland, A. (1991). Eigenfaces for recognition. *Journal of Cognitive Neuroscience*, *13*(1), 71–86. doi:10.1162/jocn.1991.3.1.71 PMID:23964806

Ullman, S., Vidal-Naquet, M., & Sali, E. (2002). Visual features of intermediate complexity and their use in classification. *Nature Neuroscience*, *5*(7), 682–687. PMID:12055634

Vapnik, V. (1998). *Statistical learning theory*. New York: John Wiley and Sons.

Wang, D., & Kong, S. (2012). Feature selection from high-order tensorial data via sparse decomposition. *Pattern Recognition Letters*, *33*(13), 1695–1702. doi:10.1016/j.patrec.2012.06.010

Wei, X., Zhou, C., & Zhang, Q. (2010). ICA-based features fusion for face recognition. *International Journal of Innovative Computing, Information, & Control*, *6*(10), 4651–4662.

Wiskott, L., Fellous, J. M., Kruger, N., & Malsburg, C. (1997). Face recognition by elastic bunch graph matching. *IEEE Transactions on Pattern Analysis and Machine Intelligence*, *19*(7), 775–779. doi:10.1109/34.598235

Zhang, B., Gao, Y., Zhao, S., & Liu, J. (2010). Local Derivative Pattern Versus Local Binary Pattern: Face Recognition With High-Order Local Pattern Descriptor. *IEEE Transactions on Image Processing*, *19*(2), 533–544. doi:10.1109/TIP.2009.2035882 PMID:19887313

Zhang, L., Li, S. Z., Qu, Z.-Y., & Huang, X. (2004). Boosting Local Feature Based Classifiers for Face Recognition. In *Proceedings of Conference on Computer Vision and Pattern Recognition Workshops*, (pp. 87-92). Academic Press.

Zhang, W., Shan, S., Chen, X., & Gao, W. (2007). Local Gabor Binary Patterns Based on Kullback–Leibler Divergence for Partially Occluded Face Recognition. *IEEE Signal Processing Letters*, *14*(11), 875–878. doi:10.1109/LSP.2007.903260

Zhang, W., Shan, S., Gao, W., Chen, X., & Zhang, H. (2005). Local Gabor binary pattern histogram sequence (LGBPHS): A novel non-statistical model for face representation and recognition. In *Proceedings of International Conference on Computer Vision*, (pp. 786–791). Academic Press.

Zou, J., Ji, Q., & Nagy, G. (2007). A Comparative Study of Local Matching Approach for Face Recognition. *IEEE Transactions on Image Processing*, *16*(10), 2617–2628. doi:10.1109/TIP.2007.904421 PMID:17926941

KEY TERMS AND DEFINITIONS

Discrete Transforms: They are mathematical transforms of signals across discrete domains, such as from discrete time to discrete frequency. Many common integral transforms used in signal processing (such as the Fourier Transform) have their discrete counterparts.

Entropy: It is a quantity that is interpreted as a measure of disorder present in any physical system. In image processing, the entropy measures the amount of uncertainty or information found in an image. The image entropy can also be though as the amount of information which must be coded for by a compression algorithm.

Feature Dimensionality Reduction: Feature extraction draws out data in a high-dimensional space, so that a very large feature vector is constructed to represent the original object. In order to reduce the dimension of the original feature space, while preserving the most of its representativeness, both linear and non-linear approaches are used. They map points in the high dimensional space onto points laying in the low dimensional one, trying to preserve their topological relationships.

Holistic Method: Pattern recognition approaches are commonly grouped into two classes, that are holistic methods and analytical approaches. Holistic techniques analyze the whole image in order to recognize a subject, while analytical approaches work on different local parts of the image.

Neural Network: It is an information processing technique, whose purpose is to simulate biological neural networks to solve pattern recognition problems. The idea underlying a neural network is to acquire information from the real world, process it and return a result in the form of an impulse.

Texture Coarseness: It is the quality of roughness or graininess and is related to the perception humans have of a texture. There are also many quantitative measures to evaluate texture coarseness, which differ in their robustness against the variation of other image features, like brightness, contrast, noise and size of the image.

Texture Regularity: It is related to the spatial relationships between intensities of pixels and the distance between repetitive units. In regular textures, each pixel shows dependencies and steady changes with respects to pixels surrounding it.

Wavelet: It is a wave-like oscillation, whose amplitude starts at zero, increases, and then decreases back to zero. It is commonly used to extract features from many different kinds of data, such as images and audio signals. A set of "complementary" wavelets is used to decompose data without gaps or overlap, thus the decomposition process is mathematically reversible.

Chapter 10
Fusion of Face Recognition Classifiers under Adverse Conditions

Norman Poh
University of Surrey, UK

Chi Ho Chan
University of Surrey, UK

Josef Kittler
University of Surrey, UK

ABSTRACT

A face acquired by recognition systems is invariably subject to environmental and sensing conditions, which may change over time. This may have a significant negative impact on the accuracy of recognition algorithms. In the past, these problems have been tackled by building in invariance to the various changes, by adaptation, and by multiple expert systems. More recently, the possibility of enhancing the pattern classification system robustness by using auxiliary information has been explored. In particular, by measuring the extent of degradation, the resulting sensory data quality information can be used to combat the effect of the degradation phenomena. This can be achieved by using the auxiliary quality information as features in the fusion stage of a multiple classifier system, which uses the discriminant function values from the first stage as inputs. Data quality can be measured directly from the sensory data. Different architectures are suggested in this chapter for decision making using quality information. Examples of these architectures are presented and their relative merits discussed. The problems and benefits associated with the use of auxiliary information in sensory data analysis are illustrated on the problem of personal identity verification used in biometrics.

DOI: 10.4018/978-1-4666-5966-7.ch010

1. INTRODUCTION

Recognising faces under adverse conditions is one of the most important challenges for practical face recognition system because unfavourable imaging conditions affect the quality of face image. In data analysis, this problem is called data drift. By drift we understand that the observe feature vectors are subject to a number of transformations which include factors affecting data acquisition as a special case. Depending on the nature of the data, these factors relate to changes in the camera characteristics (e.g. for visible, infrared, or thermal camera), the unconstrained environmental conditions (illumination, background noise, clutter, atmospheric conditions), and / or the behaviour of the imaged object during data acquisition process (e.g. pose, motion, deformation, biological evolution such as aging).

One of the possible solutions is to develop condition-invariant face descriptor for recognition, but it is impossible to be robust to all conditions. Another solution is to collect face images in all the possible conditions that may be envisaged during the system operation. This approach ensures that the image that serves as a basis for solving the classification problem remains representative in future operation. This is somewhat difficult to accomplish, as, at the outset, it is not always possible to predict all the possible types of changes in advance. An alternative solution is to apply a suitable normalisation procedure by evaluating the factor causing a data drift. Various normalization procedures proposed in the literature have been shown to be very effective in stabilizing the data(Poh, Kittler, & Bourlai, 2010).

Another effective approach to dealing with the data drift is to use multiple experts. In other words, a set of solutions to the same classification problem is used instead of the individually best solution. It is well known that, if these experts provide diverse opinions about the points to be classified, the classification accuracy of the solution is improved. It is less well known that multiple classifier systems also improve the robustness of the solution to adverse conditions.

In this chapter, we pursue this particular approach to the data drift problem. We show that the effectiveness of the multiple expert approach can be enhanced by making the use of information about the data quality. By data quality we mean an objective measure of the data departure from its nominal characteristic. As already indicated, data drift is caused by various factors which will be reflected in the properties of the sensory signals. One can view these signal changes as changes in signal quality. In the normalization approach discussed earlier we attempt to reverse the signal changes by the application of preprocessing algorithms that aim to stabilize the data to be classified. In the multiple classifier system approach the idea is to express signal changes in the form of quality measures. These quality measures can then be used as auxiliary features in the multiple classifier system fusion. As a result, the fused system decision is influenced not only by the expert opinions regarding the respective hypotheses, but also by measures of the signal quality. We formulate the problem of multiple expert decision-making which incorporates quality information. We then show that the use of this auxiliary information leads to further improvement of the system performance under data drift. This is illustrated on data relating to personal identity authentication using facial biometric.

The chapter is organized as follows. In the next section we develop a theoretical framework for the quality based fusion of multiple classifier systems. In the formulation adopted the quality information is used as additional features. Accordingly, the decision making in the fusion stage of the resulting multiple classifier system is realized in an augmented feature space. In Section 3, we demonstrate this approach on a two class problem of face verification, where the data drift is caused by illumination changes. We show that the use of multiple experts results in performance gains over the best performing expert. These gains are further enhanced by incorporating quality information in the fusion process. Conclusions are drawn in Section 4.

2. THEORETICAL FRAMEWORK

2.1 Problem Formulation

In order to facilitate the discussion, we shall first present some notation.

- $k \in [1, \cdots, K]$ is the class label (or object types), and there are K classes.
- $\mathbf{y} = \mathrm{F}(\mathbf{x})$ Is a vector output of a classifier F of K dimensions, typically estimating the posterior probabilities of all K class membership given

$$\mathbf{x}, \mathbf{y} \equiv [y_1, y_2, \cdots, y_K]^{\mathrm{T}} =$$
$$[\mathrm{P}(k=1|\mathbf{x}), \mathrm{P}(k=2|\mathbf{x}), \cdots, \mathrm{P}(k=K|\mathbf{x})]^{\mathrm{T}}$$

where "T" denotes the matrix transpose operator. The classifier will assign $\mathbf{x}$ to the class

$$k_* = \max_k \mathrm{P}(k|\mathbf{x}). \tag{1}$$

An example of classifier F giving $\mathbf{y}$ as posterior probabilities of class membership is a neural network with the *softmax* activation function at its output layer (Bishop, 1995). Although our interpretation of y is probabilistic, it is not restricted to this. Other classifier architectures, e.g., support vector machines (SVM) and classifiers outputting ratios of two competing hypotheses (e.g., discriminant functions) can also be used as F, as long as the decision rule in Equation 1 is applicable. In all cases, the score vector $\mathbf{y}$ can be seen as a measurement in the class hypothesis space.

- $\mathbf{q} \in \Re^L$ is a vector of quality measures output by L quality detectors. A quality detector is an algorithm designed to assess the quality of the signal from which pattern vector $\mathbf{x}$ originates. If the signal is an image, the measures may include, e.g., resolution, the number of bits per pixel, contrast and brightness as defined by the MPEG standards. These measurements aim directly to measure the quality of the acquired signal. More examples will be given in Section 2-E. In general, these measures will be closely linked to the classifier, F, and will have to be designed with the classifier in mind.

There are several points to note. First, in the presence of data draft affecting $\mathbf{x}$, the measurement $\mathbf{y}$ will also be affected. This will manifest in an increase in the *entropy* of $\{y_k | k = 1, \cdots, K\}$, defined as

$$entropy(\mathbf{y}) = \mathrm{E}_k[\log(y_k)],$$

where $\{y_k | k = 1, \cdots, K\}$ are elements in $\mathbf{y}$.

Second, the hypothesis space $\mathbf{y}$ does not need to reflect probabilities. For instance, one can apply the *logit* transform. or its generalized version, to each of the elements in $\mathbf{y}$. This is a one-to-one order preserving transformation. The generalized logit transform is defined as (Dass, Zhu, & Jain, 2006):

$$\hat{y}_k = \log\left(\frac{y_k - a}{b - y_k}\right) \tag{2}$$

for an output variable y_k bounded in $[a, b]$. An important advantage of this transformation is that the processed vector $\hat{\mathbf{y}}$ appears to be much more normally distributed, rather than skewed as in the probability space. This can significantly improve the design of a fusion classifier in any subsequent stage of decision making (stacked generalizer). Figure 1 shows the effect of this transformation.

In the multiple expert paradigm, one would construct multiple estimates of $\mathbf{y}$. Let i be the index of the i-th expert and let there be $i = 1, \cdots, N$ experts. We shall introduce $\mathbf{y}_i = \mathrm{F}_i(\mathbf{x})$ as the output of expert F_i (each observing the same data sample, $\mathbf{x}$). At this point, it is also convenient to define $\mathbf{Y} = [\mathbf{y}_1, \cdots, \mathbf{y}_N]^{\mathrm{T}}$ as a concatenation of the outputs of all N experts. Note that an element of $\mathbf{Y}$, Y_{ik}, indicates the output of the i-th expert for the k-th class hypothesis. In order to integrate the opinions of the respective experts, we need to design a fusion mechanism capable of handling the output of multiple experts along with the quality measures:

$$G : \mathbf{Y}, \mathbf{q} \rightarrow \mathbf{y}^{com} \qquad (3)$$

where $\mathbf{y}^{com} \in \Re^K$. G is also known as *quality-based* fusion.

The function of G estimates the posterior probability of the respective hypotheses, where the element in $\mathbf{y}^{com}$, y_k^{com}, is estimated by:

$$\mathbf{y}_k^{com} = \mathrm{P}\left(k \middle| \mathbf{Y}, \mathbf{q}\right) \qquad (4)$$

Two possible architectures for realizing G are shown in Figure 2. In the first approach (Figure 2(a)), the quality measures are used to normalize each individual expert output $\mathbf{y}_i$:

$$\mathbf{y}_i^{norm} = G_i\left(\mathbf{y}_i, \mathbf{q}\right), \forall i \qquad (5)$$

The normalized outputs are then combined using another classifier or a fixed rule (sum or product) in order to obtain $\mathbf{y}^{com}$. A typical example of the latter case is the sum fusion

$$\mathbf{y}^{com} = \sum_i \mathbf{y}_i^{norm}$$

The second approach (see Figure 2(b)) solves (3) directly. In the absence of the quality measures, both approaches reduce to the conventional fusion (i.e. without quality measures), shown in Figure 2(c). In Section 3, we will show that under changing test conditions, the quality-based fusion

Figure 1. The effect of applying the generalized logit transformation to two expert outputs

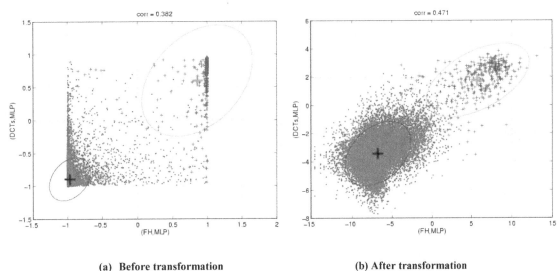

(a) **Before transformation**   (b) **After transformation**

Figure 2. (a) and (b): Two possible architectures for implementing quality-based fusion. (c): Fusion scheme without quality assessment. These three architecture types are also referred to as Architecture I, II and III, respectively.

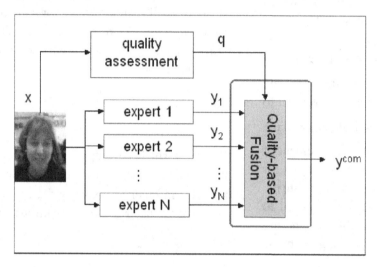

(a) Quality normalization-based fusion

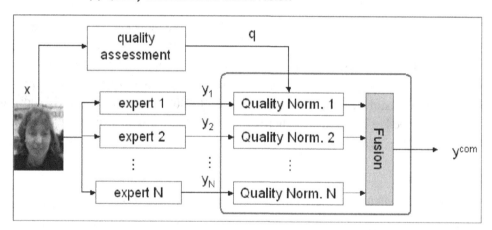

(b) Direct design of quality-based fusion

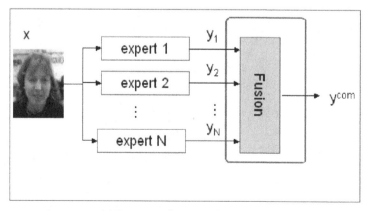

(c) Fusion without quality assessment

systematically outperforms the conventional one (J. Kittler, et al., 2007).

The first approach, combined with a fixed rule, offers an attractive modular solution in the sense that each expert output is processed individually. Effectively, the dimension of the quality augmented hypothesis space is *K+L* (the sum of length of the vectors $\mathbf{y}_i$ and $\mathbf{q}$). This is significantly smaller than that of the second approach, which is *K×N+L* (the sum of dimensions of **Y** and **q**), or that of the conventional fusion scheme (i.e., without quality measures) where the dimensionality is *K×N*.

The increased dimensionality in the second approach can be seen as a weakness because many more parameters need to be estimated at the same time. This weakness is, however, outweighed by an important advantage: the ability to handle the dependency among the system outputs. Since each expert observes the same input sample x, their outputs are necessarily dependent.

2.2 Quality-Based Fusion: A Generative Perspective

This section aims to estimate Equation 4, bearing in mind that any classifier, even those that do not output probabilities (e.g., SVM) can be used after an appropriate normalization. We shall explore two different approaches: generative and discriminative.

In order to facilitate the discussion for the generative approaches, we shall use graphical models (Bishop, 2006), also known as Bayesian networks (Jensen, 1996). A graphical model is a graph with directed arrows representing conditional probabilities. A node in the graph is a variable. An arrow from variable *A* to variable *B* specifies their causal relationship, i.e., the conditional probability of *B* given *A*, i.e., p(*B*|*A*).

Two possible graphical models for modelling the relationship between y (noting that the index for each expert *i* is not used here for simplicity) and **q** are shown in Figure 3. The first model

(Nandakumar, Chen, Dass, & Jain, 2008), as depicted in Figure 3(a), attempts to characterize the following joint density

$$p(\mathbf{y},\mathbf{q},k) = p(\mathbf{y},\mathbf{q}|k)P(k) \qquad (6)$$

whereas the second model (Figure 3(b)) achieves this slightly differently:

$$p(\mathbf{y},\mathbf{q},k) = p(\mathbf{y}|k,\mathbf{q})p(\mathbf{q}|k)P(k) \qquad (7)$$

Note that the second model involves the density of quality measures conditioned on class label *k*. However, as the signal quality is independent of the class label *k*, i.e., the quality measures cannot be used to distinguish among different classes of objects. In other words, modelling p(**q**|*k*) is unnecessary because this term is not discriminative. More importantly, an impending problem with the implementation of the second model is the need to estimate the conditional density p(**y**|*k*,**q**). Because the conditioning variable **q** is multivariate and continuous, one has to use a multivariate regression algorithm. In comparison, the first approach needs only to estimate p(**y**,**q**|*k*), a problem which is well understood (e.g., using Gaussian Mixture Model), since the conditioning variable in this case is discrete.

Although the first approach is preferable, there is an alternative. The third approach (Poh, Heusch, & Kittler, 2007), attempts to model **q** by introducing a latent discrete variable $Q \in [1,\cdots,Q]$ (see Figure 3(c)). The idea is first to classify **q** into Q discrete clusters. Then, the modelling of p(**y**|**q**,*k*) can be achieved as follows:

$$p(\mathbf{y}|\mathbf{q},k) = \sum_Q p(\mathbf{y},Q|\mathbf{q},k) = \sum_Q p(\mathbf{y}|Q,k)P(Q|\mathbf{q}) \qquad (8)$$

where P(Q|**q**) is the posterior probability of cluster *Q* given the quality measures **q**. The cluster-based

*Figure 3. Three graphical models that capture the relationship between match score y, quality measures q and the class label **k** in different ways.*

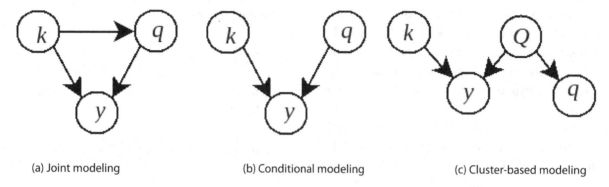

(a) Joint modeling   (b) Conditional modeling   (c) Cluster-based modeling

approach can effectively provide a simpler method of implementing the second approach.

If one uses a mixture of Gaussian (Bishop, 1995) as a clustering algorithm, modelling p(**q**) as:

$$p(\mathbf{q}) = \sum_{Q} p(\mathbf{q}|Q) P(Q), \qquad (9)$$

then the posterior probability p(Q|**q**) can be estimated via the Bayes rule:

$$P(Q|\mathbf{q}) = \frac{p(\mathbf{q}|Q) P(Q)}{p(\mathbf{q})} \qquad (10)$$

Once the density p(**y**,**q**|k) (for the first approach) or p(**y**|**q**,k) (for the second and third approach) is estimated, for the generative model, the posterior probability of class membership can be obtained by using the Bayes rule:

$$P(k|\mathbf{y},\mathbf{q}) = \frac{p(\mathbf{y},\mathbf{q}|k) P(k)}{\sum_{k'} p(\mathbf{y},\mathbf{q}|k') P(k')} \qquad (11)$$

The second and third model can be estimated similarly by replacing the term p(**y**,**q**|k) with p(**y**|**q**,k).

Extending this concept to estimating P(k|**Y**,**q**), in the context of multiple classifiers, is straightforward. Following the discussion in Section Theoretical Framework-A, one can employ the normalization-based strategy or the joint modelling strategy. For the first strategy, one can employ the sum rule, or the Naïve Bayes principle, i.e., by estimating p(**Y**, **q**|k) as $p(\mathbf{Y},\mathbf{q}|k) = \prod_{i} p(\mathbf{y}_{i},\mathbf{q}|k)$, and then applying the Bayes rule in order to obtain P(k|**Y**, **q**). For the second strategy, one simply replaces every appearance of **y** by **Y** in this section.

2.3 Quality-Based Fusion: A Discriminative Approach

As an alternative to the generative approach, one can estimate P(k|**y**,**q**) directly, i.e., without using the Bayes rule as shown by Equation 11. Two possible approaches to do so are shown by the graphical models in Figure 4.

The main difference between these models compared to those shown in Figure 3 is on how the relationship between the score variable y and the class label k is modelled. In Figure 3, the conditional score density is modelled whereas here, the posterior class probability is directly modelled.

We shall refer to the first approach, shown in Figure 4(a), as *feature-based* discriminative ap-

Figure 4. Discriminative graphical models that capture the relationship between match scores y, quality measures q and the class label k: (a) without clustering and (b) via the quality cluster Q.

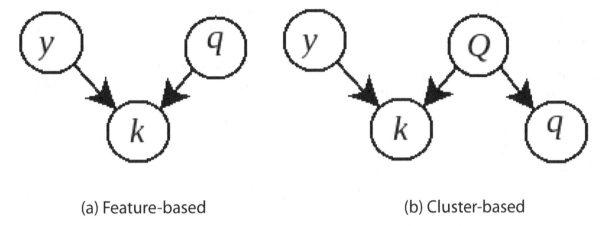

(a) Feature-based   (b) Cluster-based

proach whereas (b) as *cluster-based* discriminative approach.

The feature-based approach attempts directly to learn the relationship between **y** and **q** from the data. If the relationship of these is very complex, a non-linear classifier will be needed. The only means of controlling the complexity of the classifier is by controlling the number of parameters to be optimized.

For instance, if the posterior probability P(k|**y**,**q**) (for all K classes) is estimated using a multilayer perceptron with a softmax output layer (Bishop, 1995), than, one needs to choose the number of hidden units carefully. Alternatively, for non-probabilistic classifiers, if one uses a multi-class SVM, then, it is important to choose the correct parameterization of the kernel matrix, e.g., the width of the Gaussian kernels.

Rather than attempting to model the relationship between **y** and **q** directly, the cluster-based approach would first rely on a clustering algorithm to discover the number of clusters actually present from the training data. Ideally, the training data would be collected from an actual or trial operational data. Since no further processing is needed (apart from running an unsupervised/clustering algorithm), often the required data for this purpose are readily available in abundance.

Once the clusters are found, the cluster-based approach would then model the relationship between the expert output **y** and the quality measure **q** via the found clusters Q. This approach is therefore a divide-and-conquer solution. As will be supported by the results of our experiments, the cluster-based approach can scale to a potentially very high dimension of quality measures without suffering from the estimation problem affected by the curse of dimensionality, as would be faced by the feature-based approach.

For the cluster-based approach, the posterior probability of class k given **Y** and **q** can be modelled as follows:

$$P\left(k\middle|\mathbf{Y},\mathbf{q}\right)=\sum_{Q}P\left(k\middle\|\mathbf{Y},Q\right)P\left(Q\middle|\mathbf{q}\right) \qquad (12)$$

where the posterior probability of cluster Q, P(Q|**q**) is obtained using

$$P\left(Q\middle|\mathbf{q}\right)=\frac{p\left(\mathbf{q}\middle|Q\right)P\left(Q\right)}{p\left(\mathbf{q}\right)}$$

The sum over all the states in Q is necessary since Q is not observed. A simplification to (12) is to choose the state that maximizes P(Q|$\mathbf{q}$), say $Q_* = \arg\max_Q \mathrm{P}\left(Q\,\middle|\,\mathbf{q}\right)$, and then use the corresponding P(k|$\mathbf{Y}$,Q_*) as an approximation to P(k|$\mathbf{Y}$,$\mathbf{q}$).

2.4 Incorporation of Expert Knowledge in Clustering / Inference

In order to use the clustering solution, implemented using either a discriminative framework, i.e., Equation 12 or via a generative framework as in Equation 8, it is often helpful to guide the clustering process. In many real problems, often additional expert knowledge may be available about the data. For instance, by simply observing a data sample, it is immediately apparent that a data is of certain quality. For instance, in the face recognition problem that we will use as an illustration shortly (see Figure 5), the principal source of degradation is change in lighting. It is immediately apparent that one can assist the clustering process by first dividing the data into two groups: one under the normal operating condition (with front lighting) and the other under non-ideal condition (with strong side illumination as in our case). For our problem here, there is no further need to distinguish left or right illumination because the noise influence is symmetric. For instance, a light source of −25% or +25% of deviation in panning from an on-looking face would cause

the same amount of degradation in verification/recognition performance.

However, it is of interest to further identify *sub-clusters* of data for each of the two groups of data (normal versus non-ideal conditions) already classified by the expert. The existence of the sub-clusters is not only necessarily related to the data quality, but may also be attributed to the characteristic of the object one attempts to classify. For instance, a quality measure that calculates the brightness of an image may consistently give lower value for ethnic groups with dark skins. Therefore, ethnicity may *correlate* with the brightness quality measure.

In practice, as in any clustering problem, it is often difficult to assign a label to an automatically defined clusters or sub-clusters. However, whenever such additional expert knowledge is available, it should be fully exploited in assisting the clustering process. An advantage of "assisted clustering" is that during testing, such expert knowledge is not required. However, if it is available, it can still be used during inference (testing). In the following, we shall describe a procedure to do so.

Let us denote $C \in \left[1, \cdots, C\right]$ to be the clusters identified by the expert and there are C such clusters. In order to estimate the unconditional density of $\mathbf{q}$, one should divide the observations of quality measurements (Bishop, 1995; Cardinaux et al., 2006; Dass et al.; Gross & Brajovic, 2003;

Figure 5. Frontal and side illumination of a subject taken from the XM2VTS database

(a) Well illumination   (b) Right illumination   (c) Left illumination

Jensen, 1996; Kittler et al., 2000; Nandakumar et al., 2008; Poh et al., 2010; Reynolds, 2000) into C groups. For each group, one runs a clustering algorithm, hence obtaining the conditional density

$$\mathrm{p}\big(\mathbf{q}\big|C\big) = \sum_Q \mathrm{p}\big(\mathbf{q}\big|Q,C\big)\mathrm{P}\big(Q\big|C\big) \text{ for each } C,$$

where $\mathrm{P}(Q|C)$ is the prior probability of the sub-cluster Q conditioned on the expert-identified cluster C. The unconditioned density of $\mathbf{q}$, for all C expert-identified clusters is:

$$\mathrm{p}\big(\mathbf{q}\big) = \sum_C \mathrm{p}\big(\mathbf{q}\big|C\big)\mathrm{P}\big(C\big)$$

$$= \sum_C \sum_Q \mathrm{p}\big(\mathbf{q}\big|Q,C\big)\mathrm{P}\big(Q\big|C\big)\mathrm{P}\big(C\big) \qquad (13)$$

$$= \sum_C \sum_Q \mathrm{p}\big(\mathbf{q}\big|Q,C\big)\mathrm{P}\big(Q,C\big)$$

$$= \sum_C \sum_Q \mathrm{p}\big(\mathbf{q}\big|Q'\big)\mathrm{P}\big(Q'\big) \qquad (14)$$

where we introduced Q' as a *joint variable* of (Q,C).

When the expert knowledge is available during inference (testing), this information can be exploited. Let $C=C_*$ be the state the expert has chosen. Once can then set $\mathrm{P}(C=C_*)=1$ and then set $\mathrm{P}(C)=0$ for $C\neq C_*$. In this case, one needs to evaluate $\sum_Q \mathrm{p}\big(\mathbf{q}\big|Q,C_*\big)\mathrm{P}\big(Q\{C_*\}\big)$, giving p(q| C_*). Conversely, when the expert knowledge is not available (during inference as well as training), then one can use Equation 13 instead, which is exactly equivalent to Equation 9, Our previous study (Poh et al., 2010) shows that the availability of the expert knowledge during inference can result in statistically significantly increased in performance. Therefore, the expert knowledge for assisted clustering as well as inference should be used whenever possible.

2.5 Data Quality Assessment

The quality of sensory signal giving rise to data point **x**, respectively y is multifaceted and cannot be captured by a single quality measure. Instead, a collection of quality measures, $q_1, ..., q_p$ should be computed, as implied in the formulation given in Section 2-A. For instance, there are many measures that have been proposed to characterize image quality. These include focus, resolution, image size, uniformity of illuminations, background noise, object pose, etc. If all these measures are treated as separate features augmenting the dimensionality of the score space, then its size may grow disproportionately, potentially leading to over training problems. The likelihood of poor generalization is high, especially in view of the fact that quality measures themselves do not convey discriminatory information. This may further be aggravated by the small sample size problems plaguing some classification applications.

Second, signal quality is not an absolute concept. Suppose a classification system is designed using a set of training data acquired with a Web camera, but an operational test is conducted using images captured with a camera of much better quality. From the point of view of the classification algorithm, the better quality image will actually appear as degradation. Thus a quality assessment should be carried out in the context of a reference defined by the system design conditions. In fact the situation is even worse; as the existing approaches to quality based fusion do not take into account the properties of the classification algorithms. For instance, if one system uses an algorithm that can correct for illumination or object pose problems, then the supplied image quality information will be misleading and may affect the performance of the system adversely. On the other hand, for algorithms that cannot compensate for changes in illumination and pose the quality information is likely to be crucial. Thus signal quality assessment cannot be algorithm independent either. This raises a fundamental question how signal quality should be defined, whether it can be measured directly from the sensory data, or whether it should be derived by the classification algorithm itself using the internal knowledge about its capabilities.

3. AN ILLUSTRATION OF THE BENEFITS OF THE QUALITY BASED FUSION

3.1 Database, Systems and Quality Measures

We illustrate the benefit of quality based fusion in the presence of data drift on the problem of identity verification using face biometrics. The experiments are conducted on the XM2VTS database (Matas et al., 2000) and its degraded section (Messer et al., 2006). The problem is illustrative of data drift caused by the changing conditions of the acquisition environment and hence the quality of the data. The original database which was used for training the class models contains mugshot images with well controlled illumination. The darkened section contains images taken under strong side illumination, which is known to degrade significantly face verification performance (Messer et al., 2006). Examples of these images are shown in Figure 5. The database contains 295 subjects, which includes 200 subjects selected to be clients, 25 to be impostors for the algorithm development (training), 70 to be impostors for algorithm evaluation (testing). For each subject, the face images are acquired in four sessions; the first three are used for training the classifiers and the last one for testing. We consider the dark dataset with left illumination as the "fifth session" and the one with right illumination as the "sixth" session.

We used a set of proprietary quality measures developed by Omniperception Ltd[1] for the face image quality assessment. These measures are:

1. **Frontal quality:** The amount of deviation from the frontal face as given by the facial symmetry
2. **Rotation:** The in-plane rotation, which is zero since each image has been cropped and transformed via an affine transformation according to the eye coordinates
3. **Reflection**
4. **Illumination:** The average amount of pixel intensity of the detected face
5. **Spatial resolution:** Inter-ocular distance, i.e., the width in terms of pixel between two detected eye centers.
6. **Bit per pixel:** The resolution of pixel intensity
7. **Focus:** The sharpness of the image as a result of adjusting the camera focus
8. **Contrast:** The degree of balance between the bright area and the dark area of the image, which is also proportionate to the entropy of the pixel intensity distribution of the image
9. **Brightness:** The average intensity of the image
10. **Reliability:** The confidence of the detected face
11. **Overall quality:** The output of a trained classifier using all the above quality measures

It should be noted that none of these quality detectors were designed specifically to distinguish the three strong dominant quality states of the face images in the XM2VTS database: Using the above quality measures, instead of the ones specifically designed for this data set, makes the problem of quality-dependent fusion more challenging.

The classifiers used for the face experts in this chapter can be found in (Heusch, Rodriguez, & Marcel, 2006). There are two classifiers with three types of preprocessing, hence resulting in a matrix of six classifiers. The two classifiers used are Linear Discriminant Analysis (LDA) with correlation as a measure of similarity (Josef Kittler, Li, & Matas, 2000) and Gaussian Mixture Model

(GMM) with maximum a posteriori adaptation, described in (Reynolds, n.d.). The use of the GMM in face authentication can be found in (Cardinaux et al., 2006). The face pre-processing algorithms used include the photometric normalization as proposed by Gross and Brajovic (Gross & Brajovic, 2003), histogram equalization and local binary pattern (LBP) as reported in (Heusch et al., 2006). The feature extraction and classification algorithms are implemented using the opensource Torch Vision Library[2].

Since this is a binary classification problem (a person is either a genuine user or an impostor), logistic regression was used to approximate the posterior probabilities of class membership in all cases.

For performance evaluation, we used Equal Error Rate (EER). This error is often used in the face recognition community to handle the case of highly unbalanced class priors. EER is the performance of an operating point where the probability of falsely accepting the alternative hypothesis (often called False Acceptance Rate (FAR) or false alarm rate) is the same as the probability of falsely rejecting the hypothesis of interest (called False rejection Rate, (FRR) or miss detection rate).

3.2 Experiments

We shall perform experiments in order to illustrate three points:

1. **The impact of architectural choice:** The benefit of the direct design of quality-based fusion (i.e., joint-processing) over normalization-based fusion when the experts are correlated.

2. **The robustness of fusion to data drift:** The benefit of quality-based fusion, with or without quality assessment under normal and non-ideal conditions (with data drift).

3. **The impact of the number of quality measures on quality-based fusion:** The benefit of cluster-based approach over feature-based approach in quality-based fusion when the number of quality measures is high.

We therefore designed three experiments to illustrate each of the points above. The system configuration used for each of these experiments is shown in Table 1.

The objective of Experiment I is to compare the three architecture types shown in Figures 2 on common ground. As a result, the type of classifier, fusion algorithm and quality measures are fixed (see the first row of Table 1). A subset of quality measures are used in order to avoid the estimation problem related to large number of quality measures, as explained in Section 2.

The goal of Experiment 2 is to illustrate the effectiveness of fusion under the normal and the non-ideal conditions.

The goal of experiment 3 is to compare the merit of the feature-based and the cluster-based approach (see Figure 4).

Acronyms: LR=logistic regression, QM=quality measures, Architectures I, II and III correspond to normalization-based quality, joint processing of quality and conventional fusion (without quality measures), respectively (as shown in Figure 2). "All" in the above entry includes: feature-based quality fusion, cluster-based quality fusion, and conventional fusion without quality assessment. "Subset" above refers to the use of 2

Table 1. System configuration used in experiments

Exp	Architecture	Fusion Approach	QM	Classifier
I	I,II and III	Feature	Subset	LR
II	II	Feature	Subset	LR
III	II	All	Complete	LR

out of 11 quality measures and "complete" refers to the usage of all 11 measures.

The three fusion approaches in Table 1 are explained below:

1. **Feature-based fusion:** Logistic regression combining $\mathbf{Y}$ and $\mathbf{q}$. Since logistic regression is a linear classifier, in order to introduce non-linearity, we expanded the features via polynomial expansion [4], hence considering all pairwise products between an element in $\mathbf{Y}$ and an element in $\mathbf{q}$ in the process.

2. **Cluster-based fusion:** This is a mixture of logistic regressions as shown by (12). For this classifier, a logistic regression is constructed for each cluster of quality measures. The total number of clusters is limited to three per condition (front illumination or side illumination). Note that the clustering process is assisted since the knowledge about quality of data is used. For the purpose of discovering the clusters of quality measures, only 10% of the impostor data was used.

3. **Fusion without quality assessment:** Logistic regression combining only the expert outputs $\mathbf{Y}$, without employing the quality measures.

Prior to conducting Experiments 1 and 2, we identified two out of 11 quality measures that are likely to be useful for quality-based fusion. This is done by ranking the merit of each quality measure in distinguishing the normal condition from the non-ideal one (with data drift). The chosen quality measures are bit per pixel and brightness.

Figure 6 shows the effectiveness of the two quality measures in distinguishing between well-illuminated and side-illuminated face images. Both types of images represent the normal and drifted data, respectively. It is obvious from this figure that brightness can better distinguish between the normal and drifted conditions than bit per pixel.

1. **Experiment 1 - The Impact of Architectural Choice:** With the availability of six face experts, we performed exhaustive fusion, each time combining 2, 3, etc., experts until all 6 are used. This results in 63 combinations of fusion tasks. For each fusion task, three architecture types are implemented using logistic regression as the common classifier. The results of these fusion tasks are shown in Figure 7. Figure 7(a) plots the performance of Architecture I [Y-axis] versus that of Architecture III [X-axis]. Figure 7(b) plots the performance of Architecture II versus that of Architecture III (hence, establishing the baseline performance on the X-axis). Each point in Figures 7(a) and (b) corresponds to one of the 63 fusion tasks.

Two observations can be made. First, the performance of Architecture 1 [normalization-based fusion] is better than that of Architecture III [fusion without quality assessment] for the majority of the 63 fusion tasks. Second, the performance of Architecture 2 [joint-processing/direct design of quality-based fusion] is even better than that of Architecture 1. In fact, the average observed relative improvement of robustness to data drift by using Architecture 2, as compared to Architecture III is about 25% but up to 40% can be attained. The reason for which the quality-based normalization approach is inferior to the joint processing approach is that there is significant correlation, ranging from 0.65 to 0.92, among the six expert outputs. The correlation are readily observable in Figure 8, and is much more pronounced for the positive class, i.e., genuine user class (Figure 8(b)), than the negative one (impostor user). The data points plotted here contains both the normal and drifted data. However, the expert outputs provide absolutely no clue whatsoever to the presence/absence of data drift.

Figure 6. Distribution of the two quality measures used, as gauged by a GMM for each of the two conditions, i.e., well vs. side illumination. Black continuous (resp. red dashed) ovals are the Gaussian components of the well-illuminated (resp. side-illumined) face data. They represent data quality under normal and drifted conditions, respectively. The density in this bi-variate quality measure space is modeled using (13), i.e., with the expert knowledge of the conditions.

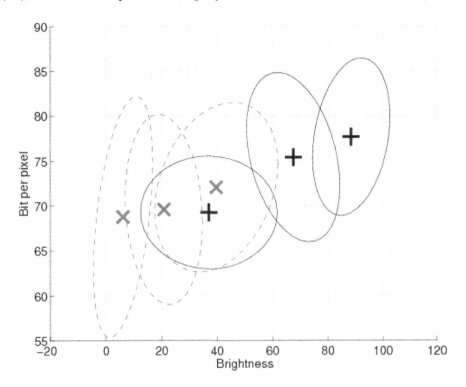

Figure 7. Comparison of (a) quality based normalization [Architecture 1] and (b) joint processing [Architecture 2] (both in the Y-axes) with respect to the baseline system without using quality [Architecture III] (in the X-axes) Each point in these figures are the EER (%) of one of the possible 63 fusion tasks. In both figures, the numbers in the legend correspond to the number of experts involved in a fusion task.

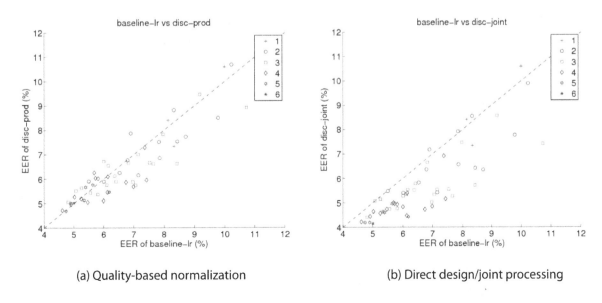

(a) Quality-based normalization   (b) Direct design/joint processing

2. **Experiment 2- The Robustness of Fusion to Data Drift:** The goal of Experiment 2 is two-fold: First, it analyzes the impact of data drift on each of the constituent experts. Second, it compares how the following three fusion approaches are robust to data drift to varying extents. It is expected that fusion approaches I and I to be better than that of 3, since quality measures are not used in the latter approach. To satisfy the first goal, we shall use the result of the cluster-based fusion approach. Six clusters were automatically found per condition (subjecting to being normal or non-ideal) based on the two selected quality measures, as depicted in Figure 6. Three of the clusters correspond to quality measures of the normal condition; and, the remaining three to the non-ideal condition (with data drift).

For each cluster Q, Figure 9 plots the marginal score distribution $p(y_i|k,Q)$ for each of the six experts, conditioned on the class label k and quality cluster Q. In this figure, the clusters are denoted as {normal C1, normal C2, normal C3, drift C1, drift C2, drift C3}. Each cluster has its corresponding two sets of scores: the positive (client) class, denoted by "+"; and the negative (impostor) class, denoted by "−."

By analyzing the scores distribution, two observations can be made. The first one is expected but not the second one. First, under drift, the scores of the positive and negative classes are more severely overlapped. This implies degradation in performance under data drift.

Second, under the normal condition, the score distribution of the cluster "normal +C1" is remarkably different from that of "normal +C2" or "normal +C3." This suggests that even under the normal operating condition, there is variation in signal quality, as gauged by the cluster "normal C1." Finding exactly the source of variation is beyond the scope of this study. Recall that the experiments have been designed to control the effect of well illumination versus side illumination. In practice, there are a myriad other number of factors which is naturally out of our control, e.g., the confidence of automatically detected face varies from one image to another, user habituation, the time-lapse between the user, gender, age, the "other-race" effect, etc.

In order to confirm the first observation above, we assessed the performance of the six experts using a Detection Error Trade-off (DET) curve for three condition types: normal, non-ideal (drift) and a mix of both conditions. The results are shown in Figure 10.

Figure 8. Pair-wise scatter plot of the six expert outputs conditioned on the two classes. Each panel in Figure (a) and (b), from left to right as well as from top to bottom, corresponds the following classifiers: lda-gross, lda-heq, lda-lbp, gmm-gross, gmm-heq and gmm-lbp.

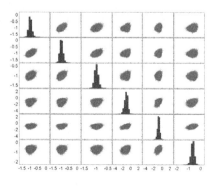

(a) Imposters

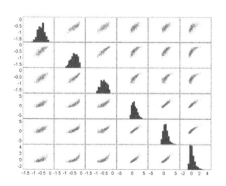

(b) Genuine users

Figure 9. Distribution of scores conditioned on each hidden component of each class (positive or negative) under normal and drifted conditions. C1, C2 and C3 indicates the values of the (latent) cluster state Q. Incidentally, in this case, there are three latent components for each class.

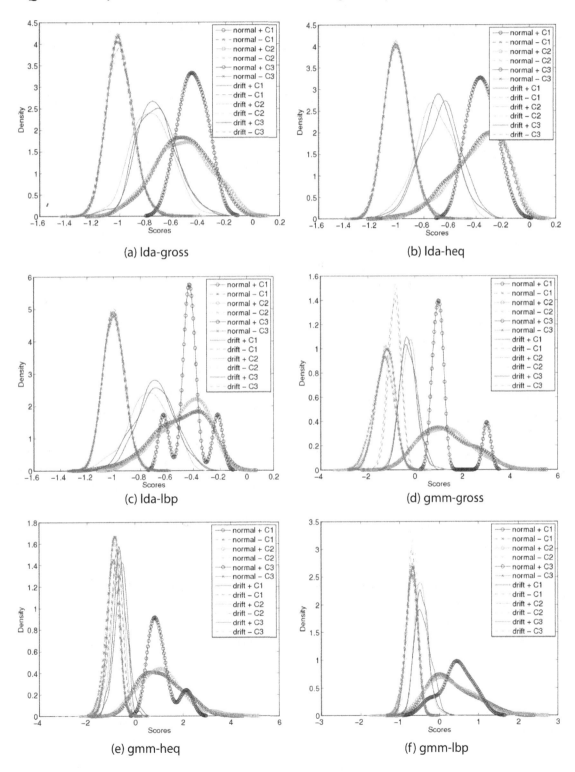

(a) lda-gross

(b) lda-heq

(c) lda-lbp

(d) gmm-gross

(e) gmm-heq

(f) gmm-lbp

Figure 10. Performance under drifting

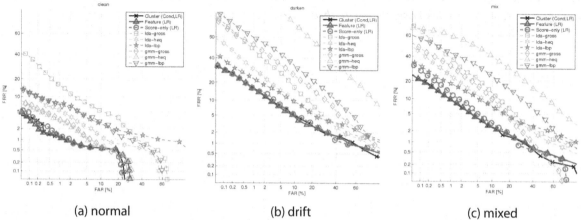

| (a) normal | (b) drift | (c) mixed |

As can be observed, under the normal condition, all experts perform well but under the non-ideal condition, all experts degrade in performance. However, the amount of degradation is not the same for all the systems.

An ordered list of the best performing systems, for both the conditions are listed in Table 2. From this table, it can be observed that while "gmm-heq" is the best system under the normal condition, it is also the worst system under the non-ideal condition. This implies that maintaining the same weight, a strategy used by the fusion without quality measures [Architecture 3] is definitely suboptimal.

In order to objectively assess the merit of quality-based fusion (i.e., the fusion approaches I and II) versus the conventional fusion without quality assessment (approach III), we again used the 63 exhaustive fusion tasks. For each fusion task, we compared the performance of the best single system and the three fusion approaches in terms of EER. In this way, we obtained 63×4 EER values per condition types; and there are three condition types, corresponding to normal, non-ideal and a mixed of the two[3].

A compact way of presenting the above experimental results is to use the *relative change*

of EER with respect to fusion approach III. It is defined as:

$$\text{rel. change of EER} = \frac{\text{EER}_{method} - \text{EER}_{III}}{\text{EER}_{III}}$$

where *method* is either fusion approach I, II or the best single expert in the pool.

Figure 11 plots the relative change of EER. Each bar contains 63 statistics, summarizing the distribution of relative change of EER at {2.5%, 25%, 50%, 75%, 97.5%} percentile. Note that a negative value of this statistic means improvement, whereas a positive value implies worse performance than approach III.

Table 2. The Ranking of the best performing system, in terms of EER, under both the normal and non-ideal conditions

Normal Condition:	Non-Ideal Condition:
1) gmm-heq	1) lda-lbp
2) gmm-gross	2) lda-heq
3) lda-heq	3) lda-gross
4) lda-lbp	4) gmm-gross
5) gmm-lbp	5) gmm-lbp
6) lda-gross	6) gmm-heq

Figure 11. Boxplots of the relative change of system performance under normal, non-ideal (with data drift) and a mixture of the two conditions. A box is bounded by the first and the third quartile of the statistics. The middle line of the box is the median value. The extents of the statistics within 95% of confidence are plotted in dashed lines. "best" denotes the statistic of the best expert in the pool; "Feature" corresponds to that of Approach I; "Cluster" corresponds to that of Approach II; and, "Score-only" corresponds to that of Approach III.

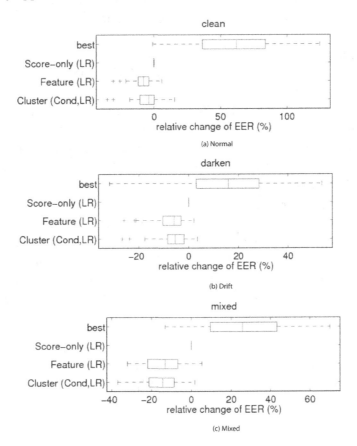

Two observations can be made from Figure 11. First, in all three condition types, all fusion approaches are better than the best expert in the pool. Second, quality-based fusion is better than fusion without quality assessment.

3. **Experiment 3:** The Impact of Large Number of Quality Measures on Fusion Approaches: In this final experiment, we shall vary the number of quality measures and compare the following two quality-based fusion: feature-based and cluster-based. The fusion without quality assessment, i.e., Approach 3, is also included in order to establish the baseline performance. This experiment configuration involves the combinatorial of $11CL$, i.e., choosing L out of 11 quality measures, and L varies from 1 to 11.

The results of this experiment are summarized in Figure 12. This figure shows that at first, the feature-based approach gets better as one increases the number of quality measures. However, this benefit is quickly diminished when the number of quality measures is increased from 7 to 8. By increasing the number of quality measures, the feature-based approach is directly affected because the number of parameters increases in the same proportion.

In comparison, the cluster-based approach exhibits certain robustness as the number of quality measures increases. In fact, as more quality measures are used, the better it performs. It is worth noting that the complexity of this fusion approach is not directly related to the number of quality measures, but the number of clusters. In this experiment, we enforced that the maximum number of clusters per condition type to be three. This illustrates two advantages of the cluster-based approach: First, one can explicitly control the classifier by controlling the number of clusters. Second, one also exploits the knowledge of the data, i.e., the annotation about the quality of the data, which is used to provide initial (supervised) clustering. The second level of clustering is unsupervised, as explained in Section 2-D. In comparison, the feature-based approach cannot exploit the prior knowledge about the data quality even if this information is available.

4. CONCLUSION

A data drift caused by changes of the environment, sensor characteristics and object representation in image acquisition can seriously degrade the accuracy of face recognition systems. We proposed a solution which is based on the protective measures against data drift offered by the paradigm of multiple classifier systems. We showed that by incorporating image quality information in the fusion stage of the multiple classifier system, considerable robustness to data drift can be achieved. A framework for quality assisted fusion of multiple experts has been developed and its

Figure 12. Comparison of feature-based and cluster-based fusion as the number of quality measures vary in term of EER. " Feature-based LR" corresponds to Approach I; "Cluster-based LR" corresponds to Approach II; and, "Score-only LR" corresponds to Approach II. All methods are based on logistic regression (hence the acronym "LR").

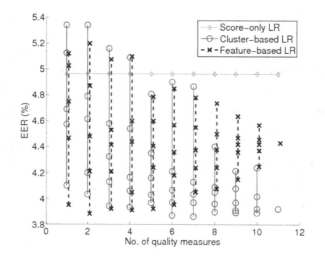

variants discussed. The proposed approach has been demonstrated on the problem of personal identity verification using facial biometrics. The improvement in handling a data drift caused by illumination changes in face image acquisition was 25% on average and could be as high as 40%.

REFERENCES

Bishop, C. M. (1995). *Neural networks for pattern recognition*. Oxford: Clarendon Press, Oxford University Press.

Bishop, C. M. (2006). *Pattern recognition and machine learning*. New York: Springer.

Cardinaux, F., Sanderson, C., & Bengio, S. (2006). User authentication via adapted statistical models of face images. *IEEE Transactions on Signal Processing*, *54*(1), 361–373. doi:10.1109/TSP.2005.861075

Dass, S. C., Zhu, Y. F., & Jain, A. K. (2006). Validating a biometric authentication system: Sample size requirements. *IEEE Transactions on Pattern Analysis and Machine Intelligence*, *28*(12), 1902–1913. doi:10.1109/TPAMI.2006.255 PMID:17108366

Gross, R., & Brajovic, V. (2003). An image preprocessing algorithm for illumination invariant face recognition. *Audio-and Video-Based Biometric Person Authentication*, *2688*, 10–18. doi:10.1007/3-540-44887-X_2

Heusch, G., Rodriguez, Y., & Marcel, S. (2006). *Local Binary Patterns as an Image Preprocessing for Face Authentication*. Paper presented at the 7th International Conference on Automatic Face and Gesture Recognition. New York, NY.

Jensen, F. V. (1996). *An introduction to Bayesian networks*. New York: Springer.

Kittler, J., Li, Y., & Matas, J. (2000). *On Matching Scores for LDA-based Face Verification*. Paper presented at the BMVC. Retrieved from http://dblp.uni-trier.de/db/conf/bmvc/bmvc2000.html#KittlerLM00

Kittler, J., Poh, N., Fatukasi, O., Messer, K., Kryszczuk, K., & Richiardi, J. etal. (2007). Quality dependent fusion of intramodal and multimodal biometric experts. *Biometric Technology for Human Identification*, *4*, 6539.

Matas, J., Hamouz, M., Jonsson, K., Kittler, J., Li, Y., Kotropoulos, C., et al. (2000). Comparison of face verification results on the XM2VTS database. In *Proceedings of 15th International Conference on Pattern Recognition*, (Vol. 4, pp. 858-863). Academic Press.

Messer, K., Kittler, J., Short, J., Heusch, G., Cardinaux, F., & Marcel, S. etal. (2006). Performance characterisation of face recognition algorithms and their sensitivity to severe illumination changes. *Advances in Bioethics*, *3832*, 1–11.

Nandakumar, K., Chen, Y., Dass, S. C., & Jain, A. K. (2008). Likelihood ratio-based biometric score fusion. *IEEE Transactions on Pattern Analysis and Machine Intelligence*, *30*(2), 342–347. doi:10.1109/TPAMI.2007.70796 PMID:18084063

Poh, N., Heusch, G., & Kittler, J. (2007). On combination of face authentication experts by a mixture of quality dependent fusion classifiers. *Multiple Classifier Systems*, *4472*, 344–356. doi:10.1007/978-3-540-72523-7_35

Poh, N., Kittler, J., & Bourlai, T. (2010). Quality-Based Score Normalization With Device Qualitative Information for Multimodal Biometric Fusion. *IEEE Transactions on Systems Man and Cybernetics Part a-Systems and Humans, 40*(3), 539-554.

Reynolds, D. A. (n.d.). *Speaker Verification Using Adapted Gaussian Mixture Models. Academic Press.*

KEY TERMS AND DEFINITIONS

Cluster-Based Fusion: A quality-based fusion strategy that treats quality measures as control variables. Quality measures are clustered so that the resultant clusters are used to determine how the classifier outputs should be combined.

Data Drift: Changes in feature vectors due to unfavourable imaging conditions and other factors causing them to differ from the normal expected ones.

Data Quality: An objective measure of the possible data departure from its nominal characteristic.

Feature-Based Fusion: A quality-based fusion strategy that treats quality measures and classifier outputs as features.

Fixed Rule Fusion: Information fusion that involves simple operators such as mean, sum, min, and max.

Latent Discrete Variables: Variables those are not observable (often used in probabilistic models).

Multiple Expert Decision-Making: An approach to decision that makes use multiple classifiers.

Quality-Based Fusion: An information fusion strategy that combines quality measures or signal quality and the outputs of several classifiers.

Quality Based Normalization: An information fusion strategy that combines quality measures with the output of a classifier. Quality based normalization is different from quality based fusion in that the former involves only one classifier whereas the latter involves more than one classifiers.

Quality Measure: Measurements that are designed to characterize (biometric) sample quality.

ENDNOTES

[1] http://www.omniperception.com

[2] Available at http://torch3vision.idiap.ch. See also a tutorial at http://www.idiap.ch/~marcel/labs/faceverif.php.

[3] Rather than just showing EER values, the complete set of DET plots of the three fusion approaches, for all the 63 fusion tasks, subjecting to the three condition types, can be found in http://personal.ee.surrey.ac.uk/Personal/Norman.Poh/data/expe/BNqj

Chapter 11
Recognizing Face Images with Disguise Variations

Neslihan Kose
EURECOM, France

Jean-Luc Dugelay
EURECOM, France

Richa Singh
IIIT – Delhi, India

Mayank Vatsa
IIIT – Delhi, India

ABSTRACT

Challenges in automatic face recognition can be classified in several categories such as illumination, image quality, expression, pose, aging, and disguise. In this chapter, the authors focus on recognizing face images with disguise variations. Even though face recognition with disguise variations is a major challenge, the research studies on this topic are limited. In this study, first disguise variations are defined followed by an overview of the existing databases used for disguise analysis. Next, the studies that are dedicated to the impact of disguise variations on existing face recognition techniques are introduced. Finally, a collection of several techniques proposed in state-of-the-art which are robust against disguise variations is provided. This study shows that disguise variations have a significant impact on face recognition; hence, more robust approaches are required to address this important challenge.

1. INTRODUCTION

Face recognition is used with diverse security contest such as surveillance, border security and forensic investigation. Face recognition is a process in which an individual is identified or verified based on facial characteristics. There have been

several researches for face recognition in the presence of pose, expression, and illumination variations (Zhao et al., 2003; Li & Jain, 2005; Wechsler, 2006; Delac & Grgic, 2007). In recent face recognition studies, the results show that under normal changes in constrained environment, the performance of existing face recognition systems

DOI: 10.4018/978-1-4666-5966-7.ch011

is greatly enhanced. However, in most real world applications, there can be several problems such as using images of low quality or non-cooperative users or temporal variations and dissimilarities in facial characteristics that are created using disguise accessories.

Challenges in face recognition can be listed as illumination, image quality, expression, pose, aging, and disguise. Among these challenges, recognition of faces with disguise is a major challenge and has been recently addressed by several researchers (Alexander & Smith, 2003;Ramanathan et al., 2004;Silva & Rosa, 2003;Singh et al., 2008). Disguise accessories can be used to alter the appearance of an individual, to impersonate another person, or to hide one's identity. In the book chapter (Singh et al., 2008), some studies on disguise variations are explained. According to this chapter, (Ramanathan et al., 2004) studied facial similarity for several variations including disguise by forming two eigenspaces from two halves of the face, one using the left half and other using the right half. From the test image, optimally illuminated half face is chosen and is projected into the eigenspace. This algorithm has been tested on the AR face database (Martinez & Benavente, 1998) and the National Geographic database (Ramanathan et al., 2004) which consists of variations in smile, glasses, and illumination. An accuracy of around 39% for best two matches is reported on the AR database. Silva and Rosa (2003) uses Eigen-eyes to handle several challenges of face recognition including disguise. Using the Yale face database (Belhumer et al., 1997), the algorithm was able to achieve an accuracy of around 87.5%. The advantage of the algorithm is that alterations in facial features excluding the eye region do not affect the accuracy. Pamudurthy et al. (2005) proposed a face recognition algorithm which uses dynamic features obtained from skin correlation and the features are matched using nearest neighbor classifier. On a database of 10 individuals, authors reported that this approach gives accurate results. Alexander and Smith (2005)

used PCA based algorithm with Mahalanobis angle as the distance metric. The results show an accuracy of 45.8% on the AR database. The limitation of these algorithms is that the performance degrades when important regions such as the eye and mouth are covered. Moreover, in Singh et al. (2008), it is stated that the AR and Yale databases do not contain many images with disguise and therefore are not ideal for validating algorithms under comprehensive disguise scenarios.

In this chapter, initially, we identify different types of disguise accessories that can be used to alter facial information. Next, we explain the specifications of several existing databases for disguise variations and show the impact of disguise variations on face recognition. Finally, we introduce techniques in state-of-the-art which are robust against disguise variations.

In Singh et al. (2008), the impact of disguise variations is evaluated on several face recognition techniques using one database. Whereas, in the present chapter, the specifications of several existing databases including disguise variations are explained. Also, the impact analysis of disguise variations are tested with more algorithms and robust techniques against disguise variations are proposed.

Experimental results suggest that the performances of existing algorithms are not sufficient enough against disguise variations. Thus, face recognition with disguise variations is still a major challenge.

2. TYPES OF DISGUISE VARIATIONS

In this study, disguise variations are grouped as minimal variations, variations in hair style, variations due to make-up, variations due to beard and moustache, variations due to facial accessories (occlusion), variations due to aging and wrinkles, variations due to plastic surgery, and variations due to multiple changes.

2.1 Minimal Variations

Two face images captured at different time instances can have minimal variations in appearance and features. In such cases, face recognition algorithms usually yield correct results.

2.2 Variations in Hair Style

Hair style can be used to alter the appearance of a face image or hide facial features (Figure 1). Although hair does not have an impact directly on face, it can alter facial appearance and features in some parts of the face. Hence, it may affect the performance of some recognition algorithms.

2.3 Variations due to make-up

Make-up has an impact on automatic face recognition as explained in Eckert et al. (2013) and Dantcheva et al. (2012). The impact of makeup on face recognition is correlated with the amount of the applied make-up on face. Figure 2 shows an example for several degrees of makeup.

2.4 Variations due to Beard and Mustache

Facial hair such as beard and moustache can alter the facial appearance and features in the lower half of the face, specifically near mouth and chin regions (Figure 3).

Figure 1. Face images with variation in hair style. Figure is taken from (Singh et al., 2008).

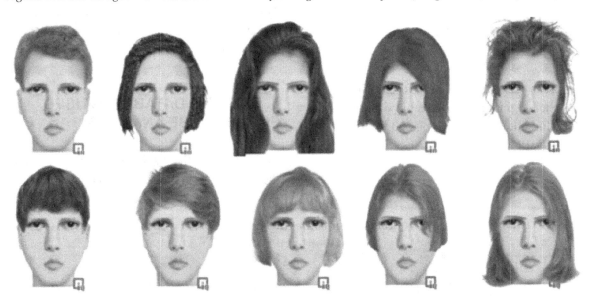

Figure 2. Reference image and makeup series images in their original form

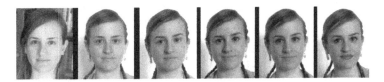

Figure 3. Ben Affleck with/without beard and moustache. Figures are taken from (Daily News, 2013).

2.5 Variations due to Facial Accessories

Min et al. (2011) shows that variations due to facial accessories (occlusions) have a significant impact on face recognition. Figure 4 shows an example of images with occlusion from the AR face database.

2.6 Variations Due to Aging and Wrinkles

Aging can be both natural and artificial. The effect of artificial aging can be obtained by using makeup tools. In both the cases, aging and wrinkles can severely affect the performance of face recogni-

tion algorithms. Figure 5 shows an example of face images with aging and wrinkle variations.

2.7 Variations Due to Plastic Surgery

The impact of plastic surgery on 2D face recognition is first analyzed in (Singh et al., 2009) using the plastic surgery database proposed in the same study. This study shows that plastic surgery has a significant impact on face recognition.

In Erdogmus et al. (2012), a 2D+3D nose alteration database is simulated using FRGC v1.0 (Figure 6) and the impact of nose alteration is evaluated on both 2D and 3D face recognition. This study shows that nose alteration has a significant impact on both 2D and 3D face recognition.

2.8 Variations Due to Multiple Changes

This group is based on the combination of several types of variations explained in this section (Figure 7).

3. EXISTING DATABASES USED FOR DISGUISE ANALYSIS

In this section, the databases which are used for the evaluations in the next sections are explained.

Figure 4. Example of images for occlusion from the AR Face Database

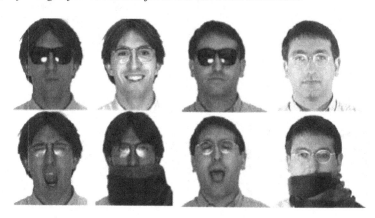

Figure 5. Example of aging and wrinkle variations. Figure is taken from (Singh et al., 2008).

Figure 6. Two examples of nose alterations with and without textures from the nose alteration simulations in (Erdogmus et al., 2012) (upper row: originals lower row: altered)

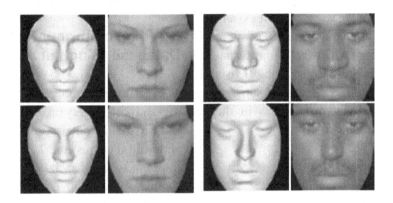

Figure 7. Face images of an individual with multiple disguise variations. Figure is taken from (Singh et al., 2008).

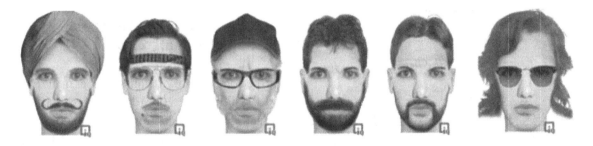

3.1 Heterogeneous Face Database and Face Disguise Database (Singh et al., 2008)

In the book chapter (Singh et al., 2008), two databases are used which are the heterogeneous face database and the face disguise database.

3.1.1 Heterogeneous Face Database

For evaluating the performance on a large database with challenging intra-class variations, images are combined from multiple face databases and a heterogeneous database of 882 subjects is created. According to Singh et al. (2008), the CMU-AMP face database contains images with large expression variations while the CMU-PIE dataset (Sim et al., 2003) contains images with variation in pose, illumination and facial expressions. The Equinox face database (Equinox: Face database, 2004) has images captured under different illumination conditions with accessories and expressions. The AR face database (Martinez & Benavente, 1998) contains face images with varying illumination and accessories, and the FERET database (Philips et al., 2000) has face images with different variations over a time interval of 3-4 years. The Faces in the Wild database (Huang et al., 2007) contains real world images of celebrities and popular individuals. It contains images of more than 1600 subjects from which 294 subjects that have at least 6 images are selected. Table 1 lists the databases used and the number of subjects selected from the individual databases in the heterogeneous face database.

3.1.2 Face Disguise Database (Singh et al., 2008)

This database contains real and synthetic face images from 125 subjects. The database contains real face images of 25 individuals with 15 - 25 different disguise variations of each individual.

Table 1. Composition of the heterogeneous face database

Face Database	Number of Subjects
CMU-AMP	13
CMU-PIE	65
Equinox	90
AR	120
FERET	300
Faces in the Wild	294
Total	882

Since the goal is to evaluate the performance of the face recognition algorithms against disguise, the database contains frontal face images with variations due to illumination, expression and pose. Figure 8 shows an example of sample disguise variations of the same image from the synthetic face database. Also, for this study, FACES software (faces software) was used to generate 4000 frontal face images of 100 subjects with a comprehensive set of variations for disguise. The complete face disguise database is used to evaluate the performance under disguise variations.

3.2 Plastic Surgery Face Database (Singh et al., 2010)

The plastic surgery face database comprises 1800 pre- and post-surgery images corresponding to 900 subjects with frontal pose, proper illumination, and neutral expression. The database consists of different types of facial plastic surgery such as rhinoplasty (nose surgery), blepharoplasty (eyelid surgery), brow lift, skin peeling, and rhytidectomy (face lift). The database contains 519 image pairs corresponding to local surgeries and 381 cases of global surgery.

3.3 Nose Alteration Database (Erdogmus et al., 2012)

In the nose alteration database, noses in the FRGC v1.0 (Philips et al., 2005) database are replaced by randomly chosen ones from different subjects. The aim is to change nasal regions in the database as realistically as possible to create nose variations for all subjects. The details of how the nose alterations are simulated are explained in (Erdogmus et al., 2012).

The original database FRGC v1.0 consists of 943 multimodal samples from 275 subjects and

Figure 8. Sample disguise variations of the same image from the synthetic face database. Figure is taken from the book chapter (Singh et al., 2008).

the simulated 3D database is of the same size. For simulated samples in 2D, the synthesized 3D models with the corresponding original texture mapped on are used. Due to some mismatches in 2D and 3D samples in the original database, 39 samples had to be removed, leaving with a database of 904 samples from 268 subjects.

The nose alteration database consists of both the original databases in 2D and 3D (DB-o2 and DB-o3), and the simulated nose alteration databases in 2D and 3D (DB-s2 and DB-s3). Two examples of nose alterations with and without textures from this database are shown in Figure 6.

3.4 Kinect Face Database (Huynh et al., 2012)

In Huynh et al. (2012), authors proposed a Kinect Face database (http://rgb-d.eurecom.fr) of images of different facial expressions in different lighting and occlusion conditions. The database consists of the multimodal facial images of 52 people (14 females, 38 males) obtained by Kinect. The data is captured in two sessions at different time periods. In each session, the dataset provides the facial images of each person in nine states of different facial expressions, lighting and occlusion conditions: neutral, smile, open mouth, left profile, right profile, occlusion eyes, occlusion mouth, occlusion paper and light on (Figure 9). All the images are provided in three sources of information: RGB color image, depth map, and 3D. The dataset comes with the manual landmarks.

3.5 IIITD In and Beyond Visible Spectrum Disguise Database (Dhamecha et al., 2013)

The IIITD In and Beyond Visible Spectrum Disguise face database contains visible and thermal spectrum images of 75 participants with disguise variations. The number of images per person varies from 6 to 10. For every subject, there is at least one frontal neutral face image and at least five frontal disguised face images. For each spectrum, there are 681 images. All the face images are captured under (almost) constant illumination with neutral expression and frontal pose. The disguise variations included in the database are categorized into the following categories: (1) without disguise: neutral image, (2) variations in hair styles: different styles and colors of wigs, (3) variations due to beard and mustache: different styles of beard and mustaches, (4) variations due to glasses: sunglasses and spectacles, (5) variations due to cap and hat: different kinds of

caps, turbans, veil (also known as hijab which covers hair), and bandanas, (6) variation due to mask: disposable doctor's mask, and (7) multiple variations: a combination of disguise accessories.

3.6 Facial Cosmetics Database (Eckert et al., 2013)

The persons in the facial cosmetics database belong mainly to the Caucasian race and are between 20 and 30 years old. The database contains frontal facial images with little expression variations. It contains one reference image and one or more progressive makeup series per person (Figure 2). The reference image does not belong to any makeup series and is taken in another setup which results in different illumination, skin and hair conditions.

To collect this database, makeup tutorial videos are used as source. Most of the videos are found on YouTube, some on Websites of facial cosmetic companies. More information about this database is available at http://fcd.eurecom.fr/.

The database contains 389 images. Among these images, 50 images are reference images and 339 images belong to makeup series. In this database, 109 of the makeup series images are classified into the makeup category 'no make-up', 147 into 'slight make-up', 54 into 'intermediate make-up', and 79 into 'heavy makeup' categories.

Figure 9. Illustration of different facial variations in the Kinect database: (a) neutral face; (b) smiling; (c) mouth open; (d) strong illumination; (e) occlusion by sunglasses; (f) occlusion by hand; (g) occlusion by paper; (h) right profile face and (i) left profile face. (Upper: the RGB images. Lower: the depth maps aligned with the above RGB images).

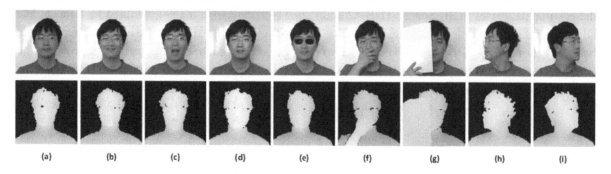

4. IMPACT ANALYSIS OF DISGUISE VARIATIONS ON FACE RECOGNITION

Different kinds of accessories and disguise variations have different effect on the performance of face recognition. This section discusses in detail the impact of individual variations on face recognition.

4.1 Impact Analysis for Several Disguise Variations (Singh et al., 2008)

In the book chapter (Singh et al., 2008), the experiments are divided into two parts. In the first part, the performance of face recognition algorithms is evaluated using the heterogeneous face database (Section 3.1) that contains variations due to pose, expression and illumination. The performance obtained with this experiment is considered as the baseline performance. The second experiment is performed using the face disguise database (Section 3.1) to evaluate the performance of face recognition algorithms in the presence of disguise variations.

For both the experiments, images are partitioned into two sets: the training set is used to train the face recognition algorithms and the test set is used to evaluate the performance of the recognition algorithms. The training set comprises of randomly selected three images of each subject and the remaining images are used as the test data for performance evaluation. This train-test partitioning is repeated 20 times (cross validation) and the Receiver Operating Characteristics (ROC) curves are generated by computing the genuine accept rates (GAR) over these trials at different false accept rates (FAR). The two experiments performed to demonstrate the impact of nose alterations on face recognition are as follows:

- **Experiment 1- Performance on the Heterogeneous Face Database:** This experiment is conducted to evaluate the effect of pose, expression, and illumination on the performance of face recognition. The first plot in Figure 10 shows the ROC plot and Table 2 illustrates the verification accuracies at 0.01% FAR.

- **Experiment 2- Performance on the Face Disguise Database:** The performance of face recognition algorithms is analyzed for each disguise category using the face disguise database. The ROC curves in the second plot in Figure 10 and Table 3 summarizes the performance of face recognition algorithms.

For evaluations, eight face recognition algorithms are selected which can be investigated in three groups as appearance based, feature based, and texture based algorithms.

1. **Appearance based algorithms:** Three appearance based algorithms are used in experiments which are: Principal Component Analysis (PCA) algorithm with Mahalanobis distance (Alexander & Smith, 2005), Half-face based algorithm (Ramanathan et al., 2004), and Eigen-eyes based algorithm (Silva & Rosa, 2003). The details of these algorithms are given in the Introduction section of this chapter.

2. **Feature based algorithms:** Two feature based algorithms are selected which are Geometrical Feature (GF) (Cox et al., 1996) and Local Feature Analysis (LFA) (Penev & Atick, 1996). GF uses mixture distances of the facial features for matching. This algorithm works on the distance between geometrical features. Facial features such as nose, mouth, eyes, and ears are extracted

Figure 10. ROC to evaluate the performance of face recognition algorithms on the (a) heterogeneous face database and (b) face disguise database. Figures are taken from (Singh et al., 2008).

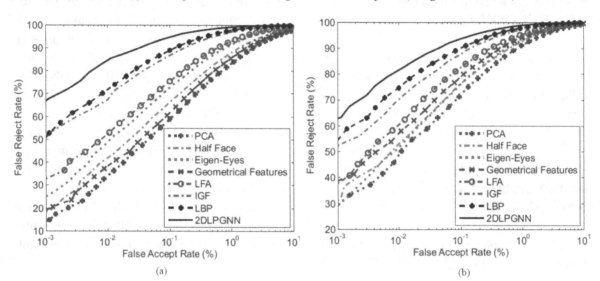

(a) (b)

and their shape information is computed. For matching two images, this shape information is matched using the Euclidean distance measure. Hence, the algorithm depends on the correspondence between the facial features and works only in cases when this information is preserved. If the facial features are occluded using accessories such as glasses, beard, moustache, and scarf, then the performance decreases. LFA refers to a class of algorithms that extract a set of geometrical metrics and distances from facial images and use these features as the basis for representation and comparison. The recognition performance depends on the environment and quality of the image.

3. **Texture based algorithms:** Three texture based algorithms are selected namely Independent Gabor Features (IGF) (Liu & Wechsler, 2003), Local Binary Pattern (LBP) (Ahonen et al., 2006), and 2D-log polar Gabor transform and Neural Network (2DLPGNN) (Singh et al., 2008). IGF extracts Gabor features from the face image and

then reduces the dimensionality using PCA. Independent Gabor features are obtained from the reduced dimensionality feature vector by applying Independent Component Analysis. These independent Gabor features are classified using Bayes classifier and then matched using the Manhattan distance measure. LBP technique extracts textural feature from the face images. In this algorithm, a face image is divided into several regions and weighted LBP features are extracted to generate a feature vector. Matching of two LBP feature vectors is performed using weighted Chi square distance. 2DLPGNN technique uses dynamic neural network architecture to extract the phase features from face images using 2D log polar Gabor transform. The phase features are divided into frames which are matched using hamming distance.

Table 2 and 3 show the results using eight recognition techniques for Experiment 1 and Experiment 2, respectively.

Table 2. Verification rates at 0.01% FAR of the selected algorithms for Experiment 1

Algorithms	Pose	Expression	Illumination	Overall
PCA	31.9	35.5	35.3	34.4
Half-face	36.6	42.1	45.2	41.8
Eigen-eyes	29.7	78.6	45.8	49.3
GF	35.4	38.2	41.7	38.9
LFA	50.1	52.3	53.5	52.7
IGF	60.7	69.8	68.6	67.3
LBP	73.2	68.6	70.9	72.1
2D-LPGNN	75.3	67.3	86.5	84.2

Table 3. Verification rates at 0.01% FAR of the selected algorithms for Experiment 2

Algorithms	Minimal Variations	Hair	Beard, Moustache	Glasses	Cap, Hat	Lip, nose, eyebrow	Aging, Wrinkles	Multiple Variations	Overall
PCA	60.3	56.8	32.2	41.4	55.7	56.3	49.6	14.7	48.2
Half-face	59.5	61.4	34.1	44.6	56.8	59.2	53.9	16.4	52.9
Eigen-eyes	63.1	57.2	60.5	6.9	50.4	47.7	41.6	30.3	51.1
GF	61.3	61.9	53.2	52.4	58.9	49.1	51.8	31.6	58.0
LFA	63.7	63.1	54.5	53.8	61.4	56.3	54.9	32.0	60.4
IGF	74.2	73.8	58.7	57.6	71.0	70.9	55.1	32.8	70.1
LBP	85.5	85.1	61.0	62.5	80.4	78.6	70.3	50.3	74.7
2D-LPGNN	96.9	96.4	77.3	81.9	86.3	89.2	80.8	65.6	82.0

The key results of Experiment 1 are summarized below:

- From Table 2, it can be observed that variations in pose cause a large reduction in verification accuracy compared to expression and illumination.
- Results suggest that texture based algorithms yield better accuracy compared to appearance and feature based algorithms. This is because pose, expression and illumination variations can cause substantial changes in appearance and spurious/missing features, thereby reducing the verification performance.

- Among all the algorithms, 2D-LPGNN yields the best verification accuracy of 84.2%, which is at least 12% better than other algorithms. 2D-LPGNN algorithm effectively encodes textural features that can handle minor to moderate variations in pose, expression and illumination.

The key results of Experiment 2 are explained below:

- For most of the disguise variations, appearance based algorithms yield lower verification accuracy because these algorithms use facial appearance to determine the identity, and the makeup tools and accessories significantly alter the facial information. Similarly, feature based algorithms suffer due to feature alterations that are caused by disguise accessories.

- Texture based algorithms provide significantly better verification accuracy compared to appearance based algorithms. Conversely, these algorithms do not yield good verification accuracy with moderate to large disguise variations.

- 2D-LPGNN yields the best verification performance. However, for the challenging scenarios of multiple disguise variations, the accuracy is only 65.6% but still outperforms other algorithms. This shows that existing algorithms are not efficient enough to handle large degrees of disguise variations.

From Tables 2 and 3, it is quite evident that multiple disguise variations is the most difficult challenge to handle (e.g. 2D-LPGNN yields accuracies in the range of 75-86% for pose, expression and illumination whereas for multiple disguise variations, it is only 65%). These comprehensive experimental results indicate that further research is needed to address high degree of disguise variations.

4.2 Impact Analysis for Variations Due to Local and Global Plastic Surgery (Singh et al., 2010)

Singh et al. (2010) performed a detailed analysis of local and global plastic surgery cases using the database explained in Section 3.2. They observed that for global surgeries such as face lift, facial features and texture are drastically altered after surgery which causes differences between the pre- and post-surgery images of the same individual. Therefore, face recognition algorithms do not yield good performance. However, there are some surgeries such as minor skin resurfacing that have relatively closer resemblance in pre- and

post-surgery images, and most of the recognition algorithms are able to perform correct classification. Similarly, it is also observed that dermabrasion is another common surgical procedure that affects the face recognition performance.

4.3 Impact Analysis for Variations Due to Nose Alterations (Erdogmus et al., 2012)

In Erdogmus et al. (2012), the impact of the applied nose alterations on face recognition performances are evaluated in both 2D and 3D using the database explained in Section 3.3. For the analysis, initially, the original databases (DB-o) and the simulated databases (DB-s) in 2D and 3D in nose alteration database are partitioned in non-overlapping training and testing datasets. Randomly selected 40% of subjects are used for training, while remaining subjects are used for testing. The partitioning is repeated 10 times and verification performances are computed over these 10 trials. For verification, each image in the test set is compared with all other images in the test set and a similarity score is obtained for each image pair.

Figures 11 and 12 show the ROC curves which plot Verification Rates (VR) as a function of False Acceptance Rates for 2D and 3D face recognition, respectively.

Two experiments are performed to show the impact of nose alterations on face recognition systems.

- **Experiment 1 – Performance on the original database:** It is important to compute the performance on the original datasets in terms of having a baseline performance. For this purpose, 2D and 3D algorithms are evaluated on DB-o where the similarities are calculated between each original image pair.

- **Experiment 2 – Performance on the simulated database:** In this scenario, the similarity scores between.

Figure 11. Verification rates of 2D FR algorithms for Experiment 1 (left) and Experiment 2 (right)

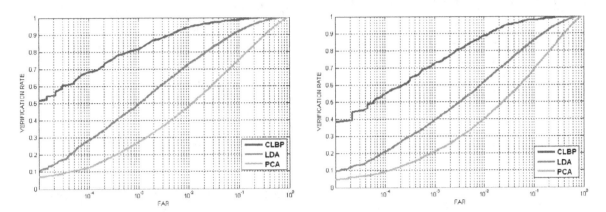

Figure 12. Verification rates of 3D FR algorithms for Experiment 1 (left) and Experiment 2 (right)

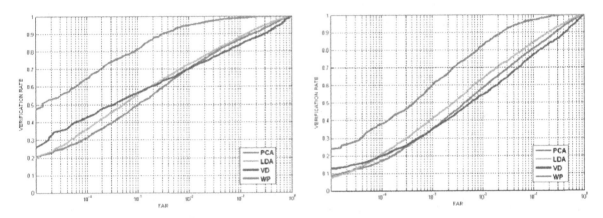

Every DB-o and DB-s sample pairs are calculated and used to evaluate the recognition performances. For each subject selected for the training set, half of the corresponding images are taken from DB-o and the rest from DB-s. Experiment 2 is identical to Experiment 1, except the probe images are now replaced by their modified versions.

4.3.1 Evaluation on 2D Face Recognition Algorithms

In Erdogmus et al. (2012), three methods are chosen for 2D face recognition: PCA, LDA (Belhumer et al., 1997), and Circular Local Binary Pattern (CLBP) (Ahonen et al., 2006). PCA and LDA are appearance-based approaches which are used for

dimensionality reduction and feature extraction. LBP is a texture-based algorithm for describing local structures. Similarity between each image pair is computed by using cosine distance metric for PCA and LDA and by using chi-square distance metric for CLBP.

According to Table 4, the best performance is obtained using CLBP. This shows that for nose alteration, texture based method is more robust than appearance based methods such as PCA and LDA. With CLBP, the percentage change between the results of Experiment 1 and 2 is 12.01%. The robustness of LDA is observed to be higher than PCA, with ~20% decrease in the performance of LDA whereas PCA suffers from 22.98% loss in verification accuracy.

Table 4. Verification rates at 0.001 FAR for 2D face recognition algorithms for Experiments 1 and 2

Algorithm	Exp.1	Exp.2
PCA	27.50%	21.18%
LDA	50.69%	40.11%
CLBP	81.51%	71.72%

4.3.2 Evaluation on 3D Face Recognition Algorithms

For evaluating 3D face recognition, four algorithms are selected in which the facial surfaces are represented as depth maps or point clouds (Erdogmus et al., 2012). Depth maps can be involved in most of the existing 2D techniques, including subspace methods. Therefore, similar to the 2D evaluations, PCA and LDA are selected. Additionally, two different approaches are implemented for 3D face recognition using point clouds. In the first technique, the faces are aligned with a generic face model using three landmark points (two outer eye corners and the nose tip) and then the depth values are regularly sampled. The similarity between two faces is obtained by averaging the z-distances of all the vertices. In this way, the volume difference (VD) between two facial surfaces is approximated. For the second approach, a warping parameters (WP) based method (Erdogmus & Dugelay, 2012), was adopted. The facial surfaces are first aligned with a generic face model using the landmark points. The alignment is then improved by the Iterative Closest Point method (Besl et al., 1992). 140 previously selected points on the generic model are then coupled with the closest vertices on the face under analysis and Thin Plate Splines (Bookstein, 1989) warping is applied thereby resulting in warping parameters of size 140x3. Finally, the distance between two face models is computed by taking the median of the cosine distances between the corresponding feature vectors.

The verification rates at 0.001 FAR by all the algorithms on databases DB-o3 and DB-s3 are given in Table 5. The analysis on these rates reveals that LDA and WP are least affected from nose alterations. The results further show that the evaluated algorithms are not robust to the variations caused by nose alterations. Furthermore, comparing the verification performances of 2D and 3D algorithms show that 3D is much more vulnerable against nose variations.

4.4 Impact Analysis for Variations due to Make-Up (Eckert et al., 2013)

In Eckert et al. (2013), the impact of facial cosmetics on face recognition is evaluated using the facial cosmetics database explained in Section 3.6. In this study, the accuracy of the face recognition algorithm is measured in terms of the identification rate (IDR). The IDR indicates the percentage of correctly identified persons. The face recognition is conducted by applying LBP with a block size of 10×10 pixels and a neighborhood with (P; R) = (8; 2), where P is the number of neighbors around a circle of radius R.

The identification rates resulting from the tests are presented below. For the first test, reference images with no makeup are used in the gallery. In the second test, the reference images in the gallery are replaced by a subset of intermediate makeup images in the database.

Table 5. Verification rates at 0.001 FAR for 3D face recognition algorithms for Experiments 1 and 2

Algorithm	Exp.1	Exp.2
PCA	49.85%	35.22%
LDA	56.67%	42.18%
VD	56.97%	38.23%
WP	81.18%	60.79%

1. **Test for which Reference Images are Selected from No Makeup Images:** The database contains 50 reference images with no makeup. Each of them are taken in different setting compared to the makeup images. As shown in Figure 13, the ability to identify a person's face decreases with increasing amount of makeup. The results are in line with the expectations. Slight makeup test images achieve a little lower IDR than no makeup images. Slight makeup maintains a natural look and has little effect on human perception. Intermediate makeup in contrast is clearly visible and therefore provides a lower IDR. Heavy makeup makes a significant change in person's appearance and is perceived as mask-alike. Hence, the IDR for faces with heavy makeup reaches only two-third of the IDR for faces with no makeup. In Figure 13, it is clear that there is an almost linear decrease for slight and heavy makeup whereas there is a little local peak in the intermediate makeup. This result shows that intermediate makeup plays an extraordinary role in face recognition. Therefore, in the second test, reference images are selected from intermediate makeup images.

2. **Test for which Reference Images are Selected from Intermediate Makeup Images:** Images with intermediate makeup are used as the reference images. The database provides makeup series for 23 persons containing intermediate makeup. The remaining makeup series only provide images belonging to the makeup categories 'no', 'slight' or 'heavy'. Therefore, the evaluation is performed with 23 reference images originating from makeup series. Since the reference images are from the same session, it is less realistic compared to the first test and this is why almost perfect result (100%) is obtained in Figure 14 for intermediate images. 175 test images are available for the specified 23 persons. 51 of them are classified into the makeup category 'no', 54 into 'slight', 30 into 'intermediate', and 40 into 'heavy'.

The IDR curve in Figure 14 with intermediate makeup reference images is higher compared to the one resulting from no makeup reference images. First reason is the feature enhancing effect in the reference images due to intermediate makeup. Second reason is the similarity of the reference images to the test images (the same makeup series as origin). Here, increasing makeup does not lead

Figure 13. IDR when the reference images are selected from no makeup images. Figure is taken from (Eckert et al., 2013).

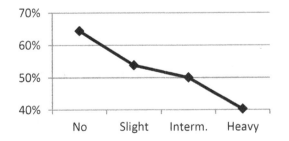

Figure 14. IDR when the reference images are selected from intermediate makeup. Figure is taken from (Eckert et al., 2013).

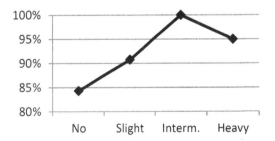

to decreasing IDRs. The IDRs for the categories 'no', 'slight' and 'heavy' are almost linearly increasing, while the one for the makeup category 'intermediate' results in a high peak as shown in Figure 14. Facial images with intermediate makeup have the highest IDR, namely 100%. Images where no makeup is applied result in the lowest IDR.

5. TECHNIQUES ROBUST AGAINST DISGUISE VARIATIONS

5.1 Face Recognition Robust Against Facial Accessories (Min et al., 2011) & (Min et al., 2013)

The focus of Min et al. (2011) is on facial occlusions, and particularly on how to improve the recognition of faces occluded by sunglasses and scarf. They divide the image into two equal components. The upper part is used to analyze the presence of sunglasses whereas the lower part is used to analyze scarfs. After dividing the image into components, Gabor wavelet features are extracted from each component. The feature vector is then subject to dimensionality reduction. An SVM classifier is used to detect the presence of occlusion in each component. Next, the face images are

divided into 64 blocks and the LBP histograms are extracted using $LBP_{8,2}^{u2}$ in Min et al. (2011). This yields a feature histogram of 3776 bins. In case of non-occluded faces, all 3776 bins are used for matching. For occluded faces, however, the feature vector histograms are extracted only from the non-occluded parts as shown in Figure 15. The occluded faces are thus represented with histograms of 1888 bins, corresponding to the 32 non-occluded blocks. This means that when a face is occluded by a scarf, the upper 32 blocks are selected, while the lower 32 blocks are used when the face is occluded by sunglasses.

In the experiments, authors selected 240 non-occluded faces from session 1 of the AR database as template images. These non-occluded faces correspond to 80 subjects (40 males and 40 females), with 3 images per subject under neutral expression, smile and anger. For evaluation, they considered the corresponding 240 non-occluded faces from session 2, 240 faces with sunglasses from session 1 and 240 faces with scarf from session 1, under three different conditions of illumination.

Table 6 shows the results of occlusion detection as a confusion matrix. Note that only 2 images from the non-occluded faces are wrongly classified as faces with scarf. This shows the efficiency of this occlusion detection method.

Figure 15. Examples of extracting the LBP histogram from the non-occluded facial regions. Figure is taken from (Min et al., 2011).

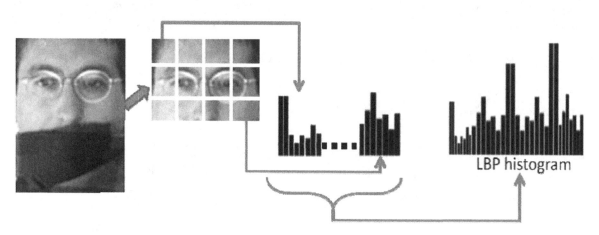

Table 6. Results obtained with occlusion detection method

	No-Occlusion	**Scarf**	**Sunglass**	**Detection Rate**
no-occlusion	238	2	0	99.17%
Scarf	0	240	0	100%
Sunglass	0	0	240	100%

Figure 16 shows the performance of this approach on three different test sets: non-occluded faces, faces occluded with scarf, and faces occluded with sunglasses. For comparison, the results of eigenfaces (PCA) and basic LBP methods are also computed. Since PCA and LBP do not address occlusion detection, a third baseline approach is implemented for comparison. The occlusion detection module is combined with eigenfaces and named as FA-PCA (facial accessories robust PCA). In FA-PCA, three eigenspaces are computed during the training stage. The first one is computed using the whole face images, while the second and third eigenspaces are computed using the upper and lower facial regions, respectively. During the recognition phase, the non-occluded components are projected into the corresponding eigenspace when partial occlusions are detected.

The results (i.e. rank-1 identification rates) in Figure 16 clearly show that the approach significantly outperforms all other methods. On the non-occluded faces, this approach and LBP yields equal performance (94.83%) while the Eigenface method (with and without occlusion detection) yields much lower performance (75.83%). On the test set of faces with scarves and sunglasses, the proposed approach gave best results (92.08%) and (75.83%), respectively. Note that LBP performed quite well even under occlusion, thus confirming the earlier findings stating that local feature-based methods are more robust against occlusion than holistic methods.

Figure 16. Recognition performance of different methods on three test sets: non-occluded faces, face occluded with scarf and faces occluded with sunglasses. Figure is taken from (Min et al., 2011).

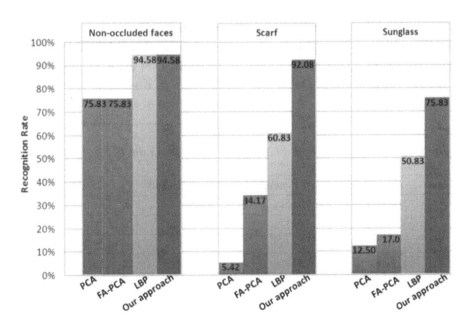

The same authors performed another study (Min et al., 2013) which is based on facial occlusion analysis for robust face recognition using the Kinect face database explained in Section 3.4. They propose to use heterogeneous cues (3D→2D) to improve face recognition in the presence of occlusions. The occlusion probability of each facial region is estimated based on the 3D information (depth map) and the estimated occlusion probability is used to improve Local Gabor Binary Patterns (LGBP) based face recognition using RGB image. In comparison to LGBP based face recognition that exploits the intensity information for occlusion analysis (Zhang et al., 2007), this method yields better recognition results.

Similar to Zhang et al. (2007), the authors adopt LGBP for face representation. LGBP operator generates $\mu \times \lambda$ LGBP images (μ scales and λ orientations for the Gabor wavelet decomposition) from a single input. Each LGBP image is then divided into R local regions, from which local histograms are extracted to summarize the LGBP codes. Next, the authors propose an occlusion estimation method based on the observation that a face surface is behind its occluding object, and therefore assume that the depth value of an occluded pixel is statistically deviated from the ones without occlusion. The occlusion probability for local regions are computed and they associate a set of weights to local regions. Finally, all local histograms of different LGBP images are concatenated into one feature vector to build the global face representation H.

In their experiment, 156 non-occluded faces (52 people with 3 expression variations) of session 1 are selected as gallery faces and 52×3 faces occluded by sunglasses, hand and paper from the same session are selected for the probe set.

The recognition performance of LGBP for RGB and depth based face recognition is also compared with four other techniques: (1) 2D occlusion analysis for 2D based face recognition, P^{RGB}-LGBP(2D); (2) 3D occlusion analysis for 2D based face recognition, P^D-LGBP(2D) (the proposed approach); (3) 2D occlusion analysis for 3D based face recognition, P^{RGB} LGBP(3D); and (4) 3D occlusion analysis for 3D based face recognition, P^D-LGBP(3D).

Table 7 shows that the proposed approach yields the best results in most cases. The obtained results also support that 3D information has more advantages over 2D for occlusion analysis in face recognition.

5.2 Face Recognition Robust Against Nose Alterations (Kose et al., 2012)

In Kose et al. (2012), the authors focus on developing a new approach which reduces the impact of nose alterations on recognition performance using the nose alteration database explained in Section 3.3. The proposed approach is based on local description. PCA, LDA and CLBP are applied generally over the whole image to extract image features. In Kose et al. (2012), these techniques are applied to extract features at block level.

Table 7. Recognition Rates of LGBP, P^{RGB}-LGBP and P^D-LGBP on the EURECOM KinectFaceDB

Face Information	Algorithm	Sunglasses	Hand	Paper	Overall
RGB (2D)	LGBP	92.31%	96.15%	86.54%	91.62%
	P^{RGB}-LGBP	94.23%	90.38%	92.31%	92.31%
	P^D-LGBP	88.46%	96.15%	94.23%	92.95%
DEPTH (3D)	LGBP	67.31%	42.31%	17.31%	42.31%
	P^{RGB}-LGBP	65.38%	44.23%	28.85%	46.15%
	P^D-LGBP	88.46%	55.77%	28.85%	53.21%

Figure 17 shows an example by using an original image in the gallery (Image#1), another image of the same person (Image#2), and a synthetic image which is in fact Image#2 after nose alteration (Image#3). The figure shows dissimilarity results, which are computed using PCA to extract the block features, for each of 36 blocks from cropped images. Dissimilarity results between the blocks of Image#1 and Image#2 are computed for original (Or.) image vs. original image comparison. Dissimilarity results between the blocks of Image#1 and Image#3 are computed for original image vs. synthetic (S.) image comparison. From Figure 17, it is clear that dissimilarity results for the two comparisons are similar for almost all the blocks except the ones which have undergone nose alteration. For instance, very high dissimilarity is obtained for Or. vs. S. compared to Or. vs. Or. comparison at Block#15 which shows the nose region is effected from nose alteration. Also Figure 17 shows that the lowest dissimilarities are observed at the blocks which represent just the skin part (e.g. Block#18) and higher dissimilarities are observed usually at the dense-textured blocks (e.g. Block#8). According to these observations, the approach in this study is developed.

In the proposed approach, the dissimilarities are computed for each block pair and sorted from minimum to maximum. D_i represents the ith minimum dissimilarity result inside the total 36 dissimilarity results. Equation 1 shows how the results are obtained inside the proposed approach.

$$RD(k) = \frac{1}{k}\sum_{i=1}^{k} D_i, \qquad k = 1,...,36$$

(1)

For the first computation (k=1), only the block pair with minimum dissimilarity (D_1) is involved in the resultant dissimilarity computation between an image pair, which is represented as RD in Equation 1. For the next computations (k>1), each time, the next minimum dissimilarity is added to the array and the resultant dissimilarity is computed as the mean of dissimilarities in this array. This means that at the last computation (k=36), the dissimilarity results computed for all the block pairs ($D_1,...,D_{36}$) are used in Equation 1 to compute the resultant dissimilarity between an image pair. The resultant dissimilarities are computed for each image pair and 36 recognition performances are evaluated from these results. Finally, the maximum recognition performance

Figure 17. Dissimilarity results obtained for original vs. original comparison between Image#1 and Image#2 and original vs. synthetic comparison between Image#1 and Image#3. Figure is taken from (Kose et al., 2012).

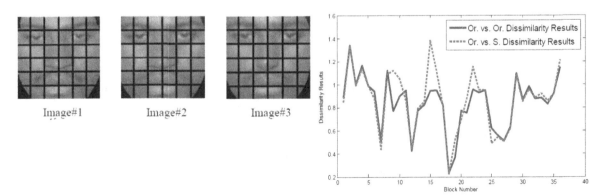

obtained after successive computations is selected as the resultant performance rate of the system. In this way, the impact of blocks with higher dissimilarities are eliminated while computing the resultant recognition rate which leads to an increase in the recognition performance.

The results of Experiments 1 and 2 are reported using both the proposed approach and the holistic approach, for which the key techniques (PCA, LDA, CLBP) are used. These methods are applied over the image blocks for the proposed approach; whereas they are applied over the whole image for the holistic approach.

Table 8 shows the results when PCA, LDA and CLBP are applied on texture images (2D face recognition) both for holistic and proposed approaches. The results show that with the proposed approach, the performance of PCA is almost doubled. Similarly, there is significant improvement in the performance of LDA and CLBP. It can also be observed that using the proposed approach, the decrease in the performance due to facial alterations is lower compared to the results obtained with the holistic approach for all three techniques. This proves that the proposed approach increases the recognition performances and also provides more robust results against facial alterations compared to the holistic approach.

Table 9 shows the results when PCA and LDA are applied on depth maps both for holistic and proposed approaches. In this table, LDA provides better performing and more robust result compared

to PCA. Similar to analysis on texture images, the proposed approach provides both better performance and more robust results compared to the holistic approach. This proves the superiority of the approach on depth maps as well. From the analysis on both texture and range images, performance decrease is visible for all the methods. With the proposed approach, results on texture and range images are closer for PCA.

5.3 Face Recognition Robust Against Plastic Surgery (Bhatt et al., 2013)

Bhatt et al. (2013) presents a multi-objective evolutionary granular computing based algorithm for recognizing faces altered due to plastic surgery. As shown in Figure 18, the proposed algorithm starts with generating non-disjoint face granules where each granule represents different information at varying size and resolution. Further, two feature extractors, namely Extended Uniform Circular Local Binary Pattern (EUCLBP) (Bhatt et al., 2010) and Scale Invariant Feature Transform (SIFT) (Lowe, 2004), are used for extracting discriminating information from face granules. Finally, different responses are unified in an evolutionary manner using a multi-objective genetic approach for improved performance. The experiments are performed on the plastic surgery database explained in Section 3.2. and the performance of the proposed algorithm is compared with a commercial-off-the-shelf face recognition

Table 8. Verification rates at 0.001 FAR for 2D FR using the holistic and proposed approaches for Experiments 1 and 2

Algorithms	Holistic Approach		Proposed Approach	
	Exp. 1	Exp. 2	Exp. 1	Exp. 2
PCA	31.75%	21.06%	69.29%	52.75%
Performance Decrease	33.67%		23.87%	
LDA	55.54%	41.60%	70.27%	57.86%
Performance Decrease	25.10%		17.66%	
CLBP	60.74%	53.30%	72.39%	66.26%
Performance Decrease	12.25%		8.47%	

Table 9. Verification rates at 0.001 FAR for 3D FR using the holistic and proposed approaches for Experiments 1 and 2

Algorithms	Holistic Approach		Proposed Approach	
	Exp. 1	Exp. 2	Exp. 1	Exp. 2
PCA	47.91%	31.86%	71.24%	54.34%
Performance Decrease	33.50%		23.72%	
LDA	54.56%	39.61%	72.49%	60.35%
Performance Decrease	27.40%		16.75%	

Figure 18. Steps pertaining to the multi-objective evolutionary granular computing based algorithm. Figure is taken from (Bhatt et al., 2013).

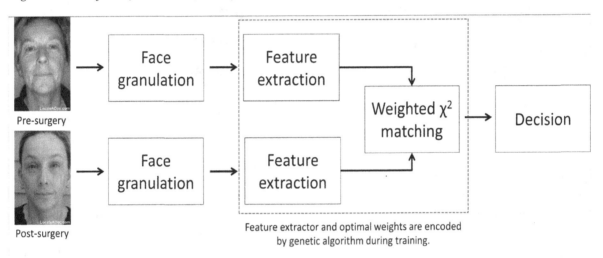

system (COTS) for matching surgically altered face images against large scale gallery. The results obtained by the proposed algorithm are state-of-the-art on the plastic surgery database.

5.4 Disguise Detection and Face Recognition in Visible and Thermal Spectrums (Dhamecha et al., 2013)

Dhamecha et al. (2013) assert that modelling the process of disguise is very challenging. They hypothesize that the facial part or patches which are under the effect of disguise (or occluded in most of the cases) are not only un-useful for face recognition, but may also provide misleading information. It is this misleading information that

a person uses to hide his/her own identity and/or to impersonate someone else. Using this intuition, they propose a framework for recognizing faces with variations in disguise using multi-spectrum images. As illustrated in Figure 19, there are two cascaded stages in the proposed framework. The first stage is patch classification which comprises dividing face image into patches and classifying them into biometric or non-biometric classes. The second stage is patch based face recognition which performs LBP based face recognition using only those patches which are found to be biometric during the patch classification stage. The proposed approach improves verification accuracy over direct application of LBP, COTS, and SRC. It is also observed that for both patch

Figure 19. Steps pertaining to the multi-spectral face recognition algorithm. Figure is taken from (Dhamecha et al., 2013).

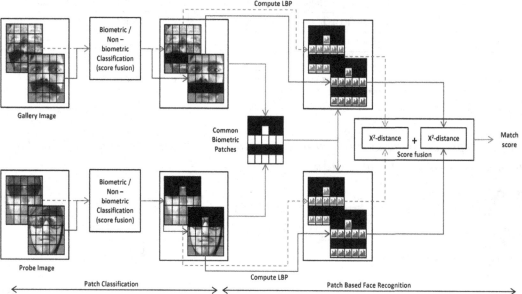

classification and face recognition, the score fusion of visible and thermal spectrum match scores leads to improvements.

6. CONCLUSION

In this chapter, initially several disguise variations and the existing databases for disguise analysis are explained. Then the impact of disguise variations on face recognition is analyzed. The results in this study show that face recognition systems are not robust against disguise variations. This is why, finally we provide a collection of techniques proposed in the literature which are robust against these variations.

Disguise variations are diverse. They have different impacts on automatic face recognition systems. For example facial accessories such as scarf or sunglasses have stronger impact on recognition systems compared to variations in hair style. Although the impact of each variation is different, the studies on disguise variations show that all these variations cause a significant impact on face recognition.

Today, there exists a very limited number of databases that allow researchers and engineers to test robustness against disguise variations. In this chapter, we provide the specifications of some existing databases including disguise images. In this study, the impact of disguise variations and robust techniques against these variations are analyzed using these databases. The analysis in this chapter further shows that the most efficient way to counter-attack disguise variations consists of two steps. The first step is pre-detection of disguise variations and the second step is proposing face recognition techniques which focus on non-affected areas using local analysis.

The future research direction in this area is to analyse the differences between human perception and computer vision for disguise variations. For example, hair style may have a strong impact on human perception. However, the impact of hair style as a disguise variation is very limited on existing automatic face recognition techniques.

Several techniques have been proposed in the literature to recognize face images with disguise variations, however, the current state-of-the-art is not satisfactory. Therefore more robust techniques have to be designed for occlusion detection and face recognition with disguise variations.

REFERENCES

Ahonen, T., Hadid, A., & Pietikäinen, M. (2006). Face description with local binary patterns: Application to face recognition. *IEEE Transactions on Pattern Analysis and Machine Intelligence, 28*(12), 2037–2041. doi:10.1109/TPAMI.2006.244 PMID:17108377

Alexander, J., & Smith, J. (2003). Engineering privacy in public: Confounding face recognition, privacy enhancing technologies. In *Proceedings of International Workshop on Privacy Enhancing Technologies* (pp. 88–106). Academic Press.

Belhumer, P. N., Hespanha, J., & Kriegman, D. (1997). Eigenfaces vs. fisherfaces: Recognition using class specific linear projection. *IEEE Transactions on Pattern Analysis and Machine Intelligence, 17*(7), 711–720. doi:10.1109/34.598228

Besl, P., & McKay, N. (1992). A Method For Registration of 3-D Shapes. *IEEE Transactions on Pattern Analysis and Machine Intelligence, 14*(2), 239–256. doi:10.1109/34.121791

Bhatt, H., Bharadwaj, S., Singh, R., & Vatsa, M. (2013). Recognizing Surgically Altered Face Images Using Multi-objective Evolutionary Algorithm. *IEEE Transactions on Information Forensics and Security, 8*(1), 89–100. doi:10.1109/TIFS.2012.2223684

Bhatt, H. S., Bharadwaj, S., Singh, R., & Vatsa, M. (2010). On matching sketches with digital face images. In *Proceedings of International Conference Biometrics: Theory Applications and Systems* (pp. 1–7). Academic Press.

Bookstein, F. L. (1989). Principal warps: Thin-Plate Splines and Decomposition of Deformations. *IEEE Transactions on Pattern Analysis and Machine Intelligence, 11*(6), 567–585. doi:10.1109/34.24792

Cox, I. J., Ghosn, J., & Yianilos, P. N. (1996). Feature-based face recognition using mixture distance. In *Proceedings of International Conference on Computer Vision and Pattern Recognition* (pp. 209-216). Academic Press.

Daily News. (2013). Retrieved from http://www.nydailynews.com/entertainment/gossip/ben-affleck-loses-grizzly-beard-oscars-win-article-1.1273919

Dantcheva, A., Chen, C., & Rosant, A. (2012). Can Facial Cosmetics Affect the Matching Accuracy of Face Recognition Systems. In *Proceedings of IEEE Fifth International Conference on Biometrics: Theory, Applications and System* (pp. 391-398). IEEE.

Delac, K., & Grgic, M. (2007). *Face recognition*. I-TECH Education and Publishing. doi:10.5772/38

Dhamecha, T. I., Nigam, A., Singh, R., & Vatsa, M. (2013). Disguise Detection and Face Recognition in Visible and Thermal Spectrum. In *Proceedings of IAPR International Conference on Biometrics* (pp. 1-8). IAPR.

Eckert, M.-L., Kose, N., & Dugelay, J.-L. (2013). Facial Cosmetics Database and Impact Analysis on Automatic Face Recognition. In *Proceedings of IEEE International Workshop on Multimedia Signal Processing*. IEEE.

Equinox. (2004). *Face database*. Retrieved from www.equinoxsensors.com/products/HID.html

Erdogmus, N., & Dugelay, J.-L. (2012). On Discriminative Properties of TPS Warping Parameters for 3D Face Recognition. In *Proceedings of International Conference on Informatics, Electronics & Vision* (pp. 225-230). Academic Press.

Erdogmus, N., Kose, N., & Dugelay, J.-L. (2012). Impact analysis of nose alterations on 2D and 3D face recognition. In *Proceedings of IEEE International Workshop on Multimedia Signal Processing* (pp. 354-359). IEEE.

Huang, G. B., Ramesh, M., Berg, T., & Learned-Miller, E. (2007). *Labeled faces in the wild: A database for studying face recognition in unconstrained environments (technical report)*. Amherst, MA: University of Massachusetts.

Huynh, T., Min, R., & Dugelay, J.-L. (2012). An Efficient LBP-based Descriptor for Facial Depth Images applied to Gender Recognition using RGB-D Face Data. In *Proceedings of ACCV Workshop on Computer Vision with Local Binary Pattern Variants* (pp. 133-145). ACCV.

Kose, N., Erdogmus, N., & Dugelay, J.-L. (2012). Block based face recognition approach robust to nose alterations. In *Proceedings of IEEE International Conference on Biometrics: Theory, Applications and Systems* (pp. 121-126). IEEE.

Li, S., & Jain, A. (2005). *Handbook of face recognition*. New York: Springer.

Liu, C., & Wechsler, H. (2003). Independent component analysis of Gabor features for face recognition. *IEEE Transactions on Neural Networks*, *14*(4), 919–928. doi:10.1109/TNN.2003.813829 PMID:18238070

Lowe, D. G. (2004). Distinctive image features from scale-invariant keypoints. *International Journal of Computer Vision*, *60*(2), 91–110. doi:10.1023/B:VISI.0000029664.99615.94

Martinez, A., & Benavente, R. (1998). *The AR face database*. Computer Vision Center.

Min, R., & Dugelay, J.-L. (2013). Kinect Based Facial Occlusion Analysis for Robust Face Recognition. In *Proceedings of IEEE International Workshop on Hot Topics in 3D*. IEEE.

Min, R., Hadid, A., & Dugelay, J.-L. (2011). Improving the recognition of faces occluded by facial accessories. In *Proceedings of IEEE Conference on Automatic Face and Gesture Recognition* (pp. 442-447). IEEE.

Pamudurthy, S., Guan, E., Mueller, K., & Rafailovich, M. (2005). Dynamic approach for face recognition using digital image skin correlation. In *Audio- and Video based Biometric Person Authentication* (pp. 1010–1018). Academic Press. doi:10.1007/11527923_105

Penev, P., & Atick, J. (1996). Local feature analysis: a general statistical theory for object representation. *Network (Bristol, England)*, *7*, 477–500. doi:10.1088/0954-898X/7/3/002

Phillips, P. J., Flynn, P. J., Scruggs, T., Bowyer, K. W., Jin, C., & Hoffman, K. … Worek, W. (2005). Overview of the face recognition grand challenge. In *Proceedings of IEEE Computer Society Conf. on Computer Vision and Pattern Recognition*, (vol. 1, pp. 947-954). IEEE.

Phillips, P. J., Moon, H., Rizvi, S., & Rauss, P. J. (2000). The FERET evaluation methodology for face recognition algorithms. *IEEE Transactions on Pattern Analysis and Machine Intelligence*, *22*(10), 1090–1104. doi:10.1109/34.879790

Ramanathan, N., Chowdhury, A., & Chellappa, R. (2004). Facial similarity across age, disguise, illumination and pose. In *Proceedings of International Conference on Image Processing*, (vol. 3, pp. 1999–2002). Academic Press.

Silva, P., & Rosa, A. S. (2003). Face recognition based on eigeneyes. *Pattern Recognition and Image Analysis*, *13*(2), 335–338.

Sim, T., Baker, S., & Bsat, M. (2003). The CMU pose, illumination, and expression database. *IEEE Transactions on Pattern Analysis and Machine Intelligence*, *25*(12), 1615–1618. doi:10.1109/TPAMI.2003.1251154

Singh, R., Vatsa, M., Bhatt, H., Bharadwaj, S., Noore, A., & Noorezayadan, S. S. (2010). Plastic Surgery: A New Dimension to Face Recognition. *IEEE Transactions on Information Forensics and Security*, *5*(3), 441–448. doi:10.1109/TIFS.2010.2054083

Singh, R., Vatsa, M., & Noore, A. (2008). Face recognition with disguise and single gallery images. *Image and Vision Computing*, *27*(3), 245–257. doi:10.1016/j.imavis.2007.06.010

Singh, R., Vatsa, M., & Noore, A. (2008). Recognizing Face Images with Disguise Variations. In *Recent Advances in Face Recognition*. Academic Press. doi:10.5772/6399

Singh, R., Vatsa, M., & Noore, A. (2009). Effect of Plastic Surgery on Face Recognition: A Preliminary Study. In *Proceedings of IEEE Computer Society Conf. on Computer Vision and Pattern Recognition Workshops* (pp. 72-77). IEEE.

Wechsler, H. (2006). *Reliable Face Recognition Methods: System Design, Implementation and Evaluation*. Springer.

Zhang, W., Shan, S., Chen, X., & Gao, W. (2007). Local gabor binary patterns based on kullback leibler divergence for partially occluded face recognition. *IEEE Signal Processing Letters*, *14*(11), 875–878. doi:10.1109/LSP.2007.903260

Zhao, W.-Y., Chellappa, R., Phillips, P. J., & Rosenfeld, A. (2003). Face recognition: A literature survey. *ACM Computing Surveys*, *35*(4), 399–458. doi:10.1145/954339.954342

KEY TERMS AND DEFINITIONS

2D Face Recognition: Authenticating or identifying the identity of an individual using 2D face images.

3D Face Recognition: Authenticating or identifying the identity of an individual using 3D face information.

Disguise Variations: Variations due to disguise accessories performed generally performed to hide one's own identity or impersonate someone else's identity.

Face Recognition: Identifying or authenticating the identity of an individual by matching face information of the probe individual corresponding to a gallery database.

Plastic Surgery: Surgical or non-surgical medical procedures to change the appearance of a body part.

Chapter 12
Using Ocular Data for Unconstrained Biometric Recognition

Hugo Proença
University of Beira Interior, Portugal

Gil Santos
University of Beira Interior, Portugal

João C. Neves
University of Beira Interior, Portugal

ABSTRACT

There are several scenarios where a full facial picture cannot be obtained nor the iris properly imaged. For such cases, a good possibility might be to use the ocular region for recognition, which is a relatively new idea and is regarded as a good trade-off between using the whole face or the iris alone. The area in the vicinity of the eyes is designated as periocular and is particularly useful on less constrained conditions, when image acquisition is unreliable, or to avoid iris pattern spoofing. This chapter provides a comprehensive summary of the most relevant research conducted in the scope of ocular (periocular) recognition methods. The authors compare the main features of the publicly available data sets and summarize the techniques most frequently used in the recognition algorithms in this chapter. In addition, they present the state-of-the-art results in terms of recognition accuracy and discuss the current issues on this topic, together with some directions for further work.

DOI: 10.4018/978-1-4666-5966-7.ch012

1. INTRODUCTION

The face and the iris are among the most popular traits for biometric recognition, and are – together with the fingerprint – the most frequently reported in the specialized literature (Bowyer, Hollingsworth, & Flynn, 2008; Zhao et al. 2000).

The iris has a predominantly randotypic morphogenesis, unique for each individual, and allows very high recognition accuracy. Also, it is a protected organ visible from the exterior, justifying the efforts on "relaxing" its acquisition setup (Santos & Hoyle, 2012; Shin et al., 2012; Tan, Zhang, Sun, & Zhang, 2012).

The face has been traditionally regarded as the main trait to perform recognition under less controlled conditions. However, several drawbacks significantly decrease the effectiveness of face-based recognition systems: 1) due to its 3D structure, substantial differences in appearance are expected with respect to subjects' poses; 2) large regions of the face are often occluded, in case of non-orthogonal data acquisition; 3) facial expressions notoriously affect the appearance of the face; 4) disguising is particularly easy.

According to the above, growing attention has been paid to other traits potentially useful for biometric recognition. Among these, the use of information in the vicinity of the eye (the periocular region) has been gaining in popularity. Being particularly useful on less constrained scenarios, when image acquisition is unreliable, or to avoid iris pattern spoofing, the periocular region does not require constrained close capturing or user cooperation, it's relatively stable, when compared to the whole face, and rarely occluded. Due to the proximity with the iris, both can be easily acquired with a single camera and fused at the score level to compensate for environmental adversities and uncooperative subjects.

The usage of periocular information has even proven itself to be of importance in scenarios where the face has been *reshaped* (*e.g.* plastic surgery), with interesting results (Jillela & Ross, 2012; Bhatt, Bharadwaj, Singh, & Vatsa, 2013).

The idea of *periocular recognition* came from the ability of humans to recognize someone by his / her eyes, which are known to provide substantial amounts of discriminating information that is relatively stable over lifetime. Hence, the term periocular biometrics refers to the development of recognition methods that analyze not only the iris structure, but also the shape of eyelids, the distribution of eyelashes, the texture of the sclera and of the skin surrounding the eye to perform recognition.

This chapter provides an overview of the most relevant attempts to perform biometric recognition in uncontrolled acquisition environments, using information in the periocular area. We summarize the most relevant methods in the literature and compare the techniques most frequently reported for each of the typical processing phases: segmentation, quality assessment, feature encoding and matching. Next, we describe the data sets that are publicly available and used in the evaluation of algorithms, and report the state-of-the-art recognition rates that act as reference values for further improvements on this technology.

The remainder of this chapter is organized as follows: Section 2 overviews the anatomic and biological features of the periocular region. Section 3 compares the main characteristics of the data sets used in periocular recognition experiments. A comprehensive review of the most relevant papers published in this scope is given in Section 4. Section 5 reports the current state-of-the-art results and Section 6 discusses the issues and challenges that are currently associated to the periocular recognition process. Finally, Section 7 concludes this chapter.

2. PERIOCULAR ANATOMY AND STRCTURES

Not only the superficial features of the skin determine the facial appearance, but also the concavities and convexities conferred by the underlying bones and muscles play a significant role. In particular, the periocular region comprises many anatomic features and landmarks that potentially fit for recognition purposes (Figure 1).

Centered on the eye, which is located on the orbital aperture, the periocular region has its creases and sulcus decided essentially by four bones: 1) the frontal bone, ending with the supraorbital process where the eyebrow is located and which affects its appearance; 2) the nasal bone, defining the upper part of the nose; 3) the lacrimal bone, that forms the cavity for the tear gland; and 4) the zygomatic bone, also known as cheek bone.

Although bone structure directly impacts facial appearance, most of the studied features rely more on muscle and skin specifications, and less on

bone level properties, which would be less prone to both natural (*e.g.* aging) and external changes (*e.g.* plastic surgery).

Eyebrows constitute the foundation for eyelids, and are straighter on men and more arched on women. Eyebrow thickness changes among ethnicities and, with the aging process, their orientation and height also change. Concerning the eyelids, their contours depend on gender, ethnic group and age, and dimension intervals are defined in previous studies (Tan, Oh, Priel, & Korn, 2011).

Even considering this richness of ocular elements, the features actually being used on periocular biometrics algorithms are quite simple and can be divided into two levels, as suggested by Woodard, Pundlik, Lyle, and Miller (2010a): 1) the first level comprises eyelids, eye folds, and eye corners, and 2) the second level comprises skin texture, wrinkles, color and pores. This simplicity might be due to the relative novelty of the field: having passed only a couple of years since the first relevant study on periocular recognition, the earliest recognition algorithms firstly employed classical techniques in the computer vision domain-of-knowledge, before attempting more sophisticated / specific methods.

3. DATA SETS

Due to the novelty of the use of the periocular region to perform biometric recognition, only a few data are publicly available. Hence, an issue is the lack of datasets specifically designed for the development of periocular recognition methods. Due to this, researchers usually resort to face and iris databases, being the most relevant given on Table 1 and illustrated on Figure 2. We report the number of images and subjects available per dataset, the dimensions of the images and the

Figure 1. Anatomic features on the periocular region

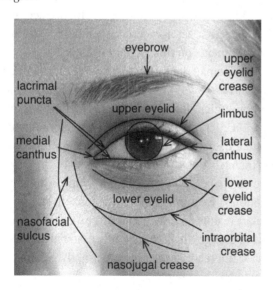

Table 1. Summary of dataset specifications. Variations abbreviations refer to Distance (D), Expression (E), Illumination (I), Occlusion (O) and Pose (P)

Name	# of Images	# of Subj.	Image Dimension	Variations
FERET	14051	1199	512×768	E, I, P
FRGC	36818	741	$\approx 1200 \times 1400$	E, I
MBGC	149 AVI	114	2048×2048	D, E, I, O, P
UBIRIS.v2	11102	261	800×600	D, O, I
UBIPr	10950	261	Multiple	D, O, I, P
FG-NET	1002	82	$\approx 400 \times 500$	D, E, I, P

Figure 2. Sample images that illustrate the datasets typically in the evaluation of periocular algorithms

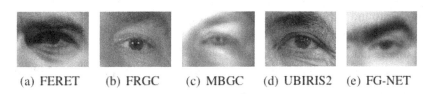

(a) FERET   (b) FRGC   (c) MBGC   (d) UBIRIS2   (e) FG-NET

main variability factors in each one, which play an extremely important role in the evaluation of the robustness of recognition algorithms.

- **FERET:** The Facial Recognition Technology (FERET) database (Phillips, Moon, Rizvi, & Rauss, 2000), designed as a standard for developing face recognition methods, was acquired at George Mason University over eleven sessions and a three years period (1993 to 1996). It was initially released as low resolution (256×384 pixels) grayscale data, and only later a high-resolution color version was also disclosed. Contains a total of 14051 images, gathered from 1199 different subjects within a semi-controlled acquisition protocol with strict expression, pose and illumination changes.

- **FRGC:** Collected at the University of Notre Dame, the Face Recognition Grand Challenge (FRGC) database (Phillips et al., 2005) consist of high resolution ($\approx 1200 \times 1400$ pixels) color still images, captured on both controlled and uncon-

trolled environments. The controlled setup was assembled at a studio with uniform illumination, where subjects were requested to stand still, look strait at the camera, and essay sequentially both neutral and smiling expressions. As for the uncontrolled acquisition, images were shoot in different scenarios, disregarding both background and illumination.

- **UBIRIS.v2:** The UBIRIS.v2 is a unconstrained iris database (Proença, Filipe, Santos, Oliveira, & Alexandre, 2010), captured on the visible wavelength from moving subjects, at different distances and challenging illumination conditions, thus simulating realistic acquisition issues and the related noise factors. Data from both eyes is separately available, as well as the surrounding periocular data, thus allowing to stress out periocular methods, and even their fusion with iris recognition techniques.

- **UBIPr:** As an effort to advance periocular biometric research, the UBI Periocular

Recognition (UBIPr) dataset (Padole & Proença, 2012) allows to evaluate periocular methods at "higher levels of heterogeneity," as noise factors were actually introduced on the acquisition setup: varying acquisition distance, irregular illumination, pose and occlusion. In addition, manual database annotation includes regions-of-interest and essential landmarks. Image dimensions vary accordingly to the acquisition distance, and range from 501×401 pixels (at 8m) to 1001×801 pixels (at 4m).

- **FG-NET:** The FG-NET is a facial aging database with around one thousand images from 82 subjects, up to 69 years old. Captured at different acquisition setups and many years apart, it is clear how subjects were shoot under very irregular illumination, pose and expression conditions.
- Images are 400×500 pixels in size, captured on the visible wavelength, and for each one a 68 landmark points annotation is also provided.

Recently, Cardoso et al. (2013) developed an algorithm for synthesizing degraded ocular images. Considering that the collection of data for biometric experiments is particularly hard due to security / privacy concerns of volunteers and the substantial amounts of data required, they described a stochastic method able to generate a practically infinite number of iris images with a singular characteristic: simulating image acquisition under uncontrolled conditions. Hence, the generated images have eight varying factors: optical defocus, motion blur, iris occlusions, gaze, pose, distance, levels of iris pigmentation and

lighting conditions (Figure 3). Particular attention was paid for mimicking the dynamic conditions in uncontrolled lighting environments, by using "cube-maps" that replicate different environments that (potentially) surround the simulated subjects. Also, authors announced the availability of an online platform[1] where anyone has the possibility to adjust the levels of variability desired for each of the above factors, and define the main properties of the artificial data sets. This tool might constitute a valuable resource for the evaluation of the robustness of iris segmentation / recognition algorithms, and is available in a completely free and anonymous way.

4. RELEVANT RESEARCH

In this section we summarize the most relevant techniques published in the scope of periocular recognition. Also, we overview the algorithms published in adjacent areas, that can potentially be used to improve periocular recognition algorithms, such as iris segmentation, image quality assessment, feature extraction and matching on ocular data.

4.1 Periocular Recognition

The pioneering approach for periocular biometrics dates back to Park, Ross, & Jain (2009), proposing to extract features at two different levels: local and global, as information concerns patches of the periocular area, or is extracted from the whole image. For global feature extraction, images are properly aligned, using the location of the iris and its dimensions as reference, and defining a 7

Figure 3. Examples of artificial images of the ocular region generated by the NOISYRIS platform

× 5 grid of square regions-of-interest. Although authors acknowledge eye corners to be more fit for such task (Park, Jilela, Ross, & Jain, 2011), they claim that such points cannot be reliably determined. Then, two well-known distribution-based descriptors, namely Histogram of Oriented Gradients (HOG) (Dalal & Triggs, 2005) and Local Binary Patterns (LBP) (Ojala, Pietikäinen, & Harwood, 1996; Ojala, Pietikäinen, & Harwood, 1994), are computed for each region-of-interest independently, and quantized into 8-bin histograms combining shape and texture information. The array comprising such histograms is easily matchable to an identical one (from another image), by simply computing the Euclidean distance. As for the local features, Scale-Invariant Feature Transform — SIFT (Lowe, 2004) allows the detection of a set of key-points, encoded with their surrounding pixels information, and compared against their counterparts from another image. This descriptor offers invariance to translation, scaling and rotation. The authors conducted their tests over a "small" (899 images, 30 subjects, 2 sessions) database of frontal periocular images acquired in the visible wavelength of the electromagnetic spectrum, and reported performances ranging from 62.5% using only HOG features to 80.8% when fusing them with SIFT results. Curiously, combining the three features didn't improved those results, setting joint performance at 80%. Recognition using the whole face, for the same database, achieved 100% Rank-1 accuracy.

On a later work, Park, Jilela, Ross and Jain (2011) went further on stressing periocular recognition by analyzing performance impact of several factors: eyebrow inclusion or disguising, automatic segmentation, side information, iris and sclera masking and expression variation. Their results showed that adding eyebrow information improved SIFT results in almost 19%, although automatic OpenCV segmentation exhibited better performance with "eyebrow-less" data. Face side information, by other side, is almost irrelevant, with performance variations of about 1%. From the stressed variations, expression has a significant impacting over periocular recognition potential, except for SIFT, because of its robustness to distortion. On the other side, this descriptor was the most disfavored on iris/sclera occlusion. Top accuracy for single classifiers was 79.45%, achieved using SIFT over unmasked data, manually segmented and including the eyebrow, when compared to images from the same side and expression. Compared to their previous work (Park et al., 2009), score level fusion didn't present a significant improvement. Recognition over non-ideal situations was also a concern, and authors compared their results with FaceVACS[2] face recognition system marks — 99.77% recognition accuracy on "clear" facial images. Occlusions, for instance, led to significant performance drops (about 60% when occluding the lower part of the face), even for small occlusions on the periocular area. Without score fusion, the encoding methods singlehanded led to accuracies no greater than 25.97%, 20.51% and 10.12% respectively for 10%, 20% and 30% of periocular occlusion. Eyebrow modifications were also subject of testing, using the TAAZ[3] tool to simulate makeover, and leading to 7.5% (LBP) to 10% (other descriptors) performance decay.

When facing subjects shoot with 15° to 30° head rotation, a 35% to 45% performance deterioration was registered. Finally, authors pointed out another issue associated with the periocular region — its lack of stability over time. Images captured three months apart from each other appear to perform 15% worst, and 30% when captured with half-year gap. As further work, authors suggest several possible improvements: better alignment and matching methods; multi-spectral analysis; and the possibility of fusion with iris (or face) recognition methods.

Miller, Rawls, Pundlik, and Woodard (2010b) analyzed the skin texture by applying an Uniform-LBP (ULBP), with further insights on each region's impact on the recognition process. This LBP-based approach achieves "improved rotation invariance with uniform patterns and finer quantization on the angular space" (Ojala, Pietikainen, & Maenpaa, 2002). Similarly to the previous approach, the periocular region is cropped proportionally to intra-eye distance, scaled to 100×160 pixels, and divided in a 7×4 region-of-interest grid. To avoid iris and sclera information influencing the results, an elliptical neutral mask is overlapped to the image. After histogram normalization, ULBP is computed for each region on an 8-pixel neighborhood, producing 59 possible results that populate a histogram and the periocular signature array. Finally, Manhattan distance is used for matching. Experiments were conducted on subjects of FRGC and FERET datasets, for both eyes separately and combined, reporting 84% and 71% and 90% and 74% recognition rates respectively.

The impact of image quality was addressed by Miller, Lyle, Pundlik, & Woodard, 2010a, over three factors: blur, resolution and illumination. Image preprocessing included a similar periocular crop and resizing (251×251 pixels), grayscale conversion, histogram equalization and eye masking, but instead of ULBP a base LBP was used. When blurring the data with a Gaussian filter convolution, the periocular performance over face was evidenced for high blur levels. A similar conclusion was reached when down sampling to 40% of the original size. As for uncontrolled illumination conditions, performance degrades to low levels, as local approaches (*e.g.* LBP) are not suited for irregular lighting conditions.

The authors also compared the discriminant capabilities of the different color channels. The green channel leads to higher differentiation (23% higher accuracy than the red channel), and has similar texture information as the blue channel. Globally, authors concluded that performance achieved on the periocular region was better than using the whole face, having suggested the use of different classification methods, in particular Support Vector Machines (SVM) (Savvides et al., 2006).

Adams et al. (2010) extended Miller et al. (2010b) work, having used a Genetic & Evolutionary Computing (GEC) method to optimize the original feature set, namely the Steady-State Genetic Algorithm (SSGA) as implemented by *NASA's eXploration Toolset for Optimization of Lauch and Space Systems*[4] (X-TOOLSS). Authors reported 86% accuracy for either eye on the FRGC dataset and 80% on FERET data, and top results of 85% and 92% for those databases respectively. Using only 49~52% of the original features improved on, at least, 10%. Nonetheless, the chosen algorithm was not proven to be the optimal for that specific periocular features.

Inspired by Park et al. (2009), Juefei-Xu et al. (2010) expanded their experiments to less ideal imaging environments, having analyzed the performance of different feature schemes on the FRGC dataset.

In addition to LBP and SIFT, both local and global feature extraction schemes were stressed: Walsh masks (Beer, 1981); Laws' masks (Laws, 1980); Direct Cosine Transform (DCT) (Ahmed, Natarajan, & Rao, 1974); Discrete Wavelet Transform (DWT) (Mallat, 1989); Force Fields (Hurley, Nixon, & Carter, 2000); Speed Up Robust Features (SURF) (Bay, Ess, Tuytelaars, & Van Gool, 2008); Gabor Filters (Clausi & Jernigan, 1996) and Laplacian of Gaussian (LoG). The LBP itself was fused with other methods, yielding the results given in Table 2.

Table 2. Rank-1 identification accuracy obtained with the fusion of LBP with other methods (Juefei-Xu et al., 2010)

Fused Methods	Accuracy (%)
LBP + LBP	42.5
Walsh Masks + LBP	52.9
Laws' Masks + LBP	51.3
DCT + LBP	53.1
DWT + LBP	53.2
Force Field Transform + LBP	41.7
Gabor Filters + LBP	12.8
LoG filters + LBP	30.9

Authors show local descriptors to register better results, with the post-application of LBP translated into a performance boost. Although top accuracy was attained with DWT + LBP (53.2%), results were very similar when using DCT and Walsh or Laws' masks. SIFT and SURF verification rate was surprisingly low (<1%), most likely due to low image resolution.

Juefei-Xu, Luu, Savvides, Bui, and Suen (2011) addressed the aging effect on periocular recognition, previously reported as an issue (Park et al. (2011)). Their approach starts by performing two types of corrections: pose, using Active Appearance Models (AAM); and illumination, through anisotropic diffusion model. The periocular region was normalized from the provided landmark points, and features extracted using Walsh-Hadamard transform encoded LBP (WLBP). On a final stage, the unsupervised discriminant projection (UDP) technique (J. Yang, Zhang, Yang, & Niu, 2007) boosted results to very high performance levels. This method was tested on the FG-NET database, with images taken years apart at different acquisition setups (non-uniform illumination, pose and expression). The reported results showed improvements in performance by 20%, and WLBP to perform 15% better than raw pixel intensity matching. UDP also delivers better accuracy (up to 40%) than Principal Component Analysis (PCA) or Locally Preserving Projections (LPP). All the stages together resulted in 100% identification accuracy.

Bharadwaj, Bhatt, Vatsa, and Singh (2010) research on periocular biometrics was focused on unconstrained visible wavelength captured data (UBIRIS.v2 dataset), and tackled the question combining ULBP with a global matcher — GIST — consisting on the combination of five perceptual scene descriptors (Oliva & Torralba, 2001): naturalness, openness, roughness, expansion and ruggedness.

ULBP was computed over 64 patches of the original image and, for the GIST, local contrast normalization was achieved with Fourier trans-

form and the special envelope computed using a set of Gabor filters. For match computation, X2 distance and min-max normalized results from both eyes are fused by a weighted sum. GIST gave best performance than ULBP, and fusing both results led to 73.65% rank-1 accuracy.

To establish the slice of the electromagnetic spectrum that most favor periocular recognition, Woodard, Pundlik, Lyle, and Miller (2010a) evaluated second level features on both NIR (MBGC) and visible-wavelength (FRGC) data. To avoid biased results, an elliptical mask was overlapped to the eye, removing the iris and sclera information. On both datasets texture information was encoded using LBP over a ROI grid, and on the visible wavelength data this information was fused at score level with color information drawn from the red and green channels histograms. At the matching stage Manhatan distance was used for LBP histograms, and Bhattacharya distance for color histograms. Results suggest texture information to be more discriminant, and only a slight improvement was registered after the fusion. As for the electromagnetic spectrum, visible wavelength data delivered better results (88~90% accuracy) than NIR (81~87%).

Subsequently, Woodard, Pundlik, Miller, Jillela, and Ross (2010b) assessed how periocular texture information could improve iris data reliability, so that difficulties when dealing with non-ideal imaging could be dealt with. Tests were conducted over MBGC data, which although being a NIR dataset, had challenging conditions for iris recognition. Iris processing was as of Daugman (1993), except with manual segmentation, and after encoding texture information as above described, information from both traits was fused with a simple weighted sum after min-max normalization. Their work showed how iris' low performance on such difficult data benefits from periocular fusion, raising rank-1 accuracy in over 80%, to 96.5%.

In Woodard, Pundlik, Miller, and Lyle (2011), both studies were unified and extended, providing a closer insight to their previous results. Once again, authors conclude periocular region performance to be comparable to the one obtained using similar features on the whole face.

Jillela and Ross (2012) take advantage of periocular region features to improve the identification performance of two commercial face recognition software over subjects that have submitted to plastic surgery. Inspired by Park et al. (2009), authors also use SIFT and LBP, even though this last one is computed for all color channels. Fusion is achieved at score-level, where all outputs are combined after a single score for LBP is averaged from individual color scores.

Tests were conducted over a plastic surgery database (Singh et al., 2010) consisting of images downloaded from plastic surgery information Websites, and thus with considerable changes in resolution, scale and expression. Results show periocular methods to have 63.9% rank-1 accuracy, and even though face recognition software overcomes that with 85.3%, the best result is obtained when fusing both: 87.4%.

On stressing noise factors impact on periocular recognition, Padole and Proença (2012) tested on images with four inherent variations: subjects' pose, distance to the camera (4m to 8m), iris pigmentation and occlusion. Choosing Park et al. (2009) method, they introduced some slight variations: the ROI was defined based on eye-corner position instead of iris center, which led to most significant improvements since unconstrained biometrics favor gaze variations; and at fusion stage both linear (logistic regression (Hosmer & Lemeshow, 2000)) and non-linear methods (Multi Layer Perceptron — MLP) were tested. Both fusing techniques produced similar results, being MLP slightly better though.

Interestingly, closer acquiring distances didn't seem to lead to better performance. In fact, worst results came from comparisons between subjects imaged at 4 meters, being the "optimal" distance 7m. Not so surprising was pose variation impact on recognition, with higher tilting angles resulting in

lower accuracy values. Similar observations were found for the occlusion trials. Iris pigmentation was reported to also impact periocular recognition performance, with darker eyes leading to poorer results and medium pigmented irises the best ones. Subjects' gender was also reported to impact recognition rates, being female more easily identified through their periocular features. The Human ability to use contextual information and "disregard" most of noise factors, adapting itself to surrounding conditions is outstanding, marking it a hard task for machines to mimic. In fact, when designed recognition algorithms we should rather try to figure out its way of working, seeking alternate strategies to tackle the same issues.

Hollingsworth, Bowyer, and Flynn (2010) aimed at identifying which ocular elements humans find more useful for the periocular recognition task. On their essay, an iris camera was used to acquire NIR data from 120 subjects, being visible the periocular region closer to the eye although some features were missing (*e.g.* incomplete eyebrows). The iris were completely masked, to avoid biased responses, iris was masked with a circular patch, and 80 pairs of images were presented to 25 human observers, who were asked to tell apart pairs belonging to the same or different persons, indicating their degree of certainty. Further to that, subjects had to individually rate each feature's helpfulness in a three level scale.

Results pointed eyelashes to be the most helpful periocular feature, closely followed by the medial canthus and the eye shape. Participants based their responses on eyelash clusters, density, direction, length and intensity. To the inquired observers, skin was actually the less useful.

Average human accuracy on such setup was 92%.

To extend that analysis to the visible spectrum, new factors and a wider dataset, another study was conducted by Hollingsworth et al. (2012). This time, periocular (Park et al., 2009) and iris (IrisBEE biometric system from ICE (Phillips et al., 2010) recognition algorithms were also used for comparison.

Imaging 210 subjects on a controlled environment, 140 pairs of images were presented to 56 observers for each one of four setups: NIR and visible wavelength, periocular and iris data. Test subjects could then rank their certainty on a five level scale, specifying how helpful individual features were ("eye shape," "tear duct," "outer corner," "eyelashes," "skin," "eyebrow," "eyelid," "color," "blood vessels" and "other"). Due to the different pairing system and limited observation time, NIR accuracy dropped to 78.8%, and it was set on 88.4% for the visible wavelength. Machine performance was similar, within 1% difference on overall accuracy. As for the feature discrimination capacity, results were similar to the previous ones (Hollingsworth et al., 2010) for NIR data, with some differences on the visible spectrum where blood vessels, skin and eye shape were reported to be more helpful than eyelashes. Skin details are in fact more perceptible on visible wavelength data, as NIR camera illumination caused frequent skin saturation. In general, visible band was found to be preferable for periocular recognition tasks.

Human perception of iris features is greater on NIR images, with 85.6% accuracy against 79.3 on the visible wavelength. However, and unlike periocular, machine performance was 13% better than humans', with 100% and 90.7% accuracy for those same bands.

4.2 Iris Segmentation

Considering that many techniques for segmenting the iris are based on Hough-transform parameterization, Junli et al. (2013) developed a robust ellipse fitting technique robust to noisy edge-maps that likely result of degraded data. Their algorithm starts by selecting a subset of the edge points that are deemed to be more accurate. Then, considering that squaring the fitting residuals magnifies the contributions of these extreme data points, their algorithm replaces it with the absolute residuals to reduce this influence. The resulting mixed l1-

l2 optimization problem is derived as a second-order cone programming one and solved by the computationally efficient interior-point methods.

Specifically concerned about the segmentation of iris images acquired at large distances, Tan and Kumar (2012) were based in the concept of Grow-cut algorithm that is able to discriminate between foreground (iris) and background (non-iris) data. The results from this phase are refined by post-processing operations: iris center estimation, boundary refinement, pupil masking and refinement, eyelashes and shadow removal and eyelid localization. Experiments were performed in well known datasets (UBIRIS.v2, FRGC and CASIA. v4 Distance) and confirmed the effectiveness of this approach. Moreover, the computational burden of the method appears to be substantially lower than of similar strategies.

Alonso-Fernandez and Bigun (2012) perform the segmentation of the iris based on the Generalized Structure Tensor algorithm. The key point of this strategy is that, using complex filters, authors are able to obtain both magnitude and orientation information for each edge pixel. This provides an additional amount of information that enables to more appropriately discriminate between the edges that are deemed to belong to one of the iris boundaries and spurious edges.

Xinyu et al. (2012) addressed the problem of less intrusive iris image acquisition, in terms of a segmentation algorithm able to work at very different image resolutions (from 50 to 350 pixels in iris diameter). Authors start by detecting a set of edges (Canny detector), which non-connected components are considered nodes of a graph. Next, based on the normalized cuts criterion, they discriminate between the most probable circle-like shapes that correspond to the iris boundaries.

4.3 Noise Detection

In most iris recognition methods, it is particularly important to have an estimate of the regions of the iris that are occluded by other types of information (e.g., eyelids, eyelashes or reflections), and hence should not be considered in the feature encoding phase. When such type of information is erroneously considered, most frequently the false rejection rates augment, but even the number of false acceptances can raise, if no adaptive thresholds with respect to the amount of un-occluded irises are not used.

According to the above observations, several authors addressed the problem of discriminating the useful parts of the iris images. Having considered that previous approaches are rule-based and have questionable effectiveness, Li and Savvides (2012) used Gaussian Mixture Models to model the probabilistic distributions of noise-free and noisy regions of the irises. The idea is to adjust the number of Gaussians for a distribution, by eliminating Gaussians which are not supported by the observations. Based on their experiments, authors propose Gabor filters as basic features, optimized by a simulated annealing process.

4.4 Quality Assessment

Zuo and Schmid (2013) propose three methods to improve the performance of a biometric recognition system, according to quality indexes: 1) quality-of-sample; 2) confidence in matching scores; and 3) quality sample and template features. The first two methods adaptively filter the probe biometric data and matching scores based on predicted values of Quality of Sample index (defined here as d-prime) and Confidence in matching Scores, respectively. The last method, considers that image quality measures as features for discriminating between genuine and imposter matching scores. The proposed algorithm has the advantage of being generic (suitable for other biometric modalities).

4.5 Iris Recognition

Ross et al. (2012), addressed the problem of recognizing degraded iris images, having authors considered five factors: 1) non-uniform illumination, 2) motion, 3) defocus blur, 4) off-axis gaze, and 5) nonlinear deformations. The key insight the proposed method is that a single-feature encoding schema doesn't appropriately handle all these variations, and propose three feature extraction / matching strategies: 1) gradient orientation histograms, 2) scale invariant feature transforms and a 3) probabilistic deformation model. The information extracted by each descriptor is matched independently and results are combined at the score level, using the classical sum-rule. Experiments on the FOCS and FRGC data sets encourage further work on this kind of hybrid techniques.

As with other biometric traits, most difficulties in iris recognition result from less controlled acquisition setups, that lead to severely degraded images. In this context, an interesting possibility might be to fuse periocular recognition to iris recognition algorithms that work on visible wavelength data. It has been claimed that acquire discriminating data from the iris at visible wavelengths might be to hard, due to the pigments of the human iris (brown-black Eumelanin (over 90%) and yellow-reddish Pheomelanin (Meredith & Sarna (2012) that have most of their radiative fluorescence under visible light, but this significantly varies with respect to the levels of iris pigmentation. Even though previous technology evaluation initiatives (Proença & Alexandre, 2010, 2012) confirmed the possibility of recognizing human beings in visible wavelength real-world data, the state-of-the-art algorithms have only a moderately satisfactory performance (decidability indexes of 2.5 at most). The approach that currently outperforms was developed by Tan, Zhang, Sun, and Zhang (2012) and makes fuses global color-based features and local ordinal measures to extract discriminating data from the iris region. Wang, Zhang, Li, Dong, Zhou, and Yin (2012) used an adaptive boosting algorithm to build a strong iris classifier from a set of bi-dimensional Gabor-based features, each corresponding to a specific orientation and scale and operating locally. Given the fact that the pupillary boundary is especially difficult to segment in visible wavelength data, the authors trained two distinct classifiers: one for irises deemed to be accurately segmented and another for cases in which the pupillary boundary is expected to be particularly hard to segment. Li, Liu, and Zhao (2012) used a novel weighted co-occurrence phase histogram to represent local textural features, which is claimed to model the distribution of both the phase angle of the image gradient and the spatial layout and overcomes the major weakness of the traditional histogram. A matching strategy based on the Bhattacharyya distance measures the goodness of match between irises. Marsico, Nappi, and Richio (2012) proposed the use of implicit equations to approximate both the pupillary and the limbic iris boundaries and to perform image normalization. They exploited local feature extraction techniques such as linear binary patterns and discriminating textons to extract information from vertical and horizontal bands of the normalized image.

4.6 Oculomotor-Based Recognition

One of the most original branches in the ocular biometrics domain, might be the recent attempts in performing recognition using as discriminating information the eye movements. In this scope, the work of Komogortsev, Karpov, Holland, and Proenca (2012) should be highlighted. These authors propose to fuse at the score level the oculomotor plant characteristic and the iris texture. From the eye-movement perspective, their results point out that the proposed schemes provide discriminating information between individuals. From the iris perspective, the main conclusion is that very low error rates can be obtained, even when operating on data with resolution substantially lower that the ISO/IEC 19794-6 recommendation. An extremely interesting feature of their experiments was that they were performed using low-cost COTS Webcams. Another interesting work on this scope is due to Rigas, Economou, and Fotopoulos (2012), that used cues that reflect the individual idiosyncrasies

of eye movements for augmenting the robustness of the resulting pattern recognition system. Their method is based on multivariate Wald-Wolfowitz test, that compares the distributions of saccadic velocity and acceleration features. The observed identification rates reveal the efficiency of the method, even though error rates are still far of the obtained with the classical biometric traits (e.g., iris and face). To narrow this gap in effectiveness with respect to other traits, authors plan to use more dynamic features, as the combination of time and spatial information provided by eye movements.

A competition on eye-movements biometric strategies was recently conducted by Kasprowski (2012). According to the observed results, the organizers concluded that is particularly important to be very careful in terms of the position of eyes during data capturing and also to camera calibration. Even though, further work in this scope is encouraged, having authors compared the observed recognition effectiveness to the results attained by the earliest face recognition algorithms.

5. RESULTS AND DISCUSSION

Table 3 summarizes the results obtained by the most relevant periocular recognition methods. We give the types of features extracted and the classification scheme used by each algorithm. Also, the data sets used in the experiments are summarized, together with the observed accuracy. As we can see, recently developed methods focus mainly on texture analysis and key-point extraction, and even simple algorithms lead to fair performance levels, with a noteworthy response of LBP based methods. Periocular fitness for more relaxed setups is also corroborated by these results, favoring the visible wavelength over NIR.

However, and facing the heterogeneity between test data, it's yet difficult to assess methods' relative performance in-between themselves. To bring some enlightenment on that subject, methods should be tested on the same data and

Table 3. Overview of periocular recognition methods

Approach	Features	Extract	Classifier	Dataset	Reported accuracy
(Park et al., 2009)	Shape, Texture, Key-Points	HOG, LBP, SIFT	Euclidean distance, SIFT matcher	899 images, 30 subjects, 2 sessions, visible wavel.	HOG: 62.5% LBP: 70.0% SIFT: 74.2% Best: 80.8%
(Miller et al., 2010b)	Texture	ULBP	Manhattan distance	FRGC, FERET	FRGC: 89.8% FERET: 85.1%
(Adams et al., 2010)	Texture	LBP+GEFE	Manhattan Distance	FRGC, FERET	FRFC: 92.2% FERET: 85.1%
(Woodard, Pundlik, Lyle, & Miller, 2010a)	Color, Texture	R&G ch. color hist., LBP	Bhattacharya distance, Manhattan distance	FRGC, MBGC	L FRGC: 90% R FRGC: 88% L MBGC: 81% R MBGC: 87%
(Woodard, Pundlik, Miller, Jillela, & Ross, 2010b)	Texture	Daugman's iriscode, LBP	Hamming distance, Manhattan distance	MBGC	L Iris: 13.8% R Peri: 92.5% L Fusion: 96.5% R Iris: 10.1% R Peri: 88.7% R Fusion: 92.4%
(Juefei-Xu et al., 2010)	Texture, Key-Points	Walsh Masks, Laws' masks, DCT, DWT, Force Fields, Gabor filters, LBP, SIFT, SURF	Cosine distance, Euclidean distance, Manhattan distance	FRGC	DWT+LBP: 53.2% DCT+LBP: 53.1% Walsh+LBP: 52.9% Laws' + LBP: 51.3% …
(Juefei-Xu et al., 2011)	Texture	WLBP+UDP	Cosine distance	FG-NET	100%
(Bharadwaj et al., 2010)	Naturalnes, Openness, Roughness, Expansion, Ruggedness, Texture	GIST, ULBP	X^2 distance	UBIRIS.v2	GIST: 70.82% ULBP: 63.77% Fusion: 73.65%
(Hollingsworth et al., 2010)	Human	Human	Human	NIR images, 120 subjects	92%
(Hollingsworth et al., 2012)	Human	Human	Human	NIR & visible, 210 subjects	NIR Peri: 78.8% V Peri: 88.4% NIR Iris: 85.6% V Iris: 79.3%

results analyzed side by side. Implementations of each method should reproduce papers' algorithm description as close as possible, and eventually omitted parameter chosen to maximize overall performance. As most of the literature reports results against the FRGC, that dataset is a good candidate for the evaluation stage. A total of 6225 images were selected, with the right-side peri-ocular region manually cropped to avoid further errors, resulting in over 250 thousand matching trials with a 1:2 intra- inter-class ratio. Results from those trials can be seen at Table 4.

Some papers reported multiple results from different setups. As so, values from Table 4 may differ from the ones on Table 3, since we now chose to display the ones best fitting our test conditions.

Table 4. Tested periocular recognition methods performance indicators: Area Under ROC Curve (AUC), Equal Error Rate (EER), Computed (CA) and Reported Accuracy (RA) and Original testing dataset

Approach	Features	AUC	EER	CA	RA	Dataset
(Park et al., 2009)	LBP	0.84	0.24	88.92%	70.00%	899 images,
	HOG	0.82	0.25	88.92%	62.50%	30 subjects,
	SIFT	0.83	0.23	88.66%	74.20%	2 sessions,
	Fusion	0.86	0.21	89.69%	80.80%	visible wav.
(Miller et al., 2010b)	ULBP	0.82	0.24	89.69%	89.80%	FRGC
(Woodard, Pundlik, Lyle, & Miller, 2010a)	ULBP	0.83	0.22	89.69%	83.40%	FRGC
	Color	0.62	0.41	35.57%	74.20%	
	Fusion	0.83	0.23	89.69%	87.10%	
(Woodard, Pundlik, Miller, Jillela, & Ross, 2010b)	LBP	0.82	0.24	90.21%	88.70%	MBGC
	Iriscode	0.75	0.30	69.07%	10.10%	
	Fusion	0.83	0.23	88.66%	92.40%	
(Bharadwaj et al., 2010)	ULBP	0.76	0.30	88.40%	54.30%	UBIRIS.v2
	GIST	0.87	0.21	89.18%	63.34%	
	Fusion	0.88	0.19	87.37%	73.65%	

Having Park et al. (2009) pioneering approach as comparison term, we can see how the subsequent developed algorithms introduce in fact some improvements, either by using more robust procedures (*e.g.* ULBP *vs.* LBP), by proposing different image pre-processing and ROI definition Woodard, Pundlik, Lyle, and Miller's (2010a) LBP *vs.* Park et al. (2009) LBP, or by bringing in new techniques (*e.g.* GIST). However, method performances are quite similar, with rank-1 accuracy around 89%.

The major discrepancy between reported results and ours occur when color information is used (Woodard, Pundlik, Lyle, & Miller, 2010a). Although images from the same database were used for testing, we weren't able to reproduce such scores, and even if obtaining better accuracy on ULBP, fusing it with the color descriptors didn't bring any improvements. That happens because the score level fusion optimization technique (logistic regression) didn't give color information enough weight to make itself representative. Nonetheless, if we attend at the correlation coefficients between features, the more contrasting one is color, followed by iris and SIFT.

6. ISSUES AND PROBLEMS

Being an emerging and relatively new biometric trait, several issues arise from the use of this type of data for recognition purposes. These were grouped into five topics, based on the criteria suggested by Park, Jillela, Ross, and Jain (2011).

The first one is related with the *imaging* stage, and determining the optimal spectrum for periocular biometrics. As former research usually prefers near-infrared data, expectations aim towards the visible wavelength, where unconstrained recognition is favored. However, wouldn't the fusion from data acquired at different wavelengths, yielding multispectral data, result in relevant advantages?

The next concern is about the actual *boundaries* of the periocular region, which are yet to be settled. Even though we observe the inclusion of some traces like the eyebrows, iris or sclera, to improve overall performance, researchers sometimes disagree on whether those elements should rather be masked or cropped to avoid biased results.

Moving on to the *feature encoding* stage, new questions arise: which features are the most representative when aiming at discriminating this region? Also, the heterogeneity of the components in the periocular region may suggest that more elaborate feature schemes are required to describe such different types of information.

After settling the features, a feature *matching* scheme should be determined. We must take into account the techniques most suitable to handle data variations inherent to the less controlled acquisition process, and how to optimally handle the variations in the traditional data variation factors.

At last, how would periocular biometrics benefit from the *fusion* with other features? Even considering that the use of multiple traits might be important to compensate for acquisition adversities, and iris being a fit candidate for score level fusion during periocular recognition, the way of maximize the outcome of this (or other) association is yet to be clearly established.

Apart from the imaging, encoding, matching and fusion alternatives detailed on the previous sections, Bakshi, Sa, and Majhi (2013) addressed the *boundary* definition issue by actually studying its proportions impact on the recognition performance and the trade-off with computational cost, and proposing an *optimized* ROI with minimal template size and maximal recognition accuracy.

7. CONCLUSION

This chapter addressed the use of information in the vicinity of the eye (periocular region) to perform biometric recognition. Particularly for uncontrolled data acquisition scenarios, the periocular region is regarded as an interesting trade-off between using the entire face or using exclusively the iris. Information inside the periocular area is considered to be highly different between individuals and relatively stable over lifetime.

According to the above properties, several research groups have been concentrating their efforts in developing algorithms for periocular recognition, that usually profit of the heterogeneous types of information in this region: shapes of eyelids, texture of the skin and iris, distribution

of eyelashes and skin key points (e.g., spots). This heterogeneity propitiates the fusion at different levels (data, features or scores), from various types of recognition algorithms, which is known to potentially increase robustness against degraded data.

Having presenting the publicly available data sets where experiments are being carried out, we also summarized the most relevant research on this topic and compared the state-of-the-art results in terms of recognition performance. Also, we discussed the issues and directions for further work on this topic.

REFERENCES

Adams, J., Woodard, D. L., Dozier, G., Miller, P., Bryant, K., & Glenn, G. (2010). *Genetic-Based Type II Feature Extraction for Periocular Biometric Recognition: Less is More*. Paper presented at the Pattern Recognition (ICPR), 2010 20th International Conference on. doi:10.1109/ICPR.2010.59

Ahmed, N., Natarajan, T., & Rao, K. R. (1974). Discrete Cosine Transform. *IEEE Transactions on Computers*, *C-23*(1), 90–93. doi:10.1109/T-C.1974.223784

Alonso-Fernandez, F., & Bigun, J. (2012). Iris boundaries segmentation using the generalized structure tensor: A study on the effects of image degradation. In *Proceedings of the 2012 IEEE Fifth International Conference on Biometrics: Theory, Applications and Systems*, (pp. 426-431). IEEE.

Bakshi, S., Sa, P. K., & Majhi, B. (2013). Optimized Periocular Template Selection for Human Recognition. *BioMed Research International*, *14*. doi: doi:10.1155/2013/481431 PMID:23984370

Bay, H., Ess, A., Tuytelaars, T., & Van Gool, L. (2008). Speeded-Up Robust Features (SURF). *Computer Vision and Image Understanding*, *110*(3), 346–359. doi:10.1016/j.cviu.2007.09.014

Beer, T. (1981). Walsh transforms. *American Journal of Physics*, *49*(5), 466–472. doi:10.1119/1.12714

Bharadwaj, S., Bhatt, H. S., Vatsa, M., & Singh, R. (2010). *Periocular biometrics: When iris recognition fails*. Paper presented at the Biometrics: Theory Applications and Systems (BTAS), 2010 Fourth IEEE International Conference on. doi:10.1109/BTAS.2010.5634498

Bhatt, H. S., Bharadwaj, S., Singh, R., & Vatsa, M. (2013). Recognizing Surgically Altered Face Images Using Multiobjective Evolutionary Algorithm. *IEEE Transactions on Information Forensics and Security*, *8*(1), 89–100. doi:10.1109/TIFS.2012.2223684

Bowyer, K. W., Hollingsworth, K., & Flynn, P. J. (2008). Image understanding for iris biometrics: A survey. *Computer Vision and Image Understanding*, *110*(2), 281–307. doi:10.1016/j.cviu.2007.08.005

Cardoso, L., Barbosa, A., Silva, F., Pinheiro, A. M. G., & Proença, H. (2013). Iris Biometrics: Synthesis of Degraded Ocular Images. *IEEE Transactions on Information Forensics and Security*, *8*(7), 1115–1125. doi:10.1109/TIFS.2013.2262942

Clausi, D. A., & Jernigan, M. (1996). *Towards a Novel Approach for Texture Segmentation of SAR Sea Ice Imagery*. Paper presented at the 26th International Symposium on Remote Sensing of Environment and 18th Annual Symposium of the Canadian Remote Sensing Society. Vancouver, Canada.

Dalal, N., & Triggs, B. (2005). *Histograms of Oriented Gradients for Human Detection*. Paper presented at the CVPR. New York, NY.

Daugman, J. G. (1993). High confidence visual recognition of persons by a test of statistical independence. *IEEE Transactions on Pattern Analysis and Machine Intelligence*, *15*(11), 1148–1161. doi:10.1109/34.244676

Hollingsworth, K., Bowyer, K. W., & Flynn, P. J. (2010). *Identifying useful features for recognition in near-infrared periocular images*. Paper presented at the Biometrics: Theory Applications and Systems (BTAS), 2010 Fourth IEEE International Conference on. doi:10.1109/BTAS.2010.5634529

Hollingsworth, K. P., Darnell, S. S., Miller, P. E., Woodard, D. L., Bowyer, K. W., & Flynn, P. J. (2012). Human and Machine Performance on Periocular Biometrics Under Near-Infrared Light and Visible Light. *IEEE Transactions on Information Forensics and Security*, *7*(2), 588–601. doi:10.1109/TIFS.2011.2173932

Hosmer, D. W., & Lemeshow, S. (2000). *Applied logistic regression*. Wiley-Interscience Publication. doi:10.1002/0471722146

Hurley, D. J., Nixon, M. S., & Carter, J. N. (2000). *A new force field transform for ear and face recognition*. Paper presented at the Image Processing (ICIP), 2009 16th IEEE International Conference on. doi:10.1109/ICIP.2000.900883

Jillela, R., & Ross, A. (2012). *Mitigating effects of plastic surgery: Fusing face and ocular biometrics*. Paper presented at the Biometrics: Theory, Applications and Systems (BTAS), 2012 IEEE Fifth International Conference on. doi:10.1109/BTAS.2012.6374607

Juefei-Xu, F., Cha, M., Heyman, J. L., Venugopalan, S., Abiantun, R., & Savvides, M. (2010). *Robust local binary pattern feature sets for periocular biometric identification*. Paper presented at the Biometrics: Theory Applications and Systems (BTAS), 2010 Fourth IEEE International Conference on. doi:10.1109/BTAS.2010.5634504

Juefei-Xu, F., Luu, K., Savvides, M., Bui, T. D., & Suen, C. Y. (2011). *Investigating age invariant face recognition based on periocular biometrics*. Paper presented at the Biometrics (IJCB), 2011 International Joint Conference on. doi:10.1109/IJCB.2011.6117600

Junli, L., Miaohua, Z., Ding, L., Xianju, Z., Ojowu, O., & Kexin, Z., Zhan, Li., & Han, L. (2013). Robust Ellipse Fitting Based on Sparse Combination of Data Points. *IEEE Transactions on Image Processing, 22*(6), 2207–2218. doi:10.1109/TIP.2013.2246518 PMID:23412616

Komogortsev, O. V., Karpov, A., Holland, C. D., & Proenca, H. (2012). Multimodal ocular biometrics approach: A feasibility study. In *Proceedings of the 2012 IEEE Fifth International Conference on Biometrics: Theory, Applications and Systems*, (pp. 209-216). IEEE.

Laws, K. I. (1980). *Rapid Texture Identification*. Paper presented at the Proc. SPIE Conf. Image Processing for Missile Guidance. doi:10.1117/12.959169

Li, P., Liu, X., & Zhao, N. (2012). Weighted Co-occurrence Phase Histogram for Iris Recognition. *Pattern Recognition Letters, 33*(8), 1000–1005. doi:10.1016/j.patrec.2011.06.018

Li, Y.-H., & Savvides, M. (2012). An Automatic Iris Occlusion Estimation Method Based on High Dimensional Density Estimation. *IEEE Transactions on Pattern Analysis and Machine Intelligence, 35*(4), 784–796. doi:10.1109/TPAMI.2012.169 PMID:22868651

Lowe, D. G. (2004). Distinctive Image Features from Scale-Invariant Keypoints. *International Journal of Computer Vision, 60*(2), 91–110. doi:10.1023/B:VISI.0000029664.99615.94

Lyle, J. R., Miller, P. E., Pundlik, S. J., & Woodard, D. L. (2010). *Soft biometric classification using periocular region features*. Paper presented at the Biometrics: Theory Applications and Systems (BTAS), 2010 Fourth IEEE International Conference on. doi:10.1109/BTAS.2010.5634537

Mallat, S. G. (1989). A theory for multiresolution signal decomposition: the wavelet representation. *IEEE Transactions on Pattern Analysis and Machine Intelligence, 11*(7), 674–693. doi:10.1109/34.192463

Marsico, M., Nappi, M., & Riccio, D. (2012). Noisy Iris Recognition Integrated Scheme. *Pattern Recognition Letters, 33*(8), 1006–1011. doi:10.1016/j.patrec.2011.09.010

Meredith, P., & Sarna, T. (2006). The physical and chemical properties of eumelanin. *Pigment Cell Research, 19*, 572–594. doi:10.1111/j.1600-0749.2006.00345.x PMID:17083485

Merkow, J., Jou, B., & Savvides, M. (2010). *An exploration of gender identification using only the periocular region*. Paper presented at the Biometrics: Theory Applications and Systems (BTAS), 2010 Fourth IEEE International Conference on. doi:10.1109/BTAS.2010.5634509

Miller, P. E., Lyle, J. R., Pundlik, S. J., & Woodard, D. L. (2010a). *Performance evaluation of local appearance based periocular recognition*. Paper presented at the Biometrics: Theory Applications and Systems (BTAS), 2010 Fourth IEEE International Conference on. doi:10.1109/BTAS.2010.5634536

Miller, P. E., Rawls, A. W., Pundlik, S. J., & Woodard, D. L. (2010b). Personal identification using periocular skin texture. In *Proceedings of the 2010 ACM Symposium on Applied Computing*. New York, NY: ACM. doi:10.1145/1774088.1774408

Ojala, T., Pietikainen, M., & Harwood, D. (1994). Performance evaluation of texture measures with classification based on Kullback discrimination of distributions. In Proceedings of Pattern Recognition, 1994. doi: doi:10.1109/ICPR.1994.576366

Ojala, T., Pietikainen, M., & Harwood, D. (1996). A comparative study of texture measures with classification based on featured distributions. *Pattern Recognition, 29*(1), 51–59. doi:10.1016/0031-3203(95)00067-4

Ojala, T., Pietikainen, M., & Maenpaa, T. (2002). Multiresolution gray-scale and rotation invariant texture classification with local binary patterns. *IEEE Transactions on Pattern Analysis and Machine Intelligence, 24*(7), 971–987. doi:10.1109/TPAMI.2002.1017623

Oliva, A., & Torralba, A. (2001). Modeling the Shape of the Scene: A Holistic Representation of the Spatial Envelope. *International Journal of Computer Vision, 42*, 145–175. doi:10.1023/A:1011139631724

Padole, C. N., & Proença, H. (2012). *Periocular recognition: Analysis of performance degradation factors.* Paper presented at the Biometrics (ICB), 2012 5th IAPR International Conference on. doi:10.1109/ICB.2012.6199790

Park, U., Jillela, R. R., Ross, A., & Jain, A. K. (2011). Periocular Biometrics in the Visible Spectrum. *IEEE Transactions on Information Forensics and Security, 6*(1), 96–106. doi:10.1109/TIFS.2010.2096810

Park, U., Ross, A., & Jain, A. K. (2009). *Periocular biometrics in the visible spectrum: A feasibility study.* Paper presented at the Biometrics: Theory, Applications, and Systems, 2009. doi:10.1109/BTAS.2009.5339068

Phillips, P. J., Flynn, P. J., Scruggs, T., Bowyer, K. W., Chang, J., Hoffman, K., et al. (2005). *Overview of the face recognition grand challenge.* Paper presented at the Computer Vision and Pattern Recognition, 2005. doi:10.1109/CVPR.2005.268

Phillips, P. J., Moon, H., Rizvi, S. A., & Rauss, P. J. (2000). The FERET evaluation methodology for face-recognition algorithms. *IEEE Transactions on Pattern Analysis and Machine Intelligence, 22*(10), 1090–1104. doi:10.1109/34.879790

Phillips, P. J., Scruggs, W. T., O'Toole, A. J., Flynn, P. J., Bowyer, K. W., Schott, C. L., & Sharpe, M. (2010). FRVT 2006 and ICE 2006 Large-Scale Experimental Results. *IEEE Transactions on Pattern Analysis and Machine Intelligence, 32*(5), 831–846. doi:10.1109/TPAMI.2009.59 PMID:20299708

Proença, H., & Alexandre, L. A. (2010). Introduction to the Special Issue on the Segmentation of Visible Wavelength Iris Images Captured At-a-distance and On-the-move. *Elsevier Image and Vision Computing, 28*(2), 213–214. doi:10.1016/j.imavis.2009.09.004

Proença, H., & Alexandre, L. A. (2012). Editorial of the Special Issue On the Recognition of Visible Wavelength Iris Images Captured At-a-distance and On-the-move. *Elsevier Pattern Recognition Letters, 33*, 963–964. doi:10.1016/j.patrec.2012.03.003

Proença, H., Filipe, S., Santos, R., Oliveira, J., & Alexandre, L. A. (2010). The UBIRIS.v2: A Database of Visible Wavelength Iris Images Captured On-the-Move and At-a-Distance. *IEEE Transactions on Pattern Analysis and Machine Intelligence, 32*(8), 1529–1535. doi:10.1109/TPAMI.2009.66 PMID:20558882

Rigas, I., Economou, G., & Fotopoulos, S. (2012). Human eye movements as a trait for biometrical identification. In *Proceedings of the 2012 IEEE Fifth International Conference on Biometrics: Theory, Applications and Systems*, (pp. 217-222). IEEE.

Ross, A., Jillela, R., Smereka, J. M., Boddeti, V. N., Kumar, B. V. K. V., & Barnard, R. ... Plemmons, R. (2012). Matching highly non-ideal ocular images: An information fusion approach. In *Proceedings of the 2012 5th IAPR International Conference on Biometrics* (ICB), (pp. 446-453). IAPR.

Santos, G., & Hoyle, E. (2012). A fusion approach to unconstrained iris recognition. *Pattern Recognition Letters*, *33*(8), 984–990. doi:10.1016/j.patrec.2011.08.017

Savvides, M., Abiantun, R., Heo, J., Park, S., Xie, C., & Vijayakumar, B. V. K. (2006). *Partial Holistic Face Recognition on FRGC-II data using Support Vector Machine*. Paper presented at the Computer Vision and Pattern Recognition Workshop, 2006. CVPRW '06. Conference on. doi:10.1109/CVPRW.2006.153

Shin, K. Y., Nam, G. P., Jeong, D. S., Cho, D. H., Kang, B. J., Park, K. R., & Kim, J. (2012). New iris recognition method for noisy iris images. *Pattern Recognition Letters*, *33*(8), 991–999. doi:10.1016/j.patrec.2011.08.016

Singh, R., Vatsa, M., Bhatt, H. S., Bharadwaj, S., Noore, A., & Nooreyezdan, S. S. (2010). Plastic Surgery: A New Dimension to Face Recognition. *IEEE Transactions on Information Forensics and Security*, *5*(3), 441–448. doi:10.1109/TIFS.2010.2054083

Tan, C.-W., & Kumar, A. (2012). Efficient iris segmentation using Grow-Cut algorithm for remotely acquired iris images. In *Proceedings of the 2012 IEEE Fifth International Conference on Biometrics: Theory, Applications and Systems*, (pp. 99-104). IEEE.

Tan, K. S., Oh, S. R., Priel, A., & Korn, B. S. (2011). *Surgical Anatomy of the Forehead, Eyelids, and Midface for the Aesthetic Surgeon*. Master Techniques. doi:10.1007/978-1-4614-0067-7_2

Tan, T., Zhang, X., Sun, Z., & Zhang, H. (2012). Noisy iris image matching by using multiple cues. *Pattern Recognition Letters*, *33*(8), 970–977. doi:10.1016/j.patrec.2011.08.009

Wang, Q., Zhang, X., Li, M., Dong, X, Zhou, Q., & Yin, Y. (2012). *Adaboost and multi-orientation 2D Gabor-based accurate noisy iris recognition*, *33*(8), 978-983.

Woodard, D., Pundlik, S., Miller, P., & Lyle, J. (2011). Appearance-based periocular features in the context of face and non-ideal iris recognition. *Signal. Image and Video Processing*, *5*, 443–455. doi:10.1007/s11760-011-0248-2

Woodard, D. L., Pundlik, S., Miller, P., Jillela, R., & Ross, A. (2010b). *On the Fusion of Periocular and Iris Biometrics in Non-ideal Imagery*. Paper presented at the Pattern Recognition (ICPR), 2010 20th International Conference on. doi:10.1109/ICPR.2010.58

Woodard, D. L., Pundlik, S. J., Lyle, J. R., & Miller, P. E. (2010a). *Periocular region appearance cues for biometric identification*. Paper presented at the Computer Vision and Pattern Recognition Workshops (CVPRW), 2010 IEEE Computer Society Conference on. doi:10.1109/CVPRW.2010.5544621

Xinyu, H., Bo, F., Changpeng, T., Tokuta, A., & Ruigang, Y. (2012). Robust varying-resolution iris recognition. In *Proceedings of the 2012 IEEE Fifth International Conference on Biometrics: Theory, Applications and Systems*, (pp. 47-54). IEEE.

Yang, J., Zhang, D., Yang, J.-Y., & Niu, B. (2007). Globally Maximizing, Locally Minimizing: Unsupervised Discriminant Projection with Applications to Face and Palm Biometrics. *IEEE Transactions on Pattern Analysis and Machine Intelligence*, *29*(4), 650–664. doi:10.1109/TPAMI.2007.1008 PMID:17299222

Zhao, W., Chellappa, R., Phillips, P., & Rosenfeld, A. (2000). Face Recognition: A Literature Survey. *ACM Computing Surveys*, *35*(4), 399–458. doi:10.1145/954339.954342

Zuo, J., & Schmid, N. A. (2013). Adaptive Quality-Based Performance Prediction and Boosting for Iris Authentication: Methodology and Its Illustration. *IEEE Transactions on Information Forensics and Security*, *8*(6), 1051–1060. doi:10.1109/TIFS.2013.2259157

KEY TERMS AND DEFINITIONS

Commercial Off-the-Shelf (COTS): Usually refers to products that are commercially available and can be bought and used as they are, in a plug-and-play setting.

Histograms of Oriented Gradients (HOG): Texture descriptor highly popular in computer vision, to efficiently describe a broad range of images. It consists in extracting the oriented gradients in images patches, to quantize and group them into local histograms that are considered the feature sets.

IrisCode: Refers to the biometric signature extracted from the unoccluded iris ring, after segmentation and normalization. The most popular approach consists in the convolution between a set of Gabor filters and the normalized data, from where the sign of coefficients is used.

Local Binary Patterns (LBP): Extremely efficient texture descriptor, that summarizes in a single value the relationship between each pixel and its surroundings, in terms of relative intensity. Usually, histograms of these values are built and considered the feature descriptors.

Oculomotor Recognition: Emerging trait for biometric recognition, based in the observation that the movement of each subject's eyes is singular and relatively stable over lifetime.

Periocular Recognition: Emerging biometric trait that complements the iris texture, in degraded data acquisition environments. The idea is that, for bad quality data, additional discriminating information can be obtained from the shape of eyelids, and eyelashes, eyebrows and the skin texture.

Region-of-Interest (ROI): It is the first phase of any periocular recognition algorithm. After detecting the ocular components, a rectangular is superimposed in the vicininity of the eye, from where the biometric signature is extracted.

Scale-Invariant Feature Transform (SIFT): It attempts to find particular regions (keypoints) in the image that are singular, in terms of their statistical properties. It also refers to a matching strategy that tries to find correspondences among keypoints in different images.

ENDNOTES

1   http://iris.di.ubi.pt/ NOISYRIS
2   FaceVACS SDK available at http://www.cognitec-systems.de
3   Free virtual makeover tool, available at http://www.taaz.com
4   http://nxt.ncat.edu/

Section 3
Example Applications

Chapter 13
Face in Person Re-Identification

Andrea F. Abate
University of Salerno, Italy

Stefano Ricciardi
University of Salerno, Italy

Genoveffa Tortora
University of Salerno, Italy

ABSTRACT

The face represents one of the most diffused and established biometrics for both identity verification and recognition with a large corpus of research focused on advancing the accuracy, the robustness, and the response speed of face recognition systems by means of 2D, 3D, and hybrid approaches. One of the new research lines emerging in this field during the last years is face-based people re-identification, namely the task of recognizing new occurrences of an individual's face once it has been detected and initialized at a given time on the same location or eventually at other locations covered by a network of non-overlapping cameras. In this chapter, the main issues and challenges specifically related to face-based people re-identification are described, and the most promising techniques and results proposed on this topic so far are presented and discussed.

INTRODUCTION

About twelve years after September 11th 2001, the diffusion of person identification and verification systems has reached a worldwide dimension, as anyone travelling overseas has probably experimented while waiting in a queue for immigration control procedures. Biometric systems exploiting face, fingerprint, iris, etc. have progressively become part of everyday life as predicted by pioneers of this technology, covering a growing number of applications in which the access to information, to services or even to physical locations is granted by the recognition of user's biometric traits. With regard to face, precision of recognition and robustness to changes in pose and expressions have represented the major concerns for researchers and developers so far, performances have been steadily improved as witnessed by the various editions of face recognition contests organized in the last decade like the FRVT- Face Recognition Vendor Test (Phillips et al., 2007) and the FRGC - Face

DOI: 10.4018/978-1-4666-5966-7.ch013

Recognition Grand Challenge (Phillips et al., 2006); nevertheless new technical and applicative challenges are still open. Among these challenges, face-based person re-identification represents an active and interesting topic that has the potential to further extend the range of application of face as a biometric.

In general, person re-identification involves identifying new occurrences of a given subject previously detected at a different location and time across a network of sensors covering a large area by non-overlapping fields of view, but there are other declinations of this topic like recognizing an individual each time he/she is visible by the same camera over time, or even counting the number of occurrences of a given person in a video file/ stream in an off-line approach. Re-identification is particularly useful in all the situations in which a large crowd gather, a kind of event more and more common in everyday life due to architectural (tall buildings, huge commercial centers, airports and stations which usually contain several thousands persons) and social reasons (e.g. big entertainment events) among the others. Consequently, it is easy to understand the interest of authorities and government agencies (which often monitor remotely these scenarios) in detecting and re-identifying subjects of interests during their movements across sensitive locations or in using automated surveillance systems able to recognize reported persons. Main obstacles in performing the above mentioned goals include multiple viewpoints and different object poses, wide lighting variations among cameras or over time, unpredictable trajectories, lack of camera coverage and also changes in clothing. Most of the approaches proposed so far to address the aforementioned issues rely on human appearance-based models (Yu et al., 2007; Gray & Tao, 2008; Farenzena et al., 2010; Doretto et al., 2011) to perform various kinds of pattern analysis to find recurrent relationships among clusters of pixels eventually classified as person's head, body or clothes. Nevertheless, biometric descriptors have also been proposed and, under the right conditions, they could represent a viable approach to the person re-identification problem. To this aim, face is particularly interesting since it can operate at a distance as it is inherently a contactless biometric. In the following pages, the main aspects of using face biometric for re-identification purposes will be presented and analyzed, together with a detailed description of the contributions published so far on this.

FROM FACE RECOGNITION TO FACE RE-IDENTIFICATION: ISSUES AND CHALLENGES

As already recalled before, the research on face recognition conducted in the last two decades produced a great number of algorithms and methodologies (Belhumeur et al., 1997; Etemad & Chellappa, 1997; Wiskott et al., 1997; Moghaddam, 2000; Bartlett et al., 2002, Wright et al., 2009). The first objective was mainly in raising the upper limit of recognition accuracy in controlled conditions (one of the explicit goals of FRGC) also because most of the first publicly available reference datasets for face recognition like the FERET (Phillips et al., 1998) and the YaleB (Georghiades et al., 2001) were acquired in studio with controlled settings and cooperative subjects.

However, after the first wave of approaches resulted in higher and higher recognition precision, the efforts were focused on improving performances in the presence of Pose, Illumination and Expression (PIE) variations, three issues extremely common in real world applications which could degrade significantly the accuracy of the results. That said, the re-identification problem poses even more compelling challenges (Chellappa et al., 2012) that can be resumed as:

- Subject-sensor distance
- Image quality
- Unconstrained Pose/Expression/Illumination
- Partial occlusions and facial hair/ware

Subject-Sensor Distance

In face recognition applications, the average distance between the subject to be acquired and the sensing device is typically in the range of one meter or less. Face re-identification is in most cases a remote identification problem (Tistarelli et al. 2009), with a subject-camera distance eventually in the range of up to tens meters. Consequently, the average dimension of a face, in terms of its representation in pixels on the captured frame, can be (depending on the camera's Field-Of-View and sensor's resolution) so small to result unusable for recognition purposes.

A common way to quantify the resolution of a face crop for recognition is to measure the distance between the pupils of the captured subject (for almost frontal shots). A distance of 20-30 pixels is generally considered a lower limit for reliable recognition, while 50+ pixels represent a more realistic measure. Let us consider the hardware related aspects of these requirements. By using a typical surveillance camera, capturing 640x480 pixels per frame and equipped with a "normal" lens providing a 45° FOV (Field Of View), we could have face crops with 55-60 pixels of intra-pupils spacing at about one meter of subject-camera distance, 27-30 pixels at 2 meters and only 10 pixels around 9 meters according to: (1) $N_{IS} = Res_H / ((2\sin(FOV_H/2)D_{C-S})/I_S)$ where N_{IS} is the inter-pupils spacing in pixels, Res_H is the horizontal resolution of captured frame, FOV_H is the horizontal field of view of the camera's lens, D_{C-S} is the camera-subject distance and I_S is the average intra-pupils spacing (6,5-7,5 cm). The situation is even worse in case of wide-angle lenses (common in ceiling or elevated camera installations), as the resulting face crops would be much smaller and, probably, difficult to use

for recognition purposes. Obviously, we can get larger crops by increasing sensor resolution and/ or decreasing the lens' FOV (higher focal length). In the first case this comes at the price of a more expensive device and of a much greater overhead both in terms of processing power/computing time required to analyze the larger frame and of a much greater video throughput (a 1280x720 sensor produces almost fourfold the pixels per frame outputted by a standard 640x480 device, while a Full HD 1920x1080 sensor has almost seven times more pixels). In the second case, decreasing the FOV means to use a greater fraction of the captured image, but this implies that the probability a subject will stay framed is much smaller for a fixed camera. To this regard the use of software controlled Pan, Tilt and Zoom (PTZ) cameras (possibly capable to follow the subject while zooming in/out when required to get more detailed face crop) could be of interest, though it would increase the complexity and the overall cost of the system.

With regard to the image processing approaches to cope with low resolution resulting from remote face capturing, most methods proposed so far exploits super-resolution techniques (Gunturk et al., 2003; Jia & Gong, 2005; Hennings et al., 2008) which output recovered high resolution images from low resolution input samples, but often at the price of strong artifacts. Other methods exploits coupled metric learning (Li et al., 2010), dictionaries (Shekhar et al., 2011) or multidimensional scaling (Biswas et al., 2010), but all these techniques tend to degrade their performance in presence of PIE variations.

Image Quality

Whatever its size, if the captured facial image results of low quality the chances of a reliable identification are reduced. Factors like image noise and blur, indeed, may degrade the discriminant information in acquired images, thus lowering considerably the recognition performance. This is particularly true for face re-identification that mostly operates at a distance. Image noise is partly related to the characteristics of the typically small sized CCD/CMOS sensing device (in general, the smaller the physical pixel dimension the stronger the noise produced due to mutual interference effects, particularly in low light) but it is also due to compression artifacts, common in case of video capturing.

Blur (i.e. image defocusing) represents another cause of image degradation and loss of details. It results from incorrect focalization of the image on the focal/sensor plane (at a local and/or global level) due to optical defects or insufficient depth of field with respect to the camera-subject distance. As depth of field decreases as focal length increases, it is easy to understand why using telephoto lens to zoom in subjects may result in more critical focusing and higher percentage of blurred frames. On the contrary, wide-angle lenses have very ample depth of field.

Apart from optical issues, image may be affected by another kind of defocusing effect, known as "motion blur" and related to the dynamic aspects of frame capturing. Motion blur is due to the insufficient frame capturing rate in presence of rapid subject or camera movements and it results in image blurring along the motion direction. Of course, the higher the capturing rate, the smaller the motion blur effect.

In outdoor scenarios, also weather conditions may involve additional factors eventually affecting image quality. Rain, fog, haze and snow may contribute in reducing image's dynamic range while increasing noise. In a typical re-identification scenario all the aspects mentioned before are inter-dependent at some extents, indeed face re-identification typically involves recognition at a distance which is likely to be performed by medium-to-long focal length camera optics with limited depth of field and prone to exhibit motion blur artifacts in case the subject moves rapidly across the FOV width. Furthermore, as larger imaging sensors require much costly and

bulkier optics to achieve the same focal length and aperture, the sensor's size would probably be small, therefore featuring a greater average level of noise and a narrower dynamic range.

From all these considerations, a clear need emerges for objectively quantifying image quality in facial images taken at a distance through a specific metric to assess their usability for recognition. To this aim, in (Tistarelli et al., 2009) a signal-to-noise ratio estimator is proposed by correlating signal-to-noise estimation and noise level to the statistics of image edge intensity. Experimental evidence proves that this estimator is directly correlated to the recognition accuracy of a face recognition system so that it represents a trustable measure of image quality useful to filter out unsuitable incoming images.

Unconstrained Pose/ Illumination/Expression

As in the introduction, PIE variations represent one of the most active research topics for face recognition, as the combination of these factors often transforms a face's appearance so as to result less similar to its neutral version than to other faces belonging to completely different individuals. Consequently, uncontrolled pose, expression and illumination may easily lead to both false positive and false negative recognition.

Therefore, face recognition literature is rich of proposals specifically targeted to cope with pose variations by means of a number of approaches such as morphable models (Blanz & Vetter, 2003), face appearance (Gross et al., 2004), tied factor analysis (Prince et al., 2008), stereo matching (Castillo & Jacobs, 2009), albedo estimation (Biswas & Chellappa, 2010). Robustness to illumination variations has been approached by exploiting spherical harmonics (Basri & Jacobs, 2003) quotient image (Wang et al., 2004), total variation models (Chen et al., 2006); stereoscopic images (Zhou et al., 2007); albedo (Biswas et al., 2009) and dictionaries (Patel et al., 2011), while expression weighting mask (Abate et al., 2005), canonical image (Bronstein et al., 2006) iso-geodesic stripes (Berretti & Del Bimbo, 2011) represents a few among the many methods developed toward the goal of expression invariant face representation.

Though many advances have been registered over the years with regard to these topics, most of the solutions proposed so far either do not perform at their best in all three regards or they are not suited to or are difficult to use for re-identification. This is partly due to the operational constraints typical of remote identification scenario (e.g. 3D methods need a sensing technology often limited to indoor/close-range usage) and partly to the specific challenges faced for outdoor re-identification, where the subject's freedom of movement and complexity of motion patterns is potentially much greater than in a typical indoor face verification scenario, the intensity and the effects of illumination can be extreme (direct sunlight, strong sharp shadows, environmental reflections, etc.) and facial expression may have an even stronger impact due to low resolution or long range issues in facial image quality.

Partial Occlusions and Facial Hair

A further challenge for face recognition in general and for face re-identification in particular is represented by the partial lack of information eventually due to occluding objects. These may be clothing elements (hats, scarves, sunglasses, etc.) worn by the subject to be identified, other persons or even architectural elements positioned between the subject-camera line-of-sight. In both cases the face descriptors resulting from capture may lack important features that possibly affect the reliability of recognition.

Sparse representation (Wright et al., 2009) has proved to be suited to address this issue, while robust principal component analysis has also been exploited with interesting results (Candès et al., 2011). Typical face re-identification scenarios might involve severe occlusion conditions, as the width of movements, the probability of a subject wearing sunglasses and the variety of objects and persons eventually hiding part of the captured face are much more relevant than in "conventional" face recognition.

Beard and facial hair in general are (along with facial expressions) among the "user-factors" which may affect face recognition performance (Tistarelli et al., 2009). These variations of facial appearance have also been addressed by a number of works like for instance (Abate et al., 2006; Mittal & Sasi, 2006; Wright et al., 2009) but their impact on remote outdoor face re-identification can be greater than for controlled indoor situations because average image quality, and resolution are likely to be lower.

USING FACE FOR PERSON RE-IDENTIFICATION: SOME EXAMPLES

From the overall analysis of problems and difficulties related to face recognition at a distance and outdoor, it is understandable why only in the very last years the research on this topic has started to provide solutions. In the following lines we report some of the most recent approaches to face-based person re-identification available in the literature so far.

In their paper "Multi-Pose Face Recognition for Person Retrieval in Camera Networks" (Bauml et al., 2010) the authors study the use of facial appearance features for the off-line re-identification of persons using distributed camera networks in a realistic surveillance scenario. They choose to rely on face instead of using features based on whole body appearance, as commonly seen in literature, because face offers an important advantage, common to biometric identifiers, of stability over large amount of time. This can make the difference in case the recognition has to be performed on images captured over several days (one of the goals of the proposed system), during which there are very high chances that a person's clothes will change, thus leading most appearance/color based methods to a failure. Another objective is the capability to locate a person by analyzing in near real time (5 to 10 seconds) video footage recorded within the last ten minutes by multiple disjoint cameras.

The advantages of using face biometric come at the price of dealing with low-resolution images and strong variations in pose and illumination. To this regard, the authors claim that the proposed method is able to work with face crop of just 18x18 pixels and is robust to out-of-plane rotations of up to 60 degrees. These performances are possible by tracking faces in real time across pose changes (see Figure 1) to increase the amount of available training data and to improve persons' identification by means of temporal association, even when recording conditions are unfavorable for multiple frames.

In brief, the method is articulated into different stages including face tracking, feature extraction, model training and track scoring. Face tracking is based on multiple Modified Census Transform (MCT) face detectors operating at increasing levels of out-of-plane rotation which result robust to illumination variations and can be performed in real time as they are embedded in particle filter framework to evaluate them only at candidate locations. For each face captured a specific particle filter is associated to it, so it is crucial that particles, which propagate according to independently drawn noise from normal distributions, do not merge onto the same target in case of occlusion. To this aim each track's center deflects particles belonging to other tracks.

A drawback of this technique is that it is not robust to large amount of occlusion, as the occluded track will be destroyed. As long as the tracker provides the location of a face within a particular

Figure 1. Image captured by a surveillance system based on four cameras, featuring face tracking and head pose estimation. By means of tracking data, challenging side views can be associated to other views to gather a broad range of training data useful to improve the accuracy of retrieval.

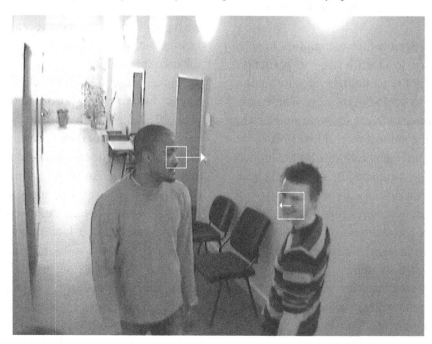

frame, pose alignment and feature extraction can be performed resulting in a feature vector.

Pose alignment firstly exploits rough pose estimation provided by the tracker to normalize all non frontal view (yaw-angle wise), then eyes and mouth are detected by boosted cascades of MCT feature histograms (previously trained on annotated images from the FERET database) and finally a further normalization based on affine transformation is performed resulting in a fixed face-crop size and pose. Discrete cosine transform (DCT) is therefore applied to 48 disjoint sub-regions of the face image leading to a 240 dimensional feature vector.

When a query set (gathering one or more live/recorded tracks of a single person) is provided, a matching score is calculated for all tracks available in the database and the results eventually above a user-defined threshold are returned. The matching score computation results from a person-specific classifier, a Support Vector Machine, trained using the features from the query set on the whole database content.

Besides operating in a fully automated way, the proposed approach allows the user to provide interactive feedback on the three highest scores and on the two lowest results to achieve progressive model re-training in subsequent rounds. The system has been evaluated on a proprietary dataset of surveillance footage, captured by means of a set of four cameras featuring 797 tracks of 92 different individuals. Overall, on this challenging dataset recorded in an indoor environment, the authors reported promising results. A mean average precision of 0.60 was achieved for inter-camera retrieval using just a single track as query set, and up to 0.86 after four rounds of relevance feedback provided by an operator.

A multi-cue approach to people re-identification is presented in (Corvee et al., 2012), based on associating people appearance with head and face features in multi camera network scenario. The underlying idea is that in most networks, cameras sometimes cannot provide the full people

appearance view due to occlusions and faces can even be not visible or partly occluded. The approach proposed is aimed to allow the user to scan throughout a network of surveillance cameras the best matching candidates and to perform the tracking of people of interest throughout this network. In general simplified Local Binary Patterns (LBP) features are exploited to detect people, head and face, while Mean Riemannian Covariance Grid (MRCG) is used to model appearance of tracked people to obtain highly discriminative human signature.

More in detail, the recognition pipeline is composed by a detection-tracking stage, temporal trajectory analysis, appearance based re-identification and face recognition. For what concerns the detection phase, the authors propose a novel simplified LBP (SLBP) providing a feature vector with dimensionality reduced from 256 to 16. Cell features are trained across a people image database by means of an Adaboost training scheme. This scheme is implemented on a multiple scale by progressively increasing the SLBP cell dimensions over both width and height. The same training algorithm is then applied to head and face image datasets for head and face detection. Overlapping candidates are eventually fused and stand-alone noisy candidates are eliminated according to a rule-based strategy. After the detection and tracking have been performed (see Figure 2), the subsequent stage is aimed to recognize the subject at a person level by means of the MRCG-based human signature that has proved to be highly discriminant and suited to work on low resolution frames and in case of inter-person occlusions, when detecting body parts may fail. This robustness results from the dense representation produced by dividing the image into overlapping cells whose spatial correlation is retained. The mean covariance matrix contains important information about the appearance modification over time with regard to a particular cell and the grid composed by all MRC cells (the MRCG) can be used to match the same appearances between different camera views.

Figure 2. A) Person, Head and Face detection. B) People, face tracking and re-identification. Face tracks are analysed by a face re-identififcation algorithm, while person tracks are analysed by a person re-identification algorithm.

A: Person, Head and Face detection

B+C: People, face tracking and re-identification
Face tracks are analysed by a
face re-identification algorithm
Person tracks are analysed by a
person re-identification algorithm

C: Iris re-identification
When a person enters a user drawn zone,
and when this person's face is detected,
a high definition camera takes multiple shots
of the person's iris for iris re-identification

The next step is to extract facial features from the candidates whose appearances match between different camera views. The face model adopted considers four specific signatures (left eye, right eye, nose and mouth), each of which is represented by a set of SLBP histograms normalized over a selected SLBP feature value. Finally, facial signatures are matched according to a similarity distance resulting from the mean similarity distance of the four facial part signatures.

The overall system and the underlying approach and algorithms have been tested on the INRIA human dataset, which contains 1132 human images and 453 background images without humans. The experimental results compared to other high performing approaches in literature describe state-of-the art performance for people detection and promising results for appearance+face based re-identification. As discussed in the previous section, one of the challenges in face re-identification is related to the camera-subject distance of acquisition in most surveillance systems combined with the freedom of movement within the controlled area which translates in a reduced chance to capture face frontally or, in other words, a high probability of wide posing variations.

This typical situation makes the frontal-to-side recognition an important element of the face-based re-identification problem. In (Dantcheva and Dugelay, 2012) the authors focus on this aspect and propose a novel approach considering color-and-texture based soft biometric traits, like those derived from patches of hair, skin and clothes to improve frontal-to-side recognition rate.

To this aim, they started studying the way humans recognize people coping with the lack of a frontal face view by using other visual cues like hair, skin and clothes color. Consequently, by understanding the reasons behind the relevance of these traits, they propose to analyze color and texture of the skin-hair-clothes patches and correlate their intensity to build a robust combined classifier capable of re-identifying a person from side view (see Figure 3). To this purpose the authors present an empirical study about the error probability for extraction and classification of a system based on the above described color soft biometric patches. The system performs patches retrieval first, operating on probe and gallery images whose pose differs by roughly 90 degrees. The retrieval of hair, skin and clothes patches is guided by the coordinates of face and eyes. Patch size is chosen according to inter-ocular distance, while patch placement (both horizontally and vertically) follows a set of empirical alignment rules. After the patches retrieval, features including color and texture are extracted and represented by the corresponding feature vectors.

The authors underline that the whole system's reliability, in term of probability of false identification of a randomly chosen person out of a random set of subjects, can be directly related to three fundamental factors: the number of categories that the system can identify; the accuracy of features / categories in representing the chosen set of subjects on which the identification has to be performed; how robustly these categories can be detected. Furthermore, also the number N of subjects affects reliability, as a higher N involves identifying a person among an increasingly large set of possibly similar-looking people.

With regard to the first factor, the approach proposed associates to each soft biometric trait specific trait-instances (e.g. the color of the hair) which sum up in determining the total number of categories. The higher this number, the greater the system's reliability due to a better distinctiveness. As the key to unambiguous recognition of a person is by associating he/her to an exclusive category, it is important to avoid collisions (i.e. multiple associations to the same category). This risk can be reduced by considering more distinctive or multiple traits. Ultimately, the robustness of categories estimation depends on a general error probability that includes the probabilities of collision errors and of classification errors.

The proposed classifier, combining all described traits boosted by the AdaBoost.MH algorithm, shows stronger classification accuracy than single trait classifiers, but experiments conducted on a subset of the FERET database achieved error probability of 0.1 in an authentication group of 4 subjects, which is a figure too high for a robust re-identification system. This non-optimal performance is due to traits inter-correlations (hair color–skin color or skin color–skin texture. To improve this performance the amount of sub-classifiers could be further extended. Nevertheless, the system in its current configuration can be usefully exploited as a pruning system for more robust systems or as an additional system for multi-trait biometric systems. A different formulation of face re-identification problem has been investigated in the context of video-retrieval by (Fisher et. al., 2012). In this case, the goal is to

Figure 3. Frontal (gallery) to side (probe) association of regions of interests for hair, skin and clothes (soft) biometrics traits

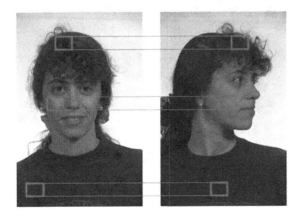

find all the occurrences of a face selected by the user within one or more videos. The peculiarity of this scenario poses a great challenge to the re-identification system. Firstly there is lack of any previously collected training data. In second place, no person-specific models can be trained in advance. Finally, the query data is limited to the image that the user clicks on. This makes it very difficult to find other occurrences of the person because they might be taken under very different lighting conditions, view the face under a different pose, have different facial expressions, etc. The choice of using face instead than relying

on appearance models, much more diffused in surveillance scenarios, is even more compelling in this context, because in many videos, particularly in TV series or movies, persons change their clothing often and sometimes only a small part of the body is visible while the faces of the actors are well visible most of the time (see Figure 4).

The approach proposed starts analyzing a video by means of a shot boundary detection and face-tracking component and then extracts features exploited for the retrieval of matching candidates. All these steps are performed offline, storing the results in a database. The user watch-

Figure 4. Examples of query (a) and retrieval results (b-f) under wide PIE variations

ing the video can then click on an actor's face at any point in the video, and the system retrieves shots from the same or a different video in which the same actor is present. If he is not yet satisfied with the number of returned results, he can assist in the retrieval process by confirming face images depicting the queried person among a small number of candidate images presented to him by the system. The query is then continued using the user-provided selections, yielding more results than before.

The system employs a face tracker that can successfully track persons across pose changes based on (Fisher, 2008) exploiting this information to extract frontal and non-frontal face images. There is a clear advantage in doing that, since in most videos there is a relevant number of shots where only profile views of an actor are available, consequently these shots could not be retrieved using only frontal faces. Tracks are matched by using a Discrete Cosine Transform local appearance-based algorithm (Eleken & Stiefelhagen, 2006). Third, the retrieval process itself works differently from usual approaches. First, a query set is built by collecting all face images that have been selected by clicking on a face image. Then the system searches for very close matches to any image in the query set. The resulting matches and the tracks they belong to are then directly added to the query set, then a new search is performed using the enlarged query set, and so on, until no more matches can be found automatically. The enlarged query set is then presented to the user.

This approach allows the system to increase the variation in the query set and this way close the gap from the pose of the face in the query image to the different poses in the target images, by leveraging the temporal association provided by the tracker and by enlarging the query set automatically using results that have a high confidence. Finally, the system allows the user to assist in the retrieval process.

Using this additional query data, the search process is restarted and yields more results. The proposed system has been evaluated quantitatively in experiments on two labeled episodes of the TV series Coupling. Intra-episode and inter-episode retrieval as well the effect of user interaction on the system performance are evaluated. The results indicate that the system works very well, given the difficult data. The fully automatic retrieval provides a reliable basis for further improvement through interactive user feedback. Even for small amounts of user feedback, very high recall rates can be achieved. For instance, with five rounds of user feedback, the recall already reaches over 80% at 95% precision. With ten rounds, the recall further increases to around 90%. This is the case both for within-episode and cross-episode retrieval.

Robustness to background and illumination variations represents the main focus of the study conducted in (Ma et al., 2012) aimed at both person and face re-identification. They propose, indeed, a new image representation on the combination of Biologically Inspired Features (BIF) and covariance descriptors (BiCov), enabling to measure effectively the similarity between two persons/faces without requiring any pre-processing steps like background subtraction or body part segmentation.

Covariance descriptors can capture shape, location and color information, and their performances have been shown to be better than other methods in many situations, as changes in rotation and illumination are absorbed by the covariance matrix.

The proposed method includes two stages. In the first stage, Biologically Inspired Features (BIF) are extracted through the use of Gabor filters (S1 layer) and MAX operator (C1 layer). In the second stage, the Covariance descriptor is applied to compute the similarity of BIF features at neighboring scales. While the Gabor filters and the Covariance descriptors improve the robustness to the illumination variation, the MAX operator increases the tolerance to scale changes and image shifts. Furthermore, by measuring the similarity of neighboring scales the influence of the background is limited. By overcoming illumination, scale and background changes, the performance of person re-identification and face verification is greatly improved.

Experiments to validate the proposed method were conducted on two well established public datasets for person re-identification: VIPeR and ETHZ which are among the most challenging ones, since they contain a wide range of combined issues (pose changes, viewpoint and lighting variations, occlusions, etc.). Regarding face verification, the popular Labeled Faces in the Wild (LFW) dataset is used, allowing comparisons with many recently published approaches. The results achieved have shown that, in the unsupervised setting, the proposed BiCov representation and the related recognition algorithm achieve state-of-the-art performance.

We briefly resume the main features of the methods for face-based person re-identification presented above in Table 1.

FUTURE PROSPECTS AND CONCLUSION

Face-based re-identification represents a challenging research topic but also an opportunity to improve the level of active safety in a number of situations in which a network of surveillance cameras is available to remotely monitor persons of interests in an unconstrained fashion. In the previous sections most of the difficulties related to this computer vision task have been described and a few of the approaches emerged so far have been presented.

The overall picture is that there is a clear limit to the accuracy that can be achieved at this moment in face re-identification due to hardware (surveillance camera sensor size, image resolution, frame rate, etc.) and software limits (robustness of algorithms to wide PIE variations, low resolution and occlusions; sub real-time or offline computing time; lower performance in unsupervised operation; etc.).

Table 1. Resume of previously described approaches to face-based person re-identification. The RT column shows either the method is capable of real time operation or not, while the MC column reports if multiple cues, besides face, are used for recognition.

Main Works on Face in Person Re-Identification				
Authors	**Dataset**	**RT**	**MC**	**Approach**
Bauml et alii	Proprietary	Y	N	multiple detectors based on Modified Census transform
Chellappa et alii	Proprietary	Y	N	Sparse Representation-based Classification (SRC)
Corvée et alii	INRIA, proprietary	Y	Y	LBP, ADAboost, Mean Riemannian Covariance Grid (MRCG)
Dantcheva and Dugelay	FERET	N	Y	AdaBoost applied to hair, skin and clothes patches
Fischer et alii	TV-series	N	N	facial appearance, assisted retrieval refinement
Ma et alii	VIPeR, ETHZ	Y	N	Biologically Inspired Features (BIF) and covariance descriptor

Nevertheless many technological improvements in surveillance camera are near to come, as affordable hires high frame-rate camera sensors becoming more and more diffused in other fields could easily boost re-identification system performances. With regard to algorithms, re-identification approaches are expected to take advantage among others of: a deeper integration level of recognition and tracking; temporal reasoning and spatial layout of the different cameras for pruning the set of candidate matches; brightness transfer function between different cameras to track individuals over multiple non-overlapping cameras; smart controlled pan/tilt/zoom cameras to overcome poor capturing quality.

Further help to handle image variability comes from on-line evidence accumulation characteristic of closed–loop control, e.g., explore and exploit using sequential importance sampling (SIS). Learning and adaptation using both labeled and unlabeled data using statistical learning, in general, and semi-supervised learning, in particular, might provide further help with re-identification. One particular learning strategy of interest is co-training, where only a small amount of labeled data is required to learn and the use of unlabeled data improves performance over time. Advances toward the solution of the re-identification problem would make a significant contribution to a wide range of real world applications.

REFERENCES

Abate, A. F., Nappi, M., Ricciardi, S., & Sabatino, G. (2005). Fast 3d face recognition based on normal map. In *Proceedings of IEEE International Conference on Image Processing*, (Vol. 2, pp. 946-949). IEEE.

Bartlett, M., Movellan, J., & Sejnowski, T. (2002). Face recognition by independent component analysis. *IEEE Transactions on Neural Networks*, 13(6), 1450–1464. doi:10.1109/TNN.2002.804287 PMID:18244540

Basri, R., & Jacobs, D. W. (2003). Lambertian reflectance and linear subspaces. *IEEE Transactions on Pattern Analysis and Machine Intelligence*, 25(2), 218–233. doi:10.1109/TPAMI.2003.1177153

Bauml, M., Bernardin, K., Fischer, M., & Ekenel, H. K. (2010). Multi-pose face recognition for person retrieval in camera networks. In *Proceedings of IEEE Int. Conf. on Advanced Video and Signal Based Surveillance (AVSS)*, (pp. 441-447). IEEE.

Belhumeur, P., Hespanda, J., & Kriegman, D. (1997). Eigenfaces versus fisherfaces: Recognition using class specific linear projection. *IEEE Transactions on Pattern Analysis and Machine Intelligence*, 19(7), 711–720. doi:10.1109/34.598228

Berretti, S., Del Bimbo, A., & Pala, P. (2010). 3D Face Recognition Using Isogeodesic Stripes. *IEEE Transactions on Pattern Analysis and Machine Intelligence*, 32(12), 2162–2177. doi:10.1109/TPAMI.2010.43 PMID:20975115

Biswas, S., Aggarwal, G., & Chellappa, R. (2009). Robust estimation of albedo for illumination-invariant matching and shape recovery. *IEEE Transactions on Pattern Analysis and Machine Intelligence*, 29(2), 884–899. doi:10.1109/TPAMI.2008.135 PMID:19299862

Biswas, S., & Chellappa, R. (2010). Pose-robust albedo estimation from a single image. In *Proceedings of IEEE Conf. on Computer Vision and Pattern Recognition (CVPR)* (pp. 2683–2690). IEEE.

Blanz, V., & Vetter, T. (2003). Face recognition based on fitting a 3D morphable model. *IEEE Transactions on Pattern Analysis and Machine Intelligence, 25*, 1063–1074. doi:10.1109/TPAMI.2003.1227983

Bronstein, A. M., Bronstein, M. M., & Kimmel, R. (2006). Robust expressioninvariant face recognition from partially missing data. In *Proc. European Conference on Computer Vision.* Gratz, Austria: Academic Press.

Candès, E. J., Li, X., Ma, Y., & Wright, J. (2011). Robust principal component analysis. *Journal of the ACM, 58*(3). doi:10.1145/1970392.1970395

Castillo, C., & Jacobs, D. (2009). Using stereo matching with general epipolar geometry for 2D face recognition across pose. *IEEE Transactions on Pattern Analysis and Machine Intelligence, 31*(12), 2298–2304. doi:10.1109/TPAMI.2009.123 PMID:19834149

Chellappa, R., Ni, J., & Patel, V. M. (2012). Remote identification of faces: Problems, prospects, and progress. *Pattern Recognition Letters, 33*, 1849–1859. doi:10.1016/j.patrec.2011.11.020

Chellappa, R., Ni, J., & Patel, V. M. (2012). Remote identification of faces: Problems, prospects, and progress. *Pattern Recognition Letters, 33*, 1849–1859. doi:10.1016/j.patrec.2011.11.020

Chen, T., Yin, W., Zhou, X. S., Comaniciu, D., & Huang, T. S. (2006). Total variation models for variable lighting face recognition. *IEEE Transactions on Pattern Analysis and Machine Intelligence, 28*(9), 1519–1524. doi:10.1109/TPAMI.2006.195 PMID:16929737

Corvée, E., Bak, S., & Brémond, F. (2012). People Detection and Re-identification for Multi Surveillance Camera. In *Proceedings of VISAPP* (pp. 82-88). SciTePress.

Dantcheva, A., & Dugelay, J. (2011). Frontal-to-side face re-identification based on hair, skin and clothes patches. In *Proceedings of IEEE International Conference on Advanced Video and Signal-Based Surveillance,* (pp. 309-313). IEEE.

Doretto, G., Sebastian, T., Tu, P., & Rittscher, J. (2011). Appearance-based person reidentification in camera networks: Problem overview and current aspects. *J. Ambient Intell. Human Comput., 2*(2), 1–25.

Ekenel, H. K., & Stiefelhagen, R. (2006). Analysis of local appearance-based face recognition: Effects of feature selection and feature normalization. In *Proc. of the CVPR Biometrics Workshop* (pp. 34–41). CVPR.

Etemad, K., & Chellappa, R. (1997). Discriminant analysis for recognition of human face images. *Journal of the Optical Society of America, 14*, 1724–1733. doi:10.1364/JOSAA.14.001724

Ethz, A. Ess, B-Leibe, & Gool. (2007). *Depth and appearance for mobile scene analysis.* Retrieved from http://www.vision.ee.ethz.ch/~aess/iccv2007/

Farenzena, M., Bazzani, L., Perina, A., Murino, V., & Cristani, M. (2010). Person Re-Identification by Symmetry-Driven Accumulation of Local Features. In *Proc. of IEEE Computer Society Conference on Computer Vision and Pattern Recognition,* (pp. 2360-2367). IEEE.

FERET. (n.d.). *Face Recognition Technology Database.* Retrieved from http://www.itl.nist.gov/iad/humanid/feret/

Fischer, Ekenel, & Stiefelhagen. (2011). Person re-identification in TV series using robust face recognition and user feedback. *Multimedia Tools and Applications, 55*(1), 83–104. doi:10.1007/s11042-010-0603-2

Fischer, M. (2008). *Automatic identification of persons in TV series*. Diplomarbeit, Interactive Systems Labs, Universitat Karlsruhe (TH).

Georghiades, A. S., Belhumeur, P. N., & Kriegman, D. J. (2001). From few to many: Ilumination cone models for face recognition under variable lighting and pose. *IEEE Transactions on Pattern Analysis and Machine Intelligence, 23*(6), 643–660. doi:10.1109/34.927464

Gray, D., & Tao, H. (2008). Viewpoint invariant pedestrian recognition with an ensemble of localized features. In *Proc. of Europ. Conf. on Computer Vision*. Marseille, France: Academic Press.

Gunturk, B., Batur, A., Altunbasak, Y., Hayes, M. H. I., & Mersereau, R. (2003). Eigenfacedomain super-resolution for face recognition. *IEEE Transactions on Image Processing, 12*(5), 597–606. doi:10.1109/TIP.2003.811513 PMID:18237935

Hennings-Yeomans, P., Baker, S., & Kumar, B. (2008). Simultaneous super-resolution and feature extraction for recognition of low-resolution faces. In *Proceedings of IEEE Conf. on Computer Vision and Pattern Recognition*, (pp. 1–8). IEEE.

INRIA. (n.d.). *Person Dataset*. Retrieved from http://pascal.inrialpes.fr/data/human/

Jia, K., & Gong, S. (2005). Multi-modal tensor face for simultaneous super-resolution and recognition. In *Proceedings of Tenth IEEE Internat. Conf. on Computer Vision ICCV*, (vol. 2, pp. 1683–1690). IEEE.

LFW. (n.d.). *Labeled Faces in the Wild face dataset*. Retrieved from http://vis-www.cs.umass.edu/lfw/

Li, B., Chang, H., Shan, S., & Chen, X. (2010). Low-resolution face recognition via coupled locality preserving mappings. *IEEE Signal Processing Letters, 17*(1), 20–23. doi:10.1109/LSP.2009.2031705

Ma, B., Su, Y., & Jurie, F. (2012). BiCov: a novel image representation for person re-identification and face verification. In *Proceedings of British Machine Vision Conference* (pp. 57.1-57.11). Academic Press.

Mittal, G., & Sreela, S. (2006). Robust Preprocessing Algorithm for Face Recognition. In *Proceedings of Canadian Conference on Computer and Robot Vision*, (pp. 57-65). Academic Press.

Moghaddam, B. (2000). Bayesian face recognition. *Pattern Recognition, 33*, 1771–1782. doi:10.1016/S0031-3203(99)00179-X

Patel, V. M., Wu, T., Biswas, S., Phillips, P. J., & Chellappa, R. (2011). Illumination robust dictionary-based face recognition. In *Proc. Internat. Conf. on Image Processing*. Academic Press.

Phillips, P. J., Flynn, P. J., Scruggs, T., Bowyer, K. W., & Worek, W. (2006). Preliminary face recognition grand challenge results. In *Proc. International Conference on Automatic Face and Gesture Recognition*, (pp. 15–24). Academic Press.

Phillips, P. J., Scruggs, T., O'Toole, A. J., Flynn, P. J., Bowyer, K. W., Schott, C. L., & Sharpe, M. (2007). *FRVT 2006 and ICE 2006 large-scale results*. National Institute of Standards and Technology.

Prince, S., Warrell, J., Elder, J., & Felisberti, F. (2008). Tied factor analysis for face recognition across large pose differences. *IEEE Transactions on Pattern Analysis and Machine Intelligence, 30*(6), 970–984. doi:10.1109/TPAMI.2008.48 PMID:18421104

Shekhar, S., Patel, V. M., & Chellappa, R. (2011). Synthesis-Based Low Resolution Face Recognition. In *Proceedings of International Joint Conference on Biometrics*, (pp. 1-6). Academic Press.

Tistarelli, M., Li, S. Z., & Chellappa, R. (2009). *Handbook of Remote Biometrics: for Surveillance and Security*. Springer Publishing Company Inc. doi:10.1007/978-1-84882-385-3

VIPeR. (n.d.). *Viewpoint Invariant Pedestrian Recognition*. Retrieved from http://vision.soe.ucsc.edu/?q=node/178

Wang, H., Li, S. Z., & Wang, Y. (2004). Generalized quotient image. In *Proc. Internat. Conf. Computer Vision and Pattern Recognition* (pp. 498-505). Academic Press.

Wiskott, L., Fellous, J.-M., Krger, N., & Malsburg, C. V. D. (1997). Face recognition by elastic bunch graph matching. *IEEE Transactions on Pattern Analysis and Machine Intelligence, 19*, 775–779. doi:10.1109/34.598235

Wright, J., Ganesh, A., Yang, A., & Ma, Y. (2009). Robust face recognition via sparse representation. *IEEE Transactions on Pattern Analysis and Machine Intelligence, 31*, 210–227. doi:10.1109/TPAMI.2008.79 PMID:19110489

Yu, Y., Harwood, D., Yoon, K., & Davis, L. S. (2007). Human appearance modelling for matching across video sequences. *Machine Vision and Applications, 18*(3-4), 139–149. doi:10.1007/s00138-006-0061-z

Zhou, S. K., Aggarwal, G., Chellappa, R., & Jacobs, D. W. (2007). Appearance characterization of linear Lambertian objects, generalized photometric stereo, and illumination-invariant face recognition. *IEEE Transactions on Pattern Analysis and Machine Intelligence, 29*(2), 230–245. doi:10.1109/TPAMI.2007.25 PMID:17170477

KEY TERMS AND DEFINITIONS

Charge-Coupled Device (CCD): The first and most diffused type of semiconductor based imaging device, at the heart of almost any digital camera system and capturing the entire image at once into a frame store.

Complementary Metal Oxide Semiconductor (CMOS): In the context of this chapter this term actually refers to CMOS "active pixel" image sensor technology, generally less prone to blooming effects in case of light overload compared to CCD, but capturing a row at time.

Field Of View (FOV): A key parameter of any lens (and related camera system), measuring the angular width of the truncated-pyramid shaped region of space captured through the lens by the sensing device. It can be measured according to horizontal, vertical or diagonal axis of the pyramid's base.

Motion Blur: A type of image defocusing typically due to a high relative velocity of the captured subject respect to the imaging device causing a particular blur oriented in the direction of motion.

Occlusion: Refers to any kind of object or subject partially or totally covering the region of interest within the captured image.

Pan, Tilt, Zoom (PTZ): Refers to a type of video capturing device able to interactively modify the way the surrounding environment is framed by controlling rotation around its vertical (pan) axis, rotation around the horizontal (tilt) axis and the magnifying power of the camera lens.

Pose, Illumination, Expression (PIE): Refers to the three main issues affecting the comparison of multiple images of the same face acquired in different moments and different environmental conditions.

Chapter 14
Methods and Perspectives in Face Tracking Based on Human Perception

Vittoria Bruni
Sapienza University of Rome, Italy & National Research Council, Italy

Domenico Vitulano
National Research Council, Italy

ABSTRACT

This chapter aims at analyzing the role of human early vision in image and video processing, with particular reference to face perception, recognition, and tracking. To this aim, the change of perspective in approaching image processing-based problems where the decoder (human eye) plays a central role is analysed and discussed. In particular, the main topics of this contribution are some important neurological results that have been successfully used in face detection and recognition, as well as those that seem to be promising in giving new and powerful tools for face tracking, which remains a less investigated topic from this new standpoint.

INTRODUCTION

The objective of target tracking is to estimate the trajectory of an object as it moves around a scene from a sequence of images acquired by a video-camera. The efficient tracking of features in complex environments is a challenging task, especially for real time applications, such as video surveillance, traffic monitoring, motion based recognition, monitoring systems, robotics, and also for computer vision. In fact, the increasing and recent diffusion of video cameras and high powered computers allowed the use of computer vision techniques in this field and the development of new ones.

The whole tracking process consists of

- The detection of the target in the first frame of the analysed video,
- Its representation and localization in subsequent frames, and
- The interpretation of its trajectory for high level processing such as recognition, warnings etc.

DOI: 10.4018/978-1-4666-5966-7.ch014

We are interested in the first two steps, with particular regard to the second one. Key points of this latter step are *target representation* through efficient features that are able to give a faithful and distinctive description of target appearance, and a proper similarity measure for finding the most probable target location in the analysed frame. The Chapter focuses on a specific target category, namely *human faces*, and gives an overview of some novel and effective features for the description of face appearance as well as some distance measures useful for face tracking. The main theme of the study is the use of perception rules for addressing the specific problem, respectively *face representation* and *face tracking*. This interest has been mainly motivated by the great benefits that the research of the last few decades received thanks to the use of the laws of visual perception in the solution of classical problems based on image/video processing. Human perception, indeed, has been at least threefold advantageous:

- It allowed offering new solutions to some important problems, also improving the achievable results in some fields. Significant examples are novel image quality assessment metrics that gave objective distance measures that correlate with Human Visual System better than classical and widely used measures depending on the Mean Square Error (MSE), as it is shown in Figure 1.

- It gave skills to make algorithms completely automatic, without requiring user's intervention. This enabled the diffusion of a lot of algorithms and applications as well as the construction of tools usable by non-expert people in Computer Science, allowing the use of computer aided solutions and frameworks in different fields like medicine, biology, cultural heritage, telecommunications, etc.. As a further consequence, it allowed to allocate more time for more complex operations, as interpretation, allowing the definition of real time operations;

- It allowed a considerable reduction of the computing time of several algorithms thanks to the possibility of using less information for getting the same goals. One example for all is *fixation points* that seem to effectively code all image information using very few points: very few features are then required for describing the most important (visual) image information.

Figure 1. Original Einstein image (leftmost) corrupted by three different kinds of distortions (respectively change of luminance mean, jpeg compression and blurring --- images kindly provided by Prof. Zhou Wang of Waterloo University - Canada). The MSE value is quite the same for the three corrupted images whereas they are visually different. On the contrary, the values of MSSIM (mean structural similarity index (Wang, 2004)) are closer to the visual quality of the same images: the second image is more similar to the original one than the last two, whose visual quality is definitely worse.

MSE=0, MSSIM=1   MSE=144, MSSIM=0.988   MSE=142, MSSIM=0.662   MSE=144, MSSIM=0.694

On the other hand, faces are the most important social stimuli for humans and the primary means by which we perceive the identity and the state of the observed person (Webster, 2011). That is why face perception is important in understanding the process of human perception mechanisms at both early and high level vision (Cerf, 2007). In order to perform visual search under natural conditions, humans use high-speed eye movements (*saccades*) to direct the highest resolution region of the retina, the *fovea*, toward potential target locations in the environment. Many studies proved that fast *saccades* and few *fixations* are enough for scene understanding and any other additional *fixation* is redundant. Even though it may seem surprising, it is consistent with survival needs. For example, the necessity of detecting dangers as soon as possible even in complicated environments, strongly influenced the natural evolution of Human Visual System. That is why the use of a more perceptual point of view in the development of tracking systems is twofold advantageous. It allows a faithful and easy tracking in agreement with human attention and, at the same time, it automatically allows a considerable reduction of the computing time, making trackers suitable for real time applications.

The Chapter is organized as follows. The first Section gives a brief overview of the main approaches to face detection and tracking problems. The second Section describes the contribution of the rules of Human Visual System in the solution of some important image processing problems. The third Section focuses on those visual concepts applied to face perception and representation, with particular attention to those features that can be useful for their tracking in subsequent frames. This Section not only analyzes existing results and their advantages, but it especially focuses on future perspectives and potential future applications of some novel theoretical results in face tracking. Concluding remarks are finally drawn in the last Section.

A SHORT REVIEW ABOUT FACE DETECTION AND TRACKING

As it is well-known, target tracking usually involves more than one operation. Adopting a classical representation in the literature, tracking can be split into two main phases (Comaniciu, 2003):

- Target representation and Localization, and
- Filtering and Data Association.

The first part is probably the most difficult since it deals with the appearance of the target and its modification in the video sequence. It is mainly based on object (face) detection and all problems tied to it. On the contrary, the second phase, i.e. *Filtering and Data Association*, is a top-down process accounting for the dynamics of the object in the scene. The next two subsections try to give a very short overview of the plethora of approaches involved in these two main phases, mainly focusing on the face tracking problem.

Face Detection

This phase is probably the most important part when dealing with faces (De Carlo, 2000) --- with respect to other applications like aerial video surveillance etc.. The first action of face detection in a video sequence is its detection within the first frame. Though many tracking papers assume this operation already accomplished, in practice it is one of the most challenging. Face detection has been mainly developed in Pattern Recognition with different approaches and different applications --- see Samal (1992), Chellappa (1995), Yang (2002), and Hjelm (2001) for pioneering and more recent reviews. In fact, face detection can also be seen as a two-class recognition problem where each image region can be classified as 'face' or 'non face' one (Hsu, 2002).

Before starting the review, we give the definition of face detection as in (Yang, 2002): *To determine whether or not there are faces in a given image and, if so, to give location and extent of each face.* Due to the complexity of scenes in any surveillance situation, it is arguable that this is an as interesting as challenging objective. Main difficulties stem from *Pose, Presence of structural components, Facial expression, Occlusion, Image conditions.* In particular, *Pose* plays a fundamental role in the image appearance as coming from a 3D space to a 2D representation (first frame), while the angle of the face (frontal, profile etc.) with respect to the camera is also crucial for an effective face detection. Another important aspect is the *Presence of structural* (but potentially changing) *components* like mustaches, beards, glasses etc. with all variability factors they involve. Even a very natural aspect like *Facial expression,* which is immediately recognized by a human observer, may cause many difficulties in designing an automatic face detector because of its high variability in many little details of different face components. *Occlusions* also play a key role. Again, there are many situations where eliminating just a small region of the face under study may produce very different results in detection and recognition. Finally, last but not least, *Image acquisition conditions* may definitely inficiate the detection result because of factors like light conditions, camera features etc., can drastically change the appearance of the same face. Historically, face detection approaches can be coarsely split into four classes: *Knowledge based methods, Feature invariant approaches, Template matching methods, Appearance-based methods.*

Knowledge based methods try to encode the 'human representation' of face information by looking for facial features and their relationships (Yang, 1994; Kotropoulos, 1997; Kanade, 1973). In other words, it is well known that a face is composed of a nose, two eyes (in symmetric locations) and a mouth --- supposing that a frontal acquisition without occlusion has been performed. Looking for them, their locations and distances may yield to detect and recognize similar (or the same) faces. The difficulty of finding neither too strict nor too large rules led researchers to propose a multiresolution approach where face is represented at different details levels (from coarser scales to finer ones). At each scale level, the rule is changed and the candidates set cardinality is then reduced. Approaches belonging to this class have good performances, even though they need a work window suitably located on the face to drastically reduce false alarms and they do not deal with the multiple faces case.

Feature invariant approaches are oriented to simulate what human beings do: to detect and recognize a face without any effort and with a great robustness to environment conditions. Though the objective is very interesting (and very close to the aim of this chapter) it results, at the same time, very challenging. The problem of looking for features that are invariant to pose, light conditions etc. is very difficult. Among the plethora of approaches belonging to this class, the main research guidelines have been the following ones. One way may be to detect image edges (along with their relationships), to group them in order 'to understand' whether they compose a face --- and eventually to compare them with another group of edges of a query face, in case of recognition. Some approaches belonging to this class are for instance (Leung, 1995; Yow, 1997; Takacs, 1995), where interestingly the last two ones exploit perceptual considerations and human visual system. Another way may be to identify face textures like skin, hair etc. to input to a suitable supervised classifier (see for instance Dai (1996)). In alternative, skin color modeled by a mixture of Gaussians can be used for a fast and effective detection (Yang, 1996; McKenna, 1998). Though several proposals have been provided to make approaches belonging to this class more effective in the presence of different lighting conditions, changing background etc., they remain (as well as the approaches belonging to the other two classes) not too robust alone. In other words, it seems that just one feature (color, texture etc.) is not sufficient to fully describe face information. That's why the last class of approaches is based on combining more than one feature (global like color etc. and local like nose etc.) leading to more robust frameworks (Kjeldsen, 1996; Viola, 2004).

Template matching methods are based on first finding out a pattern useful to describe standard face information. The successive detection is then achieved by performing a correlation between the input image and the standard pattern. This class of approaches is characterized by a high implementation simplicity. A classic example can be found in Craw (1992), where after an edge detection via the Sobel filter, the resulting edges (i.e. the input template) are compared to the standard pattern in order to determine if there is a candidate face. The process goes on at a different scale level where features relative to nose, eyes etc. are checked to confirm the face presence. Though the use of a multiresolution approach, this kind of approaches may fail in case of different pose, scale etc.. This is the reason why there have been some improvements oriented to propose deformable templates as in [Latinis95], where a combination of a Point Distribution Model on the sampled edges (nose, eyes etc.) and an Active Shape Model search is performed on the deformed template.

The class of *appearance-based methods* exploits models or templates learned from a set of typical face images. The latter can produce both probability density functions and discriminant functions able to detect face regions within an input image. Inheriting all experience from machine learning, this class contains a lot of different approaches such as Eigenface (i.e. Eigenvectors of the image autocorrelation matrix) combined with neural networks (Turk, 1991), Gaussian p.d.f.s

and multilayer perceptron (Sung, 1998), neural networks applied on luminance-based or edge-based features (Rowley, 1998), Support Vector Machine with polynomial vector (Osuna, 1997), Bayes classifiers (Schneiderman, 1998), Hidden Markov models (Rajagopalan, 1998), and finally some theoretic information based approaches that especially use the Kullback-Leibler divergence (Lew, 1996; Colmenarez, 1997).

Face Tracking

Despite the wide research for detecting faces within a single image inherited from pattern recognition, there are relatively fewer approaches explicitly oriented to face tracking (Shan, 2010).

That is why there are some approaches in literature that share face tracking and recognition (Zhou, 2002a, 2002b; Kim, 2008) or recognition on a roughly localized image (Kim, 2007). In fact, even though also videos have the same problems of still images (sensitivity to low resolution, pose variations, partial occlusion etc.), it is well-known that the wider information contained in a video may help to drastically reduce the aforementioned inconveniences. In addition, video sequences also contain facial dynamics that play a fundamental role in face identification (Knight, 1997; O'Toole, 2002). However, face tracking still remains a challenging topic.

A really effective face tracking is difficult because of face appearance variations caused by the non-rigid structure, occlusions, 3D motion and environmental changes (e.g., illumination) (Shan, 2010). These factors strongly influence classical tools for tracking, like particle filtering (Arulampalam, 2002) and mean shift (Bradski, 1998; Comaniciu, 2000a). In order to face with this problem, adaptive schemes able to deal with changing target appearance and scene conditions have been proposed. An interesting approach in this sense is contained in (Ross, 2008) where the target is updated in an adaptive manner using the images tracked in the previous frames. Another example is in Grabner (2006), where an online boosting for tracking allows online updating of the discriminative features of the target object. The risk arising from this kind of adaptation is that the current target is led to gradually adapt to non-targets, as the target model is built from the previous tracked results. This problem is well known as *drift*. In order to overcome it, some strategies have been proposed. For instance in Kim (2008), some global constraints usually based on factors like variations in pose, illumination, and expression suitably trained from a set of face images have been proposed. In particular, Kim (2008) proposes two main constraints based on a set of facial pose manifolds and a Support Vector Machine as discriminator. Another approach to reduce drifting has been proposed in Grabner (2008), where an online semi-supervised boosting allows the use of the labeled data as a prior and the data collected during tracking as unlabeled samples. Finally, in (Doulamis, 2010) an *automatic tracking recovery* tool has been proposed.

It improves the performance of any tracking algorithm whenever the results are not acceptable by means of non-linear object modeling tools that label image regions to object classes.

HUMAN VISUAL SYSTEM IN FACE DETECTION AND TRACKING: RESULTS, ADVANTAGES AND PERSPECTIVES

In the last years there has been a growing interest in the use of Human Visual Perception (HVP) to solve Image Processing based problems. This interest mainly derived from the simple observation that the final receiver of image information is human eye. Hence, acting as human eye does can be the key issue for novel and effective solutions of some classical problems involving both still images and videos (see Figure 2). In the next two Sections we will review the main contributions of HVP in information processing, with particular attention to face recognition and tracking.

Figure 2. A scheme of the perceptual information processing. Image kindly provided by Prof. Zhou Wang of Waterloo University – Canada.

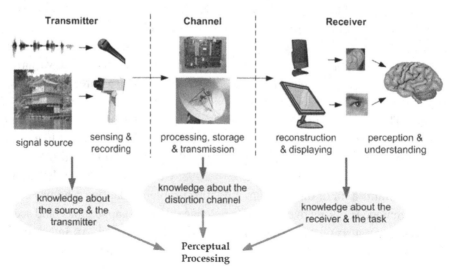

The Role of Human Visual System in Information Processing

The interest toward HVP in information processing mainly derives from a change of perspective in approaching information processing problems: from the actual (functional perspective) to the perceived (visual perspective) information. The main theoretical contribution in this sense is represented by the Minimum Description Length (Rissanen, 2007) that, thanks to the studies of Kolmogorov (Kolmogorov, 1965), (Cover, 1989), (Li, 1997) concerning the concept of complexity, provided a formal equivalence between *coding* and *learning*, also in agreement with the Occam razor for which "*the simplest solution is more likely to be the best*." As a result, if one considers that human eye is the final receiver of image information, the early vision mechanisms can be used for efficiently *coding* and *learning* the observed image, allowing a fruitful model selection in several information processing-based problems.

For example, Human Perception now guides digital restoration according to the concept of Just Noticeable Detection threshold (Pappas, 2000; Winkler, 2005; Bruni, 2012a), that fixes the limit of visibility of a given object in a given context i.e., the ability of human eye in discriminating an object from its surrounding information. It turns out that it is enough to hide degradation rather than completely remove it from the image (see Figure 3). That is why digital restoration

algorithms now reduce the visual contrast of image anomaly till it is masked by its surrounding information (Agaian, 2007; Bruni, 2009,2011a. 2013, 2006b;Greenblatt, 2008). The visual contrast is measured, using different mathematical tools, as a proper ratio between object information and the one of its local neighborhood (Winkler, 2005).

Similar concepts are applied to image and video coding, especially for tuning the quantization step (Watson, 1993; Hontsch, 2002; Wang, 2013): more visible points are quantized using a finer bin since humans are more sensitive to distortions in those regions; on the contrary, a coarser quantization step is adopted for less visually attractive points (i.e., low contrast points, tails of the contrast sensitivity function, masked regions, etc.).

Human Perception also allows the automatic detection of image anomalies as they capture human attention at first sight (Bruni, 2004, 2006a). The rationale is that since they are visually different from the remaining image content, they are perceived as foreign objects in the scene (see Figure 4).

Human Perception contributed much more and in an effective manner in the definition of novel image quality assessment measures based on the fact that existing objective measures, like PSNR (Peak Signal to Noise Ratio), SNR (Signal to Noise Ratio), do not well correlate with the perceived image quality (see Figure 5). Some of the most popular and effective measures are SSIM (Structural SIMilarity Index) and its modifications

Figure 3. Examples of images restored using perception-based models: degradation has not been completely removed from the degraded images but human eye is not able to perceive it in the restored images

Figure 4. Examples of semitransparent degradation detected using perception-based models: the original image is projected into a space where degradation is more visible than the remaining image content --- the original images have been kindly provided by Fratelli Alinari s.r.l

Original image

Optimal projection space

Global detection mask

(Wang, 2004a, 2004b, 2006, 2011), that embeds three main properties of vision i.e., luminance adaptation, contrast masking and spatial correlation (Winkler, 2005); VIF (Visual Information Fidelity index) that measures the mutual information between two images in proper multiscale projection spaces (Sheikh, 2006); VSNR (Visual Signal to Noise Ratio) (Chandler, 2007), that is based on near and supra threshold of human vision. The former is related to the visibility of distortion, the latter is related to the amount of visibility that is measured as the Euclidean distance in the distortion-contrast space. Figure 5 is a clear example of why it is necessary to have new image quality assessment metrics. In a noisy image, PSNR gives the same score to both flat and textured regions, even though noise is more visible in the flat region than in the textured one. On the contrary, noise masking effect in the textured regions is properly accounted for by the corresponding SSIM values.

This change of perspective in image analysis necessarily leads to the definition of new representations of image content: from the most to the less visible. Such kind of representation is called bottom-up since it is referred to observations without a searching task. *Saliency maps* are a representative example of such bottom-up schemes (see Figure 6). They are topographical oriented maps of the scene, where the most significant positions are the ones that are more different from their neighbors (higher contrast) in terms of color, intensity, orientation, movement, depth, etc. (Itti, 1998; Wang, 2010). More recently, this basic principle has been expressed in slightly different terms, including the definition of salient locations as those containing spatial outliers that may be more surprising in a Bayesian sense (Rosenholtz, 1999; Itti, 2006; Bruce, 2006), or context-aware saliency, which detects the important parts of the scene based on both local and global low-level considerations, visual organizational rules, and high-level factors (Goferman, 2012).

Human perception is assuming a significant role also in object detection and tracking in video sequences, even in the case of small objects (Yang, 2011; Makantasis, 2013). With regard to this topic, it is interesting to consider those papers that deal with the correlation between the mechanism that regulates eye movements during the analysis of a scene and the ability of detecting and tracking objects of interest (Javal, 1879; Lamare, 1892; Buswell, 1995; Rayner, 1998; Rajashekar, 2006; Najemnik, 2008; Rayner, 2009; Salmon, 2001). Taking into account that a *saccade* is a rapid eye movement that allows a jump from one location to another in order to direct a small part of our visual field into fovea for a closer inspection i.e.,

Figure 5. Example of visual quality assessment of a degraded frame using the Structural Similarity index. Top) original image; Bottom left) noisy image corrupted with zero-mean additive Gaussian noise; Bottom right) SSIM image: lighter points indicate higher visual quality; darker points indicate lower visual quality.

Figure 6. Saliency maps (bottom) of the three images (top) of LIVE database (Sheikh) computed using the algorithm in (Itti, 1998)

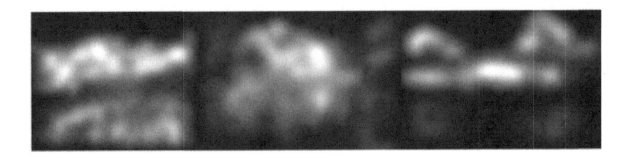

fixation., these papers show that very few points in the image are able to attract HVP in the pre-attentive phase. These points are not randomly sampled but they are effective at solving problems in visual cognition; in addition, these *fixation points* are foveated i.e., human attention decreases as one moves away from them. It means that, despite the multiscale aspect of vision, human eye uses a spatially-varying resolution. That is why classical linear multiscale transforms alone are not able to precisely model human vision. On the contrary, foveated transforms are able to cover a wide field of view, to guarantee high resolution on regions of interest, and to allow processing and bandwidth savings. Hence, they can contribute to the improvement of systems requiring automatic target acquisition, tracking, and recognition. For example, in (Dubuque, 2009) mutual information (in the sense of Information Theory (Cover, 1991) between a known but hidden target and the observed image is used for selecting fovea placements in order to detect and track that specific target. The fovea is centered at the pixel that realizes the maximum of the mutual information between the target and the observations. The results are very interesting for both acquisition and tracking. In fact, on the one hand, they showed that under a set of simplifying assumptions, a foveated acquisition system can outperform full resolution systems that require the same bandwidth. Hence, if the acquisition system is limited by communication bandwidth or computational complexity, foveated acquisition systems may be more convenient and successful since they allow to gather more information. On the other hand, a simple variation of the Kalman filter, common in most of existing trackers that optimally fuses observations from a foveated camera is able to greatly improve tracking performance thanks to a reduction of the error in estimated positions as the frame rate increases. In fact, the latter dominates the effects of increased downsampling more than the observation variance, number of targets and peripheral sampling. This kind of results are in some sense confirmed by

the studies in Raj (2005), Boot (2009), and Watson (2010) concerning the link between strategy instructions for visual search and the eye movements made during search. In particular, they give evidence of the fact that passive instructions lead the observers to *see* i.e., to process the information available in a *fixation*, whereas active instructions lead observers to *look* i.e., to make *saccades* to new locations. Hence, efficient passive searchers are those who use the information available from their longer initial *fixations* to guide subsequent search, limiting the number of *saccades* but, at the same time, allowing more direct *saccades* to the target. On the contrary, if the goal is not to search for a particular target, then an effective strategy is to peak successive *fixations* that maximally reduce the total contrast uncertainty about the image content.

The Role of Human Visual System in Face Detection and Tracking

A lot of the research of the last years concerning the use of HVP also for face processing focused on face detection and recognition, whereas very little has been specifically done for face tracking. For a successful tracking, it is fundamental not only to represent faces through efficient features, able to give a faithful and distinctive description of their appearance; it is also important to select a proper similarity measure to use for finding out the most probable face location in subsequent frames. It is then interesting to exploit HVP concepts also for deriving or selecting a proper distance that may facilitate and improve tracking performance.

Unfortunately, the problem is not trivial at all. Even though there exist several neurological studies on the mechanisms guiding human vision, especially, at its early stage, it is often not so easy to translate such studies and knowledge into efficient and faithful mathematical/computer based models. The goals and challenges from these points of view are numerous and include:

- **The selection of saccades and fixations:** What is the best way to reproduce the decision process of human eye during the observation process? How do eyes move during both scene observation and understanding processes? Can *fixations* be selected through Bayesian modeling or is it better to maximize the gained information measured in terms of entropy?

- **The characterization of fixations:** What is the measure that better characterizes *fixations*: contrast, luminance, colors, edges or all of them? In this latter case, have they the same importance?

- **The selection of a proper similarity metric for tracking:** What is the best measure able to assess the similarity between two objects in different frames/images, according to HVS?

From a more formal point of view, these ambitious and challenging goals can be summarized as follows:

- To give a mathematical formulation (characterization) of *fixation points* that includes the definition of a proper feature space for faces (image space, multiresolution, contrast sensitivity);

- To define a distance in this feature space to use for tracking.

Even though the subjective aspect in human vision cannot be predictable, it is subjected to some basic rules, especially the early vision, that can be modeled by well-defined and objective schemes. Studies carried out in Wang (2004b), Mante (2005), Raj (2005), and Frazor (2006), using tools and different skills, confirm that human eye selects some appropriate observation points from which getting information about the whole image content; any other additional information is redundant for the interpretation of the scene. More precisely, a *saccade* is a rapid eye movement that

occurs up to three times per second and allows a jump from one location to another. Its purpose is to concentrate visual attention into the fovea in order to perform closer inspections i.e., define *fixations*. The active selection performed during *saccades* is based on both bottom-up and top-down control mechanisms. The bottom-up attentional selection is linked to involuntary attention so as it is fast, involuntary, and stimulus-driven. For example, face perception seems to be an instinctive and simple action that humans do since their first few days of life. For a search without specific task, observers unconsciously tend to select central locations of the image in order to catch the potentially most important visual information (Fecteau, 2006). On the contrary, for a task oriented search, human vision relies extensively on the ability to make saccadic eye movements to orient the high-acuity fovea region of the eye over the targets of interest in the visual scene (Tatler, 2005; Rajashekar, 2007). Despite the complexity of face recognition process, very few *fixation* points are necessary for face detection and recognition in the pre-attentive phase (first 250ms of observation) and all of them are concentrated just below the eyes, in correspondence to the nose, with the first one moved toward the left (Hsiao, 2008). However, even though two *fixations* are enough, they are relatively long *fixations*. The same area is used in different illumination conditions. The only difference consists of the additional time spent by the observer for scene interpretation. However, the precise location of *fixation* points is not always the same for different individuals. In fact, even though visibility deteriorates in the periphery, the way it degrades, in terms of steepness, total amount and directionality, depends on the specific individual, that has its own upper, lower and horizontal visual fields (Abrams, 2012; Peterson, 2013). In some sense humans have the ability of maximizing task performance through optimal eye movement according to their specific visibility map as well as specific human experience and knowledge. It is obvious that this is a more complicated topic to be straightforwardly embedded in automatic algorithms unless one includes information regarding, for example, the age of the observers. For instance, babies (newborns) perceive a completely diffuse world and they are able to perceive and recognize faces just from their contours. This topic is strictly related to the holistic processing of facial features (Gauthier, 2002) that allows humans to recognize familiar faces in very low resolution images so that high-frequency information is not only useless but also insufficient for face recognition.

Inspired by biological understanding of human attention to meaningful objects, such as faces, the works in Cerf (2007) and Sharma (2009) developed new models for computing an improved saliency map which is more consistent with gaze deployment in natural images containing faces than previously studied models. They are mainly based on the fact that faces always attract attention and

gaze, independently of the task and image content, and then they are part of the bottom-up saliency pathway (Cerf, 2007). Based on this assumption, three well known algorithms for visual saliency, namely Saliency Map (SM) (Itti, 1998) (that consists of a multiscale combination of three low level features: color, intensity and orientation), GAFFE (Rajashekar, 2008) (that selects *fixations* as those points in proximity of which luminance, contrast and their bandpass get their highest values and proves that it is not so in image patches selected at random) and GBSV (Harel, 2006) (that defines activation maps on some selected feature channels that are suitably normalized), have been modified including face saliency using a variant Ada Boost algorithm (see some examples in Figure 7). In all the three cases the performance of the algorithm for visual saliency greatly improves. In particular, a face detection channel improves *fixation* prediction in images with faces, while it is useless in

Figure 7. Original image (left); Saliency map obtained using the GBVS (Harel, 2006) algorithm (middle) and the Itti et al. algorithm (Itti, 1998) (right)

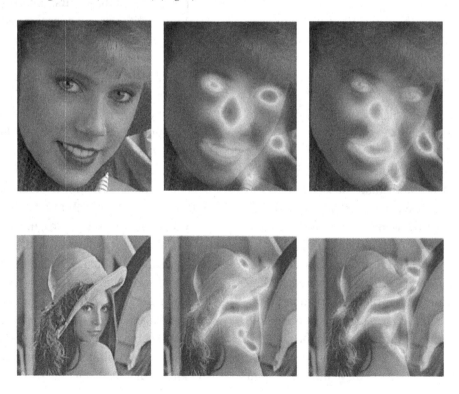

image without faces. Such results are confirmed by the work in (Marat, 2013) that concerns visual saliency in video frames. It shows that a face saliency map, properly combined with static (single frame) and dynamic (including moving objects) saliency maps, greatly improves the prediction of eye movements in frames containing faces.

By focusing on newborns vision (Slater, 2001; Johnson, 2001) and the holistic processing of facial features (Sinha, 2006), face curves have been used in (Mario, 2009) as face features for developing a face recognition algorithm that uses the Hough transform for detecting candidate curves and a PCA algorithm for selecting the interesting ones having not negligible visual importance. Also in this case the framework greatly outperforms competitive approaches since it is also consistent with the studies concerning the asymmetry of brain hemispheres in face perception. The right hemisphere is proved to process low spatial frequencies (Sergent, 1992) that are important for face processing (Tarr, 2000; Rossion, 2003; Evans, 1995) and it has direct access to the left side of the face. That is why for face stimuli humans tend to have their initial *saccade* direction to the left side (Leonards, 2005) (see, for example Figure 8), while it is not so for landscapes, fractals or inverted faces. This kind of results would indicate

smoothed spaces, for example the ones defined by multiscale transforms or kernel-based transforms, as good and appropriate spaces for addressing face processing problems.

By testing the preference for eye and nose regions and evaluating the time of *fixation* (Figure 7), in (Choi, 2012) weights maps are created according to the time spent for each *fixation*: the longer *fixation* the more time is spent by the observer for interpreting the visual stimulus and this time is not independent of changing illumination conditions. These maps have been used for weighting the salient regions embedded in the well-known Local Gabor Binary Pattern (LGBP) (Zhang, 2005) face recognition algorithm that works on the histogram of a locally thresholded Gabor wavelet image representation. The correction of the saliency map in agreement with the face *fixation* process, allows the recognition algorithm to address the problem of change of illumination. A similar concept is used by *iMap* in (Caldara, 2011). It is a robust method for the analysis of eye movement data in terms of number of *fixations*, total duration and path length, and it performs a statistical analysis that is exactly based on weighting the probability density functions of *fixations* by means of their duration.

Figure 8. Original facial image (left). Saliency map (given by GBVS (Harel, 2006) algorithm) superposed to a frontal facial image: the redder area includes the nose and its left part (right).

 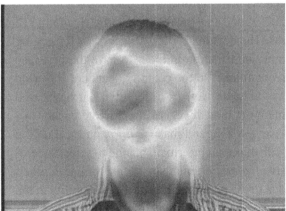

The NIM model (Lacroix, 2006) uses *fixation*-based face fragments as points in a vector space and compares the currently perceived fragments to the stored fragments for face identification: the larger the distance between the two representations in the vector space, the harder the memory can be successfully recollected. Its Bayesian and more general version, namely NIMBLE (Barrington, 2008), greatly outperforms the original model by using new kernels for density estimation. However, if on the one hand, the model was able to give a correct face identification with a small number of *fixations*; on the other hand, the probability of successful recognition increased with an increasing number of *fixations* that is not consistent with human vision. Nonetheless, quite surprisingly, in (Hsiao, 2013) it has been shown that if NIMBLE uses the center of the nose as *fixation* point, it was able to achieve its best performance with very few *fixations* and more *fixations* did not further improve it. This result turns us back to the definition of saliency maps. The original NIMBLE model is based on a visual saliency model (Yamada, 1995) that sets eye *fixation* locations as the most attractive part of human faces. On the contrary, as mentioned above, several studies proved that the first and second human *fixations* are in very close locations (around the center of the nose). A reasonable explanation is the following: because of the familiarity with faces and according to the fact that the visual acuity drops from fovea to periphery, the nose (first *fixation*) represents the center of the information (295 ms (Henderson, 2003)) and the successive nearby *fixation* (315 ms (Henderson, 2003)) is necessary for getting more information in order to have the best face recognition. On the contrary, standard Bayesian methods, as well as differential entropy based methods that disregard the foveated nature of visual system and make *fixation* on local region with maximal information, tend to select successive *fixation* points that are far from each other, due to the maximization of the probability in the first case and contrast entropy in the second. It is then more interesting to consider the predictions given by a Bayesian (foveated) ideal observer in (Najamnik, 2005; Peterson, 2012; Geisler, 2011) that integrates face information constrained to the decrease in resolution and sensitivity from the fovea toward the periphery, to the limited memory of retina during the visual search (just a couple of preceding *fixations*), and to the principle of '*inhibition of return*' for which it tends not to fixate locations that has been already fixated.

It is interesting to observe that these results are in some sense supported by those neurological studies (Mante, 2005; Frazor, 2006) concerning natural images that establish a sort of independence between luminance mean and contrast of *fixations*. Luminance mean and contrast are, in fact, the essential measures made by human eye during the observation process; they mainly depend on the first two image statistics and their spatial correlation has a fast decay. More precisely, the correlation between local contrast in correspondence to *fixations* decreases rapidly with increasing distance of *fixations*; then, the measure of local contrast is predictable only for very close observation points. The same happens for the correlation of local luminance but the correlation decay is slower. These findings seem to give value to a searching strategy that admits the selection of neighboring successive *fixation* points, in agreement with human vision.

These results are important also in the tracking phase, where human perception becomes task specific. In this case, target features, sensitivity to motion and strategy search are fundamental. In particular, search strategy plays a dominant role. In fact, the main aim in visual search is not to choose *fixations* containing features that maximize target feature, but it is to choose successive locations that will result in maximum information gain. It turns out that the vision path, that substantially guides the learning (understanding) process of a scene, is strictly related to (or constrained to) a coding process, whose aim is to get higher information at lower rate.

The equivalence between *coding* and *learning* established by the MDL and the modeling of the vision process as a coder/decoder system, create a strong link between classical Information Theory concepts and the vision process. Very recent studies proved a close relationship between Information Theory concepts and the main rules that guide HVP, especially in the early vision (Bruni, 2013c). The main representative and interesting example surely is image quality assessment, whose aim is to establish to what extent two images can be considered equal/similar from HVS point of view (Wang, 2002; Chono, 2008; Soundarajan, 2012a, 2012b). For example, natural scene statistics (NSS) based methods (Wang, 2005), (Sheihk, 2005) measure deviations of certain statistics of a distorted signal from the expected statistics, assuming that the deviations from the NSS capture a loss of visual naturalness. To this aim they quantify the amount of loss of visual information that occurs in the distorted signal with respect to a presumably distortionless reference, through information theoretic quantities. Image similarities are therefore measured as the amount of the mutual information between the two images (VIF) (Sheikh, 2006), or through the normalized information/compression distance (NID/NCD) (Nikvand, 2013), or using the Jensen-Shannon divergence (Bruni, 2013b). On the other hand we cannot neglect that tracking process is usually performed through Bayesian map a posteriori based methods (Najamnik, 2005; Rajashekar, 2006; Geisler, 2011; Peterson, 2012) that, in turn, are strictly linked to the concept of the Minimum Description Length and then to the concept of information coding. As a result image quality assessment metrics that are based on information theory concepts seem to be proper means for assessing the similarity between two objects using the minimum amount of information i.e., the one that better expresses the significant feature of the object of interest. Hence, they can be useful and effective also in face tracking.

Some studies, even though not always specific for face tracking, provided some interesting results in this sense. For example, as mentioned in the previous section, in (Dubuque, 2009) a Kalman filter was used to auto-regressively estimate target position and velocity using a foveated system in multiple target tracking.

The foveated system is based on the mutual information between a known but hidden target and the input image. In order to fuse fovea and peripheral observations, the Update step of the Kalman filter, that guides the gain of the filter by weighting the influence of the previous state and new observations, has been modified by allowing the observation variance to change according to the resolution at the position of the observation. The resulting foveated Kalman filter has been shown to be quite robust in multi-target tracking tasks.

In (Comaniciu, 2000b), a kernel-based object tracking (KbOT), that uses the mean shift algorithm, has been proposed. It uses the Bhattacharyya distance as similarity metric, that has theoretical connections with the Fisher measure of information, and it is invariant to the scale of the target since it only depends on the uncertainty in the density estimates. In addition, it also includes a weighted face model that is consistent with foveated imagery and the mean value of the gradient magnitude at the face border to improve face localization. Finally, the work in (Bruni, 2012b, 2013d) gave a more perceptual interpretation to the KbOT (Comaniciu, 2003) algorithm in order to assess to what extent a deeper dependence on perception rules can contribute to its improvement in terms not only of faithfulness of tracking but also in terms of reduction of the computational effort of the whole tracking procedure. To this aim, perception rules are expressed in terms of a visual contrast based feature space, a foveated kernel density for target features and the Jensen Shannon divergence as similarity metric that has been proved to well correlate with visual contrast. The results showed that the use of a metric that better correlates with HVS can significantly improve tracking performance of existing trackers, also allowing a reduced computational effort. For example, a less number of iterations are necessary for the convergence of the mean-shift algorithm.

FUTURE RESEARCH DIRECTIONS

The limited number of *fixations* necessary to capture all significant information, the use of the concept of Kolmogorov complexity for efficiently coding information, its link with the Minimum Description Length that strongly correlates the concept of *coding* with the one of *learning*, and finally the definition of Bayesian ideal searcher that aims at finding the target quickly, necessarily lead the future research to investigate more in depth on information theoretic concepts and their relations with human vision. In particular, it is author's opinion that the use of the concept of Normalized Information Distance (NID) can really improve the development of promising and powerful tracking models. One of the main reasons for this belief is that NID is a universal and valid measure for assessing the similarity between two objects (Cilibrasi, 2005). It measures the shortest program whose output is the string *s* if the input is the string *t* and vice versa (Li, 2004). It depends on the Kolmogorov complexity K(.), that measures the length of the shortest program that gives (.), and it is defined as

$$NID(s,t) = \frac{\max(K(s \mid t), K(t \mid s))}{\max(K(s), K(t))}. \qquad (1)$$

Although its main drawback is its incomputability, it gives impressive results if a compressor (coding algorithm) is used in place of the Kolmogorov complexity. This empirical approximation has been successfully used in several applications (medicine, biology, music, literature, etc.) since it seems able to capture the essential distinctive features of the objects to compare, independently of their nature (source) (Li, 2004, 2008). As a matter of fact, whenever Kolmogorov complexity can be approximated by Shannon entropy, NID has a close relationship with the concept of mutual information that, in turn, is a computable and significant quantity in natural scene statistics (NSS) and foveated imagery. In fact, the vision path, that guides the understanding process of a scene, is nothing else that a coding process, whose aim is to get higher information at lower rate. As a result, independently of face appearance, the Shannon entropy version of NID seems to be able to capture those distinctive points (features) that activate neurons in the recognition of a given target since it quantifies the ability of human eye in coding the candidate target in the current frame just using the information contained in the reference target in the previous frame of the analysed video sequence. More specifically, assuming two random variables *s* (*reference face*) and *t* (*candidate face*) with probability density functions respectively *p* and *q*, it holds

$$NID(p,q) = \frac{\max(H(p \mid q), H(q \mid p))}{\max(H(p), H(q))} \qquad (2)$$

that is equivalent to

$$NID(p,q) = 1 - \frac{I(p,q)}{\max(H(p), H(q))}, \qquad (3)$$

where $I(p,q) = H(p)-H(p|q)=H(q)-H(q|p)$ is the mutual information between *p* and *q* and $H(p|q) = H(p,q)-H(q)$ while $H(q|p) = H(p,q)-H(p)$. Hence, the more the reference and the candidate face share information, the closer to 0 NID is. It means that we can succinctly describe the candidate face given the reference one.

It is worth observing that Kolmogorov complexity and Shannon entropy have a slightly different meaning, since the latter deals with probability density functions instead of strings of symbols. That is why previous considerations are valid whenever the Kolmogorov complexity can be approximated by a compressor, whose capability in coding a given string is bounded by the corresponding Shannon entropy. Nonetheless, some theoretical findings, as the one in (Li, 2004),

(Teixeira, 2011), establish strong relationships between these two concepts of complexity that allow to exploit some theoretical properties of information theoretic metrics for addressing the problem of NID incomputability (see (Topsoe, 2000]) for details). These results would enable to successfully use NID in face tracking algorithms. Actually, this is one of the arguments that can be used in the interpretation of the results of KbOT algorithm (Comaniciu, 2000, 2003). In fact, it is possible to provide bounds for the Bhattacharyya distance that depend on the Jensen-Shannon divergence. The latter has been proved to well correlate with visual contrast and to have close relationships with both NID and concepts of information transmission rate.

CONCLUSION

This chapter has presented some hints and cues oriented to embed human perception into face tracking. As already outlined, this combination has received minor interest so far in this specific research field, even though human perception has several merits whenever employed in different areas of image and video processing. It is able to simply make automatic, faster and easier (i.e. user friendly for even non expert people) frameworks that were much more complicated before its introduction. This is the reason why a crucial topic like face tracking should take advantage of novel models based on visual perception. Specifically, face tracking may become the topic where human perception can give the stronger contribution, accounting for the role played by human face information in the Darwin evolution of human visual system --- both pre-attentive and not. It turns out that, if on the one hand the use of human perception can help to design more effective face tracking frameworks; on the other hand, a deeper

study of face recognition and tracking could also help to better understand and make clearer some aspects of human perception that still are partially obscure. As a result, face tracking and human perception might take a reciprocal advantage, similarly to what is happening for Information Theory and visual perception.

REFERENCES

Abrams, J., Nizam, A., & Carrasco, M. (2012). Isoeccentric locations are not equivalent: The extent of the vertical meridian asymmetry. *Vision Research*, *52*, 70–78. doi:10.1016/j.visres.2011.10.016 PMID:22086075

Agaian, S. S., Silver, B., & Panetta, K. A. (2007). Transform coefficient histogram-based image enhancement algorithms using contrast entropy. *IEEE Transactions on Image Processing*, *16*(3), 741–758. doi:10.1109/TIP.2006.888338 PMID:17357734

Arulampalam, M., Maskell, S., Gordon, N., & Clapp, T. (2002). A tutorial on particle filters for online nonlinear/non-gaussian bayesian tracking. *IEEE Transactions on Signal Processing*, *50*(2), 174–189. doi:10.1109/78.978374

Barrington, L., Marks, T., Hsiao, J. H., & Cottrell, G. W. (2008). NIMBLE: A kernel density model of *saccade*-based visual memory. *Journal of Vision (Charlottesville, Va.)*, *8*(14), 1–14. doi:10.1167/8.14.17 PMID:19146318

Boot, W. R., Becic, E., & Kramer, A. F. (2009). Stable individual differences in search strategy?: The effect of task demands and motivational factors on scanning strategy in visual search. *Journal of Vision (Charlottesville, Va.)*, *9*, 1–16. doi:10.1167/9.3.7 PMID:19757946

Bradski, G. (1998). Computer vision face tracking for use in a perceptual user interface. *Intel Technology Journal (Q2)*.

Bruce, N., & Tsotsos, J. K. (2006). Saliency Based on Information Maximization. *Advances in Neural Information Processing Systems, 18*, 155–162.

Bruni, V., Crawford, A., Kokaram, A., & Vitulano, D. (2013). Semi-transparent Blotches Removal from Sepia Images Exploiting Visibility Laws. *Signal Image and Video Processing, 7*(1), 11–26. doi:10.1007/s11760-011-0220-1

Bruni, V., Crawford, A., Vitulano, D., & Stanco, F. (2006). Visibility based detection and removal of semi-transparent blotches on archived documents. In *Proceedings of VISAPP06 International Conference on Computer Vision Theory and Applications,* (pp. 64-71). VISAPP.

Bruni, V., Crawford, A. J., & Vitulano, D. (2006). Visibility based detection of complicated objects: a case study. [IEE.]. *Proceedings of the IEE CVMP, 06*, 55–64.

Bruni, V., Ramponi, G., Restrepo, A., & Vitulano, D. (2009). *Context-Based Defading of Archive Photographs*. EURASIP Journal on Image and Video Processing, Special Issue on Image and Video Processing for Cultural Heritage.

Bruni, V., Rossi, E., & Vitulano, D. (2011). Optimal Image Restoration Using HVS-Based Rate-Distortion Curves. In *Proceedings of International Conference on Computer Analysis of Images and Patterns* (LNCS), (Vol. 6855, pp. 269-276). Berlin: Springer.

Bruni, V., Rossi, E., & Vitulano, D. (2012). On the Equivalence between Jensen-Shannon Divergence and Michelson Contrast. *IEEE Transactions on Information Theory, 58*(7), 4278–4288. doi:10.1109/TIT.2012.2192903

Bruni, V., Rossi, E., & Vitulano, D. (2012). Perceptual object tracking. In *Proceedings of IEEE Workshop on Biometric Measurements and Systems for Security and Medical Applications (BIOMS)*. IEEE.

Bruni, V., Rossi, E., & Vitulano, D. (2013). Jensen-Shannon divergence for visual quality assessment. *Signal Image and Video Processing, 7*(3).

Bruni, V., & Vitulano, D. (2004). A Generalized Model for Scratch Detection. *IEEE Transactions on Image Processing, 13*(1), 44–50. doi:10.1109/TIP.2003.817231 PMID:15376956

Bruni, V., & Vitulano, D. (2013). A perception-based interpretation of the Kernel-based Object Tracking. In *Proc. of ACIVS 2013* (LNCS), (vol. 8192, pp. 596-60). Berlin: Springer.

Bruni, V., Vitulano, D., & Wang, Z. (2013). Special Issue on Human Vision and Information Theory. *Signal Image and Video Processing, 7*(3), 389–390. doi:10.1007/s11760-013-0447-0

Buswell, G. T. (1935). *How people look at pictures: A study of the psychology of perception in art*. Chicago: University of Chicago Press.

Caldara, R., & Miellet, S. (2011). *iMap*: a novel method for statistical fixation mapping of eye movement data. *Behav Res, Springer, 43*, 864–878. doi:10.3758/s13428-011-0092-x PMID:21512875

Cerf, M., Harel, J., Einhauser, W., & Koch, C. (2007). Predicting human gaze using low-level saliency combined with face detection. In J. Platt, D. Koller, Y. Singer, & S. Roweis (Eds.), *Advances in Neural Information Processing Systems* (NIPS 2007), (pp. 241–248). Cambridge, MA: Academic Press.

Chandler, D. M., & Hemami, S. S. (2007). VSNR: A Wavelet-based Visual Signal-to-Noise Ratio for Natural Images. *IEEE Transactions on Image Processing, 16*(9), 2284–2298. doi:10.1109/TIP.2007.901820 PMID:17784602

Chellappa, R., Wilson, C. L., & Sirohey, S. (1995). Human and Machine Recognition of Faces: A survey. *Proceedings of the IEEE, 83*(5), 705–740. doi:10.1109/5.381842

Choi, E., Lee, S. W., & Wallraven, C. (2012). Face Recognition with Enhanced Local Gabor Binary Pattern from Human Fixations. In *Proceedings of IEEE International Conference on Systems, Man, and Cybernetics.* IEEE.

Chono, K., Lin, Y., Varodayan, D., Miyamoto, Y., & Girod, B. (2008). Reduced-reference image quality estimation using distributed source coding. In *Proceedings of IEEE International Conference on Multimedia and Expo,* (pp. 609-612). IEEE.

Cilibrasi, R., & Vitanyi, P. (2005). Clustering by compression. *IEEE Transactions on Information Theory, 51*(4), 1523–1545. doi:10.1109/TIT.2005.844059

Colmenarez, A. J., & Huang, T. S. (1997). Face Detection with Information-based Maximum Discrimination. In *Proceedings of IEEE Conference on Computer Vision and Pattern Recognition,* (pp. 782-787). IEEE.

Comaniciu, D., Ramesh, V., & Meer, P. (2000). Real-time tracking of non-rigid objects using mean shift. In *Proceedings of IEEE Conference on Computer Vision and Pattern Recognition* (CVPR), (pp. 142-149). IEEE.

Comaniciu, D., Ramesh, V., & Meer, P. (2000). Robust detection and tracking of human faces with an active camera. In *Proceedings of IEEE Conference on Visual Surveillance.* IEEE.

Comaniciu, D., Ramesh, V., & Meer, P. (2003). Kernel-based object tracking. *IEEE Transactions on Pattern Analysis and Machine Intelligence, 25*(2), 564–577. doi:10.1109/TPAMI.2003.1195991

Cover, T., Gacs, P., & Gray, M. (1989). Kolmogorov's contributions to information theory and algorithmic complexity. *Annals of Probability, 17,* 840–865. doi:10.1214/aop/1176991250

Cover, T. M., & Thomas, J. A. (1991). *Elements of information Theory.* New York: Wiley. doi:10.1002/0471200611

Craw, I., Tock, D., & Bennett, A. (1992). Finding Face Features. In *Proceedings of the Second European Conference on Computer Vision,* (pp. 92-96). Academic Press.

Dai, Y., & Nakano, Y. (1996). Face-Texture Model based on SGLD and its Application in Face Detection in a Color Scene. *Pattern Recognition, 29*(6), 1007–1017. doi:10.1016/0031-3203(95)00139-5

De Carlo, D., & Metaxas, D. (2000). Optical flow constraints on deformable models with applications to face tracking. *International Journal of Computer Vision, 38*(2), 99–127. doi:10.1023/A:1008122917811

Doulamis, A. (2010). Dynamic tracking readjustment: a method for automatic tracking recovery in complex visual environments. *Journal of Multimedia Tools and Applications, 50*(1), 49–73. doi:10.1007/s11042-009-0368-7

Dubuque, S., Coffman, T., McCarley, P., Bovik, A. C., & Thomas, C. W. (2009). A comparison of foveated acquisition and tracking performance relative to uniform resolution approaches. In *Proceedings of SPIE* (Vol. 7321). SPIE. doi:10.1117/12.818716

ECCV 2008 (LNCS), (vol. 5302, pp. 234–247). Berlin: Springer.

Evans, J. J., Heggs, A. J., Antoun, N., & Hodges, J. R. (1995). Progressive prosopagnosia associated with selective right temporal lobe atrophy: a new syndrome? *Brain*, *118*, 1–13. doi:10.1093/brain/118.1.1 PMID:7894996

Fecteau, J. H., & Munoz, D. P. (2006). Salience, relevance, and firing: a priority map for target selection. *Trends in Cognitive Sciences*, *10*, 382–390. doi:10.1016/j.tics.2006.06.011 PMID:16843702

Frazor, R., & Geisler, W. (2006). Local luminance and contrast in natural images. *Vision Research*, *46*, 1585–1598. doi:10.1016/j.visres.2005.06.038 PMID:16403546

Gauthier, I., & Tanaka, J. W. (2002). Configural and holistic face processing: The Whole story. *Journal of Vision (Charlottesville, Va.)*, *2*(7), 616–616. doi:10.1167/2.7.616

Geisler, W. S. (2011). Contributions of ideal observer theory to vision research. *Vision Research*, *51*, 771–781. doi:10.1016/j.visres.2010.09.027 PMID:20920517

Goferman, S., Zelnik-Manor, L., & Tal, A. (2012). Context-Aware Saliency Detection. *IEEE Transactions on Pattern Analysis and Machine Intelligence*, *34*(10), 1915–1926. doi:10.1109/TPAMI.2011.272 PMID:22201056

Grabner, H., Grabner, M., & Bischof, H. (2006). Real-time tracking via on-line boosting. In *Proceedings of British Machine Vision Conference* (BMVC), (pp. 47-56). BMVC.

Grabner, H., Leistner, C., & Bischof, H. (2008). *Semi-supervised on-line boosting for robust tracking*.

Greenblatt, A., Panetta, K., & Agaian, S. (2008). Restoration of semi-transparent blotches in damaged texts, manuscripts and images through localized, logarithmic image enhancement. In *Proceedings of ISCCSP '08*. ISCCSP.

Harel, J., Koch, C., & Perona, P. (2006). Graph-based visual saliency. In *Proceedings of Advances in Neural Information Processing Systems* (NIPS 2006), (pp. 545-552). NIPS.

Henderson, J. (2003). Human gaze control during real-world scene perception. *Trends in Cognitive Sciences*, *7*, 498–504. doi:10.1016/j.tics.2003.09.006 PMID:14585447

Hjelm, E., & Low, B. K. (2001). Face Detection: A Survey. *Computer Vision and Image Understanding*, *83*(3), 236–274. doi:10.1006/cviu.2001.0921

Hontsch, I., & Karam, L. (2002). Adaptive Image Coding with Perceptual Distortion Control. *IEEE Transactions on Image Processing*, *11*(3), 213–222. doi:10.1109/83.988955 PMID:18244625

Hsiao, J. H. (2013). *Eye Movements in Face Recognition*. Intech Book.

Hsiao, J. H., & Cottrell, G. W. (2008). Two fixations suffice in face recognition. *Psychological Science*, *9*(10), 998–1006. doi:10.1111/j.1467-9280.2008.02191.x PMID:19000210

Hsu, R.-L., Abdel-Mottaleb, M., & Jain, A. K. (2002). Face Detection in Color Images. *IEEE Transactions on Pattern Analysis and Machine Intelligence*, *24*(5), 696–706. doi:10.1109/34.1000242

Itti, L., & Baldi, P. (2006). Bayesian Surprise Attracts Human Attention. *Advances in Neural Information Processing Systems*, 19.

Itti, L., Koch, C., & Niebur, E. (1998). A model of saliency based visual attention for rapid scene analysis. *IEEE Transactions on Pattern Analysis and Machine*, *20*, 1254–1259. doi:10.1109/34.730558

Javal, É. (1879). Essai sure la physiologie de la lecture. *Annales d'Oculistique*, *82*, 242–253.

Johnson, M. H. (2001). The development and neural basis of face recognition: Comment an speculation. *Infant and Child Development*, *10*(1-2), 31–33. doi:10.1002/icd.243

Kanade, T. (1973). *Picture Processing by Computer Complex and Recognition of Human Face.* (PhD thesis). Kyoto University.

Kim, M., Kumar, S., Pavlovic, V., & Rowley, H. (2008). Face tracking and recognition with visual constraints in real-world videos. In *Proceedings of IEEE Conference on Computer Vision and Pattern Recognition* (CVPR), (pp. 1-8). IEEE.

Kim, T. K., Kittler, J., & Cipolla, R. (2007). Discriminative learning and recognition of image set classes using canonical correlations. *IEEE Transactions on Pattern Analysis and Machine Intelligence*, *29*(6), 1005–1018. doi:10.1109/TPAMI.2007.1037 PMID:17431299

Kjeldsen, R., & Kender, J. (1996). Finding Skin in Color Images. In *Proceedings of the Second International Conference on Automatic Face and Gesture Recognition*, (pp. 312-317). Academic Press.

Knight, B., & Johnson, A. (1997). The role of movement in face recognition. *Visual Cognition*, *4*(3), 265–273. doi:10.1080/713756764

Kolmogorov, A. N. (1965). Three Approaches to the Quantitative Definition of Information. *Problems of Information Transmission*, 157–168.

Kotropoulos, C., & Pitas, I. (1997). Rule-based Face Detection in Frontal Views. In *Proceedings of the International Conference on Acoustic, Speech and Signal Processing*, (vol. 4, pp. 2537-2540). Academic Press.

Lacroix, J. P. W., Murre, J. M. J., Postma, E. O., & Van den Herik, H. J. (2006). Modeling recognition memory using the similarity structure of natural input. *Cognitive Science*, *30*, 121–145. doi:10.1207/s15516709cog0000_48 PMID:21702811

Lamare, M. (1892). Des mouvements des yeux dans la lecture. *Bulletins et Memoires de la Société Francaise d'Ophtalmologie*, *10*, 354–364.

Latinis, A., Taylor, C. J., & Cootes, T. F. (1995). An Automatic Face Identification System using Flexible Appearance Models. *Image and Vision Computing*, *13*(5), 393–401. doi:10.1016/0262-8856(95)99726-H

Leonards, U., & Scott-Samuel, N. E. (2005). Idiosyncratic initiation of saccadic face exploration in humans. *Vision Research*, *45*, 2677–2684. doi:10.1016/j.visres.2005.03.009 PMID:16042969

Leung, T. K., Burl, M. C., & Perona, P. (1995). Finding Faces in Cluttered Scenes using Random Labeled Graph Matching. In *Proceedings of the fifth IEEE International Conference on Computer Vision*, (pp. 637-644). IEEE.

Lew, M. S. (1996). Information Theoretic View-based and Modular Face Detection. In *Proc. Second Int. Conf. Automatic Face and Gesture Recognition*, (pp. 198-203). Academic Press.

Li, M., Chen, X., Li, X., Ma, B., & Vitanyi, P. (2004). The similarity metric. *IEEE Transactions on Information Theory*, *50*(12), 3250–3264. doi:10.1109/TIT.2004.838101

Li, M., & Vitanyi, P. (1997). *An introduction to Kolmogorov complexity and its applications* (2nd ed.). New York: Springer-Verlag. doi:10.1007/978-1-4757-2606-0

Li, M., & Vitanyi, P. (2008). *An introduction to Kolmogorov Complexity and its applications* (3rd ed.). Springer. doi:10.1007/978-0-387-49820-1

Makantatis, K., Doulamis, A., & Doulamis, A. (2013). Vision-based maritime surveillance system using fused visual attention maps and online adaptable tracker. In *Proceedings of 14th International Workshop on Image Analysis for Multimedia Interactive Services* (WIAMIS). Academic Press.

Mante, V., Frazor, R., Bonin, V., Geisler, W., & Carandini, M. (2005). Independence of luminance and contrast in natural scenes and in the early visual system. *Nature Neuroscience*, *8*(12). doi:10.1038/nn1556 PMID:16286933

Marat, S., Rahman, A., Pellerin, D., Guyader, N., & Houzet, D. (2013). Improving visual saliency by adding Face Feature Map and Center Bias. *Cognitive Computation*, *5*, 63–75. doi:10.1007/s12559-012-9146-3

Mario, I., Chacon, M., & Pablo Rivas, P. (2009). Face Recognition Based on Human Visual Perception Theories and Unsupervised ANN. In *State of the Art in Face Recognition*. I-Tech.

McKenna, S., Gong, S., & Raya, Y. (1998). Modelling Facial Color and Identity with Gaussian Mixture. *Pattern Recognition*, *31*(12), 1883–1892. doi:10.1016/S0031-3203(98)00066-1

Najemnik, J., & Geisler, W. S. (2005). Optimal eye movement strategies in visual search. *Nature*, *434*, 387–391. doi:10.1038/nature03390 PMID:15772663

Najemnik, J., & Geisler, W. S. (2008). Eye movement statistics in humans are consistent with an optimal search strategy. *Journal of Vision (Charlottesville, Va.)*, *8*(3), 1–14. doi:10.1167/8.3.4 PMID:18484810

Nikvand, N., & Wang, Z. (2013). Image Distortion Analysis Based on Normalized Perceptual Information Distance. *Signal Image and Video Proc., 7*(3).

O'Toole, A., Roark, D., & Abdi, H. (2002). Recognizing moving faces: A psychological and neural synthesis. *Trends in Cognitive Sciences*, *6*(6), 261–266. doi:10.1016/S1364-6613(02)01908-3 PMID:12039608

Osuna, E., Freund, R., & Girosi, F. (1997). Training Support Vector Machines: An Application to Face Detection. In *Proc. IEEE Conf. Computer Vision and Pattern Recognition*, (pp. 130-136). IEEE.

Pappas, T. N., & Safranek, R. J. (2000). Perceptual criteria for image quality evaluation. In *Handbook of Image and Video Processing* (pp. 669–684). Academic Press.

Peterson, M., & Eckstein, M. P. (2012). *Looking just below the eyes is optimal across face recognition tasks* (P. N. A. S. Early, Ed.).

Peterson, M., & Eckstein, M. P. (2013). Individual Differences in Eye Movements During Face Identification Reflect Observer-Specific Optimal Points of Fixation. *Psychological Science*. doi:10.1177/0956797612471684 PMID:23740552

Raj, R., Geisler, W. S., Frazor, R. A., & Bovik, A. C. (2005). Contrast statistics for foveated visual systems: fixation selection by minimizing contrast entropy. *Journal of the Optical Society of America. A, Optics, Image Science, and Vision*, *22*(10). doi:10.1364/JOSAA.22.002039 PMID:16277275

Rajagopalan, A., Kumar, K., Karlekar, J., Manivasakan, R., Patil, M., Desai, U., et al. (1998). Finding Faces in Photographs. In *Proceedings of the. Sixth IEEE International Conference on Computer Vision*, (pp. 640-645). IEEE.

Rajashekar, U., Bovik, A. C., & Cormack, L. K. U. (2006). Visual search in noise: Revealing the influence of structural cues by gaze-contingent classification image analysis. *Journal of Vision (Charlottesville, Va.)*, *6*, 379–386. doi:10.1167/6.4.7 PMID:16889476

Rajashekar, U., van der Linde, I., Bovik, A. C., & Cormack, L. K. G. (2008). A gaze-attentive fixation finding engine. *IEEE Transactions on Image Processing*, *17*(4), 564–573. doi:10.1109/TIP.2008.917218 PMID:18390364

Rajashekar, U., van der Linde, I., Bovik, A. C., & Cormack, L. K. U. (2007). Foveated analysis of image features at fixations. *Vision Research*, *47*, 3160–3172. doi:10.1016/j.visres.2007.07.015 PMID:17889221

Rayner, K. (1998). Eye movements in reading and information processing: 20 years of research. *Psychological Bulletin*, *124*, 372–422. doi:10.1037/0033-2909.124.3.372 PMID:9849112

Rayner, K. (2009). Eye movements and attention in reading, scene perception, and visual search. *Quarterly Journal of Experimental Psychology*, *62*, 1457–1506. doi:10.1080/17470210902816461 PMID:19449261

Rissanen, J. (2007). *Information and Complexity in Statistical Modeling*. Springer.

Rosenholtz, R. (1999). A simple saliency model predicts a number of motion popout phenomena. *Vision Research*, *39*, 3157–3163. doi:10.1016/S0042-6989(99)00077-2 PMID:10615487

Ross, D., Lim, J., Lin, R. S., & Yang, M. H. (2008). Incremental learning for robust visual tracking. *International Journal of Computer Vision*, *77*(1-3), 125–141. doi:10.1007/s11263-007-0075-7

Rossion, B., Joyce, C. A., Cottrell, G. W., & Tarr, M. J. (2003). Early lateralization and orientation tuning for face, word, and object processing in the visual cortex. *NeuroImage*, *20*, 1609–1624. doi:10.1016/j.neuroimage.2003.07.010 PMID:14642472

Rowley, H., Baluja, S., & Kanade, T. (1998). Neural Network-based Face Detection. *IEEE Transactions on Pattern Analysis and Machine Intelligence*, *20*(1), 23–38. doi:10.1109/34.655647

Salmon, T. O. (2001). *Fixational eye movement, VS III: Ocular Motility and Binocular Vision*. NE State University.

Samal, A., & Iyengar, P. A. (1992). Automatic Recognition and Analysis of Human Faces and Facial Expressions: A Survey. *Pattern Recognition*, *25*(1), 65–77. doi:10.1016/0031-3203(92)90007-6

Schneiderman, H., & Kanade, T. (1998). Probabilistic Modeling of Local Appearance and Spatial Relashionships for Object Recognition. In *Proc. IEEE Conference on Computer Vision and Pattern Recognition*, (pp. 45-51). IEEE.

Sergent, J. (1982). The cerebral balance of power: Confrontation or cooperation? *Journal of Experimental Psychology. Human Perception and Performance*, *8*, 253–272. doi:10.1037/0096-1523.8.2.253 PMID:6461721

Shan, C. (2010). Face Recognition and Retrieval. In *Video Search and Mining* (pp. 235–260). SCI. doi:10.1007/978-3-642-12900-1_9

Sharma, P., Cheikh, F. A., & Hardeberg, J. Y. (2009). Face Saliency in Various Human Visual Saliency Models. In *Proceedings of the 6th International Symposium on Image and Signal Processing and Analysis*. Academic Press.

Sheikh, H. R., & Bovik, A. C. (2006). Image Information and Visual Quality. *IEEE Transactions on Image Processing*, *15*(2). doi:10.1109/TIP.2005.859378 PMID:16479813

Sheikh, H. R., Bovik, A. C., & Cormack, L. (2005). No-reference quality assessment using natural scene statistics: JPEG2000. *IEEE Transactions on Image Processing, 14*(11), 1918–1927. doi:10.1109/TIP.2005.854492 PMID:16279189

Sheikh, H. R., Wang, Z., Cormack, L., & Bovik, A. C. (n.d.). *Live Image Quality Assessment Database Release 2*. Retrieved from http://live.ece.utexas.edu/research/quality

Sinha, P., Balas, B., Ostrovsky, Y., & Russell, R. (2006). Face recognition by humans: Nineteen results all computer vision researchers should know about. *Proceedings of the IEEE, 94*(11), 1948–1962. doi:10.1109/JPROC.2006.884093

Slater, A., & Quinn, P. C. (2001). Face recognition in the newborn infant. *Infant and Child Development, 10*(1), 21–24. doi:10.1002/icd.241

Soundararajan, R., & Bovik, A. (2012). RRED Indices: Reduced Reference Entropic Differencing for Image Quality Assessment. *IEEE Transactions on Image Processing, 21*(2), 517–526. doi:10.1109/TIP.2011.2166082 PMID:21878414

Soundararajan, R., & Bovik, A. C. (2007). Survey of Information Theory in Visual Quality Assessment. *Signal Image and Video Processing, 7*(3).

Sung, K.-K., & Poggio, T. (1998). Example-based Learning for View-based Human Face Detection. *IEEE Transactions on Pattern Analysis and Machine Intelligence, 20*(1), 39–51. doi:10.1109/34.655648

Takacs, B., & Wechsler, H. (1995). Face Location using a Dynamic Model of Retinal Feature Extraction. In *Proc. First Int. Workshop Automatic Face and Gesture Recognition*, (pp. 243-247). Academic Press.

Tarr, M. J., & Gauthier, I. (2000). FFA: A flexible fusiform area for subordinate-level visual processing automatized by expertise. *Nature Neuroscience, 3*, 764–769. doi:10.1038/77666 PMID:10903568

Tatler, B. W., Baddeley, R. J., & Gilchrist, I. D. (2005). Visual correlates of fixation selection: effects of scale and time. *Vision Research, Elsevier, 45*, 643–659. doi:10.1016/j.visres.2004.09.017 PMID:15621181

Teixeira, A., Matos, A., Souto, A., & Antunes, L. (2011). Entropy measures vs Kolmogorov Complexity. *Entropy Journal, 13*, 595–611. doi:10.3390/e13030595

Topsøe, F. (2000). Some Inequalities for Information Divergence and Related Measures of Discrimination. *IEEE Transactions on Information Theory, 46*(4). doi:10.1109/18.850703

Turk, M., & Pentland, A. (1991). Eigenfaces for Recognition. *Journal of Cognitive Neuroscience, 3*(1), 71–86. doi:10.1162/jocn.1991.3.1.71 PMID:23964806

Viola, P., & Jones, M. J. (2004). Robust real-time face detection. *International Journal of Computer Vision, 57*(2), 137–154. doi:10.1023/B:VISI.0000013087.49260.fb

Wang, S., Rehman, A., Wang, Z., Ma, S., & Gao, W. (2013). Perceptual Video Coding Based on SSIM-Inspired Divisive Normalization. *IEEE Transactions on Image Processing, 22*(4). PMID:23221823

Wang, W., Wang, Y., Huang, Q., & Gao, W. (2010). Measuring Visual Saliency by Site Entropy Rate. In *Proc. of CVPR '10*, (pp. 2368-2375). CVPR.

Wang, Z., & Bovik, A. C. (2006). *Modern Image Quality Assessment*. Morgan and Claypool Publishers.

Wang, Z., Bovik, A. C., Sheikh, H. R., & Simoncelli, E. P. (2004). Image quality assessment: From error measurement to structural similarity. *IEEE Transactions on Image Processing*, *13*(4), 600–612. doi:10.1109/TIP.2003.819861 PMID:15376593

Wang, Z., & Li, Q. (2011). Information content weighting for perceptual image quality assessment. *IEEE Transactions on Image Processing*, *20*(5), 1185–1198. doi:10.1109/TIP.2010.2092435 PMID:21078577

Wang, Z., Lu, L., & Bovik, A. (2004). Video Quality Assessment based on Structural Distortion Measurement. *Signal Processing Image Communication*, *19*(2), 121–132. doi:10.1016/S0923-5965(03)00076-6

Wang, Z., Sheikh, H. R., & Bovik, A. C. (2002). No-Reference Perceptual Quality Assessment of JPEG Compressed Images. In *Proceedings of IEEE Int. Conf. on Image Processing*. Rochester, NY: IEEE.

Wang, Z., & Simoncelli, E. P. (2005). Reduced-Reference Image Quality Assessment using a Wavelet-Domain Natural Image Statistic Model. In *Proc. of SPIE Human Vision and Electronic Imaging X*, (pp. 149-159). SPIE.

Watson, A. B. (1993). DCTune: A technique for visual optimization of DCT quantization matrices for individual images. *Soc. Inf. Display Dig. Tech. Papers*, *24*, 946–949.

Watson, M. R., Brennan, A. A., Kingstone, A., & Enns, J. T. (2010). Looking versus seeing: Strategies alter eye movements during visual search. *Psychonomic Bulletin & Review*, *17*(4), 543–549. doi:10.3758/PBR.17.4.543 PMID:20702875

Webster, M. A., & MacLeod, D. I. A. (2011). Visual adaptation and face perception. *Philosophical Transactions of the Royal Society of London. Series B, Biological Sciences*, *366*, 1702–1725. doi:10.1098/rstb.2010.0360 PMID:21536555

Winkler, S. (2005). *Digital Video Quality, Vision Models and Metrics*. Wiley. doi:10.1002/9780470024065

Yamada, K., & Cottrell, G. W. (1995). A model of scan paths applied to face recognition. In *Proceedings of the Seventeenth Annual Cognitive Science Conference*, (pp. 55-60). Mahwah, NJ: Lawrence Erlbaum.

Yang, G., & Huang, T. S. (1994). Human Face Detection in Complex Background. *Pattern Recognition*, *27*(1), 53–63. doi:10.1016/0031-3203(94)90017-5

Yang, H., Shao, L., Zheng, F., Wang, L., & Song, Z. (2011). Recent advances and trends in visual tracking: A review. *Neurocomputing*, *74*, 3823–3831. doi:10.1016/j.neucom.2011.07.024

Yang, J., & Waibel, A. (1996). A Real-Time Face Tracker. In *Proc. Third Workshop Applications of Computer Vision*, (pp. 142-147). Academic Press.

Yang, M.-H., Kriegman, D., & Ahuja, N. (2002). Detecting Faces in Images: A Survey. *IEEE Transactions on Pattern Analysis and Machine Intelligence*, *24*(1), 34–58. doi:10.1109/34.982883

Yow, K. C., & Cipolla, R. (1997). Feature-based Human Face Detection. *Image and Vision Computing*, *15*(9), 713–735. doi:10.1016/S0262-8856(97)00003-6

Zhang, W., Shan, S., Gao, W., Chen, X., & Zhang, H. (2005). Local Gabor Binary Pattern Histogram Sequence: A Novel Non-statistical Model for Face Representation and Recognition. In *Proc. IEEE International Conference on Computer Vision*, (pp. 786-791). IEEE.

Zhou, S., & Chellappa, R. (2002). Probabilistic human recognition from video. In ECCV 2002 (LNCS), (vol. 2352, pp. 681–697). Springer.

Zhou, S., Krueger, V., & Chellappa, R. (2002). Face recognition from video: A condensation approach. In *Proceedings of IEEE International Conference on Automatic Face & Gesture Recognition (FG)*, (pp. 221-226). IEEE.

KEY TERMS AND DEFINITIONS

Bhattacharyya Distance: It measures the similarity of two discrete or continuous probability distributions. It is closely related to the Bhattacharyya coefficient which is a measure of the amount of overlap between two statistical samples or populations.

Differential Entropy: It extends the idea of (Shannon) entropy to continuous probability distributions.

Drift: In predictive analytics and machine learning, the concept drift means that the statistical properties of the target variable, which the model is trying to predict, change over time in unforeseen ways. This causes problems because the predictions become less accurate.

Early Vision: It concerns the visual pre-attentive processing (first 150-200 ms), i.e. the unconscious accumulation of information from the environment.

Encoder-Decoder System: It is the system composed of encoder, transmission channel, decoder. The encoder is a device, circuit, transducer, software program, algorithm or person that converts information from one format or code to another; the transmission channel conveys an information signal from one or several *senders* to one or several *receivers;* the decoder is a device which does the reverse operation of the encoder so that the original information can be retrieved.

Face Detection: To determine whether or not there are faces in a given image and, if so, to give location and extent of each face.

Face Tracking: It concerns the estimation of the (spatial) trajectory of a face in a sequence of images.

Fixation Point: It is the point in the visual field that is fixated by the two eyes in normal vision and for each eye is the point that directly stimulates the fovea of the retina.

Fixations (Visual Fixation): Maintaining of the visual gaze on a single location.

Fovea: Part of the eye which is located in the center of the macula region of the retina and which is responsible for sharp central vision (necessary in any activity where visual detail is of primary importance).

Foveated Imagery: It is a digital image processing technique in which the image resolution, or amount of detail, varies across the image according to one or more fixation points.

Human Visual System: All the physiological components involved in vision.

Ideal Observer: An ideal observer is a hypothetical device that performs optimally in a perceptual task given the available information. The theory of ideal observers has proven to be a powerful and useful tool in vision research, which has been applied to a wide range of problems.

Kalman Filtering: It is an algorithm that uses a series of measurements observed over time, containing noise (random variations) and other inaccuracies, and produces estimates of unknown variables that tend to be more precise than those based on a single measurement alone. The Kalman filter operates recursively on streams of noisy input data to produce a statistically optimal estimate of the underlying system state.

Kolmogorov Complexity: The Kolmogorov complexity of an object, such as a piece of text, is a measure of the computability resources needed to specify the object.

Jensen-Shannon Divergence: It measures the distance between two probability density functions. It is based on the Kullback–Leibler divergence, it is symmetric and it is always a finite value. The square root of the Jensen–Shannon divergence is a metric.

Just Noticeable Detection Threshold: In psychophysics, a just-noticeable difference is the smallest detectable difference between a starting and secondary level of a particular sensory stimulus.

Mean-Shift: Mean shift is a powerful method for non parametric clustering and optimization. It iteratively moves each data point to its local mean until convergence.

Minimum Description Length: It is an important concept in information theory and computational learning theory. It is a formalization of Occam's razor in which the best hypothesis for a given set of data is the one that leads to the best compression of the data.

Mutual Information: In probability theory and information theory, the mutual information of two random variables is a measure of the variables' mutual dependence. It is a measure of the amount of information one random variable contains about another.

Natural Scene Statistics (NSS): Natural Scene statistics is concerned with the statistical regularities related to natural scenes. It is based on the premise that a perceptual system is designed to interpret scenes and that biological perceptual systems have evolved in response to physical properties of natural environments. Natural scene statistics are useful for defining the behavior of an ideal observer in a natural task, typically by incorporating signal detection theory, information theory, or estimation theory.

Normalized Compression Distance (NCD): It is the normalized information distance where the Kolmogorov complexity (that is incomputable) is approximated by a real world compressor (for example "gzip", "bzip2", "PPMZ").

Normalized Information Distance (NID): It is way of measuring the similarity between two objects (documents, letters, music scores, languages, pictures, systems, genomes, etc.) using the Kolmogorov complexity.

Particle Filters: Particle filters or Sequential Monte Carlo (SMC) methods are a set of online posterior density estimation algorithms that estimate the posterior density of the state-space by directly implementing the Bayesian recursion equations. SMC methods use a grid-based approach, and use a set of particles to represent the posterior density. These filtering methods make no restrictive assumption about the dynamics of the state-space or the density function.

Quantization: It is the process of mapping a large set of input values to a (countable) smaller set – such as rounding values to some unit of precision.

Saccades: It is a rapid eye movement that allows a jump from one location to another in order to direct a small part of our visual field into fovea for a closer inspection.

Saliency Map: It is topographical oriented map of the scene, where the most significant positions are the ones that are more different from their neighbors (higher contrast) in terms of color, intensity, orientation, movement, depth, etc.

Shannon Entropy: In information theory, it measures the uncertainty in a random variable and quantifies the expected value of the information contained in a message. It is typically measured in bits, nats, or bans. Shannon entropy provides an absolute limit on the best possible lossless encoding or compression of any communication, assuming that the communication may be represented as a sequence of independent and identically distributed random variables.

Similarity Measure: In computer science, a similarity measure or similarity function is a real-valued function that quantifies the similarity between two objects.

SSIM: The Structural SIMilarity (SSIM) index is a method for measuring the similarity between two images. The SSIM index can be viewed as a quality measure of one of the images being compared, provided the other image is regarded as of perfect quality.

Visual Contrast: It is the difference in luminance and/or color that makes an object (or its representation in an image or display) distinguishable.

Visual Perception: It is the ability to interpret the surrounding environment by processing information that is contained in visible light.

Chapter 15
Human Face Region Detection Driving Activity Recognition in Video

Anastasios Doulamis
Technical University of Crete, Greece

Athanasios Voulodimos
National Technical University of Athens, Greece

Theodora Varvarigou
National Technical University of Athens, Greece

ABSTRACT

Automatic recognition of human actions from video signals is probably one of the most salient research topics of computer vision with a tremendous impact for many applications. In this chapter, the authors introduce a new descriptor, the Human Constrained Pixel Change History (HC-PCH), which is based on PCH but focuses on the human body movements over time. They propose a modification of the conventional PCH that entails the calculation of two probabilistic maps based on human face and body detection, respectively. These HC-PCH features are used as input to an HMM-based classification framework, which exploits redundant information from multiple streams by employing sophisticated fusion methods, resulting in enhanced activity recognition rates.

INTRODUCTION

Identification of events from visual cues is in general a very arduous task because of complex motion, cluttered backgrounds, occlusions, and geometric and photometric variances of the physical objects. Services regarding identification of events from visual signals are of vital importance for large-scale enterprises like industrial plants or public infrastructure organizations. For example, an event identification service is used for quality assurance, i.e. adherence to predefined procedures for production or services, or security and safety purposes, namely prevention of actions that may lead to hazardous situations (Doulamis et al., 2008).

DOI: 10.4018/978-1-4666-5966-7.ch015

Recently several supervision systems have been presented; however, for most of them the supervision service is manually performed which is insufficient and subjective. The inefficiency stems from the fact that the videos from many cameras are displayed on monitors that switch between cameras, thus no 100% monitoring is possible, even if we assume that the operators are constantly concentrated on their task. Regarding subjectivity, recent studies have proven that the attention of the operators of current surveillance systems is mainly attracted by the appearance of monitored individuals and not by their behaviour (Smith, 2004).

The recent research advances in computer vision and pattern recognition have stimulated the development of a series of innovative algorithms, tools and methods for salient object detection and tracking in still images/video streams. All these research methods can be considered as initial steps towards the ultimate goal for behaviour/event understanding. However, automatic comprehension of someone's behaviour within a scene or even automatic supervision of workflows (e.g., industrial processes) is a complex research field of great attention but with limited results so far, since we need to map the extracted low level visual features to high level concepts, such as human actions performed within a scene. An example of an architecture, able to recognize events from visual signals, is presented in (Doulamis et al., 2008) and developed by the European Union funded project SCOVIS ("Self Configurable Cognitive Video Supervision- www.scovis.eu). This research was one of the first results for large scale automatic video supervision of complex industrial processes.

Apart from the research work of SCOVIS, other approaches have been also proposed in the literature for automatic event identification from video information, as described in the Related Work Section. The common point of all these works is the extraction of a set of visual descriptors that capture spatial and temporal variations in an image sequence [such as Motion History Image (Davis,

2001) or Pixel Change History (Xiang & Gong, 2006)], which are then fed to classifier to detect the events and human actions, such as Hidden Markov Models or Neural Networks. However, these descriptors are very generic and thus classification accuracy can be robust and reliable for event detection only in cases of well structured actions executed under noise-free environments, or in cases where the visual recordings are restricted to specific visual domains (like sports and news) [see the Background Section]. To improve reliability of human actions recognition process under complex industrial workflows but structured environments, (Doulamis et al., 2008) modifies the traditional Pixel Change History (PCH) descriptor of (Xiang and Gong, 2006), which is in fact a visual map, to incorporate Zernike moments on PCH descriptors (Zernike, 1934). Still, however, the results suffer from accuracy especially when abrupt background changes take place stemming from manufacturing assembly processes. This is mainly due to the fact that PCH considers whole image alterations meaning that abrupt luminosity changes or severe motion in the background can affect the event identification process.

In order to overcome this problem, (Voulodimos et al., 2012) and (Kosmopoulos et al., 2012) propose a rectification mechanism that ameliorates the performance of the classifiers by taking into account information coming from expert users. The latter evaluate the supervision outcomes of the classifier and the evaluation results are fed back to the system to improve its performance at next iterations of the algorithm. Such an approach, however, moves the complexity from the system to the user side involving the user in the loop and therefore making the supervision process semi-automatic (semi-supervised).

In this Chapter, we propose a new methodology that is suitable for detecting human actions and events from video recordings. Our algorithm introduces a Human Constrained Pixel Change History descriptor, hereby called HC-PCH, in order to eliminate background effect on human action detection. We assume that the majority of the crucial actions occurring in video data are manifestations of activities that humans execute.

In particular, initially a face detector algorithm is applied exploiting probabilistic theory on two chrominance colour components. The algorithm roughly identifies facial regions in real-time. Then, an approximate detection of the human body takes place exploiting biometric measures as regards human body location beneath the facial region. Again, probabilistic theory is exploited to roughly localize these two regions. This way, we form a probabilistic map that describes how probable it is for a pixel to be located within a human region.

As we have mentioned above, a significant element towards reliable human action recognition is the incorporation of the temporal factor in the description process. This represents how a region of interest is modified through time and how such modification affects the outcome of the analysis. To include the temporal factor in our case, we stack the rough human face and body probabilistic detector map through time as we do when we stack the changes of a pixel through time in the PCH descriptor. This way, we introduce a temporally fluctuated descriptor which represents the spatial localization of a human within the image. That is, as the wavelet transform simultaneously discriminates the frequency and temporal components of a signal, the proposed HC-PCH temporally represents the spatial variations of a human (or humans) identified within an image. Then, through this localization we can discriminate human actions or activities.

This Chapter is organized as follows: After briefly reviewing existing literature on visual descriptors and action recognition methods, we present our proposed descriptor, the Human Constrained Pixel Change History (HC-PCH). Subsequently, we describe the HMM-based classification framework which uses as input the HC-PCH descriptions of the video images and classifies video segments as activities of the observed industrial workflow. The proposed

methods are experimentally validated on a real world surveillance dataset. Finally, we briefly summarize future research directions pertaining to the topic of the Chapter, and conclude with a summary of findings.

BACKGROUND KNOWLDEGE: RELATED WORK

The first step towards a semantic image analysis is the extraction of appropriate visual descriptors (Bastan et al., 2010; Kim & Kim, 2012; Doulamis et al., 2000; van Gool et al., 2001; Spala et al., 2012). Generally, holistic and local descriptors are applied. The former represent the image content as a whole, losing particular local details, while the latter focuses more on local information but they lose the whole picture. Hybrid approaches have been also applied in the literature structuring the descriptors so as to identify common patterns within the visual content and finding the correspondences among them. In addition, adaptive mixture background models are commonly used to memorise and maintain the background pixel distribution of a dynamic scene (Ng & Gong, 2001; Stauffer & Grimson, 2000). The foreground pixels detected by adaptive mixture models correspond to pixel-level changes that are either short term; caused by (1) instant moving alien objects, or long term; caused by (2) localised movements of alien objects, (3) introduction of static alien objects or (4) the removal of background objects. However, they cannot differentiate their differences. Adaptive mixture background models are insensitive to persistent movements of background objects such as waving tree leaves (Xiang et al, 2002).

Then, all these descriptors are fed as inputs to non-linear classifiers to detect the objects and track their position within a space (Liu et al., 2011; Miao et al., 2011; Doulamis & Makantasis, 2011). Most of the algorithms applied towards this direction concentrate on localizing the objects onto the projected 2D image plane. When complicated visual effects, like severe occlusions, 3D positioning and concurrent movement of multiple objects towards diverse directions are encountered, they face serious difficulties in their performance and computational complexity. Algorithms in the current state-of-the-art in computer vision study constrained visual environments, like the ones within a research laboratory or of real-like sequences of one or a few objects. To handle these bottlenecks, in the recent years, several research efforts have been also published using complicated visual environments, like the ones of outdoors surveillance of multiple persons (pedestrians), crowded conditions, aerial monitoring, teleconferences rooms, sports events, and daily activities within houses, like the kitchen.

Regarding 3D capturing, passive methods are based on disparity estimation by finding correspondences in images captured by cameras in different views. Their performance relies on efficient disparity estimation and the resolution of the cameras. On the other hand, active methods exploit ToF technology, by using ToF cameras and structured light techniques. ToF cameras can measure depth maps at video rate, while they don't interfere with the scene in the visual spectrum. However, they present very low resolution and random noise behaviour. To overcome these limitations, the work of Ciu et al. (2010) combines resolution enhancement using the ToF superresolution method of (Schuon et. al., 2009) and multiple ToF scans alignment resulting to high resolution 3D points cloud suitable to be used for 3D modelling.

Regarding event detection and human action and activity recognition, a variety of methods have been proposed. These include semilatent topic models (Wang & Mori, 2009), spatial-temporal context (Hu et al., 2010), optical flow and kinematic features (Ali & Shah, 2010), and random trees and Hough transform voting (Yao et al., 2010). Wada and Matsuyama (2000) employ a non-deterministic finite automaton as a sequence analyzer to present an approach for multiobject

behaviour recognition based on behaviour driven selective attention. Other works focus on more specific domains, e.g. event detection in sports (Hung & Hsieh, 2008), retrieving actions in movies (Laptev & Perez, 2007), and automatic discovery of activities (Hamid et al., 2007). Models might be previously trained and kept fixed (Wang et al., 2008; Antonakaki et al., 2009) or adapted over time (Breitenstein et al., 2009) to cope with changing conditions. A broad variety of image feature extraction methods are used, such as global scene 3D motion (Padoy et al., 2009), object trajectories (Johnson & Hogg, 1996) or other object based approaches (Fusier et al., 2007) which require accurate detection and tracking. Other machine learning and statistical methods that have been used for activity recognition include clustering (Boiman & Irani, 2005) and density estimation (Johnson & Hogg, 1996). A very popular approach is hidden Markov models (HMMs) (Ivanov & Bobick, 2000; Padoy et al., 2009), due to the fact that they can efficiently model stochastic time series at various time scales. An alternative approach to the HMM for the analysis of complex dynamical systems is the Echo State Networks (ESNs) (Jaeger et al., 2007). ESNs have been recently used for industrial activity recognition in workflows using part of the same dataset that we are using (Veres et al., 2010). A limitation of ESNs is that all significant variations of activity order in a given workflow have to be learnt to provide good classification results. As will be shown in the experimental section through comparisons, our approach outperforms ESN based methods. Other approaches for industrial activity recognition have also been proposed, involving sensors and wearable computing, (Stiefmeier et al., 2008). A recent comprehensive literature review regarding action and activity recognition can be found in (Poppe, 2010).

As far as multiple cameras are concerned, the work that investigates fusion of time series resulting from holistic image representation is limited. Some typical approaches seek to solve the problem of position or posture extraction in 3D or on ground coordinates, (Antonakaki et al., 2009; Lao et al., 2009). However, camera calibration or homography estimation is required and in most cases there is still dependency on tracking or on extraction of foreground objects and their position, which can be easily corrupted by illumination changes and occlusions. Later in the chapter, several fusion schemes using HMMs are discussed and their applicability to our scenario is scrutinised.

Finally, adaptive strategies can be applied through the incorporation of the user in the learning process so as to improve human action recognition accuracy. In particular, an expert user can verify the efficiency of the proposed scheme in terms of performance accuracy and then the system automatically updates its performance so that a better classification of the actions is achieved at the ensuing human actions recognition stages. Kosmopoulos et al. (2012) proposes such as a system in recognizing complex multiple industrial processes.

In this chapter we overcome the aforementioned drawbacks by proposing a new visual descriptor that exploits human face variations with pixel changes. The new descriptor is appropriate to detect complex human actions in which human regions play a significant role.

HUMAN CONSTRAINED PIXEL CHANGE HISTORY

In this section, we describe the new modified Pixel Change History (PCH) which is constrained on human regions. For clarity of presentation, we discuss in the following subsection the conventional PCH descriptor while in next subsection the proposed Human constrained PCH (HC-PCH).

Pixel Change History

To implement an efficient human action recognition system, we need to develop a visual descriptor able to detect the presence of pixel level changes at temporal scales. In general, a pixel-level change of different temporal scales can have different significance in the semantic concept that an image represents. In particular, a short term change is most probably caused by instant moving objects, a medium term change is most likely to be caused by the localized moving objects, while long term change are due to the appearance of new static objects in the scene or the hiding of some of the objects from others (objects disappearance). All these properties can be well represented by Pixel Change History (PCH) descriptor, a single, unified multi-scale temporal representation that can capture and differentiate changes of such different rates/scales at the pixel level (Xiang & Gong, 2006).

In particular, let us denote as (x,y) the position of one pixel in an image $I(t)$ at a time t and let us represent as $F(x,y,t)$ the foreground object of a frame. PCH descriptor is independent of the type of the algorithm applied to subtract the foreground from the background. Then, we define the PCH descriptor, say $P_{\sigma,\tau}(x,y,t)$, as shown in Box 1.

In Equation (1), σ and τ are two factors indicating pixel accumulation and decay respectively. Equation (1) means that when we are at the foreground region, the values of the descriptor gradually increase depending on the accumulation factor. In addition, in case there is no significant pixel level change at the examined location (x,y), the respective pixels are treated as a part of the background and PCH starts to decay. Factor τ defines the speed of such decay. In particular, large values of σ and τ imply that the history of visual change at (x, y) is considered over a longer backward temporal window. On the contrary, the ratio between σ and τ determines how much weight is put on the recent change.

Box 1.

$$P_{\sigma,\tau}(x,y,t) = \begin{cases} \min\left(P_{\sigma,\tau}(x,y,t-1) + \dfrac{255}{\sigma}, 255\right) & \text{if } F(x,y,t) = 1 \\[2ex] \max\left(P_{\sigma,\tau}(x,y,t-1) - \dfrac{255}{\tau}, 0\right) & \text{otherwise} \end{cases} \tag{1}$$

According to (Xiang and Gong, 2006), a simple method to derive the foreground object is to subtract two successive frames and then take the absolute values between them. Then, the PCH descriptor can be used to detect the medium and long term pixel changes within an image. Motion History Image is a special case of PCH when the factor σ is set to 1.

Human Constrained Pixel Change History

In this section, we constrain the aforementioned descriptor focusing on detection of humans. This is due to the fact that most of the actions taking place within a video stream are in fact consequences of human actions being executed within a particular time window. Thus, concentrating on human objects we aspire to improve efficiency and performance in actions recognition since abrupt background changes will be ignored by the new descriptor.

Human Face Detection: To achieve this, we initially apply a probabilistic human face detector algorithm on image pixels. The goal of the algorithm is to derive a gray-scale valued map of the same size with the examined frame, which represents the probability of locating human faces within the scene. Our goal is to extract a rough map on where human faces may be located within the image. In this Chapter, human face detection is accomplished by exploiting the two chrominance components of a pixel since it is verified in

(Wang & Chang, 1997) that the two chrominance components of a human face are located on a very small colour space.

In particular, let us denote as $\mathbf{c}(x,y) = [c_r(x,y)\ c_b(x,y)]^T$ the two-dimensional vector of the two chrominance components of a pixel at position (x, y), where $c_r(x,y)$, $c_b(x,y)$ correspond to the first and the second chrominance component respectively, while symbol T defines the transpose of a vector. Then, we can model the histogram of the chrominance values, corresponding to the face area, as a two dimensional (2D) Gausssian probability density function (pdf). Then, the probability of a pixel at position (x, y) to be part of the face region is given in Box 2. where μ_f and $\mathbf{S}_f$ are the mean vector and variance matrix of the pdf respectively. The parameters of (1) can be estimated based on several training data of face images and using the maximum likelihood algorithm.

The probabilistic map constructed in Equation (2) indicates that a pixel at position (x,y) belongs to a facial region if the respective probability is high. Instead, pixels of low probability are classified as non-face pixels. This way, we obtain a density mask that indicates the probability of each pixel belonging to a human face region.

To eliminate false alarms in the human face detection process, shape constraints are also adopted in the proposed scheme. The shape constrains take into account biometric properties as regards the aspect ratio of the human face so as to exclude erroneous regions. This is mainly due to the ex-

Box 2.

$$\Pr(\mathbf{c}(x,y) \mid \text{face}) = \frac{\exp\left(-\dfrac{1}{2}(\mathbf{c}(x,y) - \boldsymbol{\mu}_f)^T \cdot \mathbf{S}_f^{-1} \cdot (\mathbf{c}(x,y) - \boldsymbol{\mu}_f)\right)}{(2\pi)\left|\mathbf{S}_f\right|^{1/2}} \tag{2}$$

Box 3.

$$\Pr(\mathbf{r}(x,y) \mid body) = \frac{\exp\left(-\dfrac{1}{2\sigma_x^2}(r_x - \mu_x)^2\right)\exp(-\dfrac{1}{2\sigma_y}(r_y - \mu_y)^2)}{(2\pi)\sigma_x\sigma_y} \tag{3}$$

istence background regions with colors similar to the face region's colours. For this reason, in this Chapter, as shape constraints we use the anatomical aspect ratio of human face. In particular, it is impossible for the outline of a human face to have an aspect ratio (height over width) of 3 to1, or 1 to 3, if we do not consider face regions in video created by special effects. Other constraints are from the attributes of video. For example, the size of the video frames sets the upper bound of the largest face regions that our algorithm can detect (Wang & Chang, 1997).

Human Body Detection: The next step is the detection of the human body from the facial regions. Again, a probability mask is created the centre $\mathbf{e} = [e_x\ e_y]^T$, height h and width w of which is defined by the centre and the location of the face region. In particular, let us denote as $\mathbf{r}(x,y) = [r_x\ r_y]^T$ the distance between the (x,y) pixel and the origins. In our case, fixed origins are defined as the up left corner of the image. These origins should be the same as human face location algorithm. Then, we create a product of two independent one dimensional Gaussian pdfs to model the probability of a pixel to belong to the human body region. In particular, we have

what is shown in Box 3.where μ_x μ_y, σ_x and σ_y express the parameters of the human body location model; these are calculated based on information derived from the face detection task, taking into account the relationship between human face and body. In our simulations, the parameters in (3) are estimated with respect to the face region as follows

$$\mu_x = e_x, \mu_y = e_y + h/2, \ \sigma_x = w, \ \sigma_y = w/2 \tag{4}$$

Parameters in Equation (4) we have defined using extensive experiments on annotated data of SCOVIS sequence. They are actually define biometric properties on where the human body should be roughly located having detected the face and assuming an upright position for the human. We should stress that the goal of Equation (3) is to provide a rough approximate localization of the human body instead of a precise one. The main purpose is the selected regions to be with high confidence human body regions while the excluded ones can either human body or other regions as well.

Similarly to the human face detection task, a pixel belongs to a human body if the respective probability, $\Pr(\mathbf{r}(x,y) \mid body)$ is high, otherwise the probability is low (thresholding). Then, we create a grey-scale mask that includes the probabilities for the image pixels to belong to the human area. Let us denote as $HP(x,y,t)$ this probabilistic map, where (x,y,t) indicates the probability for a pixel at position (x,y) and time t of belonging to the human area.

Human Constrained Pixel Change History Descriptor: One simple and naïve way to incorporate human face and body regions within the PCH descriptors is to substitute the foreground regions involved in Equation (1), with the human face and body areas. This will improve the robustness of the visual description for activity recognition, especially when these activities are caused by human actions.

Another more robust way, which is proposed in this Chapter, is to incorporate the human area probability map within the descriptors by multiplying each image pixel with the respective probability to belong to a human area. In other words pixels outside the human area are suppressed since their probabilities take low values. On the contrary, pixels inside the human area are enhanced since the respective probabilities are high. We modify the PCH descriptor in Box 4.

This new descriptor, called HC-PCH is used in our paper for human action recognition.

To represent the images as vectors preserving the most important content we use the Zernike moments, which are among the most popular choices as shape descriptors (Flussel et al., 2009). Zernike moments representation is selected due to its efficiency in noise and its reconstruction capability. Moments of low order keep the coarse information while the ones of higher order keep the fine details. However, the more detailed the region representation is, the more processing power will be required, so a balance between accuracy of representation and processing power is desirable.

ACTIVITY CLASSIFICATION

The goal of automatic activity recognition may be viewed as the recovery of a specific learned behavior (class or visual task) from the sequence of observations O. Each camera frame is associated with one observation vector and the observations from all cameras will be later combined in a fusion framework to exploit complementarity of the different views. The sequence of observations from each camera composes a separate camera-specific information stream, which can be modeled by camera-specific models such as the Hidden Markov Model or neural networks such as the echo state network (ESN).

Single Stream Classification

The HMM framework entails a Markov chain comprising a number of, say, N states, with each state being coupled with an observation emission

Box 4.

$$P_{\sigma,\tau}(x,y,t) = \begin{cases} \min\left(P_{\sigma,\tau}(x,y,t-1) * HP(x,y,t-1) + \dfrac{255}{\sigma}, 255\right) & \text{if } HP(x,y,t) > Thr \\ \max\left(P_{\sigma,\tau}(x,y,t-1) * HP(x,y,t-1) - \dfrac{255}{\sigma}, 0\right) & \text{otherwise} \end{cases} \tag{5}$$

distribution. An HMM defines a set of initial probabilities $\left\{\pi_k\right\}_{k=1}^{N}$ for each state, and a matrix A of transition probabilities between the states; each state is associated with a number of observations O (input vectors). Gaussian mixture models are typically used for modeling the observation emission densities of the HMM hidden states. The EM (or Baum-Welch) algorithm is very popular

for training HMMs under a maximum- likelihood framework; it involves four main steps, iterated until convergence (see Algorithm 1 in Box 5 and Figure 1). Moreover, given a trained HMM, probability assignment for an observation sequence is performed by simply conducting the two first steps of the HMM training process using the given test sequence.

Box 5. Algorithm 1: Outline of the EM algorithm for HMM training

---

1. The observation model Θ used to represent the observation emission likelihoods is employed to calculate the observation emission probabilities of each training sequence $O = \{ot\}Tt=1$ with respect to (a) the model states (result is the matrix **B**) and (b) the component densities of the model states, in case a mixture model-based observation model is considered (resulting in matrix ^Bm).
2. The forward-backward algorithm is executed to calculate the assignment posterior probability (γ) of each observation of each given input sequence to the model states. Moreover, the posterior probabilities of the observations with regard to the mixture model components are also computed $^{(\gamma}m)$. Furthermore, the corresponding state transition posterior probabilities ξ, and the input sequence likelihoods are calculated. In all these computations, the outputs of the previous step as well as the state priors $\{\pi_k\}^N k = 1$, the transition matrix (**A**) and the component priors matrix (**M**) are used.
3. The updates of $\{\pi_k\}^N_{k=1}$, **A**, **M**, and Θ are calculated using (γ) and ξ.
4. The updated observation model is calculated using γ_m and O.

---

*Figure 1. The HMM treated using the EM framework. The inputs-outputs are assumed in matrix form and in parentheses are given their dimensions. After initialization, model training comprises iteration over the steps 1-4 of Algorithm 1 until convergence. Model testing consists of one execution of steps 1 and 2 of Algorithm 1. O is the input sequence, Θ the full postulated observation model, **B** the observation likelihoods given the model state, and **B**$_m$ the observation likelihoods given the model state and the mixture model component. **M** are the mixture priors, π the state priors, **A** the transition matrix, and **M**, π, **A** the respective estimated values. ξ is the posterior probability of being in state i at time t and in state j at t+1. γ and γ_m are the state and state/mixture component posterior probabilities at time t.*

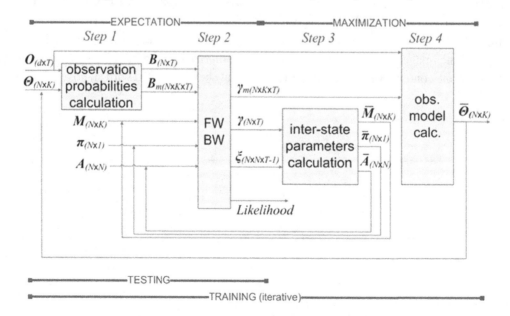

The HMM framework is very appropriate for the needs of automatic activity recognition in complex environments. The complexity is linear in the number of states and observations. The training is very fast by employing the Baum Welch and Viterbi algorithms. Moreover the framework is applicable in online classification schemes with appropriate modifications (Rabiner, 1989).

Disambiguation Using Multiple Streams

One of the weaknesses of holistic image-based methods for activity recognition is their dependence on the viewpoint, and thus their vulnerability to occlusions. This can be alleviated by deploying multiple cameras so that the occlusions are minimized by appropriately placing the cameras. Each camera input can be used to generate a stream of observations. Multi-camera fusion aims at attaining better recognition results than the ones obtained by employing single stream recognition.

In the following section, we will analyze the fusion methods that we have implemented within the HMM framework. We will provide details on how we have extended the typical EM framework to implement them with respect to Algorithm 1 and Figure 1. More specifically we are going to examine the following fusion schemes:

- Feature fusion

- Synchronous HMM
- Parallel HMM
- HMM coupling state and interstream observation

Feature Fusion

Among existing approaches feature fusion is the simplest; it assumes that the observation streams are synchronous. This synchronicity is a valid assumption for cameras that have overlapping fields of view and support synchronization. The related architecture is displayed in Figure 2. For streams from C cameras and respective observations at time t given by $o_{1t}, ..., o_{Ct}$, the proposed scheme defines the full observation vector as a simple concatenation of the individual observations:

$$o_t = \left\{ o_{ct} \right\}_{c=1}^{C} \tag{6}$$

Then, the observation emission probability of the state $s_t = i$ of the fused model, when considered as a k-component mixture model, yields:

$$P\left(O_t | s_t = i\right) = \sum_{k=1}^{K} w_{ik} P\left(O_t | \theta_{ik}\right) \tag{7}$$

where w_{ik} denotes the weights of the mixtures and θ_{ik} the parameters of the kth component density

Figure 2. The feature HMM fusion framework for two streams

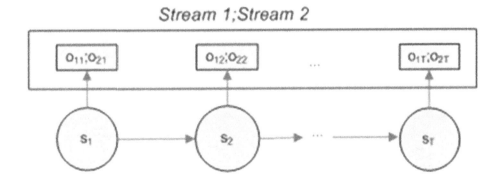

of the ith state (e.g., mean and covariance matrix of a Gaussian pdf). Both training and testing are performed in the typical way using the obtained concatenated vectors.

Synchronous HMM

In the state-synchronous multistream HMM (see Figure 3) the streams are assumed to be synchronized. Each stream is modeled using an individual HMM; the postulated streamwise HMMs share the same state dynamics (identical states, state priors, transition matrices, component priors).

Then, the likelihood for one observation is given by the product of the observation likelihood of each stream c raised to an appropriate positive stream weight r_c (Dupont and Leuttin, 2000):

$$P(O_t|s_t = i) = \prod_{c=1..C} \left[\sum_{k=1}^{K} w_{ik} P(O_{ct}|, _{ik}) \right]^{r_c}$$

(8)

The weight r_c is associated with the reliability of the information carried by the c-th stream. For example, a camera that does not capture the moving target very well due to occlusions should be weighted less.

Training is performed differently from the standard HMM in the following sense:

- Step 1 of *Algorithm 1* is performed for all C input streams $\{o_c\}_{c=1}^{C}$ separately, using the respective streamwise HMMs. Thus, the streamwise observation probabilities with respect to the model states, $\boldsymbol{B}_c$, and with respect to the model mixture components, $\boldsymbol{B}_{cm}$, are calculated.

- Similar to the standard method, step 2 uses the inputs $\boldsymbol{B}$, $\boldsymbol{B}_m$, which now express the fused observation probabilities per state and state component.

- The latter matrices are calculated as inner products over the corresponding streamwise matrices.

Figure 3. The synchronous HMM fusion framework for two streams

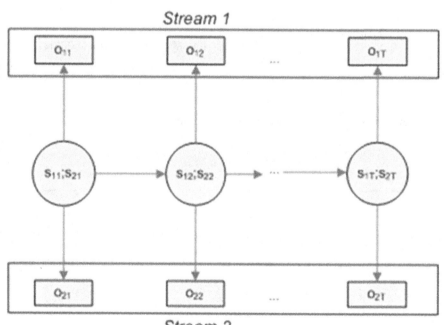

- Finally, step 4 of the algorithm is performed C times, separately for each stream. Test sequence probability estimation comprises in essence the first two steps of the training algorithm.

Parallel HMM

Another alternative is the parallel HMM (see Figure 4); it assumes that the streams are independent of each other, and, hence we can train one individual HMM for each stream in the typical way. This HMM-type model can be applied to cameras (or other sensors) that may not be synchronized and may operate at different acquisition rates. Similar to the synchronous case, each stream c may have its own weight r_c depending on the reliability of the source.

Classification is performed by selecting the class that maximizes the weighted sum of the classification probabilities from the stream-wise HMMs. In other words, class assignment is conducted by picking the class with:

$$l = argmax_l \left(\sum_{c=1}^{C} r_c \log P\left(o_1..o_T \mid \lambda_{cl}\right) \right) \quad (9)$$

where λ_{cl} are the parameters of the postulated streamwise HMM of the cth stream that corresponds to the lth class.

HMM Coupling State and Interstream Observation

The multistream fused HMM (MFHMM) is another promising method for modeling of multistream data (Zeng et. al., 2008) (Figure 5) with several desirable features:

- State transitions do not necessarily happen simultaneously, which makes the method appropriate for both synchronous and asynchronous camera networks;

Figure 4. The parallel HMM fusion framework for two streams

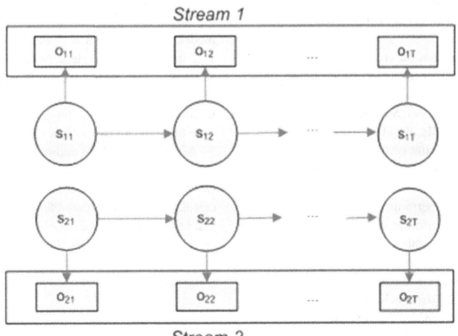

Figure 5. Multistream fused HMM using coupling between states and observations of all streams

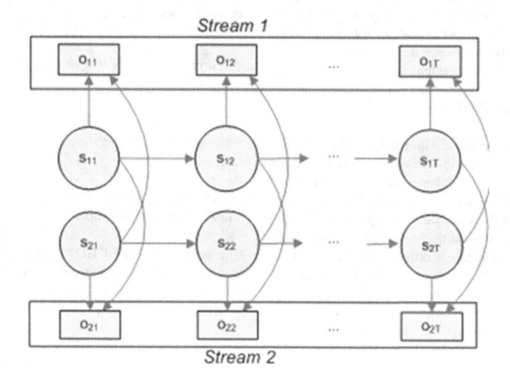

- It has simple and fast training and inference algorithms;
- If one of the component HMMs fails due to noise or some other reason, the rest of the constituent HMMs can still work properly; and
- It still retains the crucial information about the interdependencies between the multiple data streams, which coupled HMMs tend to neglect. Similar to the case of parallel HMMs, the class that maximizes the weighted sum of the log-likelihoods over the streamwise models is the winner.

Training is performed as follows. Step 1 of *Algorithm 1* is performed for all C input streams $\{o_c\}C$ separately; this way a set of initial streamwise HMMs is obtained. Then, the emitting HMM states sequence corresponding to the training sequence of each streamwise model is extracted by means of the standard Viterbi algorithm. Having

the emitting state sequences available, we compute for each stream c the probabilities $\boldsymbol{B}_{fc}$ of the observations of all the other observable streams given the state sequence of the cth stream; thus, we obtain, in essence, an interstream probability model. Then, the input $\boldsymbol{B}$ of step 2 of *Algorithm 1* is the fused observation probability defined as $\boldsymbol{B}=\oplus_{c=1\ldots C}\{\boldsymbol{B}_c \oplus \boldsymbol{B}_{fc}\}$, where $\oplus$ is the symbol of the inner product. The rest of the training is performed using the stream-specific parameters as in the standard case (*Algorithm 1*).

After training, likelihood-based classification can be subsequently performed by using the first two steps of the described training algorithm to calculate the log-likelihood for each stream. On that basis, similar to the case of parallel HMMs, the class that maximizes the weighted sum of the log-likelihoods over the streamwise models is the winner.

EXPERIMENTAL VALIDATION

We experimentally validated the proposed methods with video sequences obtained from a real assembly line of an automobile manufacturer. The workflow on this line included picking several parts from racks and placing them on a designated welding cell. Each of the above activities/tasks was regarded as a class of behavioral patterns that had to be recognized. Two cameras with partially overlapping views were used. We evaluated the overall efficiency of the proposed system, as well as the framework's different alternative constituent components.

The workspace configuration and the camera positions are depicted in Figure 6. According to the manufacturing requirements each workflow consists of the following seven activities/tasks, which are not necessarily executed sequentially:

Task 1: A part from Rack 1 (upper) is placed on the welding spot by worker(s).

Task 2: A part from Rack 2 is placed on the welding spot by worker(s).

Task 3: A part from Rack 3 is placed on the welding spot by worker(s).

Task 4: Two parts from Rack 4 are placed on the welding spot by worker(s).

Task 5: A part from Rack 1 (lower) is placed on the welding spot by worker(s).

Task 6: A part from Rack 5 is placed on the welding spot by worker(s).

Task 7: Worker(s) grab(s) the welding tools and weld the parts together.

Dataset-1 from the SCOVIS datasets (Voulodimos et al., 2012) is used for the experiments. Each dataset contains 20 segmented sequences representing full assembly cycles/workflows.

Figure 6. Depiction of workcell along with the position of the cameras and racks #1-5

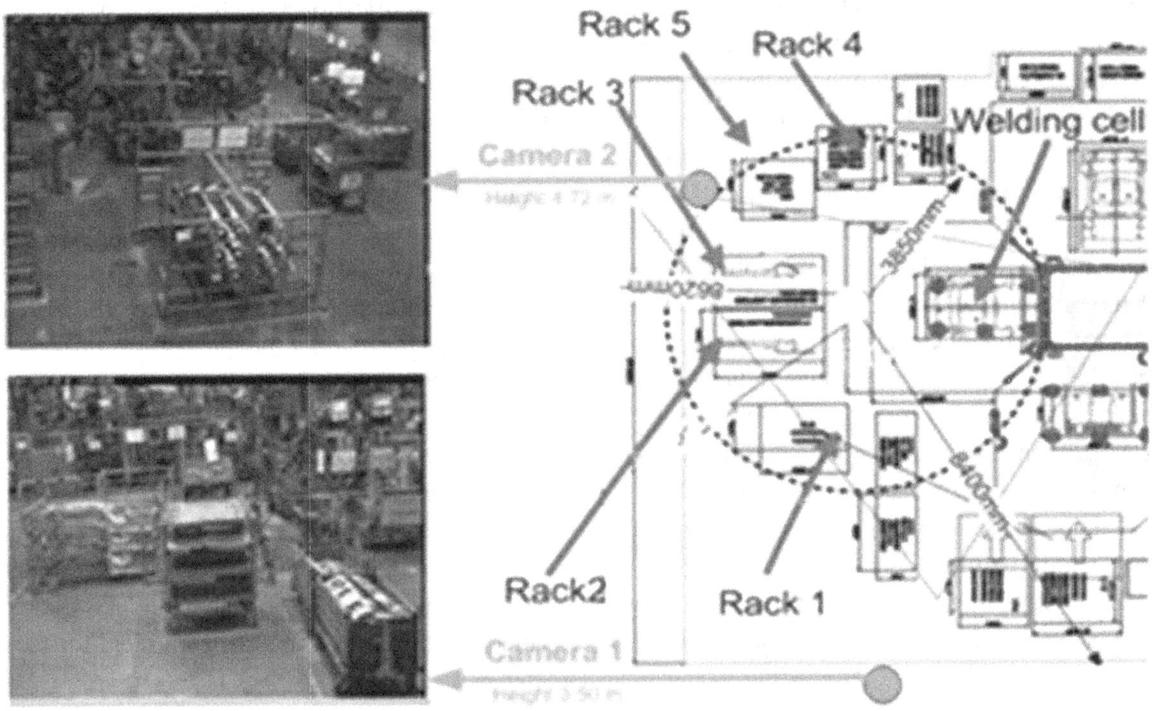

Table 1. Results obtained using i) individual HMMs to model information from Stream 1 (HMM1); ii) individual HMMs to model information from Stream 2 (HMM2); iii) feature fusion; iv) state-synchronous HMMs; v) parallel HMMs; and vi) multistream fused HMMs.

Model	HMM 1	HMM 2	Feature Fusion	Synchronous	Parallel	Multistream Fused
Accuracy	63.4%	68.7%	54.2%	64.8%	69.3%	72.6%

We used three-state HMMs with a single Gaussian mixture component per state to model each of the seven tasks described above, which is a good trade-off between performance and efficiency. The testing sequences were then tested against each of the seven trained HMMs; the HMM yielding the highest likelihood was considered to correspond to the task executed in the sequence. The sequence was thus classified to one of the seven activities. For the mixture model representing the interstream interactions in the context of the multistream fused HMM we used mixture models of two component distributions. Full covariance matrices were employed for the observation models. The stream weights r_c in the fusion models were selected according to the reliability of the individual streams, that is in proportion to the classification accuracy attained by the respective single stream HMM. Ten workcycles were used for training of the HMMs and the other ten were used for testing.

The results we obtained show that the proposed method provides a relatively good representation of the observed scenes, especially when taking into account the challenging nature of the dataset. More specifically, the results indicated that the individual HMM corresponding to camera 2 (HMM2) tended to yield better recognition rates than HMM1, which can be explained by the better viewpoint of the former, in terms of less occlusions and proximity to the scene.

By looking at the results of Table 1 we draw the conclusion that information fusion provides added value when implemented in the form of multistream fused HMM. This can be put down to the multistream fused model's capability of capturing the state interdependencies, without assuming strict synchronicity. The parallel HMM approach provided slightly better success rates in comparison to the best individual streamwise model. This approach considers the streams to be totally asynchronous and is thus unable to make use of state interdependencies. On the other hand, accuracy rates deteriorated when assuming perfect synchronicity by employing the state-synchronous approach, reflecting the fact that our cameras were indeed not perfectly synchronized.

An example of a frequently occurring erroneous classification was the misclassification of a "task 1" sequence for a "task 5" sequence. The reason behind this is the significant visual resemblance of the activities, since both involve picking up a part from the same rack, although from a different shelf of the rack. The viewpoint of camera 1 was such, that it made discerning the shelf from which the part is picked up very difficult. In this case, the use of fusion with camera 2 improved the recognition rates in several cases.

Although other methods of representation (such as the ones presented in Voulodimos et al. (2012) and Veres et al. (2010)) achieve higher accuracy rates in activity recognition, we consider this effort to be a promising start for the Human Constrained Pixel Change History descriptor that we have introduced. The fact that the surveillance videos of the dataset are far from ideal for face region detection (which constitutes the first step of the descriptor calculation), i.e. distance between cameras and persons, low resolution, leads to the conclusion that the proposed descriptor might be significantly more effective in cases where the face region is clear.

FUTURE RESEARCH DIRECTIONS

As was mentioned above, the first future step would be to apply the proposed Human Constrained Pixel Change History to other datasets that offer better chances of detecting the human face and body; we have reasons to believe that the overall performance will be significantly improved in those cases. It would be also interesting to apply the descriptor on different recognition frameworks as well, such as the Echo State Networks, or in the context of adaptive strategies used to enhance recognition performance through relevance feedback. Finally, a thorough comparison of HC-PCH with PCH, Motion History Images (MHI), etc. would be useful to show the strengths and weaknesses of each descriptor.

CONCLUSION

Activity recognition from video sequences is one of the most interesting research fields in computer vision today. We hereby introduced a new descriptor that focuses on the human silhouette, the Human Constrained Pixel Change History. This descriptor is derived by "enriching" the conventional Pixel Change History with information from a probabilistic map that is obtained using human face and body detection algorithms. The features based on this descriptor are fed into an HMM-based classification framework which allows for exploitation of multiple camera streams to solve occlusions through the use of fusion methods, such as synchronous, parallel and multistream fused HMMs. The experimental results show that the

proposed descriptor provides a good representation of the scenes and the activity recognition framework attains good accuracy rates, especially in the case of multistream fusion. It is reasonable to assume that the performance of HC-PCH will be significantly better in video sequences where the human face and body are easier discernible than in the case of the industrial dataset used for validation in this chapter.

REFERENCES

Ali, S., & Shah, M. (2010). Human action recognition in videos using kinematic features and multiple instance learning. *IEEE Transactions on Pattern Analysis and Machine Intelligence*, *32*(2), 288–303. doi:10.1109/TPAMI.2008.284 PMID:20075459

Antonakaki, P., Kosmopoulos, D., & Perantonis, S. (2009). Detecting abnormal human behaviour using multiple cameras. *Signal Processing*, *89*(9), 1723–1738. doi:10.1016/j.sigpro.2009.03.016

Bastan, M., Cam, H., Gudkbay, U., & Ulusoy, O. (2010). Bilvideo-7: an MPEG-7-compatible video indexing and retrieval system. *IEEE MultiMedia*, *17*(3), 62–73. doi:10.1109/MMUL.2010.5692184

Boiman, O., & Irani, M. (2005). *Detecting irregularities in images and in video (ICCV)*. Paper presented at the IEEE International Conference on Computer Vision. Beijing, China.

Brand, M., Oliver, N., & Pentland, A. (1997). *Coupled hidden Markov models for complex action recognition (CVPR)*. Paper presented at the IEEE Conference on Computer Vision and Pattern Recognition. San Juan, Puerto Rico.

Breitenstein, M., Grabner, H., & van Gool, L. (2009). *Hunting nessie - real-time abnormality detection from Webcams (ICCV Workshops)*. Paper presented at the IEEE International Conference on Computer Vision Workshops. Kyoto, Japan.

Cui, Y., Schuon, S., Chan, D., Thrun, S., & Theobalt, C. (2010). *3D shape scanning with a time-of-flight camera (CVPR)*. Paper presented at the IEEE Conference on Computer Vision and Pattern Recognition. San Francisco, CA.

Davis, J. (2001). *Hierarchical Motion History Images for Recognizing Human Motion*. Paper presented at the IEEE Workshop on Detection and Recognition of Events in Video. Vancouver, Canada.

Doulamis, A., Doulamis, N., & Kollias, S. (2000). A fuzzy video content representation for video summarization and content-based retrieval. *Signal Processing, 80*(6), 1049–1067. doi:10.1016/S0165-1684(00)00019-0

Doulamis, A., Kosmopoulos, D., Sardis, M., & Varvarigou, T. (2008). *An architecture for a self configurable video supervision*. Paper presented at the ACM International Conference on Multimedia. Vancouver, Canada.

Doulamis, A., & Makantasis, K. (2011). *Iterative Scene Learning In Visually Guided Persons' Falls Detection (EUSIPCO)*. Paper presented at the 19th European Conference on Signal Processing. Barcelona, Spain.

Dupont, S., & Luettin, J. (2000). Audio-visual speech modeling for continuous speech recognition. *IEEE Transactions on Multimedia, 2*(3), 141–151. doi:10.1109/6046.865479

Flusser, J., Zitova, B., & Suk, T. (2009). *Moment Functions in Image Analysis: Theory and Applications*. Wiley.

Fusier, F., Valentin, V., Bremond, F., Thonnat, M., Borg, M., Thirde, D., & Ferryman, J. (2007). Video understanding for complex activity recognition. *Machine Vision and Applications, 18*, 167–188. doi:10.1007/s00138-006-0054-y

Hamid, R., Maddi, S., Bobick, A., & Essa, M. (2007). *Structure from statistics - unsupervised activity analysis using suffix trees (ICCV)*. Paper presented at the IEEE International Conference on Computer Vision. Rio de Janeiro, Brazil.

Hu, Q., Qin, L., Huang, Q., Jiang, S., & Tian, Q. (2010). *Action recognition using spatial-temporal context (ICPR)*. Paper presented at the 20th International Conference on Pattern Recognition. Istanbul, Turkey.

Hung, M.-H., & Hsieh, C.-H. (2008). Event detection of broadcast baseball videos. *IEEE Transactions on Circuits and Systems for Video Technology, 18*(12), 1713–1726. doi:10.1109/TCSVT.2008.2004934

Ivanov, Y., & Bobick, A. (2000). Recognition of visual activities and interactions by stochastic parsing. *IEEE Transactions on Pattern Analysis and Machine Intelligence, 22*(8), 852–872. doi:10.1109/34.868686

Jaeger, H., Maass, W., & Principe, J. (2007). Special issue on echo state networks and liquid state machines. *Neural Networks, 20*(3), 287–289. doi:10.1016/j.neunet.2007.04.001

Johnson, N., & Hogg, D. (1996). Learning the distribution of object trajectories for event recognition. *Image and Vision Computing, 14*(8), 609–615. doi:10.1016/0262-8856(96)01101-8

Kim, W., & Kim, C. (2012). Background Subtraction for Dynamic Texture Scenes Using Fuzzy Color Histograms. *IEEE Signal Processing Letters, 19*(3), 127–130. doi:10.1109/LSP.2011.2182648

Kosmopoulos, D., Doulamis, N., Voulodimos, A., & Varvarigou, T. (2012). Online Behavior Recognition in Workflows allowing for User Feedback. *Computer Vision and Image Understanding, 116*(3), 422–434. doi:10.1016/j.cviu.2011.09.006

Kosmopoulos, D. I., Voulodimos, A., & Doulamis, A. D. (2013). A system for multicamera task recognition and summarization for structured environments. *IEEE Transactions on Industrial Informatics*, *9*(1), 161–171. doi:10.1109/TII.2012.2212712

Lao, W., Han, J., & de With, P. H. N. (2009). Automatic video-based human motion analyzer for consumer surveillance system. *IEEE Transactions on Consumer Electronics*, *55*(2), 591–598. doi:10.1109/TCE.2009.5174427

Laptev, I., & Perez, P. (2007). *Retrieving actions in movies (ICCV)*. Paper presented at the IEEE International Conference on Computer Vision. Minneapolis, MN.

Liu, C., Yuen, J., & Torralba, A. (2011). SIFT Flow: Dense Correspondence across Scenes and Its Applications. *IEEE Transactions on Pattern Analysis and Machine Intelligence*, *33*(5), 978–994. doi:10.1109/TPAMI.2010.147 PMID:20714019

(2001). Local Features for Image Retrieval. InVeltkamp, R. C., Burkhardt, H., & Kriegel, H.-P. (Eds.), *State-of-the-Art in Content-Based Image and Video Retrieval* (pp. 21–41). Kluwer Academic Publishers.

Makris, A. Kosmopoulos, Perantonis, & Theodoridis, S. (2007). *Hierarchical feature fusion for visual tracking (ICIP)*. Paper presented at the IEEE International Conference on Image Processing. San Antonio, TX.

Miao, Q., Wang, G., Shi, C., Lin, X., & Ruan, Z. (2011). A new framework for on-line object tracking based on SURF. *Pattern Recognition Letters*, *32*(13), 1564–1571. doi:10.1016/j.patrec.2011.05.017

Nefian, A., Liang, L., Pi, X., Xiaoxiang, L., Mao, C., & Murphy, K. (2002). *A coupled hmm for audio-visual speech recognition (ICASSP)*. Paper presented at the IEEE International Conference on Acoustics, Speech, and Signal Processing. Orlando, FL.

Ng, J., & Gong, S. (2001, September). *Learning pixel-wise signal energy for understanding semantics (BMVC)*. Paper presented at the British Machine Vision Conference. Manchester, UK.

Ostendorf, M., & Singer, H. (1997). HMM topology design using maximum likelihood successive state splitting. *Computer Speech & Language*, *11*(1), 17–41. doi:10.1006/csla.1996.0021

Padoy, N., Mateus, D., Weinland, D., Berger, M.-O., & Navab, N. (2009). *Workflow monitoring based on 3D motion features*. Paper presented at the IEEE International Conference on Computer Vision Workshops. Kyoto, Japan.

Poppe, R. (2010). A survey on vision-based human action recognition. *Image and Vision Computing*, *28*(6), 976–990. doi:10.1016/j.imavis.2009.11.014

Rabiner, L. R. (1989). A tutorial on hidden Markov models and selected applications in speech recognition. *Proceedings of the IEEE*, *77*(2), 257–286. doi:10.1109/5.18626

Schuon, S., Theobalt, C., Davis, J., & Thrun, S. (2009). Lidarboost: Depth superresolution for ToF 3D shape scanning. In *Proceedings of IEEE Computer Vision Pattern Recognition Conference*. Miami, FL: IEEE.

Smith, G. J. D. (2004). Behind the screens: Examining constructions of deviance and informal practices among CCTV control room operators in the UK. *Surveillance & Society*, *2*(2/3), 376–395.

Spala, P., Malamos, A., Doulamis, A., & Mamakis, G. (2012). Extending MPEG-7 For Efficient Annotation of Complex Web 3D Scenes. *Multimedia Tools and Applications, 59*(2), 463–504. doi:10.1007/s11042-011-0790-5

Stauffer, C., & Grimson, W. (2000). Learning patterns of activity using real-time tracking. *IEEE Trans. PAMI, 22*(8), 747–758. doi:10.1109/34.868677

Stiefmeier, T., Roggen, D., Troster, G., Ogris, G., & Lukowicz, P. (2008). Wearable activity tracking in car manufacturing. *IEEE Pervasive Computing / IEEE Computer Society [and] IEEE Communications Society, 7*(2), 42–50. doi:10.1109/MPRV.2008.40

Veres, G., Grabner, H., Middleton, L., & van Gool, L. (2010). *Automatic workflow monitoring in industrial environments (ACCV).* Paper presented at the Asian Conference on Computer Vision. New York, NY.

Voulodimos, A., Doulamis, N., Kosmopoulos, D., & Varvarigou, T. (2012). Improving multi-camera activity recognition by employing neural network based readjustment. *Applied Artificial Intelligence, 26*(1-2), 97–118. doi:10.1080/0883 9514.2012.629540

Voulodimos, A., Kosmopoulos, D., Vasileiou, G., Sardis, E., Doulamis, A., & Anagnostopoulos, V. etal. (2011). A threefold dataset for activity and workflow recognition in complex industrial environments. *IEEE MultiMedia, 19*(3), 42–52. doi:10.1109/MMUL.2012.31

Wada, T., & Matsuyama, T. (2000). Multi-object behavior recognition by event driven selective attention method. *IEEE Transactions on Pattern Analysis and Machine Intelligence, 22*(8), 873–887. doi:10.1109/34.868687

Wang, H., & Chang, S.-F. (1997). Highly Efficient System for Automatic Face Region Detection in MPEG Video Sequences. *IEEE Trans. on Circuits and Syst. for Video Technol, 7*(4), 615–628. doi:10.1109/76.611173

Wang, X., Ma, K.-T., Ng, G.-W., & Grimson, W. (2008). *Trajectory analysis and semantic region modeling using a nonparametric bayesian model (ICPR).* Paper presented at the IEEE Conference on Computer Vision and Pattern Recognition. Anchorage, AK.

Wang, Y., & Mori, G. (2009). Human action recognition by semilatent topic models. *IEEE Transactions on Pattern Analysis and Machine Intelligence, 31*(10), 1762–1774. doi:10.1109/TPAMI.2009.43 PMID:19696448

Xiang, T., & Gong, S. (2006). Beyond tracking: modelling activity and understanding behaviour. *International Journal of Computer Vision, 67,* 21–51. doi:10.1007/s11263-006-4329-6

Xiang, T., Gong, S., & Parkinson, D. (2002). *Autonomous Visual Events Detection and Classification without Explicit Object-Centred Segmentation and Tracking (BMCVC).* Paper presented at the British Machine Vision Conference. Cardiff, UK.

Yao, A., Gall, J., & van Gool, L. (2010). *A hough transform-based voting framework for action recognition (CVPR).* Paper presented at the IEEE Conference on Computer Vision and Pattern Recognition. San Francisco, CA.

Zeng, Z., Tu, J., Pianfetti, B., & Huang, T. (2008). Audio-visual affective expression recognition through multistream fused HMM. *IEEE Transactions on Multimedia, 10*(4), 570–577. doi:10.1109/TMM.2008.921737

Zernike, F. (1934). Beugungstheorie des Schneidenverfahrens und Seiner Verbesserten Form, der Phasenkontrastmethode. *Physica I, 1*(8), 689–704. doi:10.1016/S0031-8914(34)80259-5

KEY TERMS AND DEFINITIONS

Activity Classification: A process which applies machine learning algorithms on visual data so as to identify key actions, events and activities taking place within a visual scene.

Aspect Ratio: The aspect ratio of an image describes the proportional relationship between its width and its height.

Background Modeling: Visually modeling the complexity of the background.

Echo Sate Networks: An architecture and supervised learning principle for recurrent neural networks (RNNs).

EM: Expectation- Minimization Algorithm.

Face Detection: A process that automatically assigns image pixels to a face and non-face area.

Face Recognition: A process that automatically identifies to whom person a face belongs.

Feature Fusion: The merging of information from heterogeneous sources with differing conceptual, contextual and typographical representations. It is used in data mining and consolidation of data from unstructured or semi-structured resources.

Hidden Markov Model (HMM): A statistical Markov model in which the system being modeled is assumed to be a Markov process with unobserved (hidden) states.

HMM Coupling State and Interstream Observation: The multistream fused HMM (MFHMM) is performs intelligent fusion of multi-stream data.

Homography: In projective geometry, a homography is an isomorphism of projective spaces, induced by an isomorphism of the vector spaces from which they are derived.

Human Constrained Pixel Change History: A descriptor based on Pixel Change History that also incorporates the probability of a pixel corresponding to a human face or body region.

Human Constrained Pixel Change History (HC-PCH): A modification of the PCH to take into account human regions.

Mixture Models: A probabilistic model for representing the presence of subpopulations within an overall population, without requiring that an observed data set should identify the sub-population to which an individual observation belongs.

Multidimensional Gaussian: In probability theory and statistics, the multivariate normal distribution or multivariate Gaussian distribution, is a generalization of the one-dimensional (univariate) normal distribution to higher dimensions.

Multistream Classification: A process able to identify events exploiting multi-streams.

Multistream Fused Hidden Markov Model: An HMM fusion architecture which is appropriate for modelling two streams of observations and whose main advantage lies in its capability of capturing the crucial information about the interdependencies between the multiple data streams.

Parallel HMM: It assumes that the streams are independent of each other, and, hence we can train one individual HMM for each stream in the typical way. This HMM-type model can be applied to cameras (or other sensors) that may not be synchronized and may operate at different acquisition rates.

Pixel Change History (PCH): A motion based holistic global visual descriptor that maps for each image pixel the intensity caused by stacking up previous pixels at the same location.

PDF: Probability density function.

SCOVIS: Self Configurable Cognitive Video Supervision: an FP7 European Union funded project.

Single Stream Classification: A process able to identify events using single video streams.

Synchronous HMM: In the state-synchronous multistream HMM (see Figure 3) the streams are assumed to be synchronized.

ToF: Time of Flight Cameras.

Visual Cues: Implementation of image analysis tools so as to identify critical image regions which are useful in an application.

Chapter 16
Automatic Face Image Tagging in Large Collections

Silvio Barra
University of Cagliari, Italy

Maria De Marsico
Sapienza University of Roma, Italy

Chiara Galdi
University of Salerno, Italy

ABSTRACT

In this chapter, the authors present some issues related to automatic face image tagging techniques. Their main purpose in user applications is to support the organization (indexing) and retrieval (or easy browsing) of images or videos in large collections. Their core modules include algorithms and strategies for handling very large face databases, mostly acquired in real conditions. As a background for understanding how automatic face tagging works, an overview about face recognition techniques is given, including both traditional approaches and novel proposed techniques for face recognition in uncontrolled settings. Moreover, some applications and the way they work are summarized, in order to depict the state of the art in this area of face recognition research. Actually, many of them are used to tag faces and to organize photo albums with respect to the person(s) presented in annotated photos. This kind of activity has recently expanded from personal devices to social networks, and can also significantly support more demanding tasks, such as automatic handling of large editorial collections for magazine publishing and archiving. Finally, a number of approaches to large-scale face datasets as well as some automatic face image tagging techniques are presented and compared. The authors show that many approaches, both in commercial and research applications, still provide only a semi-automatic solution for this problem.

DOI: 10.4018/978-1-4666-5966-7.ch016

INTRODUCTION

Face image tagging is the process of assigning an identification code (e.g. a personal name) to a face image according to the depicted persons, and is traditionally made by hand. This supports both indexing/classification and retrieval operations. In general, the task is not that demanding when it pertains to personal collections, e.g., the photos of participants in a social network. However, it can become very challenging too. An example is the huge work of cruise photographers, who take hundreds, if not thousands, of passengers photos during the day, and try to organize them during the night to sell them the day after to interested customers. A similar problem, with different time constraints, is addressed when organizing and keeping updated the usually huge photo collection of a magazine editorial office. When related operations can be performed in a totally automatic way, we speak of automatic face tagging. Of course, there is a tight relationship between automatic face tagging and face recognition. In general, face recognition requires comparing a sample image (or a template extracted from it) with a set of images (or templates) of known (enrolled) subjects to establish or verify the sample identity. Automatic face tagging is a particular application of face recognition: its aim is to identify the same person or group of persons in different images or video frames, with the purpose of organizing an archive accordingly, or of tracking the activities of a person. After an initial assignment of labels/tags performed by hand, the process of assigning an identity to a new incoming face and to classify the related image is performed automatically by the face recognition engine instead of a human operator. Clusters of images containing the same face are managed by the system, and new incoming images must be inserted in the correct cluster. Further applications for automatic face image tagging can also address video indexing and retrieval in large collections. Of course in all cases the accuracy of an automatic face image tagging system strongly depends on the face recognition algorithm used, and on its robustness to a variety of distortions (typically PIE – Pose, Illumination, Expression, but also ageing and other demographics). In particular, face tagging is a typical example of face recognition "in the wild" (Huang *et al.*, 2007), due to the complete lack of control over the acquisition settings. Furthermore, tagging is typically performed at a time later the sample acquisition, so that in case of failure to recognize no kind of adjustment and re-acquisition is possible in any case, as for example in authentication applications. In this chapter we present some approaches to face recognition that seem better suited to address this problem. As we will see, automatic face tagging is a complex issue and this is the reason why this kind of systems have not reached a large distribution yet, and are not used in critical (security) settings. Some of the solutions to automatic face image tagging proposed are described in more detail, in order to give to the reader an overview of the state of the art.

Face recognition techniques may undergo different classifications. In Zhao et al. (2003) psychophysicists and neuroscientists theories are taken into account to identify three classes: holistic, which use the whole face region as input to the recognition system; feature-based methods, which first extract local features such as the eyes, nose, and mouth and then use their locations and local statistics for classification; hybrid, which work just as the human perception system is deemed to do, using both local features and the whole face region for recognition. A different classification was used in Abate *et al.* (2007), which mostly takes into account the main techniques underlying the literature approaches: linear/nonlinear projection methods (for dimensionality reduction), neural networks, Gabor filters and wavelets, fractals and Iterated Function Systems (IFSs), use of thermal and hyperspectral images. 3D face recognition is also often discussed, but it requires special equipment and/or computationally expensive processing, which is not appropriate for the kind of operations which we are addressing here. A detailed discussion of the methods in literature is out of the scope of this chapter, but the interested reader can find details in the cited works, and also in Nappi and Riccio (2008) and Jafri and Arabnia (2009).

Notwithstanding the adopted classification, it is widely accepted that a mixture of local and global methods often seems the most appropriate and PIE-robust approach to address the problem of face recognition and, as a consequence, of automatic face tagging. However, it is to consider that even the most traditional methods underwent research efforts to improve their robustness to uncontrolled settings. A first example is related to PCA (Principal Component Analysis), an application of the Karhunen-Loeve procedure for space dimensionality reduction. Kirby and Sirovich (1990) were among the first to adopt the PCA in characterizing human faces. The addition to the database of images pertaining to a new face appears to be very fast, because PCA-related procedure is only performed for the training phase of the system. However, when a large number of new subjects is added to the system, it is necessary to train the system again (retraining). Moreover, the method suffers from a high sensitivity to PIE variations and occlusions. A possible solution to address such limitations was presented in Acosta et al. (2002), where PCA is used in a modified version intended to address the complexity of recognizing a person in a video frame, with multiple views of the same face. More details about their method are given later in this chapter in the section about state of the art. Proposed as a better alternative to PCA, LDA (Linear Discriminant Analysis) (Martinez & Kak, 2001; Lu et al., 2003) expressly provides a better discrimination between the classes. However, LDA too achieves poor robustness to PIE variations to be used in uncontrolled settings. Despite this, in Lee and Kim (2004) the authors claim to use an enhanced combination of PCA/LDA for the face recognition process in a video summarization and retrieval system. For details

about the adopted method they refer to a working document of ISO/IEC JTC1/SC29/WG11 which seems no longer available (W.Y. Kim, J.H. Lee, H.S. Park, and H.J. Lee: PCA/LDA Face Recognition Descriptor using Pose Transformation, ISO/IEC JTC1/SC29/WG11 MPEG2002/M8934 -2002.). However, from the description of the exploited face recognition descriptors, which is available from a further document by International Organization For Standardization (2004), it seems confirmed that the basis of such descriptors is the projection of the linearized vector of the normalized face image onto a reduced space. Still in the context of proposals for MPEG-7 face recognition descriptors, a further proposal involving LDA was presented by Kim et al. (2005). They devise a component-based LDA representation which allows to enhance the generalization capability of the LDA representation with respect to changes underrepresented in the training data. In practice, the face is divided into a number of facial regions and a separate LDA is learnt for each region. As a matter of fact, this is an example of how local processing can even improve the performance of more classical approaches.

Neural Networks are a nonlinear solution to the pattern recognition problem. The basic idea of face recognition based on neural networks is to associate each neuron of the net with each pixel in the image, but because of the high number of neurons needed, a dimensionality reduction technique is first performed and neural networks are trained on the reduced image space. In practice, the vector representing the input image is often first submitted to a first neural network that reduces it to a (much) shorter vector h. Afterwards, the vector h is submitted to the second net (classification) for recognition. Actually, the neural network approach is not suited for massive face recognition tasks in uncontrolled conditions, but related methods can give good results in preliminary face region detection instead. For instance, in Garcia and Delakis (2002) a convolutional neural network architecture was presented to recognize highly variable face

Figure 1. Examples of the appearance of the basis elements computed for the different kinds of subspaces: (a) Eigenfaces, (b) Fisherfaces, and (c) Laplacianfaces

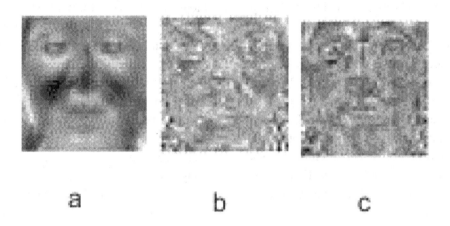

a   b   c

patterns with no preprocessing. Detection and precise localization of semi-frontal human faces is performed making no assumption on colors, on the illumination conditions, or on the size of the face. As we will further discuss, face detection is the first crucial step for a reliable recognition, so that methods allowing to achieve good results for this task are important as well for tagging.

The approach of using Laplacianfaces for recognition was first introduced by He *et al.* (2005). Laplacianface use Locality Preserving Projection (LPP) to learn a locality preserving subspace. Its aim is to capture the intrinsic geometry of the data and its local structure. Each face image is mapped onto the computed subspace that is characterized by a set of feature images, called Laplacianfaces. The basis functions obtained with the original Laplacianface approach are not orthogonal, making it difficult to reconstruct the data. For this reason Cai *et al.* (2006) developed the OLPP method that produces orthogonal basis functions that preserve the metric structure of the face space and achieves more locality preserving power than LPP.

Figure 1 shows some example elements belonging to the bases identified by the different space reduction methods.

Among traditional feature based methods, Elastic Bunch Graph Matching (EBGM), first introduced by Wiskott *et al.* (1997) is very popular. It is an extension of Elastic Graph Matching for object classes with a common structure, for example faces in the same pose. It uses an approach based on Gabor Wavelets. A two-dimensional face image is represented by a full connected graph in which fiducial points on the face (pupils, mouth, etc.) are the nodes. Each node is then described by linear combinations of a set of wavelets named jets, and each arc is labeled with the distance between the two nodes it connects. A jet describes a small set of gray values (the local texture) around a certain pixel and then is stored in a feature vector that is further used for recognition. From these individual graphs a bunch graph (Face Bunch Graph - FBG) with the same structure is created, with the nodes representing local textures of any face in the class, e.g. all the detected variants of a left eye, and the edges represent the mean distances between the node locations, e.g. the mean distance between the two eyes. A bunch graph represents classes rather than individual objects. Comparison is performed in two steps: a rigid alignment of the grid is performed to handle global transformations, such as translations and scale, then the local misplacement of nodes is evaluated by a Graph Similarity Function. EBGM-based recognition requires that the objects share a common structure. As for faces, this means to match faces in frontal pose, sharing a common set of landmarks. Therefore EBGM can only handle small pose changes. Larger pose differences excessively modify the local features, and, some of them may also be occluded. To address this limitation, it is possible to create bunch graphs for different poses and match all of them to the probe image. This method is robust with respect to variations in pose and illumination, and does not require retraining (unlike Eigenfaces) when new graphs are added. On the other hand, the training as well as the recognition phases are quite slow. Westphal and Würtz (2009) have later proposed a graph dynamics that allows an object representations emerge from a collection of arbitrary objects. The underlying idea is to extract typical local texture arrangements from the objects and provide the rules to compose them as needed to represent new objects.

The consideration stemming from this brief introduction is that face recognition in uncontrolled settings has spurred significant research even in connection with more traditional approaches. However, even if low accuracy can be emended, this often requires complex training/re-training and/or high computational costs. In the following, we will survey some more efficient methods suitable to be exploited in automatic tagging.

OVERVIEW OF PRESENT FACE TAGGING APPLICATIONS

The advent of digital cameras has deeply revolutionized the habits of million people. The traditional analog photographic process took time and money, even because it was not possible to select "good" photos in advance. Moreover, the only way to remotely share photos was to duplicate and send them by mail or, more recently, to scan them and send them by email. Digital capture has dramatically changed this, since one can take

thousand shots at no expense, and store and share them in electronic format in seconds. Digital photo albums were formerly stored in personal computers. Afterwards, the increasing spreading of personal Web pages, blogs, digital albums, and more recently the rise of social networks, like Facebook, Instagram, Twitter and Flickr, has further spurred an exponential growth of the use of digital cameras and smartphones aimed at sharing more than at personal enjoyment of captured images. People from all over the world use to share a huge amount of photos over the net. Moreover, with the rising of Web 2.0, tagging has become a very popular tool to handle one's own albums. Tagging turns out to be a very effective approach to simplify the management and sharing of photos, as it can add additional information to the picture (the place where it was taken, people in it, etc.), which supports making more flexible and efficient the typical operations performed on a large collection of images. In other words, as specified in Cui *et al.* (2007) tagging enriches the photo with a "semantic" annotation, with the aim to simplify tasks such as indexing, searching and browsing. In this scenario, identities of depicted people are one of the most used tagging information, and face recognition can support a (semi) automatic handling of related operations. Face tagging is a typical example of face recognition "in the wild" (Huang *et al.*, 2007). The complete lack of control over the acquisition settings and the non-repeatability of the capture allows to share related approaches with applications used in more critical uncontrolled settings (e.g., re-identification in video-surveillance), with the difference to allow a higher error rate, and therefore less demanding techniques. The schema of a generic face tagging system is shown in Figure 2. Then we sketch some typical applications of face tagging.

Digital photo management: As mentioned above, with the new devices, such as digital cameras and more recently camera-equipped smartphones, taking photos has become an ubiquitous, easy operation with an immediately visible result,

Figure 2. Diagram of a generic face tagging system

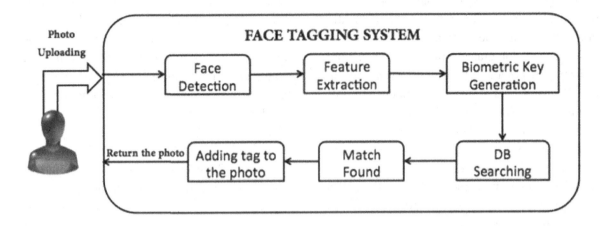

so that the user can also quickly choose which photos to keep in memory and which ones to delete. The result is that in a single day one can take hundreds of photo, and in such large collection of images, photo annotation becomes the most challenging task. Many of the more sophisticated photo management systems implement face detection, but often each detected face still needs to be annotated individually to record the identity of the captured subjects. As observed in Liu *et al.* (2011), from the user point of view, tagging is a labor-intensive and time consuming activity, while simply entering tags for the whole album, instead of annotating each single photo, leads to unsatisfying results. Automatic tagging of photos becomes extremely appealing, even to support a more efficient automatic management of albums, through the annotation of a number of interesting features (caption, description, identities in the image, geolocalization, kind of scene, event, etc.). As an example, nowadays most advanced cameras, even compact ones, provide automatic geolocalization (see below), which is one of the relevant image features. With automatic face tagging, the owner has only to provide an initial image-identity association. Afterwards photos can be annotated automatically by the system through automatic face recognition. In an alternative strategy, even

without the initial association, clustering may be performed on the collection in order to speed up the annotation process.

Smart Album Creation: Following the image annotation, many useful operations can be accomplished. One of these is the creation of a smart image gallery. In the specific case, a smart album is a collection of photos which meet the same criteria. For instance, a user would be able to cluster all the photos in which his parents or his friends appear, in order to create collections of images containing specific people. Once the face tagging has been accomplished, this kind of activity can be achieved in an extremely fast way and with the least number of operations. Moreover, a smart album can be integrated with other information, depending on the kind of device used to take images. For instance, Qin et al. (2012) show how a smartphone can add geographic information to a photo, simply keeping the GPS antenna switched on during the snapshot. Actually, GPS based location coordinates are quite rough and hardly meaningful for a human user, so that they are not suited for a meaningful location-based photo store and search, e.g., to quickly identify all photos in St. Peter in Rome. It would be much more useful to provide a semantic form of location, such as the name of a town, or of a specific place. In practice, a reverse lookup on the GPS coordinates should be possible, through some database or remote service, which is presently not largely available. The authors describe an architecture to integrate the photo with even more information (weather conditions, event, scene, etc…), thanks, for instance, to the detection of "companion" devices held by other friends in the same venue, in order to obtain an image with a very rich semantic annotation. As mentioned above, nowadays even the latest digital cameras launched on the market are equipped with GPS antenna, so as to add, on the spot, geolocation information to the pictures. Therefore, a similar processing would be possible. However, one of the most useful information, i.e. the identity of persons in a photo, provided by a fully automatic face tagging, is still mostly out of reach.

Editorial Board for Magazines: Another field in which automatic face tagging can be very useful is managing an Editorial Board. In the past images of a particular person have to be found manually in huge archives. Classical systems for digital image retrieval require the user to submit a textual query, such as a set of keywords corresponding to the images to be found. Of course, this requires that the stored images must have been preliminarily annotated, using the same set of keywords, or exploiting a thesaurus strategy to establish a correspondence among equivalent terms. Images are treated as ancillary data, while image retrieval by content is still an open research topic. More advanced systems may rather require the user to submit an image similar to the one to be found. Comprehensive surveys can be found in De Marsico *et al.* (1997) and Rui *et al.* (1999), while further literature addresses specific problems (e.g., video indexing). Both these approaches can be somehow related to automatic face tagging. In the case of a textual query, as already noticed, the keywords should have already been associated with the images. Automatic face tagging can avoid, or lighten at least, the tedious task of doing it manually. Moreover, the exploited strate-

gies can support both classification (tagging) and content-based query. However, the approach based on image queries not only shares solutions, but also problems of automatic tagging, which does not always ensure to retrieve images of the same person or even images of persons. As a matter of fact, query by example is still a generally open problem, and face identification is a specialized instance of it.

Video indexing: Acosta *et al.* (2002) and Lee and Kim. (2004) present some techniques for detecting and labeling faces in video, in which tagging is involved. The obtained information can be later used for video retrieval or video summary. However, tagging faces in a video is a very complex and expensive in terms of time, even because the same faces may appear in a high number of frames yet with different poses and illumination. In general, the first step is searching for faces in each video frame (for example via skin detectors or similar approaches). Abate *et al.* (2011) and De Marsico *et al.* (2012) present a solution to the problems due to variations in pose and illumination by including a face normalization module in their systems for automatic face tracking and tagging in video. The solution is also suitable for video surveillance. These approaches are presented in more detail later in this chapter. In their present state, the systems only identify the same subject in different frames, however the extension to precisely identify a person is quite straightforward, and only requires to submit one of the best subject templates (with respect to PIE distortions) to an identification system.

SOME METHODS FOR FACE RECOGNITION IN TAGGING

Generic face recognition systems aim at identifying a subject, comparing his presently captured face image with the one acquired in a previous enrollment phase. The first prototypes presented in literature were soon able to achieve good performance, but in well controlled settings: frontal pose, neutral expression and uniform illumination. In forensics and in homeland security, face recognition systems are mainly used in order to identify criminals, and this biometrics is also often exploited to authenticate people. Even in this case, the processed images are mostly acquired in controlled settings, e.g. mugshots in police stations or photos for identification cards. In the last decades similar systems made relevant advances, and developers started to apply these techniques for many kinds of applications. As one of the most recent examples, advanced applications for the smartphones should allow to recognize users from any captured photo. However, this requires the possibility to rely on much more robust techniques. Unfortunately, face recognition in uncontrolled settings is still a great challenge in the biometric research community; changes and distortions in pose, illumination and expression (PIE) can significantly affect performances of face recognition system. Illumination variations are influenced by the skin reflectance properties in relation with the intensity of the light in the ambient where the acquisition is recorded. The situation may even worsen if the acquisition process happens in an outdoor space. Pose, instead, and also some expressions, most of all very marked ones, can affect the face image because they can introduce different kinds of deformations, including projective ones, self-occlusions, as well as shadow problems caused, for example, by the nose. Besides PIE, adverse conditions also include the "natural" occlusions like those by hair or beard, or occlusions by objects like eyeglasses or scarfs, which can dramatically influence the performance of a face recognition system, in particular if they are located in the upper part of the face. As underlined above, tagging "in the wild" is a typical example of recognition in adverse conditions.

In traditional applications, the problem of a reliable recognition mainly arises because in the enrollment phase, i.e. when the *gallery* or the set of reference identities of the system is created, the images are usually acquired in controlled settings, in which pose and illumination are standardized and set ad hoc for the capture process and the subject is asked to take a neutral expression. Also the camera is in a predefined position, so that no kind of occlusion can affect the image of the face. During *probe* capture, instead, usually several kinds of restrictions are relaxed, and this increases the intra-class variability, since uncontrolled pose, illumination, as well as expression and occlusions, may affect in a significant way the good result of image capture process. The problem is even worse in modern applications requiring identification/ re-identification, like video-surveillance or also tagging, where even the initial acquisition may not be performed in optimal conditions. In other words, the model too might be distorted, therefore the problem of recognition becomes even more difficult to address. In some cases, depending on the kind of application, it might be useful to first identify the "best" templates, i.e. those presenting the best capture conditions, to use them as "seeds" for the following processing of the collection.

In most recent research, several solutions have been devised to address PIE variations and occlusions, and thanks to them it is often possible to use face recognition systems in uncontrolled settings too, especially in non-critical applications, without decreasing performance beyond an acceptable point. The following paragraphs describe some techniques used by the face-based biometric systems, both in the preprocessing phase, in order to correct an image affected by bad lighting condition, bad pose or occlusion, and in the coding phase, so that matching and score assignment can appropriately return the distance between gallery and probe images. In particular, since the focus is on face recognition in adverse conditions, the mentioned techniques deal with the local information of the image, rather than on the global one. Local approaches are preferable because they allow a more flexible consideration of geometric relation between the elements of the face (eyes, mouth, nose, chin, etc...), are more robust to occlusion as well as local distortions, and offer higher reliability in terms of illumination variations and image rotations with respect to the global ones.

A very important issue to consider is that, in order to allow any possibility of a correct recognition, a reliable face detection must be first performed. The same factors affecting recognition, have an early influence on detection too. Besides this, artifacts reproducing a specific shape/structure (a face, in our case) can be erroneously passed to the recognition phase, with the consequence of a waste of time: As an example, Figure 3 shows a correct and an incorrect face detection performed by the popular iPhoto application. At present, most systems presented in literature use Viola-Jones algorithm (Viola & Jones, 2001) to detect regions of interest (ROIs) containing faces.

Scale Invariant Feature Transform

SIFT (*Scale Invariant Feature Transform*) features are used to perform reliable matching between images of the same object taken from different points of view, therefore it is really suitable for recognizing faces of the same person with difference in pose. Moreover, it also lends itself to address expression variations, even if it is not very robust to illumination changes. This kind

of features is orientation and scale independent, so they are highly distinctive of the image. As described in Lowe (2004), the SIFT algorithm is composed of four stages of computation:

- **Detection of the points of interest:** The keypoints (as they are called in the SIFT framework) are extracted by applying a set of Difference of Gaussian filters at different scales all over the image; for each octave of scale space, the initial image is repeatedly convolved with Gaussians to produce the set of scale space images (Figure 4); adjacent Gaussian images are subtracted to produce the difference-of-Gaussian images; after each octave, the obtained Gaussian image is down-sampled by a factor of 2, and the process repeated;

- **Unreliable keypoints removal:** Low contrast points are discarded; the $\left| O\left(x, y, \sigma^2\right) \right|$ value (representing the convolution of the image *I(x, y)* with $\sigma^2 \nabla^2 G$, which is calculated in the previous step) is evaluated at each point extracted in first stage; if this value is below a predefined threshold, which means that the structure has low contrast, the keypoint will be removed;

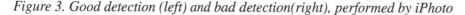

Figure 3. Good detection (left) and bad detection(right), performed by iPhoto

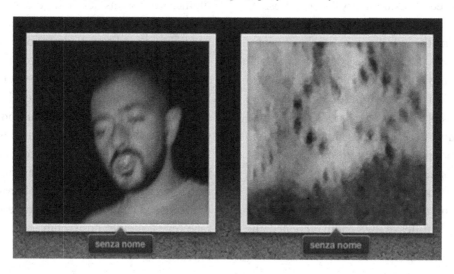

Figure 4. The Gaussian pyramids of two face images (o=octave, s=scale)

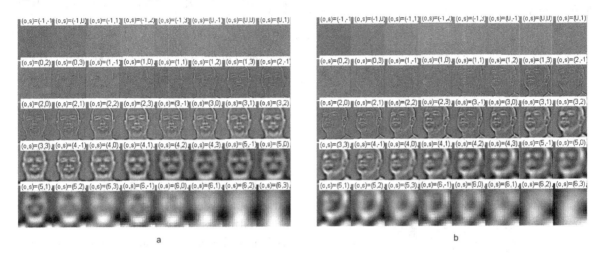

a

b

- **Orientation assignment:** An orientation based on local image gradient is assigned at each keypoint (Figure 5);
- **Keypoint descriptor:** A descriptor based on the local image gradient is computed at each key point; the final descriptor is a 128 bits vector that is highly distinctive of the neighbors around the point.

Figure 6 shows the matching between pairs of points in the descriptors for the two images in the example.

SIFT features have been applied in several face-based biometric systems; notably, their reliability is exploited in different kinds of applications. In Luo et al. (2007), SIFT features are used to match characteristics in faces with expression variation.

Figure 5. Keypoints gradient vectors; length of arrows is proportional to the module

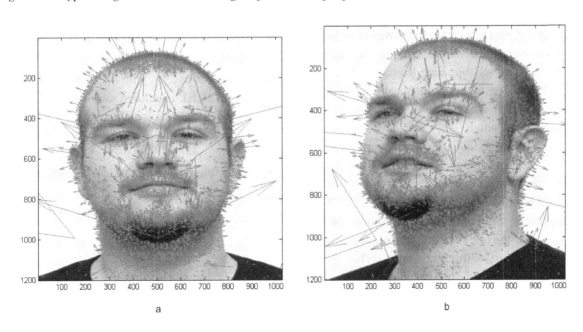

a

b

Figure 6. Keypoints matching for the two images in the example

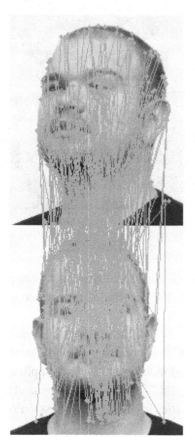

In particular, a new matching strategy, based on local and global features, is proposed in order to get more robust matching operations and making the score more reliable. Bicego *et al.* (2006) also use SIFT features for face authentication; *minimum pair distance* is the methodology used to assign a score to the match.

Going further along this approach, Geng and Jiang (2009) developed new types of SIFT-based approaches, acting on different stages of the SIFT computation process. The Volume-SIFT (VSIFT) is applied on the second stage of the computation process, i.e. the one regarding the removal of the extracted points with low contrast. While SIFT algorithm removes the less reliable points according to the value produced by the computation of

$\left| O\left(x, y, \sigma^2\right) \right|$, VSIFT uses the volume of the blob structure $V\left(x, y, \sigma^2\right) = \sigma^2 \left| O\left(x, y, \sigma^2\right) \right|$, which is evaluated at the location of each keypoint: if this value is below a predefined threshold, the keypoint is removed. In the same work the authors present the Partial Descriptor SIFT (PDSIFT). PDSIFT is used in case the keypoints cannot be described due to the limitation of the image (for example, keypoints detected at large scales or near face boundaries). The original descriptor F is a 128 dimensional vector. PDSIFT defines a 128×128 diagonal matrix M in which the diagonal elements indicate if the block is valid (completely within the face image) or not. A suitable similarity measure is also defined.

Local Binary Pattern

Also techniques based on LBP (*Local Binary Pattern*), first introduced in (Ojala *et al.*, 1996) belong to the family of Local Feature Analysis (LFA) algorithms. Approximately 80% of the works dealing with face recognition under uncontrolled settings exploits LBP for extracting features from the images. In its basic formulation, LBP works as follows (Figure 7):

- The image is divided into non overlapping cells of the same dimension;
- For each pixel p_c with coordinates (x_c, y_c) in a cell, LBP is defined as an ordered binary sequence of color intensity comparisons (1=greater, 0=lower) between the pixel and its eight adjacent neighbors;
- The decimal form of the resulting 8-bit word (LBP-Code) is derived;
- A histogram shows the frequencies of the decimal values in the cell and describes the texture of the image.

The approach is extended in Ojala *et al.* (2002) introducing a variable size neighborhood (multi-

Figure 7. How LBP works

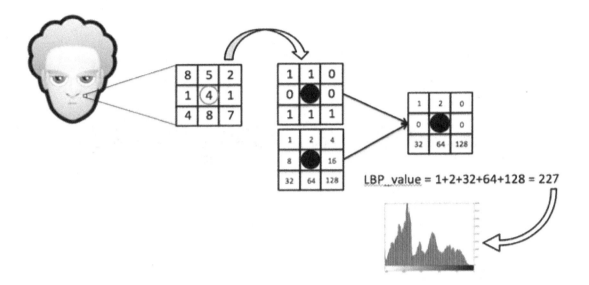

resolution) and the concept of *uniform* pattern. Ahonen *et al*. (2006) apply LBP to face recognition; in this specific application the face area is divided into small regions and the LBP histograms, one for each region, are concatenated together; the resulting histogram is used to represent the image. The recognition is performed using a nearest neighbour classifier in the computed feature space with Chi square as dissimilarity measure.

Among the systems using LPB, we can mention EasyAlbum (Cui et al., 2007), which will be discussed later in the chapter, which extracts the facial features and builds a cluster of photos, according to a face in input.

Tan and Triggs (2010) propose further adaptations of LBP to address face recognition in difficult lighting conditions. In particular, they propose Local Ternary Patterns, where the binary coding is substituted by a ternary one, adding value -1.

STASM

Many approaches which rely on relevant points in the face use STASM (Milborrow & Nicolls, 2008) to locate a set of landmarks . STASM,

which is also provided as an open source software implementation, is based on Active Shape Model (ASM). In a first step, a face detector is used to localize the region of interest (ROI) containing a face. Then, the identified regions are given as input to STASM, which searches for landmarks on the face, using a model (*shape model*), precomputed over a wide set of training images. The algorithm locates 68 points of interest. In De Marsico *et al.* (2013) STASM landmark identification is used by FACE (Face Analysis for Commercial Entities) to achieve a robust face recognition in uncontrolled settings. A fixed set of 13 out of such points are used for the correction of the pose, before extracting a face template (Figure 8).

- The centers of the eyes are used to measure the head rolling;
- The distances between the external corners of the left and right eyes and the tip of the nose are used to determine the best half of the face, i.e. the better exposed one, which is used to create the normalized complete face, and also the amount of yaw;

Figure 8. STASM landmark location

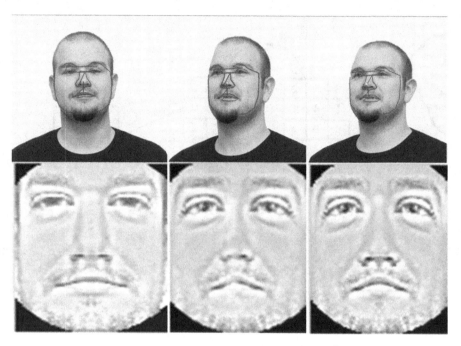

- After an appropriate transformation (usually stretching) to have relevant points in fixed positions, the best half face is mirrored to have a complete one.

The points located at the center of the mouth, on the chin and on the tip of the nose are used to measure the head pitch. The amount of roll, pitch and yaw can be used to compute a measure of the pose distortion to possibly discard too "hard" images. Further implementation of ASM algorithm are also tested: OpenASM and ASMLibrary. In the work presenting FACE, it is observed that the point location provided by STASM is about 10% more precise than that offered by the other two implementations.

Table 1 lists the most popular face recognition and face detection argorithms, which are compared based on their robustness to variation of face expression, illumination, pose and occlusions, conditions that may affect the image on which a tagging system has to work.

SOME EXAMPLES OF STATE OF THE ART APPLICATIONS

Examples of Semi-Automatic Tagging

Automatic tagging, ending with a fully automatic assignment of a name to a face in a photo, is still to come. At the best of present systems, similarity clustering can be achieved, followed by a final human refinement step. Of course, in many cases this is still much better than a fully manual annotation.

We start from two examples of semi-automatic tagging, which still require user interaction. We can assume that popular commercial products, like Google Picasa, Apple iPhoto and Adobe Photoshop Elements, follow a similar approach, though using different algorithms for similarity matching and clustering/classification.

One of the first proposals for face annotation in family photo management can be found in Chen and (2003). The goal of the system is to provide a semi-automatic face annotation in a

Table 1. Comparison among different face recognition and detection algorithm. See (Abate at al., 2007) for more details for some af the algorithms listed above.

Face Recognition					
Authors	Method	Expr.	Ill.	Pose	Occl.
Kirby and Sirovich (1990)	PCA		No	No	No
Swets andWeng (1996)	LDA		No	No	No
Belhumeur et al. (1997)	Fisherfaces	Yes	Yes	No	No
Barlett Marian et al. (2002)	ICA	Yes	No	No	No
Wiskott et al. (1997)	EBGM	Yes		Yes	
Perronnin and Dugelay (2003)	HMM	Yes	No	No	No
Luo et al. (2007)	SIFT	Yes	Yes	Yes	Yes
Ahonen et al. (2004)	LBP	Yes	Yes	Yes	
De Marsico et al. (2013)	FACE		Yes	Yes	No
Face Detection					
Viola and Jones (2001)	Viola Jones		Yes	Yes	No
Milborrow and Nicolls (2008)	STASM		Yes	Yes	No
Zhu and Ramanan (2012)	Face detection "in the wild"	Yes		Yes	
Rowley et al. (1998)	Neural network-based f. d.			No	

typical family setting, where a digital photo album usually contains at most 10-50 different people appearing frequently. When a face is detected in a photo, the system calculates a candidate list of names according to the similarities to the already annotated faces. The user can either accept a name from the recommendation set, or decide a new name. To capture the structural information of the face, the authors test the use of local regional features to capture spatial information. A facial area is represented in terms of 4×2 blocks and the features are extracted from these local blocks. A comparison of features, including color moments and eigenface values, shows that the best alternatives are the 8-block wavelet based texture, and 8-block correlogram (Huang et al., 1997), with 144 and 2048 dimensions respectively. As for the first, each block is decomposed into 10 de-correlated sub-bands through 3-level wavelet transform. In each sub-band, the standard deviation of the wavelet coefficients is extracted. As for the second, they quantize the RGB color

space into $4 \times 4 \times 4 = 64$ colors. Then they use the distance set D $=\{1; 3; 5; 7\}$ for computing the auto-correlogram to build a 256-dimension feature. Feature extraction is combined with a Bayesian learning framework to suggest a list of candidates for a new image classification. In particular, Nearest Neighbor (NN) and K-Nearest Neighbor (KNN) are tested.

A more recent approach is presented in Cui *et al.* (2007), where a management system for large photo collections is presented. The system combines face recognition technology and interactive user operations through UI functions. It still requires users to tag their photos but, unlike other existing systems, it also provides interesting features that strongly reduce the user annotation workload. Photos are automatically clustered based on present faces or similar scenes, so that they are not tagged one by one but in clusters. However, due to the limitations of current clustering and face recognition algorithms, a face cluster cannot be automatically related to a person actual identity (name) without user interaction. Due to the same limitations, the faces of the same person may be scattered in several clusters, or different persons may be found in the same cluster. Therefore, final face annotation is achieved through a set of cluster operations, i.e., cluster annotation, merging and splitting, which are provided by the system. In this way user can directly manipulate a group of photos instead of annotating them individually. The system uses a three-stage process, including offline preprocessing, online clustering, and online interactive labeling. During offline preprocessing, face features are extracted after face detection though Viola-Jones algorithm (Viola & Jones, 2001), and an alignment procedure (Zhou *et al.,* 2003, 2005). One of the facial features is based on LBP. The online clustering stage relies on an enhanced version of spectral clustering algorithm (Bach & Jordan, 2003). Finally, user interaction is intended to refine clustering results.

EasyAlbum further provides a context-sensitive environment that automatically adapts to the user's actions. As the user selects a certain photo or cluster, the remaining ones are re-ranked according to the content of the photo/cluster selected, in order to improve user experience. For example if the user selects a photo of a particular person, the system assumes that he/she is interested in photos containing that person and shows those photos before others. Finally the system provides an "ad hoc annotation" mechanism: as the user tags photos, annotation information is accumulated gradually and then used to progressively and dynamically improve the clustering and search results of unlabeled data. According to the reported results, when compared with Photoshop Elements, EasyAlbum allows to drastically reduce the annotation workload as the size of the album to be annotated increases. It only uses less than 25% percent of time for annotation (from more than 2000 secs to less than 500 secs) when the album contains 400 photos.

Clustering of Face Images

As we have seen above, clustering algorithms can play a key role in addressing the face image tagging problem. After aggregating similar face images, it would be possible to tag the entire cluster with an identity and speed up the annotation process. However, most clustering algorithms require to fix in advance the number of classes, like K-means, or to learn a distance matrix, like spectral clustering. In massive applications this may be an extremely hard constraint.

In Nappi *et al.* (2013) Entropy based Aggregative Clustering (E-AC) is presented. It is based on a revisiting of Shannon Entropy. In image processing, this is traditionally used as an estimate of the degree of randomness of pixels in an image. A novel formulation is used in this case, to measure the amount of information (representativeness) of the templates in a gallery. The core idea is to consider the similarity among templates as a kind of probability that they belong to the same subject. This information is used in turn to evaluate the difference of a subject from a population. Both the feature extraction technique and the derived distance measure are not fixed in advance, therefore the E-AC approach is suitable to any kind of classifier. Differently from the most used K-Means, E-AC does not need to fix the number of classes a priori. The input templates are sorted in a list according to representativeness (calculated by the introduced entropy measure). The templates in the terminal part of the list are very similar to each other. This means that they can represent the same person, so the last *m* are selected and moved in a cluster. The remaining templates are then considered starting from the last one: each one is compared with those in the newly created cluster via Pearson's correlation, and added to the cluster until they achieve a defined amount of correlation. Afterwards the overall procedure is repeated on the remaining templates, since template removal generally changes the entropy of the set. When the process ends, it is possible that templates of the same person are placed in different cluster, so an aggregating phase is performed, based again on Pearson's correlation, to merge similar clusters. An illustration of the E-AC approach is presented in Figure 9.

Video Indexing

A specific application of massive automatic or semi-automatic tagging is the indexing of video sequences according to the subjects captured in the clips. In Acosta *et al.* (2002) an automatic face detection and recognition system for video indexing applications is presented. The system is composed essentially of two blocks, the first one performing face detection on video frames and the second one performing face recognition via PCA. Face detection includes a number of steps. First, skin detection is performed using a simple color map in the YCbCr color space. Then segmentation is performed both on chrominance and luminance information with an algorithm which combines pixel and region based color segmentation techniques. The result of the previous step is a set of connected skin regions which are iteratively merged together according to an adjacency criterion to form potential face candidates (FC). From this set of candidates the ones that do not fit the constrains of shape and size to be a face are removed. To improve the accuracy of the face detector, a criterion based on texture is also introduced. In the recognition step a modified PCA is used. To address the complexity of recognizing a person in a video frame, with possibly multiple views of its face, during the training phase the PCA is applied for each different subject on a set of its face views, obtaining different sets of eigenfaces. Then test images are projected and reconstructed for each set of the different eigenfaces. When the reconstruction error for a particular set of eigenfaces is minimum, the test image is matched. The main problem of this approach is training, which may result in poor performance in massive applications when the testing set is huge and highly dynamic.

VIVIE (Video Surveillance Indexer Via Identity Extraction) is a completely automatic face recognition system designed for video-surveillance presented in Abate et al. (2011). It can be defined as a first step towards a complete automatic face tagging system, since in its present implementation it does not assign the real identity of a person to a

Figure 9. Entropy based aggregative clustering

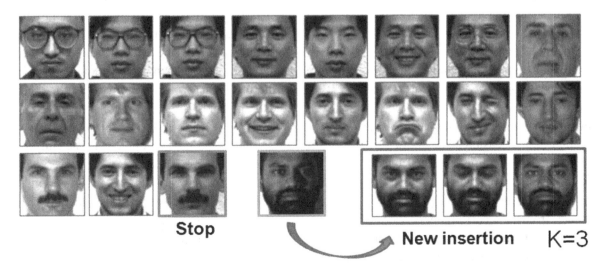

Stop   **New insertion**   K=3

face image, but rather assigns different ID codes to samples of different faces, and the same ID to the same face in different views (reidentification). It is a modular system performing a sequence of steps:

1. Detection and location of all possible faces in a frame via Viola-Jones' algorithm, with recording of their position, dimension, and quality;
2. Tracking, through which position information for each face is submitted to the tracking module; STASM software, presented before in this chapter, is used to obtain face fiducial points, and the coordinates of the nose tip are used to track a face in different frames: in practice, if the distance of the nose tip of two faces in two consecutive frames is lower than a threshold th_{nose} (spatial coherence), the same temporary identity is assigned to the two samples; in this way, and until a face is detected in the scene, a list is created containing all the samples associated to the same temporary identity;
3. Normalization, as well as feature extraction and matching, are performed by exploiting the FACE approach discussed earlier in this chapter and addresses the different pose and illumination issues;
4. Feature extraction;
5. Face classification;
6. Face clustering.

The last steps deserve some more details. When a face is not detected in the scene anymore, the temporary identity associated to it must be mapped onto a permanent identity, or a new permanent identity must be created if such mapping is not feasible. The set of samples of the temporary identity generated by the tracking module is compared with the all the sets of samples of existing permanent identities. If the distance from the set of samples of one permanent identity, measured according to an appropriate metric, is lower than a threshold, the temporary

and the permanent sets are merged together and the most representatives samples are maintained while the remaining ones are discarded, otherwise a new permanent identity is created. After the video has been completely processed, it would be possible to extract the best sample (according to PIE criteria) for each permanent identity, and then perform a true identification by comparing them with a gallery of possibly enrolled subjects.

Faces "In the Wild"

Working with faces "in the wild" is an extremely challenging problem, due to the high degree of variability of a face. In fact, there are many factors that affect the model of a face and decrease critically the performance of a face recognition system. An Internet image search for a celebrity yields thousands of photos, that differ from each other in pose (frontal and profile), illumination (indoor, outdoor, with flash or not), exposure (varying color balance, resolution, zoom levels and other parameters that differ from one photo to the next), expression, aging, facial hair etc. In light of this extreme variability, no single reconstruction can be consistent with the whole set of images. Several works deal with this problem, addressing different aspects of it.

The work in Kemelmacher-Shlizerman and Seiz (2011) shows an approach to reconstruct a face starting from a set of images of the same person, using a 3D shape of the person. They define a model that is locally consistent with a large set of photos, so that it captures the dominant trends in the input data for different parts of the face. The algorithm is based on the following steps:

1. Fiducial points extraction from each image; a 3D shape is initialized;
2. Pose normalization by using the points extracted in the previous step, leading to a canonical frontal pose; each image is warped to frontal using the current shape;

3. Solution for initial shape and lighting using a photometric stereo approach;
4. Application of local view selection: each image is used to reconstruct a different part of the face;
5. Shape integration;
6. Iteration of the algorithm from step 2 until convergence, i.e. the matrix of the warped images does not change significantly.

Zhu and Ramanan (2012) rather enhance the state of the art in face detection, pose estimation and landmark localization implementing an approach based on a mixture of tree-structured part models, and test their approach with "in the wild" images from Flickr.

In the state of the art, it is mandatory to talk about Facebook and the face recognition in a social context. Earlier in the chapter, we mentioned the fact that tagging is a labor intensive and time consuming operation for the user. Nevertheless, in Stone *et al.* (2010) it is noticed how the social context – and Facebook in particular – gives a social incentive to the tagging that can be leveraged to obtain significant quantities of labeled facial images "in the wild" of millions of individuals. In particular, the authors make an empirical study to propose a computational method for using these images. In particular, they deal with the issue of labeling a face in a photo with an identity chosen from a set of possible ones, which is built starting from:

1. The image data (appearance of each face);
2. The image metadata (geotag, timestamp, photograph identity, caption…);
3. Social network structure (relationships between individuals in the image).

Social network context is an important tool for assembling scalable recognition systems and the ever increasing growth of online social networks, the improving of social tagging systems and the increasing interconnectivity of the Web have the potential to enhance the ability of the research to improve face recognition. This aspect arises from the fact that the huge amount of data available in an online social context and the imbalance between the numbers of intra and extra personal image pairs make the preparation of a suitable training set, usually a non-trivial step for any face recognition system, far less complicated. With regard to this, Zhou et al. (2009) underline the importance of having large datasets. They propose a classification framework for large-scale face recognition systems, consisting of two components:

1. A data sampling strategy, aimed at dealing with the imbalance within the large amount of training data when image pairs are sampled for features extraction;
2. A modified version of KFD (Kernel Fisher Discriminant) suited to deal with large datasets.

TagSense

Is image processing strictly required to tag images, in particular personal photos? In Qin et al. (2012) an alternative way to address the photo tagging issue is presented. It is interesting because it is an example of an orthogonal approach, where information comes from different sources than images themselves. Of course, it heavily relies on a kind of equipment, e.g. a smartphone, which, though hugely spread, is not suited for all kinds of applications, but only for personal photo tagging on the fly. Most of the current approaches leverages pattern recognition techniques to tag subjects or scenes in a photo. These approaches work on information contained in the images. In TagSense, other kinds of information are obtained instead from mobile phones equipment and used to tag photos. This information comes, during acquisition, from both the device capturing the images and from the surrounding mobile devices. Examples of information used in the tagging process are: date, weather, location, indoor/outdoor, people in the photo, what people in the photo are doing. Deducing the first four information from a mobile phone is trivial (GPS). To understand who is in the photo and what he is doing, information from the other mobile devices and sensors is used, in particular three aspects are considered: (1) accelerometer based motion signatures, since a subject posing for a photo is assumed to move into a specific posture in preparation for the picture, to stay still during the picture-click, and then to move again to resume normal behavior, (2) complementary compass directions, since TagSense makes the assumption that people in the picture roughly face the direction of the camera, and hence, the direction of their compasses will be roughly complementary to the camera's facing direction, and (3) motion correlation across visual and accelerometer/compass, since TagSense relies on a multi-dimensional sensing heuristic to identify the moving subjects from multiple snapshots from the camera.

Tag information produced by this system may be considered as complementary to the ones usually exploited by people. The following is an example of tags expressed by a human compared whit those extracted by TagSense:

- **Human:** Many people, smiling, standing;
- **TagSense:** November 21st afternoon, Nasher Museum, indoor, Romit, Sushma, Naveen, Souvik, Justin, Vijay, Xuan, standing, talking.

CONCLUSION

As we have seen in this chapter, there is still much to do in order to obtain a fully automatic system for automatic face image tagging. As stated before, we consider as fully automatic, a system which automatically detects faces in static images or in video frames, and tags them with an identity comparing the detected faces with templates contained in a database. However, systems we have mentioned, and Facebook too, still require user interaction to manually associate an identity to a face in a picture or to correct a misclassification. On the other hand, the video indexing solutions presented, are closer than the other works presented to the concept of automatic face tagging. In fact the system presented in Acosta et al. (2002) is fully automatic. However methods chosen for face detection (skin-detection based) and for face recognition (PCA) that are not very robust to PIE variations, making it not suitable for the application "in the wild." The VIVIE system (Abate et al., 2011), even if intended for video-surveillance, can be easily converted into an automatic face image tagging system. It already associate in a totally automatic way different Ids to different faces in a video sequence, and it would be trivial to modify the system to associate the real identity by matching the detected face with the face templates stored in a database. We also presented clustering methods and solutions for face recognition or reconstruction "in the wild" that, tough not representing a complete automatic face image tagging system, could play a key role in improving the system accuracy and performance. The widespread use of smart phones that incorporate acquisition devices with ever increasing resolution will certainly make the process of tagging of photos easier, for personal collections at least, both because a higher resolution is likely to facilitate face recognition, and mainly because it is possible to leverage the additional information provided by smart devices. Moreover many approaches for face image clustering or large scale dataset management can be easily adapted to automatic face image tagging.

REFERENCES

Abate, A. F., De Marsico, M., Nappi, M., & Riccio, D. (2011). VIVIE: A Video-Surveillance Indexer Via Identity Extraction. In *Proceedings of International Conference on Multimedia and Expo,* (pp. 1-6). Barcelona, Spain: ICME.

Abate, A. F., Nappi, M., Riccio, D., & Sabatino, G. (2007). 2D and 3D Face Recognition: A survey. *Pattern Recognition Letters, 28*(14), 1885–1906. doi:10.1016/j.patrec.2006.12.018

Acosta, E., Torres, L., Albiol, A., & Delp, E. (2002). An Automatic Face Detection and Recognition System for Video Indexing Applications. In *Proceedings of IEEE International Conference on Acoustics, Speech and Signal Processing (ICASSP 2002).* IEEE.

Ahonen, T., Hadid, A., & Pietikäinen, M. (2006). Face Description with Local Binary Patterns: Application to Face Recognition. *IEEE Transactions on Pattern Analysis and Machine Intelligence, 28*(12), 2037–2041. doi:10.1109/TPAMI.2006.244 PMID:17108377

Bach, F., & Jordan, M. (2003). Learning spectral clustering. In Advances of Neural Info. Processing Systems, (pp. 305-312). Academic Press.

Bicego, M., Lagorio, A., Grosso, E., & Tistarelli, M. (2006). On the Use of SIFT Features for Face Authentication. In *Proceedings of Conference on Computer Vision and Pattern Recognition Workshop, 2006.* CVPRW.

Cai, D., He, X., Han, J., & Zhang, H.-J. (2006). Orthogonal Laplacianfaces for Face Recognition. *IEEE Transactions on Image Processing, 15*(11), 3608–3614. doi:10.1109/TIP.2006.881945 PMID:17076419

Chen, L., & Hu, B (2003). Face annotation for family photo album management. *International Journal of Image and Graphics, 3*(1), 1-14.

Cui, J., Wen, F., Xiao, R., Tian, Y., & Tang, X. (2007). EasyAlbum: an interactive photo annotation system based on face clustering and re-ranking. In *Proceedings of the SIGCHI Conference on Human Factors in Computing Systems* (CHI '07) (pp. 367-376). ACM.

De Marsico, M., Cinque, L., & Levialdi, S. (1997). Indexing pictorial documents by their content: a survey of current techniques. *Image and Vision Computing, 15*(2), 119–141. doi:10.1016/S0262-8856(96)01114-6

De Marsico, M., Doretto, G., & Riccio, D. (2012). M-VIVIE: a Multi-thread Video Indexer Via Identity Extraction. *Pattern Recognition Letters, 33*(14), 1882–1890. doi:10.1016/j.patrec.2012.03.005

De Marsico, M., Nappi, M., Riccio, D., & Wechsler, H. (2013). Robust Face Recognition for Uncontrolled Pose and Illumination Changes. *IEEE Transactions on Systems, Man, and Cybernetics. Systems, 43*(1), 149–163.

Garcia, C., & Delakis, M. (2002). A neural architecture for fast and robust face detection. In *Proceedings of 16th International Conference on Pattern Recognition,* (vol. 2, pp. 44-47). ICPR.

Geng, C., & Jiang, X. (2009). Face recognition using sift features. In *Proceedings of 16th IEEE International Conference on Image Processing (ICIP),* (pp. 3313-3316). IEEE.

He, X., Yan, S., Hu, Y., Niyogi, P., & Zhang, H.-J. (2005). Face recognition using Laplacianfaces. *IEEE Transactions on Pattern Analysis and Machine Intelligence, 27*(3), 328–340. doi:10.1109/TPAMI.2005.55 PMID:15747789

Huang, G. B., Ramesh, M., Berg, T., & Learned-Miller, E. (2007). *Labeled Faces in the Wild: A Database for Studying Face Recognition in Unconstrained Environments.* Amherst, MA: University of Massachusetts.

Huang, J., Kumar, S. R., Mitra, M., Zhu, W. J., & Zabih, R. (1997). Image indexing using color correlograms. In *Proceedings of IEEE Conf. Computer Vision and Pattern Recognition,* (pp. 762-768). IEEE.

International Organization For Standardization. (2004). *ISO/IEC JTC1/SC29/WG11 Coding Of Moving Pictures And Audio.* ISO/IEC JTC1/SC29/WG11 N6828. Retrieved from http://mpeg.chiariglione.org/sites/default/files/files/standards/docs/w6828_mp7_Overview_v10.zip

Jafri, R., & Arabnia, H. R. (2009). A Survey of Face Recognition Techniques. *Journal of Information Processing Systems, 5*(2), 41–68. doi:10.3745/JIPS.2009.5.2.041

Kemelmacher-Shlizerman, I., & Seitz, S. M. (2011). Face Reconstruction in the wild. In *Proceedings of IEEE International Conference on Computer Vision,* (pp. 1746-1753). IEEE.

Kim, T.-K., Kim, H., Hwang, W., & Kittler, J. (2005). Component-based LDA face description for image retrieval and MPEG-7 standardization. *Image and Vision Computing, 23*(7), 631–642. doi:10.1016/j.imavis.2005.02.005

Kirby, M., & Sirovich, L. (1990). Application of the Karhunen-Loeve procedure for the characterization of human faces. *IEEE Transactions on Pattern Analysis and Machine Intelligence, 12*(1), 103–108. doi:10.1109/34.41390

Lee, J.-H., & Kim, W.-Y. (2004). Video Summarization and Retrieval System Using Face Recognition and MPEG-7 Descriptors. In P. K. Enser (Ed.), *CIVR 2004 - Image and Video Retrieval, (LNCS)* (Vol. 3115, pp. 170–178). Dublin, Ireland: Springer. doi:10.1007/978-3-540-27814-6_23

Liu, D., Wang, M., Hua, S.-J., & Zhang, H.-J. (2011). Semi-Automatic Tagging of Photo Albums via Exemplar Selection and Tag Inference. *IEEE Transactions on Multimedia, 13*(1), 82–91. doi:10.1109/TMM.2010.2087744

Lowe, D. G. (2004). Distinctive Image Features from Scale-Invariant Keypoints. *International Journal of Computer Vision, 60*(2), 91–110. doi:10.1023/B:VISI.0000029664.99615.94

Lu, J., Plataniotis, K. N., & Venetsanopoulos, A. N. (2003). Face recognition using LDA-based algorithms. *IEEE Transactions on Networks, 14*(1), 195–200. doi:10.1109/TNN.2002.806647 PMID:18238001

Luo, J., Ma, Y., Takikawa, E., Lao, S., Kawade, M., & Lu, B.-L. (2007). Person-Specific SIFT Features for Face Recognition. In *Proceedings of IEEE International Conference on Acoustics, Speech and Signal Processig2007* (vol. 2, pp. 593-596). IEEE.

Martinez, A. M., & Kak, A. C. (2001). PCA versus LDA. *IEEE Transactions on Pattern Analysis and Machine Intelligence, 23*(2), 228–233. doi:10.1109/34.908974

Milborrow, S., & Nicolls, F. (2008). Locating Facial Features with an Extended Active Shape Model. In *Proceedings of the 10th European Conference on Computer Vision* (vol. 4, pp. 504-513). Academic Press.

Nappi, M., & Riccio, D. (2008). *Moderne Tecniche di Elaborazione di Immagini e Biometria.* CUA.

Nappi, M., Riccio, D., & De Marsico, M. (2013). Entropy Based Biometric Template Clustering. In *Proceedings of International Conference on Pattern Recognition Applications and Methods,* (pp. 560-563). Academic Press.

Ojala, T., Pietikainen, M., & Harwood, D. (1996). A comparative study of texture measures with classification based on feature distributions. *Pattern Recognition, 29*(1), 51–59. doi:10.1016/0031-3203(95)00067-4

Ojala, T., Pietikainen, M., & Maenpaa, T. (2002). Multiresolution gray-scale and rotation invariant texture classification with local binary patterns. *IEEE Transactions on Pattern Analysis and Machine Intelligence, 24*(7), 971–987. doi:10.1109/TPAMI.2002.1017623

Qin, C., Bao, X., Choudhury, R., & Nelakuditi, S. (2012). TagSense: Leveraging Smartphones for Automatic Image Tagging. *IEEE Transactions on Mobile Computing.* doi: doi:10.1109/TMC.2012.235

Rowley, H. A., Baluja, S., & Kanade, T. (1998). Neural network-based face detection. *IEEE Transactions on Pattern Analysis and Machine Intelligence, 20*(1), 23–38. doi:10.1109/34.655647

Rui, Y., Huang, T. S., & Chang, S. F. (1999). Image retrieval: Current techniques, promising directions, and open issues. *Journal of Visual Communication and Image Representation, 10*(1), 39–62. doi:10.1006/jvci.1999.0413

Stone, Z., Zickler, T., & Darrell, T. (2010). Toward Large scale face recognition using social network context. *Proceedings of the IEEE, 98*(8), 1408–1415. doi:10.1109/JPROC.2010.2044551

Swets, D. L., & Weng, J. J. (1996). Using Discriminant Eigenfeatures for Image Retrieval. *IEEE Transactions on Pattern Analysis and Machine Intelligence, 18*(8), 831–836. doi:10.1109/34.531802

Tan, X., & Triggs, B. (2010). Enhanced Local Texture Feature Sets for Face Recognition Under Difficult Lighting Conditions. *IEEE Transactions on Image Processing, 19*(6), 1635–1650. doi:10.1109/TIP.2010.2042645 PMID:20172829

Viola, P., & Jones, M. (2001). Rapid object detection using a boosted cascade of simple features. In *Proceedings of IEEE Conf. on Computer Vision and Pattern Recognition*, (vol. 1, pp. 511–518). IEEE.

Westphal, G., & Würtz, R. P. (2009). Combining feature-and correspondence-based methods for visual object recognition. *Neural Computation, 21*(7), 1952–1989. doi:10.1162/neco.2009.12-07-675 PMID:19292649

Wiskott, L., Fellous, J.-M., Kuiger, N., & Von der Malsburg, C. (1997). Face recognition by elastic bunch graph matching. *IEEE Transactions on Pattern Analysis and Machine Intelligence, 19*(7), 775–779. doi:10.1109/34.598235

Zhao, W., Chellappa, R., Phillips, P. J., & Rosenfeld, A. (2003). Face recognition: A literature survey. [CSUR]. *ACM Computing Surveys, 35*(4), 399–458. doi:10.1145/954339.954342

Zhou, Y., Gu, L., & Zhang, H.-J. (2003). Bayesian tangent shape model: Estimating shape and pose parameters via bayesian inference. In *Proceedings of IEEE Conf. on Computer Vision and Pattern Recognition, CVPR 2003*. IEEE.

Zhou, Y., Zhang, W., Tang, X., & Shum, H. (2005). A bayesian mixture model for multi-view face alignment. In *Proceedings of IEEE Conference on Computer Vision and Pattern Recognition (CVPR'05)* (vol. 2, pp. 741-746). IEEE.

Zhou, Z., Chindaro, S., & Deravi, F. (2009). A Classification Framework for Large-Scale Face Recognition Systems. In N. M. Tistarelli M. (Ed.), Advances in Biometrics (LNCS), (vol. 5558, pp. 337-346). Berlin: Springer.

Zhu, X., & Ramanan, D. (2012). Face detection, pose estimation, and landmark localization in the wild. In *Proceedings of IEEE Conference on Computer Vision and Pattern Recognition (CVPR)*, (pp. 2879-2886). IEEE.

KEY TERMS AND DEFINITIONS

Annotation: An external information added to a (possibly digital) document for comment, explanation or classification (indexing).

Automatic Image Tagging: The process performed by a computer to automatically assign metadata to digital images for organization (indexing) and retrieval for a digital archive or database.

Face Image Tagging: To annotate an image using the identities (names) of the depicted subjects.

Tagging: Attaching short annotations, i.e. labels, keywords or metadata, to someone or something for the purpose of identification, classification, or to give some other information.

Uncontrolled Setting: A capture setting where neither environment conditions (illumination, distance from the capture device, orientation) nor subject presentation (pose, expression) are set in advance or controlled in any way.

Chapter 17
Secure Face Recognition for Mobile Applications

Brian C. Lovell
The University of Queensland, Australia

Daniel F. Smith
The University of Queensland, Australia

ABSTRACT

Biometric systems are generally restricted to specialist deployments and require expensive equipment. However, the world has recently experienced the widespread rollout of cheap biometric devices in the form of smart phones and tablets. One of the main drivers for mainstream adoption of biometric technologies is the need to address continuing problems with authenticating to online systems. These mobile devices may now be suitable to provide biometric-based authentication to a wide user population. This chapter discusses the different ways that face recognition can be used on smart mobile devices. The authors highlight the online authentication problem and show how three-factor authentication can address many pressing issues. They also discuss the ways that such a system could be attacked, and focus on replay attacks which have yet to be seriously addressed in the literature. The authors conclude with a brief examination of the current research into addressing replay attacks.

INTRODUCTION

Biometrics has been studied for several decades but widespread use is still yet to occur outside of specialist security deployments. Holding back the wider usage of biometrics is the lack of ubiquitous biometric sensors and systems, driven primarily by cost factors. Moreover, to date, there has been no compelling use case to motivate such a universal rollout.

What if, suddenly, every user had a biometric device available to them at no additional cost? Would this be enough to see the use of biometrics finally reach that elusive tipping point?

It appears that the world is indeed on the cusp of just such a tipping point. Biometric devices, in the form of hand-held smart mobile devices, are being purchased in increasingly large numbers. How could these now ubiquitous devices be leveraged into a gigantic biometric system?

DOI: 10.4018/978-1-4666-5966-7.ch017

This chapter examines the use of commodity smart mobile devices as biometric sensors. More specifically, we focus on using the video camera to support facial recognition applications. Mobile face recognition raises two important questions. What is the application driver that will ensure the widespread adoption of such a biometric system? What are the security issues that must still be resolved before smart mobile devices can successfully act as biometric sensors?

BIOMETRICS

Biometrics has been defined as "The automated use of physiological or behavioral characteristics to determine or verify identity" (International Biometric Group, 2013) and has been studied for over 100 years (Bertillon, 1893). Jain *et al.* (1999) is an excellent introduction to the field of Biometrics.

Examples of the many modes of biometric systems include fingerprints, face recognition, voice recognition, iris scanning, retina scanning, hand geometry, ear patterns, gait recognition, vein patterns, written signature, keystroke dynamics, and DNA.

Immigration and border protection services are among the early adopters of automated bio-

metric systems. The USA originally used hand geometry in their INSPASS program, and then moved to face recognition and fingerprints in the upgraded US-VISIT program. This current system is manually driven, and very labour intensive. Australia and New Zealand use face recognition in their SmartGate system that is coupled to the passenger's biometric enabled passport. This system uses automated booths, but there is still significant staff oversight to prevent security breaches and to facilitate passenger movement. Figure 1 shows examples of each of these biometric border protection systems.

Other uses for biometrics are personal identification of persons of interest (iris scanning), building/restricted space access control (face, voice, fingerprint), and crime scene investigation (DNA). More recently, biometrics have started to appear in laptop and desktop computers (face, fingerprint), but these are primarily used for local access to that computer system only.

Outside of such deployments, biometric systems are not commonly used by the general public. One of the primary challenges to widespread adoption is that the biometric sensor technology must be readily available in the location where it is expected to be used. An examination of the many different types of biometrics above shows that only a small subset of biometric modes could

Figure 1. Border protection biometric systems - INSPASS, US-VISIT, and SmartGate

be supported in a practical system or the number of different sensors would continue to grow out of all proportion.

According to Jain *et al.* (2000) a suitable biometric should have the following characteristics:

- **Universality:** All users should possess the biometric;
- **Distinctiveness:** It should be possible to use the biometric to distinguish between any two different people;
- **Permanence:** The biometric should not change significantly over time;
- **Collect-ability:** It should be relatively easy to collect the biometric signal quantitatively;
- **Acceptability:** Users need to accept the biometric system.

Each of the biometric modes above supports these characteristics to varying degrees. So, if only one biometric mode could be used, which one should be chosen? They each have their strengths and weaknesses. The answer lies, not so much in their characteristics, but which mode allows for the most cost-effective deployment of sensors for a given use case. Like all security systems, cost is almost always the primary driver for the choice of technology, with acceptability/usability next, followed by security (Herley, van Oorschot, & Patrick, 2009).

User acceptance has a number of components. Requiring users to perform unnatural acts in public (*e.g.,* making specific face gestures, being subjected to intensive personal inspection, speaking certain words) will be far less accepted than if the user can interact with the biometric system in a natural way (looking at a screen, typing on a keyboard).

Speed of operation is also a factor. Systems that take many seconds to make a decision can act as a bottleneck. A state-of-the-art iris-in-motion border protection system uses specialised processors, sensors, and infrared panels that operate at multiple wave lengths to increase processing speed. This system can recognise up to 50 persons per minute, allowing the user to simply walk through a gate at normal speed (EyeLock, 2013). However, such a system is also quite expensive, limiting broad adoption.

Biometric features for identification have significant drawbacks as well. They are not really "secrets" as they are either displayed publicly (*e.g.,* face, photos), or traces of them may be left everywhere people go (*e.g.,* fingerprints, DNA). Once a biometric for a user is compromised, it is very difficult to revoke and replace it.

Even worse, biometric matching is not exact, as opposed to the way that traditional computer authentication mechanisms operate. Two pictures of a person's face can vary widely, including changes in lighting, pose, expression, make-up, glasses, hair, and aging. Such variations require the system to perform a fuzzy match, with a variable degree of tolerance (Zhao, Chellappa, Phillips, & Rosenfeld, 2003).

One of the most widely deployed biometric sensing devices is the CCTV camera. Thousands of these cameras are deployed in cities around the world. The limitations of resolution from these cameras restricts the biometric choice to face recognition - often via human face recognition since automated face matching is problematic on low resolution images of non-cooperative subjects. Being recognised via CCTV is certainly very unobtrusive for the user - all they need do is simply walk past the camera. However, what is the benefit to the user other than nebulous and disputed claims of increased safety? This lack of perceived benefit to the biometric user often encourages complaints regarding invasion of privacy.

The next section discusses how mobile devices may have a significant impact on choosing face recognition as the primary biometric modality. It could be argued that biometric technology is simply a solution waiting for an important problem to solve. If a universally useful application could be identified and user concerns addressed, then user acceptance will be increased.

It turns out that there is a major universal use case for biometrics already – addressing cybersecurity and identity fraud. The section on Authentication introduces the topic of users logging into their online accounts, and the significant problems that surround this action. Biometrics authenticates real people, not things or knowledge, promising to dramatically improve authentication. They are difficult for users to forget or lose as they are measured from human characteristics that are permanently present, which means that biometric systems (should) require the actual person to be present to complete the authentication.

The pairing of reliable face recognition with smart mobile devices has the potential to offer an alternative solution to online authentication for banking and other activities. The choice of face recognition is very natural, based upon how users generally interact with their smart devices (see the next section for discussion). Authenticating using face recognition also has the added benefit that humans can later verify the matches in a natural way. This provides a powerful mechanism for auditing *who* performed the transaction.

Face Detection and Face Recognition

The first step in creating a face recognition system is to detect the face within a photograph or video. Several techniques have been provided to achieve this, as discussed in (Rowley, Baluja, & Kanade, 1998; Viola & Jones, 2004; Zhu & Ramanan, 2012). Google's Android 4.0 (Android Open Source Project, 2011) and Apple's iOS (Apple Inc., 2012) operating systems for mobile phones now provide Application Programming Interfaces (APIs) that provide face detection facilities to developers.

Face recognition systems have progressed significantly due to continued research. Although the focus of this chapter is not to describe face

recognition systems *per se*, the reader is referred to (Chellappa, Du, Turaga, & Zhou, 2011; Turk & Pentland, 1991; Zhao et al., 2003) for further details.

SMART MOBILE DEVICES

The last decade has seen an explosion in mobile device usage. Mobile phones are no longer just a phone, but a complete online client system that is capable of executing sophisticated applications.

Coupled with the improvements in mobile devices, mobile networks have kept pace, with the introduction of GPRS, then 3G, and now 4G networks. Today's device users are now highly mobile and always connected.

The Australian Communications and Media Authority recently reported that nearly half of adult Australians now possess a smart phone (ACMA, 2013). The Pew Research Center's Internet & American Life Project also report similar numbers for the United States of America (Smith, 2013).

Smart mobile devices (smart phones, tablets, laptops) are becoming the required tools for living daily life. The functionality they now provide is sufficiently mature that they are used as client devices in many enterprises. Several organisations are allowing users to bring their own smart devices for use at work (Bring Your Own Device, or BYOD). In addition, these mobile devices are now small enough to be carried everywhere, and the widespread network access allows them to remain connected for the majority of the time. This creates a highly mobile and always connected user base, with each user provisioned with a personally owned (or allocated) smart device.

It is, therefore, a logical choice to examine these smart mobile devices to determine if they have capabilities that can be used as a universal biometric sensor.

Smart mobile devices come armed with a wide array of inbuilt sensors and output devices. Many devices include the following:

- Global Positioning System (GPS);
- Compass;
- Ambient light sensor;
- On-screen or hardware based keyboard/keypad;
- Accelerometer;
- Low resolution front-facing digital camera, with the ability to capture live video;
- High resolution rear-facing digital camera, with the ability to capture live video;
- Microphone;
- Speaker;
- Display screen.

However, most mobile devices currently do not have a single, ubiquitously deployed biometric sensor. Until a universal, secure, biometric interface is provided by all phone manufacturers, it will be necessary to leverage common existing device interfaces.

GPS location data, ambient light readings, sounds from the speaker, and compass data provide no measure of user characteristics. Therefore, they are not suitable for use as biometric information.

The keyboard or keypad might be used to perform keystroke analysis (Clarke & Furnell, 2007). However, users sometimes consider small hardware keyboards too clumsy to use to be able to get an effective measure. In addition, the on-screen keyboards performing error correction may skew the results to introduce additional verification errors.

Studies on gait recognition using accelerometers (Kwapisz, Weiss, & Moore, 2010) have shown some promising results, but these require that the mobile device be in a certain position on the body (such as in a pocket). To use this system requires the user to carry the device on their body while they walk or run. Operating a mobile device while walking around is not safe, and this reduces acceptability. In addition, gait recognition is simply not possible once the user stops walking. Thus the system must remember the user identity for a period of time, which could allow

an imposter to take the device and impersonate the authenticated user.

Voice verification, in ideal conditions, can be suitably robust. However, in noisy environments (*e.g.,* railway stations, airports, and public spaces) performance will decrease. Although work has been undertaken to improve performance in noisy environments, the results are often poor (Lee, Kang, Han, & Kim, 2012). Voice systems suffer when people read or pronounce words differently from what was requested or intended (*e.g.,* reading "one-two" instead of "twelve") (Jansen, 2003). In addition, using mobile phones for voice communication in public places is starting to be viewed negatively as it intrudes on other's personal space. For example, some trains have designated *quiet carriages* where travellers are asked to "refrain from having loud conversations, using mobile phones and noisy musical devices" (Queensland Rail, 2013).

This essentially leaves the video camera as the sole remaining biometric sensor. There are numerous possibilities for using the on-board camera, including:

- Face recognition;
- Iris scanning;
- Retina scanning;
- Ear patterns.

Retinal and iris scans often require specialised devices (*e.g.,* near-infrared light sources and capture equipment in very close proximity to the eye). Current mobile device cameras tend not to have sufficient resolution nor the near-infrared illumination sources to successfully perform this scanning unless used in very close proximity to the face (for example, the CASIA database (National Laboratory of Pattern Recognition (NLPR), 2010) uses images that are 320x280 pixels which would require a significant portion of a 720p video stream. However, some work has been performed in this area (Cho, Park, Rhee, Kim, & Yang, 2006; Jeong,

Park, Park, & Kim, 2005; Park, Park, Kang, Lee, & Jeong, 2008).

Although ear recognition is possible, the requirement for someone to hold the mobile device to video their ear, or moving their head blindly into a suitable position, reduces the acceptability of this biometric for users.

Therefore, the practical conclusion is to use the video camera on the smart mobile device for face recognition. This could be the camera that faces the user as they normally use the mobile device, or could be a standard Webcam connected to a desktop or laptop computer. Using the camera in this way requires little cooperation from, or interaction with, the user other than to have them continue looking at the screen during the authentication process. This non-cooperative solution addresses many of the usability concerns raised by Bonneau *et al.* (2012).

Recent mobile phone releases include a suitable camera that faces the user. Figure 2 shows the trend of improvement in the capabilities of some Apple and Samsung mobile phones over the last few years. The purpose of this analysis is to illustrate the trend of rapid improvement in mobile phone capabilities over the past few years. Video resolutions (solid black line in Figure 2) of 480p have been available since 2010, 720p since 2011, and 1080p since 2013. During that time, screen resolutions have increased from 480x800 to 1080x1920 pixels. However, it can be argued that video capture resolutions will not increase much past 1080p@30fps, so this is a good baseline to work with.

Figure 2. Capability trends for iPhone and Samsung phones. Data retrieved Nov-2013 from Apple and Samsung. © 2013, Daniel F. Smith. Used with permission.

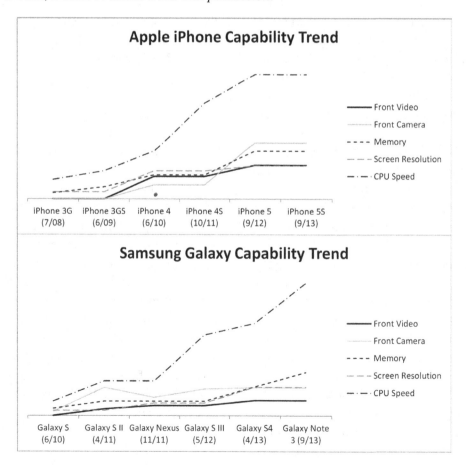

However, using a mobile device as a biometric reader is not as simple as it may appear. These devices, rich in functionality, have also become a target for intruders. Malicious software (commonly referred to as *malware*) exists for many smart mobile devices (RSA, 2012). Sophisticated security attacks will continue to improve as the widespread use of these devices only makes them a bigger target.

The recently released Apple iPhone 5s shipped with a Touch ID fingerprint sensor built into the Home button. It can be argued that this sensor was more designed for convenience rather than security, since it is disabled if the phone is rebooted or remains locked for more than 48 hours. Apple claims that "more than 50 percent of smartphone users don't use a passcode" (Apple, 2013a) and state that "Touch ID is designed to minimize the input of your passcode, but your passcode will be needed for additional security validation..." (Apple, 2013b). However, this did not prevent users claiming to have "bypassed the biometric security" within a day of the phone becoming available (Chaos Computer Club, 2013). Restricting the use of the fingerprint reader to a supervised mode of operation would resolve this issue, but that is not the general use case for mobile devices. Regardless, using the fingerprint security is still a convenient improvement over using weak or no PIN security to protect the phone.

The inclusion of a fingerprint scanner in the iPhone is a new trend and has served to highlight the emerging use of biometrics in devices destined for the general public rather than specialised deployments. The security of biometrics on mobile devices will continue to receive close attention in the coming years.

USE CASES ON SMART MOBILE DEVICES

If the choice is to use a mobile device as a biometric sensor, then the next decision is *how* applications will use that biometric most effectively and be of benefit to the greatest number of users. A number of options exist from a standalone system, to one where the device is simply a biometric reader and the processing of the biometric data is performed on another system.

Example Use Cases

This section outlines three example use cases of biometrics on a mobile device.

Stand Alone Application

The first case is using a biometric in a standalone application on a smart device. This was one of our group's first applications of biometrics on mobile devices as it was easier to provide a fully self-contained application rather than to integrate more deeply with the device. The core of our Advanced Surveillance research group's Face Recognition Engine (Lovell, Bigdeli, & Mau, 2011) and parts of the OpenCV library (OpenCV, 2013) were cross-compiled to develop the face recognition application infrastructure for iOS on the Apple iPhone and iPad. This led to the EyeContact face recognition app for iPhone which was released in August, 2011 (see Figure 3 for an example). Eye-Contact used photos associated with the iPhone contact list as the face gallery. The user could then lookup a contact based on their face image rather than their name. The app could potentially use the phone camera to scan a crowded room to identify faces stored within the iPhone contact list. It may even be useful as an *aide-mémoire* if you are in the common, but nonetheless embarrassing, situation where you have forgotten a colleague's name. You just need to unobtrusively capture their face from a distance. The app may even be used as an alternative to name tags at business meetings. A more conventional security example would be a self-contained watch list of faces that could be used by security officers to identify persons of interest.

Searching databases of faces and performing near-real time matching has not been possible in the past without significant computing power.

Figure 3. Example interface from EyeContact app. © 2013, Brian C. Lovell. Used with permission.

However, the newer mobile devices contain faster processors and more memory. Some recent devices even contain GPUs that can be conveniently accessed via tools like OpenCL (Khronos Group, 2013).

Local Authentication

The second case is to use the biometric to authenticate the user to the actual mobile device. This could be to unlock the device, login to privileged functionality, or to access restricted data. The possible choices of biometric to use here are somewhat broader, and could include face recognition, fingerprint, voice, gait, iris, keystroke, or even hand writing. This would restrict the device to only a small set of authorised users. As each different user authenticates, they might be presented with their own personal profile which sets up the device according to personal preferences.

A minor expansion of this scenario is that the mobile device performs all of the biometric processing, and communicates its authentication decision to a remote service. However, this means that if the unsupervised and uncontrolled mobile device is compromised, then the security decisions can no longer be trusted.

A "Low security, experimental" face recognition system is provided by Android 4.0 on a variety of phones. This system allows the user to unlock their device using their face image. However, the system failed to operate correctly during the product launch (The Telegraph UK, 2011), and when the users attempts to enable it, the system warns users that "Face Unlock is less secure than a pattern, PIN, or password." The system was easily defeated by a spoofing attack using a simple photograph.

Android 4.1 added a liveness check by requiring the user blink after the initial scan. However, this too was easily defeated.

Remote Authentication

The third and emerging case is to use the mobile device as the biometric sensor, providing the biometric data to a remote system or service to process and authenticate the user. This requires the mobile device to be connected to the network at the time of authentication.

This type of system reduces the trust requirement for the mobile device. Provided the back-end system is confident that it is receiving a valid biometric signal, it can then do all of the security checking itself rather than relying on a decision by an unknown device.

A number of software development kits (SDKs) are starting to appear that provide face recognition. One example is from KeyLemon (KeyLemon Inc., 2013) which also provides some liveness detection facilities to defeat spoofing attacks.

Continuous Authentication

One interesting challenge for authentication systems is that the authentication process typically occurs at a single point in time, often at the beginning of a transaction. However, there is a desperate need to prove that the authenticated user is the same one that actually completes the transaction.

Most practical authentication schemes authenticate objects, not the person. Since a strong connection between the authenticated session and the actual user is not available, it is possible to replace the user with another user during the transaction and the service will not be aware of this switch.

Consider the following scenario in a bricks and mortar bank. You walk up to the bank counter to withdraw cash from your account. The bank teller requests a suitable level of identification (such as your bank card and/or PIN) before authorising the transaction. In the meantime, you leave the bank counter and someone else takes your place to receive the cash at the end of the transaction.

In a physically-based transaction such as the one just outlined, it is difficult to achieve this attack as the bank teller would probably not complete the transaction under those circumstances.

However, when the user is remote, how can the service provider know that the session has been hijacked and taken over by an attacker?

Security systems must not only successfully complete the authentication, but must then manage the entire session until the transaction has completed to ensure that the user is still the same authenticated user. This is not as easy as it might seem when using remote uncontrolled client systems over the Internet (such as a Web browser).

Recently, an attack against session management cookies was successfully demonstrated. The tool, called *firesheep* (Butler, 2010), was able to obtain access to unprotected session cookies after the user had authenticated. This allowed the attacker to hijack the session and continue the transaction under their control.

Ideally, not only is the client device authenticated, but also the actual user. Once the user is authenticated, the system should render it very difficult to replace the user with a different user during the transaction. This could be achieved by requiring the user to authenticate to the system on a continual basis throughout the lifetime of the entire transaction. In the physical case, this is easy as the user's physical presence maintains a continual contact with the service provider.

In a remote online situation, asking the user to continually prove who they are could be extremely annoying. Imagine a system which insists that you type in your password, or swipe your finger for a fingerprint scan, every second throughout the lifetime of the transaction. Even continually speaking words for voice recognition would become onerous very quickly.

Yet with forward facing cameras on mobile devices (and desktop Webcams), continual authentication could be more easily achieved without annoying the users. By continually obtaining a face image and performing face recognition, the remote service system can gain a level of assurance that the user is the same user that authenticated at the beginning of the transaction. If the user walks away out of range from the camera, the transaction can be aborted.

Continuous authentication has the potential to significantly increase the security of online transactions, and would also hamper a wide variety of online attacks.

AUTHENTICATION

Mobile devices are now deployed sufficiently widely, and have sufficient capabilities and capacity, to act as a universal biometric sensor. Moreover, face currently appears to be the bio-metric of choice.

As shown in the section on Use Cases, the face biometric can be used in a number of ways. Applications such as a local face recognition database are simple and available now, but it will take more than these types of human-assist applications to act as a compelling driver for the widespread deployment and adoption of face recognition on mobile devices.

What will be the use case that drives widespread biometric adoption? There are a number of issues to be resolved, but authentication to online services is a known problem area where widely deployed biometrics has the potential to make significant improvements in both convenience and security. Unlike human-assist applications where there is a small potential user base, on-line services are universally required so biometric technologies could have billion person user bases.

This section outlines current online authentica-tion techniques, and why users are still struggling with using them effectively.

Background to Authentication

Authentication is the foundation upon which many other security decisions are made. Accurately authenticating someone or something is necessary to decide what is, and what is not, allowed. Some simple examples include:

- Residents deciding who may enter their homes;
- Parents deciding who may pick up their children from school;
- Service providers validating the identity of clients before providing the service;
- Requiring and validating tickets to enter a ballet performance.

Face recognition is the primary means for humans to authenticate each other. Human babies learn to recognise their mother's voice in-utero (Lee, 2010). After birth, they learn to recognise faces quickly, and respond to them (Bushnell, 1982; Pascalis, de Schonen, Morton, Deruelle, & Fabre-Grenet, 1995).

Traditionally, authentication systems rely on three basic methods, or factors (Browne, 1972):

- Something you *have*, such as a key to an office, identification badge, or authentica-tion token;
- Something you *know*, such as a secret, password, or PIN;
- Something you *are*, such as recognising a person by their face, fingerprints, or DNA.

Requirements for Online Authentication

In the early days of mainframe computers, people were authorised to access the computer by being physically allowed to access the console in the computer room. As networks, remote access, and time-sharing were introduced, a mechanism was required to authenticate users that were physically separated from the computer room.

Two primary drivers for authenticating users were the need to keep users and their data sepa-rated from each other (*access control* (Saltzer, 1974)), and the desire to account or charge for expensive computer time (one of the uses for *auditing* (Bishop, 2005)). These drivers soon expanded beyond access control and auditing, to *non-repudiation* (Caelli, Longley, & Shain, 1994). To successfully perform their roles, services such as access control, auditing, and non-repudiation rely on robust authentication to validate the identity of client users.

As time has progressed, more and more of our daily lives exist online. It is important to be able to authenticate the person engaging in the transaction. In a business model, not only do the different parties desire to authenticate each other before performing a business transaction but, after the transaction is complete, they often wish to be able to prove that a transaction has taken place. For example, once the customer pays for goods and takes delivery, the merchant will wish to be able to prove that the customer received the goods and the customer will wish to be able to prove that the merchant received the payment. This concept of proving that an action has taken place is termed *non-repudiation*.

Proving participation in a transaction is fairly easy when the transaction is face-to-face, but in remote transactions, such as online shopping where the two parties may never have met, it is very hard to prove participation.

Current Techniques for Online Authentication

Passwords

The first factor of authentication is *Something You Know*. Online authentication is generally performed using a shared secret, known as a *password*. Passwords have been used since the very early days of computing.

It is primarily cost and usability drivers that have led to the widespread adoption of passwords as the authentication mechanism of choice by service providers (Bonneau et al., 2012). Passwords may have been relatively cheap and easy to implement, but they are not necessarily easy or secure to use.

Surprisingly, despite extensive literature on the inherent weaknesses of the password scheme (Bishop & Klein, 1995; Klein, 1990; Morris & Thompson, 1979; Spafford & Weeber, 1991; Zviran & Haga, 1990), passwords remain the most widely used authentication scheme today - simply due to cost and convenience.

Problems with Password Systems

Increasing attacks against password systems have led to necessary security improvements, such as:

- Encrypting the stored passwords in the password file;
- Providing system generated passwords;
- Salting the encrypted passwords;
- Making the encrypted passwords unreadable to non-privileged users.

Despite these protection mechanisms in the password systems, users continue to contribute to the password problem. It was discovered that users tend to pick poor passwords, and will continue to do so unless forced to do otherwise (Florêncio & Herley, 2007). The increasing attacks against password schemes have driven a constant cycle of proposed improvements to strengthen the chosen passwords (Jobusch & Oldehoeft, 1989a, 1989b). As a result, rules governing the complexity of passwords were implemented to strengthen passwords. These rules included:

- Preventing the use of dictionary-based words;
- Enforcing minimum password lengths;
- Enforcing password complexity rules;
- Forcing regular changes to the password;
- Preventing the reuse of passwords;
- Providing instant feedback to users on password strength;
- Using passphrases.

This has led to users trying to work around the rules, so the rules were strengthened further. As computer power increased, brute force attacks of six, then seven, then eight character passwords became feasible, so the minimum length of passwords was increased. The result is the need for complex passwords that are very difficult to remember. Indeed, Coskun and Herley (2008) argue that for a secret sharing authentication scheme to contain sufficient entropy to resist brute-force attacks, it has become too complex for human minds to conveniently use.

Regardless of the size and complexity passwords, they may still be compromised through other means and subsequently reused by an intruder. Some common attacks are:

- Brute-force guessing of passwords;
- Sniffing from the network due to the lack of encryption in transit;
- Keystroke loggers on compromised client systems;
- Users writing passwords down and leaving them open to discovery;
- Using the same password on multiple computer systems, especially where these systems apply different levels of diligence in securing passwords.

At the same time, users are accruing more and more accounts and passwords, seemingly without end. Florêncio and Herley (2007) discovered that users average more than 20 different accounts, type eight passwords a day, and maintain 6.5 different passwords. Each of these passwords is often constructed using different, and sometimes conflicting, sets of enforced rules.

The accumulation of so many passwords coupled with the conflicting password complexity rules leads to users constantly forgetting their passwords, requiring the help of support personnel to reset the password. This resultant increased cost of support has led to systems where users could reset the passwords themselves by answering a set of "personal questions" to provide a secondary form of authentication. However, studies have shown that the use of these questions generally *reduces* the security of the system (Rabkin, 2008; Schechter, Brush, & Egelman, 2009).

A major problem with passwords is that, once compromised, they can be used over and over again, possibly without detection. In other words,, they can be *replayed* (Coskun & Herley, 2008).

Shared secrets, such as personal details, may also be compromised easily when there is a lack of mutual authentication. Usually, an entity proves that they are in possession of the shared secret by uttering it. When a service requests the shared secret from a client, there is no proof that the service is in possession of the shared secret initially. After the client reveals the shared secret, the service will be in possession of it whether they are authorised to or not.

An example of this is when fraudsters pretend to be from the bank and contact unsuspecting customers to request account details (Kirda & Kruegel, 2006).

As passwords became increasingly complex to keep secure, they became harder to use and remember. In particular, there was a desire to have passwords that could only be used once (a *one-time password*) so that, if they were captured, they could not be used again. However, one-time passwords can be very complex to calculate and use.

Token-Based Authentication

The second factor of authentication is *Something You Have*. Throughout history, authentication has been performed with physical artefacts such as mechanical keys, called tokens in the security literature. Anyone possessing such a token is granted access and permissions accordingly. In addition to cost, the risk of tokens being stolen or lost is one of the major problems with this security model. Another problem in an increasingly mobile world is the need to carry the token whenever it is needed. However tokens also possess certain delegation advantages over passwords since they can be given to another person to provide temporary privileges which are then revoked when the token is returned. For example, a hotel provides a key to a guest room for a short period of stay and once the key is returned to the hotel desk, the guest may no longer access the room.

Two-Factor Authentication

To prevent the unauthorised use of tokens, usage is often combined with a secret of some form (either a password or PIN). By combining two authentication factors, a *two-factor authentication* (2FA) scheme can benefit from the strengths of one factor to address the weaknesses in the other factor. A common example of this technique is the use of the Automatic Teller Machine (ATM) card to withdraw cash - *both* the card and its corresponding PIN must be used to authenticate successfully (imagine the problem if anyone that found your lost wallet could withdraw cash from your account just by using your ATM card alone).

Reducing the overall cost of solutions is a key contributor to deployment success. Rather than supply specialised tokens for Internet banking, more recently some banks have deployed solutions that use SMS codes sent to the user's mobile phone to provide single-use passwords for higher risk transactions (RSA, 2002). This has resulted in a cheaper, remotely deliverable form of two-factor authentication (SMS plus password) where the solution leverages an existing device (mobile phone) rather than requiring new hardware tokens. However, there are drawbacks since the mobile phone service is not under the bank's control, so the bank is relying heavily on a third party for their security (*i.e.,* mapping the mobile phone number to a particular user). It is expected

that attacks against such systems will continue to improve (RSA, 2012).

If the required token is not available at the time its use is needed, then authentication cannot take place (consider the inconvenient situation when you arrive at your office on a weekend only to discover that you have left your office keys at home).

Passwords/PINs and tokens can also suffer from an attack known as the *Man-in-the-Middle (MITM)* attack (Oppliger, Rytz, & Holderegger, 2009). If an active attacker can masquerade as the service provider (such as an online banking Website), they can capture the authentication sequence presented by the user, and then use this sequence themselves to access the account.

Electronic Token-Based Authentication

There are also electronic tokens that can perform complex cryptographic computations, or provide a sequence of passwords that may only be used once, in an effort to circumvent replay attacks against multi-use passwords. However, if a token is lost or stolen it could be used to authenticate to the system by anyone who possesses it. Although a token is generally used by only one person at a time (unlike shared passwords), the token can easily be used by other people once they take possession of it.

Electronic hardware tokens for user accounts do not enjoy widespread use due to the increased cost of deployment (Herley et al., 2009). Replacing 20 or more user accounts with 20 or more tokens becomes expensive and inconvenient for both users and providers - (*e.g.,* look at how many keys are on your key rings).

An obvious solution is to use one smart mobile device (*e.g.,* phone) to provide the functionality of multiple electronic tokens, often implemented as small applications. In this way, the user needs only to carry one device (which they often already carry on their person). An example of such a technique is provided in van Thanh, Jørstad, Jønvik, and van Thuan (2009).

Biometrics

The third factor of authentication is *Something You Are*. This is usually implemented using some form of biometrics which identifies people based upon their behavioural or biological characteristics.

Current online authentication systems have several problems. The significant weakness of password and token based schemes is that they authenticate knowledge of a secret, or possession of a device. That is, the token and shared secret can be passed on to another person for use. This results in not being able to be completely sure who is performing the authentication. As a result of this doubt, users can argue that they were not responsible for certain actions that were performed using their authenticated identity. Without the ability to authenticate the actual user, non-repudiation is not easily supported.

By introducing biometrics, it becomes possible to authenticate the actual person. This opens a number of potential advantages, such as:

- Limiting the ability to use another person's token or password to masquerade as them;
- Enforcing non-repudiation on transactions;
- Providing continuous authentication for the lifetime of the complete transaction.

These capabilities will significantly enhance the security of online transactions.

BIOMETRIC SYSTEM ATTACKS

Despite their advantages, biometric systems are not a "silver bullet" (Furnell & Clarke, 2005) that can magically solve all of the problems with authentication. Biometric systems are also subject to a number of serious attacks.

Furthermore, biometrics must be used very carefully or they open a new range of attacks. This section discusses attacks against biometric systems, and how some of these attacks can be remediated. It also focuses on one specific attack that has currently received little attention.

In 2001, Ratha *et al.* documented eight attack points within biometric systems (Ratha, Connell, & Bolle, 2001a). The different attack points in Figure 4 are identified as (Ambalakat, 2005; Ratha et al., 2001a):

1. Spoofing attacks;
2. Replay attacks;
3. Compromised feature extraction;
4. False template provided to the matcher;
5. Compromised matcher;
6. Compromised stored templates;
7. False stored template provided to the matcher;
8. Compromised decision from the matcher.

Figure 4. Attack points in biometric systems. © 2001, Springer-Verlag. Adapted from (Ratha et al., 2001a)).

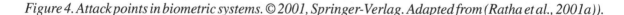

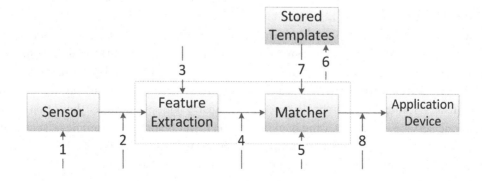

Spoofing Attacks

Attack point 1 shows the position where an attacker can use a spoofing attack. Spoofing attacks occur when a fake biometric is presented to the sensor prior to being read and converted into its digital representation.

The specific spoofing technique will vary, depending on the mode of the chosen biometric system.

In fingerprint systems, the attacker may attempt to use a fake fingerprint that has been retrieved elsewhere (Matsumoto, Matsumoto, Yamada, & Hoshino, 2002; van der Putte & Keuning, 2000). Other fingerprint spoofing attacks involve spraying the sensor with some special material to activate a previous fingerprint, or using the finger from a deceased person (Drahanský, 2011).

For voice recognition systems, the attacker may have previously recorded the victim's conversation and either reconstructed the voice characteristics or pasted together select words to construct a specific phrase (Vielhauer, 2006).

Face recognition systems have previously been defeated by using photographs, videos, or face masks of the victim (Anjos & Marcel, 2011). Significant research has been undertaken to detect these forgeries (Ambalakat, 2005; Chingovska, Anjos, & Marcel, 2012; De Marsico, Nappi, Riccio, & Dugelay, 2012; Määttä, Hadid, & Pietikäinen, 2011; Tan, Li, Liu, & Jiang, 2010).

Recent face recognition systems have been shown effective at detecting live faces in front of the camera, while not easily being fooled by holding a photograph or a video in front of the camera. One of the more robust techniques for performing this detection is based upon Local Binary Patterns (LBP) (Chingovska et al., 2012; Määttä et al., 2011). Figure 5 shows an example of attempting to spoof the face recognition system using a cut-out photograph of a face.

One generic solution to defeating spoofing attacks is to ensure that fake biometrics are not presented to the sensor (Matsumoto et al., 2002),

Figure 5. Unsuccessful spoofing attempt using a photo. (2013, Daniel F. Smith. Used with permission.

for example, by supervising the user as they use the system to ensure that they are not trying to present artificial biometric features. Operating the biometric system in this supervised mode can act as a deterrent against such attacks.

However, operating in this manner can also be very expensive and intrusive.

Biometric features are not secrets, so they cannot be protected in the way that secrets often are. Users broadcast their biometrics (*e.g.,* displaying their face, the way they walk, or speaking), or leave traces of their biometric behind (*e.g.,* latent fingerprints, DNA). Once the biometric is compromised, it is very difficult to revoke, unlike a password which is easy to change. Users generally only have one face, two eyes, and ten fingers (Ratha, Connell, & Bolle, 2001b). Hence, there is a pressing need for liveness testing.

Replay Attacks

Attack point 2 shows the position where an attacker can compromise biometric data after it has been captured by the biometric sensor and converted into a digital form. This compromise may involve copying the biometric data, or injecting false biometric data that had either been previously captured, or carefully crafted.

Biometric systems need the ability to determine if a digital representation of a biometric signal was captured in real-time. A number of techniques have been proposed to do this, including supervised operations (see the discussion on spoofing attacks above), intelligent sensors that can perform complex encryption or challenge/response operations, encrypted communication paths, or time-stamp watermarking the data in some manner.

The excellent LBP-based systems above were evaluated to determine their ability to withstand a replay attack. Unfortunately, all tested systems were immediately compromised by feeding a video from a file into a virtual Webcam device. Such a compromise could be performed with a sophisticated malware attack. The biometric systems were unable to determine that the fake video signal had not been captured live from a real Webcam.

Although the current literature discusses replay attacks as being of major concern, there appears to be little empirical research to address the problem.

In the scenario of using a Webcam on a smart mobile device, the Webcam does not currently possess any intelligent capabilities to defeat replay attacks. All it can provide is an unaltered image of what is being observed in its field of view. To use smart mobile devices for face recognition, additional security features are critical to combat replay attacks. These security features cannot be provided by the mobile device itself, as they could be easily defeated by the attacker.

Without solutions to replay attacks, the widespread deployment of biometrics on uncontrolled mobile devices cannot be trusted, and further progress in authentication will continue to be impeded.

Figure 6 illustrates the difference between Spoofing Attacks and Replay Attacks in an example face recognition system.

Figure 6. Spoofing attacks vs. replay attacks in a face recognition system. © 2013, Daniel F. Smith. Used with permission. Image constructed from sub-images obtained from http://openclipart.org.

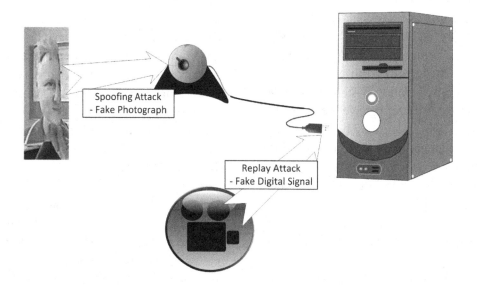

Compromised Feature Extraction

Once the biometric signal has been captured and converted into a digital form, it is often processed to extract its identifying features. Attack point 3 is where the feature extraction process is compromised, so that the resulting extracted features do not accurately represent the supplied biometric signal.

A number of techniques already exist to combat this attack, including system integrity checks, closed system designs, code control, and multi-path processing. For open and uncontrolled systems (in this case, a smart mobile device), attack points 3-8 are a real threat. This reduces the effectiveness of many of the use cases that were outlined in that section.

However, in the use case where the mobile device is acting only as a biometric sensor before providing the biometric signal to a back-end system for further processing, then attack points 3-8 will be located within the secure back-end system, where they can be more effectively mitigated.

False Template Provided to the Matcher

At attack point 4, if the communications channel between the feature extractor and the matcher is not secure, then an attacker could supply a false feature set for matching. This is similar to the replay attack, except that the communications path is located deeper within the service, possibly further away from the attacker.

As discussed in attack point 3, this attack will be much more difficult to achieve in systems that have a closed back-end component, rather than a fully open system.

Compromised Matcher

The correct operation of the biometric system requires the correct operation of each of its components. At attack point 5, if the matcher can be modified to bias its decision, or the decision can be over-ridden, then the overall system will fail. Again, a closed system design will make this attack much harder to achieve.

Compromised Stored Templates

Attack points 6 and 7 relate to the enrolment components, rather than the authentication or matching components. To use a biometric system for authenticating users, each user must first be enrolled into the system. This is usually done by validating their identity through some external mechanism (such as requiring a number of different items of identification) before capturing their biometric, processing it to extract the features to create the user's template, and storing that template in the biometric system.

If the attacker can change this template to one of their own before or during storage, then it may allow false matching in later authentication attempts. The first part of this attack is more a failure in the enrolment process rather than a failure in the system, and is no different for any other system that fails to adequately verifying the identity of its users during the enrolment process.

A secondary attack would be where the database of stored templates is compromised by an attacker, and the biometric data copied or modified. A suitably secure enrolment and storage system, which includes the appropriate use of transmission and storage encryption, can help prevent this attack.

Another form of this attack is where the attacker uses a captured template to recreate a facsimile of the original biometric (Adler, 2003; Ross, Shah,

& Jain, 2007). This ends up being very similar to the spoofing attack at attack point 1.

False Stored Template Provided to the Matcher

Whether the stored template is incorrect, or the connection to the matcher is insecure, if an attacker can provide a false template for matching against a purported identity, then it may be possible that the matcher will erroneously confirm the match by using the wrong template for that user.

Attack points 6 and 7 show that the enrolment system and template storage must also be protected against compromise if the biometric system is to operate correctly.

Compromised Decision from the Matcher

Attack point 8 is where the attacker either compromises the integrity of the matching process, or alters the final decision that is output from the matcher before the requesting entity can observe the original decision.

As for attack point 3, a closed system is harder to compromise than a fully open system.

Attacking Face Recognition on Mobile Devices

In the use case where the face recognition is contained within a self-contained application that operates entirely on the mobile device, all eight attack points are possible. Therefore, in an uncontrolled and open system, malicious software such as viruses and trojan horses can be very effective at compromising the biometric system, making it untrusted.

If the application is to perform a biometric match on the device such as fingerprint, voice, or face matching, and then supply a yes/no answer

to an authentication system, then the security of the system places significant trust in the correct operation of the application. If the application is modified to provide an incorrect answer, then the security of the whole system is compromised.

If the biometric is used to authenticate the user only to the local device (*e.g.,* to unlock the screen or decrypt some data) then, again, this system might not be secure if the application is modified.

For systems where the mobile device acts as a biometric sensor only, and the captured biometric signal is then transmitted to an online authentication service for further authentication analysis, then attack points 3-8 are moved away from the uncontrolled mobile device and located in a back-end system. Provided the back-end system is suitably secure (*e.g.,* by providing a range of standard information security mechanisms including self-integrity checking, reduced attack surfaces, and encrypted communications), then these attack points are much harder to compromise by the intruder.

Enrolment services and processes must also be robust, as for any other online system. The casual enrolment of users without suitable identity checking will always undermine any authentication system. This is shown as attack points 6 and 7 in Figure 4.

There are good solutions being proposed for these attack points, such as encrypted and authenticated data channels, closed system design, system integrity protection, privacy-preserving data storage, and cancellable biometrics (Bhargav-Spantzel et al., 2007; Cavoukian, Chibba, & Stoianov, 2012; Erkin et al., 2009; Newton, Sweeney, & Malin, 2005; Rathgeb & Uhl, 2011).

This leaves attack points 1 (spoofing) and 2 (replay) which will still be located within the open, uncontrolled, mobile device. As noted, recent research has greatly improved the resilience against spoofing attacks, by improving liveness testing. However, replay attacks are still a significant threat. The section on proposed solutions discusses systems designed to withstand replay attacks. Current research is evaluating the feasibility of these systems.

Privacy Issues

One of the biggest objections by users to using biometric systems is their concern about privacy, and that their biometric data could be reused to gain unauthorised access to systems. Part of this problem is exacerbated because biometric data are not secrets, and are often displayed in full view for anyone to capture.

The threat is not that the biometric data is captured, but that it is able to be reused in the system. If the system can perform suitable liveness testing, as well as protect against replay attacks by verifying when the biometric signal was captured, then this will significantly reduce the threat of reuse of biometric data.

If the replay attack problem can be solved, this will remove a major obstacle to the widespread use of biometrics in online transactions as well as helping to allay the concerns of users about reuse of their biometric information. The next section examines proposed systems that could provide one of the first widespread deployments of biometrics that have security features included for defeating a number of serious attacks.

PROPOSED SOLUTIONS TO FACE RECOGNITION REPLAY ATTACKS

Replay attacks remain a serious threat. Without solutions to replay attacks, users continue to be cautious about biometric systems due to privacy concerns.

Research is currently underway in our group to address replay attacks for face recognition on mobile devices, without requiring additional specialised hardware. Due to the desire to use the generic Webcam in the mobile device, it is not

possible to utilise techniques such as challenge-response to the sensor or encrypting the biometric data at the time of capture to defeat replay attacks. As well, given the typical usage of mobile devices, it is not desirable to use such a system in a supervised manner.

Candidate techniques being researched in our group to defeat the replay attack problem involve digitally watermarking the captured face images.

Face Reflection Technique

One method displays images on the screen of the device, and then observes the reflection of those images in the user's face. This does not involve any cooperation from the user.

For our purposes, it is very convenient that the display screen is positioned very close to the front-facing camera on most devices. If the user is facing the screen, this ensures that reflections from the screen mainly occur in the facial region. Simple face detection techniques can be used to identify the face, and then further analysis applied to determine the reflected colour.

By displaying a set pattern of images on the screen, it may be possible to determine that the video was captured at a certain point in time by looking for patterns in the reflections. The displayed pattern would be a subtle *challenge*, and the eye reflections are the *response*. These screen reflections would be included in the images that are supplied to the back-end face recognition system, and represent a digital watermark of the face images. In a well-designed system this continual challenge and response could be performed without user cooperation or, possibly, even awareness.

Current results are promising, but further research is required to increase the robustness of the classifier. The technique degrades if the user does not keep their head relatively still throughout the displayed colour cycle. The cameras used to date also exhibit quite different characteristics, making a generic solution somewhat challenging. These characteristics include the automatic setting of

Figure 7. Face recognition system with proposed replay attack protection. © 2013, Daniel F. Smith. Used with permission. Image constructed from sub-images obtained from http://openclipart.org.

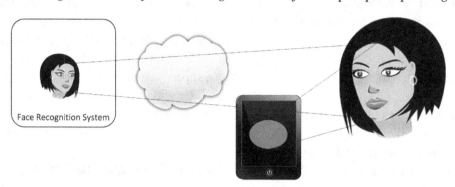

white-balance, focus, contrast, brightness, gain, and saturation. Extensive testing has shown that determining a manual setting that applies across multiple cameras is extremely difficult, and any techniques used would benefit from letting the camera perform its own automatic adjustments.

Figure 7 shows how the light from the screen can be reflected from the user's face, and observed in the captured image by the back-end system.

Face Positioning Technique

A second method involves displaying a region on the screen and requesting the user to move their head and/or phone to manipulate their recorded face image so that it falls within the designated region on the screen. This movement can be performed in three dimensions which not only include left/right and up/down, but also in/out for scaling.

A mobile device is designed specifically to capture the face image during device interaction to support services such as mobile video-conferencing. Some mobile devices now ship with face detection and tracking included. However, the validation of finding the face within a larger image should be performed on a back-end system as the mobile device cannot be trusted to report the correct settings. Therefore, features such as "follow my face" should be disabled during the alignment process.

The entire captured image should be sent to the back-end system, and the frames searched to identify the facial region of interest. Provided the face falls within the designated area, then the challenge has been successfully completed as the user has responded by positioning their face correctly.

Figure 8 shows a sample screen capture during the process where the user is aligning their face into the challenge region on the screen.

Figure 8. Face recognition system with proposed face alignment replay attack protection. © 2013, Daniel F. Smith. Used with permission. Image constructed from sub-images obtained from http://openclipart.org).

These two techniques may be combined to increase the security of the entire system.

Once it has been determined that the images have been captured "live," further processing can then proceed to determine if there is a spoofing attempt (*e.g.,* a photograph with the eyes cut out, or using curved mirrors to mimic the eyes), before finally authenticating the user using the face recognition system.

Combining face recognition with existing authentication techniques could lead to the first widespread deployment of three-factor authentication. Several challenges remain to be resolved, but results to date look promising.

The future looks bright and, soon, authenticating for online transactions could be as simple as looking at your mobile device, and yet more secure and convenient than the current authentication systems today, rather than less secure.

CONCLUSION

To date, biometrics has not enjoyed widespread usage outside of small, fixed installations. Cost and usability factors have been primary limiters. However, the explosion in use of smart mobile devices equips a significant proportion of the population with a biometric reader. As consumer transactions increasingly move online, authentication systems are being identified as inadequate to authenticate real users. Biometrics has the potential to authenticate the actual user, rather than only their possession of a secret or a device. If smart mobile devices are to be used as biometric sensors, face recognition looks to be one of the more acceptable biometric methods for users. However, despite significant research into resolving spoofing attacks, replay attacks remain a serious threat.

Current research is now examining techniques to combat replay attacks. If this research is successful, it will open opportunities for face recognition systems to be used on smart mobile devices to securely authenticate users to online transactions.

This, in turn, will open additional opportunities for the wider deployment of biometric systems that use smart mobile devices as the user interaction platform.

REFERENCES

ACMA. (2013). *Smartphones and tablets - Take-up and use in Australia.* Melbourne, Australia: Australian Communications and Media Authority.

Adler, A. (2003). *Sample images can be independently restored from face recognition templates.* Paper presented at the Canadian Conference on Electrical and Computer Engineering (CCECE). Montreal, Canada.

Ambalakat, P. (2005). *Security of Biometric Authentication Systems.* Paper presented at the 21st Annual Computer Science Seminar. Hartford, CT.

Android Open Source Project. (2011). *Android 4.0 APIs.* Retrieved 12 Nov, 2013, from http://developer.android.com/about/versions/android-4.0.html

Anjos, A., & Marcel, S. (2011). *Counter-Measures to Photo Attacks in Face Recognition: a public database and a baseline.* Paper presented at the International Joint Conference on Biometrics (IJCB). Washington, DC.

Apple. (2013a). *iPhone 5s: About Touch ID security.* Retrieved 07 Nov, 2013, from http://support.apple.com/kb/HT5949

Apple. (2013b). *iPhone 5s: Using Touch ID.* Retrieved 07 Nov, 2013, from http://support.apple.com/kb/HT5883

Apple Inc. (2012). *Core Image Reference Collection*. Retrieved 12 Nov, 2013, from https://developer.apple.com/library/ios/documentation/GraphicsImaging/Reference/CoreImagingRef/_index.html

Bertillon, A. (1893). *Identification Anthropométrique, instructions signalétiques*. Melun, France: Imprimerie administrative, nouvelle édition.

Bhargav-Spantzel, A., Squicciarini, A. C., Modi, S., Young, M., Bertino, E., & Elliott, S. J. (2007). Privacy preserving multi-factor authentication with biometrics. *Journal of Computer Security*, *15*(5), 529–560.

Bishop, M. (2005). *Introduction to Computer Security*. Boston, MA: Addison-Wesley.

Bishop, M., & Klein, D. V. (1995). Improving system security via proactive password checking. *Computers & Security*, *14*(3), 233–249. doi:10.1016/0167-4048(95)00003-Q

Bonneau, J., Herley, C., van Oorschot, P. C., & Stajano, F. (2012). *The Quest to Replace Passwords: A Framework for Comparative Evaluation of Web Authentication Schemes*. Paper presented at the IEEE Symposium on Security and Privacy. San Francisco, CA.

Browne, P. S. (1972). Computer Security: a Survey. *SIGMIS Database*, *4*(3), 1–12. doi:10.1145/1017536.1017537

Bushnell, I. W. R. (1982). Discrimination of Faces by Young Infants. *Journal of Experimental Child Psychology*, *33*(2), 298–308. doi:10.1016/0022-0965(82)90022-4 PMID:7069368

Butler, E. (2010). *Firesheep*. Retrieved 04 Sep, 2012, from http://codebutler.com/firesheep

Caelli, W. J., Longley, D., & Shain, M. (1994). *Information Security Handbook*. Basingstoke, UK: Macmillan.

Cavoukian, A., Chibba, M., & Stoianov, A. (2012). Advances in Biometric Encryption: Taking Privacy by Design from Academic Research to Deployment. *The Review of Policy Research*, *29*(1), 37–61. doi:10.1111/j.1541-1338.2011.00537.x

Chaos Computer Club. (2013). *Chaos Computer Club breaks Apple TouchID*. Retrieved 06 Nov, 2013, from http://www.ccc.de/en/updates/2013/ccc-breaks-apple-touchid

Chellappa, R., Du, M., Turaga, P., & Zhou, S. K. (2011). Face Tracking and Recognition from Video. In S. Z. Li, & A. K. Jain (Eds.), *Handbook of Face Recognition* (2nd ed., pp. 323–351). London: Springer. doi:10.1007/978-0-85729-932-1_13

Chingovska, I., Anjos, A., & Marcel, S. (2012). *On the Effectiveness of Local Binary Patterns in Face Anti-spoofing*. Paper presented at the International Conference of the Biometrics Special Interest Group (BIOSIG). Darmstadt, Germany.

Cho, D.-H., Park, K. R., Rhee, D. W., Kim, Y., & Yang, J. (2006). *Pupil and Iris Localization for Iris Recognition in Mobile Phones*. Paper presented at the Seventh ACIS International Conference on Software Engineering, Artificial Intelligence, Networking, and Parallel/Distributed Computing (SNPD). Las Vegas, NV.

Clarke, N. L., & Furnell, S. M. (2007). Advanced user authentication for mobile devices. *Computers & Security*, *26*(2), 109–119. doi:10.1016/j.cose.2006.08.008

Coskun, B., & Herley, C. (2008). *Can Something You Know Be Saved?* Paper presented at the Information Security Conference (ISC08). Taipei, Taiwan.

De Marsico, M., Nappi, M., Riccio, D., & Dugelay, J.-L. (2012). *Moving Face Spoofing Detection via 3D Projective Invariants*. Paper presented at the 5th IAPR International Conference on Biometrics (ICB). New Delhi, India.

Drahanský, M. (2011). Liveness Detection in Biometrics. In *Advanced Biometric Technologies* (pp. 179–198). InTech-Open Access Publisher. doi:10.5772/17205

Erkin, Z., Franz, M., Guajardo, J., Katzenbeisser, S., Lagendijk, I., & Toft, T. (2009). *Privacy-Preserving Face Recognition*. Paper presented at the 9th International Symposium on Privacy Enhancing Technologies (PETS). Seattle, WA.

EyeLock. (2013). *HBOX®*. Retrieved 09 Aug, 2013, from http://www.eyelock.com/Products/HBOX%C2%AE.aspx

Florêncio, D., & Herley, C. (2007). *A Large-Scale Study of Web Password Habits*. Paper presented at the 16th International World Wide Web Conference (WWW2007). Banff, Canada.

Furnell, S., & Clarke, N. (2005). Biometrics: no silver bullets. *Computer Fraud & Security*, (8): 9–14. doi:10.1016/S1361-3723(05)70243-8

Herley, C., van Oorschot, P. C., & Patrick, A. S. (2009). *Passwords: If We're So Smart, Why Are We Still Using Them?* Paper presented at the 13th International Conference on Financial Cryptography and Data Security (FC). Accra Beach, Barbados.

International Biometric Group. (2013). *How is Biometrics Defined?* Retrieved 31 May, 2013, from https://ibgWeb.com/products/reports/free/biometrics-definition

Jain, A. K., Bolle, R., & Pankanti, S. (1999). *Biometrics: Personal identification in networked society*. Boston, MA: Kluwer. doi:10.1007/b117227

Jain, A. K., Hong, L., & Pankanti, S. (2000). Biometric Identification. *Communications of the ACM*, *43*(2), 90–98. doi:10.1145/328236.328110

Jansen, W. A. (2003). *Authenticating Users on Handheld Devices*. Paper presented at the 15th Annual Canadian Information Technology Security Symposium (CITSS). Ottawa, Canada.

Jeong, D. S., Park, H.-A., Park, K. R., & Kim, J. (2005). *Iris Recognition in Mobile Phone Based on Adaptive Gabor Filter*. Paper presented at the Advances in Biometrics. New York, NY.

Jobusch, D. L., & Oldehoeft, A. E. (1989a). A Survey of Password Mechanisms: Weaknesses and Potential Improvements: Part 1. *Computers & Security*, *8*(7), 587–604. doi:10.1016/0167-4048(89)90051-5

Jobusch, D. L., & Oldehoeft, A. E. (1989b). A Survey of Password Mechanisms: Weaknesses and Potential Improvements: Part 2. *Computers & Security*, *8*(8), 675–689. doi:10.1016/0167-4048(89)90006-0

KeyLemon Inc. (2013). *KeyLemon*. Retrieved 12 Nov, 2013, from https://www.keylemon.com/

Khronos Group. (2013). *The open standard for parallel programming of heterogeneous systems*. Retrieved 01 Aug, 2013, from http://www.khronos.org/opencl/

Kirda, E., & Kruegel, C. (2006). Protecting Users against Phishing Attacks. *The Computer Journal*, *49*(5), 554. doi:10.1093/comjnl/bxh169

Klein, D. V. (1990). *Foiling the Cracker: A Survey of, and Improvements to, Password Security*. Paper presented at the USENIX Security Workshop. Portland, OR.

Kwapisz, J. R., Weiss, G. M., & Moore, S. A. (2010). *Cell Phone-Based Biometric Identification*. Paper presented at the Fourth IEEE International Conference on Biometrics: Theory Applications and Systems (BTAS). Washington, DC.

Lee, G. H., Kang, S. J., Han, C. W., & Kim, N. S. (2012). *Feature Enhancement Error Compensation for Noise Robust Speech Recognition*. Paper presented at the International Multi-Conference on Systems, Signals and Devices (SSD). Chemnitz, Germany.

Lee, G. Y. C. (2010). Fetal and Newborn Auditory Processing of the Mother's and Father's Voice. (Master of Science MR70279). Queen's University, Kingston, Ontario, Canada. ProQuest Dissertations & Theses (PQDT) database.

Lovell, B. C., Bigdeli, A., & Mau, S. (2011). *Embedded Face and Biometric Technologies for National and Border Security*. Paper presented at the IEEE Computer Society Conference on Computer Vision and Pattern Recognition Workshops (CVPRW). Colorado Springs, CO.

Matsumoto, T., Matsumoto, H., Yamada, K., & Hoshino, S. (2002). *Impact of Artificial Gummy Fingers on Fingerprint Systems*. Paper presented at the Optical Security and Counterfeit Deterrence Techniques IV. San Jose, CA.

Morris, R., & Thompson, K. (1979). Password Security: A Case History. *Communications of the ACM*, *22*(11), 594–597. doi:10.1145/359168.359172

Määttä, J., Hadid, A., & Pietkäinenen, M. (2011). *Face Spoofing Detection From Single Images Using Micro-Texture Analysis*. Paper presented at the International Joint Conference on Biometrics (IJCB). Washington, DC.

National Laboratory of Pattern Recognition (NLPR). (2010). *Biometrics Ideal Test*. Retrieved 15 Nov, 2013, from http://www.idealtest.org/index.jsp

Newton, E., Sweeney, L., & Malin, B. (2005). Preserving Privacy by De-identifying Facial Images. *IEEE Transactions on Knowledge and Data Engineering*, *17*(2), 232–243. doi:10.1109/TKDE.2005.32

Open, C. V. (2013). *OpenCV (Open Source Computer Vision)*. Retrieved 01 Aug, 2013, from http://opencv.org/

Oppliger, R., Rytz, R., & Holderegger, T. (2009). Internet Banking: Client-Side Attacks and Protection Mechanisms. *Computer*, *42*(6), 27–33. doi:10.1109/MC.2009.194

Park, K. R., Park, H.-A., Kang, B. J., Lee, E. C., & Jeong, D. S. (2008). A Study on Iris Localization and Recognition on Mobile Phones. *EURASIP Journal on Advances in Signal Processing*, *20*. doi: doi:10.1155/2008/281943

Pascalis, O., de Schonen, S., Morton, J., Deruelle, C., & Fabre-Grenet, M. (1995). Mother's Face Recognition by Neonates: A Replication and an Extension. *Infant Behavior and Development*, *18*(1), 79–85. doi:10.1016/0163-6383(95)90009-8

Queensland Rail. (2013). *Queensland Rail Quiet Carriage*. Retrieved 17 Jul, 2013, from http://queenslandrail.com.au/quietcarriage

Rabkin, A. (2008). *Personal knowledge questions for fallback authentication: Security questions in the era of Facebook*. Paper presented at the 4th Symposium on Usable Privacy and Security (SOUPS). Pittsburgh, PA.

Ratha, N. K., Connell, J. H., & Bolle, R. M. (2001a). *An Analysis of Minutiae Matching Strength*. Paper presented at the Third International Conference on Audio- and Video-Based Biometric Person Authentication (AVBPA). Halmstad, Sweden.

Ratha, N. K., Connell, J. H., & Bolle, R. M. (2001b). Enhancing security and privacy in biometrics-based authentication systems. *IBM Systems Journal*, *40*(3), 614–634. doi:10.1147/sj.403.0614

Rathgeb, C., & Uhl, A. (2011). A survey on biometric cryptosystems and cancelable biometrics. *EURASIP Journal on Information Security*, (1), 1-25. doi: 10.1186/1687-417X-2011-3

Ross, A. A., Shah, J., & Jain, A. K. (2007). From Template to Image: Reconstructing Fingerprints from Minutiae Points. *IEEE Transactions on Pattern Analysis and Machine Intelligence, 29*(4), 544–560. doi:10.1109/TPAMI.2007.1018 PMID:17299213

Rowley, H. A., Baluja, S., & Kanade, T. (1998). Neural Network-Based Face Detection. *IEEE Transactions on Pattern Analysis and Machine Intelligence, 20*(1), 23–38. doi:10.1109/34.655647

RSA. (2002). *RSA Security Unveils Innovative Two-Factor Authentication Solution for the Consumer Market.* Retrieved 13 Sep, 2012, from http://www.rsa.com/press_release.aspx?id=1370

RSA. (2012). *RSA 2012 Cybercrime Trends Report: EMC Corporation.* RSA.

Saltzer, J. H. (1974). Protection and the Control of Information Sharing in Multics. *Communications of the ACM, 17*(7), 388–402. doi:10.1145/361011.361067

Schechter, S., Brush, A. J. B., & Egelman, S. (2009). *It's No Secret. Measuring the Security and Reliability of Authentication via Secret Questions.* Paper presented at the IEEE Symposium on Security and Privacy. Oakland, CA.

Smith, A. (2013). *Smartphone Ownership - 2013 Update.* Washington, DC, USA: Pew Research Center.

Spafford, E. H., & Weeber, S. A. (1991). *User Authentication and Related Topics: An Annotated Bibliography.* West Lafayette, IN: Purdue University.

Tan, X., Li, Y., Liu, J., & Jiang, L. (2010). *Face Liveness Detection from a Single Image with Sparse Low Rank Bilinear Discriminative Model.* Paper presented at the European Conference on Computer Vision (ECCV). Crete, Greece.

The Telegraph UK. (2011). *Technology fail: Google's Galaxy nexus suffers embarrassing failure at Samsung launch.* Retrieved 12 Nov, 2013, from http://youtu.be/eBy3gXpDVes

Turk, M., & Pentland, A. (1991). Eigenfaces for Recognition. *Journal of Cognitive Neuroscience, 3*(1), 71–86. doi:10.1162/jocn.1991.3.1.71 PMID:23964806

van der Putte, T., & Keuning, J. (2000). *Biometrical Fingerprint Recognition: Don't Get Your Fingers Burned.* Paper presented at the Fourth Working Conference on Smart Card Research and Advanced Applications. Bristol, UK.

van Thanh, D., Jørstad, I., Jønvik, T., & van Thuan, D. (2009). *Strong authentication with mobile phone as security token.* Paper presented at the 6th International Conference on Mobile Adhoc and Sensor Systems (MASS). Macau, China.

Vielhauer, C. (2006). Biometric User Authentication for IT Security. In S. Jajodia (Ed.), *Advances in Information Security* (Vol. 18, p. 287). New York, NY: Springer-Verlag.

Viola, P., & Jones, M. J. (2004). Robust Real-Time Face Detection. *International Journal of Computer Vision, 57*(2), 137–154. doi:10.1023/B:VISI.0000013087.49260.fb

Zhao, W., Chellappa, R., Phillips, P. J., & Rosenfeld, A. (2003). Face Recognition: A Literature Survey. [CSUR]. *ACM Computing Surveys, 35*(4), 399–458. doi:10.1145/954339.954342

Zhu, X., & Ramanan, D. (2012). *Face Detection, Pose Estimation, and Landmark Localization in the Wild.* Paper presented at the IEEE Conference on Computer Vision and Pattern Recognition (CVPR). Providence, RI.

Zviran, M., & Haga, W. J. (1990). *Passwords Security: An Exploratory Study.* Monterey, CA: Naval Postgraduate School.

ADDITIONAL READING

Adler, A. (2008). Biometric System Security. In A. Jain, P. Flynn, & A. Ross (Eds.), *Handbook of Biometrics* (pp. 381–402). Springer, US. doi:10.1007/978-0-387-71041-9_19

Bao, W., Li, H., Li, N., & Jiang, W. (2009, 11-12 April 2009). A Liveness Detection Method for Face Recognition Based on Optical Flow Field. Paper presented at the International Conference on Image Analysis and Signal Processing (IASP), Taizhou, China.

Bolle, R. M., Connell, J. H., & Ratha, N. K. (2002). Biometric perils and patches. *Pattern Recognition*, *35*(12), 2727–2738. doi:10.1016/S0031-3203(01)00247-3

Bringer, J., & Chabanne, H. (2008). An Authentication Protocol with Encrypted Biometric Data. Paper presented at the Progress in Cryptology – AFRICACRYPT, Casablanca, Morocco.

de Freitas Pereira, T., Anjos, A., De Martino, J. M., & Marcel, S. (2013, 5-6 Nov 2012). LBP − TOP based countermeasure against face spoofing attacks. Paper presented at the Computer Vision - ACCV 2012 Workshops, Daejeon, Korea.

Doddington, G., Liggett, W., Martin, A., Przybocki, M., & Reynolds, D. (1998). Sheep, Goats, Lambs and Wolves: A Statistical Analysis of Speaker Performance in the NIST 1998 Speaker Recognition Evaluation. Paper presented at the International Conference on Spoken Language Processing (ICSLP), Sydney, Australia.

Frischholz, R. W., & Werner, A. (2003, 17 Oct 2003). Avoiding Replay-Attacks in a Face Recognition System using Head-Pose Estimation. Paper presented at the International Workshop on Analysis and Modeling of Faces and Gestures (AMFG), Nice, France.

Garfinkel, S. L. (2005). *Design Principles and Patterns for Computer Systems That Are Simultaneously Secure and Usable. (Doctor of Philosophy)*. Boston, MA, USA: Massachusetts Institute of Technology.

Hao, F., Anderson, R., & Daugman, J. (2006). Combining Crypto with Biometrics Effectively. *IEEE Transactions on Computers*, *55*(9), 1081–1088. doi:10.1109/TC.2006.138

Hocking, C. G., Furnell, S., Clarke, N., & Reynolds, P. L. (2010, 23-25 Aug 2010). A Distributed and Cooperative User Authentication Framework. Paper presented at the Sixth International Conference on Information Assurance and Security (IAS), Atlanta, GA, USA.

Hyppönen, K. (2009). Secure *Identity Management and Mobile Payments Using Hand-Held Devices.* (PhD Doctoral dissertation), University of Kuopio, Kuopio, Finland.

Jee, H.-K., Jung, S.-U., & Yoo, J.-H. (2006). Liveness Detection for Embedded Face Recognition System. *International Journal of Biological and Medical Sciences*, *1*, 235–238.

Kasprowski, P., & Ober, J. (2004). Eye Movements in Biometrics. In D. Maltoni, & A. K. Jain (Eds.), *Biometric Authentication* (Vol. 3087, pp. 248–258). Springer Berlin Heidelberg. doi:10.1007/978-3-540-25976-3_23

Kaushik, N. (2012). What Happens When Telco's Declare SMS 'Unsafe'? Retrieved from http://blog.talkingidentity.com/2012/11/what-happens-when-telcos-declare-sms-unsafe.html

Khan, M. K., Zhang, J., & Alghathbar, K. (2011). Challenge-response-based biometric image scrambling for secure personal identification. *Future Generation Computer Systems*, *27*(4), 411–418. doi:10.1016/j.future.2010.05.019

Kim, Y., Yoo, J.-H., & Choi, K. (2011). A Motion and Similarity-Based Fake Detection Method for Biometric Face Recognition Systems. *IEEE Transactions on Consumer Electronics, 57*(2), 756–762. doi:10.1109/TCE.2011.5955219

Lee, E. C., Park, K. R., & Kim, J. (2006, 5-7 Jan 2006). *Fake Iris* Detection *by Using Purkinje Image*. Paper presented at the International Conference on Biometrics (ICB), Hong Kong, China.

Li, J., Wang, Y., Tan, T., & Jain, A. K. (2004, 12 Apr 2004). Live Face Detection Based on the Analysis of Fourier Spectra. Paper presented at the Biometric Technology for Human Identification, Orlando, FL, USA.

Nishino, K., & Nayar, S. K. (2004, 27 Jun - 2 Jul 2004). The World in an Eye. Paper presented at the 2004 IEEE Computer Vision and Pattern Recognition (CVPR), Washington, DC, USA.

Nixon, K. A., Aimale, V., & Rowe, R. K. (2008). Spoof Detection Schemes. In A. K. Jain, P. Flynn, & A. A. Ross (Eds.), *Handbook of Biometrics* (pp. 403–423). Springer, US. doi:10.1007/978-0-387-71041-9_20

O'Gorman, L. (2003). Comparing Passwords, Tokens, and Biometrics for User Authentication. *Proceedings of the IEEE, 91*(12), 2021–2040. doi:10.1109/JPROC.2003.819611

Pacut, A., & Czajka, A. (2006). Aliveness Detection for Iris Biometrics. Paper presented at the IEEE International Carnahan Conference on Security Technology (ICCST), Lexington, KY, USA.

Pan, G., Sun, L., Wu, Z., & Wang, Y. (2011). Monocular camera-based face liveness detection by combining eyeblink and scene context. *Telecommunication Systems, 47*(3-4), 215–225. doi:10.1007/s11235-010-9313-3

Roberts, C. (2007). Biometric Attack Vectors and Defences. *Computers & Security, 26*(1), 14–25. doi:10.1016/j.cose.2006.12.008

Schneier, B. (1999). Inside Risks: The Uses and Abuses of Biometrics. *Communications of the ACM, 42*(8), 136. doi:10.1145/310930.310988

Schnieders, D., Fu, X., & Wong, K.-Y. K. (2010, 13-18 June 2010). Reconstruction of Display and Eyes from a Single Image. Paper presented at the IEEE Conference on Computer Vision and Pattern Recognition (CVPR), San Francisco, CA, USA.

Soutar, C. (2002). Biometric System Security White Paper, Bioscrypt, http://www.bioscrypt.com: Bioscrypt, Inc.

Thalheim, L., Krissler, J., & Ziegler, P.-M. (2002). Body check: Biometric Access Protection Devices and their Programs Put to the Test. c't, 11.

Toth, B. (2005). Biometric Liveness Detection. *Information Security Bulletin, 10*(8), 291–297.

Uludag, U., & Jain, A. K. (2004). Attacks on Biometric Systems: A Case Study in Fingerprints. Paper presented at the Security, Steganography and Watermarking of Multimedia Contents VI, San Jose, CA, USA.

Uludag, U., Pankanti, S., Prabhakar, S., & Jain, A. K. (2004). Biometric Cryptosystems: Issues and Challenges. *Proceedings of the IEEE, 92*(6), 948–960. doi:10.1109/JPROC.2004.827372

Van Norren, D., & Tiemeijer, L. F. (1986). Spectral Reflectance of the Human Eye. *Vision Research, 26*(2), 313–320. doi:10.1016/0042-6989(86)90028-3 PMID:3716223

Whitten, A., & Tygar, J. D. (1998). *Usability of Security: A Case Study* (p. 41). (S. C. Science, Trans.). Pittsburgh, PA, USA: Carnegie Mellon University.

KEY TERMS AND DEFINITIONS

Challenge/Response: A security technique where the entity being authenticated must response to a challenge by giving the correct response. Spy movies show this by using phrase/counter-phrase or a photo torn in half.

Continuous Authentication: When we shop in person, we remain present to accept the goods once the payment has been completed. In an online transaction, it is possible that once the payment has been processed, an attacker could intervene seamlessly to complete the transaction. Continuous authentication is a technique where the user must prove their identity not only at the start of the transaction, but at key points throughout the life of the transaction. This technique is not widely used currently.

Liveness Testing: The process of identifying if the biometric that is entered into the system (*e.g.*, fingerprint, face image, voice sample) has been obtained from a living person, or artificially created (*e.g.*, fake fingerprints, photo of a face, video of a face, recorded voice).

Mobile Device: For the purposes of this chapter, mobile devices can include smart phones (ones that can run applications, such as Android, iPhone, or Windows phones), tablets (such as Android or iPad), or traditional laptops. However, the techniques described within for these devices can also be applied to the old desktop computer if they have a suitable Webcam (either in-built into the monitor, or as a separate USB device). Each device will require a connection to the Internet.

Online Authentication: Many business services are now delivered online and accessed via the Internet. This often requires an account and password to access the system. Businesses require users to prove who they are before engaging in a transaction (such as ordering a product). This process is *authentication*, and is most commonly performed by typing in your account and password.

Replay Attack: A replay attack is where a biometric signal has been captured, and an attempt is made to use it again at a later date. Although this appears to be similar to the spoofing attack, there are differences. The spoofing attack is generally performed outside of the biometric system, and the replay attack is performed inside. Within computer systems, replay attacks can be easily used by hackers or viruses.

Spoofing Attack: A spoofing attack is an attempt to fool a biometric system by presenting a fake form of the biometric. This could be a finger made from gelatine, a photograph, or a recorded voice. Liveness testing has been used to prevent spoofing attacks. For face recognition systems, techniques based upon Local Binary Patterns appear to be effective at discriminating between live faces and printed photographs.

Three-Factor Authentication (3FA): Authentication generally consists of one or more of three different factors: something you *have* (*e.g.*, a key or ATM card), something you *know* (*e.g.*, a password or PIN), or something you *are* (*e.g.*, a biometric such as a face image or fingerprint). Most online authentication systems use a single factor (password). Combining two factors together into a two-factor authentication (2FA) system (such as the ATM card combined with the PIN) significantly improves the strength of the authentication, but still only authenticates that a person possesses the correct token or knows the password. A three-factor authentication (3FA) system combines all three factors, which requires the actual user to be present to complete the authentication.

Section 4
Future Research Directions

The concluding chapter is devoted to a bird's-eye survey of the main achievements in the field of face recognition and on sketching the most promising research lines.

Chapter 18
Face Recognition in Adverse Conditions:
A Look at Achieved Advancements

Maria De Marsico
Sapienza University of Rome, Italy

Michele Nappi
University of Salerno, Italy

ABSTRACT

In this chapter, the authors discuss the main outcomes from both the most recent literature and the research activities summarized in this book. Of course, a complete review is not possible. It is evident that each issue related to face recognition in adverse conditions can be considered as a research topic in itself and would deserve a detailed survey of its own. However, it is interesting to provide a compass to orient one in the presently achieved results in order to identify open problems and promising research lines. In particular, the final chapter provides more detailed considerations about possible future developments.

INTRODUCTION

The aim of this book is to discuss the main open issues regarding face recognition. While results in controlled settings are quite satisfying, the most interesting challenges are presently related to adverse/uncontrolled conditions. New and most accurate sensors can be part of the solution. As 3D techniques become more affordable, both computationally and economically, they are more and more often proposed as a viable alternative as well as complement to 2D approaches. However, 3D is not always available or feasible. New models

are being investigated to identify features allowing to better address recognition problems in noisy environments and with unaware/non cooperative users, even in 2D. Such models often imply local approaches to recognition, whereas global ones seem to suffer more for Pose, Illumination and Expression (PIE) distortions commonly found in real uncontrolled situations. Suitable normalization procedures, for pose or illumination, can be applied both in global and local approaches. However, disguise variations, e.g. variations due to plastic surgery or make-up, seem to be better addressed through local approaches. A promising

DOI: 10.4018/978-1-4666-5966-7.ch018

line of research implies using more classifiers, with different strengths and flaws, or even more biometric traits, to improve the final accuracy through intelligent information fusion.

Given the list of possible solutions to present problems, it is also interesting to consider the set of advanced applications that can take advantage of the new face recognition performance. Ambient intelligence, tracking in critical environments, automatic tagging of large image collections, advanced mobile facilities are only examples, while new applications may rise as technology advances. Regarding this, the Chapter "Real world applications: a Literature Survey" by Tistarelli and Lin has provided a sample of the challenging application of face recognition in present real world scenarios. This necessarily short overview has provided a shortlist of interesting applications, which may be useful to orientate those who are approaching this research field. Even though the study of face recognition techniques has been initially spurred by problems related to security and access control, nowadays the analysis of human faces can further support law enforcement, foster a more natural man-machine interaction, and also provide an aid to disabled people. Among emerging applications, a crucial requirement is to facilitate a better interaction. Therefore, also due to the specific operational settings where security is not the main issue, it is often the case that a high recognition accuracy may be sacrificed to rather achieve a higher flexibility and capability to deal with minimally constrained environments.

THE ROLE OF POSE

Pose variation is one of the great challenges for robust face recognition. We can divide techniques to address this problem in two broad categories: those only relying on 2D images and those using 3D models.

Methods based on 2D images were the first to be investigated (see for example Reisfeld and Yeshurun, 1998). In their simplest basic versions, those methods perform face normalization based on the location of the eyes and mouth. A two dimensional affine transformation is uniquely determined by three points. *Warp* is defined as the affine mapping of a face image determined by the location of the eyes and mouth in the given image and by the usual standard locations. In a more general case, if two given samples are well aligned, there exists an approximated linear mapping between the two images of the person captured under variable poses. In order for this mapping to be consistent for all subjects, it is required that their facial images are aligned pixel-wise. Since this kind of alignment is a problem in itself, the one actually performed usually relies on very few facial landmarks, such as the two eye centers. However, in this way face images are aligned quite coarsely, so that the assumption of linear mapping no longer holds theoretically.

A popular solution for dealing with the pose variations is to rely on real (or synthetized, i.e. virtual) multiple views of the subject face. Along this line we can mention the work by Vetter and Poggio (1997) who exploit a 2D example-based view synthesis approach to generate novel virtual views under multiple poses. Prior face knowledge is represented by different 2D views of prototype faces. The method assumes that the 3D shape of an object as well as its 2D projections can be represented by a linear combination of prototype objects. According to this, a rotated view of an object is a linear combination of the rotated views of the prototype objects. Thy exploit the concept of Linear Object Classes (LOC) to synthesize rotated views of facial images from a single example view. In particular, in LOC approach a facial image is first separated into a shape vector and a texture vector, and then LOC is applied to them separately to generate the virtual rotated images. These virtual views are highly dependent on the correspondence between the images. Again, building accurate pixel-wise correspondence between facial images is a difficult problem.

The approach by Chai *et al.* (2007) aims at addressing the inability of global linear methods in the case of coarse alignment. Starting from LOC approach, they present a piecewise linear solution, locally linear regression (LLR), to provide a satisfying approximation to the ground-truth nonlinear mapping. The method relies on the observation that linearity of the mapping can be increased on the patches obtained by partitioning the whole face surface, thanks to the consistency of the normal to the surface within the single patch, and to the possibility to achieve a better local alignment. A different approach is adopted in (Gonzalez-Jimenez & Alba-Castro, 2007). It uses a training set of sparse face meshes (62 points per image) to build a Point Distribution Model. The interesting elements of such model are the parameters controlling the perceived changes in shape due to turning and nodding of the head. Before comparing two meshes, either the pose parameters from both can be set to typical values of a frontal face, or one mesh adopts the pose parameters of the other one.

A different single image-based strategy is exploited by Face Analysis for Commercial Entities (FACE), proposed by De Marsico *et al.* (2013b). Here the extended Active Shape Model (STASM) algorithm (Milborrow and Nicolls, 2008) is used to extract a fixed subset of 14 landmark points, which are relevant for the kind of processing adopted, out of the 68 returned. STASM algorithm minimizes a global distance between candidate image points and their homologues located on a general model, which is learned during a training phase. The located points are used to reconstruct a "canonical" form for the face, to be better compared during recognition. The precision of the STASM location results depends on the amount of face distortion, therefore some aberrations are sometimes possible in the reconstruction of a frontal-like face, therefore FACE and similar

approaches may take advantage from improvements in this task.

A common problem of the above methods is that the nature of 2D linear transformations hardly captures variations due to 3D rotations, unless very limited.

The seminal work of Blanz and Vetter (1999) proposes to exploit a morphable to synthetize 3D faces and then be able to simulate their pose changes. This model was also evaluated during the Face Recognition Vendor Test (FRVT2002, Phillips *et al.*, 2003), and achieved good results. Later proposals, e.g., the one by Chai *et al.* (2005) and that by Asthana *et al.* (2011) extend this method using only sparse feature points. In general, 3D methods exploit sparse correspondences between 2D facial feature points and 3D model vertices, to densely map the non-frontal images onto the 3D textured model, and then rotating it to frontal view. To solve the pose-dependency of the required correspondences with 3D vertices, the approach by Asthana *et al.* (2011) exploits hand labeling to set up a pose-specific look-up table. As a further advancement, the work by Ding *et al.* (2012) presents a pose normalization algorithm that can handle continuous pose variations without manual operation. The hand labeling is avoided. An automatic method is first used to find pose-dependent correspondences between 2D facial feature points and 3D face model. The method is based on a multi-view version of random forest embedded active shape model (RFE- ASM, Wang *et al.*, 2011). The RFE-ASM automatically locates 88 facial feature points, and is claimed to allow a more robust texture representation than traditional active shape model. Then the algorithm densely maps each pixel in the face image onto the 3-D face model and rotates it till to reach the frontal view. Facial symmetry is finally exploited to fill possibly occluded face regions.

The problem of methods based on 3D models is still their computational cost, so that they are hardly suited for real time, online applications, like continuous re-identification or subject tracking in videosurveillance. In real practical situations, pose invariance remains one of the hardest challenges for uncontrolled face recognition. Directly or indirectly, this problem is connected to many chapters of this book, since it is common in many kinds of biometric applications involving face, and because a change of pose, besides distorting the appearance of a face, may also cause a change in illumination of some of its parts as well as a kind of self-occlusion.

THE ROLE OF ILLUMINATION

It has been proven since long, both experimentally (see for example Adini *et al.* (1997)) and theoretically (see for example Zhao and Chellappa (1999)) that the differences due to illumination variations can heavily influence, and degrade, face recognition performance. Not only the earliest methods, including for example Eigenface and Fisherface, but also SVM (Guo *et al.*, 2000) are highly sensitive to this kind of variations. Several algorithms have been proposed to address this problem. Among them, we can mention the methods based on the concept of Illumination Cone (Belhumeur & Kriegman, 1998; Georghiades *et al.*, 2001), special representations based on spherical harmonic (see for example Ramamoorthi and Hanrahan, 2001), and approaches based on quotient images (Shashua & Riklin-Raviv, 2001). On one hand, the performances of most of these methods are still not completely satisfying. On the other hand, many of them require assumptions about the light source, or in alternative need a large number of training samples. In order to reduce the impact of these two issues, variations have been proposed especially for the last class of methods. They include quotient image relighting (QIR) (Shan *et al.*, 2003), self-quotient image (SQI) (Wang *et al.*, 2004), and the total variation quotient image (TVQI) model (Chen *et al.*, 2005). In a comparison presented in the last referred work, the authors demonstrate the advantages of their

method which does not require training images, makes no assumption about the light source, and

does not require any alignment between images for illumination normalization, though achieving very good performance. Actually, alignment is a serious problem for many approaches. While a number of methods used for face recognition are based on wavelets transform (see for example Cao *et al.* (2012)), the work by Du and Ward (2005) exploits wavelets also in the pre-processing phase for normalizing illumination variations of face images prior to the automatic recognition. Wavelet decomposition provides different band information of face images, and the different band coefficients are manipulated separately. Differently from the popular histogram equalization method, it takes into account both contrast and edge enhancements simultaneously. Similar considerations are exploited in the work by Sellahewa and Jassim (2010). As a further example, the method for illumination compensation and normalization presented in (Chen *et al.*, 2006) uses Discrete Cosine Transform (DCT) in logarithmic domain. The Chapter "Illumination Invariant Face Recognition: A Survey" by Chan *et al.* has presented an extensive and up-to-date survey of the existing techniques to address these problems. It discusses both the conventional *passive* techniques, that attempt to solve the illumination problem by studying the visible light images in which face appearance has been affected by illumination variations, and the *active* techniques, that investigate face image modalities invariant to environmental illumination.

THE ROLE OF EXPRESSION

The third PIE factor, namely expression, is as hard, if not harder, than the others. It requires considering that the relevant subjects can often be captured in non-neutral expressions, most of all in uncontrolled settings such as videosurveillance, automatic face tagging, or continuous re-identification (to be sure for example that in a plane cockpit the place of the captain is not taken by an intruder). One way to address expression variation is to consider the amount of facial asymmetry in different individuals. Liu *et al.* (2003) classify the factors affecting facial symmetry as intrinsic, such as growth, injury, and age, and extrinsic, such as viewing orientation, illuminations, shadows, and highlights. In their work they investigate if intrinsic asymmetry is robust for automatic identification under expression variation. Differently from the other factors, expression variations might be interesting in themselves. As an example, one of the most interesting features of affective computing (Picard, 2003; Tao & Tan, 2005) is the ability of the system to automatically assess user reactions, also based on facial expressions, and to adapt its behavior accordingly in order to better address users' needs and preferences. As a matter of fact, automatic facial expression analysis has become a quite active research area, with applications in human–computer interaction, realistic synthesis of virtual faces (e.g., talking heads), image retrieval and automated analysis of human emotion during specific tasks or activities. Besides reflecting emotions, facial expressions also support social interaction (as communication backchannels, see Krauss *et al.*, 1977) and can reveal important physiological signals. An interesting survey by Fasel and Luettin (2003) discusses a number of methods for automatic facial expression analysis. A first important distinction reported therein is the one between facial expression recognition and emotion recognition. First of all, facial expressions are not only generated by emotions, and in a similar way emotions are not only revealed by facial expressions. Facial expression recognition aims at classifying facial motion and the (consequent) facial feature deformation in order to deal with classes that are purely based on visual appearance. On the other hand, human emotions result from both internal and external factors, and expression is only one of the channels through which they may (or may not) be externalized, which also include

voice, pose, gestures, special ways of directing gaze (e.g., as a sign of embarrassment or when lying). In practice, emotion recognition is rather an interpretation task, trying to assign a meaning to external appearance. Different approaches can be adopted for facial motion and deformation extraction, which have to address issues such as face normalization, facial expression dynamics and facial expression intensity, but also be robust towards environmental changes. In particular, in the mentioned work Fasel and Luettin introduce as key elements the location of facial actions, their intensity and their dynamics. Among these, due to significant inter-personal variations, facial expression intensities are difficult to determine in an absolute way without a reference to an image of the same subject with neutral expression. Also dynamics are quite difficult to determine, since as in all dynamic processes, like gesture and speech, it is sometimes difficult to determine in a continuous flow when the facial expression starts to arise and when the next one is to be considered. In particular, onset (attack), apex (sustain), and onset (relaxation) temporal parameters are relevant. This extends to the process of facial action recognition.

One of the seminal works in the field of facial action recognition is that by Ekman and Friesen (1978), which formalizes the so called Facial Action Coding System (FACS). FACS is a method, also used in psychological research, aiming at standardizing the description of changes in the facial expression in terms of (visually observable) activations of facial muscles. The changes are described with FACS in terms of action units (AUs), each of which corresponds to a distinct muscle or muscle group in a specific face region. It is assumed that AUs can be considered as facial phonemes, which once assembled form facial expressions. FACS also provides the rules for AU detection in a face image. According to authors' intentions, FACS is designed for human experts having a formal related training (FACS coders). Using its rules, a FACS coder should encode a facial expression in terms of the AUs that produce it. On the other hand, achieving a reliable AUs recognition by a computer using a 2D image is still a challenge, since AUs can occur in more than 7000 different combinations, many of which are difficult to detect in a still image (e.g., bulges caused for example by the tongue pushed under one of the lips, or a jetted jaw). Many works addressing the problem of AU recognition exploit sequence of images and/or recognize subsets of anatomically close sets of AUs. In the work by Tian *et al.* (2001) lip tracking, template matching and NNs are used to recognize 16 AUs occurring alone or in combination in sequences of nearly frontal face images. In the work by Bartlett *et al.* (2006) 20 AUs occurring in spontaneous expressions during discourse are recognized using either support vector machines or AdaBoost. For both classifiers, the output margin predicts action unit intensity. Another example is the work by Kapoor *et al.* (2003) which deals the AUs related to the upper part of the face (eyes and eyebrows), using pupil location and tracking. Differently from these, the work by Pantic and Rothkrantz (2004) approaches the problem in a different way, by using static images in both frontal and profile view. Going further along this line, Chapter "Facial Action Recognition in 2D and 3D" by Valstar *et al.* has extended facial action recognition in 2D and 3D.

UNCONSTRAINED FACE RECOGNITION: WHERE ARE WE? TECHNIQUES AND MODELS

As we have often underlined, face recognition research has a long history. However, most work prior to the last decade was focused on fully or relatively constrained environments. The same equipment was exploited to capture a whole dataset, and the above discussed PIE, as well as background variations, were either completely absent, or they were controlled at least, to the aim of studying in known conditions the factors possibly hindering recognition. Popular examples,

ordered when possible for increasing amount of distortion in captured images, are the following well-known datasets (all accessed 12/01/2013):

- **The Database of Faces (formerly The ORL Database of Faces):** http://www.cl.cam.ac.uk/research/dtg/attarchive/face-database.html
- **Yale Face Database:** http://vision.ucsd.edu/content/yale-face-database
- **CVL Face Database:** http://www.lrv.fri.uni-lj.si/facedb.html
- **The CMU Multi-PIE Face Database:** http://www.multipie.org/
- **AR Face Database:** http://www2.ece.ohio-state.edu/~aleix/ARdatabase.html
- **The Facial Recognition Technology (FERET) Database:** http://www.itl.nist.gov/iad/humanid/feret/feret_master.html
- **The FRGC Data Set:** http://www.nist.gov/itl/iad/ig/frgc.cfm
- **SCface - Surveillance Cameras Face Database:** http://scface.org
- **Labeled Faces in the Wild (LWF):** http://vis-www.cs.umass.edu/lfw/

Further emerging challenges regard the influence of demographics (see for example Klare *et al.*, 2012; De Riccio *et al.*, 2012), and of temporary as well as permanent face appearance variations due to makeup (Chen *et al.*, 2013) or plastic surgery (Singh *et al.*, 2009b, 2010). New datasets have been explicitly prepared to test recognition systems in such conditions:

- **EGA (Ethnicity, Gender, Age) Face Database:** http://biplab.unisa.it/EGA.html
- **Plastic Surgery Face Database:** http://research.iiitd.edu.in/groups/lab/facedatabases.html
- **Makeup In the Wild (MIW) Database:** http://www.antitza.com/makeup-datasets.html

The rise of the Internet, of social networks and of new kinds of applications requiring image tagging have made it possible, from one side, to gather larger and larger collections of face images in completely uncontrolled conditions. On the other side, the availability of such images and the new requirements related to them has raised the need for much more robust recognition techniques. Such collections are often referred to as "in the wild," from the first and still most popular database of this kind (Labeled Faces in the Wild – LWF – Huang *et al.*, 2007) which has been used for algorithm assessment. In such collections, faces come from a wide variety of sources, therefore from different capture devices, and most of all images were not acquired for the purpose of research. As a consequence, PIE variations as well as background, setting (indoor vs. outdoor), clothing, ethnicity, gender age, camera features, and other factors are not determined in advance. Moreover, any kind of grouping of different subjects in the same image makes the face location task even more challenging.

Many approaches use low-level visual features. For instance, we can mention Scale-Invariant Feature Transform (SIFT, see for example Luo *et al.*, (2007)), Histograms of Oriented Gradients (HOG, see for example Albiol *et al.*, 2004) or Local Binary Patterns (LBP, see for example Ahonen *et al.*, (2007)) and their variations that transforms raw pixels values into a better form for subsequent processing. Notwithstanding the often remarkable results which are achieved using such features, it is worth mentioning the spreading interest for biologically-inspired approaches, aiming at building artificial visual systems able to capture relevant aspects of the computational architecture of the brain, in order to try

mimicking its recognition abilities. The efforts to discover how visual computation is performed by the brain have a long history, starting from Fukushima's Neocognitron (1980) and proceeding with the study of visual cortex mechanisms performed by Poggio and his collaborators (among

the most recent works, see for example Serre *et al.*, (2007)). Along this line, the work by Cox and Pinto (2011) attempts a strategy to explore the range of possible "biologically-inspired" feature representations: an efficient screening approach chooses the best performing models for unconstrained face recognition, as represented by the LFW test set. Regarding features used for recognition, it is worth mentioning that a significant amount of research has been devoted to model their identification looking at the saccade pattern during human browsing of a scene, of an object or of a face. Among the first works, it is worth mentioning those by Takács and Wechsler (1998) and by Smeraldi *et al.* (1999). This research line is still active. Among the most recent works we can mention (Wei & Li, 2013).

Model used for face recognition play a crucial role in addressing unconstrained face recognition. We can roughly identify descriptor-based methods (e.g., the above mentioned SIFT, HOG or LBP), and subspace-based methods (in the wide literature, see for example Belkin and Niyogi, (2003), Liu *et al.* (2006), and Wang and Tang (2004)) as two extremely representative appearance-based approaches. While the descriptor-based methods aim at extracting discriminative information from the facial structure, the subspace-based algorithms rather aim at learning an optimal subspace for recognition. The common aspect of most appearance-based methods is the tradeoff between the discriminative ability and the invariance to intra-personal variation. The latter is often addressed by prior knowledge. As an example, the approach by Blanz and Vetter (2003) uses the prior morphable 3D models to simulate the 3D appearance transformation of the input face. Kumar *et al.* (2009) organize an extra identity data set as prior knowledge. In their work, similarity relations between identities are exploited to build a kind of high-level face representation, Simile Classifiers. This and similar methods do not consider the setting of the input faces, therefore still hardly deal with varying settings. To solve this flaw, Yin *et al.* (2011) compute an Associate-Predict model for each person. For each input face, they select a few most similar faces to train a specific classifier for the person, aiming at predicting her/his appearance in different settings and to use this information for recognition.

Chapters "Unconstrained Face Recognition" by Zafeiriou *et al.* and "Face recognition methods for uncontrolled settings" by Wechsler have presented an interesting review of approaches addressing this very challenging topics.

A possible solution to the problem of recognition in (adverse) uncontrolled conditions is to collect face images in all the possible conditions that may be anticipated to occur during normal system operation. This approach is expected to ensures that the "right" image for the correct recognition is always available in the system. This is the principle of galleries containing more templates for the same subject, possibly the most representative ones, i.e., those increasing the amount of information about the subject (De Marsico *et al.*, 2013a). This is somewhat difficult to accomplish, since it is not always possible either to predict all the possible distortions in advance, or to capture the necessary images. Alternative solution rely on suitable normalization or "canonicalization" procedure (De Marsico *et al.*, 2013b). However, the higher the distortion, the easier to obtain some "aberration" in the result. A further approach is to use multiple experts. The individually best solution is substituted by a set of solutions to the same recognition problem. Multi-expert fusion can be addressed in different ways, e.g., by combining all results or by selecting only the best before combination. It can be demonstrated that even better accuracy can be achieved if the experts collaborate with each other according to information exchange protocols (De Marsico *et al.*, 2012). In Chapter "Fusion of face recognition classifiers under adverse conditions" by Poh *et al.*, a quality-based multi-expert fusion approach (Poh *et al.*, 2010; Poh & Kittler, 2012) is adopted for face recognition.

3D-BASED TECHNIQUES: ACCURACY VS. COST?

As widely assessed, 3D information may offer great support for improving recognition performance. As a matter of fact, in (Xu *et al.*, 2004) the authors demonstrated that (3D) depth maps a more robust face representation, less affected by illumination changes, than (2D) intensity images. A 3D model, either built exploiting range data or by a polygonal mesh, retains much more information about the complete face geometry, in particular local and global curvatures that make up the real signature which identifies a specific person. The two most commonly used face models in 3D applications are 2.5D and 3D images. A 2.5D image (a popular name for range images) is a two-dimensional representation of a set of 3D points in the form (x, y, z): each pixel in the X-Y plane stores the depth value z, like in a grey-scale image. The final 2.5D image depends both on the subject appearance as well as environmental conditions. The whole head model results from taking several scans from different viewpoints. The 3D images are instead a global representation of the head, where the facial surface is related to the internal anatomical structure. 2.5D and 3D images also differ because the latter are not affected by self-occlusions of the face, when the pose is not full-frontal. The simplest 3D face representation is a 3D polygonal mesh, consisting of a list of points (vertices) connected by edges; vertices and edges from the polygons. The most popular ways to build a 3D mesh are combining several 2.5D images, exploiting a morphable model or using a 3D scanner. Despite the asserted robustness of 3D models, it is to say that aligning them might be computationally very expensive, and that the assertion that 3D data acquisition is light independent is questionable; 3D sensors could be affected by a strong light source or by reflective surfaces, so it is reasonable to expect that different light sources might generate quite different 3D data sets. Among the methods exploiting 3D, we can distinguish those which are still based on comparisons among 2D intensity images, yet supported by some 3D data to increase the system robustness (Blanz & Vetter, 2003), those purely based on 3D facial representations, like range images or meshes, where the first problem to address is alignment (e.g., methods exploiting Iterative Closest Point – ICP, such as Cook et al. (2004)), and those combining 2D and 3D image information. The main problem with ICP is its computational cost and, when the models are strongly unaligned, it may also lack convergence. A possible alternative was presented by Abate et al. (2007), who use Pyramidal Normal map Metric to achieve fast £D face alignment. Among the first systematic attempts to asses the combined 2D-3D strategy, we can mention the work by Chang et al. (2003a), where 2D and 3D data are used in a kind of multi-biometric scheme. The chapter "3D Face Recognition in the Presence of Partial Data: A Semi-Coupled Dictionary Learning Approach" by Chu et al. has presented a new technique for computing the distance between two biometric signatures with insufficient training data available, or with gallery images originating from one side of the face while the probe images originates from the other one. Chapter "3D Face Recognition using Spatial Relations" by Berretti *et al.* has briefly surveyed of the main methodologies for 3D face recognition, shortly reviewing the related literature by distinguishing between global and local approaches, in order to introduce an original proposal. The presence of occlusions is, together with pose variations, one of the main factors hindering face recognition. Significant alterations of the geometry complicate the identification process by affecting all involved processes such as face detection, landmark localization, coarse and fine registration, and feature extraction. Chapter "Robust 3D Face Identification in the Presence of Occlusions" by Alyuz *at al.* has presented both available datasets and a case study to better illustrate this specific problem.

The main problem with 3D-based approaches is that the accuracy of most 3D reconstruction techniques depends on both the cooperation of the subjects to be recognized, and on an accurate calibration and synchronization of all the elements of the system. Of course both requirements are hardly met in most uncontrolled settings, e.g. video surveillance applications or automatic tagging of large image collections, where sometimes only an intensity 2D image of the face is available for recognition. Many approaches try to exploit mixed strategies. The effort underlying many research approaches is focused on devising flexible methods to integrate 2D (always available) and 3D (possibly available only at enrollment) information. A possible solution relies on geometric invariants (Riccio & Dugelay, 2007). A further one relies on Partial Principal Component Analysis (P^2CA) proposed Rama and Tarrés in 2005 and improved in following papers (Rama *et al.*, 2006, 2008). As in conventional PCA the dimensionality of the face images is reduced through the projection onto a set of M optimal vectors. The main difference is that the whole image is represented as a 2D matrix instead of a 1D vector arrangement. Therefore requiring to reformulate the optimization problem for finding the projection vectors. The method uses 3D data for the description of the images on the database but may process faces using either 3D or 2D in the recognition stage. However, it requires to compute a cylindrical representation of the 3D face data for training and therefore including new subjects in the database. The work by Yang *et al.* (2008) rather uses the canonical correlation analysis (CCA, Hotelling, 1936) to learn the mapping between the 2D face image and 3D face model. The method includes two phases. In the learning phase, PCA is applied on both 2D face image and 3D face model making the pair of training data for each subject. Afterwards, the CCA regression is performed between features of 2D-3D in the PCA subspaces previously determined. The learnt regression is exploited in the recognition phase, when, given an input 2D face image as probe, the correlation between the probe and the gallery is computed using it. Despite the attempt to avoid the use of 3D data during recognition, this is necessary in a preliminary phase at least, and this heavily limits the use of these techniques in cases like re-identification and tagging of large image collections (see Chapters "Face in Person Re-Identification" by Abate *et al.*, and "Automatic face image tagging in large collections" by Barra *et al.*) where no preliminary enrollment of relevant subjects is generally possible, and training can only rely on faces which are not necessarily those that will be involved in recognition.

GLOBAL VS. LOCAL APPROACHES

Face recognition methods can be generally divided into two gross categories: global (or holistic) methods and local (or component-based) methods. Global approaches use the whole face region as the input to a recognition system. The practical principle is to construct a subspace to be used for projection of probes and matching. Among the most popular methods we can mention Principal Component Analysis (PCA, for the pioneering works see Kirby and Sirovich (1990), and Turk and Pentland (1991)), Linear Discriminant Analysis (LDA, see Etemand and Chellappa, 1997), Independent Component Analysis (ICA, see Bartlett *et al.* (2002)) and all their variations which have been proposed along the years in order to improve their performance in presence of PIE distortions. We can also mention different projection methods, like Neighborhood Preserving Embedding (NPE, He *at al*,), which aim at preserving the local neighborhood structure on the data manifold instead of the global Euclidean structure of the subspace. On the other hand, a number of research results seem to indicate that the face images possibly reside on a nonlinear submanifold, as for example the work by Roweis and Saul (2000) introducing Locally Linear Embedding (LLE). Locality Preserving Projections (LPP, He and Niyogi (2004)) share many of the data representation properties of non-linear techniques such LLE though being linear.

Given the problems affecting global methods, local matching approaches have also been investigated. The achieved results seem quite promising, not only in face recognition (Martinez, 2002; Ahonen *et al.*, 2004; Kim *et al.*, 2005). The idea underlying local matching methods is to first locate facial components, extract features from them, and then classify the faces by comparing and combining the corresponding local statistics. Heisele *et al.* (2003) directly compared local and global approaches focusing on the pose problem, and observed that the former significantly outperform the latter. The increasing interest in local methods has also inspired surveys like the one by Zou *et al.* (2007). It is to underline that multicomponent approaches inherit issues like normalization, fusion, and reliability of single responses. Most researches stop once regions and fusion modalities have been fixed, and limit results to certifying the superiority of component-based approaches. A partial exception is the work by Harandi *et al.* (2007). They explore the hierarchical combination of a global system with a component-based one: the latter activates when the former cannot return a response with a sufficient score; the limit is that the component-based step is not started if the first system chooses the wrong class, yet with high confidence. Along a similar line, the work by Su *et al.* (2009) investigates the use of a hierarchical ensemble of global and local classifiers. The work by De Marsico *et al.* (2009) goes further, by proposing to process each face component as a separate biometrics. To this aim, it systematically investigates the possibilities to combine single scores produced by facial components, in terms of fusion levels, integration schemes, and reliability margins. The paper therefore defines a framework integrating the main concepts of both component-based facial recognition and of multimodal authentication. Chapter "Local vs global: Intelligent Local Face Recognition" by Riccio *et al.* has offered further discussion about this aspect of face recognition.

UNVOLUNTARY OR MALICIOUS DISGUISE

Enhancing one's appearance by make-up, hairstyle or headdress is something that goes back to the mists of time. The desire to feel and appear more attractive or more threatening has inspired thousands of strategies and accessories, including make-up for women and beards and mustaches for men. Even more tricks have been devised to conceal ones identity to escape or to commit crimes. Notwithstanding the human ability to recognize a known person, these factors may make recognition difficult also in familiar settings. Among the first works addressing the problem of disguise in face recognition we can mention that by Alexander and Smith (2003). They build a system that treats training images as vectors, stacked into a matrix, and estimates eigenvectors for such matrix using the classical principal component analysis (PCA). Probe images are projected into the "face space." The distance metric used is the "Mahalanobis angle," which takes the "cosine" similarity measure and scales each axis in face space according to the actual variance in the data along that axis. Silva and Rosa (2003) propose Eigen-eyes to handle different problems found in face recognition including disguise. Ramanathan *et al.* (2004) address face variations including disguise by treating the two halves of the face separately, by forming two eigenspaces from them. The best illuminated half face from a probe is chosen and is projected onto the eigenspace. Singh *et al.* (2008, 2009a) classify variations (excluding minimal ones due to time elapse) in those due to hair style, to beard and moustache, to glasses, to cap and hat, to lips, eyebrows and nose, to aging and wrinkles, or to a combination. They also create a synthetic face disguise database to simulate these kinds of variations and test their methods on them. Recent works also focus on the effect of make-up: for example Chen *et al.* (2013) address this problem and also propose to use a database collected from Internet makeup tutorials to assess the robustness of algorithms with respect to this element. Furthermore, nowadays the so called beautification process has gone digital. It is possible to improve the look of a person in a photo by appropriate software algorithms, as discussed for example by Leyvand *et al.* (2008). Beautification performed on celebrities photographs, e.g., by ADOBE PHOTOSHOP, may hinder their automatic tagging, i.e., the automatic recognition to label, say, the photographical archive of a magazine editorial office. This kind of beautification operation often produce just a gentle smoothing of unpleasantly and maybe temporarily marked features (e.g. wrinkles, or dark rings under one's eyes). On the other hand, beautification performed through plastic surgery has concrete and definitive effects, which may significantly hinder also security controls. The taxonomy made by Singh *et al.* (2209b, 2010) categorizes the apparent effects ("regions affected and how") of this kind of operations. The experimental results in the work by De Marsico *et al.* (2011) support the hypothesis that local approaches can better address also this kind of variations. Chapter "Recognizing Face Images With Disguise Variations" by: Kose *et al.* has provided a discussion about this topic and a review of existing databases supporting related research.

MULTIMODAL SOLUTIONS

Systems relying on a single biometrics suffer from a number of problems related to the trait they process (for instance, PIE variations hindering face recognition, or alterations due to a cold for voice recognition, or the possible non-universality of that biometric feature, e.g., voice recognition with deaf-mute subjects) as well as to acquisition errors, or limitations of the algorithms they implement. Moreover, they are also more vulnerable to possible spoofing and disguise attacks. In a multimodal system, flaws of a single-biometric subsystem can be compensated by the others.

Specific architectures can combine more recognition modules into multimodal systems. Dealing with any mixed combination of physical as well as behavioral traits. The choice of biometrics, the kind of performed normalization of results and the protocol used for integration are the main issues to address. The most natural candidates for a multimodal system including face, are those traits that can be captured in a single operation. Since we focus on the strategies to perform recognition under uncontrolled data acquisition conditions (ideally fully covert ones), it is out of our scope to mention all those multimodal proposals which would imply an aware user participation, e.g. recognition involving some combination of face with fingerprint, or palmprint, or signature (notice that almost any combination is present in literature). While these systems are obviously able to significantly increase performance of identification for aware and somehow collaborative users, they are of course not feasible for the kind of settings that we are addressing here. The systems that we will shortly describe rather join face recognition with ear or gait, which can be acquired even at a reasonable distance without user participation. In many cases, the true novelty of presented methods is in the kind of fusion they adopt, rather than in the techniques exploited for the single modalities. Fusion in a multibiometric system may be performed at feature-level, by combining different (compatible) templates, and training a specific system on the obtained combination. This approach is the most expensive one, but fully preserves all the original information. Fusion at matching score or ranking level is the preferred solution, because already existing unimodal systems can be exploited . Moreover, enough information is still present in the result (e.g., a list of scores or ranks). Finally, fusion can be performed at decision level, which is the cheapest one, but lacks any useful information to possibly identify possible problems from any system.

Among the first results of combining face and ear biometrics we find those in the work by Chang *et al.* (2003b). Combination experiments exploit a very simple feature-level combination technique. The images of the ear and face are normalized are concatenated to form a combined face-plus-ear image. These new images undergo PCA processing. A similar approach is used by Yuan *et al.* (2007), with the difference that users are chimeric ones, i.e. faces and ears come from different databases. This was a quite common practice when multimodal databases were lacking. Feature vectors are extracted from chained images using Full-Space Linear Discriminant Analysis (FSLDA).

Face and ear are matched separately in (Kisku et al., 2009), and face is captured in frontal pose. For localization of ear region, relevant points are detected manually on ear image, and then used to apply a complete ear localization technique. Both face and ear are cropped from the respective images. After geometric normalization and histogram equalization, face and ear images are convolved with Gabor wavelet filters to extract spatially enhanced Gabor features for both.

Face and 3D ear are fused by Cadavid *at al.* (2009). For the 2D face recognition, a set of facial landmarks is extracted using Active Shape Model technique. A series of Gabor filters are applied at the locations of facial landmarks, and the responses are calculated. The Gabor features are stored in the database as the face model, and are compared with those extracted from a probe image during testing. The match scores of the ear recognition and face recognition are fused at score level using a weighted sum to fuse the results after normalizing them.

The work presented in (Javadtalab *et al.*, 2011) addresses identification during video conferences using face and ear. Face features include color features, computed in Hue, Saturation and Value (HSV) color space, and 2D wavelet based features, approximated by Generalized Gaussian Density (GGD). For ear, only GGD is used. The Kullback-Leibler Distance (KLD) is used to match GGD features from both traits on probe and gallery templates. Fusion exploits min-max normalization and sum rule.

Profile face image may contain less discriminant information than frontal view. Nevertheless, it contains the ear, which can be used as well if the system includes this possibility, and also some complementary features with respect to frontal ones (e.g., the profile shape of the nose). Among the works addressing ear and profile phase fusion, one of the earliest is presented by Yuan *et al.* (2006). There is no need for a fusion step, since the face profile silhouette is already combined with the ear in a single image. Actually, considering also the ear region is a way to overcome the limitation of many recognition techniques based on face profile. Such techniques usually rely on a number of fiducial points and on their relations. However, their reliability decreases with special features such as a concave nose, protruding lips, or a flat chin. Furthermore, the number and position of fiducial points may vary with expression changes even for the same person. Full-Space Linear Discriminant Analysis (FSLDA) is therefore applied here to the profile image containing the ear region too.

A mixed solution between fully controlled settings and the relaxation of some related constraint is an equipped "'biometric tunnel'", like the University of Southampton Multi-Biometric Tunnel (Seely *et al.*, 2008). It is a constrained environment designed to address the requirements of airports and other high throughput settings. It can acquire a number of contactless biometrics in a nonintrusive manner and with not much participation by the user, who is aware of the acquisition process anyway. The system uses synchronized cameras to capture gait and additional cameras to capture images from the face and one ear, as an individual walks through the tunnel. The path allowed to the subject is quite narrow and inside a volume where illumination and other conditions are controlled.

Ear, face and gait are exploited by Yazdanpanah *et al.* (2010). For each modality, feature extraction creates a Gabor wavelet representation, processed by principal component analysis (PCA). During matching step, after normalization, fusion is performed at score level.

In their proposal, Monwar *et al.* (2011), fuse face, ear and iris scores using a fuzzy approach. In the identification phase, the input face and ear images are compared with the gallery images by Fisherfaces and Fisherears, and measuring the Euclidian distance, while for iris the Hamming distance between the iris codes is computed. In each of the three cases, the first five identifiers are obtained as output that will be ranked according to their distances. These are then passed to a fuzzy fusion module along with their normalized scores. A further contribution comes from the normalized scores from soft biometrics on the face, namely gender, ethnicity and color of the eyes. During identification, the soft biometric information of input identifiers is fed into the fusion module.

The work by Muramatsu *et al.* (2013) exploits a walking video sequences to combine multiple hard and soft biometrics. As a matter of fact, face and gait, which are often fused in multimodal systems, are also complemented with subject's height. Single frames contain all three information. On the other hand, the availability of more frames in the same sequence is exploited to set-up a multi-view face recognition as well as multi-view gait recognition, therefore merging in a unifying approach the multi-view and the multi-modal strategies.

Following a complementary trend, a quite recent research line focuses on using the periocular region. Even in this case, the aim is to address problems related to face distortions. The choice for this specific area in the vicinity of the eye is due to a number of factors: it does not require either constrained or close capturing, or user cooperation, recent tests report that it is relatively stable, when compared to the whole face, and it is naturally rarely occluded. It can also be easily acquired with a single camera together with iris, and fused at the score level to compensate for environmental adversities and uncooperative subjects. Periocular information has even proven helpful in scenarios where the face has been *reshaped* (*e.g.* plastic surgery), with interesting results (Jillela & Ross, 2012; Bhatt, Bharadwaj, Singh, & Vatsa, 2013).

Chapter "Using Ocular Data for Unconstrained Biometric Recognition" by Proença *et al.* has presented a review of present approaches to the use of periocular region in biometric recognition.

ADVANCED AND EMERGING APPLICATIONS

On one side, the increasing availability of quite cheap capture equipment has encouraged both the research in new fields and the implementation of novel methodologies for biometric recognition. On the other side it has also inspired new expectations from users, which in turn continuously spur new research lines therefore closing a virtuous circle. Face recognition plays a significant role in this scenario, due to the possibility to capture face images even at a distance and without user collaboration. It is more and more often used for authentication and security applications, like for example recognition of relevant subjects (white as well as black lists) or subject tracking in video-surveillance. However, it is also becoming a privileged approach also for applications in the field of affective computing and ambient intelligence. Moreover, again thanks to technological advancements, face recognition is going mobile, so that a number of useful tools, like home banking, can migrate on devices like smart phones or tablets.

Real-time detection and tracking of human faces in videos is often a key component of automatic video surveillance and monitoring systems (Lipton *et al.*, 2000). In general, an appearance model is joined to a statistical model to anticipate possible variations of the subject appearance in the following frames. Its role is usually to feed

higher-level processing such as access control, or re-identification, or also the analysis and classification of human activities. The latter has long interested researchers (Aggarwal & Cai, 1997; Gavrila, 1999). An example is the work by Comaniciu and Ramesh (2000). Tracking and re-identification are addressed in Gandhi and Trivedi (2007) and Hamdoun et al. (2008). Re-identification based on face recognition is addressed in Chapter "Face in Person Re-Identification" by Abate *et al.* Moreover, Chapter "Methods and perspectives in face tracking based on human perception" by Bruni and Vitulano analyzes the role of human early vision in face perception, recognition and tracking, particularly focusing on some neurological results that have been successfully used in face detection and recognition.

We have already outlined some considerations about affective computing. Very interesting surveys about this topic can be found in Tao and Tan (2007) and in Pantic et al. (2007). Affective computing aims at making computers able to reproduce some (elementary) human-like abilities of observation, interpretation and generation of affective interaction features. Actually, it sounds strange to link the term "affect" to machines, however a number of disciplines, such as psychology, cognitive sciences, physiology and computer sciences, try to create a multidisciplinary background. This should suggest inference rules to capture and decode various sensors information, to attempt an interpretation of human's feeling and to mimic an intelligent response. This makes foresee a wide spectrum of promising applications in different areas such as advanced human-computer interaction, virtual reality and surveillance. Emotional speech processing, interpretation of facial expression, body gesture and movement, and affect understanding and generating, are key technologies as well as research fields to achieve the mentioned goals. Advanced "intelligent" interfaces should go well beyond the traditional keyboard and mouse to reach natural, human-like communication channels and interactive functions.

The latter ones include understanding and emulating certain human behaviors such as affective and social signaling (backchannels). In practice, information about human behavioral signals, like language prosody, nonlinguistic conversational signal, like face expression, and in summary emotion, attitude, mood, should be appropriately processed, analyzed, and possibly reproduced in similar interaction situations. In this context, facial expression plays an important role.

Like affective computing, even the concept of "ambient intelligence" involves the convergence of several computing areas (Shadbolt, 2003). Ubiquitous or pervasive computing contributes to the development of ad hoc networking capabilities that exploit highly portable, possibly numerous, very-low-cost computing devices. Intelligent systems research provides learning algorithms and pattern matchers, able to perform speech recognition, language translation, gesture classification, but also possibly user recognition. Context awareness allows detecting and tracking objects of all types and representing objects' interactions among them and with their environments. A special role is deserved by user recognition, since it allows a fine-grain personalization of a number of ambient services/actions/reactions based on the identity of the (registered) subject identified in the equipped ambient from time to time. Due to its ability to work at a distance and in uncontrolled conditions, face recognition is a privileged tool (Cook *et al.*, 2009). Chapter "Human face region detection driving activity recognition in video" by Doulamis *et al.* deals with the problem of face region detection driving activity recognition in video.

A further emerging kind of applications is based on automatic face tagging in large/very large collections of photos. The main use of them in the context of social networks is to organize personal photo galleries. In this case, the amount of samples to process might be reasonably limited, and most of all related to an equally limited number of classes (persons). If the social network server automatically provides this service, the identity of the photographer, who is the person who usually stored a photo, the recognition system can exploit this person's surrounding social context to reduce the set of possible candidate identity labels that is considered for each detected face in each photo. Moreover, co-occurrence of an individual's friends in past photos may be relevant for predicting co-occurrence in new photos. Using real photo collections from volunteers who are members of a popular online social network, Stone et al. (2010) asses the availability of resources to support the improvement of face recognition and discuss techniques relying on the application of these resources. On the other hand, if the same kind of task is carried out in the context of the editorial photo collection of a magazine publishing company, this is much more demanding and error-prone, though exploiting advanced clustering and recognition techniques, due to the concurrent significant growth of both the collection size and of the number of relevant subjects. Chapter "Automatic face image tagging in large collections" by Barra *et al.* deals with these topics.

Nowadays mobile devices (in this context we refer to smart phones and tablets) maintain a lot of private information, from personal photographs to personal notes till to payment information. In some countries, (Near Field Communication), both thanks to NFC, technology and to Web-based banking services, people are starting to use cellular phones as means of payment. Therefore, security and authentication have become an issue to be addressed as in desktop equipment. A good password should be complicated and long enough to assure security, however it is troublesome for users to type such a long password, especially on keys of limited size. To solve both security and usability problem simultaneously, various types of biometric solutions have been proposed. Among these, thanks to the presence of on-board cameras in all smart phones, face recognition is one of the most appreciated ones (Ijiri *et al.,* 2006).

Mobile devices, and in particular smart phones and tablets, represent a challenging setting for face recognition. As a matter of fact, despite the continuous improvement of hardware equipment and of computational resources, their possible achievable performance cannot be compared with that of desktop or server processing devices yet. Therefore, from one side implementation of (face) authentication techniques on them can usually rely on user cooperation. However, the reverse side of the medal is that most techniques must be adapted to a setting with reduced resources. Nowadays, this still dramatically limits the range of approaches that can be reasonably ported on mobile devices. The recent MOBIO (Mobile Biometry) challenge (Marcel *et al.*, 2010) just aimed at evaluating face and speaker verification on mobile devices. Chapter "Secure Face Recognition for Mobile Applications" by Lovell and Smith discusses the different ways that face recognition can be used on smart mobile devices.

CONCLUSION

This closing chapter has presented a bird's eye view on the main issues related to face recognition, focusing on uncontrolled conditions, as well as on the emerging fields where related techniques are playing a more and more important role. As results evident form the topics addressed throughout the book, many problems are still open in this area. PIE variations are still a very rich source for research, and further the investigation of new factors emerge, like ethnicity (Klare *et al.*, 2012; De Marsico *et al.*, 2013c) and disguise. Technology moves forward, and therefore hardware becomes more and more reliable and capture devices produce samples of higher and higher quality. However, just for this reason, and given that "appetite comes with eating," as solutions to old problems are found, more challenges raise from new needs and from new research hypotheses. Our aim was to spur the emergence of the latter. Now that we have an

idea of the present state of the art, the obvious questions is "Where do we go from here?" The search for an answer is a challenge in itself. It will depend day by day from unpredictable scientific discoveries, both in the filed of new materials and technologies, and in the field of new mathematical and algorithmic approaches to present and future problems.

REFERENCES

Abate, A. F., Nappi, M., Ricciardi, S., & Sabatino, G. (2007). Fast 3D Face Alignment and Improved Recognition Through Pyramidal Normal map Metric. In *Proceedings of IEEE International Conference on Image Processing, ICIP 2007* (vol. 1, pp. 157-160). IEEE.

Adini, Y., Moses, Y., & Ullman, S. (1997). Face recognition: The problem of compensating for changes in illumination direction. *IEEE Transactions on Pattern Analysis and Machine Intelligence, 19*(7), 721–732. doi:10.1109/34.598229

Aggarwal, J. K., & Cai, Q. (1997). Human motion analysis: A review. In *Proceedings of IEEE Nonrigid and Articulated Motion Workshop* (pp. 90-102). IEEE.

Ahonen, T., Hadid, A., & Pietikainen, M. (2004). Face recognition with local binary patterns. In *Proceedings of European Conference on Computer Vision, ECCV 2004* (pp. 469–481). ECCV.

Ahonen, T., Hadid, A., & Pietikainen, M. (2006). Face Description with Local Binary Patterns: Application to Face Recognition. *IEEE Transactions on Pattern Analysis and Machine Intelligence, 28*(12), 2037–2041. doi:10.1109/TPAMI.2006.244 PMID:17108377

Albiol, A., Monzo, D., Martin, A., Sastre, J., & Albiol, A. (2008). Face recognition using HOG–EBGM. *Pattern Recognition Letters, 29*(10), 1537–1543. doi:10.1016/j.patrec.2008.03.017

Alexander, J., & Smith, J. (2003). Engineering privacy in public: Confounding face recognition, privacy enhancing technologies. In *Proceedings of International Workshop on Privacy Enhancing Technologies*, (pp. 88–106). Academic Press.

Alyuz, N., Gokberk, B., & Akarun, L. (2008). A 3D Face Recognition System for Expression and Occlusion Invariance. In *Proceedings of 2nd IEEE International Conference on Biometrics: Theory, Applications and Systems, 2008. BTAS 2008* (pp. 1-7). IEEE.

Alyuz, N., Gokberk, B., Spreeuwers, L., Veldhuis, R., & Akarun, L. (2012). Robust 3D face recognition in the presence of realistic occlusions. In *Proceedings of 2012 5th IAPR International Conference on Biometrics (ICB)* (pp. 111-118). IAPR.

Asthana, A., Marks, T. K., Jones, M. J., & Tieu, K. H. (2011). Fully automatic pose-invariant face recognition via 3D pose normalization. In *Proceedings of 2011 IEEE International Conference on Computer Vision, ICCV* (pp. 937–944). IEEE.

Bartlett, M. S., Littlewort, G., Frank, M., Lainscsek, C., Fasel, I., & Movellan, J. (2006). Fully Automatic Facial Action Recognition in Spontaneous Behavior. In *Proceedings of 7th International Conference on Automatic Face and Gesture Recognition*, (pp. 223-230). Academic Press.

Bartlett, M. S., Movellan, J. R., & Sejnowski, T. J. (2002). Face recognition by independent component analysis. *IEEE Transactions on Neural Networks*, *13*(6), 1450–1464. doi:10.1109/TNN.2002.804287 PMID:18244540

Belhumeur, P. N., & Kriegman, D. J. (1998). What is the set of images of an object under all possible lighting conditions? *International Journal of Computer Vision*, *28*(3), 245–260. doi:10.1023/A:1008005721484

Belkin, M., & Niyogi, P. (2003). Laplacian eigenmaps for dimensionality reduction and data representation. *Neural Computation*, *15*(6), 1373–1396. doi:10.1162/089976603321780317

Bhatt, H. S., Bharadwaj, S., Singh, R., & Vatsa, M. (2013). Recognizing Surgically Altered Face Images Using Multiobjective Evolutionary Algorithm. *IEEE Transactions on Information Forensics and Security*, *8*(1), 89–100. doi:10.1109/TIFS.2012.2223684

Blanz, V., & Vetter, T. (1999). A morphable model for the synthesis of 3D faces. [ACM.]. *Proceedings of SIGGRAPH*, *1999*, 187–194.

Blanz, V., & Vetter, T. (2003). Face recognition based on fitting a 3D morphable model. *IEEE Transactions on Pattern Analysis and Machine Intelligence*, *25*(9), 1063–1074. doi:10.1109/TPAMI.2003.1227983

Cadavid, S., Mahoor, M. H., & Abdel-Mottaleb, M. (2009). Multi-modal biometric modeling and recognition of the human face and ear. In *Proceedings of IEEE International Workshop on Safety, Security & Rescue Robotics - SSRR 2009* (pp. 1–6). IEEE.

Cao, X., Shen, W., Yu, L. G., Wang, Y. L., Yang, J. Y., & Zhang, Z. W. (2012). Illumination invariant extraction for face recognition using neighboring wavelet coefficients. *Pattern Recognition*, *45*(4), 1299–1305. doi:10.1016/j.patcog.2011.09.010

Chai, X., Qing, L., Shan, S., Chen, X., & Gao, W. (2005). Pose invariant face recognition under arbitrary illumination based on 3D face reconstruction. In Audio- and Video-Based Biometric Person Authentication (pp. 956–965). Academic Press.

Chai, X., Shan, S., Chen, X., & Gao, W. (2007). Locally linear regression for pose-invariant face recognition. *IEEE Transactions on Image Processing*, *16*(7), 1716–1725. doi:10.1109/TIP.2007.899195 PMID:17605371

Chang, K., Bowyer, K., & Flynn, P. (2003a). Face Recognition using 2D and 3D facial data. In *Proceedings of ACM Workshop on Multimodal User Authentication* (pp. 25–32). ACM.

Chang, K., Victor, B., Bowyer, K. W., & Sarkar, S. (2003b). Comparison and Combination of Ear and Face Images in Appearance-Based Biometrics. *IEEE Transactions on Pattern Analysis and Machine Intelligence, 25*(8), 1160–1165. doi:10.1109/TPAMI.2003.1227990

Chen, C., Dantcheva, A., & Ross, A. (2013). Automatic facial makeup detection with application in face recognition. In *Proceedings of International Conference on Biometrics, ICB 2013* (pp. 1-8). ICB.

Chen, T., Yin, W., Zhou, X. S., Comaniciu, D., & Huang, T. S. (2005). Illumination normalization for face recognition and uneven background correction using total variation based image models. In *Proceedings of IEEE Computer Society Conference on Computer Vision and Pattern Recognition,* (vol. 2, pp. 532-539). IEEE.

Chen, W., Er, & Wu. (2006). Illumination compensation and normalization for robust face recognition using discrete cosine transform in logarithm domain. *IEEE Transactions on Systems, Man, and Cybernetics. Part B, Cybernetics, 36*(2), 458–466. doi:10.1109/TSMCB.2005.857353 PMID:16602604

Comaniciu, D., & Ramesh, V. (2000). Robust detection and tracking of human faces with an active camera. In *Proceedings Third IEEE International Workshop on Visual Surveillance, 2000* (pp. 11-18). IEEE.

Cook, D. J., Augusto, J. C., & Jakkula, V. R. (2009). Ambient intelligence: Technologies, applications, and opportunities. *Pervasive and Mobile Computing, 5*(4), 277–298. doi:10.1016/j.pmcj.2009.04.001

Cook, J., Chandran, V., Sridharan, S., & Fookes, C. (2004). Face recognition from 3D data using iterative closest point algorithm and Gaussian mixture models. In *Proceedings of International Symposium on 3D Data Processing, Visualization and Transmission, 3DPVT 2004* (pp. 502-509). 3DPVT.

Cox, D., & Pinto, N. (2011). Beyond simple features: A large-scale feature search approach to unconstrained face recognition. In *Proceedings of 2011 IEEE International Conference on Automatic Face & Gesture Recognition and Workshops (FG 2011)* (pp. 8-15). IEEE.

De Marsico, M., Nappi, M., & Riccio, D. (2009). A Self-tuning People Identification System from Split Face Components. In *Proceedings of Advances in Image and Video Technology - Third Pacific Rim Symposium, PSIVT 2009,* (LNCS) (vol. 5414, pp. 1–12). Berlin: Springer.

De Marsico, M., Nappi, M., & Riccio, D. (2012). CABALA—Collaborative architectures based on biometric adaptable layers and activities. *Pattern Recognition, 45*(6), 2348–2362. doi:10.1016/j.patcog.2011.12.005

De Marsico, M., Nappi, M., Riccio, D., & Tortora, G. (2013a). Entropy Based Template Analysis in Face Biometric Identification Systems. *Journal of Signal. Image and Video Processing, 7*(3), 493–505. doi:10.1007/s11760-013-0451-4

De Marsico, M., Nappi, M., Riccio, D., & Wechsler, H. (2011). Robust Face Recognition after Plastic Surgery Using Local Region Analysis. In *Proceedings of International Conference on Image Analysis and Recognition* (LNCS), (Vol. 6754, pp. 191-200). Berlin: Springer.

De Marsico, M., Nappi, M., Riccio, D., & Wechsler, H. (2013b). Robust face recognition for uncontrolled pose and illumination changes. *IEEE Transactions On Systems, Man. Cybernetics and Systems, 43*(1), 149–163.

De Marsico, M., Nappi, M., Riccio, D., & Wechsler, H. (2013c). Demographics versus Biometric Automatic Interoperability. In *Proceedings of International Conference on Image Analysis and Processing, ICIAP 2013* (LNCS), (vol. 8156, pp. 472-481). Berlin: Springer.

Ding, L., Ding, X., & Fang, C. (2012). Continuous pose normalization for pose-robust face recognition. *IEEE Signal Processing Letters, 19*(11), 721–724. doi:10.1109/LSP.2012.2215586

Du, S., & Ward, R. (2005). Wavelet-based illumination normalization for face recognition. In *Proceedings of IEEE International Conference on Image Processing,* (vol. 2, pp. 954-957). IEEE.

Ekman, P., & Friesen, W. V. (1978). *The Facial Action Coding System: A Technique for Measurement of Facial Movement.* Consulting Psychologists Press.

Etemad, K., & Chellappa, R. (1997). Discriminant analysis for recognition of human face images. *Journal of the Optical Society of America. A, Optics, Image Science, and Vision, 14*(8), 1724–1733. doi:10.1364/JOSAA.14.001724

Fasel, B., & Luettin, J. (2003). Automatic facial expression analysis: a survey. *Pattern Recognition, 36*(1), 259–275. doi:10.1016/S0031-3203(02)00052-3

Fukushima, K. (1980). Neocognitron: A self-organizing neural network model for a mechanism of pattern recognition unaffected by shift in position. *Biological Cybernetics, 36*(4), 193–202. doi:10.1007/BF00344251 PMID:7370364

Gandhi, T., & Trivedi, M. (2007). Person tracking and reidentification: Introducing Panoramic Appearance Map (PAM) for feature representation. *Machine Vision and Applications, 18*(3), 207–220. doi:10.1007/s00138-006-0063-x

Gavrila, D. M. (1999). The visual analysis of human movement: A survey. *Computer Vision and Image Understanding, 73*(1), 82–98. doi:10.1006/cviu.1998.0716

Georghiades, A. S., Belhumeur, P. N., & Kriegman, D. J. (2001). From few to many: Illumination cone models for face recognition under differing pose and lighting. *IEEE Transactions on Pattern Analysis and Machine Intelligence, 23*(6), 643–660. doi:10.1109/34.927464

Gonzalez-Jimenez, D., & Alba-Castro, J. L. (2007). Toward pose-invariant 2-D face recognition through point distribution models and facial symmetry. *IEEE Transactions on Information Forensics and Security, 2*(3), 413–429. doi:10.1109/TIFS.2007.903543

Guo, G., Li, S. Z., & Chan, K. (2000). Face recognition by support vector machines. In *Proceedings of Fourth IEEE International Conference on Automatic Face and Gesture Recognition,* (pp. 196-201). IEEE.

Hamdoun, O., Moutarde, F., Stanciulescu, B., & Steux, B. (2008). Person re-identification in multi-camera system by signature based on interest point descriptors collected on short video sequences. In *Proceedings of Second ACM/IEEE International Conference on Distributed Smart Cameras,* (pp. 1-6). ACM/IEEE.

Harandi, M. T., Ahmadabadi, M. N., & Araabi, B. N. (2007). A hierarchical face identification system based on facial components. In *Proceedings of IEEE/ACS International Conference on Computer Systems and Applications* (pp. 669–675). IEEE.

He, X., Cai, D., Yan, S., & Zhang, H.-J. (2005). Neighborhood preserving embedding. In *Proceedings of Tenth IEEE International Conference on Computer Vision, ICCV 2005* (vol. 2, pp. 1208-1213). IEEE.

He, X., & Niyogi, P. (2003). Locality Preserving Projections. In *Proceedings of Advances in Neural Information Processing Systems 16: Proceedings of the 2003 Conference* (pp. 153-160). Academic Press.

Heisele, B., Ho, P., Wu, J., & Poggio, T. (2003). Face recognition: Component- based versus global approaches. *Computer Vision and Image Understanding, 91*(1), 6–12. doi:10.1016/S1077-3142(03)00073-0

Hotelling, H. (1936). Relations between two sets of variates. *Biometrika, 28*, 321–377. doi:10.1093/biomet/28.3-4.321

Huang, G. B., Mattar, M., Berg, T., & Learned-Miller, E. (2007). *Labeled Faces in the Wild: A Database for Studying Face Recognition in Unconstrained Environments* (Technical Report 07-49). University of Massachusetts.

Ijiri, Y., Sakuragi, M., & Lao. (2006). Security Management for Mobile Devices by Face Recognition. In *Proceedings of 7th International Conference on Mobile Data Management,* (pp. 49-49). MDM.

Javadtalab, A., Abbadi, L., Omidyeganeh, M., Shirmohammadi, S., Adams, C. M., & El-Saddik, A. (2011). Transparent non-intrusive multimodal biometric system for video conference using the fusion of face and ear recognition. In *Proceedings of Ninth Annual International Conference on Privacy, Security and Trust - PST 2011* (pp. 87–92). PST.

Jillela, R., & Ross, A. (2012). Mitigating effects of plastic surgery: Fusing face and ocular biometrics. In *Proceedings of IEEE Fifth International Conference on Biometrics: Theory, Applications and Systems - BTAS 2012* (pp. 402–411). IEEE.

Kapoor, A., Qi, Y., & Picard, R. W. (2003). Fully automatic upper facial action recognition. In *Proceedings of IEEE International Workshop on Analysis and Modeling of Faces and Gestures, AMFG 2003* (pp. 195-202). IEEE.

Kim, T.-K., Kim, H., Hwang, W., & Kittler, J. (2005). Component-Based LDA face description for image retrieval and MPEG-7 standardisation. *Image and Vision Computing, 23*, 631–642. doi:10.1016/j.imavis.2005.02.005

Kirby, M., & Sirovich, L. (1990). Application of the Karhunen–Loeve procedure for the characterization of human faces. *IEEE Transactions on Pattern Analysis and Machine Intelligence, 12*(1), 103–108. doi:10.1109/34.41390

Kisku, D. R., Sing, J. K., & Gupta, P. (2009). Multibiometrics Belief Fusion. In *Proceedings of Second International Conference on Machine Vision - ICMV 2009* (pp. 37–40). ICMV.

Klare, B. F., Burge, M. J., Klontz, J. C., Vorder Bruegge, R. W., & Jain, A. K. (2012). Face Recognition Performance: Role of Demographic Information. *IEEE Transactions on Information Forensics and Security, 7*(6), 1789–1801. doi:10.1109/TIFS.2012.2214212

Krauss, R. M., Garlock, C. M., Bricker, P. D., & McMahon, L. E. (1977). The role of audible and visible back-channel responses in interpersonal communication. *Journal of Personality and Social Psychology, 35*(7), 523–529. doi:10.1037/0022-3514.35.7.523

Kumar, N., Berg, A. C., Belhumeur, P. N., & Nayar, S. K. (2009). Attribute and simile classifiers for face verification. In *Proceedings of 2009 IEEE 12th International Conference on Computer Vision* (pp. 365-372). IEEE.

Lerner, T. (2013). *Mobile Payment*. Springer Fachmedien Wiesbaden.

Leyvand, T., Cohen-Or, D., Dror, G., & Lischinski, D. (2008). Data-Driven Enhancement of Facial Attractiveness. In *Proceedings of ACM SIGGRAPH 2008*. ACM.

Lipton, A., Kanade, T., Fujiyoshi, H., Duggins, D., Tsin, Y., Tolliver, D., & Wixson, L. (2000). *A system for video surveillance and monitoring* (Vol. 2). Pittsburgh, PA: Carnegie Mellon University, the Robotics Institute.

Liu, Q., Tang, X., Lu, H., & Ma, S. (2006). Face recognition using kernel scatter-difference-based discriminant analysis. *IEEE Transactions on Neural Networks, 17*(4), 1081–1085. doi:10.1109/TNN.2006.875970 PMID:16856670

Liu, Y., Schmidt, K. L., Cohn, J. F., & Mitra, S. (2003). Facial asymmetry quantification for expression invariant human identification. *Computer Vision and Image Understanding, 91*(1), 138–159. doi:10.1016/S1077-3142(03)00078-X

Luo, J., Ma, Y., & Takikawa, E. Lao, Kawade, M., & Lu. (2007). Person-Specific SIFT Features for Face Recognition. In *Proceedings of IEEE International Conference on Acoustics, Speech and Signal Processing, ICASSP 2007*, (vol. 2, pp. 593-596). IEEE.

Marcel, S., McCool, C., Matejka, P., Ahonen, T., Cernocky, J., & Chakraborty, S. … Kittler, J. (2010). On the results of the first mobile biometry (MOBIO) face and speaker verification evaluation. In Proceedings of Recognizing Patterns in Signals, Speech, Images and Videos (LNCS), (vol. 6388, pp. 210-225). Berlin: Springer.

Martinez, A. M. (2002). Recognizing imprecisely localized, partially occluded, and expression variant faces from a single sample per class. *IEEE Transactions on Pattern Analysis and Machine Intelligence, 24*(6), 748–763. doi:10.1109/TPAMI.2002.1008382

Milborrow, S., & Nicolls, F. (2008). Locating facial features with an extended active shape model. In *Proceedings of European Conference on Computer Vision – ECCV 2008* (pp. 504–513). ECCV.

Monwar, M. M., Gavrilova, M., & Yingxu. (2011). A novel fuzzy multimodal information fusion technology for human biometric traits identification. In *Proceedings of 10th IEEE International Conference on Cognitive Informatics & Cognitive Computing* (pp. 112–119). IEEE.

Muramatsu, D., Iwama, H., Makihara, Y., & Yagi, Y. (2013). Multi-view multi-modal person authentication from a single walking image sequence. In *Proceedings of International Conference on Biometrics, ICB 2013* (pp. 1-8). ICB.

Pantic, M., Pentland, A., Nijholt, A., & Huang, T. S. (2007). Human computing and machine understanding of human behavior: a survey. In *Proceedings of Artificial Intelligence for Human Computing, (LNCS)* (Vol. 4451, pp. 47–71). Berlin: Springer. doi:10.1007/978-3-540-72348-6_3

Pantic, M., & Rothkrantz, L. J. M. (2004). Facial action recognition for facial expression analysis from static face images. *IEEE Transactions on Systems, Man, and Cybernetics. Part B, Cybernetics, 34*(3), 1449–1461. doi:10.1109/TSMCB.2004.825931 PMID:15484916

Phillips, P. J., Grother, P., Micheals, R. J., Blackburn, D. M., Tabassi, E., & Bone, J. M. (2003). *FRVT 2002: Overview and Summary*. Retrieved October 25, 2013 from http://biometrics.nist.gov/cs_links/face/frvt/FRVT_2002_Overview_and_Summary.pdf

Picard, R. W. (2003). Affective computing: challenges. *International Journal of Human-Computer Studies, 59*(1–2), 55–64. doi:10.1016/S1071-5819(03)00052-1

Poh, N., & Kittler, J. (2012). A Unified Framework for Biometric Expert Fusion Incorporating Quality Measures. *IEEE Transactions on Pattern Analysis and Machine Intelligence, 34*, 3–18. doi:10.1109/TPAMI.2011.102

Poh, N., Kittler, J., & Bourlai, T. (2010). Quality-Based Score Normalization With Device Qualitative Information for Multimodal Biometric Fusion. *IEEE Transactions on Systems, Man, and Cybernetics. Part A, Systems and Humans, 40*(3), 539–554. doi:10.1109/TSMCA.2010.2041660

Rama, A., & Tarrés, F. (2005). P²CA: A new face recognition scheme combining 2D and 3D information. In *Proceedings of IEEE International Conference on Image Processing,* (vol.3, pp. 776-779). IEEE.

Rama, A., Tarres, F., Onofrio, D., & Tubaro, S. (2006). Mixed 2D-3D Information for Pose Estimation and Face Recognition. In *Proceedings. 2006 IEEE International Conference on Acoustics, Speech and Signal Processing,* (vol.2, pp. 14-19). IEEE.

Rama Calvo, A., Tarrés Ruiz, F., Rurainsky, J., & Eisert, P. (2008). 2D-3D Mixed Face Recognition Schemes. In K. Delac, M. Grgic, & M. Stewart Bartlett (Eds.), *Recent Advances in Face Recognition* (pp. 125–148). InTech. doi:10.5772/6398

Ramamoorthi, R., & Hanrahan, P. (2001). On the relationship between radiance and irradiance: Determining the illumination from images of a convex lambertian object. *Journal of the Optical Society of America. A, Optics, Image Science, and Vision, 18*(10), 2448–2459. doi:10.1364/JOSAA.18.002448 PMID:11583261

Ramanathan, N., Chowdhury, A., & Chellappa, R. (2004). Facial similarity across age, disguise, illumination and pose. In *Proceedings of International Conference on Image Processing,* (Vol. 3, pp. 1999–2002). Academic Press.

Reisfeld, D., & Yeshurun, Y. (1998). Preprocessing of face images: detection of features and pose normalization. *Computer Vision and Image Understanding, 71*(3), 413–430. doi:10.1006/cviu.1997.0640

Riccio, D., & Dugelay, J.-L. (2007). Geometric invariants for 2D/3D face recognition. *Pattern Recognition Letters, 28*(14), 1907–1914. doi:10.1016/j.patrec.2006.12.017

Riccio, D., Tortora, G., De Marsico, M., & Wechsler, H. (2012). EGA - Ethnicity, Gender and Age, a pre-annotated face database. In *Proceedings of 2012 IEEE Workshop on Biometric Measurements and Systems for Security and Medical Applications, BioMS 2012* (pp. 38-45). IEEE.

Roweis, S. T., & Saul, L. K. (2000). Nonlinear Dimensionality Reduction by Locally Linear Embedding. *Science, 290*(5500), 2323–2326. doi:10.1126/science.290.5500.2323 PMID:11125150

Seely, R. D., Samangooei, S., Lee, M., Carter, J. N., & Nixon, M. S. (2008). The University of Southampton Multi-Biometric Tunnel and introducing a novel 3D gait dataset. In *Proceedings of 2nd IEEE International Conference on Biometrics: Theory, Applications and Systems, BTAS 2008* (pp.1–6). IEEE.

Sellahewa, H., & Jassim, S. A. (2010). Image-Quality-Based Adaptive Face Recognition. *IEEE Transactions on Instrumentation and Measurement, 59*(4), 805–813. doi:10.1109/TIM.2009.2037989

Serre, T., Wolf, L., Bileschi, S., Riesenhuber, M., & Poggio, T. (2007). Robust Object Recognition with Cortex-Like Mechanisms. *IEEE Transactions on Pattern Analysis and Machine Intelligence, 29*(3), 411–426. doi:10.1109/TPAMI.2007.56 PMID:17224612

Shadbolt, N. (2003). Ambient intelligence. *IEEE Intelligent Systems*, *18*(4), 2–3. doi:10.1109/MIS.2003.1200718

Shan, S., Gao, W., Cao, B., & Zhao, D. (2003). llumination normalization for robust face recognition against varying lighting conditions. In *Proceedings of IEEE International Workshop on Analysis and Modeling of Faces and Gestures, AMFG 2003*. IEEE.

Shashua, A., & Riklin-Raviv, T. (2001). The quotient image: Class-based re-rendering and recognition with varying illuminations. *IEEE Transactions on Pattern Analysis and Machine Intelligence*, *23*(2), 129–139. doi:10.1109/34.908964

Silva, P., & Rosa, A. S. (2003). Face recognition based on eigeneyes. *Pattern Recognition and Image Analysis*, *13*(2), 335–338.

Singh, R., Vatsa, M., Bhatt, H. S., Bharadwaj, S., Noore, A., & Nooreyezdan, S. S. (2010). Plastic surgery: A new dimension to face recognition. *IEEE Transactions on Information Forensics and Security*, *5*(3), 441–448. doi:10.1109/TIFS.2010.2054083

Singh, R., Vatsa, M., & Noore, A. (2008). Recognizing Face Images with Disguise Variations. In K. Delac, M. Grgic, & M. Stewart Bartlett (Eds.), *Recent Advances in Face Recognition* (pp. 149–160). InTech. doi:10.5772/6399

Singh, R., Vatsa, M., & Noore, A. (2009a). Face recognition with disguise and single gallery images. *Image and Vision Computing*, *27*(3), 245–257. doi:10.1016/j.imavis.2007.06.010

Singh, R., Vatsa, M., & Noore, A. (2009b). Effect of plastic surgery on face recognition: A preliminary study. [CVPRW.]. *Proceedings of Computer Vision and Pattern Recognition Workshops, CVPRW, 2009*, 72–77.

Smeraldi, F., Capdevielle, N., & Bigun, J. (1999). Facial features detection by saccadic exploration of the Gabor decomposition and Support Vector Machines. In *Proceedings of 11th Scandinavian Conference on Image Analysis, SCIA 1999* (vol. 1, pp. 39-44). SCIA.

Stone, Z., Zickler, T., & Darrell, T. (2010). Toward Large-Scale Face Recognition Using Social Network Context. *Proceedings of the IEEE*, *98*(8), 1408–1415. doi:10.1109/JPROC.2010.2044551

Su, Y., Shan, S., Chen, X., & Gao, W. (2009). Hierarchical Ensemble of Global and Local Classifiers for Face Recognition. *IEEE Transactions on Image Processing*, *18*(8), 1885–1896. doi:10.1109/TIP.2009.2021737 PMID:19556198

Takács, B., & Wechsler, H. (1998). A Saccadic Vision System for Landmark Detection and Face Recognition. *Face Recognition*, *163*, 627–636. doi:10.1007/978-3-642-72201-1_42

Tao, J., & Tan, T. (2005). Affective computing: A review. In *Proceedings of Affective Computing and Intelligent Interaction, First International Conference, ACII 2005*, (LNCS), (vol. 3784, pp. 981-995). Berlin: Springer.

Tian, Y. I., Kanade, T., & Cohn, J. F. (2001). Recognizing action units for facial expression analysis. *IEEE Transactions on Pattern Analysis and Machine Intelligence*, *23*(2), 97–115. doi:10.1109/34.908962

Turk, M., & Pentland, A. (1991). Eigenfaces for recognition. *Journal of Cognitive Neuroscience*, *13*(1), 71–86. doi:10.1162/jocn.1991.3.1.71 PMID:23964806

Vetter, T., & Poggio, T. (1997). Linear object classes and image synthesis from a single example image. *IEEE Transactions on Pattern Analysis and Machine Intelligence*, *19*(7), 733–742. doi:10.1109/34.598230

Wang, H., Li, S. Z., & Wang, Y. (2004). Generalized quotient image. In *Proceedings of IEEE International Conference on Computer Vision and Pattern Recognition, CVPR 2004* (vol. 2, pp. 498-505). IEEE.

Wang, L., Ding, L., Ding, X., & Fang, C. (2011). 2D face fitting-assisted 3D reconstruction for pose-robust face recognition. *Soft Computing, 15*(3), 417–428. doi:10.1007/s00500-009-0523-0

Wang, X., & Tang, X. (2004). A unified framework for subspace face recognition. *IEEE Transactions on Pattern Analysis and Machine Intelligence, 26*(9), 1222–1228. doi:10.1109/TPAMI.2004.57 PMID:15742896

Wei, X., & Li, C. T. (2013). Fixation and Saccade Based Face Recognition from Single Image per Person with Various Occlusions and Expressions. In *Proceedings of 2013 IEEE Conference on Computer Vision and Pattern Recognition Workshops, CVPRW* (pp.70-75). IEEE.

Xu, C., Wang, Y., Tan, T., & Quan, L. (2004). Depth vs. intensity: Which is more important for face recognition? In *Proceedings of International Conference on Pattern Recognition*, (Vol. 4, pp. 342–345). ICPR.

Yang, F., & Paindavoine, M. (2003). Implementation of an RBF neural network on embedded systems: Real-time face tracking and identity verification. *IEEE Transactions on Neural Networks, 14*(5), 1162–1175. doi:10.1109/TNN.2003.816035 PMID:18244568

Yang, W., Yi, D., Lei, Z., Sang, J., & Li, S. Z. (2008). 2D–3D face matching using CCA. In *Proceedings of 8th IEEE International Conference on Automatic Face & Gesture Recognition*. IEEE.

Yazdanpanah, A. P., Faez, K., & Amirfattahi, R. (2010). Multimodal biometric system using face, ear and gait biometrics. In *Proceedings of 10th International Conference on Information Science, Signal Processing and their Applications, ISSPA 2010* (pp. 251- 254). ISSPA.

Yin, Q., Tang, X., & Sun, J. (2011). An associate-predict model for face recognition. In *Proceedings of 2011 IEEE Conference on Computer Vision and Pattern Recognition (CVPR)* (pp. 497-504). IEEE.

Yuan, L., Mu, Z.-C., & Xu, X.-N. (2007). Multimodal recognition based on face and ear. In *Proceedings of International Conference on Wavelet Analysis and Pattern Recognition - ICWAPR 2007* (vol. 3, pp. 1203–1207). ICWAPR.

Yuan, L., Zhichun, M. Z., & Liu, Y. (2006). Multimodal recognition using face profile and ear. In *Proceedings of 1st International Symposium on Systems and Control in Aerospace and Astronautics - ISSCAA 2006* (pp.887–891). ISSCAA.

Zhao, W., & Chellappa, R. (1999). *Robust face recognition using symmetric shape-from-shading*. University of Maryland. Retrieved October 23, 2013, from ftp://ftp.cfar.umd.edu/TRs/CVL-Reports-1999/TR4036-zhao.ps.gz

Zou, J., Ji, Q., & Nagy, G. (2007). A Comparative Study of Local Matching Approach for Face Recognition. *IEEE Transactions on Image Processing, 16*(10), 2617–2628. doi:10.1109/TIP.2007.904421 PMID:17926941

KEY TERMS AND DEFINITIONS

Active Shape Models: ASMs are statistical models of the shape of objects which iteratively deformed to fit to an example of the object in a new image. The shape of an object is represented by a set of points which are controlled by the shape model. All the shapes are constrained to vary only in ways compatible with a training set of labelled examples.

Adverse Conditions: When referred to the acquisition of images for biometric recognition, the term refers to conditions that can seriously compromise the quality of the sample, e.g., a strong shadow or motion blur. In such settings, most samples might be especially problematic to process.

COTS: The term (Commercial off-the-shelf) refers to products that are commercially available and can be bought and used as they are.

Face Detection: A process that automatically assigns image pixels to a face and non-face area.

Face Recognition: A process that automatically identifies to whom person a face belongs.

Feature Dimensionality Reduction: Feature extraction usually draws out data in a high-dimensional space, so that a very large feature vector is built to represent the original object. For this reason a number of reduction techniques are used to decrease the dimension of the original feature space, while preserving the most of its representativeness. Both linear and non-linear approaches are used. They map points in the high dimensional space onto points laying in the low dimensional one, trying to preserve their topological relationships.

Hidden Markov Model (HMM): A statistical Markov model in which the system being modeled is assumed to be a Markov process with unobserved (hidden) states.

Holistic vs. Analytical Methods: Pattern recognition approaches are commonly grouped into two classes, that are holistic methods and analytical approaches. Holistic techniques analyze the whole image in order to recognize a subject, while analytical approaches work on different local parts of the image.

Local Binary Patterns (LBP): Very popular texture descriptor, that summarizes in a single value the relationship between each pixel and its surroundings, in terms of relative intensity. Histograms of these values are generally built and used as feature descriptors.

Morphable Models: In the original approach, starting from an example set of 3D face models, it is possible to derive a Morphable Face Model by transforming the shape and texture of the examples into a vector space representation. From this, new faces and expressions can be modeled by computing linear combinations of the prototypes. Shape and texture constraints are derived from the statistics of the example faces. These are used to guide manual modeling or automated matching algorithms.

Mixture Models: A probabilistic model for representing the presence of subpopulations within an overall population, without requiring that an observed data set should identify the sub-population to which an individual observation belongs.

Multimodal Systems: In multimodal systems, face recognition accuracy can be improved by adopting either multi-classifier or multi-sample approaches, as well as exploiting multiple biometric traits, and fusing the obtained results.

Neural Network: it is an information processing technique, whose purpose is to simulate biological neural networks to solve pattern recognition problems. The idea underlying a neural network is to acquire information from the real world, process it and return a result in the form of an impulse.

Pose, Illumination, Expression (PIE): The acronym ( ) refers to the three main issues affecting the comparison of multiple images of the same face acquired in different moments and different environmental conditions.

Region-of-Interest (ROI): It is the first phase of many recognition algorithms. After detecting the required components, a rectangular area is superimposed on them.

Scale-Invariant Feature Transform (SIFT): Attempts to find particular regions (keypoints) in the image that are singular in terms of their statistical properties. The related matching strategy tries to find correspondences among keypoints in different images.

Uncontrolled Settings: When referred to the acquisition for biometric recognition, the term refers to settings where it is not possible to control critical factors like illumination, pose, expression, acquisition distance, etc. As a consequence, there is no guarantee on the characteristics of the obtained sample and on the possibility to successfully process it.

Wavelet: It is a wave-like oscillation, whose amplitude starts at zero, increases, and then decreases back to zero. It is commonly used to extract features from many different kinds of data, such as images and audio signals. A set of "complementary" wavelets is used to decompose data without gaps or overlap, thus the decomposition process is mathematically reversible.

Compilation of References

(2001). Local Features for Image Retrieval. In Veltkamp, R. C., Burkhardt, H., & Kriegel, H.-P. (Eds.), *State-of-the-Art in Content-Based Image and Video Retrieval* (pp. 21–41). Kluwer Academic Publishers.

3DMD: 3d Imaging Systems and Software. (2012). Author.

Abate, A. F., De Marsico, M., Nappi, M., & Riccio, D. (2011). VIVIE: A Video-Surveillance Indexer Via Identity Extraction. In *Proceedings of International Conference on Multimedia and Expo,* (pp. 1-6). Barcelona, Spain: ICME.

Abate, A. F., Nappi, M., Ricciardi, S., & Sabatino, G. (2005). Fast 3d face recognition based on normal map. In *Proceedings of IEEE International Conference on Image Processing,* (Vol. 2, pp. 946-949). IEEE.

Abate, A. F., Nappi, M., Ricciardi, S., & Sabatino, G. (2007). Fast 3D Face Alignment and Improved Recognition Through Pyramidal Normal map Metric. In *Proceedings of IEEE International Conference on Image Processing, ICIP 2007* (vol. 1, pp. 157-160). IEEE.

Abate, A. F., Nappi, M., Riccio, D., & Sabatino, G. (2007). 2D and 3D face recognition: A survey. *Pattern Recognition Letters, 28*(14), 1885–1906. doi:10.1016/j.patrec.2006.12.018

Abate, A. F., Ricciardi, S., & Sabatino, G. (2007). 3D face recognition in a ambient intelligence environment scenario. In K. Delac, & M. Grgic (Eds.), *Face recognition.* I-Tech.

Abrams, J., Nizam, A., & Carrasco, M. (2012). Isoeccentric locations are not equivalent: The extent of the vertical meridian asymmetry. *Vision Research, 52,* 70–78. doi:10.1016/j.visres.2011.10.016 PMID:22086075

ACMA. (2013). *Smartphones and tablets - Take-up and use in Australia.* Melbourne, Australia: Australian Communications and Media Authority.

Acosta, E., Torres, L., Albiol, A., & Delp, E. (2002). An Automatic Face Detection and Recognition System for Video Indexing Applications. In *Proceedings of IEEE International Conference on Acoustics, Speech and Signal Processing (ICASSP 2002).* IEEE.

Adams, J., Woodard, D. L., Dozier, G., Miller, P., Bryant, K., & Glenn, G. (2010). *Genetic-Based Type II Feature Extraction for Periocular Biometric Recognition: Less is More.* Paper presented at the Pattern Recognition (ICPR), 2010 20th International Conference on. doi:10.1109/ICPR.2010.59

Adini, Y., Moses, Y., & Ullman, S. (1997). Face recognition: The problem of compensating for changes in illumination direction. *IEEE Transactions on Pattern Analysis and Machine Intelligence, 19*(7), 721–732. doi:10.1109/34.598229

Adler, A. (2003). *Sample images can be independently restored from face recognition templates.* Paper presented at the Canadian Conference on Electrical and Computer Engineering (CCECE). Montreal, Canada.

Agaian, S. S., Silver, B., & Panetta, K. A. (2007). Transform coefficient histogram-based image enhancement algorithms using contrast entropy. *IEEE Transactions on Image Processing, 16*(3), 741–758. doi:10.1109/TIP.2006.888338 PMID:17357734

Aggarwal, J. K., & Cai, Q. (1997). Human motion analysis: A review. In *Proceedings of IEEE Nonrigid and Articulated Motion Workshop* (pp. 90-102). IEEE.

Aharon, M., Elad, M., & Bruckstein, A. M. (2005). *K-SVD And Its Non-Negative Variant For Dictionary Design*. Paper Presented At The Proc. Spie Wavelets Xi. New York, NY.

Ahmad, M., Natarajan, T., & Rao, K. R. (1974). Discrete Cosine Transform. *IEEE Transactions on Computers*, *23*(1), 90–94. doi:10.1109/T-C.1974.223784

Ahonen, T., Hadid, A., & Pietikainen, M. (2004). Face recognition with local binary patterns. *Computer Vision - Eccv 2004, Pt 1, 3021*, 469-481.

Ahonen, T., Rahtu, E., Ojansivu, V., & Heikkila, J. (2008). Recognition of blurred faces using local phase quantization. In *Proceedings of 19th International Conference on Pattern Recognition*. Academic Press.

Ahonen, T., Hadid, A., & Pietikäinen, M. (2004). Face recognition with local binary patterns. In *Proceedings of Computer Vision-ECCV* (pp. 469–481). ECCV.

Ahonen, T., & Pietikainen, M. (2006). Face Description with Local Binary Patterns: Application to Face Recognition. *IEEE Transactions on Pattern Analysis and Machine Intelligence*, *28*(12), 2037–2041. doi:10.1109/TPAMI.2006.244 PMID:17108377

Al-Allaf, O. N. A., Tamimi, A. A., & Alia, M. A. (2013). Face Recognition System Based on Different Artificial Neural Networks Models and Training Algorithms. *International Journal of Advanced Computer Science and Applications*, *4*(6), 40–47.

Albiol, A., Monzo, D., Martin, A., Sastre, J., & Albiol, A. (2008). Face recognition using HOG–EBGM. *Pattern Recognition Letters*, *29*(10), 1537–1543. doi:10.1016/j.patrec.2008.03.017

Alexander, J., & Smith, J. (2003). Engineering privacy in public: Confounding face recognition, privacy enhancing technologies. In *Proceedings of International Workshop on Privacy Enhancing Technologies* (pp. 88–106). Academic Press.

Ali, S., & Shah, M. (2010). Human action recognition in videos using kinematic features and multiple instance learning. *IEEE Transactions on Pattern Analysis and Machine Intelligence*, *32*(2), 288–303. doi:10.1109/TPAMI.2008.284 PMID:20075459

Allison, T., Puce, A., & McCarthy, G. (2000). Social perception from visual cues: role of the STS region. *Trends in Cognitive Sciences*, *4*, 267–278. doi:10.1016/S1364-6613(00)01501-1 PMID:10859571

Almaev, T., & Valstar, M. F. (2013). Local Gabor binary patterns from three orthogonal planes for automatic facial expression recognition. In *Proceedings of the International Conference on Affective Computing and Intelligent Interaction*. Academic Press.

Alonso-Fernandez, F., & Bigun, J. (2012). Iris boundaries segmentation using the generalized structure tensor: A study on the effects of image degradation. In *Proceedings of the 2012 IEEE Fifth International Conference on Biometrics: Theory, Applications and Systems*, (pp. 426-431). IEEE.

Alyuz, N., Gokberk, B., & Akarun, L. (2008). A 3D Face Recognition System for Expression and Occlusion Invariance. In *Proceedings of 2nd IEEE International Conference on Biometrics: Theory, Applications and Systems, 2008. BTAS 2008* (pp. 1-7). IEEE.

Alyuz, N., Gokberk, B., & Akarun, L. (2012). Adaptive model based 3D face registration for occlusion invariance. In *Proceedings of European Conference on Computer Vision - Workshops - Benchmarking Facial Image Analysis Technologies*.

Alyuz, N., Gokberk, B., Spreeuwers, L., Veldhuis, R., & Akarun, L. (2012). Robust 3D face recognition in the presence of realistic occlusions. In *Proceedings of 2012 5th IAPR International Conference on Biometrics (ICB)* (pp. 111-118). IAPR.

Alyuz, N., Gokberk, B., & Akarun, L. (2010). Regional registration for expression resistant 3-D face recognition. *IEEE Trans. on Information Forensics and Security*, *5*(3), 425–440.

Alyuz, N., Gokberk, B., & Akarun, L. (2013). 3D Face Recognition under Occlusion using Masked Projection. *IEEE Trans. on Information Forensics and Security*, *8*(5), 789–802. doi:10.1109/TIFS.2013.2256130

Ambadar, Z., Cohn, J. F., & Reed, L. I. (2009). All smiles are not created equal: Morphology and timing of smiles perceived as amused, polite, and embarrassed/nervous. *Journal of Nonverbal Behavior*, *33*, 17–34. doi:10.1007/s10919-008-0059-5 PMID:19554208

Ambady, N., & Rosenthal, R. (1992). Thin slices of expressive behavior as predictors of interpersonal consequences: a meta-analysis. *Psychological Bulletin, 111*(2), 256–274. doi:10.1037/0033-2909.111.2.256

Ambalakat, P. (2005). *Security of Biometric Authentication Systems.* Paper presented at the 21st Annual Computer Science Seminar. Hartford, CT.

Amberg, B. (2011). *Editing Faces in Videos.* (PhD Thesis).

Amberg, B., Blake, A., & Vetter, T. (2009). On compositional image alignment, with an application to active appearance models. In *Proceedings of IEEE Conference on Computer Vision and Pattern Recognition* (CVPR). IEEE.

Amberg, B., Knothe, R., & Vetter, T. (2008). SHREC'08 Entry: Shape Based Face Recognition with a Morphable Model. In *Proceedings of IEEE International Conference on Shape Modeling and Applications,* (pp. 253-254). IEEE.

Android Open Source Project. (2011). *Android 4.0 APIs.* Retrieved 12 Nov, 2013, from http://developer.android.com/about/versions/android-4.0.html

Anjos, A., & Marcel, S. (2011). *Counter-Measures to Photo Attacks in Face Recognition: a public database and a baseline.* Paper presented at the International Joint Conference on Biometrics (IJCB). Washington, DC.

Antonakaki, P., Kosmopoulos, D., & Perantonis, S. (2009). Detecting abnormal human behaviour using multiple cameras. *Signal Processing, 89*(9), 1723–1738. doi:10.1016/j.sigpro.2009.03.016

Apple Inc. (2012). *Core Image Reference Collection.* Retrieved 12 Nov, 2013, from https://developer.apple.com/library/ios/documentation/GraphicsImaging/Reference/CoreImagingRef/_index.html

Apple. (2013a). *iPhone 5s: About Touch ID security.* Retrieved 07 Nov, 2013, from http://support.apple.com/kb/HT5949

Apple. (2013b). *iPhone 5s: Using Touch ID.* Retrieved 07 Nov, 2013, from http://support.apple.com/kb/HT5883

Arulampalam, M., Maskell, S., Gordon, N., & Clapp, T. (2002). A tutorial on particle filters for online nonlinear/non-gaussian bayesian tracking. *IEEE Transactions on Signal Processing, 50*(2), 174–189. doi:10.1109/78.978374

Asthana, A., Marks, T. K., Jones, M. J., & Tieu, K. H. (2011). Fully automatic pose-invariant face recognition via 3D pose normalization. In *Proceedings of 2011 IEEE International Conference on Computer Vision, ICCV* (pp. 937–944). IEEE.

Asthana, A., Zafeiriou, S., Cheng, S., & Pantic, M. (2013). Robust discriminative response map fitting with constrained local models. In *Proceedings of IEEE Conference on Computer Vision and Pattern Recognition* (CVPR), (pp. 3444-3451). IEEE.

Bach, F., & Jordan, M. (2003). Learning spectral clustering. In Advances of Neural Info. Processing Systems, (pp. 305-312). Academic Press.

Bach, F., Thibaux, R., & Jordan, M. I. (2004). Computing regularization paths for learning multiple kernels. Advances in Neural Information Processing Systems (NIPS), 17.

Bailly-Bailli, E., Bengio, S., Bimbot, R., et al. (2003). *The BANCA database and evaluation protocol.* Paper presented at the 4th international conference on Audio- and video-based biometric person authentication. New York, NY.

Bakshi, S., Sa, P. K., & Majhi, B. (2013). Optimized Periocular Template Selection for Human Recognition. *BioMed Research International, 14.* doi: doi:10.1155/2013/481431 PMID:23984370

Balas, B. J., & Sinha, P. (2003). *Dissociated Dipoles: Image representation via non-local comparisons.* Paper presented at the CBCL Paper #229/AI Memo #2003-018. Cambridge, MA.

Balas, B. J., & Sinha, P. (2006). Region-based representations for face recognition. *ACM Transactions on Applied Perception, 3*(4), 354–375. doi:10.1145/1190036.1190038

Balasubramanian, V., Chakraborty, S., & Panchanathan, S. (2009). Generalized query by transduction for online active learning. In *Proceedings of Computer Vision Workshop (CVW) (12th Int. Conf. on Computer Vision).* Kyoto, Japan: CVW.

Barlow, H. B. (1989). Unsupervised learning. *Neural Computation, 1,* 295–311. doi:10.1162/neco.1989.1.3.295

Barrington, L., Marks, T., Hsiao, J. H., & Cottrell, G. W. (2008). NIMBLE: A kernel density model of *saccade-based* visual memory. *Journal of Vision (Charlottesville, Va.)*, *8*(14), 1–14. doi:10.1167/8.14.17 PMID:19146318

Barr, J. R., Bowyer, K. W., Flynn, P. J., & Biswas, S. (2012). Face Recognition From Video: A Review. *International Journal of Pattern Recognition and Artificial Intelligence*, *26*(5). doi:10.1142/S0218001412660024

Bartlett, M. S., Littlewort, G., Frank, M., Lainscsek, C., Fasel, I., & Movellan, J. (2006). Fully Automatic Facial Action Recognition in Spontaneous Behavior. In *Proceedings of 7th International Conference on Automatic Face and Gesture Recognition,* (pp. 223-230). Academic Press.

Bartlett, M. S., Littlewort, G., Frank, M., Lainscsek, C., Fasel, I., & Movellan, J. (2006). Automatic recognition of facial actions in spontaneous expressions. *Journal of Multimedia*, *1*(6), 22–35. doi:10.4304/jmm.1.6.22-35

Bartlett, M. S., Movellan, J. R., & Sejnowski, T. J. (2002). Face recognition by independent component analysis. *IEEE Transactions on Neural Networks*, *13*(6), 1450–1464. doi:10.1109/TNN.2002.804287 PMID:18244540

Basri, R., & Jacobs, D. (2001). Lambertian reflectance and linear subspaces. In *Proceedings of Eighth IEEE International Conference on Computer Vision,* (pp. 383-390). IEEE.

Bastan, M., Cam, H., Gudkbay, U., & Ulusoy, O. (2010). Bilvideo-7: an MPEG-7- compatible video indexing and retrieval system. *IEEE MultiMedia*, *17*(3), 62–73. doi:10.1109/MMUL.2010.5692184

Batur, A. U., & Hayes, M. H. (2001). Linear subspaces for illumination robust face recognition. In *Proceedings of IEEE Computer Society Conference on Computer Vision and Pattern Recognition,* (vol. 2, pp. 296-301). IEEE.

Bauml, M., Bernardin, K., Fischer, M., & Ekenel, H. K. (2010). Multi-pose face recognition for person retrieval in camera networks. In *Proceedings of IEEE Int. Conf. on Advanced Video and Signal Based Surveillance (AVSS),* (pp. 441-447). IEEE.

Bay, H., Ess, A., Tuytelaars, T., & Van Gool, L. (2008). Speeded-Up Robust Features (SURF). *Computer Vision and Image Understanding*, *110*(3), 346–359. doi:10.1016/j.cviu.2007.09.014

Bebis, G., Gyaourova, A., Singh, S., & Pavlidis, I. (2006). Face recognition by fusing thermal infrared and visible imagery. *Image and Vision Computing*, *24*(7), 727–742. doi:10.1016/j.imavis.2006.01.017

Beer, T. (1981). Walsh transforms. *American Journal of Physics*, *49*(5), 466–472. doi:10.1119/1.12714

Belhumeur, P. N., Hespanha, J. P., & Kriegman, D. J. (1997). Eigenfaces vs. fisherfaces: Recognition using class specific linear projection. *IEEE Transactions on Pattern Analysis and Machine Intelligence*, *19*(7), 711–720. doi:10.1109/34.598228

Belhumeur, P. N., & Kriegman, D. J. (1998). What is the set of images of an object under all possible illumination conditions? *International Journal of Computer Vision*, *28*(3), 245–260. doi:10.1023/A:1008005721484

Belkin, M., & Niyogi, P. (2003). Laplacian eigenmaps for dimensionality reduction and data representation. *Neural Computation*, *15*(6), 1373–1396. doi:10.1162/089976603321780317

Belkin, V., Niyogi, P., & Sindhwani, V. (2006). Manifold regularization: A geometric framework for learning from examples. *Journal of Machine Learning Research*, *7*, 2399–2434.

Bengio, Y. (2009). Learning deep architectures for AI. *Foundations and Trends in Machine Learning*, *2*(1), 1–127. doi:10.1561/2200000006

Berg, T., & Belhumeur, P. (2012). Tom-vs-Pete classifiers and identity-preserving alignment for face verification. In *Proc. British Machine Vision Conference (BMVC).* Guildford, UK: BMVC.

Berretti, S., del Bimbo, A., & Pala, P. (2006). Description and Retrieval of 3D Face Models using iso-Geodesic Stripes. In *Proceedings of ACM SIGMM International Workshop on Multimedia Information Retrieval* (MIR'06), (pp. 13-22). ACM.

Berretti, S., del Bimbo, A., & Pala, P. (2011). Facial Curves between Keypoints for Recognition of 3D Faces with Missing Parts. In *Proceedings of IEEE Computer Vision and Pattern Recognition Workshop on Multi Modal Biometrics,* (pp. 49-54). IEEE.

Berretti, S., del Bimbo, A., & Pala, P. (2010). 3D Face Recognition using iso-Geodesic Stripes. *IEEE Transactions on Pattern Analysis and Machine Intelligence, 32*(12), 2162–2177. doi:10.1109/TPAMI.2010.43 PMID:20975115

Berretti, S., del Bimbo, A., & Pala, P. (2012). Distinguishing Facial Features for Ethnicity based 3D Face Recognition. *ACM Transactions on Intelligent Systems and Technology, 3*(3), 1–20. doi:10.1145/2168752.2168759

Berretti, S., del Bimbo, A., & Pala, P. (2013). Sparse Matching of Salient Facial Curves for Recognition of 3D Faces with Missing Parts. *IEEE Transactions on Information Forensics and Security, 8*(2), 374–389. doi:10.1109/TIFS.2012.2235833

Berretti, S., del Bimbo, A., & Vicario, E. (2001). Efficient matching and indexing of graph models in content-based retrieval. *IEEE Transactions on Pattern Analysis and Machine Intelligence, 23*(10), 1089–1105. doi:10.1109/34.954600

Bertillon, A. (1893). *Identification Anthropométrique, instructions signalétiques.* Melun, France: Imprimerie administrative, nouvelle édition.

Besl, P. J., & Mc Kay, N. D. (1992). A method for registration of 3-D shapes. *IEEE Transactions on Pattern Analysis and Machine Intelligence, 14*(2), 239–256. doi:10.1109/34.121791

Beumier, C., & Acheroy, M. (2001). Face Verification from 3D and Grey Level Clues. *Pattern Recognition Letters, 22*(12), 1321–1329. doi:10.1016/S0167-8655(01)00077-0

Beveridge, J. R., et al. (2011). When high-quality face images match poorly. In *Proc. 9th Int'l Conf. Automatic Face and Gesture Recognition (AFGR),* (pp. 572-578). Santa Barbara, CA: AFGR.

Bharadwaj, S., Bhatt, H. S., Vatsa, M., & Singh, R. (2010). *Periocular biometrics: When iris recognition fails.* Paper presented at the Biometrics: Theory Applications and Systems (BTAS), 2010 Fourth IEEE International Conference on. doi:10.1109/BTAS.2010.5634498

Bhargav-Spantzel, A., Squicciarini, A. C., Modi, S., Young, M., Bertino, E., & Elliott, S. J. (2007). Privacy preserving multi-factor authentication with biometrics. *Journal of Computer Security, 15*(5), 529–560.

Bhatt, H. S., Bharadwaj, S., Singh, R., & Vatsa, M. (2010). On matching sketches with digital face images. In *Proceedings of International Conference Biometrics: Theory Applications and Systems* (pp. 1–7). Academic Press.

Bhatt, H. S., Bharadwaj, S., Singh, R., & Vatsa, M. (2013). Recognizing Surgically Altered Face Images using Multiobjective Evolutionary Algorithm. *IEEE Transactions on Information Forensics and Security, 8*(1), 89–100. doi:10.1109/TIFS.2012.2223684

Bicego, M., Lagorio, A., Grosso, E., & Tistarelli, M. (2006). On the Use of SIFT Features for Face Authentication. In *Proceedings of Conference on Computer Vision and Pattern Recognition Workshop, 2006.* CVPRW.

Bicego, M., Brelstaff, G., Brodo, L., Grosso, E., Lagorio, A., & Tistarelli, M. (2008). Distinctiveness of faces: a computational approach. *ACM Transactions on Applied Perception, 5*(2), 1–18. doi:10.1145/1279920.1279925

Bickel, S., Bruckner, M., & Scheffer, T. (2009). Discriminative learning under covariate shift. *Journal of Machine Learning Research, 10*, 2137–2155.

Bilgazyev, E., & Efros. (2011). *Sparse Representation-Based Super-Resolution For Face Recognition At A Distance.* Paper Presented At The British Machine Vision Conference. Dundee, UK.

Bilgazyev, E., & Kurkure. (2013). *Asie: Application-Specific Image Enhancement For Face Recognition.* Paper Presented At The Spie Biometric And Surveillance Technology For Human And Activity Identification X. Baltimore, MD. Retrieved from http://Proceedings.Spiedigitallibrary.Org/Proceeding.Aspx?Articleid=1693611

Bishop, C. M. (1995). *Neural networks for pattern recognition.* Oxford: Clarendon Press, Oxford University Press.

Bishop, C. M. (2006). *Pattern recognition and machine learning.* New York: Springer.

Bishop, M. (2005). *Introduction to Computer Security.* Boston, MA: Addison-Wesley.

Bishop, M., & Klein, D. V. (1995). Improving system security via proactive password checking. *Computers & Security, 14*(3), 233–249. doi:10.1016/0167-4048(95)00003-Q

Biswas, S., & Chellappa, R. (2010). Pose-robust albedo estimation from a single image. In *Proceedings of IEEE Conf. on Computer Vision and Pattern Recognition (CVPR)* (pp. 2683–2690). IEEE.

Biswas, S., Aggarwal, G., & Chellappa, R. (2009). Robust estimation of albedo for illumination-invariant matching and shape recovery. *IEEE Transactions on Pattern Analysis and Machine Intelligence*, 29(2), 884–899. doi:10.1109/TPAMI.2008.135 PMID:19299862

Biswas, S., Aggarwal, G., Flynn, P. J., & Bowyer, K. W. (2013). Pose-Robust Recognition of Low-Resolution Face Images. *IEEE Transactions on Pattern Analysis and Machine Intelligence*. doi:10.1109/TPAMI.2013.68

Biswas, S., Bowyer, K. W., & Flynn, P. J. (2012). Multidimensional scaling for matching low-resolution face images. *IEEE Transactions on Pattern Analysis and Machine Intelligence*, 34(10), 2019–2030. doi:10.1109/TPAMI.2011.278 PMID:22201067

Blanz, V., & Vetter, T. (1999). A morphable model for the synthesis of 3D faces. In *Proceedings of the 26th annual conference on Computer graphics and interactive techniques*. ACM Press/Addison-Wesley Publishing Co.

Blanz, V., & Vetter, T. (2003). Face recognition based on fitting a 3D morphable model. *IEEE Transactions on Pattern Analysis and Machine Intelligence*, 25(9), 1063–1074. doi:10.1109/TPAMI.2003.1227983

Bledsoe, W. W. (1964). The model method in facial recognition (Tech. rep. PRI:15). Palo Alto, CA: Panoramic research Inc.

Boiman, O., & Irani, M. (2005). *Detecting irregularities in images and in video (ICCV)*. Paper presented at the IEEE International Conference on Computer Vision. Beijing, China.

Bonneau, J., Herley, C., van Oorschot, P. C., & Stajano, F. (2012). *The Quest to Replace Passwords: A Framework for Comparative Evaluation of Web Authentication Schemes*. Paper presented at the IEEE Symposium on Security and Privacy. San Francisco, CA.

Bookstein, F. L. (1989). Principal warps: Thin-Plate Splines and Decomposition of Deformations. *IEEE Transactions on Pattern Analysis and Machine Intelligence*, 11(6), 567–585. doi:10.1109/34.24792

Boot, W. R., Becic, E., & Kramer, A. F. (2009). Stable individual differences in search strategy?: The effect of task demands and motivational factors on scanning strategy in visual search. *Journal of Vision (Charlottesville, Va.)*, 9, 1–16. doi:10.1167/9.3.7 PMID:19757946

Bowyer, K. W., Chang, K., & Flynn, P. (2004). A survey of approaches to three-dimensional face recognition. In *Proceedings of the 17th International Conference on Pattern Recognition*, (vol. 1, pp. 358-361). Academic Press.

Bowyer, K. W., Hollingsworth, K., & Flynn, P. J. (2008). Image understanding for iris biometrics: A survey. *Computer Vision and Image Understanding*, 110(2), 281–307. doi:10.1016/j.cviu.2007.08.005

Bowyer, K., Chang, K., & Flynn, P. (2006). A survey of approaches and challenges in 3D and multi-modal 3D+2D face recognition. *Computer Vision and Image Understanding*, 101(1), 1–15. doi:10.1016/j.cviu.2005.05.005

Bradski, G. (1998). Computer vision face tracking for use in a perceptual user interface. *Intel Technology Journal (Q2)*.

Brand, M., Oliver, N., & Pentland, A. (1997). *Coupled hidden Markov models for complex action recognition (CVPR)*. Paper presented at the IEEE Conference on Computer Vision and Pattern Recognition. San Juan, Puerto Rico.

Breitenstein, M., Grabner, H., & van Gool, L. (2009). *Hunting nessie - real-time abnormality detection from Webcams (ICCV Workshops)*. Paper presented at the IEEE International Conference on Computer Vision Workshops. Kyoto, Japan.

Bronstein, A. M., Bronstein, M. M., & Kimmel, R. (2006). Robust Expression Invariant Face Recognition from Partially Missing Data. In *Proceedings of European Conference on Computer Vision*, (pp. 396-408). Academic Press.

Bronstein, A. M., Bronstein, M. M., & Kimmel, R. (2005). Three Dimensional Face Recognition. *International Journal of Computer Vision*, 64(1), 5–30. doi:10.1007/s11263-005-1085-y

Browne, P. S. (1972). Computer Security: a Survey. *SIGMIS Database*, 4(3), 1–12. doi:10.1145/1017536.1017537

Bruce, N., & Tsotsos, J. K. (2006). Saliency Based on Information Maximization. *Advances in Neural Information Processing Systems*, 18, 155–162.

Bruce, V., & Young, A. W. (1986). Understanding face recognition. *The British Journal of Psychology, 77*(3), 305–327. doi:10.1111/j.2044-8295.1986.tb02199.x PMID:3756376

Bruner, I. S., & Tagiuri, R. (1954). The perception of people. In *Handbook of Social Psychology* (Vol. 2, pp. 634–654). Reading, MA: Addison-Wesley.

Bruni, V., & Vitulano, D. (2013). A perception-based interpretation of the Kernel-based Object Tracking. In *Proc. of ACIVS 2013* (LNCS), (vol. 8192, pp. 596-60). Berlin: Springer.

Bruni, V., Crawford, A., Vitulano, D., & Stanco, F. (2006). Visibility based detection and removal of semi-transparent blotches on archived documents. In *Proceedings of VISAPP06 International Conference on Computer Vision Theory and Applications,* (pp. 64-71). VISAPP.

Bruni, V., Rossi, E., & Vitulano, D. (2011). Optimal Image Restoration Using HVS-Based Rate-Distortion Curves. In *Proceedings of International Conference on Computer Analysis of Images and Patterns* (LNCS), (Vol. 6855, pp. 269-276). Berlin: Springer.

Bruni, V., Rossi, E., & Vitulano, D. (2012). Perceptual object tracking. In *Proceedings of IEEE Workshop on Biometric Measurements and Systems for Security and Medical Applications (BIOMS)*. IEEE.

Bruni, V., Rossi, E., & Vitulano, D. (2013). Jensen-Shannon divergence for visual quality assessment. *Signal Image and Video Processing, 7*(3).

Bruni, V., Crawford, A. J., & Vitulano, D. (2006). Visibility based detection of complicated objects: a case study.[IEE.]. *Proceedings of the IEE CVMP, 06*, 55–64.

Bruni, V., Crawford, A., Kokaram, A., & Vitulano, D. (2013). Semi-transparent Blotches Removal from Sepia Images Exploiting Visibility Laws. *Signal Image and Video Processing, 7*(1), 11–26. doi:10.1007/s11760-011-0220-1

Bruni, V., Ramponi, G., Restrepo, A., & Vitulano, D. (2009). *Context-Based Defading of Archive Photographs*. EURASIP Journal on Image and Video Processing, Special Issue on Image and Video Processing for Cultural Heritage.

Bruni, V., Rossi, E., & Vitulano, D. (2012). On the Equivalence between Jensen-Shannon Divergence and Michelson Contrast. *IEEE Transactions on Information Theory, 58*(7), 4278–4288. doi:10.1109/TIT.2012.2192903

Bruni, V., & Vitulano, D. (2004). A Generalized Model for Scratch Detection. *IEEE Transactions on Image Processing, 13*(1), 44–50. doi:10.1109/TIP.2003.817231 PMID:15376956

Bruni, V., Vitulano, D., & Wang, Z. (2013). Special Issue on Human Vision and Information Theory. *Signal Image and Video Processing, 7*(3), 389–390. doi:10.1007/s11760-013-0447-0

Bushnell, I. W. R. (1982). Discrimination of Faces by Young Infants. *Journal of Experimental Child Psychology, 33*(2), 298–308. doi:10.1016/0022-0965(82)90022-4 PMID:7069368

Buswell, G. T. (1935). *How people look at pictures: A study of the psychology of perception in art*. Chicago: University of Chicago Press.

Butler, E. (2010). *Firesheep*. Retrieved 04 Sep, 2012, from http://codebutler.com/firesheep

Cadavid, S., Mahoor, M. H., & Abdel-Mottaleb, M. (2009). Multi-modal biometric modeling and recognition of the human face and ear. In *Proceedings of IEEE International Workshop on Safety, Security & Rescue Robotics - SSRR 2009* (pp. 1–6). IEEE.

Caelli, W. J., Longley, D., & Shain, M. (1994). *Information Security Handbook*. Basingstoke, UK: Macmillan.

Cai, D., He, X., Han, J., & Zhang, H.-J. (2006). Orthogonal Laplacianfaces for Face Recognition. *IEEE Transactions on Image Processing, 15*(11), 3608–3614. doi:10.1109/TIP.2006.881945 PMID:17076419

Caldara, R., & Miellet, S. (2011). *iMap*: a novel method for statistical fixation mapping of eye movement data. *Behav Res, Springer, 43*, 864–878. doi:10.3758/s13428-011-0092-x PMID:21512875

Calder, A., & Young, A. (2005). Understanding the recognition of facial identity and facial expression. *Nature Reviews. Neuroscience, 6*, 641–651. doi:10.1038/nrn1724 PMID:16062171

Calder, A., Young, A., Rowland, D., Perrett, D., Hodges, J., & Etcoff, H. (1996). Facial emotion recognition after bilateral amygdala damage: Differentially severe impairment of fear. *Cognitive Neuropsychology*, *13*, 699–745. doi:10.1080/026432996381890

Candès, E. J., Li, X., Ma, Y., & Wright, J. (2011). Robust principal component analysis. *Journal of the ACM*, *58*(3). doi:10.1145/1970392.1970395

Cao, X., Wei, Y., Wen, F., & Sun, J. (2012). Face alignment by explicit shape regression. In *Proceedings of IEEE Conference on Computer Vision and Pattern Recognition* (CVPR), (pp. 2887-2894). IEEE.

Cao, X., Shen, W., Yu, L. G., Wang, Y. L., Yang, J. Y., & Zhang, Z. W. (2012). Illumination invariant extraction for face recognition using neighboring wavelet coefficients. *Pattern Recognition*, *45*(4), 1299–1305. doi:10.1016/j.patcog.2011.09.010

Cardinaux, F., Sanderson, C., & Bengio, S. (2006). User authentication via adapted statistical models of face images. *IEEE Transactions on Signal Processing*, *54*(1), 361–373. doi:10.1109/TSP.2005.861075

Cardoso, L., Barbosa, A., Silva, F., Pinheiro, A. M. G., & Proença, H. (2013). Iris Biometrics: Synthesis of Degraded Ocular Images. *IEEE Transactions on Information Forensics and Security*, *8*(7), 1115–1125. doi:10.1109/TIFS.2013.2262942

Castillo, C. D., & Jacobs, D. (2009). Using Stereo Matching with General Epipolar Geometry for 2-D Face Recognition Across Pose. *IEEE Transactions on Pattern Analysis and Machine Intelligence*, *31*(12), 2298–2304. doi:10.1109/TPAMI.2009.123 PMID:19834149

Cavalcanti, G. D. C., Ren, T. I., & Reis, J. R. (2012). Recognition of Partially Occluded Face Using Gradientface and Local Binary Patterns. In *Proceedings of IEEE International Conference on Systems, Man, and Cybernetics*, (pp. 2324-2329). IEEE.

Cavoukian, A., Chibba, M., & Stoianov, A. (2012). Advances in Biometric Encryption: Taking Privacy by Design from Academic Research to Deployment. *The Review of Policy Research*, *29*(1), 37–61. doi:10.1111/j.1541-1338.2011.00537.x

Cerf, M., Harel, J., Einhauser, W., & Koch, C. (2007). Predicting human gaze using low-level saliency combined with face detection. In J. Platt, D. Koller, Y. Singer, & S. Roweis (Eds.), *Advances in Neural Information Processing Systems* (NIPS 2007), (pp. 241–248). Cambridge, MA: Academic Press.

Chadha, A. R., Vaidya, P. P., & Roja, M. M. (2011). Face Recognition Using Discrete Cosine Transform for Global and Local Features. In *Proceedings of International Conference on Recent Advancements in Electrical, Electronics and Control Engineering*, (pp. 502-505). Academic Press.

Chai, X., Qing, L., Shan, S., Chen, X., & Gao, W. (2005). Pose invariant face recognition under arbitrary illumination based on 3D face reconstruction. In Audio- and Video-Based Biometric Person Authentication (pp. 956–965). Academic Press.

Chai, X., Shan, S., Chen, X., & Gao, W. (2007). Locally linear regression for pose-invariant face recognition. *IEEE Transactions on Image Processing*, *16*(7), 1716–1725. doi:10.1109/TIP.2007.899195 PMID:17605371

Chan, C. H., Kittler, J., & Messer, K. (2007). Multi-scale local binary pattern histograms for face recognition. *Advances in Bioethics*, *4642*, 809–818.

Chan, C. H., Tahir, M., Kittler, J., & Pietikäinen, M. (2013). Multiscale local phase quantisation for robust component-based face recognition using kernel fusion of multiple descriptors. *IEEE Transactions on Pattern Analysis and Machine Intelligence*, *35*(5), 1164–1177. doi:10.1109/TPAMI.2012.199 PMID:23520257

Chandler, D. M., & Hemami, S. S. (2007). VSNR: A Wavelet-based Visual Signal-to-Noise Ratio for Natural Images. *IEEE Transactions on Image Processing*, *16*(9), 2284–2298. doi:10.1109/TIP.2007.901820 PMID:17784602

Chang, K., Bowyer, K., & Flynn, P. (2003a). Face Recognition using 2D and 3D facial data. In *Proceedings of ACM Workshop on Multimodal User Authentication* (pp. 25–32). ACM.

Chang, K. I., Bowyer, K. W., & Flynn, P. J. (2005). An Evaluation of Multimodal 2D + 3D Face Biometrics. *IEEE Transactions on Pattern Analysis and Machine Intelligence*, *27*(4), 619–624. doi:10.1109/TPAMI.2005.70 PMID:15794165

Chang, K. I., Bowyer, K. W., & Flynn, P. J. (2006). Multiple Nose Region Matching for 3D Face Recognition under Varying Facial Expression. *IEEE Transactions on Pattern Analysis and Machine Intelligence*, 28(6), 1695–1700. doi:10.1109/TPAMI.2006.210 PMID:16986549

Chang, K., Victor, B., Bowyer, K. W., & Sarkar, S. (2003b). Comparison and Combination of Ear and Face Images in Appearance-Based Biometrics. *IEEE Transactions on Pattern Analysis and Machine Intelligence*, 25(8), 1160–1165. doi:10.1109/TPAMI.2003.1227990

Chaos Computer Club. (2013). *Chaos Computer Club breaks Apple TouchID*. Retrieved 06 Nov, 2013, from http://www.ccc.de/en/updates/2013/ccc-breaks-apple-touchid

Chapelle, O., Scholkopf, B., & Zie, A. (Eds.). (2006). *Semi-SupervisedLearning*. Cambridge, MA: MIT Press. doi:10.7551/mitpress/9780262033589.001.0001

Chellappa, R., Charles, L. W., & Saad, S. (1995). Human and machine recognition of faces: A survey. *Proceedings of the IEEE*, 83(5), 705–741. doi:10.1109/5.381842

Chellappa, R., Du, M., Turaga, P., & Zhou, S. K. (2011). Face Tracking and Recognition from Video. In S. Z. Li, & A. K. Jain (Eds.), *Handbook of Face Recognition* (2nd ed., pp. 323–351). London: Springer. doi:10.1007/978-0-85729-932-1_13

Chellappa, R., Ni, J., & Patel, V. M. (2012). Remote identification of faces: Problems, prospects, and progress. *Pattern Recognition Letters*, 33, 1849–1859. doi:10.1016/j.patrec.2011.11.020

Chen, C. P., & Chen, C. S. (2005). Lighting normalization with generic intrinsic illumination subspace for face recognition. In *Proceedings of Tenth IEEE International Conference on Computer Vision*, (pp. 1089-1096). IEEE.

Chen, C., Dantcheva, A., & Ross, A. (2013). Automatic facial makeup detection with application in face recognition. In *Proceedings of International Conference on Biometrics, ICB 2013* (pp. 1-8). ICB.

Chen, D., Cao, X., Wen, F., & Sun, J. (2013). Blessing of Dimensionality: High-dimensional Feature and Its Efficient Compression for Face Verification. *In Proceedings of IEEE Conference on Computer Vision and Pattern Recognition* (CVPR). IEEE.

Chen, H. F., Belhumeur, P. N., & Jacobs, D. W. (2000). In search of illumination invariants. In *Proceedings of IEEE Conference on Computer Vision and Pattern Recognition, Proceedings*, (pp. 254-261). IEEE.

Chen, Hu, Zhang, Li, & Zhang. (n.d.). Face annotation for family photo album management. *International Journal of Image and Graphics, 3*(1), 1-14.

Chen, L.-H., Yang, Y.-H., Chen, C.-S., & Cheng, M.-Y. (2011). *Illumination invariant feature extraction based on natural images statistics -- Taking face images as an example.* Paper presented at the 2011 IEEE Conference on Computer Vision and Pattern Recognition. New York, NY.

Chen, T., Yin, W. T., Zhou, X. S., Comaniciu, D., & Huang, T. S. (2005). Illumination normalization for face recognition and uneven background correction using total variation based image models. In *Proceedings of 2005 IEEE Computer Society Conference on Computer Vision and Pattern Recognition*, (vol. 2, pp. 532-539). IEEE.

Chen, X., Flynn, P. J., & Bowyer, K. W. (2003). *Visible-light and infrared face recognition.* Paper presented at the Proc. Workshop on Multimodal User Authentication. New York, NY.

Chen, J., Liu, X., Tu, P., & Aragones, A. (2013). Learning person-specific models for facial expressions and action unit recognition. *Pattern Recognition Letters*, 34(15), 1964–1970. doi:10.1016/j.patrec.2013.02.002

Chen, T., Yin, W., Zhou, X. S., Comaniciu, D., & Huang, T. S. (2006). Total variation models for variable lighting face recognition. *IEEE Transactions on Pattern Analysis and Machine Intelligence*, 28(9), 1519–1524. doi:10.1109/TPAMI.2006.195 PMID:16929737

Chen, W., Er, M. J., & Wu, S. (2006). Illumination compensation and normalization for robust face recognition using discrete cosine transform in logarithm domain. *Trans. Sys. Man Cyber. Part B*, 36(2), 458–466. doi:10.1109/TSMCB.2005.857353

Chew, S. W., Lucey, P., Saragih, S., Cohn, J. F., & Sridharan, S. (2012). In the pursuit of effective affective computing: The relationship between features and registration. *IEEE Transactions on Systems, Man and Cybernetics. Part B*, 42(4), 1006–1016.

Chingovska, I., Anjos, A., & Marcel, S. (2012). *On the Effectiveness of Local Binary Patterns in Face Anti-spoofing*. Paper presented at the International Conference of the Biometrics Special Interest Group (BIOSIG). Darmstadt, Germany.

Cho, D.-H., Park, K. R., Rhee, D. W., Kim, Y., & Yang, J. (2006). *Pupil and Iris Localization for Iris Recognition in Mobile Phones*. Paper presented at the Seventh ACIS International Conference on Software Engineering, Artificial Intelligence, Networking, and Parallel/Distributed Computing (SNPD). Las Vegas, NV.

Choi, E., Lee, S. W., & Wallraven, C. (2012). Face Recognition with Enhanced Local Gabor Binary Pattern from Human Fixations. In *Proceedings of IEEE International Conference on Systems, Man, and Cybernetics*. IEEE.

Chono, K., Lin, Y., Varodayan, D., Miyamoto, Y., & Girod, B. (2008). Reduced-reference image quality estimation using distributed source coding. In *Proceedings of IEEE International Conference on Multimedia and Expo*, (pp. 609-612). IEEE.

Chu, W., de la Torre, F., & Cohn, J. F. (2013). Selective transfer machine for personalized facial action unit detection. In *Proceedings of the IEEE Conference on Computer Vision and Pattern Recognition, 2013*. IEEE.

Chunyan, X., Savvides, M., & Kumar, B. V. K. V. (2005). *Quaternion Correlation Filters for Face Recognition in Wavelet Domain*. Paper presented at the Acoustics, Speech, and Signal Processing, 2005 (ICASSP '05). New York, NY.

Chyuan-Huei, T., Shang-Hong, L., & Long-Wen, C. (2002). *Robust face matching under different lighting conditions*. Paper presented at the Multimedia and Expo, 2002. ICME '02. New York, NY.

Cilibrasi, R., & Vitanyi, P. (2005). Clustering by compression. *IEEE Transactions on Information Theory, 51*(4), 1523–1545. doi:10.1109/TIT.2005.844059

Claes, P., Smeets, D., Hermans, J., Vandermeulen, D., & Suetens, P. (2011). SHREC'11 track: Robust fitting of statistical model. In *Proceedings of Eurographics Workshop on 3D Object Retrieval*, (pp. 89–95). Academic Press.

Clarke, N. L., & Furnell, S. M. (2007). Advanced user authentication for mobile devices. *Computers & Security, 26*(2), 109–119. doi:10.1016/j.cose.2006.08.008

Clausi, D. A., & Jernigan, M. (1996). *Towards a Novel Approach for Texture Segmentation of SAR Sea Ice Imagery*. Paper presented at the 26th International Symposium on Remote Sensing of Environment and 18th Annual Symposium of the Canadian Remote Sensing Society. Vancouver, Canada.

Coates, A., & Ng, A. Y. (2011). The importance of encoding versus training with sparse coding and vector quantization. In *Proc. 25th Int. Conf. on Machine Learning*. Bellevue, WA: Academic Press.

Cohn, J. F., & Ekman, P. (2005). Measuring facial actions. In *The New Handbook of Methods in Nonverbal Behavior Research* (pp. 9–64). Oxford, UK: Oxford University Press.

Cohn, J. F., & Schmidt, K. L. (2004). The timing of facial motion in posed and spontaneous smiles. *International Journal of Wavelets, Multresolution, and Information Processing, 2*(2), 121–132. doi:10.1142/S021969130400041X

Colmenarez, A. J., & Huang, T. S. (1997). Face Detection with Information-based Maximum Discrimination. In *Proceedings of IEEE Conference on Computer Vision and Pattern Recognition*, (pp. 782-787). IEEE.

Colombo, A., Cusano, C., & Schettini, R. (2011). UMB-DB: A database of partially occluded 3D faces. In *Proceedings of International Conference on Computer Vision – Workshops* (pp. 2113–2119). Academic Press.

Colombo, A., Cusano, C., & Schettini, R. (2009). Gappy PCA classification for occlusion tolerant 3D face detection. *Journal of Mathematical Imaging and Vision, 35*(3), 193–207. doi:10.1007/s10851-009-0165-y

Colombo, A., Cusano, C., & Schettini, R. (2011). Three-dimensional occlusion detection and restoration of partially occluded faces. *Journal of Mathematical Imaging and Vision, 40*(1), 105–119. doi:10.1007/s10851-010-0252-0

Comaniciu, D., & Ramesh, V. (2000). Robust detection and tracking of human faces with an active camera. In *Proceedings Third IEEE International Workshop on Visual Surveillance, 2000* (pp. 11-18). IEEE.

Comaniciu, D., Ramesh, V., & Meer, P. (2000). Real-time tracking of non-rigid objects using mean shift. In *Proceedings of IEEE Conference on Computer Vision and Pattern Recognition* (CVPR), (pp. 142-149). IEEE.

Comaniciu, D., Ramesh, V., & Meer, P. (2003). Kernel-based object tracking. *IEEE Transactions on Pattern Analysis and Machine Intelligence*, 25(2), 564–577. doi:10.1109/TPAMI.2003.1195991

Computational Biomedicine Lab Of University Of Houston. (2009). *Uhdb11 Face Database*. Author.

Cook, J., Chandran, V., & Fookes, C. (2006). 3D Face Recognition Using Log-Gabor Templates. *British Machine Vision Conference, 2*, 769-778.

Cook, J., Chandran, V., Sridharan, S., & Fookes, C. (2004). Face recognition from 3D data using iterative closest point algorithm and Gaussian mixture models. In *Proceedings of International Symposium on 3D Data Processing, Visualization and Transmission, 3DPVT 2004* (pp. 502-509). 3DPVT.

Cook, D. J., Augusto, J. C., & Jakkula, V. R. (2009). Ambient intelligence: Technologies, applications, and opportunities. *Pervasive and Mobile Computing*, 5(4), 277–298. doi:10.1016/j.pmcj.2009.04.001

Cootes, T. F., Edwards, G. J., & Taylor, C. J. (2001). Active appearance models. *IEEE Transactions on Pattern Analysis and Machine Intelligence*, 23(6), 681–685. doi:10.1109/34.927467

Cootes, T. F., Taylor, C. J., Cooper, D. H., & Graham, J. (1995). Active Shape Models-Their Training And Application. *Computer Vision and Image Understanding*, 61(1), 38–59. doi:10.1006/cviu.1995.1004

Corvée, E., Bak, S., & Brémond, F. (2012). People Detection and Re-identification for Multi Surveillance Camera. In *Proceedings of VISAPP* (pp. 82-88). SciTePress.

Cosker, D., Krumhuber, E., & Hilton, A. (2011). A FACS valid 3D dynamic action unit database with applications to 3D dynamic morphable facial modeling. In *Proceedings of the IEEE International Conference on Computer Vision*, (pp. 2296–2303). IEEE.

Coskun, B., & Herley, C. (2008). *Can Something You Know Be Saved?* Paper presented at the Information Security Conference (ISC08). Taipei, Taiwan.

Cover, T. M., & Thomas, J. A. (1991). *Elements of information Theory*. New York: Wiley. doi:10.1002/0471200611

Cover, T., Gacs, P., & Gray, M. (1989). Kolmogorov's contributions to information theory and algorithmic complexity. *Annals of Probability*, 17, 840–865. doi:10.1214/aop/1176991250

Cox, D., & Pinto, N. (2011). Beyond simple features: A large-scale feature search approach to unconstrained face recognition. In *Proc. IEEE Automatic Face and Gesture Recognition (AFGR)*. Santa Barbara, CA: IEEE.

Cox, I. J., Ghosn, J., & Yianilos, P. N. (1996). Feature-based face recognition using mixture distance. In *Proceedings of International Conference on Computer Vision and Pattern Recognition* (pp. 209-216). Academic Press.

Craw, I., Tock, D., & Bennett, A. (1992). Finding Face Features. In *Proceedings of the Second European Conference on Computer Vision*, (pp. 92-96). Academic Press.

Cui, J., Wen, F., Xiao, R., Tian, Y., & Tang, X. (2007). EasyAlbum: an interactive photo annotation system based on face clustering and re-ranking. In *Proceedings of the SIGCHI Conference on Human Factors in Computing Systems* (CHI '07) (pp. 367-376). ACM.

Cui, Y., Schuon, S., Chan, D., Thrun, S., & Theobalt, C. (2010). *3D shape scanning with a time-of-flight camera (CVPR)*. Paper presented at the IEEE Conference on Computer Vision and Pattern Recognition. San Francisco, CA.

Daily News. (2013). Retrieved from http://www.nydailynews.com/entertainment/gossip/ben-affleck-loses-grizzly-beard-oscars-win-article-1.1273919

Dai, Y., & Nakano, Y. (1996). Face-Texture Model based on SGLD and its Application in Face Detection in a Color Scene. *Pattern Recognition*, 29(6), 1007–1017. doi:10.1016/0031-3203(95)00139-5

Dalal, N., & Triggs, B. (2005). Histograms of oriented gradients for human detection. In *Proceedings of IEEE Conference on Computer Vision and Pattern Recognition (CVPR)*, (pp. 886-893). IEEE.

Dantcheva, A., & Dugelay, J. (2011). Frontal-to-side face re-identification based on hair, skin and clothes patches. In *Proceedings of IEEE International Conference on Advanced Video and Signal-Based Surveillance*, (pp. 309-313). IEEE.

Dantcheva, A., Chen, C., & Rosant, A. (2012). Can Facial Cosmetics Affect the Matching Accuracy of Face Recognition Systems. In *Proceedings of IEEE Fifth International Conference on Biometrics: Theory, Applications and System* (pp. 391-398). IEEE.

Daoudi, M., ter Haar, F., & Veltkamp, R. (2008). *SHREC contest session on retrieval of 3D face scans.* Shape Modeling International.

Darwin, C. (1872). *The Expression of the Emotions in Man and Animals.* John Murray. doi:10.1037/10001-000

Dasgupta, S., & Gupta, A. (2002). An elementary proof of a theorem of Johnson and Lindenstrauss. *Random Structures and Algorithms*, 22(1), 60–65. doi:10.1002/rsa.10073

Dass, S. C., Zhu, Y. F., & Jain, A. K. (2006). Validating a biometric authentication system: Sample size requirements. *IEEE Transactions on Pattern Analysis and Machine Intelligence*, 28(12), 1902–1913. doi:10.1109/TPAMI.2006.255 PMID:17108366

Daugman, J. G. (1993). High confidence visual recognition of persons by a test of statistical independence. *IEEE Transactions on Pattern Analysis and Machine Intelligence*, 15(11), 1148–1161. doi:10.1109/34.244676

Davis, J. (2001). *Hierarchical Motion History Images for Recognizing Human Motion.* Paper presented at the IEEE Workshop on Detection and Recognition of Events in Video. Vancouver, Canada.

Davis, J. V., Kulis, B., Jain, P., Sra, S., & Dhillon, I. S. (2007). Information theoretic metric learning. In *Proc. 24th Int. Conf. on Machine Learning (ICML).* Corvallis, OR: ICML.

De Carlo, D., & Metaxas, D. (2000). Optical flow constraints on deformable models with applications to face tracking. *International Journal of Computer Vision*, 38(2), 99–127. doi:10.1023/A:1008122917811

de la Torre, F., Campoy, J., Ambadar, Z., & Cohn, J. F. (2007). Temporal segmentation of facial behavior. In *Proceedings of the IEEE International Conference on Computer Vision*, (pp. 1–8). IEEE.

De La Torre, F., & Black, M. J. (2003). A framework for robust subspace learning. *International Journal of Computer Vision*, 54(1-3), 117–142. doi:10.1023/A:1023709501986

De Marsico, M., Nappi, M., & Riccio, D. (2009). A Self-tuning People Identification System from Split Face Components. In *Proceedings of Advances in Image and Video Technology - Third Pacific Rim Symposium, PSIVT 2009*, (LNCS) (vol. 5414, pp. 1–12). Berlin: Springer.

De Marsico, M., Nappi, M., & Riccio, D. (2010). Face: face analysis for Commercial Entities. In *Proceedings of IEEE International Conference on Image Processing (ICIP)*, (pp. 1597-1600). ICIP.

De Marsico, M., Nappi, M., Riccio, D., & Dugelay, J.-L. (2012). *Moving Face Spoofing Detection via 3D Projective Invariants.* Paper presented at the 5th IAPR International Conference on Biometrics (ICB). New Delhi, India.

De Marsico, M., Nappi, M., Riccio, D., & Wechsler, H. (2011). Robust Face Recognition after Plastic Surgery Using Local Region Analysis. In *Proceedings of International Conference on Image Analysis and Recognition* (LNCS), (Vol. 6754, pp. 191-200). Berlin: Springer.

De Marsico, M., Nappi, M., Riccio, D., & Wechsler, H. (2013c). Demographics versus Biometric Automatic Interoperability. In *Proceedings of International Conference on Image Analysis and Processing, ICIAP 2013* (LNCS), (vol. 8156, pp. 472-481). Berlin: Springer.

De Marsico, M., Cinque, L., & Levialdi, S. (1997). Indexing pictorial documents by their content: a survey of current techniques. *Image and Vision Computing*, 15(2), 119–141. doi:10.1016/S0262-8856(96)01114-6

De Marsico, M., Doretto, G., & Riccio, D. (2012). M-VIVIE: a Multi-thread Video Indexer Via Identity Extraction. *Pattern Recognition Letters*, 33(14), 1882–1890. doi:10.1016/j.patrec.2012.03.005

De Marsico, M., Nappi, M., & Riccio, D. (2012). CABALA—Collaborative architectures based on biometric adaptable layers and activities. *Pattern Recognition*, 45(6), 2348–2362. doi:10.1016/j.patcog.2011.12.005

De Marsico, M., Nappi, M., Riccio, D., & Tortora, G. (2013a). Entropy Based Template Analysis in Face Biometric Identification Systems. *Journal of Signal. Image and Video Processing*, 7(3), 493–505. doi:10.1007/s11760-013-0451-4

De Marsico, M., Nappi, M., Riccio, D., & Wechsler, H. (2013). Robust Face Recognition for Uncontrolled Pose and Illumination Changes. *IEEE Transactions on Systems, Man, and Cybernetics. Systems, 43*(1), 149–163.

De Marsico, M., Nappi, M., Ricci, D., & Wechsler, H. (2011). Robust face recognition after plastic surgery using local region analysis. In *Proc. Int. Conf. on Image Analysis and Recognition (ICIAR)*. Burnaby, Canada: ICIAR.

Delac, K., & Grgic, M. (2007). *Face recognition*. I-TECH Education and Publishing. doi:10.5772/38

Deng, W., Hu, J., Lu, J., & Guo, J. (2013). Transform-Invariant PCA: A Unified Approach to Fully Automatic Face Alignment, Representation, and Recognition. *IEEE Transactions on Pattern Analysis and Machine Intelligence*. doi:10.1109/TPAMI.2013.194 PMID:24101334

Dhamecha, T. I., Nigam, A., Singh, R., & Vatsa, M. (2013). Disguise Detection and Face Recognition in Visible and Thermal Spectrum. In *Proceedings of IAPR International Conference on Biometrics* (pp. 1-8). IAPR.

Ding, L., Ding, X., & Fang, C. (2012). Continuous pose normalization for pose-robust face recognition. *IEEE Signal Processing Letters, 19*(11), 721–724. doi:10.1109/LSP.2012.2215586

Donato, G., Bartlett, M. S., Hager, J. C., Ekman, P., & Sejnowski, T. J. (1999). Classifying facial actions. *IEEE Transactions on Pattern Analysis and Machine Intelligence, 21*(10), 974–989. doi:10.1109/34.799905 PMID:21188284

Doretto, G., Sebastian, T., Tu, P., & Rittscher, J. (2011). Appearance-based person reidentification in camera networks: Problem overview and current aspects. *J. Ambient Intell. Human Comput., 2*(2), 1–25.

Douglas-Cowie, E., Cowie, R., Cox, C., Amier, N., & Heylen, D. (2008). The sensitive artificial listener: an induction technique for generating emotionally coloured conversation. In *Proceedings of the LREC Workshop on Corpora for Research on Emotion and Affect*. LREC.

Doulamis, A., & Makantasis, K. (2011). *Iterative Scene Learning In Visually Guided Persons' Falls Detection (EUSIPCO)*. Paper presented at the 19th European Conference on Signal Processing. Barcelona, Spain.

Doulamis, A., Kosmopoulos, D., Sardis, M., & Varvarigou, T. (2008). *An architecture for a self configurable video supervision*. Paper presented at the ACM International Conference on Multimedia. Vancouver, Canada.

Doulamis, A. (2010). Dynamic tracking re-adjustment: a method for automatic tracking recovery in complex visual environments. *Journal of Multimedia Tools and Applications, 50*(1), 49–73. doi:10.1007/s11042-009-0368-7

Doulamis, A., Doulamis, N., & Kollias, S. (2000). A fuzzy video content representation for video summarization and content-based retrieval. *Signal Processing, 80*(6), 1049–1067. doi:10.1016/S0165-1684(00)00019-0

Douze, M., Jegou, H., Sandhawalia, H., Amsaleg, L., & Schmid, C. (2009). Evaluation of GIST descriptors for Web-scale image search. In *Proc. 8th ACM Int. Conf. on Image and Video Retrieval (CIVR)*. Santorini Island, Greece: ACM.

Drahanský, M. (2011). Liveness Detection in Biometrics. In *Advanced Biometric Technologies* (pp. 179–198). InTech-Open Access Publisher. doi:10.5772/17205

Drira, H., Ben Amor, B., Srivastava, A., Daoudi, M., & Slama, R. (2013). 3D Face Recognition Under Expressions, Occlusions and Pose Variations. *IEEE Transactions on Pattern Analysis and Machine Intelligence, 35*(9), 2270–2283. doi:10.1109/TPAMI.2013.48 PMID:23868784

Du, S., & Ward, R. (2005). Wavelet-based illumination normalization for face recognition. In *Proceedings of 2005 International Conference on Image Processing (ICIP)*, (pp. 2129-2132). ICIP.

Dubuque, S., Coffman, T., McCarley, P., Bovik, A. C., & Thomas, C. W. (2009). A comparison of foveated acquisition and tracking performance relative to uniform resolution approaches. In *Proceedings of SPIE* (Vol. 7321). SPIE. doi:10.1117/12.818716

Duc, B., Fischer, S., & Bigun, J. (1999). Face authentication with Gabor information on deformable graphs. *IEEE Transactions on Image Processing, 8*(4), 504–516. doi:10.1109/83.753738 PMID:18262894

Duda, R. O., Hart, P. E., & Stork, D. G. (2000). *Pattern Classification* (2nd ed.). Wiley.

Dupont, S., & Luettin, J. (2000). Audio-visual speech modeling for continuous speech recognition. *IEEE Transactions on Multimedia, 2*(3), 141–151. doi:10.1109/6046.865479

ECCV 2008 (LNCS), (vol. 5302, pp. 234–247). Berlin: Springer.

Eckert, M.-L., Kose, N., & Dugelay, J.-L. (2013). Facial Cosmetics Database and Impact Analysis on Automatic Face Recognition. In *Proceedings of IEEE International Workshop on Multimedia Signal Processing*. IEEE.

Edwards, G. J., Cootes, T. F., & Taylor, C. J. (1998). Face recognition using active appearance models. In *Proceedings of Computer Vision (ECCV)*. Springer.

Ekenel, H. K., & Stiefelhagen, R. (2005). Local appearance-based face recognition using discrete cosine transform. In *Proceedings of 13th European Signal Processing Conference*, (pp. 1-5). Academic Press.

Ekenel, H. K., & Stiefelhagen, R. (2006). Analysis of local appearance-based face recognition: Effects of feature selection and feature normalization. In *Proc. of the CVPR Biometrics Workshop* (pp. 34–41). CVPR.

Ekman, P., Friesen, W., & Hager, J.C. (2002). *Facial action coding system*. A Human Face.

Ekman, P. (2003). Darwin, deception, and facial expression. *Annals of the New York Academy of Sciences, 1000*, 205–221. doi:10.1196/annals.1280.010 PMID:14766633

Ekman, P., & Friesen, W. V. (1978). *The Facial Action Coding System: A Technique for Measurement of Facial Movement*. Consulting Psychologists Press.

Ekman, P., & Rosenberg, L. E. (2005). *What the face reveals: Basic and applied studies of spontaneous expression using the Facial Action Coding System*. Oxford University Press. doi:10.1093/acprof:oso/9780195179644.001.0001

Equinox. (2004). *Face database*. Retrieved from www.equinoxsensors.com/products/HID.html

Equinox. (n.d.). Retrieved from http://www.equinoxsensors.com/product/hid.html

Erdogmus, N., & Dugelay, J.-L. (2012). On Discriminative Properties of TPS Warping Parameters for 3D Face Recognition. In *Proceedings of International Conference on Informatics, Electronics & Vision* (pp. 225-230). Academic Press.

Erdogmus, N., & Marcel, S. (2013). Spoofing in 2D Face Recognition with 3D Masks and Anti-spoofing with Kinect. In *Proc. of IEEE Conf. on Biometrics: Theory, Applications and Systems*. IEEE.

Erdogmus, N., Kose, N., & Dugelay, J.-L. (2012). Impact analysis of nose alterations on 2D and 3D face recognition. In *Proceedings of IEEE International Workshop on Multimedia Signal Processing* (pp. 354-359). IEEE.

Erkin, Z., Franz, M., Guajardo, J., Katzenbeisser, S., Lagendijk, I., & Toft, T. (2009). *Privacy-Preserving Face Recognition*. Paper presented at the 9th International Symposium on Privacy Enhancing Technologies (PETS). Seattle, WA.

Etemad, K., & Chellappa, R. (1997). Discriminant analysis for recognition of human face images. *Journal of the Optical Society of America, 14*(8), 1724–1733. doi:10.1364/JOSAA.14.001724

Ethz, A. Ess, B-Leibe, & Gool. (2007). *Depth and appearance for mobile scene analysis*. Retrieved from http://www.vision.ee.ethz.ch/~aess/iccv2007/

Evans, J. J., Heggs, A. J., Antoun, N., & Hodges, J. R. (1995). Progressive prosopagnosia associated with selective right temporal lobe atrophy: a new syndrome? *Brain, 118*, 1–13. doi:10.1093/brain/118.1.1 PMID:7894996

Everson, R., & Sirovich, L. (1995). Karhunen–Loeve procedure for gappy data. *Journal of the Optical Society of America. A, Optics, Image Science, and Vision, 12*(8), 1657–1664. doi:10.1364/JOSAA.12.001657

Evgeniou, T., & Pontil, M. (2004). Regularized multi-task learning. In *Proc. 17th ACM SIGKDD Int. Conf. Knowledge Discovery Data Mining*, (pp. 109–117). ACM.

EyeLock. (2013). *HBOX®*. Retrieved 09 Aug, 2013, from http://www.eyelock.com/Products/HBOX%C2%AE.aspx

Faltemier, T. C., Bowyer, K. W., & Flynn, P. J. (2008). A region ensemble for 3-D face recognition. *Transactions on Information Forensics and Security, 3*(1), 62–73.

Faltemier, T. C., Bowyer, K. W., & Flynn, P. J. (2008b). Using Multi Instance Enrollment to Improve Performance of 3D Face Recognition. *Computer Vision and Image Understanding, 112*(2), 114–125. doi:10.1016/j.cviu.2008.01.004

Farenzena, M., Bazzani, L., Perina, A., Murino, V., & Cristani, M. (2010). Person Re-Identification by Symmetry-Driven Accumulation of Local Features. In *Proc. of IEEE Computer Society Conference on Computer Vision and Pattern Recognition*, (pp. 2360-2367). IEEE.

Fasel, B., & Luettin, J. (2003). Automatic facial expression analysis: a survey. *Pattern Recognition*, *36*(1), 259–275. doi:10.1016/S0031-3203(02)00052-3

Fecteau, J. H., & Munoz, D. P. (2006). Salience, relevance, and firing: a priority map for target selection. *Trends in Cognitive Sciences*, *10*, 382–390. doi:10.1016/j.tics.2006.06.011 PMID:16843702

Felzenszwalb, P. F., & Huttenlocher, D. P. (2005). Pictorial structures for object recognition. *International Journal of Computer Vision*, *61*(1), 55–79. doi:10.1023/B:VISI.0000042934.15159.49

FERET. (n.d.). *Face Recognition Technology Database*. Retrieved from http://www.itl.nist.gov/iad/humanid/feret/

Fischer, M. (2008). *Automatic identification of persons in TV series*. Diplomarbeit, Interactive Systems Labs, Universitat Karlsruhe (TH).

Fischer, Ekenel, & Stiefelhagen. (2011). Person re-identification in TV series using robust face recognition and user feedback. *Multimedia Tools and Applications*, *55*(1), 83–104. doi:10.1007/s11042-010-0603-2

Fischler, M. A., & Bolles, R. C. (1981). Random sample consensus. *Communications of the ACM*, *24*(6), 381–395. doi:10.1145/358669.358692

Fischler, M. A., & Elschlager, R. A. (1973). The representation and matching of pictorial structures. *IEEE Transactions on Computers*, *100*(1), 67–92. doi:10.1109/T-C.1973.223602

Florêncio, D., & Herley, C. (2007). *A Large-Scale Study of Web Password Habits*. Paper presented at the 16th International World Wide Web Conference (WWW2007). Banff, Canada.

Flusser, J., Zitova, B., & Suk, T. (2009). *Moment Functions in Image Analysis: Theory and Applications*. Wiley.

Frank, M. G., & Ekman, P. (1997). The ability to detect deceit generalizes across different types of high-stakes lies. *Journal of Personality and Social Psychology*, *72*(6), 1429–1439. doi:10.1037/0022-3514.72.6.1429 PMID:9177024

Fratric, I., & Ribaric, S. (2011). Local Binary LDA for Face Recognition. *Biometrics and ID Management*, 144-155.

Frazor, R., & Geisler, W. (2006). Local luminance and contrast in natural images. *Vision Research*, *46*, 1585–1598. doi:10.1016/j.visres.2005.06.038 PMID:16403546

Freund, Y., & Shapire, R. E. (1996). Experiments with a new boosting algorithm. In *Proc. 13th Int. Conf. on Machine Learning (ICML)*. Bari, Italy: ICML.

Friedman, F. H., Hastie, T., & Tibshirani, R. (2000). Additive logistic regression: A statistical view of boosting. *Annals of Statistics*, *28*, 337–407. doi:10.1214/aos/1016218223

Fukushima, K. (1980). Neocognitron: A self-organizing neural network model for a mechanism of pattern recognition unaffected by shift in position. *Biological Cybernetics*, *36*(4), 193–202. doi:10.1007/BF00344251 PMID:7370364

Furnell, S., & Clarke, N. (2005). Biometrics: no silver bullets. *Computer Fraud & Security*, (8): 9–14. doi:10.1016/S1361-3723(05)70243-8

Fusier, F., Valentin, V., Bremond, F., Thonnat, M., Borg, M., Thirde, D., & Ferryman, J. (2007). Video understanding for complex activity recognition. *Machine Vision and Applications*, *18*, 167–188. doi:10.1007/s00138-006-0054-y

Gan, J., & Xiao, J. (2011). *An Over-Complete Sparse Representation Approach For Face Recognition Under Partial Occlusion*. Paper Presented At The International Conference On System Science And Engineering. Macau, China.

Gandhi, T., & Trivedi, M. (2007). Person tracking and reidentification: Introducing Panoramic Appearance Map (PAM) for feature representation. *Machine Vision and Applications*, *18*(3), 207–220. doi:10.1007/s00138-006-0063-x

Ganek, A., & Corbi, T. (2003). The dawning of the autonomic computing era. *IBM Systems Journal, 42*(1), 5–18. doi:10.1147/sj.421.0005

Gang, H., & Akbarzadeh, A. (2009). *A robust elastic and partial matching metric for face recognition.* Paper presented at the Computer Vision, 2009 IEEE 12th International Conference on. New York, NY.

Gao, Y. S., & Leung, M. K. H. (2002). Face recognition using line edge map. *IEEE Transactions on Pattern Analysis and Machine Intelligence, 24*(6), 764–779. doi:10.1109/TPAMI.2002.1008383

Garcia, C., & Delakis, M. (2002). A neural architecture for fast and robust face detection. In *Proceedings of 16th International Conference on Pattern Recognition*, (vol. 2, pp. 44-47). ICPR.

Gates, K. A. (2011). *Our Biometric Future: Facial Recognition Technology and the Culture of Surveillance.* New York University Press.

Gauthier, I., & Tanaka, J. W. (2002). Configural and holistic face processing: The Whole story. *Journal of Vision (Charlottesville, Va.), 2*(7), 616–616. doi:10.1167/2.7.616

Gavrila, D. M. (1999). The visual analysis of human movement: A survey. *Computer Vision and Image Understanding, 73*(1), 82–98. doi:10.1006/cviu.1998.0716

Geisler, W. S. (2011). Contributions of ideal observer theory to vision research. *Vision Research, 51*, 771–781. doi:10.1016/j.visres.2010.09.027 PMID:20920517

Geng, C., & Jiang, X. (2009). Face recognition using sift features. In *Proceedings of 16th IEEE International Conference on Image Processing (ICIP)*, (pp. 3313-3316). IEEE.

Geng, X., & Zhi-Hua, Z. (2006). Image Region Selection and Ensemble for Face Recognition. *Journal of Computer Science and Technology, 21*(1), 116–125. doi:10.1007/s11390-006-0116-7

Georghiades, A. S., Belhumeur, P. N., & Kriegman, D. J. (2001). From few to many: Illumination cone models for face recognition under variable lighting and pose. *IEEE Transactions on Pattern Analysis and Machine Intelligence, 23*(6), 643–660. doi:10.1109/34.927464

Goferman, S., Zelnik-Manor, L., & Tal, A. (2012). Context-Aware Saliency Detection. *IEEE Transactions on Pattern Analysis and Machine Intelligence, 34*(10), 1915–1926. doi:10.1109/TPAMI.2011.272 PMID:22201056

Gokberk, B., Irfanoglu, M. O., & Akarun, L. (2006). 3D shape-based face representation and feature extraction for face recognition. *Image and Vision Computing, 24*(8), 857–869. doi:10.1016/j.imavis.2006.02.009

Gökberk, B., İrfanoğlu, M. O., Akarun, L., & Alpaydın, E. (2007). Learning the best subset of local features for face recognition. *Pattern Recognition, 40*(5), 1520–1532. doi:10.1016/j.patcog.2006.09.009

Gokberk, B., Salah, A. A., Akarun, L., Etheve, R., Riccio, D., & Dugelay, J. L. (2008). 3D face recognition. In D. Petrovska-Delacretaz, G. Chollet, & B. Dorizzi (Eds.), *Guide to Biometric Reference Systems and Performance Evaluation* (pp. 1–33). Springer Verlag.

Gong, P., Yr, J., & Zhang, C. (2012). Robust multi-task feature learning. In *Proc. 18th Conf. on Knowledge Discovery and Data Mining (KDD)*. Beijing, China: ACM.

Gonzalez-Jimenez, D., & Alba-Castro, J. L. (2007). Toward pose-invariant 2-D face recognition through point distribution models and facial symmetry. *IEEE Transactions on Information Forensics and Security, 2*(3), 413–429. doi:10.1109/TIFS.2007.903543

Gonzalez, R. C., & Woods, R. E. (1992). *Digital image processing.* Reading, MA: Addison-Wesley.

Gonzalez-Rodriguez, J., Rose, P., Ramos, D., Toledano, D. T., & Ortega-Garcia, J. (2007). Emulating DNA: Rigorous quantification of evidential weight in transparent and testable forensic speaker recognition. *IEEE Trans. on Audio. Speech and Language Processing, 15*(7), 2104–2115. doi:10.1109/TASL.2007.902747

Gordon, G. (1992). Face Recognition Based on Depth and Curvature Features. In *Proceedings of IEEE Conference on Computer Vision and Pattern Recognition*, (pp. 808-810). IEEE.

Gottumukkal, R., & Asari, V. K. (2003). An improved face recognition technique based on modular PCA approach. *Pattern Recognition Letters, 25*, 429–436. doi:10.1016/j.patrec.2003.11.005

Grabner, H., Grabner, M., & Bischof, H. (2006). Real-time tracking via on-line boosting. In *Proceedings of British Machine Vision Conference* (BMVC), (pp. 47-56). BMVC.

Grabner, H., Leistner, C., & Bischof, H. (2008). *Semi-supervised on-line boosting for robust tracking.*

Graham, D. B., & Allinson, N. M. (1998). Characterizing virtual eigensignatures for general purpose face recognition. *Face Recognition: From Theory to Applications, 163,* 446–456. doi:10.1007/978-3-642-72201-1_25

Gray, D., & Tao, H. (2008). Viewpoint invariant pedestrian recognition with an ensemble of localized features. In *Proc. of Europ. Conf. on Computer Vision*. Marseille, France: Academic Press.

Greenblatt, A., Panetta, K., & Agaian, S. (2008). Restoration of semi-transparent blotches in damaged texts, manuscripts and images through localized, logarithmic image enhancement. In *Proceedings of ISCCSP '08*. ISCCSP.

Grgic, M., Delac, K., & Grgic, S. (2011). *SCface - Surveillance cameras face database.*

Grgic, M., Delac, K., & Grgic, S. (2011). SCface–surveillance cameras face database. *Multimedia Tools and Applications, 51*(3), 863–879. doi:10.1007/s11042-009-0417-2

Gross, R., & Brajovic, V. (2003). *An image preprocessing algorithm for illumination invariant face recognition.* Paper presented at the 4th international conference on Audio- and video-based biometric person authentication. New York, NY.

Gross, R. (2005). Face databases. In *Handbook of Face Recognition* (pp. 301–327). Academic Press. doi:10.1007/0-387-27257-7_14

Gross, R., & Brajovic, V. (2003). An image preprocessing algorithm for illumination invariant face recognition. *Audio-and Video-Based Biometric Person Authentication, 2688,* 10–18. doi:10.1007/3-540-44887-X_2

Gross, R., Matthews, I., & Baker, S. (2005). Generic vs. person specific active appearance models. *Image and Vision Computing*. doi:10.1016/j.imavis.2005.07.009

Gross, R., Matthews, I., Cohn, J., Kanade, T., & Baker, S. (2010). Multi-pie. *Image and Vision Computing, 28*(5), 807–813. doi:10.1016/j.imavis.2009.08.002

Gu, X., Gortler, S., & Hoppe, H. (2002). *Geometry Images*. Paper Presented At The 29th International Conference On Computer Graphics And Interactive Techniques (Siggraph). San Antonio, TX.

Günther, M., Costa-Pazo, A., Ding, C., Boutellaa, E., Chiachia, G., Zhang, H., et al. (2013). The 2013 Face Recognition Evaluation in Mobile Environment. In *Proceedings of 6th IAPR International Conference on Biometrics*. IAPR.

Gunturk, B., Batur, A., Altunbasak, Y., Hayes, M. H. I., & Mersereau, R. (2003). Eigenfacedomain super-resolution for face recognition. *IEEE Transactions on Image Processing, 12*(5), 597–606. doi:10.1109/TIP.2003.811513 PMID:18237935

Guo, G., Li, S. Z., & Chan, K. (2000). Face recognition by support vector machines. In *Proceedings of Fourth IEEE International Conference on Automatic Face and Gesture Recognition,* (pp. 196-201). IEEE.

Guo, G. D., & Dyer, C. R. (2005). Learning from examples in the small sample case: Face expression recognition. *IEEE Transactions on Systems, Man, and Cybernetics. Part B, Cybernetics, 35*(3), 479–488. doi:10.1109/TSMCB.2005.846658

Guo, Z., Zhang, L., & Zhang, D. (2010). Rotation Invariant texture classification using LBP variance (LBPV) with global matching. *Pattern Recognition, 43*(3), 706–719. doi:10.1016/j.patcog.2009.08.017

Gupta, S., Markey, M. K., & Bovik, A. C. (2010). Anthropometric 3D face recognition. *International Journal of Computer Vision, 90*(3), 331–349. doi:10.1007/s11263-010-0360-8

Gutta, S., Huang, J., Phillip, P. J., & Wechsler, H. (2000). Mixtures of experts for categorization of human faces based on gender and ethnic origin and pose discrimination. *IEEE Transactions on Neural Networks, 11*(4), 948–960. doi:10.1109/72.857774 PMID:18249821

Haitao, W., Li, S. Z., & Yangsheng, W. (2004). *Face recognition under varying lighting conditions using self quotient image*. Paper presented at the Automatic Face and Gesture Recognition. New York, NY.

Hallinan, P. W. (1994). A Low-Dimensional Representation of Human Faces for Arbitrary Lighting Conditions. In *Proceedings of 1994 IEEE Computer Society Conference on Computer Vision and Pattern Recognition,* (pp. 995-999). IEEE.

Hamdoun, O., Moutarde, F., Stanciulescu, B., & Steux, B. (2008). Person re-identification in multi-camera system by signature based on interest point descriptors collected on short video sequences. In *Proceedings of Second ACM/IEEE International Conference on Distributed Smart Cameras,* (pp. 1-6). ACM/IEEE.

Hamid, R., Maddi, S., Bobick, A., & Essa, M. (2007). *Structure from statistics - unsupervised activity analysis using suffix trees (ICCV).* Paper presented at the IEEE International Conference on Computer Vision. Rio de Janeiro, Brazil.

Hamm, J., Kohler, C. G., Gur, R. C., & Verma, R. (2011). Automated facial action coding system for dynamic analysis of facial expressions in neuropsychiatric disorders. *Journal of Neuroscience Methods, 200*(2), 237–256. doi:10.1016/j.jneumeth.2011.06.023 PMID:21741407

Han, H., Klare, B., Bonnen, K., & Jain, A. K. (2013). Matching composite sketches to face photos: A component based approach. *IEEE Trans. IFS, 8*(1), 191–204.

Harandi, M. T., Ahmadabadi, M. N., & Araabi, B. N. (2007). A hierarchical face identification system based on facial components. In *Proceedings of IEEE/ACS International Conference on Computer Systems and Applications* (pp. 669–675). IEEE.

Harel, J., Koch, C., & Perona, P. (2006). Graph-based visual saliency. In *Proceedings of Advances in Neural Information Processing Systems* (NIPS 2006), (pp. 545-552). NIPS.

He, X., & Niyogi, P. (2003). Locality Preserving Projections. In *Proceedings of Advances in Neural Information Processing Systems 16: Proceedings of the 2003 Conference* (pp. 153-160). Academic Press.

He, X., Cai, D., Yan, S., & Zhang, H.-J. (2005). Neighborhood preserving embedding. In *Proceedings of Tenth IEEE International Conference on Computer Vision, ICCV 2005* (vol. 2, pp. 1208-1213). IEEE.

Heikkila, M., Pietikainen, M., & Schmid, C. (2009). Description of interest regions with Local Binary Pattern. *Pattern Recognition, 42*(3), 425–436. doi:10.1016/j.patcog.2008.08.014

Heisele, B., Ho, P., & Poggio, T. (2001). Face recognition with support vector machines: Global versus component-based approach. In *Proceedings of International Conference on Computer Vision.* Academic Press.

Heisele, B., Ho, P., Wu, J., & Poggio, T. (2003). Face recognition: Component-based versus global approaches. *Computer Vision and Image Understanding, 91*(1), 6–12. doi:10.1016/S1077-3142(03)00073-0

Heller, M., & Haynal, V. (1994). Les visages de la depression de suicide. Kahiers Psychiatriques Genevois (Medecine et Hygiene Editors), 16, 107–117.

Henderson, J. (2003). Human gaze control during real-world scene perception. *Trends in Cognitive Sciences, 7,* 498–504. doi:10.1016/j.tics.2003.09.006 PMID:14585447

Hennings-Yeomans, P., Baker, S., & Kumar, B. (2008). Simultaneous super-resolution and feature extraction for recognition of low-resolution faces. In *Proceedings of IEEE Conf. on Computer Vision and Pattern Recognition,* (pp. 1–8). IEEE.

Heo, J. G., Savvides, M., & Vijayakumar, B. V. K. (2005). Illumination tolerant face recognition using phase-only support vector machines in the frequency domain. *Pattern Recognition and Image Analysis, 3687,* 66–73.

Herley, C., van Oorschot, P. C., & Patrick, A. S. (2009). *Passwords: If We're So Smart, Why Are We Still Using Them?* Paper presented at the 13th International Conference on Financial Cryptography and Data Security (FC). Accra Beach, Barbados.

Hesher, C., Srivastava, A., & Erlebacher, G. (2002). Principal Component Analysis of Range Images for Facial Recognition. In *Proceedings of International Conference on Imaging Science, Systems, and Technology.* Academic Press.

Heusch, G., Rodriguez, Y., & Marcel, S. (2006). *Local Binary Patterns as an Image Preprocessing for Face Authentication.* Paper presented at the 7th International Conference on Automatic Face and Gesture Recognition. New York, NY.

He, X., Yan, S., Hu, Y., Niyogi, P., & Zhang, H. J. (2005). Face recognition using laplacianfaces. *IEEE Transactions on Pattern Analysis and Machine Intelligence, 27*(3), 328–340. doi:10.1109/TPAMI.2005.55 PMID:15747789

Hizem, W., Krichen, E., Ni, Y., Dorizzi, B., & Garcia-Salicetti, S. (2006). Specific sensors for face recognition. *Advances in Bioethics, 3832*, 47–54.

Hjelm, E., & Low, B. K. (2001). Face Detection: A Survey. *Computer Vision and Image Understanding, 83*(3), 236–274. doi:10.1006/cviu.2001.0921

Ho, H. T., & Chellappa, R. (2013). Pose-Invariant Face Recognition Using Markov Random Fields. *IEEE Transactions on Image Processing, 22*, 1573–1584. doi:10.1109/TIP.2012.2233489 PMID:23247858

Hollingsworth, K., Bowyer, K. W., & Flynn, P. J. (2010). *Identifying useful features for recognition in near-infrared periocular images.* Paper presented at the Biometrics: Theory Applications and Systems (BTAS), 2010 Fourth IEEE International Conference on. doi:10.1109/BTAS.2010.5634529

Hollingsworth, K. P., Darnell, S. S., Miller, P. E., Woodard, D. L., Bowyer, K. W., & Flynn, P. J. (2012). Human and Machine Performance on Periocular Biometrics Under Near-Infrared Light and Visible Light. *IEEE Transactions on Information Forensics and Security, 7*(2), 588–601. doi:10.1109/TIFS.2011.2173932

Hongjun, J., & Martinez, A. M. (2009). Support Vector Machines in face recognition with occlusions. In *Proceedings of IEEE Conference on Computer Vision and Pattern Recognition.* IEEE.

Hontsch, I., & Karam, L. (2002). Adaptive Image Coding with Perceptual Distortion Control. *IEEE Transactions on Image Processing, 11*(3), 213–222. doi:10.1109/83.988955 PMID:18244625

Hornak, J., Rolls, E., & Wade, D. (1996). Face and voice expression identification in patients with emotional and behavioral changes following ventral frontal lobe damage. *Neuropsychologia, 34*, 173–181. doi:10.1016/0028-3932(95)00106-9

Ho, S. S., & Wechsler, H. (2008). Query by transduction. *IEEE Transactions on Pattern Analysis and Machine Intelligence, 30*(9), 1557–1571. doi:10.1109/TPAMI.2007.70811 PMID:18617715

Ho, S. S., & Wechsler, H. (2010). A Martingale framework for detecting changes in the data generating model in data streams. *IEEE Transactions on Pattern Analysis and Machine Intelligence, 32*(12), 2113–2127. doi:10.1109/TPAMI.2010.48 PMID:20975112

Hosmer, D. W., & Lemeshow, S. (2000). *Applied logistic regression.* Wiley-Interscience Publication. doi:10.1002/0471722146

Hotelling, H. (1936). Relations between two sets of variates. *Biometrika, 28*, 321–377. doi:10.1093/biomet/28.3-4.321

Hsiao, J. H. (2013). *Eye Movements in Face Recognition.* Intech Book.

Hsiao, J. H., & Cottrell, G. W. (2008). Two fixations suffice in face recognition. *Psychological Science, 9*(10), 998–1006. doi:10.1111/j.1467-9280.2008.02191.x PMID:19000210

Hsu, R.-L., Abdel-Mottaleb, M., & Jain, A. K. (2002). Face Detection in Color Images. *IEEE Transactions on Pattern Analysis and Machine Intelligence, 24*(5), 696–706. doi:10.1109/34.1000242

Hu, Q., Qin, L., Huang, Q., Jiang, S., & Tian, Q. (2010). *Action recognition using spatial-temporal context (ICPR).* Paper presented at the 20th International Conference on Pattern Recognition. Istanbul, Turkey.

Hua, G., Yang, M. H., Learned-Miller, E., Ma, Y., Turk, M., Kriegman, D. J., & Huang, T. S. (2011). Introduction to the special section on real-world face recognition. [PAMI]. *IEEE Transactions on Pattern Analysis and Machine Intelligence, 33*(10), 1921–1924. doi:10.1109/TPAMI.2011.182

Huang, G. B., & Learned-Miller, E. (2007). Unsupervised joint alignment of complex images. In *Proc. of IEEE International Conference on Computer Vision* (ICCV). IEEE.

Huang, G. B., Mattar, M., Berg, T., & Learned-Miller, E. (2008). Labeled faces in the wild: A database for studying face recognition in unconstrained environments. In *Proceedings of Workshop on Faces in 'Real-Life 'Images: Detection, Alignment, and Recognition*. Academic Press.

Huang, G. B., Mattar, M., Lee, H., & Learned-Miller, E. (2012). Learning to Align from Scratch. In Proceedings of Advances in Neural Information Processing Systems (NIPS). NIPS.

Huang, J., Huang, X., & Metaxas, D. (2008). Simultaneous image transformation and sparse representation recovery. In *Proceedings of IEEE Conference on Computer Vision and Pattern Recognition*. IEEE.

Huang, J., Kumar, S. R., Mitra, M., Zhu, W. J., & Zabih, R. (1997). Image indexing using color correlograms. In *Proceedings of IEEE Conf. Computer Vision and Pattern Recognition,* (pp. 762-768). IEEE.

Huang, G. B., Lee, H., & Learned-Miller, E. (2012). Learning hierarchical representations for face verification with convolutional deep belief networks. In *Proc. of Computer Vision and Pattern Recognition (CVPR)*. Providence, RI: CVPR. doi:10.1109/CVPR.2012.6247968

Humphreys, G., Donnelly, N., & Riddoch, M. (1993). Expression is computed separately from facial identity, and it is computed separately for moving and static faces: Neuropsychological evidence. *Neuropsychologia, 31*, 173–181. doi:10.1016/0028-3932(93)90045-2 PMID:8455786

Hung, M.-H., & Hsieh, C.-H. (2008). Event detection of broadcast baseball videos. *IEEE Transactions on Circuits and Systems for Video Technology, 18*(12), 1713–1726. doi:10.1109/TCSVT.2008.2004934

Hurley, D. J., Nixon, M. S., & Carter, J. N. (2000). *A new force field transform for ear and face recognition*. Paper presented at the Image Processing (ICIP), 2009 16th IEEE International Conference on. doi:10.1109/ICIP.2000.900883

Husken, M., Brauckmann, M., Gehlen, S., & Malsburg, C. (2005). Strategies and Benefits of Fusion of 2D and 3D Face Recognition. In *Proceedings of IEEE Workshop Face Recognition Grand Challenge*. IEEE.

Huynh, T., Min, R., & Dugelay, J.-L. (2012). An Efficient LBP-based Descriptor for Facial Depth Images applied to Gender Recognition using RGB-D Face Data. In *Proceedings of ACCV Workshop on Computer Vision with Local Binary Pattern Variants* (pp. 133-145). ACCV.

Ijiri, Y., Sakuragi, M., & Lao. (2006). Security Management for Mobile Devices by Face Recognition. In *Proceedings of 7th International Conference on Mobile Data Management,* (pp. 49-49). MDM.

Imtiaz, H., & Fattah, S. A. (2012). A Wavelet-Domain Local Dominant Feature Selection Scheme for Face Recognition. *ISRN Machine Vision*, 1-13.

INRIA. (n.d.). *Person Dataset*. Retrieved from http://pascal.inrialpes.fr/data/human/

International Biometric Group. (2013). *How is Biometrics Defined?* Retrieved 31 May, 2013, from https://ibgWeb.com/products/reports/free/biometrics-definition

International Organization For Standardization. (2004). *ISO/IEC JTC1/SC29/WG11 Coding Of Moving Pictures And Audio*. ISO/IEC JTC1/SC29/WG11 N6828. Retrieved from http://mpeg.chiariglione.org/sites/default/files/files/standards/docs/w6828_mp7_Overview_v10.zip

Itti, L., & Baldi, P. (2006). Bayesian Surprise Attracts Human Attention. *Advances in Neural Information Processing Systems*, 19.

Itti, L., Koch, C., & Niebur, E. (1998). A model of saliency based visual attention for rapid scene analysis. *IEEE Transactions on Pattern Analysis and Machine, 20*, 1254–1259. doi:10.1109/34.730558

Ivanov, Y., & Bobick, A. (2000). Recognition of visual activities and interactions by stochastic parsing. *IEEE Transactions on Pattern Analysis and Machine Intelligence, 22*(8), 852–872. doi:10.1109/34.868686

Jabid, T., Kabir, M. H., & Chae, O. (2012). Local Directional Pattern (LDP) for Face Recognition. *International Journal of Innovative Computing, 8*(4), 2423–2437.

Jaeger, H., Maass, W., & Principe, J. (2007). Special issue on echo state networks and liquid state machines. *Neural Networks*, *20*(3), 287–289. doi:10.1016/j.neunet.2007.04.001

Jafri, R., & Arabnia, H. R. (2009). A Survey of Face Recognition Techniques. *Journal of Information Processing Systems*, *5*(2), 41–68. doi:10.3745/JIPS.2009.5.2.041

Jain, A. K., Bolle, R., & Pankanti, S. (1999). *Biometrics: Personal identification in networked society*. Boston, MA: Kluwer. doi:10.1007/b117227

Jain, A. K., Hong, L., & Pankanti, S. (2000). Biometric Identification. *Communications of the ACM*, *43*(2), 90–98. doi:10.1145/328236.328110

Jansen, W. A. (2003). *Authenticating Users on Handheld Devices*. Paper presented at the 15th Annual Canadian Information Technology Security Symposium (CITSS). Ottawa, Canada.

Jarrett, K., Kavukcuoglu, K., Ranzato, M., & LeCun, Y. (2009). What is the best multi-stage architecture for object recognition? In *Proc. 12th Int. Conf. on Computer Vision (ICCV)*. Kyoto, Japan: ICCV.

Javadtalab, A., Abbadi, L., Omidyeganeh, M., Shirmohammadi, S., Adams, C. M., & El-Saddik, A. (2011). Transparent non-intrusive multimodal biometric system for video conference using the fusion of face and ear recognition. In *Proceedings of Ninth Annual International Conference on Privacy, Security and Trust - PST 2011* (pp. 87–92). PST.

Javal, É. (1879). Essai sure la physiologie de la lecture. *Annales d'Oculistique*, *82*, 242–253.

Jeni, L. A., Girard, J. M., Cohn, J. F., & de la Torre, F. (2013). Continuous au intensity estimation using localized, sparse facial feature space. In *Proceedings of the IEEE International Conference on Automatic Face and Gesture Recognition*. IEEE.

Jensen, F. V. (1996). *An introduction to Bayesian networks*. New York: Springer.

Jeong, D. S., Park, H.-A., Park, K. R., & Kim, J. (2005). *Iris Recognition in Mobile Phone Based on Adaptive Gabor Filter*. Paper presented at the Advances in Biometrics. New York, NY.

Jia, K., & Gong, S. (2005). Multi-modal tensor face for simultaneous super-resolution and recognition. In *Proceedings of Tenth IEEE Internat. Conf. on Computer Vision ICCV*, (vol. 2, pp. 1683–1690). IEEE.

Jiang, B., Martinez, B., Valstar, M. F., & Pantic, M. (2013). *Automatic Analysis of Facial Actions: A Survey*. Unpublished.

Jiang, B., Valstar, M. F., & Pantic, M. (2011). Action unit detection using sparse appearance descriptors in space-time video volumes. In *Proceedings of the IEEE International Conf. on Automatic Face and Gesture Recognition*, (pp. 314–321). IEEE.

Jiang, Z., Lin, Z., & Davis, L. S. (2011). *Learning A Discriminative Dictionary For Sparse Coding Via Label Consistent K-Svd*. Paper Presented At The IEEE Conference On Computer Vision And Pattern Recognition. San Francisco, CA.

Jiang, B., Valstar, M. F., Martinez, B., & Pantic, M. (2013). *Dynamic appearance descriptor approach to facial actions temporal modelling*. IEEE Transactions of Systems, Man and Cybernetics – Part B.

Jillela, R., & Ross, A. (2012). Mitigating effects of plastic surgery: Fusing face and ocular biometrics. In *Proceedings of IEEE Fifth International Conference on Biometrics: Theory, Applications and Systems - BTAS 2012* (pp. 402–411). IEEE.

Jin, H., Liu, Q., Lu, H., & Tong, X. (2004). *Face Detection Using Improved LBP under Bayesian Framework*. Paper presented at the Third International Conference on Image and Graphics. New York, NY.

Jobson, D. J., Rahman, Z. U., & Woodell, G. A. (1997a). A multiscale retinex for bridging the gap between color images and the human observation of scenes. *IEEE Transactions on Image Processing*, *6*(7), 965–976. doi:10.1109/83.597272 PMID:18282987

Jobson, D. J., Rahman, Z. U., & Woodell, G. A. (1997b). Properties and performance of a center/surround retinex. *IEEE Transactions on Image Processing*, *6*(3), 451–462. doi:10.1109/83.557356 PMID:18282940

Jobusch, D. L., & Oldehoeft, A. E. (1989a). A Survey of Password Mechanisms: Weaknesses and Potential Improvements: Part 1. *Computers & Security*, *8*(7), 587–604. doi:10.1016/0167-4048(89)90051-5

Jobusch, D. L., & Oldehoeft, A. E. (1989b). A Survey of Password Mechanisms: Weaknesses and Potential Improvements: Part 2. *Computers & Security, 8*(8), 675–689. doi:10.1016/0167-4048(89)90006-0

Johnson, M. H. (2001). The development and neural basis of face recognition: Comment an speculation. *Infant and Child Development, 10*(1-2), 31–33. doi:10.1002/icd.243

Johnson, N., & Hogg, D. (1996). Learning the distribution of object trajectories for event recognition. *Image and Vision Computing, 14*(8), 609–615. doi:10.1016/0262-8856(96)01101-8

Jones, J. P., & Palmer, L. A. (1987). An evaluation of the two-dimensional Gabor filter model of simple receptive fields in cat striate cortex. *Journal of Neurophysiology, 58*(6), 1233–1258. PMID:3437332

Juefei-Xu, F., Cha, M., Heyman, J. L., Venugopalan, S., Abiantun, R., & Savvides, M. (2010). *Robust local binary pattern feature sets for periocular biometric identification*. Paper presented at the Biometrics: Theory Applications and Systems (BTAS), 2010 Fourth IEEE International Conference on. doi:10.1109/BTAS.2010.5634504

Juefei-Xu, F., Luu, K., Savvides, M., Bui, T. D., & Suen, C. Y. (2011). *Investigating age invariant face recognition based on periocular biometrics*. Paper presented at the Biometrics (IJCB), 2011 International Joint Conference on. doi:10.1109/IJCB.2011.6117600

Jun Luo, J., Ma, Y., Takikawa, E., Lao, S., Kawade, M., & Lu, B.-L. (2007). Person-Specific SIFT Features for Face Recognition. In *Proceedings of IEEE International Conference on Acoustics, Speech and Signal Processig2007* (vol. 2, pp. 593-596). IEEE.

Junli, L., Miaohua, Z., Ding, L., Xianju, Z., Ojowu, O., & Kexin, Z., Zhan, Li., & Han, L. (2013). Robust Ellipse Fitting Based on Sparse Combination of Data Points. *IEEE Transactions on Image Processing, 22*(6), 2207–2218. doi:10.1109/TIP.2013.2246518 PMID:23412616

Kabir, H., Jabid, T., & Chae, O. (2012). Directional Pattern Variance (LDPv), A Robust Feature Descriptor for Facial Expression Recognition. *International Arab Journal of Information Technology, 9*(4), 382–391.

Kakadiaris, I.A., & Toderici. (2012). *3d-2d Face Recognition With Pose-Illumination Normalization Using A 3d Deformable Model And Bidirectional Relighting*. Academic Press.

Kakadiaris, I.A., & Passalis. (2007). Three-Dimensional Face Recognition In The Presence Of Facial Expressions: An Annotated Deformable Model Approach. *IEEE Transactions on Pattern Analysis and Machine Intelligence, 29*(4), 640–649. doi:10.1109/TPAMI.2007.1017 PMID:17299221

Kaltwang, S., Rudovic, O., & Pantic, M. (2012). Continuous pain intensity estimation from facial expressions. In *Proceedings of the International Symposium on Visual Computing*, (pp. 368–377). Academic Press.

Kanade, T. (1973). *Picture Processing by Computer Complex and Recognition of Human Face*. (PhD thesis). Kyoto University.

Kanade, T., Cohn, J. F., & Tian, Y. (2000). Comprehensive database for facial expression analysis. In *Proceedings of the IEEE International Conference on Automatic Face and Gesture Recognition*, (pp. 46–53). IEEE.

Kanade, T. (1973). *Computer recognition of human faces*. Basel, Switzerland: Birkhauser.

Kapoor, A., Qi, Y., & Picard, R. W. (2003). Fully automatic upper facial action recognition. In *Proceedings of IEEE International Workshop on Analysis and Modeling of Faces and Gestures, AMFG 2003* (pp. 195-202). IEEE.

Kelly, M. D. (1970). *Visual identification of people by computer* (Tech. rep. AI-130). Stanford AI Project.

Kemelmacher-Shlizerman, I., & Seitz, S. M. (2011). Face Reconstruction in the wild. In *Proceedings of IEEE International Conference on Computer Vision*, (pp. 1746-1753). IEEE.

KeyLemon Inc. (2013). *KeyLemon*. Retrieved 12 Nov, 2013, from https://www.keylemon.com/

Khanesar, M. A., Teshnehlab, M., & Shoorehdeli, M. A. (2007). A novel binary particle swarm optimization. In *Proceedings of Mediterranean Conference on Control & Automation*. Academic Press.

Khiyari, H., DeMarsico, M., Abate, A., & Wechsler, H. (2012). Biometric interoperability across training, enrollment, and testing for the purpose of face identification. In *Proc. IEEE Workshop on Biometric Measurements and Systems for Security and Medical Applications*. Salerno, Italy: IEEE.

Khronos Group. (2013). *The open standard for parallel programming of heterogeneous systems*. Retrieved 01 Aug, 2013, from http://www.khronos.org/opencl/

Kim, M., Kumar, S., Pavlovic, V., & Rowley, H. (2008). Face tracking and recognition with visual constraints in real-world videos. In *Proceedings of IEEE Conference on Computer Vision and Pattern Recognition* (CVPR), (pp. 1-8). IEEE.

Kim, T. K., Kittler, J., & Cipolla, R. (2007). Discriminative learning and recognition of image set classes using canonical correlations. *IEEE Transactions on Pattern Analysis and Machine Intelligence*, 29(6), 1005–1018. doi:10.1109/TPAMI.2007.1037 PMID:17431299

Kim, T.-K., Kim, H., Hwang, W., & Kittler, J. (2005). Component-based LDA face description for image retrieval and MPEG-7 standardization. *Image and Vision Computing*, 23(7), 631–642. doi:10.1016/j.imavis.2005.02.005

Kim, W., & Kim, C. (2012). Background Subtraction for Dynamic Texture Scenes Using Fuzzy Color Histograms. *IEEE Signal Processing Letters*, 19(3), 127–130. doi:10.1109/LSP.2011.2182648

Kirby, M., & Sirovich, L. (1990). Application of the Karhunen-Loeve procedure for the characterization of human faces. *IEEE Transactions on Pattern Analysis and Machine Intelligence*, 12(1), 103–108. doi:10.1109/34.41390

Kirda, E., & Kruegel, C. (2006). Protecting Users against Phishing Attacks. *The Computer Journal*, 49(5), 554. doi:10.1093/comjnl/bxh169

Kisku, D. R., Sing, J. K., & Gupta, P. (2009). Multibiometrics Belief Fusion. In *Proceedings of Second International Conference on Machine Vision - ICMV 2009* (pp. 37–40). ICMV.

Kittler, J., Hilton, A., Hamouz, M., & Illingworth, J. (2005). *3D Assisted Face Recognition: A Survey of 3D Imaging, Modelling and Recognition Approachest*. Paper presented at the 2005 IEEE Computer Society Conference on Computer Vision and Pattern Recognition (CVPR'05). New York, NY.

Kittler, J., Li, Y., & Matas, J. (2000). *On Matching Scores for LDA-based Face Verification*. Paper presented at the BMVC. Retrieved from http://dblp.uni-trier.de/db/conf/bmvc/bmvc2000.html#KittlerLM00

Kittler, J., Poh, N., Fatukasi, O., Messer, K., Kryszczuk, K., & Richiardi, J. et al. (2007). Quality dependent fusion of intramodal and multimodal biometric experts. *Biometric Technology for Human Identification*, 4, 6539.

Kjeldsen, R., & Kender, J. (1996). Finding Skin in Color Images. In *Proceedings of the Second International Conference on Automatic Face and Gesture Recognition*, (pp. 312-317). Academic Press.

Klare, B. F., Burge, M. J., Klontz, J. C., Vorder Bruegge, R. W., & Jain, A. K. (2012). Face Recognition Performance: Role of Demographic Information. *IEEE Transactions on Information Forensics and Security*, 7(6), 1789–1801. doi:10.1109/TIFS.2012.2214212

Klare, B., & Jain, A. (2013). Heterogeneous face recognition using kernel prototype similarities. *IEEE Transactions on Pattern Analysis and Machine Intelligence*, 35(6), 1410–1422. doi:10.1109/TPAMI.2012.229 PMID:23599055

Klare, B., Li, Z., & Jain, A. K. (2011). Matching forensic sketches to mug shot photos. *IEEE Transactions on Pattern Analysis and Machine Intelligence*, 33(3), 639–646. doi:10.1109/TPAMI.2010.180 PMID:20921585

Klein, D. V. (1990). *Foiling the Cracker: A Survey of, and Improvements to, Password Security*. Paper presented at the USENIX Security Workshop. Portland, OR.

Kliper-Gross, O., Hassner, T., & Wolf, L. (2012). The action similarity labeling challenge. *IEEE Transactions on Pattern Analysis and Machine Intelligence*, 34(3), 615–621. doi:10.1109/TPAMI.2011.209 PMID:22262724

Knight, B., & Johnson, A. (1997). The role of movement in face recognition. *Visual Cognition, 4*(3), 265–273. doi:10.1080/713756764

Koelstra, S., Pantic, M., & Patras, I. (2010). A dynamic texture based approach to recognition of facial actions and their temporal models. *IEEE Transactions on Pattern Analysis and Machine Intelligence, 32*(11), 1940–1954. doi:10.1109/TPAMI.2010.50 PMID:20847386

Kohonen, T. (1982). Self-organized formation of topologically correct feature maps. *Biological Cybernetics, 43*(1), 59–69. doi:10.1007/BF00337288

Kolda, T. G., & Bader, B. W. (2009). Tensor decompositions and applications. *SIAM Review, 51*(3), 455–500. doi:10.1137/07070111X

Kolmogorov, A. N. (1965). Three Approaches to the Quantitative Definition of Information. *Problems of Information Transmission,* 157–168.

Komogortsev, O. V., Karpov, A., Holland, C. D., & Proenca, H. (2012). Multimodal ocular biometrics approach: A feasibility study. In *Proceedings of the 2012 IEEE Fifth International Conference on Biometrics: Theory, Applications and Systems,* (pp. 209-216). IEEE.

Kong, S., Wang, X., Wang, D., & Wu, F. (2013). Multiple feature fusion for face recognition. In *Proceedings of 10th IEEE International Conference and Workshops on Automatic Face and Gesture Recognition,* (pp. 1-7). IEEE.

Kong, S. G., Heo, J., Abidi, B. R., Paik, J., & Abidi, M. A. (2005). Recent advances in visual and infrared face recognition: a review. *Computer Vision and Image Understanding, 97*(1), 103–135. doi:10.1016/j.cviu.2004.04.001

Kose, N., Erdogmus, N., & Dugelay, J.-L. (2012). Block based face recognition approach robust to nose alterations. In *Proceedings of IEEE International Conference on Biometrics: Theory, Applications and Systems* (pp. 121-126). IEEE.

Kosmopoulos, D. I., Voulodimos, A., & Doulamis, A. D. (2013). A system for multicamera task recognition and summarization for structured environments. *IEEE Transactions on Industrial Informatics, 9*(1), 161–171. doi:10.1109/TII.2012.2212712

Kosmopoulos, D., Doulamis, N., Voulodimos, A., & Varvarigou, T. (2012). Online Behavior Recognition in Workflows allowing for User Feedback. *Computer Vision and Image Understanding, 116*(3), 422–434. doi:10.1016/j.cviu.2011.09.006

Kotropoulos, C., & Pitas, I. (1997). Rule-based Face Detection in Frontal Views. In *Proceedings of the International Conference on Acoustic, Speech and Signal Processing,* (vol. 4, pp. 2537-2540). Academic Press.

Kotropoulos, C., Tefas, A., & Pitas, I. (2000). Frontal face authentication using morphological elastic graph matching. *IEEE Transactions on Image Processing, 9*(4), 555–560. doi:10.1109/83.841933 PMID:18255429

Kotropoulos, C., Tefas, A., & Pitas, I. (2000). Morphological elastic graph matching applied to frontal face authentication under well-controlled and real conditions. *Pattern Recognition, 33*(12), 31–43. doi:10.1016/S0031-3203(99)00185-5

Krauss, R. M., Garlock, C. M., Bricker, P. D., & McMahon, L. E. (1977). The role of audible and visible back-channel responses in interpersonal communication. *Journal of Personality and Social Psychology, 35*(7), 523–529. doi:10.1037/0022-3514.35.7.523

Kriegman, D. J., & Belhumeur, P. N. (2001). What shadows reveal about object structure. *Journal of the Optical Society of America. A, Optics, Image Science, and Vision, 18*(8), 1804–1813. doi:10.1364/JOSAA.18.001804 PMID:11488484

Križaj, J., Štruc, V., & Pavesic, N. (2010). Adaptation of SIFT features for face recognition under varying illumination. In *Proceedings of International Convention on Information and Communication Technology, Electronics and Microelectronics,* (pp. 691-694). Academic Press.

Krüger, N. (1997). An algorithm for the learning of weights in discrimination functions using A priori constraints. *IEEE Transactions on Pattern Analysis and Machine Intelligence, 19*(7), 764–768. doi:10.1109/34.598233

Kulis, B., Jain, P., & Grauman, K. (2009). Fast similarity search for learned metrics. *IEEE Transactions on Pattern Analysis and Machine Intelligence, 31*(12), 2143–2157. doi:10.1109/TPAMI.2009.151 PMID:19834137

Kumar, N., Berg, A. C., Belhumeur, P. N., & Nayar, S. K. (2009). Attribute and simile classifiers for face verification. In *Proceedings of 2009 IEEE 12th International Conference on Computer Vision* (pp. 365-372). IEEE.

Kumar, N., Berg, A. C., Belhumeur, P. N., & Nayar, S. K. (2011). Describable visual attributes for face verification and image search. *IEEE Transactions on Pattern Analysis and Machine Intelligence*, *33*(10), 1962–1977. doi:10.1109/TPAMI.2011.48 PMID:21383395

Kwapisz, J. R., Weiss, G. M., & Moore, S. A. (2010). *Cell Phone-Based Biometric Identification*. Paper presented at the Fourth IEEE International Conference on Biometrics: Theory Applications and Systems (BTAS). Washington, DC.

Lacroix, J. P. W., Murre, J. M. J., Postma, E. O., & Van den Herik, H. J. (2006). Modeling recognition memory using the similarity structure of natural input. *Cognitive Science*, *30*, 121–145. doi:10.1207/s15516709cog0000_48 PMID:21702811

Lades, M., Vorbruggen, J. C., Buhmann, J., Lange, J., Von der Malsburg, C., Wurtz, R. P., & Konen, W. (1993). Distortion invariant object recognition in the dynamic link architecture. *IEEE Transactions on Computers*, *42*(3), 300–311. doi:10.1109/12.210173

Laiyun, Q., Shiguang, S., Xilin, C., & Wen, G. (2006). *Face Recognition under Varying Lighting Based on the Probabilistic Model of Gabor Phase*. Paper presented at the Pattern Recognition. New York, NY.

Lamare, M. (1892). Des mouvements des yeux dans la lecture. *Bulletins et Memoires de la Société Francaise d'Ophtalmologie*, *10*, 354–364.

Lanitis, A., Taylor, C. J., & Cootes, T. F. (2002). Toward automatic simulation of aging effects on face images. *IEEE Transactions on Pattern Analysis and Machine Intelligence*, *24*(4), 442–455. doi:10.1109/34.993553

Lanzarini, L., La Battaglia, J., Maulini, J., & Hasperué, W. (2010). Face Recognition Using SIFT and Binary PSO Descriptors. In *Proceedings of International Conference on Information Technology Interfaces*, (pp. 557-562). Academic Press.

Lao, W., Han, J., & de With, P. H. N. (2009). Automatic video-based human motion analyzer for consumer surveillance system. *IEEE Transactions on Consumer Electronics*, *55*(2), 591–598. doi:10.1109/TCE.2009.5174427

Laptev, I., & Perez, P. (2007). *Retrieving actions in movies (ICCV)*. Paper presented at the IEEE International Conference on Computer Vision. Minneapolis, MN.

Latha, P., Ganesan, L., & Annadurai, S. (2009). Face Recognition Using Neural Networks. *International Journal on Signal Processing*, *3*(5), 153–160.

Latinis, A., Taylor, C. J., & Cootes, T. F. (1995). An Automatic Face Identification System using Flexible Appearance Models. *Image and Vision Computing*, *13*(5), 393–401. doi:10.1016/0262-8856(95)99726-H

Laws, K. I. (1980). *Rapid Texture Identification*. Paper presented at the Proc. SPIE Conf. Image Processing for Missile Guidance. doi:10.1117/12.959169

Le, Q. V., et al. (2012). Building high-level features using scale unsupervised learning. In *Proc. 29th Int. Conf. on Machine Learning (ICML)*. Edinburgh, UK: ICML.

Lee, G. H., Kang, S. J., Han, C. W., & Kim, N. S. (2012). *Feature Enhancement Error Compensation for Noise Robust Speech Recognition*. Paper presented at the International Multi-Conference on Systems, Signals and Devices (SSD). Chemnitz, Germany.

Lee, G. Y. C. (2010). Fetal and Newborn Auditory Processing of the Mother's and Father's Voice. (Master of Science MR70279). Queen's University, Kingston, Ontario, Canada. ProQuest Dissertations & Theses (PQDT) database.

Lee, J. C., & Milios, E. (1990). Matching Range Images of Human Faces. In *Proceedings of IEEE International Conference on Computer Vision*, (pp. 722-726). IEEE.

Lee, K. C., Ho, J., & Kriegman, D. (2001). Nine points of light: Acquiring subspaces for face recognition under variable lighting. In *Proceedings of 2001 IEEE Computer Society Conference on Computer Vision and Pattern Recognition*, (pp. 519-526). IEEE.

Lee, J.-H., & Kim, W.-Y. (2004). Video Summarization and Retrieval System Using Face Recognition and MPEG-7 Descriptors. In P. K. Enser (Ed.), *CIVR 2004 - Image and Video Retrieval, (LNCS)* (Vol. 3115, pp. 170–178). Dublin, Ireland: Springer. doi:10.1007/978-3-540-27814-6_23

Lee, K. C., Ho, J., & Kriegman, D. J. (2005). Acquiring linear subspaces for face recognition under variable lighting. *IEEE Transactions on Pattern Analysis and Machine Intelligence, 27*(5), 684–698. doi:10.1109/TPAMI.2005.92 PMID:15875791

Lei, Z., Sen, W., & Samaras, D. (2005). *Face synthesis and recognition from a single image under arbitrary unknown lighting using a spherical harmonic basis morphable model.* Paper presented at the Computer Vision and Pattern Recognition. New York, NY.

Leonards, U., & Scott-Samuel, N. E. (2005). Idiosyncratic initiation of saccadic face exploration in humans. *Vision Research, 45,* 2677–2684. doi:10.1016/j.visres.2005.03.009 PMID:16042969

Lerner, T. (2013). *Mobile Payment.* Springer Fachmedien Wiesbaden.

Leung, T. K., Burl, M. C., & Perona, P. (1995). Finding Faces in Cluttered Scenes using Random Labeled Graph Matching. In *Proceedings of the fifth IEEE International Conference on Computer Vision,* (pp. 637-644). IEEE.

Lew, M. S. (1996). Information Theoretic View-based and Modular Face Detection. In *Proc. Second Int. Conf. Automatic Face and Gesture Recognition,* (pp. 198-203). Academic Press.

Leyvand, T., Cohen-Or, D., Dror, G., & Lischinski, D. (2008). Data-Driven Enhancement of Facial Attractiveness. In *Proceedings of ACM SIGGRAPH 2008.* ACM.

LFW. (n.d.). *Labeled Faces in the Wild face dataset.* Retrieved from http://vis-www.cs.umass.edu/lfw/

Li, H., Huang, D., Lemaire, P., Morvan, J.-M., & Chen, L. (2011). Expression robust 3D face recognition via mesh-based histograms of multiple order surface differential quantities. In *Proceedings of International Conference on Image Processing* (pp. 3053–3056). Academic Press.

Li, S. Z., Chu, R. F., Ao, M., Zhang, L., & He, R. (2006). Highly accurate and fast face recognition using near infrared images. In *Proc. of IAPR International Conference on Biometrics* (ICB-2006), (pp. 151-158). IAPR.

Li, S. Z., Zhang, L., Liao, S. C., Zhu, X. X., Chu, R. F., Ao, M., & He, R. (2006). A near-infrared image based face recognition system. In *Proc. of 7th IEEE International Conference Automatic Face and Gesture Recognition* (FG-2006), (pp. 455-460). IEEE.

Li, Z., Imai, J., & Kaneko, M. (2010). *Robust Face Recognition Using Block-Based Bag Of Words.* Paper Presented At The International Conference On Pattern Recognition. Istanbul, Turkey.

Liang, Y., Wang, L., Liao, S., & Zou, B. (2011). Feature selection via simultaneous sparse approximation for person specific face verification. In *Proceedings of 18th IEEE International Conference on Image Processing* (ICIP), (pp. 789-792). IEEE.

Liao, S., & Jain, A. K. (2011). *Partial Face Recognition: An Alignment Free Approach.* Paper Presented At The International Joint Conference On Biometrics. Washington, DC.

Liao, S. C., Zhu, X. X., Lei, Z., Zhang, L., & Li, S. Z. (2007). Learning multi-scale block local binary patterns for face recognition. *Advances in Biometrics. Proceedings, 4642,* 828–837.

Liao, S., Law, M. W. K., & Chung, A. C. S. (2009). Dominant Local Binary Patterns for Texture Classification. *IEEE Transactions on Image Processing, 18*(5), 1107–1118. doi:10.1109/TIP.2009.2015682 PMID:19342342

Li, B., Chang, H., Shan, S., & Chen, X. (2010). Low-resolution face recognition via coupled locality preserving mappings. *IEEE Signal Processing Letters, 17*(1), 20–23. doi:10.1109/LSP.2009.2031705

Lien, J. J., Kanade, T., Cohn, J. F., & Li, C. (2000). Detection, tracking, and classification of action units in facial expression. *Robotics and Autonomous Systems, 31,* 131–146. doi:10.1016/S0921-8890(99)00103-7

Li, F., & Wechsler, H. (2005). Open set face recognition using transduction. *IEEE Transactions on Pattern Analysis and Machine Intelligence, 27*(11), 1686–1697. doi:10.1109/TPAMI.2005.224 PMID:16285369

Li, F., & Wechsler, H. (2009). Face authentication using recognition-by-parts, boosting and transduction. *Int.* [IJP-RAI]. *Journal of Artificial Intelligence and Pattern Recognition, 23*(3), 545–573. doi:10.1142/S0218001409007193

Li, M., Chen, X., Li, X., Ma, B., & Vitanyi, P. (2004). The similarity metric. *IEEE Transactions on Information Theory, 50*(12), 3250–3264. doi:10.1109/TIT.2004.838101

Li, M., & Vitanyi, P. (2008). *An introduction to Kolmogorov Complexity and its applications* (3rd ed.). Springer. doi:10.1007/978-0-387-49820-1

Li, P., Liu, X., & Zhao, N. (2012). Weighted Co-occurrence Phase Histogram for Iris Recognition. *Pattern Recognition Letters, 33*(8), 1000–1005. doi:10.1016/j.patrec.2011.06.018

Lipton, A., Kanade, T., Fujiyoshi, H., Duggins, D., Tsin, Y., Tolliver, D., & Wixson, L. (2000). *A system for video surveillance and monitoring* (Vol. 2). Pittsburgh, PA: Carnegie Mellon University, the Robotics Institute.

Li, S. Z., Chu, R., Liao, S., & Zhang, L. (2007). Illumination invariant face recognition using near-infrared images. *IEEE Transactions on Pattern Analysis and Machine Intelligence, 29*(4), 627–639. doi:10.1109/TPAMI.2007.1014 PMID:17299220

Li, S., & Jain, A. (2005). *Handbook of face recognition.* New York: Springer.

Liu, P., Wang, Y., Huang, D., & Zhang, Z. (2012). Recognizing occluded 3D faces using an efficient ICP variant. In *Proceedings of International Conference on Multimedia and Expo* (pp. 350–355). Academic Press.

Liu, C., & Wechsler, H. (2001). Shape-and-texture based enhanced Fisher classifier for face recognition. *IEEE Transactions on Image Processing, 10*(4), 598–608. doi:10.1109/83.913594 PMID:18249649

Liu, C., & Wechsler, H. (2003). Independent component analysis of Gabor features for face recognition. *IEEE Transactions on Neural Networks, 14*(4), 919–928. doi:10.1109/TNN.2003.813829 PMID:18238070

Liu, C., Yuen, J., & Torralba, A. (2011). SIFT Flow: Dense Correspondence across Scenes and Its Applications. *IEEE Transactions on Pattern Analysis and Machine Intelligence, 33*(5), 978–994. doi:10.1109/TPAMI.2010.147 PMID:20714019

Liu, D. H., Lam, K. M., & Shen, L. S. (2005). Illumination invariant face recognition. *Pattern Recognition, 38*(10), 1705–1716. doi:10.1016/j.patcog.2005.03.009

Liu, D., Wang, M., Hua, S.-J., & Zhang, H.-J. (2011). Semi-Automatic Tagging of Photo Albums via Exemplar Selection and Tag Inference. *IEEE Transactions on Multimedia, 13*(1), 82–91. doi:10.1109/TMM.2010.2087744

Liu, Q., Tang, X., Lu, H., & Ma, S. (2006). Face recognition using kernel scatter-difference-based discriminant analysis. *IEEE Transactions on Neural Networks, 17*(4), 1081–1085. doi:10.1109/TNN.2006.875970 PMID:16856670

Liu, Y., Schmidt, K. L., Cohn, J. F., & Mitra, S. (2003). Facial asymmetry quantification for expression invariant human identification. *Computer Vision and Image Understanding, 91*(1), 138–159. doi:10.1016/S1077-3142(03)00078-X

Li, X., & Da, F. (2012). Efficient 3D face recognition handling facial expression and hair occlusion. *Image and Vision Computing, 30*(9), 668–679. doi:10.1016/j.imavis.2012.07.011

Li, Y.-H., & Savvides, M. (2012). An Automatic Iris Occlusion Estimation Method Based on High Dimensional Density Estimation. *IEEE Transactions on Pattern Analysis and Machine Intelligence, 35*(4), 784–796. doi:10.1109/TPAMI.2012.169 PMID:22868651

Li, Z., Park, U., & Jain, A. K. (2011). A discriminative model for age invariant face recognition. *IEEE Transactions on Information Forensics and Security, 6*(3), 1028–1037. doi:10.1109/TIFS.2011.2156787

Llano, E. G., Vazquez, H. M., Kittler, J., & Messer, K. (2006). An illumination insensitive representation for face verification in the frequency domain. In *Proceedings of 18th International Conference on Pattern Recognition,* (pp. 215-218). Academic Press.

Lovell, B. C., Bigdeli, A., & Mau, S. (2011). *Embedded Face and Biometric Technologies for National and Border Security.* Paper presented at the IEEE Computer Society Conference on Computer Vision and Pattern Recognition Workshops (CVPRW). Colorado Springs, CO.

Lowe, D. (1999). *Object Recognition From Local Scale-Invariant Features.* Paper Presented At The IEEE International Conference On Computer Vision. Kerkyra, Greece.

Lowe, D. G. (2004). Distinctive image features from scale-invariant keypoints. *International Journal of Computer Vision, 60*(2), 91–110. doi:10.1023/B:VISI.0000029664.99615.94

Lu, X., & Jain, A. K. (2006). Deformation Modeling for Robust 3D Face Matching. In *Proceedings of IEEE Conference on Computer Vision and Pattern Recognition,* (pp. 1377-1383). IEEE.

Lucey, P., Cohn, J. F., Kanade, T., Saragih, J., & Ambadar, Z. (2010). The extended cohn-kanade dataset (CK+), A complete dataset for action unit and emotion-specified expression. In *Proceedings of the IEEE Conference on Computer Vision and Pattern Recognition,* (pp. 94– 101). IEEE.

Lucey, P., Cohn, J. F., Prkachin, K. M., Solomon, P. E., & Matthews, I. (2011). Painful data: The UNBC-McMaster shoulder pain expression archive database. In *Proceedings of the IEEE International Conference on Automatic Face and Gesture Recognition,* (pp. 57–64). IEEE.

Lucieer, A., Stein, A., & Fisher, P. (2005). Multivariate Texturebased Segmentation of Remotely Sensed Imagery for Extraction of Objects and Their Uncertainty. *International Journal of Remote Sensing, 26*(14), 2917–2936. doi:10.1080/01431160500057723

Lu, J., Plataniotis, K. N., & Venetsanopoulos, A. N. (2003). Face recognition using LDA-based algorithms. *IEEE Transactions on Networks, 14*(1), 195–200. doi:10.1109/TNN.2002.806647 PMID:18238001

Luo, J., Ma, Y., & Takikawa, E. Lao, Kawade, M., & Lu. (2007). Person-Specific SIFT Features for Face Recognition. In *Proceedings of IEEE International Conference on Acoustics, Speech and Signal Processing, ICASSP 2007,* (vol. 2, pp. 593-596). IEEE.

Lu, X., Jain, A. K., & Colbry, D. (2006). Matching 2.5d Face Scans to 3D Models. *IEEE Transactions on Pattern Analysis and Machine Intelligence, 28*(1), 31–43. doi:10.1109/TPAMI.2006.15 PMID:16402617

Lyle, J. R., Miller, P. E., Pundlik, S. J., & Woodard, D. L. (2010). *Soft biometric classification using periocular region features.* Paper presented at the Biometrics: Theory Applications and Systems (BTAS), 2010 Fourth IEEE International Conference on. doi:10.1109/BTAS.2010.5634537

Lyons, M. J., Budynek, J., Plante, A., & Akamatsu, S. (2000). Classifying facial attributes using a 2-d gabor wavelet representation and discriminant analysis. In *Proceedings of International Conference on Automatic Face and Gesture Recognition,* (pp. 202–207). Academic Press.

Lyons, M. J., Budynek, J., & Akamatsu, S. (1999). Automatic Classification of Single Facial Images. *IEEE Transactions on Pattern Analysis and Machine Intelligence, 21*(12), 1357–1362. doi:10.1109/34.817413

Ma, B., Su, Y., & Jurie, F. (2012). BiCov: a novel image representation for person re-identification and face verification. In *Proceedings of British Machine Vision Conference* (pp. 57.1-57.11). Academic Press.

Maeng, H., Liao, S., Kang, D., Lee, S. W., & Jain, A. K. (2012). Nighttime Face Recognition at Long Distance: Cross-distance and Cross-spectral Matching. In *Proc. of 11th Asian Conference on Computer Vision.* ACCV.

Maenpaa, T., & Pietikainen, M. (2003). Multi-scale binary patterns for texture analysis. *Image Analysis. Proceedings, 2749,* 885–892.

Mahoor, M. H., Zhou, M., Veon, K. L., Mavadati, M., & Cohn, J. F. (2011). Facial action unit recognition with sparse representation. In *Proceedings of the IEEE International Conference on Automatic Face and Gesture Recognition,* (pp. 336– 342). IEEE.

Mairal, J., Bach, F., Ponce, J., & Sapiro, G. (2008). *Supervised dictionary learning.* INRIA, Report de Recherche #6652.

Mairal, J., Bach, F., Ponce, J., & Sapiro, G. (2010). Online Learning For Matrix Factorization And Sparse Coding. *Journal of Machine Learning Research, 11,* 19–60.

Majumdar, A., & Ward, R. K. (2009). Discriminative SIFT Features for Face Recognition. In *Proceedings of Canadian Conference on Electrical and Computer Engineering,* (pp. 27-30). Academic Press.

Makantatis, K., Doulamis, A., & Doulamis, A. (2013). Vision-based maritime surveillance system using fused visual attention maps and online adaptable tracker. In *Proceedings of 14th International Workshop on Image Analysis for Multimedia Interactive Services* (WIAMIS). Academic Press.

Makris, A. Kosmopoulos, Perantonis, & Theodoridis, S. (2007). *Hierarchical feature fusion for visual tracking (ICIP)*. Paper presented at the IEEE International Conference on Image Processing. San Antonio, TX.

Mallat, S. G. (1989). A theory for multiresolution signal decomposition: the wavelet representation. *IEEE Transactions on Pattern Analysis and Machine Intelligence*, *11*(7), 674–693. doi:10.1109/34.192463

Mante, V., Frazor, R., Bonin, V., Geisler, W., & Carandini, M. (2005). Independence of luminance and contrast in natural scenes and in the early visual system. *Nature Neuroscience*, *8*(12). doi:10.1038/nn1556 PMID:16286933

Marat, S., Rahman, A., Pellerin, D., Guyader, N., & Houzet, D. (2013). Improving visual saliency by adding Face Feature Map and Center Bias. *Cognitive Computation*, *5*, 63–75. doi:10.1007/s12559-012-9146-3

Marcel, S., McCool, C., Matejka, P., Ahonen, T., Cernocky, J., & Chakraborty, S. … Kittler, J. (2010). On the results of the first mobile biometry (MOBIO) face and speaker verification evaluation. In Proceedings of Recognizing Patterns in Signals, Speech, Images and Videos (LNCS), (vol. 6388, pp. 210-225). Berlin: Springer.

Mario, I., Chacon, M., & Pablo Rivas, P. (2009). Face Recognition Based on Human Visual Perception Theories and Unsupervised ANN. In *State of the Art in Face Recognition*. I-Tech.

Marsico, M., Nappi, M., & Riccio, D. (2012). Noisy Iris Recognition Integrated Scheme. *Pattern Recognition Letters*, *33*(8), 1006–1011. doi:10.1016/j.patrec.2011.09.010

Martinez, A. M. (1998). *The AR face database*. CVC Technical Report, 24.

Martinez, A. M. (2002). Recognizing imprecisely localized, partially occluded, and expression variant faces from a single sample per class. *IEEE Transactions on Pattern Analysis and Machine Intelligence*, *24*(6), 748–763. doi:10.1109/TPAMI.2002.1008382

Martinez, A. M., & Kak, A. C. (2001). PCA versus LDA. *IEEE Transactions on Pattern Analysis and Machine Intelligence*, *23*(2), 228–233. doi:10.1109/34.908974

Martinez, A., & Benavente, R. (1998). *The AR face database*. Computer Vision Center.

Matas, J., Hamouz, M., Jonsson, K., Kittler, J., Li, Y., Kotropoulos, C., et al. (2000). Comparison of face verification results on the XM2VTS database. In *Proceedings of 15th International Conference on Pattern Recognition*, (Vol. 4, pp. 858-863). Academic Press.

Matsumoto, T., Matsumoto, H., Yamada, K., & Hoshino, S. (2002). *Impact of Artificial Gummy Fingers on Fingerprint Systems*. Paper presented at the Optical Security and Counterfeit Deterrence Techniques IV. San Jose, CA.

Matthews, I., & Baker, S. (2004). Active appearance models revisited. *International Journal of Computer Vision*, *60*(2), 135–164. doi:10.1023/B:VISI.0000029666.37597.d3

Matthews, I., Xiao, J., & Baker, S. (2007). 2d vs. 3d deformable face models: Representational power, construction, and real-time fitting. *International Journal of Computer Vision*, *75*(1), 93–113. doi:10.1007/s11263-007-0043-2

Mavadati, S. M., Mahoor, M. H., Bartlett, K., & Trinh, P. (2012). Automatic detection of non-posed facial action units. In *Proceedings of the International Conference on Image Processing*, (pp. 1817–1820). Academic Press.

McCool, C., Marcel, S., Hadid, A., Pietikäinen, M., Matějka, P., Černocký, J., et al. (2012). Bi-Modal Person Recognition on a Mobile Phone: using mobile phone data. In *Proceedings of IEEE ICME Workshop on Hot Topics in Mobile Mutlimedia*. IEEE.

McDuff, D., el Kaliouby, R., Senechal, T., Amr, M., Cohn, J. F., & Picard, R. (2013). Affectiva-MIT facial expression dataset (am-fed), Naturalistic and spontaneous facial expressions collected in-the-wild. In *Proceedings of the IEEE conference on Computer Vision and Pattern Recognition*, (pp. 881–888). IEEE.

McKenna, S., Gong, S., & Raya, Y. (1998). Modelling Facial Color and Identity with Gaussian Mixture. *Pattern Recognition*, *31*(12), 1883–1892. doi:10.1016/S0031-3203(98)00066-1

McKeown, G., Valstar, M. F., Cowie, R., Pantic, M., & Schröder, M. (2012). The SEMAINE database: Annotated multimodal records of emotionally colored conversations between a person and a limited agent. *IEEE Transactions on Affective Computing*, *3*, 5–17. doi:10.1109/T-AFFC.2011.20

Meena, K., & Suruliandi, A. (2011). Local Binary Patterns and its Variants for Face Recognition. In *Proceedings of IEEE-International Conference on Recent Trends in Information Technology*, (pp. 782-786). IEEE.

Meredith, P., & Sarna, T. (2006). The physical and chemical properties of eumelanin. *Pigment Cell Research*, *19*, 572–594. doi:10.1111/j.1600-0749.2006.00345.x PMID:17083485

Merkow, J., Jou, B., & Savvides, M. (2010). *An exploration of gender identification using only the periocular region*. Paper presented at the Biometrics: Theory Applications and Systems (BTAS), 2010 Fourth IEEE International Conference on. doi:10.1109/BTAS.2010.5634509

Messer, K., Matas, J., Kittler, J., Luettin, J., & Maitre, G. (1999). XM2VTSDB: The extended M2VTS database. In *Proceedings of Second international conference on audio and video-based biometric person authentication*, (pp. 964-966). Academic Press.

Messer, K., Kittler, J., Short, J., Heusch, G., Cardinaux, F., & Marcel, S. et al. (2006). Performance characterisation of face recognition algorithms and their sensitivity to severe illumination changes. *Advances in Bioethics*, *3832*, 1–11.

Mian, A. S., Bennamoun, M., & Owens, R. (2007). An Efficient Multi-modal 2D-3D Hybrid Approach to Automatic Face Recognition. *IEEE Transactions on Pattern Analysis and Machine Intelligence*, *29*(11), 1927–1943. doi:10.1109/TPAMI.2007.1105 PMID:17848775

Miao, Q., Wang, G., Shi, C., Lin, X., & Ruan, Z. (2011). A new framework for on-line object tracking based on SURF. *Pattern Recognition Letters*, *32*(13), 1564–1571. doi:10.1016/j.patrec.2011.05.017

Milborrow, S., & Nicolls, F. (2008). Locating facial features with an extended active shape model. In *Proceedings of European Conference on Computer Vision – ECCV 2008* (pp. 504–513). ECCV.

Milborrow, S., & Nicolls, F. (2008). Locating Facial Features with an Extended Active Shape Model. In *Proceedings of the 10th European Conference on Computer Vision* (vol. 4, pp. 504-513). Academic Press.

Miller, P. E., Lyle, J. R., Pundlik, S. J., & Woodard, D. L. (2010a). *Performance evaluation of local appearance based periocular recognition*. Paper presented at the Biometrics: Theory Applications and Systems (BTAS), 2010 Fourth IEEE International Conference on. doi:10.1109/BTAS.2010.5634536

Miller, P. E., Rawls, A. W., Pundlik, S. J., & Woodard, D. L. (2010b). Personal identification using periocular skin texture. In *Proceedings of the 2010 ACM Symposium on Applied Computing*. New York, NY: ACM. doi:10.1145/1774088.1774408

Miller, E. G., Matsakis, N. E., & Viola, P. A. (2000). Learning from one example through shared densities on transforms. In *Proc. Computer Vision and Pattern Recognition (CVPR)*. Hilton Head, SC: CVPR. doi:10.1109/CVPR.2000.855856

Min, R., & Dugelay, J.-L. (2013). Kinect Based Facial Occlusion Analysis for Robust Face Recognition. In *Proceedings of IEEE International Workshop on Hot Topics in 3D*. IEEE.

Min, R., Hadid, A., & Dugelay, J.-L. (2011). Improving the recognition of faces occluded by facial accessories. In *Proceedings of IEEE Conference on Automatic Face and Gesture Recognition* (pp. 442-447). IEEE.

Ming, Y., & Ruan, Q. (2012). Robust sparse bounding sphere for 3D face recognition. *Image and Vision Computing*, *30*(8), 524–534. doi:10.1016/j.imavis.2012.05.001

Mittal, G., & Sreela, S. (2006). Robust Preprocessing Algorithm for Face Recognition. In *Proceedings of Canadian Conference on Computer and Robot Vision*, (pp. 57-65). Academic Press.

Miura, H., Ishiwata, H., Lida, Y., Matunaga, Y., Numazaki, S., Morisita, A., et al. (1999). *A 100 frame/s CMOS active pixel sensor for 3D-gesture recognition system*. Paper presented at the Solid-State Circuits Conference, 1999. New York, NY.

Moghaddam, B. (2000). Bayesian face recognition. *Pattern Recognition*, *33*, 1771–1782. doi:10.1016/S0031-3203(99)00179-X

Monwar, M.M., Gavrilova, M., & Yingxu. (2011). A novel fuzzy multimodal information fusion technology for human biometric traits identification. In *Proceedings of 10th IEEE International Conference on Cognitive Informatics & Cognitive Computing* (pp. 112–119). IEEE.

Moreno, A. B., Sànchez, A., Vélez, J. F., & Dìaz, F. J. (2003). Face Recognition Using 3D Surface-Extracted Descriptors. In *Proceedings of Irish Machine Vision and Image Processing Conference*. Academic Press.

Morris, R., & Thompson, K. (1979). Password Security: A Case History. *Communications of the ACM*, *22*(11), 594–597. doi:10.1145/359168.359172

Moses, Y., Adini, Y., & Ullman, S. (1994). Face recognition: The problem of compensating for changes in illumination direction. In J.-O. Eklundh (Ed.), *Computer Vision — ECCV '94* (Vol. 800, pp. 286–296). Springer. doi:10.1007/3-540-57956-7_33

Muramatsu, D., Iwama, H., Makihara, Y., & Yagi, Y. (2013). Multi-view multi-modal person authentication from a single walking image sequence. In *Proceedings of International Conference on Biometrics, ICB 2013* (pp. 1-8). ICB.

Nagesh, P., & Li, B. (2009). *A Compressive Sensing Approach For Expression-Invariant Face Recognition*. Paper Presented At The IEEE Conference On Computer Vision And Pattern Recognition. Miami, FL.

Najemnik, J., & Geisler, W. S. (2005). Optimal eye movement strategies in visual search. *Nature*, *434*, 387–391. doi:10.1038/nature03390 PMID:15772663

Najemnik, J., & Geisler, W. S. (2008). Eye movement statistics in humans are consistent with an optimal search strategy. *Journal of Vision (Charlottesville, Va.)*, *8*(3), 1–14. doi:10.1167/8.3.4 PMID:18484810

Nandakumar, K., Chen, Y., Dass, S. C., & Jain, A. K. (2008). Likelihood ratio-based biometric score fusion. *IEEE Transactions on Pattern Analysis and Machine Intelligence*, *30*(2), 342–347. doi:10.1109/TPAMI.2007.70796 PMID:18084063

Nappi, M., Riccio, D., & De Marsico, M. (2013). Entropy Based Biometric Template Clustering. In *Proceedings of International Conference on Pattern Recognition Applications and Methods*, (pp. 560-563). Academic Press.

Nappi, M., & Riccio, D. (2008). *Moderne Tecniche di Elaborazione di Immagini e Biometria*. CUA.

Nappi, M., & Wechsler, H. (2012). Robust re-identification using randomness and statistical learning: Quo Vadis. *Pattern Recognition Letters*, *33*(14), 1820–1827. doi:10.1016/j.patrec.2012.02.005

National Laboratory of Pattern Recognition (NLPR). (2010). *Biometrics Ideal Test*. Retrieved 15 Nov, 2013, from http://www.idealtest.org/index.jsp

Nefian, A. (1999). *A Hidden Markov Model-based Approach for Face Detection and Recognition*. (Unpublished doctoral dissertation). Louisiana State University, Georgia Institute of Technology.

Nefian, A., Liang, L., Pi, X., Xiaoxiang, L., Mao, C., & Murphy, K. (2002). *A coupled hmm for audio-visual speech recognition (ICASSP)*. Paper presented at the IEEE International Conference on Acoustics, Speech, and Signal Processing. Orlando, FL.

Newton, E., Sweeney, L., & Malin, B. (2005). Preserving Privacy by De-identifying Facial Images. *IEEE Transactions on Knowledge and Data Engineering*, *17*(2), 232–243. doi:10.1109/TKDE.2005.32

Ng, J., & Gong, S. (2001, September). *Learning pixelwise signal energy for understanding semantics (BMVC)*. Paper presented at the British Machine Vision Conference. Manchester, UK.

Ni, Y., & Xie-Long, Y. (2002). *CMOS active differential imaging device with single in&amp,#8211,pixel analog memory*. Paper presented at the Solid-State Circuits Conference. New York, NY.

Nikvand, N., & Wang, Z. (2013). Image Distortion Analysis Based on Normalized Perceptual Information Distance. *Signal Image and Video Proc.*, *7*(3).

Ni, Y., Krichen, E., Hizem, W., Garcia-Salicetti, S., & Dorizzi, B. (2006). Active differential CMOS imaging device for human face recognition. *IEEE Signal Processing Letters*, *13*(4), 220–223. doi:10.1109/LSP.2005.863661

Nowak, E., & Jurie, F. (2007). Learning visual similarity measures for comparing never seen objects. In *Proc. Computer Vision and Pattern Recognition (CVPR)*. Minneapolis, MN: CVPR. doi:10.1109/CVPR.2007.382969

Nowruzi, F., Balafar, M. A., & Pashazadeh, S. (2012). Robust Recognition Against Illumination Variations based on SIFT. In *Proceedings of International Conference on Intelligent Robotics and Applications*, (pp. 503-511). Academic Press.

O'Toole, A. J., Harms, J., Snow, S. L., Hurst, D. R., Pappas, M. R., Ayyad, J. H., & Abdi, H. (2005). Recognizing people from dynamic and static faces and bodies: Dissecting identity with a fusion approach. *Vision Research*, *51*(1), 74–83. doi:10.1016/j.visres.2010.09.035 PMID:20969886

O'Toole, A., Roark, D., & Abdi, H. (2002). Recognizing moving faces: A psychological and neural synthesis. *Trends in Cognitive Sciences*, *6*(6), 261–266. doi:10.1016/S1364-6613(02)01908-3 PMID:12039608

Ocegueda, O., & Fang. (2013). 3d-Face Discriminant Analysis Using Gauss-Markov Posterior Marginals. *IEEE Transactions On Pattern Analysis And Machine Intelligence, 35*(3), 728-739. Doi: Http://Dx.Doi.Org/10.1109/Tpami.2012.126

Ojala, T., Pietikainen, M., & Harwood, D. (1994). Performance evaluation of texture measures with classification based on Kullback discrimination of distributions. In Proceedings of Pattern Recognition, 1994. doi: doi:10.1109/ICPR.1994.576366

Ojala, T., Pietikainen, M., & Harwood, D. (1996). A comparative study of texture measures with classification based on featured distributions. *Pattern Recognition*, *29*(1), 51–59. doi:10.1016/0031-3203(95)00067-4

Ojala, T., Pietikäinen, M., & Mäenpää, T. (2002). Multiresolution Gray-Scale and Rotation Invariant Texture Classification with Local Binary Patterns. *IEEE Transactions on Pattern Analysis and Machine Intelligence, 24*(7), 971–987. doi:10.1109/TPAMI.2002.1017623

Oliva, A., & Torralba, A. (2001). Modeling the shape of the scene: A holistic representation of the spatial envelope. *International Journal of Computer Vision*, *42*(3), 145–175. doi:10.1023/A:1011139631724

Olshausen, B. A., & Field, D. A. (1996). Emergence of simple-cell receptive field properties by learning a sparse code for natural images. *Nature*, *381*, 607–609. doi:10.1038/381607a0 PMID:8637596

Open, C. V. (2013). *OpenCV (Open Source Computer Vision)*. Retrieved 01 Aug, 2013, from http://opencv.org/

Oppliger, R., Rytz, R., & Holderegger, T. (2009). Internet Banking: Client-Side Attacks and Protection Mechanisms. *Computer*, *42*(6), 27–33. doi:10.1109/MC.2009.194

Ostendorf, M., & Singer, H. (1997). HMM topology design using maximum likelihood successive state splitting. *Computer Speech & Language, 11*(1), 17–41. doi:10.1006/csla.1996.0021

Osuna, E., Freund, R., & Girosi, F. (1997). Training Support Vector Machines: An Application to Face Detection. In *Proc. IEEE Conf. Computer Vision and Pattern Recognition*, (pp. 130-136). IEEE.

Padole, C. N., & Proença, H. (2012). *Periocular recognition: Analysis of performance degradation factors*. Paper presented at the Biometrics (ICB), 2012 5th IAPR International Conference on. doi:10.1109/ICB.2012.6199790

Padoy, N., Mateus, D., Weinland, D., Berger, M.-O., & Navab, N. (2009). *Workflow monitoring based on 3D motion features*. Paper presented at the IEEE International Conference on Computer Vision Workshops. Kyoto, Japan.

Pamudurthy, S., Guan, E., Mueller, K., & Rafailovich, M. (2005). Dynamic approach for face recognition using digital image skin correlation. In *Audio- and Video based Biometric Person Authentication* (pp. 1010–1018). Academic Press. doi:10.1007/11527923_105

Pan, G., Han, S., Wu, Z., & Wang, Y. (2005). 3D Face Recognition Using Mapped Depth Images. In *Proceedings of IEEE Conference on Computer Vision and Pattern Recognition*, (Vol. 3, pp. 175-18). IEEE.

Pan, S. J., & Yang, Q. (2010). A Survey on Transfer Learning. *IEEE Transactions on Knowledge and Data Engineering*, *22*(10), 1345–1359. doi:10.1109/TKDE.2009.191

Pantic, M. (2009). Machine analysis of facial behaviour: Naturalistic and dynamic behaviour. *Philosophical Transactions of The Royal Society B: Biological sciences*, *365*(1535), 3505–3513.

Pantic, M., Valstar, M. F., Rademaker, R., & Maat, L. (2005). Web-based database for facial expression analysis. In *Proceedings on the International Conference on Multimedia & Expo*, (pp. 317–321). Academic Press.

Pantic, M., & Bartlett, M. S. (2007). Machine Analysis of Facial Expressions. In *Face Recognition* (pp. 377–416). I-Tech Education and Publishing. doi:10.5772/4847

Pantic, M., Nijholt, A., Pentland, A., & Huang, T. S. (2008). Human-centred intelligent human-computer interaction (hci2), how far are we from attaining it? *International Journal of Autonomous and Adaptive Communications Systems*, *1*(2), 168–187. doi:10.1504/IJAACS.2008.019799

Pantic, M., & Patras, I. (2006). Dynamics of facial expression: Recognition of facial actions and their temporal segments from face profile image sequences. *IEEE Trans. Systems, Man and Cybernetics. Part B, 36*, 433–449.

Pantic, M., Pentland, A., Nijholt, A., & Huang, T. S. (2007). Human computing and machine understanding of human behavior: a survey. In *Proceedings of Artificial Intelligence for Human Computing, (LNCS)* (Vol. 4451, pp. 47–71). Berlin: Springer. doi:10.1007/978-3-540-72348-6_3

Pantic, M., & Rothkrantz, L. J. M. (2004). Facial action recognition for facial expression analysis from static face images. *IEEE Transactions on Systems, Man, and Cybernetics. Part B, Cybernetics, 34*(3), 1449–1461. doi:10.1109/TSMCB.2004.825931 PMID:15484916

Pan, Z. H., Healey, G., Prasad, M., & Tromberg, B. (2003). Face recognition in hyperspectral images. *IEEE Transactions on Pattern Analysis and Machine Intelligence, 25*(12), 1552–1560. doi:10.1109/TPAMI.2003.1251148

Pan, Z., & Bolouri, H. (1999). *High speed face recognition based on discrete cosine transforms and neural networks. (Technical report)*. University of Hertfordshire.

Papandreou, G., & Maragos, P. (2008). Adaptive and constrained algorithms for inverse compositional active appearance model fitting. In *Proceedings of IEEE Conference on Computer Vision and Pattern Recognition (CVPR)*. IEEE.

Papatheodorou, T., & Rueckert, D. (2007). 3D face recognition. In K. Delac, & M. Grgic (Eds.), *Face Recognition*. I-Tech. doi:10.5772/4848

Pappas, T. N., & Safranek, R. J. (2000). Perceptual criteria for image quality evaluation. In *Handbook of Image and Video Processing* (pp. 669–684). Academic Press.

Parikh, D., & Grauman, K. (2011). Relative attributes. In *Proc. 13th Int. Conf. on Computer Vision (ICCV)*. Barcelona, Spain: ICCV.

Park, U., Ross, A., & Jain, A. K. (2009). *Periocular biometrics in the visible spectrum: A feasibility study*. Paper presented at the Biometrics: Theory, Applications, and Systems, 2009. doi:10.1109/BTAS.2009.5339068

Park, K. R., Park, H.-A., Kang, B. J., Lee, E. C., & Jeong, D. S. (2008). A Study on Iris Localization and Recognition on Mobile Phones. *EURASIP Journal on Advances in Signal Processing, 20*. doi: doi:10.1155/2008/281943

Park, U., & Jain, A. K. (2010). Face Matching and Retrieval Using Soft Biometrics. *IEEE Trans. Information Forensics and Security, 5*(3), 406–415. doi:10.1109/TIFS.2010.2049842

Park, U., Jillela, R. R., Ross, A., & Jain, A. K. (2011). Periocular Biometrics in the Visible Spectrum. *IEEE Transactions on Information Forensics and Security, 6*(1), 96–106. doi:10.1109/TIFS.2010.2096810

Park, U., & Tong, Y., & Jain, Anil K. (2010). Age-invariant face recognition. *IEEE Transactions on Pattern Analysis and Machine Intelligence, 32*(5), 947–954. doi:10.1109/TPAMI.2010.14 PMID:20299717

Pascalis, O., de Schonen, S., Morton, J., Deruelle, C., & Fabre-Grenet, M. (1995). Mother's Face Recognition by Neonates: A Replication and an Extension. *Infant Behavior and Development, 18*(1), 79–85. doi:10.1016/0163-6383(95)90009-8

Passalis, G., Kakadiaris, I. A., Theoharis, T., Toderici, G., & Murtuza, N. (2005). Evaluation of 3D Face Recognition in the Presence of Facial Expressions: An Annotated Deformable Model Approach. In *Proceedings of IEEE Workshop Face Recognition Grand Challenge Experiments*, (Vol. 3, pp. 171-179). IEEE.

Passalis, G., & Perakis. (2011). Using Facial Symmetry To Handle Pose Variations In Real-World 3d Face Recognition. *IEEE Transactions on Pattern Analysis and Machine Intelligence, 33*(10), 1938–1951. doi:10.1109/TPAMI.2011.49 PMID:21383396

Patel, V. M., Wu, T., Biswas, S., Phillips, P. J., & Chellappa, R. (2011). Illumination robust dictionary-based face recognition. In *Proc. Internat. Conf. on Image Processing*. Academic Press.

Pechyony, D., Izmailov, R., Vashist, A., & Vapnik, V. (2010). SMO-style algorithms for learning using privileged information. In Proc. Data Mining (DMIN), (pp. 235 - 241). CMIN.

Penev, P., & Atick, J. (1996). Local Feature Analysis: A General Statistical Theory for Object Representation. *Journal of Network Computation in Neural Systems, 7*(3), 477–500. doi:10.1088/0954-898X/7/3/002

Peng, Y., Ganesh, A., Wright, J., Xu, W., & Ma, Y. (2011). RASL: robust alignment by sparse and low-rank decomposition for linearly correlated images. *Transactions on Pattern Analysis and Machine Intelligence, 18*, 315–322.

Pentland, A., Moghaddam, B., & Starner, T. (1994). View-based and modular eigenspaces for face recognition. In *Proceedings of International Conference on Computer Vision and Pattern Rectognition*, (pp. 84-91). Academic Press.

Perakis, P., Passalis, G., Theoharis, T., Toderici, G., & Kakadiaris, I. A. (2009). Partial matching of interpose 3D facial data for face recognition. In *Proceedings of IEEE International Conference on Biometrics: Theory, Applications, and Systems*, (pp. 1–8). IEEE.

Peterson, M., & Eckstein, M. P. (2012). *Looking just below the eyes is optimal across face recognition tasks* (P. N. A. S. Early, Ed.).

Peterson, M., & Eckstein, M. P. (2013). Individual Differences in Eye Movements During Face Identification Reflect Observer-Specific Optimal Points of Fixation. *Psychological Science*. doi:10.1177/0956797612471684 PMID:23740552

Phillips, P. J., Flynn, P. J., Scruggs, T., Bowyer, K. W., & Worek, W. (2006). Preliminary face recognition grand challenge results. In *Proc. International Conference on Automatic Face and Gesture Recognition*, (pp. 15–24). Academic Press.

Phillips, P. J., Flynn, P. J., Scruggs, T., Bowyer, K. W., Chang, J., Hoffman, K., & Worek, W. (2005). *Overview Of The Face Recognition Grand Challenge*. Paper Presented At The IEEE Computer Society Conference On Computer Vision And Pattern Recognition. San Diego, CA.

Phillips, P. J., Grother, P., Micheals, R. J., Blackburn, D. M., Tabassi, E., & Bone, J. M. (2003). *FRVT 2002: Overview and Summary*. Retrieved October 25, 2013 from http://biometrics.nist.gov/cs_links/face/frvt/FRVT_2002_Overview_and_Summary.pdf

Phillips, P., Scruggs, W., O´Toole, A., Flynn, P., Bowyer, K., Schott, C., & Sharpe, M. (2007). FRVT 2006 and ICE 2006 large-scale results. National Institute of Standards and Technology, 7408.

Phillips, J. P., Scruggs, T. W., O'toole, A. J., Flynn, P. J., Bowyer, K. W., Schott, C. L., & Sharpe, M. (2007). *Frvt 2006 And Ice 2006 Large-Scale Results*. Gaithersburg, MD: National Institute Of Standards And Technology.

Phillips, P. J., Flynn, P. J., Beveridge, J. R., Scruggs, W. T., O'Toole, A. J., & Bolme, D. et al. (2009). Overview of the multiple biometrics grand challenge. In *Proceedings of Advances in Biometrics* (pp. 705–714). Academic Press. doi:10.1007/978-3-642-01793-3_72

Phillips, P. J., Grother, P., Micheals, R. J., Blackburn, D., Tabassi, E., & Bone, M. (2003). *FRVT 2002: Evaluation report. National Institute of Standards and Technology.* NIST.

Phillips, P. J., Moon, H., Rizvi, S. A., & Rauss, P. J. (2000). The FERET evaluation methodology for face-recognition algorithms. *IEEE Transactions on Pattern Analysis and Machine Intelligence, 22*(10), 1090–1104. doi:10.1109/34.879790

Phillips, P. J., Scruggs, W. T., O'Toole, A. J., Flynn, P. J., Bowyer, K. W., Schott, C. L., & Sharpe, M. (2010). FRVT 2006 and ICE 2006 Large-Scale Experimental Results. *IEEE Transactions on Pattern Analysis and Machine Intelligence, 32*(5), 831–846. doi:10.1109/TPAMI.2009.59 PMID:20299708

Phillips, P. J., Wechsler, H., Huang, J., & Rauss, P. J. (1998). The FERET database and evaluation procedure for face-recognition algorithms. *Image and Vision Computing, 16*(5), 295–306. doi:10.1016/S0262-8856(97)00070-X

Picard, R. W. (2003). Affective computing: challenges. *International Journal of Human-Computer Studies*, *59*(1–2), 55–64. doi:10.1016/S1071-5819(03)00052-1

Pigeon, S., & Vandendorpe, L. (1997). The M2VTS multimodal face database (release 1.00). In *Proceedings of Audio-and Video-Based Biometric Person Authentication*. Springer. doi:10.1007/BFb0016021

Poggio, T., & Smale, S. (2003). The mathematics of learning: Dealing with data. *Notices of ASM*, 537–544.

Poh, N., Kittler, J., & Bourlai, T. (2010). Quality-Based Score Normalization With Device Qualitative Information for Multimodal Biometric Fusion. *IEEE Transactions on Systems Man and Cybernetics Part a-Systems and Humans*, *40*(3), 539-554.

Poh, N., Heusch, G., & Kittler, J. (2007). On combination of face authentication experts by a mixture of quality dependent fusion classifiers. *Multiple Classifier Systems*, *4472*, 344–356. doi:10.1007/978-3-540-72523-7_35

Poh, N., & Kittler, J. (2012). A Unified Framework for Biometric Expert Fusion Incorporating Quality Measures. *IEEE Transactions on Pattern Analysis and Machine Intelligence*, *34*, 3–18. doi:10.1109/TPAMI.2011.102

Poppe, R. (2010). A survey on vision-based human action recognition. *Image and Vision Computing*, *28*(6), 976–990. doi:10.1016/j.imavis.2009.11.014

Powers, D. M. W. (2011). Evaluation: From precision, recall and f-measure to roc, informedness, markedness & correlation. *Journal of Machine Learning Technologies*, *2*(1), 37–63.

Prince, S., Warrell, J., Elder, J., & Felisberti, F. (2008). Tied factor analysis for face recognition across large pose differences. *IEEE Transactions on Pattern Analysis and Machine Intelligence*, *30*(6), 970–984. doi:10.1109/TPAMI.2008.48 PMID:18421104

Priya, K. J., & Rajesh, R. S. (2011). A Local Min-Max Binary Pattern Based Face Recognition Using Single Sample per Class. *International Journal of Advanced Science and Technology*, *36*(1), 41–50.

Proença, H., & Alexandre, L. A. (2010). Introduction to the Special Issue on the Segmentation of Visible Wavelength Iris Images Captured At-a-distance and On-the-move. *Elsevier Image and Vision Computing*, *28*(2), 213–214. doi:10.1016/j.imavis.2009.09.004

Proença, H., & Alexandre, L. A. (2012). Editorial of the Special Issue On the Recognition of Visible Wavelength Iris Images Captured At-a-distance and On-the-move. *Elsevier Pattern Recognition Letters*, *33*, 963–964. doi:10.1016/j.patrec.2012.03.003

Proença, H., Filipe, S., Santos, R., Oliveira, J., & Alexandre, L. A. (2010). The UBIRIS.v2: A Database of Visible Wavelength Iris Images Captured On-the-Move and At-a-Distance. *IEEE Transactions on Pattern Analysis and Machine Intelligence*, *32*(8), 1529–1535. doi:10.1109/TPAMI.2009.66 PMID:20558882

Qin, C., Bao, X., Choudhury, R., & Nelakuditi, S. (2012). TagSense: Leveraging Smartphones for Automatic Image Tagging. *IEEE Transactions on Mobile Computing*. doi:10.1109/TMC.2012.235

Queensland Rail. (2013). *Queensland Rail Quiet Carriage*. Retrieved 17 Jul, 2013, from http://queenslandrail.com.au/quietcarriage

Queirolo, C. C., Silva, L., Bellon, O. R. P., & Pamplona Segundo, M. (2010). 3D Face Recognition Using Simulated Annealing and the Surface Interpenetration Measure. *IEEE Transactions on Pattern Analysis and Machine Intelligence*, *32*(2), 206–219. doi:10.1109/TPAMI.2009.14 PMID:20075453

Rabiner, L. R. (1989). A tutorial on hidden Markov models and selected applications in speech recognition. *Proceedings of the IEEE*, *77*(2), 257–286. doi:10.1109/5.18626

Rabkin, A. (2008). *Personal knowledge questions for fallback authentication: Security questions in the era of Facebook*. Paper presented at the 4th Symposium on Usable Privacy and Security (SOUPS). Pittsburgh, PA.

Rahtu, E., Heikkilä, J., Ojansivu, V., & Ahonen, T. (2012). Local Phase Quantization for Blur-Insensitive Image Analysis. *Image and Vision Computing*, *30*(8), 501–512. doi:10.1016/j.imavis.2012.04.001

Rajagopalan, A., Kumar, K., Karlekar, J., Manivasakan, R., Patil, M., Desai, U., et al. (1998). Finding Faces in Photographs. In *Proceedings of the. Sixth IEEE International Conference on Computer Vision*, (pp. 640-645). IEEE.

Rajashekar, U., Bovik, A. C., & Cormack, L. K. U. (2006). Visual search in noise: Revealing the influence of structural cues by gaze-contingent classification image analysis. *Journal of Vision (Charlottesville, Va.)*, *6*, 379–386. doi:10.1167/6.4.7 PMID:16889476

Rajashekar, U., van der Linde, I., Bovik, A. C., & Cormack, L. K. G. (2008). A gaze-attentive fixation finding engine. *IEEE Transactions on Image Processing*, *17*(4), 564–573. doi:10.1109/TIP.2008.917218 PMID:18390364

Rajashekar, U., van der Linde, I., Bovik, A. C., & Cormack, L. K. U. (2007). Foveated analysis of image features at fixations. *Vision Research*, *47*, 3160–3172. doi:10.1016/j.visres.2007.07.015 PMID:17889221

Raj, R., Geisler, W. S., Frazor, R. A., & Bovik, A. C. (2005). Contrast statistics for foveated visual systems: fixation selection by minimizing contrast entropy. *Journal of the Optical Society of America. A, Optics, Image Science, and Vision*, *22*(10). doi:10.1364/JOSAA.22.002039 PMID:16277275

Rama Calvo, A., Tarrés Ruiz, F., Rurainsky, J., & Eisert, P. (2008). 2D-3D Mixed Face Recognition Schemes. In K. Delac, M. Grgic, & M. Stewart Bartlett (Eds.), *Recent Advances in Face Recognition* (pp. 125–148). InTech. doi:10.5772/6398

Rama, A., & Tarrés, F. (2005). P²CA: A new face recognition scheme combining 2D and 3D information. In *Proceedings of IEEE International Conference on Image Processing*, (vol.3, pp. 776-779). IEEE.

Rama, A., Tarres, F., Onofrio, D., & Tubaro, S. (2006). Mixed 2D-3D Information for Pose Estimation and Face Recognition. In *Proceedings. 2006 IEEE International Conference on Acoustics, Speech and Signal Processing*, (vol.2, pp. 14-19). IEEE.

Ramamoorthi, R., & Hanrahan, P. (2001). On the relationship between radiance and irradiance: determining the illumination from images of a convex Lambertian object. *Journal of the Optical Society of America. A, Optics, Image Science, and Vision*, *18*(10), 2448–2459. doi:10.1364/JOSAA.18.002448 PMID:11583261

Ramanathan, N., Chowdhury, A., & Chellappa, R. (2004). Facial similarity across age, disguise, illumination and pose. In *Proceedings of International Conference on Image Processing*, (vol. 3, pp. 1999–2002). Academic Press.

Ramanathan, V., & Wechsler, H. (2010). Robust face recognition for occlusion and disguise using holistic anthropometric and appearance-based features and boosting. *Pattern Recognition Letters*, *30*, 2425–2435. doi:10.1016/j.patrec.2010.07.011

Randive, S., & Gonde, A. (2012). A Novel Approach for Face Recognition Using Fusion of Local Gabor Patterns. [IJECE]. *International Journal of Electrical and Computer Engineering*, *2*(3), 345–352.

Rara, H. M., Farag, A. A., & Davis, T. (2011). *Model-Based 3d Shape Recovery From Single Images Of Unknown Pose And Illumination Using A Small Number Of Feature Points*. Paper Presented At The International Joint Conference On Biometrics. Washington, DC.

Ratha, N. K., Connell, J. H., & Bolle, R. M. (2001a). *An Analysis of Minutiae Matching Strength*. Paper presented at the Third International Conference on Audio- and Video-Based Biometric Person Authentication (AVBPA). Halmstad, Sweden.

Ratha, N. K., Connell, J. H., & Bolle, R. M. (2001b). Enhancing security and privacy in biometrics-based authentication systems. *IBM Systems Journal*, *40*(3), 614–634. doi:10.1147/sj.403.0614

Rathgeb, C., & Uhl, A. (2011). A survey on biometric cryptosystems and cancelable biometrics. *EURASIP Journal on Information Security*, (1), 1-25. doi: 10.1186/1687-417X-2011-3

Rayner, K. (1998). Eye movements in reading and information processing: 20 years of research. *Psychological Bulletin*, *124*, 372–422. doi:10.1037/0033-2909.124.3.372 PMID:9849112

Rayner, K. (2009). Eye movements and attention in reading, scene perception, and visual search. *Quarterly Journal of Experimental Psychology*, *62*, 1457–1506. doi:10.1080/17470210902816461 PMID:19449261

Reale, M., Zhang, X., & Yin, L. (2013). Nebula feature: a space-time feature for posed and spontaneous 4D facial behavior analysis. In *Proceedings of the IEEE International Conference on Automatic Face and Gesture Recognition*. IEEE.

Reisfeld, D., & Yeshurun, Y. (1998). Preprocessing of face images: detection of features and pose normalization. *Computer Vision and Image Understanding, 71*(3), 413–430. doi:10.1006/cviu.1997.0640

Reynolds, D. A. (n.d.). *Speaker Verification Using Adapted Gaussian Mixture Models. Academic Press.*

Ricanek, K., & Tesafaye, T. (2006). Morph: A longitudinal image database of normal adult age-progression. In Proceedings of Automatic Face and Gesture Recognition, (pp. 341-345). Academic Press.

Riccio, D., Tortora, G., De Marsico, M., & Wechsler, H. (2012). EGA - Ethnicity, Gender and Age, a pre-annotated face database. In *Proceedings of 2012 IEEE Workshop on Biometric Measurements and Systems for Security and Medical Applications, BioMS 2012* (pp. 38-45). IEEE.

Riccio, D., & Dugelay, J.-L. (2007). Geometric invariants for 2D/3D face recognition. *Pattern Recognition Letters, 28*(14), 1907–1914. doi:10.1016/j.patrec.2006.12.017

Rigamonti, R., Brown, M. A., & Lepetit, V. (2010). Are sparse representations really relevant for image classification? In *Proc. Computer Vision and Pattern Recognition (CVPR)*. Colorado Springs, CO: CVPR.

Rigas, I., Economou, G., & Fotopoulos, S. (2012). Human eye movements as a trait for biometrical identification. In *Proceedings of the 2012 IEEE Fifth International Conference on Biometrics: Theory, Applications and Systems*, (pp. 217-222). IEEE.

Rissanen, J. (2007). *Information and Complexity in Statistical Modeling.* Springer.

Rohrbach, M., Stark, M., & Schiele, B. (2011). Evaluating knowledge transfer and zero-shot learning in a large scale setting. In *Proc. Computer Vision and Pattern Recognition (CVPR)*. Colorado Springs, CO: CVPR. doi:10.1109/CVPR.2011.5995627

Romdhani, S. (2005). *Face Image Analysis using a Multiple Feature Fitting Strategy.* (PhD Thesis).

Romdhani, S., & Vetter, T. (2003). Efficient, robust and accurate fitting of a 3D morphable model. In *Proceedings of IEEE International Conference on Computer Vision (ICCV)*, (pp. 59-66). IEEE.

Romdhani, S., Blanz, V., & Vetter, T. (2002). Face identification by fitting a 3D morphable model using linear shape and texture error functions. In *Proceedings of ECCV*. ECCV.

Rosenholtz, R. (1999). A simple saliency model predicts a number of motion popout phenomena. *Vision Research, 39*, 3157–3163. doi:10.1016/S0042-6989(99)00077-2 PMID:10615487

Ross, A., Jillela, R., Smereka, J. M., Boddeti, V. N., Kumar, B. V. K. V., & Barnard, R. … Plemmons, R. (2012). Matching highly non-ideal ocular images: An information fusion approach. In *Proceedings of the 2012 5th IAPR International Conference on Biometrics* (ICB), (pp. 446-453). IAPR.

Ross, A. A., Shah, J., & Jain, A. K. (2007). From Template to Image: Reconstructing Fingerprints from Minutiae Points. *IEEE Transactions on Pattern Analysis and Machine Intelligence, 29*(4), 544–560. doi:10.1109/TPAMI.2007.1018 PMID:17299213

Ross, D., Lim, J., Lin, R. S., & Yang, M. H. (2008). Incremental learning for robust visual tracking. *International Journal of Computer Vision, 77*(1-3), 125–141. doi:10.1007/s11263-007-0075-7

Rossion, B., Joyce, C. A., Cottrell, G. W., & Tarr, M. J. (2003). Early lateralization and orientation tuning for face, word, and object processing in the visual cortex. *NeuroImage, 20*, 1609–1624. doi:10.1016/j.neuroimage.2003.07.010 PMID:14642472

Roweis, S. T., & Saul, L. K. (2000). Nonlinear Dimensionality Reduction by Locally Linear Embedding. *Science, 290*(5500), 2323–2326. doi:10.1126/science.290.5500.2323 PMID:11125150

Rowley, H., Baluja, S., & Kanade, T. (1998). Neural Network-based Face Detection. *IEEE Transactions on Pattern Analysis and Machine Intelligence, 20*(1), 23–38. doi:10.1109/34.655647

RSA. (2002). *RSA Security Unveils Innovative Two-Factor Authentication Solution for the Consumer Market.* Retrieved 13 Sep, 2012, from http://www.rsa.com/press_release.aspx?id=1370

RSA. (2012). *RSA 2012 Cybercrime Trends Report: EMC Corporation.* RSA.

Rubinstein, Y. D., & Hastie, T. (1997). Discriminative vs. informative learning. In Proceedings of Knowledge and Data Discovery (KDD), (pp. 49–53). ACM.

Rudovic, O., Pavlovic, V., & Pantic, M. (2012). Kernel conditional ordinal random fields for temporal segmentation of facial action units. In *Proceedings of the European Conference on Computer Vision.* Academic Press.

Rui, Y., Huang, T. S., & Chang, S. F. (1999). Image retrieval: Current techniques, promising directions, and open issues. *Journal of Visual Communication and Image Representation, 10*(1), 39–62. doi:10.1006/jvci.1999.0413

Salmon, T. O. (2001). *Fixational eye movement, VS III: Ocular Motility and Binocular Vision.* NE State University.

Saltzer, J. H. (1974). Protection and the Control of Information Sharing in Multics. *Communications of the ACM, 17*(7), 388–402. doi:10.1145/361011.361067

Samal, A., & Iyengar, P. A. (1992). Automatic Recognition and Analysis of Human Faces and Facial Expressions: A Survey. *Pattern Recognition, 25*(1), 65–77. doi:10.1016/0031-3203(92)90007-6

Samaria, F. S., & Harter, A. C. (1994). Parameterization of a stochastic model for human face identification. In *Proceedings of the 2nd IEEE workshop on Applications of Computer Vision.* IEEE.

Samir, C., Srivastava, A., & Daoudi, M. (2006). Three-Dimensional Face Recognition Using Shapes of Facial Curves. *IEEE Transactions on Pattern Analysis and Machine Intelligence, 28*(11), 1853–1863. doi:10.1109/TPAMI.2006.235 PMID:17063689

Sandbach, G., Zafeiriou, S., & Pantic, M. (2012a). Local normal binary patterns for 3D facial action unit detection. In *Proceedings of the IEEE International Conference on Image Processing,* (pp. 1813–1816). IEEE.

Sandbach, G., Zafeiriou, S., & Pantic, M. (2012b). Binary Pattern Analysis for 3D Facial Action Unit Detection. In *Proceedings of the British Machine Vision Conference.* Academic Press.

Sanderson, C., & Paliwal, K. K. (2003). Features for robust face-based identity verification. *Journal of Signal Processing, 83*(5), 931–940. doi:10.1016/S0165-1684(02)00497-8

Sang, N., Wu, J., & Yu, K. (2007). Local Gabor Fisher Classifier for Face Recognition. In *Proceedings of Fourth International Conference on Image and Graphics,* (pp. 620-626). Academic Press.

Santos, G., & Hoyle, E. (2012). A fusion approach to unconstrained iris recognition. *Pattern Recognition Letters, 33*(8), 984–990. doi:10.1016/j.patrec.2011.08.017

Savran, A., Alyuz, N., Dibeklioglu, H., Celiktutan, O., Gokberk, B., Sankur, B., & Akarun, L. (2008). Bosphorus database for 3D face analysis. In *Proceedings of the COST workshop on Biometrics and Identity Management,* (pp. 47–56). COST.

Savran, A., Alyuz, N., Dibeklioglu, H., Celiktutan, O., Gokberk, B., Sankur, B., & Akarun, L. (2008). Bosphorus database for 3D face analysis. In *Biometrics and Identity Management* (pp. 47–56). Academic Press. doi:10.1007/978-3-540-89991-4_6

Savran, A., Sankur, B., & Bilge, M. T. (2012a). Comparative evaluation of 3D versus 2D modality for automatic detection of facial action units. *Pattern Recognition, 45*(2), 767–782. doi:10.1016/j.patcog.2011.07.022

Savran, A., Sankur, B., & Bilge, M. T. (2012b). Regression-based intensity estimation of facial Action Units. *Image and Vision Computing, 30*(10), 774–784. doi:10.1016/j.imavis.2011.11.008

Savvides, M., Abiantun, R., Heo, J., Park, S., Xie, C., & Vijayakumar, B. (2006). *Partial & Holistic Face Recognition on FRGC-II data using Support Vector Machine.* Paper presented at the Computer Vision and Pattern Recognition Workshop, 2006. New York, NY.

Savvides, M., Kumar, B. V. K. V., & Khosla, P. K. (2004a). Corefaces - Robust shift invariant PCA based correlation filter for illumination tolerant face recognition. In *Proceedings of the 2004 IEEE Computer Society Conference on Computer Vision and Pattern Recognition,* (Vol. 2, pp. 834-841). IEEE.

Savvides, M., Kumar, B. V. K. V., & Khosla, P. K. (2004b). Eigenphases vs. Eigenfaces. In *Proceedings of the 17th International Conference on Pattern Recognition,* (vol. 3, pp. 810-813). Academic Press.

Schechter, S., Brush, A. J. B., & Egelman, S. (2009). *It's No Secret. Measuring the Security and Reliability of Authentication via Secret Questions.* Paper presented at the IEEE Symposium on Security and Privacy. Oakland, CA.

Scheenstra, A., Ruifrok, A., & Veltkamp, R. C. (2005). A survey of 3D face recognition methods. *Lecture Notes in Computer Science, 3546,* 891–899. doi:10.1007/11527923_93

Scheirer, W. J., Kumar, N., Ricanek, K., Belhumeur, P. N., & Boult, T. E. (2011). Fusing with Context: a Bayesian Approach to Combining Descriptive Attributes. In *Proc. of 1st IEEE Int.l Joint Conference on Biometrics,* (pp. 1-8). IEEE.

Scheirer, W. J., Boult, T. E., de Rezende Rocha, A., & Sapkota, A. (2013). Toward Open Set Recognition. *IEEE Transactions on Pattern Analysis and Machine Intelligence, 35*(7), 1757–1772. doi:10.1109/TPAMI.2012.256 PMID:23682001

Scheirer, W. J., Rocha, A., Parris, J., & Boult, T. E. (2012). Learning for meta-recognition. *IEEE Transactions on Information Forensics and Security, 7*(4), 1214–1224. doi:10.1109/TIFS.2012.2192430

Schneiderman, H., & Kanade, T. (1998). Probabilistic Modeling of Local Appearance and Spatial Relashionships for Object Recognition. In *Proc. IEEE Conference on Computer Vision and Pattern Recognition,* (pp. 45-51). IEEE.

Schuon, S., Theobalt, C., Davis, J., & Thrun, S. (2009). Lidarboost: Depth superresolution for ToF 3D shape scanning. In *Proceedings of IEEE Computer Vision Pattern Recognition Conference.* Miami, FL: IEEE.

Scott, W. L. (2003). *Block-level Discrete Cosine Transform Coefficients for Autonomic Face Recognition.* (Unpublished doctoral dissertation). Louisiana State University.

Seely, R. D., Samangooei, S., Lee, M., Carter, J. N., & Nixon, M. S. (2008). The University of Southampton Multi-Biometric Tunnel and introducing a novel 3D gait dataset. In *Proceedings of 2nd IEEE International Conference on Biometrics: Theory, Applications and Systems, BTAS 2008* (pp.1–6). IEEE.

Sellahewa, H., & Jassim, S. A. (2010). Image-Quality-Based Adaptive Face Recognition. *IEEE Transactions on Instrumentation and Measurement, 59*(4), 805–813. doi:10.1109/TIM.2009.2037989

Sergent, J. (1982). The cerebral balance of power: Confrontation or cooperation? *Journal of Experimental Psychology. Human Perception and Performance, 8,* 253–272. doi:10.1037/0096-1523.8.2.253 PMID:6461721

Serre, T., Wolf, L., Bileschi, S., Riesenhuber, M., & Poggio, T. (2007). Robust object recognition with cortex-like mechanisms. *IEEE Transactions on Pattern Analysis and Machine Intelligence, 29*(3), 411–426. doi:10.1109/TPAMI.2007.56 PMID:17224612

Shadbolt, N. (2003). Ambient intelligence. *IEEE Intelligent Systems, 18*(4), 2–3. doi:10.1109/MIS.2003.1200718

Shakhnarovich, G., & Moghaddam, B. (2011). Face recognition in subspaces. In *Handbook of Face Recognition.* Springer. doi:10.1007/978-0-85729-932-1_2

Shale-Schwartz, S., Wexler, Y., & Shashua, A. (2011). ShareBoost: Efficient multiclass learning with feature sharing. In *Proceedings of Advances in Neural Information Processing Systems (NIPS).* Granada, Spain: NIPS.

Shan, S. G., Gao, W., Cao, B., & Zhao, D. B. (2003). Illumination normalization for robust face recognition against varying lighting conditions. In *Proceedings of IEEE International Workshop on Analysis and Modeling of Face and Gestures,* (pp. 157-164). IEEE.

Shan, C. (2010). Face Recognition and Retrieval. In *Video Search and Mining* (pp. 235–260). SCI. doi:10.1007/978-3-642-12900-1_9

Sharma, P., Cheikh, F. A., & Hardeberg, J. Y. (2009). Face Saliency in Various Human Visual Saliency Models. In *Proceedings of the 6th International Symposium on Image and Signal Processing and Analysis*. Academic Press.

Shashua, A. (1997). On Photometric Issues in 3D Visual Recognition from a Single 2D Image. *International Journal of Computer Vision*, *21*(1-2), 99–122. doi:10.1023/A:1007975506780

Shashua, A., & Riklin-Raviv, T. (2001). The quotient image: Class-based re-rendering and recognition with varying illuminations. *IEEE Transactions on Pattern Analysis and Machine Intelligence*, *23*(2), 129–139. doi:10.1109/34.908964

Sheikh, H. R., Wang, Z., Cormack, L., & Bovik, A. C. (n.d.). *Live Image Quality Assessment Database Release 2*. Retrieved from http://live.ece.utexas.edu/research/quality

Sheikh, H. R., & Bovik, A. C. (2006). Image Information and Visual Quality. *IEEE Transactions on Image Processing*, *15*(2). doi:10.1109/TIP.2005.859378 PMID:16479813

Sheikh, H. R., Bovik, A. C., & Cormack, L. (2005). No-reference quality assessment using natural scene statistics: JPEG2000. *IEEE Transactions on Image Processing*, *14*(11), 1918–1927. doi:10.1109/TIP.2005.854492 PMID:16279189

Shekhar, S., Patel, V. M., & Chellappa, R. (2011). Synthesis-Based Low Resolution Face Recognition. In *Proceedings of International Joint Conference on Biometrics*, (pp. 1-6). Academic Press.

Shen, C., Wang, P., & Wang, H. (2012). UBoost: Boosting with the Universum. *IEEE Transactions on Pattern Analysis and Machine Intelligence*, *34*(4), 825–832. doi:10.1109/TPAMI.2011.240 PMID:22156096

Shen, L., Bai, L., Bardsley, D., & Wang, Y. (2005). Gabor Feature Selection for Face Recognition Using Improved AdaBoost Learning. *Advances in Biometric Person Authentication*, *3781*, 39–49. doi:10.1007/11569947_6

Shin, H.-C., Kim, S.-D., & Choi, H.-C. (2007). Generalized elastic graph matching for face recognition. *Pattern Recognition Letters*, *28*(9), 1077–1082. doi:10.1016/j.patrec.2007.01.003

Shin, H.-C., Park, J. H., & Kim, S.-D. (2007). Combination of warping robust elastic graph matching and kernel-based projection discriminant analysis for face recognition. *IEEE Transactions on Multimedia*, *9*(6), 1125–1136. doi:10.1109/TMM.2007.898933

Shin, K. Y., Nam, G. P., Jeong, D. S., Cho, D. H., Kang, B. J., Park, K. R., & Kim, J. (2012). New iris recognition method for noisy iris images. *Pattern Recognition Letters*, *33*(8), 991–999. doi:10.1016/j.patrec.2011.08.016

Shi, Q., Erikkson, A., Van den Hengel, A., & Shen, C. (2011). Is face recognition really a compressive sensing problem? In *Proc. Computer Vision and Pattern Recognition (CVPR)*. Colorado Springs, CO: CVPR. doi:10.1109/CVPR.2011.5995556

Short, J., Kittler, J., & Messer, K. (2004). *A comparison of photometric normalisation algorithms for face verification*. Paper presented at the Automatic Face and Gesture Recognition, 2004. New York, NY.

Short. (2006). Illumination Invariance for Face Verification. University of Surrey.

Short, J., Kittler, J., & Messer, K. (2005). Photometric Normalisation for Face Verification. In T. Kanade, A. Jain, & N. Ratha (Eds.), *Audio- and Video-Based Biometric Person Authentication* (Vol. 3546, pp. 617–626). Springer. doi:10.1007/11527923_64

Siarry, P., Berthiau, G., Durbin, F., & Haussy, J. (1997). Enhanced Simulated Annealing For Globally Minimizing Functions Of Many-Continuous Variables. *ACM Transactions on Mathematical Software*, *23*(2), 209–228. doi:10.1145/264029.264043

Silva, P., & Rosa, A. S. (2003). Face recognition based on eigeneyes. *Pattern Recognition and Image Analysis*, *13*(2), 335–338.

Sim, T., & Kanade, T. (2001). *Combining Models and Exemplars for Face Recognition: An Illuminating Example*. Paper presented at the CVPR 2001 Workshop on Models versus Exemplars in Computer Vision. New York, NY.

Sim, T., Baker, S., & Bsat, M. (2002). *The CMU Pose, Illumination, and Expression (PIE) Database*. Paper presented at the Fifth IEEE International Conference on Automatic Face and Gesture Recognition. New York, NY.

Simon, T., Nguyen, M. H., de la Torre, F., & Cohn, J. F. (2010). Action unit detection with segment-based SVMs. In *Proceedings of the IEEE Conference on Computer Vision and Pattern Recognition*, (pp. 2737–2744). IEEE.

Sim, T., Baker, S., & Bsat, M. (2003). The CMU pose, illumination, and expression database. *IEEE Transactions on Pattern Analysis and Machine Intelligence*, 25(12), 1615–1618. doi:10.1109/TPAMI.2003.1251154

Singh, R., Vatsa, M., & Noore, A. (2009). Effect of Plastic Surgery on Face Recognition: A Preliminary Study. In *Proceedings of IEEE Computer Society Conf. on Computer Vision and Pattern Recognition Workshops* (pp. 72-77). IEEE.

Singh, R., Vatsa, M., Bhatt, H. S., Bharadwaj, S., Noore, A., & Nooreyezdan, S. S. (2010). Plastic Surgery: A New Dimension to Face Recognition. *IEEE Transaction on Information Forensics and Security*, 5(3), 441–448. doi:10.1109/TIFS.2010.2054083

Singh, R., Vatsa, M., & Noore, A. (2008). Face recognition with disguise and single gallery images. *Image and Vision Computing*, 27(3), 245–257. doi:10.1016/j.imavis.2007.06.010

Singh, R., Vatsa, M., & Noore, A. (2008). Recognizing Face Images with Disguise Variations. In *Recent Advances in Face Recognition*. Academic Press. doi:10.5772/6399

Singh, R., Vatsa, M., & Noore, A. (2009b). Effect of plastic surgery on face recognition: A preliminary study. [CVPRW.]. *Proceedings of Computer Vision and Pattern Recognition Workshops, CVPRW, 2009*, 72–77.

Sinha, P. (2002). Qualitative representations for recognition. *Biologically Motivated Computer Vision*, 2525, 249–262. doi:10.1007/3-540-36181-2_25

Sinha, P., Balas, B., Ostrovsky, Y., & Russell, R. (2006). Face recognition by humans: Nineteen results all computer vision researchers should know about. *Proceedings of the IEEE*, 94(11), 1948–1962. doi:10.1109/JPROC.2006.884093

Slaney, M., & Casey, M. (2008). Locality-sensitive hashing for finding nearest neighbors. *IEEE Signal Processing Magazine*, 128–131. doi:10.1109/MSP.2007.914237

Slater, A., & Quinn, P. C. (2001). Face recognition in the newborn infant. *Infant and Child Development*, 10(1), 21–24. doi:10.1002/icd.241

Smeets, D., Keustermans, J., Vandermeulen, D., & Suetens, P. (2013). meshSIFT: Local surface features for 3D face recognition under expression variations and partial data. *Computer Vision and Image Understanding*, 117(2), 158–169.

Smeraldi, F., Capdevielle, N., & Bigun, J. (1999). Facial features detection by saccadic exploration of the Gabor decomposition and Support Vector Machines. In *Proceedings of 11th Scandinavian Conference on Image Analysis, SCIA 1999* (vol. 1, pp. 39-44). SCIA.

Smith, A. (2013). *Smartphone Ownership - 2013 Update*. Washington, DC, USA: Pew Research Center.

Smith, G. J. D. (2004). Behind the screens: Examining constructions of deviance and informal practices among CCTV control room operators in the UK. *Surveillance & Society*, 2(2/3), 376–395.

Smith, R. S., & Windeatt, T. (2011). Facial action unit recognition using filtered local binary pattern features with bootstrapped and weighted ECOC classifiers. *Ensembles in Machine Learning Applications*, 373, 1–20. doi:10.1007/978-3-642-22910-7_1

Socolinsky, D. A., & Selinger, A. (2002). *A Comparative Analysis of Face Recognition Performance with Visible and Thermal Infrared Imagery*. Paper presented at the 16 th International Conference on Pattern Recognition (ICPR'02). New York, NY.

Socolinsky, D. A., & Selinger, A. (2004a). *Thermal face recognition in an operational scenario*. Paper presented at the Computer Vision and Pattern Recognition, 2004. New York, NY.

Socolinsky, D. A., & Selinger, A. (2004b). *Thermal face recognition over time*. Paper presented at the Pattern Recognition, 2004. New York, NY.

Socolinsky, D. A., Selinger, A., & Neuheisel, J. D. (2003). Face recognition with visible and thermal infrared imagery. *Computer Vision and Image Understanding*, 91(1–2), 72–114. doi:10.1016/S1077-3142(03)00075-4

Somanath, G., Rohith, M. V., & Kambhamettu, C. (2011). VADANA: A dense dataset for facial image analysis. In *Proc. BeFIT 2011 – First IEEE International Workshop on Benchmarking Facial Image Analysis Technologies (held in conjunction with ICCV 2011)*. IEEE.

Soundararajan, R., & Bovik, A. C. (2007). Survey of Information Theory in Visual Quality Assessment. *Signal Image and Video Processing, 7*(3).

Soundararajan, R., & Bovik, A. (2012). RRED Indices: Reduced Reference Entropic Differencing for Image Quality Assessment. *IEEE Transactions on Image Processing, 21*(2), 517–526. doi:10.1109/TIP.2011.2166082 PMID:21878414

Spafford, E. H., & Weeber, S. A. (1991). *User Authentication and Related Topics: An Annotated Bibliography*. West Lafayette, IN: Purdue University.

Spala, P., Malamos, A., Doulamis, A., & Mamakis, G. (2012). Extending MPEG-7 For Efficient Annotation of Complex Web 3D Scenes. *Multimedia Tools and Applications, 59*(2), 463–504. doi:10.1007/s11042-011-0790-5

Spreeuwers, L. (2011). Fast and Accurate 3D Face Recognition. *International Journal of Computer Vision, 93*(3), 389–414. doi:10.1007/s11263-011-0426-2

Stauffer, C., & Grimson, W. (2000). Learning patterns of activity using real-time tracking. *IEEE Trans. PAMI, 22*(8), 747–758. doi:10.1109/34.868677

Stiefmeier, T., Roggen, D., Troster, G., Ogris, G., & Lukowicz, P. (2008). Wearable activity tracking in car manufacturing. *IEEE Pervasive Computing / IEEE Computer Society [and] IEEE Communications Society, 7*(2), 42–50. doi:10.1109/MPRV.2008.40

Stollnitz, E., Derose, T., & Salesin, D. (1996). *Wavelets For Computer Graphics: Theory And Applications*. Morgan Kaufmann Publishers, Inc.

Stone, Z., Zickler, T., & Darrell, T. (2010). Toward Large scale face recognition using social network context. *Proceedings of the IEEE, 98*(8), 1408–1415. doi:10.1109/JPROC.2010.2044551

Stratou, G., Ghosh, A., Debevec, P., & Morency, L.-P. (2011). Effect of illumination on automatic expression recognition: A novel 3D relightable facial database. In *Proceedings of IEEE International Conference on Automatic Face and Gesture Recognition*, (pp. 611–618). IEEE.

Sugiyama, M., Krauledat, M., & Muller, K. R. (2007). Covariate shift adaptation by importance weighted cross validation. *Journal of Machine Learning Research, 8*, 985–1005.

Sung, K.-K., & Poggio, T. (1998). Example-based Learning for View-based Human Face Detection. *IEEE Transactions on Pattern Analysis and Machine Intelligence, 20*(1), 39–51. doi:10.1109/34.655648

Suruliandi, A., Meena, K., & Rose, R. R. (2012). Local binary pattern and its derivatives for face recognition. *IET Computer Vision, 6*(5), 480–488. doi:10.1049/iet-cvi.2011.0228

Su, Y., Shan, S., Chen, X., & Gao, W. (2009). Hierarchical ensemble of global and local classifiers for face recognition. *Transactions on Image Processing, 18*(8), 1885–1896. doi:10.1109/TIP.2009.2021737 PMID:19556198

Swets, D. L., & Weng, J. J. (1996). Using Discriminant Eigenfeatures for Image Retrieval. *IEEE Transactions on Pattern Analysis and Machine Intelligence, 18*(8), 831–836. doi:10.1109/34.531802

Tahir, M. A., Chan, C. H., Kittler, J., & Bouridane, A. (2011). Face Recognition using Multi-Scale Local Phase Quantisation and Linear Regression Classifier. In *Proceedings of IEEE International Conference on Image Processing*, (pp. 765-768). IEEE.

Taigman, Y., & Wolf, L. (2011). *Leveraging billions of faces to overcome performance barriers in unconstrained face recognition*. arXiv preprint arXiv:1108.1122.

Takacs, B., & Wechsler, H. (1995). Face Location using a Dynamic Model of Retinal Feature Extraction. In *Proc. First Int. Workshop Automatic Face and Gesture Recognition*, (pp. 243-247). Academic Press.

Takács, B., & Wechsler, H. (1998). A Saccadic Vision System for Landmark Detection and Face Recognition. *Face Recognition, 163*, 627–636. doi:10.1007/978-3-642-72201-1_42

Tan, C.-W., & Kumar, A. (2012). Efficient iris segmentation using Grow-Cut algorithm for remotely acquired iris images. In *Proceedings of the 2012 IEEE Fifth International Conference on Biometrics: Theory, Applications and Systems*, (pp. 99-104). IEEE.

Tan, X., Li, Y., Liu, J., & Jiang, L. (2010). *Face Liveness Detection from a Single Image with Sparse Low Rank Bilinear Discriminative Model*. Paper presented at the European Conference on Computer Vision (ECCV). Crete, Greece.

Tan, K. S., Oh, S. R., Priel, A., & Korn, B. S. (2011). *Surgical Anatomy of the Forehead, Eyelids, and Midface for the Aesthetic Surgeon*. Master Techniques. doi:10.1007/978-1-4614-0067-7_2

Tan, T., Zhang, X., Sun, Z., & Zhang, H. (2012). Noisy iris image matching by using multiple cues. *Pattern Recognition Letters*, *33*(8), 970–977. doi:10.1016/j.patrec.2011.08.009

Tan, X., & Triggs, B. (2010). Enhanced Local Texture Feature Sets for Face Recognition Under Difficult Lighting Conditions. *IEEE Transactions on Image Processing*, *19*(6), 1635–1650. doi:10.1109/TIP.2010.2042645 PMID:20172829

Tao, J., & Tan, T. (2005). Affective computing: A review. In *Proceedings of Affective Computing and Intelligent Interaction, First International Conference, ACII 2005*, (LNCS), (vol. 3784, pp. 981-995). Berlin: Springer.

Tao, Y., & Yang, J. (2012). Fusion of Local Features for Face Recognition by Multiple Least Square Solutions. *Lecture Notes in Computer Science*, *7701*, 9–16. doi:10.1007/978-3-642-35136-5_2

Tarres, F., Rama, A., & Torres, L. (2005). A novel method for face recognition under partial occlusion or facial expression variations. In *Proceedings of ELMAR International Symposium* (pp. 163–166). ELMAR.

Tarr, M. J., & Gauthier, I. (2000). FFA: A flexible fusiform area for subordinate-level visual processing automatized by expertise. *Nature Neuroscience*, *3*, 764–769. doi:10.1038/77666 PMID:10903568

Tatler, B. W., Baddeley, R. J., & Gilchrist, I. D. (2005). Visual correlates of fixation selection: effects of scale and time. *Vision Research, Elsevier*, *45*, 643–659. doi:10.1016/j.visres.2004.09.017 PMID:15621181

Tax, M. J., Hendriks, E., Valstar, M. F., & Pantic, M. (2010). The detection of concept frames using clustering multi-instance learning. In *Proceedings of the International Conference on Pattern Recognition*, (pp. 2917–2920). Academic Press.

Tefas, A., Kotropoulos, C., & Pitas, I. (2001). Using support vector machines to enhance the performance of elastic graph matching for frontal face authentication. *IEEE Transactions on Pattern Analysis and Machine Intelligence*, *23*(7), 735–746. doi:10.1109/34.935847

Tefas, A., Kotropoulos, C., & Pitas, I. (2002). Face verification using elastic graph matching based on morphological signal decomposition. *Signal Processing*, *82*(6), 833–851. doi:10.1016/S0165-1684(02)00157-3

Teixeira, A., Matos, A., Souto, A., & Antunes, L. (2011). Entropy measures vs Kolmogorov Complexity. *Entropy Journal*, *13*, 595–611. doi:10.3390/e13030595

ter Haar, F., & Veltkamp, R. (2008). A 3D Face Matching Framework. In *Proceedings of IEEE International Conference on Shape Modeling and Applications* (pp. 103-110). IEEE.

Teuner, A. (1999). *Surveillance Sensor Systems Using CMOS Imagers*. Academic Press.

The Telegraph UK. (2011). *Technology fail: Google's Galaxy nexus suffers embarrassing failure at Samsung launch*. Retrieved 12 Nov, 2013, from http://youtu.be/eBy3gXpDVes

Tian, Y., Kanade, T., & Cohn, J. (2001). Recognizing action units for facial expression analysis. *IEEE Transactions on Pattern Analysis and Machine Intelligence*, *23*(2), 97–115. doi:10.1109/34.908962

Tistarelli, M., Lagorio, A., & Grosso, E. (2009). Face recognition by local and global analysis. In *Proceedings of International Symposium on Image and Signal Processing and Analysis*, (pp. 690-694). Academic Press.

Tistarelli, M., Li, S. Z., & Chellappa, R. (2009). *Handbook of Remote Biometrics: for Surveillance and Security.* Springer Publishing Company Inc. doi:10.1007/978-1-84882-385-3

Toderici, G., & Passalis. (2010). *Bidirectional Relighting For 3d-Aided 2d Face Recognition.* Paper Presented At The IEEE Computer Conference On Computer Vision And Pattern Recognition. San Francisco, CA.

Tong, Y., Chen, J., & Ji, Q. (2010). A unified probabilistic framework for spontaneous facial action modeling and understanding. *IEEE Transactions on Pattern Analysis and Machine Intelligence, 32*(2), 258–273. doi:10.1109/TPAMI.2008.293 PMID:20075457

Tong, Y., Liao, W., & Ji, Q. (2007). Facial action unit recognition by exploiting their dynamic and semantic relationships. *IEEE Transactions on Pattern Analysis and Machine Intelligence, 29*(10), 1683–1699. doi:10.1109/TPAMI.2007.1094 PMID:17699916

Topsøe, F. (2000). Some Inequalities for Information Divergence and Related Measures of Discrimination. *IEEE Transactions on Information Theory, 46*(4). doi:10.1109/18.850703

Torralba, A., & Efros, A. A. (2011). Unbiased look at dataset bias. In *Proc. Computer Vision and Pattern Recognition (CVPR).* Colorado Springs, CO: CVPR.

Tranel, D., Damasio, A., & Damasio, H. (1988). Intact Recognition of Facial Expression, Gender, and Age in Patients with Impaired Recognition of Face Identity. *Neurology, 38*, 690–696. doi:10.1212/WNL.38.5.690 PMID:3362363

Tsalakanidou, F., & Malassiotis, S. (2009). Robust facial action recognition from real-time 3D streams. In *Proceedings of the IEEE conference on Computer Vision and Pattern Recognition*, (pp. 4–11). IEEE.

Tsalakanidou, F., Tzovaras, D., & Strintzis, M. (2003). Use of Depth and Colour Eigenfaces for Face Recognition. *Pattern Recognition Letters, 24*(9/10), 1427–1435. doi:10.1016/S0167-8655(02)00383-5

Tsochantaridis, I., Joachims, T., Hofmann, T., & Altun, Y. (2005). Large margin methods for structured and interdependent output variables. *Journal of Machine Learning Research, 6*, 1453–1484.

Turk, M., & Pentland, A. (1991). Eigenfaces for recognition. *Journal of Cognitive Neuroscience, 3*(1), 71–86. doi:10.1162/jocn.1991.3.1.71 PMID:23964806

Tzimiropoulos, G., Alabort-i-Medina, J., Zafeiriou, S., & Pantic, M. (2013). Generic active appearance models revisited. In *Proceedings of Computer Vision–ACCV.* Springer.

Tzimiropoulos, G., Zafeiriou, S., & Pantic, M. (2012). Subspace learning from image gradient orientations. *IEEE Transactions on Pattern Analysis and Machine Intelligence, 34*(12), 2454–2466. doi:10.1109/TPAMI.2012.40 PMID:22271825

Ullman, S., Vidal-Naquet, M., & Sali, E. (2002). Visual features of intermediate complexity and their use in classification. *Nature Neuroscience, 5*(7), 682–687. PMID:12055634

Uludag, U., & Jain, A. (2006). Securing fingerprint template: Fuzzy vault with helper data. In *Proc. IEEE Workshop on Privacy Research in Vision.* New York: IEEE.

University of Notre Dame Biometrics Database. (2008). Retrieved from http://www.nd.edu/@cvrl/UNDBiometricsDatabase.html

University Of Notre Dame. (2008). *University Of Notre Dame Biometrics Database.* Author.

Valstar, M. F., & Pantic, M. (2010). Induced disgust, happiness and surprise: an addition to the MMI facial expression database. In *Proceedings of the International Conference on Language Resources and Evaluation*, (pp. 65–70). Academic Press.

Valstar, M. F., Jiang, B., Mehu, M., Pantic, M., & Scherer, K. (2011). The first facial expression recognition and analysis challenge. In *Proceedings of the IEEE International Conference on Automatic Face and Gesture Recognition.* IEEE.

Valstar, M. F., Patras, I., & Pantic, M. (2005). Facial action unit detection using probabilistic actively learned support vector machines on tracked facial point data. In *Proceedings of the IEEE Conference on Computer Vision and Pattern Recognition*, (pp. 76–84). IEEE.

Valstar, M. F., Mehu, M., Jiang, B., Pantic, M., & Scherer, K. (2012). Meta-analyis of the first facial expression recognition challenge. *IEEE Transactions in Systems, Man and Cybernetics. Part B, 42*(4), 966–979.

Valstar, M. F., & Pantic, M. (2012). Fully automatic recognition of the temporal phases of facial actions. *IEEE Transactions on Systems, Man and Cybernetics. Part B, 1*(99), 28–43.

van der Maaten, L., & Hendriks, E. (2012). Action unit classification using active appearance models and *conditional random fields. Cognitive Processing, 13*, 507–518. doi:10.1007/s10339-011-0419-7 PMID:21989609

van der Putte, T., & Keuning, J. (2000). *Biometrical Fingerprint Recognition: Don't Get Your Fingers Burned.* Paper presented at the Fourth Working Conference on Smart Card Research and Advanced Applications. Bristol, UK.

van Thanh, D., Jørstad, I., Jønvik, T., & van Thuan, D. (2009). *Strong authentication with mobile phone as security token.* Paper presented at the 6th International Conference on Mobile Adhoc and Sensor Systems (MASS). Macau, China.

Vapnik, V. (1998). *Statistical learning theory.* New York: John Wiley and Sons.

Vapnik, V. (2000). *The Nature of Statistical Learning Theory* (2nd ed.). Springer. doi:10.1007/978-1-4757-3264-1

Vapnik, V. N. (2006). *Estimation of Dependencies Based on Empirical Data: Empirical Inference Science: Afterword of 2006.* Springer.

Vasilescu, M. A. O., & Terzopoulos, D. (2002). Multilinear analysis of image ensembles: Tensorfaces. In *Proceedings of Computer Vision.* Springer.

Vedaldi, A., & Fulkerson, B. (2008). *VLFeat: An Open and Portable Library of Computer Vision Algorithms.* Retrieved from http://www.vlfeat.org/

Veres, G., Grabner, H., Middleton, L., & van Gool, L. (2010). *Automatic workflow monitoring in industrial environments (ACCV).* Paper presented at the Asian Conference on Computer Vision. New York, NY.

Vetter, T., & Poggio, T. (1997). Linear object classes and image synthesis from a single example image. *IEEE Transactions on Pattern Analysis and Machine Intelligence, 19*(7), 733–742. doi:10.1109/34.598230

Vielhauer, C. (2006). Biometric User Authentication for IT Security. In S. Jajodia (Ed.), *Advances in Information Security* (Vol. 18, p. 287). New York, NY: Springer-Verlag.

Vijayan, V., & Bowyer. (2011). Twins 3d Face Recognition Challenge. *IEEE Transactions on Pattern Analysis and Machine Intelligence*, 1–7.

Viola, P., & Jones, M. (2001). Rapid object detection using a boosted cascade of simple features. In *Proceedings of IEEE Conf. on Computer Vision and Pattern Recognition*, (vol. 1, pp. 511–518). IEEE.

Viola, P., & Jones, M. J. (2004). Robust real-time face detection. *International Journal of Computer Vision, 57*(2), 137–154. doi:10.1023/B:VISI.0000013087.49260.fb

VIPeR. (n.d.). *Viewpoint Invariant Pedestrian Recognition.* Retrieved from http://vision.soe.ucsc.edu/?q=node/178

Voulodimos, A., Doulamis, N., Kosmopoulos, D., & Varvarigou, T. (2012). Improving multi-camera activity recognition by employing neural network based readjustment. *Applied Artificial Intelligence, 26*(1-2), 97–118. doi:10.1080/08839514.2012.629540

Voulodimos, A., Kosmopoulos, D., Vasileiou, G., Sardis, E., Doulamis, A., & Anagnostopoulos, V. et al. (2011). A threefold dataset for activity and workflow recognition in complex industrial environments. *IEEE MultiMedia, 19*(3), 42–52. doi:10.1109/MMUL.2012.31

Vovk, V., Gammerman, A., & Shafer, G. (2005). *Algorithmic Learning in a Random World.* Springer.

Wada, T., & Matsuyama, T. (2000). Multi-object behavior recognition by event driven selective attention method. *IEEE Transactions on Pattern Analysis and Machine Intelligence, 22*(8), 873–887. doi:10.1109/34.868687

Wagner, A., Wright, J., Ganesh, A., Zhou, Z., Mobahi, H., & Ma, Y. (2012). Toward a practical face recognition system: Robust alignment and illumination by sparse representation. *IEEE Transactions on Pattern Analysis and Machine Intelligence, 34*(2), 372–386. doi:10.1109/TPAMI.2011.112 PMID:21646680

Wang, H., Li, S. Z., & Wang, Y. (2004). Generalized quotient image. In *Proc. Internat. Conf. Computer Vision and Pattern Recognition* (pp. 498-505). Academic Press.

Wang, Q., Zhang, X., Li, M., Dong, X, Zhou, Q., & Yin, Y. (2012). *Adaboost and multi-orientation 2D Gabor-based accurate noisy iris recognition, 33*(8), 978-983.

Wang, S., Wang, Y., Jin, M., Gu, X., & Samaras, D. (2006). 3D Surface Matching and Recognition Using Conformal Geometry. In *Proceedings of IEEE Conference on Computer Vision and Pattern Recognition*, (Vol. 2, pp. 2453-2460). IEEE.

Wang, S., Zhang, L., Liang, Y., & Pan, Q. (2012). *Semi-Coupled Dictionary Learning With Applications To Image Super-Resolution And Photo-Sketch Synthesis*. Paper Presented At The IEEE Conference On Computer Vision And Pattern Recognition. Providence, RI.

Wang, W., Wang, Y., Huang, Q., & Gao, W. (2010). Measuring Visual Saliency by Site Entropy Rate. In *Proc. of CVPR '10*, (pp. 2368-2375). CVPR.

Wang, X., Ma, K.-T., Ng, G.-W., & Grimson, W. (2008). *Trajectory analysis and semantic region modeling using a nonparametric bayesian model (ICPR)*. Paper presented at the IEEE Conference on Computer Vision and Pattern Recognition. Anchorage, AK.

Wang, Y., Chiang, M.-C., & Thompson, P. M. (2005). Mutual Information-Based 3D Surface Matching with Applications to Face Recognition and Brain Mapping. In *Proceedings of IEEE International Conference on Computer Vision* (pp. 527-534). IEEE.

Wang, Z., & Simoncelli, E. P. (2005). Reduced-Reference Image Quality Assessment using a Wavelet-Domain Natural Image Statistic Model. In *Proc. of SPIE Human Vision and Electronic Imaging X*, (pp. 149-159). SPIE.

Wang, Z., Sheikh, H. R., & Bovik, A. C. (2002). No-Reference Perceptual Quality Assessment of JPEG Compressed Images. In *Proceedings of IEEE Int. Conf. on Image Processing*. Rochester, NY: IEEE.

Wang, D., & Kong, S. (2012). Feature selection from high-order tensorial data via sparse decomposition. *Pattern Recognition Letters, 33*(13), 1695–1702. doi:10.1016/j.patrec.2012.06.010

Wang, H., & Chang, S.-F. (1997). Highly Efficient System for Automatic Face Region Detection in MPEG Video Sequences. *IEEE Trans. on Circuits and Syst. for Video Technol, 7*(4), 615–628. doi:10.1109/76.611173

Wang, L., Ding, L., Ding, X., & Fang, C. (2011). 2D face fitting-assisted 3D reconstruction for pose-robust face recognition. *Soft Computing, 15*(3), 417–428. doi:10.1007/s00500-009-0523-0

Wang, S., Rehman, A., Wang, Z., Ma, S., & Gao, W. (2013). Perceptual Video Coding Based on SSIM-Inspired Divisive Normalization. *IEEE Transactions on Image Processing, 22*(4). PMID:23221823

Wang, X., & Tang, X. (2004). A unified framework for subspace face recognition. *IEEE Transactions on Pattern Analysis and Machine Intelligence, 26*(9), 1222–1228. doi:10.1109/TPAMI.2004.57 PMID:15742896

Wang, X., & Tang, X. (2009). Face Photo-Sketch Synthesis and Recognition. *IEEE Transactions on Pattern Analysis and Machine Intelligence, 31*(11), 1955–1967. doi:10.1109/TPAMI.2008.222 PMID:19762924

Wang, Y., & Chua, C.-S. (2005). Face Recognition from 2D and 3D Images Using 3D Gabor Filters. *Image and Vision Computing, 11*(23), 1018–1028. doi:10.1016/j.imavis.2005.07.005

Wang, Y., Liu, J., & Tang, X. (2010). Robust 3D face recognition by local shape difference boosting. *IEEE Transactions on Pattern Analysis and Machine Intelligence, 32*(10), 1858–1870. doi:10.1109/TPAMI.2009.200 PMID:20724762

Wang, Y., & Mori, G. (2009). Human action recognition by semilatent topic models. *IEEE Transactions on Pattern Analysis and Machine Intelligence, 31*(10), 1762–1774. doi:10.1109/TPAMI.2009.43 PMID:19696448

Wang, Z., & Bovik, A. C. (2006). *Modern Image Quality Assessment*. Morgan and Claypool Publishers.

Wang, Z., Bovik, A. C., Sheikh, H. R., & Simoncelli, E. P. (2004). Image quality assessment: From error measurement to structural similarity. *IEEE Transactions on Image Processing, 13*(4), 600–612. doi:10.1109/TIP.2003.819861 PMID:15376593

Wang, Z., & Li, Q. (2011). Information content weighting for perceptual image quality assessment. *IEEE Transactions on Image Processing*, *20*(5), 1185–1198. doi:10.1109/TIP.2010.2092435 PMID:21078577

Wang, Z., Lu, L., & Bovik, A. (2004). Video Quality Assessment based on Structural Distortion Measurement. *Signal Processing Image Communication*, *19*(2), 121–132. doi:10.1016/S0923-5965(03)00076-6

Watson, A. B. (1993). DCTune: A technique for visual optimization of DCT quantization matrices for individual images. *Soc. Inf. Display Dig. Tech. Papers*, *24*, 946–949.

Watson, M. R., Brennan, A. A., Kingstone, A., & Enns, J. T. (2010). Looking versus seeing: Strategies alter eye movements during visual search. *Psychonomic Bulletin & Review*, *17*(4), 543–549. doi:10.3758/PBR.17.4.543 PMID:20702875

Webster, M. A., & MacLeod, D. I. A. (2011). Visual adaptation and face perception. *Philosophical Transactions of the Royal Society of London. Series B, Biological Sciences*, *366*, 1702–1725. doi:10.1098/rstb.2010.0360 PMID:21536555

Wechsler, H. (2006). *Reliable Face Recognition Methods: System Design, Implementation and Evaluation*. Springer.

Wechsler, H. (2007). *Reliable Face Recognition Methods*. Springer. doi:10.1007/978-0-387-38464-1

Wei, S. D., & Lai, S. H. (2004). Robust face recognition under lighting variations. In *Proceedings of the 17th International Conference on Pattern Recognition*, (pp. 354-357). Academic Press.

Wei, X., & Li, C. T. (2013). Fixation and Saccade Based Face Recognition from Single Image per Person with Various Occlusions and Expressions. In *Proceedings of 2013 IEEE Conference on Computer Vision and Pattern Recognition Workshops, CVPRW* (pp.70-75). IEEE.

Weinberger, K. O., Blitzer, J., & Saul, L. K. (2006). Distance metric learning for large margin nearest neighbor classifier. In *Proceedings of Advances in Neural Information Processing Systems (NIPS)*. Vancouver, Canada: NIPS.

Wei, X., Zhou, C., & Zhang, Q. (2010). ICA-based features fusion for face recognition. *International Journal of Innovative Computing, Information, & Control*, *6*(10), 4651–4662.

Wenyi, Z., & Chellappa, R. (2000). *Illumination-insensitive face recognition using symmetric shape-from-shading*. Paper presented at the Computer Vision and Pattern Recognition, 2000. New York, NY.

Weston, J., Collobert, R., Sinz, F., Bottou, L., & Vapnik, V. (2006). Inference with the Universum. In *Proc. 23rd Int. Conf. Machine Learning*, (pp. 1009–1016). Academic Press.

Westphal, G., & Würtz, R. P. (2009). Combining feature- and correspondence-based methods for visual object recognition. *Neural Computation*, *21*(7), 1952–1989. doi:10.1162/neco.2009.12-07-675 PMID:19292649

Whitehill, J., & Omlin, C. W. (2006). Haar features for FACS AU recognition. In *proceedings of the IEEE International Conference on Automatic Face and Gesture Recognition*. IEEE.

Wilder, J., Phillips, P. J., Cunhong, J., & Wiener, S. (1996). *Comparison of visible and infra-red imagery for face recognition*. Paper presented at the Automatic Face and Gesture Recognition, 1996. New York, NY.

Winkler, S. (2005). *Digital Video Quality, Vision Models and Metrics*. Wiley. doi:10.1002/9780470024065

Wiskott, L. (1997). Phantom faces for face analysis. *Pattern Recognition*, *30*(6), 837–846. doi:10.1016/S0031-3203(96)00132-X

Wiskott, L., Fellous, J. M., Kuiger, N., & Von Der Malsburg, C. (1997). Face recognition by elastic bunch graph matching. *IEEE Transactions on Pattern Analysis and Machine Intelligence*, *19*(7), 775–779. doi:10.1109/34.598235

Wolf, L., Hassner, T., & Maoz, I. (2011). Face Recognition in Unconstrained Videos with Matched Background Similarity. In *Proc. of IEEE Conf. on Computer Vision and Pattern Recognition (CVPR)*. IEEE.

Wolf, L., Hassner, T., & Taigman, Y. (n.d.). *Descriptor Based Methods in the Wild*. Paper presented at the Workshop on Faces in 'Real-Life' Images: Detection, Alignment, and Recognition. Retrieved from http://hal.inria.fr/inria-00326729

Wolf, L., Hassner, T., & Taigman, Y. (2011). Effective unconstrained face recognition by combining multiple descriptors and learned background statistics. *IEEE Transactions on Pattern Analysis and Machine Intelligence, 33*(10), 1978–1990. doi:10.1109/TPAMI.2010.230 PMID:21173442

Wolf, L., & Levy, N. (2013). The SVM-minus similarity score for video face recognition. In *Proc. Computer Vision and Pattern Recognition (CVPR)*. Portland, OR: CVPR. doi:10.1109/CVPR.2013.452

Wong, Y., Chen, S., Mau, S., Sanderson, C., & Lovell, B. C. (2011). Patch-based probabilistic image quality assessment for face selection and improved video-based face recognition. In *Proc. of IEEE Computer Vision and Pattern Recognition Workshops* (CVPRW), (pp. 74-81). IEEE.

Woodard, D. L., Pundlik, S. J., Lyle, J. R., & Miller, P. E. (2010a). *Periocular region appearance cues for biometric identification*. Paper presented at the Computer Vision and Pattern Recognition Workshops (CVPRW), 2010 IEEE Computer Society Conference on. doi:10.1109/CVPRW.2010.5544621

Woodard, D. L., Pundlik, S., Miller, P., Jillela, R., & Ross, A. (2010b). *On the Fusion of Periocular and Iris Biometrics in Non-ideal Imagery*. Paper presented at the Pattern Recognition (ICPR), 2010 20th International Conference on. doi:10.1109/ICPR.2010.58

Woodard, D., Pundlik, S., Miller, P., & Lyle, J. (2011). Appearance-based periocular features in the context of face and non-ideal iris recognition. *Signal. Image and Video Processing, 5*, 443–455. doi:10.1007/s11760-011-0248-2

Wright, J., Yang, A. Y., Ganesh, A., Sastry, S. S., & Ma, Y. (2009). Robust face recognition via sparse representation. *IEEE Transactions on Pattern Analysis and Machine Intelligence, 31*(2), 210–227. doi:10.1109/TPAMI.2008.79 PMID:19110489

Wurtz, R. P. (1997). Object recognition robust under translations, deformations, and changes in background. *IEEE Transactions on Pattern Analysis and Machine Intelligence, 19*(7), 769–775. doi:10.1109/34.598234

Xiang, S., Yuan, L., Fan, W., Wang, Y., Thompson, P. M., & Ye, J. (2013). Multi-source learning with block-wise missing data for Alzheimer's disease prediction. In *Proc. 19th Conf. on Knowledge Discovery and Data Mining (KDD)*. Chicago, IL: ACM.

Xiang, T., Gong, S., & Parkinson, D. (2002). *Autonomous Visual Events Detection and Classification without Explicit Object-Centred Segmentation and Tracking (BMCVC)*. Paper presented at the British Machine Vision Conference. Cardiff, UK.

Xiang, T., & Gong, S. (2006). Beyond tracking: modelling activity and understanding behaviour. *International Journal of Computer Vision, 67*, 21–51. doi:10.1007/s11263-006-4329-6

Xie, X., & Lam, K.-M. (2006). An efficient illumination normalization method for face recognition. *Pattern Recognition Letters, 27*(6), 609–617. doi:10.1016/j.patrec.2005.09.026

Xing, E., Ng, A., Jordan, S., & Russell, S. (2003). Distance metric learning with applications to clustering with side-information. In *Proceedings of Advances in Neural Information Processing Systems (NIPS)*. Vancouver, Canada: NIPS.

Xinyu, H., Bo, F., Changpeng, T., Tokuta, A., & Ruigang, Y. (2012). Robust varying-resolution iris recognition. In *Proceedings of the 2012 IEEE Fifth International Conference on Biometrics: Theory, Applications and Systems*, (pp. 47-54). IEEE.

Xiong, X., & De la Torre, F. (2013). Supervised Descent Method and its Applications to Face Alignment. In *Proceedings of IEEE Conference on Computer Vision and Pattern Recognition (CVPR)*. IEEE.

Xu, C., Wang, Y., Tan, T., & Quan, L. (2004). Depth vs. intensity: Which is more important for face recognition? In *Proceedings of International Conference on Pattern Recognition*, (Vol. 4, pp. 342–345). ICPR.

Xu, D., Hu, P., Cao, W., & Li, H. (2008). Shrec'08 Entry: 3D Face Recognition Using Moment Invariants. In *Proceedings of IEEE International Conference on Shape Modeling and Applications*, (pp. 261-262). IEEE.

Xu, W., Caramanis, C., & Mannor, S. (2012). Sparse algorithms are not stable: A no free-lunch theorem. *IEEE Transactions on Pattern Analysis and Machine Intelligence, 34*(1), 187–193. doi:10.1109/TPAMI.2011.177 PMID:21844627

Yager, N., & Dunstone, T. (2010). The biometric menagerie. *IEEE Transactions on Pattern Analysis and Machine Intelligence, 32*(2), 220–230. doi:10.1109/TPAMI.2008.291 PMID:20075454

Yamada, K., & Cottrell, G. W. (1995). A model of scan paths applied to face recognition. In *Proceedings of the Seventeenth Annual Cognitive Science Conference*, (pp. 55-60). Mahwah, NJ: Lawrence Erlbaum.

Yang, J., & Waibel, A. (1996). A Real-Time Face Tracker. In *Proc. Third Workshop Applications of Computer Vision*, (pp. 142-147). Academic Press.

Yang, W., Yi, D., Lei, Z., Sang, J., & Li, S. Z. (2008). 2D–3D face matching using CCA. In *Proceedings of 8th IEEE International Conference on Automatic Face & Gesture Recognition*. IEEE.

Yang, F., & Paindavoine, M. (2003). Implementation of an RBF neural network on embedded systems: Real-time face tracking and identity verification. *IEEE Transactions on Neural Networks, 14*(5), 1162–1175. doi:10.1109/TNN.2003.816035 PMID:18244568

Yang, G., & Huang, T. S. (1994). Human Face Detection in Complex Background. *Pattern Recognition, 27*(1), 53–63. doi:10.1016/0031-3203(94)90017-5

Yang, H., Shao, L., Zheng, F., Wang, L., & Song, Z. (2011). Recent advances and trends in visual tracking: A review. *Neurocomputing, 74*, 3823–3831. doi:10.1016/j.neucom.2011.07.024

Yang, J., & Wright. (2010). Image Super-Resolution Via Sparse Representation. *IEEE Transactions on Image Processing, 19*, 2861–2873. doi:10.1109/TIP.2010.2050625 PMID:20483687

Yang, J., Zhang, D., Yang, J.-Y., & Niu, B. (2007). Globally Maximizing, Locally Minimizing: Unsupervised Discriminant Projection with Applications to Face and Palm Biometrics. *IEEE Transactions on Pattern Analysis and Machine Intelligence, 29*(4), 650–664. doi:10.1109/TPAMI.2007.1008 PMID:17299222

Yang, M.-H., Kriegman, D., & Ahuja, N. (2002). Detecting Faces in Images: A Survey. *IEEE Transactions on Pattern Analysis and Machine Intelligence, 24*(1), 34–58. doi:10.1109/34.982883

Yan, P., & Bowyer, K. W. (2007). A Fast Algorithm for ICP-Based 3D Shape Biometrics. *Computer Vision and Image Understanding, 107*(3), 195–202. doi:10.1016/j.cviu.2006.11.001

Yao, A., Gall, J., & van Gool, L. (2010). *A hough transform-based voting framework for action recognition (CVPR)*. Paper presented at the IEEE Conference on Computer Vision and Pattern Recognition. San Francisco, CA.

Yazdanpanah, A. P., Faez, K., & Amirfattahi, R. (2010). Multimodal biometric system using face, ear and gait biometrics. In *Proceedings of 10th International Conference on Information Science, Signal Processing and their Applications, ISSPA 2010* (pp. 251- 254). ISSPA.

Yin, L., Chen, X., Sun, Y., Worm, T., & Reale, M. (2008). A high-resolution 3D dynamic facial expression database. In *Proceedings of the International Conference on Automatic Face and Gesture Recognition*, (pp. 1–6). Academic Press.

Yin, L., Wei, X., Sun, Y., Wang, J., & Rosato, M. (2006). A 3D facial expression database for facial behavior research. In *Proceedings of the IEEE International Conference on Automatic Face and Gesture Recognition*, (pp. 211–216). IEEE.

Yin, Q., Tang, X., & Sun, J. (2011). An associate-predict model for face recognition. In *Proceedings of 2011 IEEE Conference on Computer Vision and Pattern Recognition (CVPR)* (pp. 497-504). IEEE.

Yow, K. C., & Cipolla, R. (1997). Feature-based Human Face Detection. *Image and Vision Computing, 15*(9), 713–735. doi:10.1016/S0262-8856(97)00003-6

Yuan, L., Mu, Z.-C., & Xu, X.-N. (2007). Multimodal recognition based on face and ear. In *Proceedings of International Conference on Wavelet Analysis and Pattern Recognition - ICWAPR 2007* (vol. 3, pp. 1203–1207). ICWAPR.

Yuan, L., Zhichun, M. Z., & Liu, Y. (2006). Multimodal recognition using face profile and ear. In *Proceedings of 1st International Symposium on Systems and Control in Aerospace and Astronautics - ISSCAA 2006* (pp. 887–891). ISSCAA.

Yu, Y., Harwood, D., Yoon, K., & Davis, L. S. (2007). Human appearance modelling for matching across video sequences. *Machine Vision and Applications, 18*(3-4), 139–149. doi:10.1007/s00138-006-0061-z

Zabih, R., & Woodfill, J. (1994). Non-parametric local transforms for computing visual correspondence. In J.-O. Eklundh (Ed.), *Computer Vision — ECCV '94* (Vol. 801, pp. 151–158). Springer. doi:10.1007/BFb0028345

Zafeiriou, S. (2012). Subspace learning in Krein spaces: complete kernel fisher discriminant analysis with indefinite kernels. In *Proceedings of Computer Vision*. Springer. doi:10.1007/978-3-642-33765-9_35

Zafeiriou, S., Tefas, A., Buciu, I., & Pitas, I. (2006). Exploiting discriminant information in nonnegative matrix factorization with application to frontal face verification. *IEEE Transactions on Neural Networks, 17*(3), 683–695. doi:10.1109/TNN.2006.873291 PMID:16722172

Zafeiriou, S., Tefas, A., & Pitas, I. (2007a). The discriminant elastic graph matching algorithm applied to frontal face verification. *Pattern Recognition, 40*(10), 2798–2810. doi:10.1016/j.patcog.2007.01.026

Zafeiriou, S., Tefas, A., & Pitas, I. (2007b). Learning discriminant person-specific facial models using expandable graphs. *IEEE Transactions on Information Forensics and Security, 2*(1), 55–68. doi:10.1109/TIFS.2006.890308

Zafeiriou, S., Tzimiropoulos, G., Petrou, M., & Stathaki, T. (2012). Regularized kernel discriminant analysis with a robust kernel for face recognition and verification. *IEEE Transactions on Neural Networks and Learning Systems, 23*(3), 526–534. doi:10.1109/TNNLS.2011.2182058

Zeng, Z., Pantic, M., Roisman, G. I., & Huang, T. S. (2009). A survey of affect recognition methods: audio, visual, and spontaneous expressions. *IEEE Transactions on Pattern Analysis and Machine Intelligence, 31*(1), 39–58. doi:10.1109/TPAMI.2008.52 PMID:19029545

Zeng, Z., Tu, J., Pianfetti, B., & Huang, T. (2008). Audio-visual affective expression recognition through multistream fused HMM. *IEEE Transactions on Multimedia, 10*(4), 570–577. doi:10.1109/TMM.2008.921737

Zernike, F. (1934). Beugungstheorie des Schneidenverfahrens und Seiner Verbesserten Form, der Phasenkontrastmethode. *Physica I, 1*(8), 689–704. doi:10.1016/S0031-8914(34)80259-5

Zhang, L., & Samaras, D. (2003). Face recognition under variable lighting using harmonic image exemplars. In *Proceedings of IEEE Computer Society Conference on Computer Vision and Pattern Recognition,* (pp. 19-25). IEEE.

Zhang, L., Li, S. Z., Qu, Z.-Y., & Huang, X. (2004). Boosting Local Feature Based Classifiers for Face Recognition. In *Proceedings of Conference on Computer Vision and Pattern Recognition Workshops,* (pp. 87-92). Academic Press.

Zhang, Q., & Li, B. (2010). *Discriminative K-Svd For Dictionary Learning In Face Recognition.* Paper Presented At The IEEE Conference On Computer Vision And Pattern Recognition. San Francisco, CA.

Zhang, W., Shan, S., Gao, W., Chen, X., & Zhang, H. (2005). Local Gabor binary pattern histogram sequence (LGBPHS): A novel non-statistical model for face representation and recognition. In *Proceedings of International Conference on Computer Vision,* (pp. 786–791). Academic Press.

Zhang, X., Yin, L., Cohn, J. F., Canavan, S., Reale, M., Horowitz, A., & Liu, P. (2013). A high resolution spontaneous 3D dynamic facial expression database. In *Proceedings of the IEEE International conference on Automatic Face and Gesture Recognition,* (pp. 22-26). IEEE.

Zhang, B., Gao, Y., Zhao, S., & Liu, J. (2010). Local Derivative Pattern Versus Local Binary Pattern: Face Recognition With High-Order Local Pattern Descriptor. *IEEE Transactions on Image Processing, 19*(2), 533–544. doi:10.1109/TIP.2009.2035882 PMID:19887313

Zhang, J., Yan, Y., & Lades, M. (1997). Face recognition: Eigenface, elastic matching, and neural nets. *Proceedings of the IEEE*, *85*(9), 1423–1435. doi:10.1109/5.628712

Zhang, L., & Samaras, D. (2006). Face Recognition from a Single Training Image under Arbitrary Unknown Lighting Using Spherical Harmonics. *IEEE Transactions on Pattern Analysis and Machine Intelligence*, *28*(3), 351–363. doi:10.1109/TPAMI.2006.53 PMID:16526422

Zhang, T., Tang, Y. Y., Fang, B., Shang, Z., & Liu, X. (2009). Face recognition under varying illumination using gradientfaces. *IEEE Transactions on Image Processing*, *18*(11), 2599–2606. doi:10.1109/TIP.2009.2028255 PMID:19635700

Zhang, W., Shan, S., Chen, X., & Gao, W. (2007). Local Gabor Binary Patterns Based on Kullback–Leibler Divergence for Partially Occluded Face Recognition. *IEEE Signal Processing Letters*, *14*(11), 875–878. doi:10.1109/LSP.2007.903260

Zhang, Y., Tian, J., He, X., & Yang, X. (2007). MQI Based Face Recognition Under Uneven Illumination. In S.-W. Lee, & S. Li (Eds.), *Advances in Biometrics* (Vol. 4642, pp. 290–298). Springer. doi:10.1007/978-3-540-74549-5_31

Zhao, W., & Chellappa, R. (1999). *Robust face recognition using symmetric shape-from-shading*. University of Maryland. Retrieved October 23, 2013, from ftp://ftp.cfar.umd.edu/TRs/CVL-Reports-1999/TR4036-zhao.ps.gz

Zhao, X., & Chu. (2013). *Uhae: Minimizing Illumination Difference In 3d-2d Face Recognition Using Lighting Maps*. IEEE.

Zhao, X., & Shah. (2012). *Illumination Normalization Using Self-Lighting Ratios For 3d-2d Face Recognition*. Paper Presented At The European Conference On Computer Vision Workshop: What's In A Face. Firenze, Italy.

Zhao, X., & Shah. (2013). *Illumination Alignment Using Lighting Ratio: Application To 3d-2d Face Recognition*. Paper Presented At The 10th International Conference On Automatic Face And Gesture Recognition. Shanghai, China. Retrieved from Http://Ieeexplore.Ieee.Org/Xpl/Articledetails.Jsp?Tp=&Arnumber=6553782

Zhao, X., Dellandrea, E., Chen, L., & Samaras, D. (2010). AU recognition on 3D faces based on an extended statistical facial feature model. In *Proceedings of the International Conference on Biometrics: Theory Applications and Systems*, (pp. 1–6). Academic Press.

Zhao, G. Y., & Pietikainen, M. (2007). Dynamic texture recognition using local binary pattern with an application to facial expressions. *IEEE Transactions on Pattern Analysis and Machine Intelligence*, *2*(6), 915–928. doi:10.1109/TPAMI.2007.1110

Zhao, S., & Grigat, R.-R. (2005). An Automatic Face Recognition System in the Near Infrared Spectrum. In P. Perner, & A. Imiya (Eds.), *Machine Learning and Data Mining in Pattern Recognition* (Vol. 3587, pp. 437–444). Springer. doi:10.1007/11510888_43

Zhao, W., Chellappa, R., Phillips, P. J., & Rosenfeld, A. (2003). Face recognition: A literature survey. [CSUR]. *ACM Computing Surveys*, *35*(4), 399–458. doi:10.1145/954339.954342

Zhou, F., de la Torre, F., & Cohn, J. F. (2010). Unsupervised discovery of facial events. In *Proceedings of the IEEE Conference on Computer Vision and Pattern Recognition*. IEEE.

Zhou, S., & Chellappa, R. (2002). Probabilistic human recognition from video. In ECCV 2002 (LNCS), (vol. 2352, pp. 681–697). Springer.

Zhou, S., Krueger, V., & Chellappa, R. (2002). Face recognition from video: A condensation approach. In *Proceedings of IEEE International Conference on Automatic Face & Gesture Recognition (FG)*, (pp. 221-226). IEEE.

Zhou, Y., Gu, L., & Zhang, H.-J. (2003). Bayesian tangent shape model: Estimating shape and pose parameters via bayesian inference. In *Proceedings of IEEE Conf. on Computer Vision and Pattern Recognition, CVPR 2003*. IEEE.

Zhou, Y., Zhang, W., Tang, X., & Shum, H. (2005). A bayesian mixture model for multi-view face alignment. In *Proceedings of IEEE Conference on Computer Vision and Pattern Recognition (CVPR'05)* (vol. 2, pp. 741-746). IEEE.

Zhou, Z., Chindaro, S., & Deravi, F. (2009). A Classification Framework for Large-Scale Face Recognition Systems. In N. M. Tistarelli M. (Ed.), Advances in Biometrics (LNCS), (vol. 5558, pp. 337-346). Berlin: Springer.

Zhou, S. K., Aggarwal, G., Chellappa, R., & Jacobs, D. W. (2007). Appearance characterization of linear Lambertian objects, generalized photometric stereo, and illumination-invariant face recognition. *IEEE Transactions on Pattern Analysis and Machine Intelligence*, 29(2), 230–245. doi:10.1109/TPAMI.2007.25 PMID:17170477

Zhu, X., & Ramanan, D. (2012). Face detection, pose estimation, and landmark localization in the wild. In *Proceedings of IEEE Conference on Computer Vision and Pattern Recognition (CVPR)*, (pp. 2879-2886). IEEE.

Zhu, Y., De la Torre, F., Cohn, J. F., & Zhang, Y. (2011). Dynamic cascades with bidirectional bootstrapping for action unit detection in spontaneous facial behavior. *IEEE Transactions Affective Computing*, 2(2), 79–91. doi:10.1109/T-AFFC.2011.10

Zou, X., Kittler, J., & Messer, K. (2007). *Motion compensation for face recognition based on active differential imaging*. Paper presented at the 2007 international conference on Advances in Biometrics. New York, NY.

Zou, J., Ji, Q., & Nagy, G. (2007). A Comparative Study of Local Matching Approach for Face Recognition. *IEEE Transactions on Image Processing*, 16(10), 2617–2628. doi:10.1109/TIP.2007.904421 PMID:17926941

Zou, X. (2007). *Illumination Invariant Face Recognition based on Active Near-IR Differential Imaging*. University of Surrey.

Zou, X., Kittler, J., & Messer, K. (2005). Ambient Illumination Variation Removal by Active Near-IR Imaging. In D. Zhang, & A. Jain (Eds.), *Advances in Biometrics* (Vol. 3832, pp. 19–25). Springer. doi:10.1007/11608288_3

Zou, X., Kittler, J., & Messer, K. (2007). Illumination invariant face recognition: A survey. In *Proceedings of Biometrics: Theory, Applications, and Systems*. Academic Press.

Zuo, J., & Schmid, N. A. (2013). Adaptive Quality-Based Performance Prediction and Boosting for Iris Authentication: Methodology and Its Illustration. *IEEE Transactions on Information Forensics and Security*, 8(6), 1051–1060. doi:10.1109/TIFS.2013.2259157

Zviran, M., & Haga, W. J. (1990). *Passwords Security: An Exploratory Study*. Monterey, CA: Naval Postgraduate School.

About the Contributors

Maria De Marsico was born in Salerno, Italy, in 1963. She received the Laurea degree (cum laude) in Computer Science from the University of Salerno, Italy, in 1988. She is currently an Assistant Professor of Computer Science at Sapienza University of Rome. Her main research interests include pattern recognition, multibiometric systems, image processing, human-computer interaction. In the field of biometrics, she collaborates with BIPLab at University of Salerno. She has been member of the Program Committees of many international conferences, and is member of the Editorial Board of the *IEEE Biometris Compendium*. Maria De Marsico is a member of IEEE, ACM, and IAPR.

Michele Nappi was born in Naples, Italy, in 1965. He received the laurea degree (cum laude) in computer science from the University of Salerno, Salerno, Italy, in 1991, the M.Sc. degree in information and communication technology from I.I.A.S.S. Œ.R. Caianiello, Vietri sul Mare, Salerno, and the Ph.D. degree in Applied Mathematics and Computer Science from the University of Padova, Padova, Italy. He is currently an Associate Professor of computer science at the University of Salerno. His research interests include multibiometric systems, pattern recognition, image processing, compression and indexing, multimedia databases, and human-computer interaction. He is currently the Director of BIPLab (Biometrics and Image Processing Lab) at University of Salerno. Dr. Nappi is a member of IEEE and IAPR.

Massimo Tistarelli was born on November 11, 1962 in Genoa, Italy. He received the PhD in Computer Science and Robotics in 1991 from the University of Genoa. He is Full Professor in Computer Science (with tenure) and director of the Computer Vision Laboratory at the University of Sassari, Italy. Since 1986, he has been involved as project coordinator and task manager in several projects on computer vision and biometrics funded by the European Community. Since 1994, he has been the director of the Computer Vision Laboratory at the Department of Communication, Computer and Systems Science of the University of Genoa, and now at the University of Sassari, leading several National and European projects on computer vision applications and image-based biometrics. He is a founding member of the Biosecure Foundation, which includes all major European research centers working in biometrics. He is the Chair of the Management Committee of the European Union COST Action IC1106 "Integrating Biometrics and Forensics for the Digital Age." His main research interests cover biological and artificial vision (particularly in the area of recognition, three-dimensional reconstruction, and dynamic scene analysis), pattern recognition, biometrics, visual sensors, robotic navigation, and visuo-motor coordination. He is co-author of more than 100 scientific papers in peer-reviewed books, conferences, and international journals. He is the principal editor for the Springer book *Handbook of Remote Biometrics*, published in June 2009. Prof. Tistarelli is one of the world-recognized leading researchers in the area of biometrics, especially in the field of face recognition and multimodal fusion. He is the Scientific Director of the Italian Platform for Biometric Technologies (established from the Italian Ministry of the University and Scientific Research), chair of the IAPR Technical Committee 4 on Biometrics, President of the Italian Chapter of the IEEE Biometrics Coucil, Member of the IEEE Biometrics Professional Certification Committee, Fellow member of IAPR, and Senior member of IEEE.

* * *

Andrea F. Abate received the Ph.D. degree in Applied Mathematics and Computer Science from the University of Pisa, Italy, in 1998. He now serves as Associate Professor of Computer Science at the University of Salerno. His research interests include Computer Graphics, Virtual and Augmented Reality, Virtual Reality Interaction, Biometrics and Multimedia Databases. He is currently the Co-Director of the VR_Lab - Virtual Reality Lab.

Lale Akarun received the B.S. and M.S. degrees in Electrical Engineering from Bogazici University, Istanbul, Turkey, in 1984 and 1986, respectively, and the Ph.D. degree from the Polytechnic University, New York, in 1992. From 1993 to the present, she has been a Faculty Member at, Bogazici University, where she serves as professor of Computer Engineering since 2001. Her research areas are biometrics; face recognition, and hand vein recognition; and human computer interaction; with emphasis on human activity and gesture analysis. Prof. Akarun has worked on the organization committees of the IEEE NSIP99, EUSIPCO 2005, eNTERFACE2007, and ICPR2010.

Nese Alyuz received the B.S. degree in Computer Engineering from Istanbul Technical University, Istanbul, Turkey, in 2005. She obtained the M.Sc. and Ph.D. degrees in Computer Engineering from Bogazici University, Istanbul, Turkey, in 2008 and 2013, respectively. Her Ph.D thesis is titled "3D Face Recognition under Occlusion Variance." She is currently a member of the Intelligent User Interfaces Laboratory, Koc University, Istanbul, Turkey. Her research areas are biometrics, computer vision, image processing, pattern recognition, and machine learning.

Silvio Barra is a PhD student at the University of Cagliari. He was born in 1985, and in 2012, he received the Laurea degree (cum laude) in Computer Science from the University of Salerno. His main research interests include: biometrics, iris segmentation and recognition, face detection, video surveillance systems, and tracking.

Stefano Berretti received the Ph.D. in Information and Telecommunications Engineering in 2001 from the University of Firenze, Italy. Currently, he is an Associate Professor at the Department of Information Engineering of the University of Firenze, Italy, and at the Media Integration and Communication Center of the same University. His current research interests are mainly focused on content modeling, retrieval, and indexing of image and 3D object databases. Recent researches have addressed 3D object retrieval and partitioning, 3D face recognition, 3D facial expression recognition. He has been visiting researcher at the Indian Institute of Technology (IIT), in Mumbai, India (2000), and visiting professor at the Institute TELECOM, TELECOM Lille 1, in Lille, France (2009), and at the Khalifa University of Science, Technology and Research, Sharjah, UAE (2013). Stefano Berretti is author of more than

100 publications appeared in conference proceedings and international journals in the area of pattern recognition, computer vision and multimedia. He is in the program committee of several international conferences and serves as a frequent reviewer of many international journals. He has been co-chair of the Fifth Workshop on Non-Rigid Shape Analysis and Deformable Image Alignment (NORDIA'12), held on October 7, 2012, in conjunction with ECCV 2012, Firenze, Italy.

Vittoria Bruni received the degree in Mathematics from the University of Rome" La Sapienza" in 2001. In January 2006, she received the PhD degree in applied mathematics from the same University, Department of Mathematical Methods and Models for Applied Sciences. Since 2010, she is researcher at the Department of SBAI - Faculty of Engineering of the same University. Her research interests include image compression, denoising, restoration and quality assessment, wavelets theory and applications, numerical anaysis, pattern recognition. She is co-author of several scientific articles published on international journals and in the proceedings of international conferences. She is also referee for various international journals. Since September 2001, she collaborates with the Institute for the Application of Calculus (IAC) of National Research Council in Rome within national and international projects.

Andrea Casanova is Assistant Professor at Department of Computer Science - University of Cagliari. Lecturer in Biometric Authentication and Software Engineering for both the Course of Study in Computer Science, Medical Informatics, and Medicine. GIRPR member (Italian research group focused on Pattern Recognition) and MILab member (Medical Image Laboratory, University of Cagliari). The current research interests are in the field of Biometric Authentication, Haptic System, Image Analysis and Processing, Human-Computer Interaction vr/ar and Computer-Aided Diagnosis.

Chi Ho Chan received the PhD degree from the University of Surrey, United Kingdom, in 2008. He is currently a research fellow at the Centre for Vision, Speech and Signal Processing, University of Surrey. From 2002 to 2004, he served as a researcher at ATR International, Japan. His research interests include image processing, pattern recognition, biometrics, and vision-based human-computer interaction.

Dat Chu has received his B.S. and M.Sc. in Computer Science from University of Houston. His interests include machine learning, face recognition, computer vision, and software engineering.

Alberto del Bimbo is Full Professor of Computer Engineering, Director of the Master in Multimedia, and Director of the Media Integration and Communication Center at the University of Florence. He was the Deputy Rector for Research and Innovation Transfer of the University of Florence from 2000 to 2006. His scientific interests are multimedia information retrieval, pattern recognition, image and video analysis, and natural human-computer interaction. He has published over 250 publications in some of the most distinguished scientific journals and international conferences, and is the author of the monograph *Visual Information Retrieval*. From 1996 to 2000, he was the President of the IAPR Italian Chapter and from 1998 to 2000, Member at Large of the IEEE Publication Board. He was the general Chair of IAPR ICIAP'97, the International Conference on Image Analysis and Processing, IEEE ICMCS'99, the International Conference on Multimedia Computing and Systems and Program Co-Chair of ACM Multimedia 2008. He is the General Co-Chair of ACM Multimedia 2010 and of ECCV 2012, the European Conference on Computer Vision. He is IAPR Fellow and Associate Editor of *Multimedia Tools and Applications, Pattern Analysis and Applications, Journal of Visual Languages and Computing*, and

International Journal of Image and Video Processing, and was Associate Editor of *Pattern Recognition, IEEE Transactions on Multimedia*, and *IEEE Transactions on Pattern Analysis and Machine Intelligence*.

Anastasios D. Doulamis (S'96, M'00) received the Diploma degree in Electrical and Computer Engineering from the National Technical University of Athens (NTUA) in 1995 with the highest honor. In 2000, he has received the PhD degree in electrical and computer engineering from the NTUA. Since September 2013, he is an Associate professor at the Technical University of Crete and from 2014 is elected as faculty member of the National Technical University of Athens. Dr. Doulamis has received several awards and prizes during his studies, including the Best Greek Student in the field of engineering in national level in 1995, the Best Graduate Thesis Award in the area of electrical engineering with A. Doulamis in 1996 and several prizes from the National Technical University of Athens, the National Scholarship Foundation and the Technical Chamber of Greece, the IEEE. He has also served as program committee in several international conferences and workshops of IEEE and ACM. He is author of more than 200 papers in the above areas in leading international journals and conferences. His research interests include, non-linear analysis, neural networks, and multimedia content description.

Jean-Luc Dugelay obtained his PhD in Information Technology from the University of Rennes in 1992. His thesis work was undertaken at CCETT (France Télécom Research) at Rennes between 1989 and 1992. He then joined EURECOM in Sophia Antipolis where he is now a Professor in the Department of Multimedia Communications. His current work focuses in the domain of multimedia image processing, in particular activities in security (image forensics, biometrics and video surveillance, mini drones), and facial image processing. He has authored or co-authored over 250+ publications in journals and conference proceedings, 1 book on 3D object processing published by Wiley, 4 book chapters, and 3 international patents. His research group is involved in several national projects and European projects. He has delivered several tutorials on digital watermarking, biometrics and compression at major international conferences such as ACM Multimedia and IEEE ICASSP. He participated in numerous scientific events as member of scientific technical committees, invited speakers or session chair. He is a fellow member of IEEE and an elected member of the EURASIP BoG. Jean-Luc Dugelay is (or was) associate editor of several international journals (IEEE Trans. on IP, IEEE Trans. on MM) and is the founding editor-in-chief of the *EURASIP journal on Image and Video Processing* (SpringerOpen). Jean-Luc Dugelay is co-author of several conference articles that received an IEEE award in 2011, 2012, and 2013. He co-organized the 4th IEEE International Conference on Multimedia Signal Processing held in Cannes, 2001 and the Multimodal User Authentication held in Santa Barbara, 2003. In 2015, he will serve as general co-chair of IEEE ICIP and EURASIP EUSIPCO.

Gianni Fenu is associate professor of Computer Science at the Department of Mathematics and Computer Science, Faculty of Sciences, University of Cagliari, Italy. During the last years, he taught several courses, including Computer Graphics, Foundations of Computer Science, Computer Networks, Network Architecture Planning Laboratory. He's Head of the degree course of Computer Science, Coordinator of Development Projects and published about 70 scientific papers on international Journals and Conferences on the following main topics: Computer Network, HCI, and Information Systems Development.

Chiara Galdi was born in 1988. She received the Laurea degree (cum laude) in Computer Science from the University of Salerno, Italy, in 2012. She is currently a PhD student at the University of Salerno. Her main research interests include biometrics, iris recognition under uncontrolled conditions.

Berk Gokberk received the B.S., M.Sc., and Ph.D. degrees in Computer Engineering from Bogazici University, Istanbul, Turkey, in 1999, 2001, and 2006, respectively. He worked as a senior scientist at Philips Research, Eindhoven between 2006 and 2008. He is currently with the Signals and Systems group of Department of Electrical Engineering Mathematics and Computer Science, University of Twente, The Netherlands. His research interests are in the areas of biometrics, computer vision, computer graphics, and pattern recognition.

Ioannis A. Kakadiaris is a Hugh Roy and Lillie Cranz Cullen University Professor of Computer Science, Electrical and Computer Engineering, and Biomedical Engineering at the University of Houston. He joined UH in August 1997 after a postdoctoral fellowship at the University of Pennsylvania. Ioannis earned his B.Sc. in physics at the University of Athens in Greece, his M.Sc. in computer science from Northeastern University and his Ph.D. at the University of Pennsylvania. He is the founder of the Computational Biomedicine Lab (www.cbl.uh.edu) and in 2008 directed the Methodist-University of Houston-Weill Cornell Medical College Institute for Biomedical Imaging Sciences (IBIS) (ibis.uh.edu). His research interests include biometrics, video analytics, computer vision, pattern recognition, and biomedical image computing. Dr. Kakadiaris is the recipient of a number of awards, including the NSF Early Career Development Award, Schlumberger Technical Foundation Award, UH Computer Science Research Excellence Award, UH Enron Teaching Excellence Award, and the James Muller Vulnerable Plaque Young Investigator Prize. His research has been featured on The Discovery Channel, National Public Radio, KPRC NBC News, KTRH ABC News, and KHOU CBS News. Selected professional service leadership positions include: General Co-Chair of the 2013 Biometrics: Theory, Applications and Systems Conference (BTAS 2013), General Co-chair of the 2014 SPIE Biometric and Surveillance Technology for Human and Activity Identification, Program Co-Chair of the 2015 International Conference on Automatic Face and Gesture Recognition Conference, and Vice-President for Technical Activities for the IEEE Biometrics Council.

Josef Kittler received the BA, PhD, and Dsc degrees from the University of Cambridge in 1971, 1974, and 1991, respectively. He heads the Centre for Vision, Speech, and Signal Processing of the Faculty of Engineering and Physical Sciences, University of Surrey. He teaches and conducts research in the subject area of machine intelligence, with a focus on biometrics, video and image database retrieval, automatic inspection, medical data analysis, and cognitive vision. He has published a Prentice Hall textbook Pattern Recognition: A Statistical Approach and several edited volumes, as well as more than 600 scientific papers, including in excess of 170 journal papers. He serves on the editorial boards of several scientific journals in pattern recognition and computer vision. He became the series editor of Springer Lecture Notes on Computer Science in 2004. He served as the president of the International Association for Pattern Recognition 1994-1996. He was elected a fellow of the Royal Academy of Engineering in 2000. In 2006, he was awarded the KS Fu Prize from the International Association for Pattern Recognition for outstanding contributions to pattern recognition. He received an honorary doctorate from the Czech Technical University in Prague in 2007 and the IET Faraday Medal in 2008.

Neslihan Kose graduated from Electrical and Electronics Engineering Department of Middle East Technical University (METU), Ankara, Turkey in 2007. She received her master's degree from the same department of METU in 2009. Her specialization field in master study is signal processing. Since November 2010, she is a PhD student at Multimedia Department of EURECOM Institute under the supervision of Prof. Jean-Luc Dugelay. Currently, she works in the European project TABULA RASA. Her PhD study is mainly based on spoofing attacks and disguise variations in face recognition and countermeasures.

Irene Kotsia received the BSc and PhD degrees from the Department of Informatics, Aristotle University of Thessaloniki, Thessaloniki, Greece, in 2002 and 2008, respectively. From 2008 to 2009, she was a Research Associate and teaching assistant in the department of Informatics at Aristotle University of Thessaloniki. From 2009 to 2011, she was a Research Associate in the department of Electronic Engineering and Computer Science of Queen Mary University of London, while from 2012 she is a Research Associate in the department of computing in Imperial College London and a Lecturer in Creative Technology and Digital Creativity in the Department of Computing Science of Middlesex University of London. She has coauthored more than 35 journal and conference publications. Her current research interests lie in the areas of image and signal processing, statistical pattern recognition especially for human actions localization and recognition, facial expression recognition from static images and image sequences as well as in the areas of graphics and animation.

Stan Li received PhD degree from Surrey University, UK. He is currently a professor at the National Laboratory of Pattern Recognition and the director of the Center for Biometrics and Security Research (CBSR), Institute of Automation (CASIA), and the director of the Center for Visual Internet of Things Research (VIOT), Chinese Academy of Sciences. He worked at Microsoft Research Asia as a researcher from 2000 to 2004. Prior to that, he was an associate professor at Nanyang Technological University, Singapore. He was elevated to IEEE Fellow for his contributions to the fields of face recognition, pattern recognition and computer vision. His research interest includes pattern recognition and machine learning, image and vision processing, face recognition, biometrics, and intelligent video surveillance. He has published over 200 papers in international journals and conferences, and authored and edited 8 books among which *Markov Random Field Models in Image Analysis* (Springer, 1st edition 1995, 2nd edition 2001, 3rd edition 2009) has been cited more than 2000 times (by Google Scholar). Other works include *Handbook of Face Recognition* (Springer, 1st edition 2005, 2nd edition 2011), and *Encyclopedia of Biometrics* (Springer Reference Work, 2010).

Brian C. Lovell was born in Brisbane, Australia in 1960. He received the BE in electrical engineering in 1982, the BSc in computer science in 1983, and the PhD in signal processing in 1991: all from the University of Queensland (UQ). Professor Lovell is Director of the Advanced Surveillance Group in the School of ITEE, UQ. He was President of the International Association for Pattern Recognition (IAPR) (2008-2010), and is Fellow of the IAPR, Senior Member of the IEEE, and voting member for Australia on the Governing Board of the IAPR. He was General Co-Chair of the IEEE International Conference on Image Processing in Melbourne, 2013 and Program Co-Chair of the International Conference of Pattern Recognition in Tampa, 2008. His interests include non-cooperative Face Recognition, Biometrics, and Pattern Recognition.

João Neves received the B.Sc. degree and the M.Sc. in Computer Science in 2011 and 2013 from University of Beira Interior, Covilhã, Portugal. His principal field of interest is Computer Vision having worked in different research projects at the SOCIA-LAB from 2010 to 2013. Currently, he is a PhD student with a particular interest in visual surveillance for unconstrained scenarios.

Pietro Pala received the Ph.D. in Information and Telecommunications Engineering in 1997 at the University of Firenze, Italy. Pietro Pala is currently an Associate Professor and the President of the committee deputed to the evaluation of quality, according to the CRUI 2011 model, for the course of Informatics Engineering. His research activity has focused on the use of pattern recognition models for multimedia information retrieval and biometrics. Former studies targeted the definition of elastic models for measuring shape similarity and support shape based retrieval in image databases. From these studies, a number of different yet related topics were investigated, including image segmentation, content-based description and retrieval of color images, multidimensional indexing structures for retrieval by color and shape, semantic content description in paintings and advertising videos, description and similarity matching of 3D models, segmentation of 3D models. Recently, the research activity focused on the study of biometric models for person recognition based on 3D facial scans. Pietro Pala serves as editor for Multimedia Systems and as reviewer for many leading scientific journals including *IEEE Trans. on Pattern Analysis and Machine Intelligence, IEEE Trans. on Multimedia, ACM Trans. on Multimedia Computing Communications,* and *Applications and Pattern Recognition.*

Maja Pantic is Professor in Affective and Behavioural Computing at Imperial College London, Department of Computing, UK, and at the University of Twente, Department of Computer Science, The Netherlands. She received various awards for her work on automatic analysis of human behaviour including the European Research Council Starting Grant Fellowship 2008 and the Roger Needham Award 2011. She currently serves as the Editor in Chief of *Image and Vision Computing Journal* and as an Associate Editor for both the *IEEE Transactions on Systems, Man, and Cybernetics Part B* and the *IEEE Transactions on Pattern Analysis and Machine Intelligence.* She is a Fellow of the IEEE. She (co-) authored more than 160 publications leading to more than 8,500 citations (h-index = 42).

Norman Poh received the PhD degree in computer science from the Swiss Federal Institute of Technology, Lausanne, Switzerland. He has been a research fellow with the Centre for Vision, Speech, and Signal Processing, University of Surrey, Guildford, Surrey, United Kingdom, since 2006. He was one of the Work-Package Leaders in the Mobile Biometry (MOBIO) project, responsible for designing adaptive multimodal biometric systems. His areas of interest are pattern recognition, video processing, biometric authentication, and information fusion, in which he has authored more than 50 peer-reviewed publications. He was the recipient of five best paper awards (AVBPA'05, ICB'09, ICPR'10, HSI'10, Pattern Recognition Journal 2006) and two fellowship research grants from the Swiss National Science

Foundation. He was the researcher of the year 2011 in the Faculty of Engineering and Physical Sciences, University of Surrey.

Hugo Proença received the B.Sc. degree from the University of Beira Interior, Portugal, in 2001, the M.Sc. degree from the Faculty of Engineering, University of Oporto, in 2004, and the Ph.D. degree from the University of Beira Interior, in 2007. His research interests are focused in the artificial intelligence, pattern recognition and biometrics. Currently, he serves as Assistant Professor in the Department of Computer Science, University of Beira Interior. He is a Senior Member of the IEEE, the area editor (ocular biometrics) of the *IEEE Biometrics Compendium Journal* and a member of the Editorial Board of the *International Journal of Biometrics*. In addition, he served as Guest Editor of special issues of the *Pattern Recognition Letters, Image and Vision Computing*, and *Signal, Image, and Video Processing* journals.

Stefano Ricciardi received the Laurea degree in Computer Science and the Laurea degree in Informatics from the University of Salerno. He has been co-founder/owner of a videogame development team focused on 3D sports simulations. He is currently a researcher at the Virtual Reality Lab of the University of Salerno. His main research interests include virtual and augmented reality, biometry, haptics systems, and human-computer interaction. He is author of about 60 research papers including international journals, book chapters, and conference proceedings.

Daniel Riccio was born in Cambridge, UK, in 1978. He received the Laurea degree (cum laude) and the Ph.D. degree in Computer Science from the University of Salerno, Salerno, Italy, in 2002 and 2006, respectively. He is currently an Assistant Professor at the University of Naples, Federico II. His research interests include biometrics, fractal image compression, and indexing. Dr. Riccio is an IEEE member since 2012. He is also a member of the Italian Group of Italian Researcher in Pattern Recognition since 2004.

Gil Santos received the B.Sc. degree in 2007, and the M.Sc. degree in 2009, both from the University of Beira Interior, Portugal, in the field of Computer Science. His research interest are focused on unconstrained biometrics, pattern recognition and signal processing. He is currently a Ph.D. student and researcher at the Soft Computing and Image Analysis Lab, University of Beira Interior, and a IEEE Student Member.

Shishir K. Shah is an Associate Professor in the Department of Computer Science at the University of Houston, which he joined in 2005. He received his B.S. degree in Mechanical Engineering, and M.S. and Ph.D. degrees in Electrical and Computer Engineering from The University of Texas at Austin. He directs research at the Quantitative Imaging Laboratory and his current research focuses on fundamentals of computer vision, pattern recognition, and statistical methods in image and data analysis with applications in multi-modality sensing, video analytics, object recognition, biometrics, and microscope image analysis. He has co-edited one book, and authored numerous papers on object recognition, sensor fusion, statistical pattern analysis, biometrics, and video analytics. Dr. Shah currently serves as an Associate Editor for *Image and Vision Computing* and the *IEEE Trans. on Biomedical Engineering*. He recently served as a Guest Editor of the special issue of *IEEE Trans. on Biomedical Engineering* on Multiscale

Biomedical Signal and Image Modeling and Analysis. He received the College of Natural Sciences and Mathematics' John C. Butler Teaching Excellence Award in 2011.

Richa Singh received the M.S. and Ph.D. degrees in computer science in 2005 and 2008, respectively, from the West Virginia University, Morgantown, USA. She is currently an Assistant Professor at the Indraprastha Institute of Information Technology (IIIT) Delhi, India. Her research has been funded by the UIDAI and DIT, India. She is a recipient of FAST award by DST, India. Her areas of interest are biometrics, pattern recognition, and machine learning. She has more than 100 publications in refereed journals, book chapters, and conferences. She is also an editorial board member of *Information Fusion*, Elsevier and *EURASIP Journal on Image and Video Processing*, Springer. Dr. Singh is a member of the CDEFFS, IEEE, Computer Society, and the Association for Computing Machinery. She is also a member of the Golden Key International, Phi Kappa Phi, Tau Beta Pi, Upsilon Pi Epsilon, and Eta Kappa Nu honor societies. She is the recipient of fourteen best paper and best poster awards in international conferences.

Daniel F. Smith has 35 years of experience in the field of Computer Security and Cryptography. He received from The University of Queensland (UQ) his BSc in computer science in 1983, P/GDipInfTech in formal methods and data security in 1991, MInfTechSt in data security and cryptography in 1994, and is currently studying for his PhD. Danny has previously been an Adjunct Professor for the School of ITEE at UQ, Director of IT Security Engineering for Sun Microsystems, Founder and Technical Director of the Australian Computer Emergency Response Team (AusCERT), and chaired the Working Group to develop the Access Control model for the X.500 directory service standards. He has worked in higher education, commercial, and government sectors in the area of enterprise level IT security, and has consulted, presented, and lectured across the globe. His current research combines the worlds of consumer level biometrics with traditional IT security.

Michel F. Valstar is a Lecturer in the Computer Vision and Mixed Reality Labs at the University of Nottingham. He was a Visiting Researcher at MIT's Media Lab, and a Research Associate in the intelligent Behaviour Understanding Group (iBUG) at Imperial College London. He received his Master's Degree in Electrical Engineering at Delft University of Technology in 2005 and his PhD in computer science with the intelligent Behaviour Understanding Group (iBUG) at Imperial College London in 2008. Currently, he is working in the fields of computer vision and pattern recognition, where his main interest is in automatic recognition of human behaviour. In 2011, he was the main organiser of the first facial expression recognition challenge, FERA 2011. In 2007, he won the BCS British Machine Intelligence Prize for part of his PhD work and his work has received popular press coverage in New Scientist and on BBC Radio and television. He (co-)authored more than 40 publications leading to more than 1,750 citations (h-index = 22).

Genoveffa Tortora is a full professor in Computer Science, at the University of Salerno, since 1990. Dean of the Faculty of Sciences. She is IEEE senior member and member of IAPR. She is in the Editorial Board of several scientific journals. Author and co-author of over 150 papers published in scientific journals or proceedings of refereed conferences, and co-editor of three books. Her research interests are in the Software Engineering and Information Systems areas, and include software development environments, human-computer interaction, visual languages, databases and geographic information systems, image processing, and biometric systems.

Theodora A. Varvarigou received the B. Tech degree from the National Technical University of Athens, Athens, Greece in 1988, the MS degrees in Electrical Engineering (1989) and in Computer Science (1991) from Stanford University, Stanford, California in 1989 and the Ph.D. degree from Stanford University as well in 1991. She is now professor at the NTUA. Prof. Varvarigou has great experience in the area of information processing, Semantic Web technologies, media streaming and casting, scheduling over distributed platforms. In this area, she has published more than 150 papers in leading journals and conferences. She is the co-ordinator several EU funded projects, such as EXPERIMEDIA, 4Caast, VISION, ANSWER (Coordinator), POLYMNIA (Coordinator), SCOVIS (Coordinator), Challenger (Coordinator), IRMOS (Technical Manager), +Space (Technical Manager), PONTE (Technical Manager), GRIA (Coordinator), GRIDLAB, MEMPHIS. She is also ICCS responsible for MKBEEB, MARIDES, DELOS, SCHEMA, FIDIS, HPC-EURORA, Next Grid, IRMOS, Ponte, and Spaces.

Mayank Vatsa received the M.S. and Ph.D. degrees in computer science in 2005 and 2008, respectively, from the West Virginia University, Morgantown, USA. He is currently an Assistant Professor at the Indraprastha Institute of Information Technology (IIIT) Delhi, India. He has more than 100 publications in refereed journals, book chapters, and conferences. His research has been funded by the UIDAI and DIT. He is the recipient of FAST award by DST, India. His areas of interest are biometrics, image processing, computer vision, and information fusion. Dr. Vatsa is a member of the IEEE, Computer Society, and Association for Computing Machinery. He is also a member of the Golden Key International, Phi Kappa Phi, Tau Beta Pi, Sigma Xi, Upsilon Pi Epsilon, and Eta Kappa Nu honor societies. He is the recipient of fourteen best paper and best poster awards in international conferences. He is also an associate editor of Information Fusion, Elsevier, area editor of IEEE Biometric Compendium, and PC Co-Chair of ICB2013 and IJCB2014.

Domenico Vitulano received the physics degree from the University of Naples "Federico II" in 1993 and M. Sc. degree (summa cum laude) in information and communication technology from IIASS "R.R. Caianiello" Institute of Vietri sul Mare, Salerno, in 1997. Since 1995, he is at Institute for the Application of Calculus of National Research Council in Rome, and since 2001, he is permanent researcher. His research interests include pattern recognition, image and data compression, indexing and computer vision. He has been involved in various national and international Research Projects concerning Cultural Heritage. He is currently head of the CNR research line entitled "Analysis and Synthesis of Heterogeneous Data for a Computer-Aided Monitoring of Cultural Heritage" (PC.P03.008), and he is the scientific coordinator of various research projects. He is currently lecturer at University of Rome "Tor Vergata," Department of Mathematics, degree in "Applied Mathematics." He is author and co-author of more than 60 scientific papers on journals, tutorials, monographs, and proceedings of international conferences and workshops. He his referee for various international conferences and Journals.

Athanasios S. Voulodimos received his Dipl.-Ing. degree from the School of Electrical and Computer Engineering of the National Technical University of Athens (NTUA) in 2007, ranking among the top 2% of his class. His diploma thesis titled "Quality of Service and Privacy Protection in Personalized

Context-Aware Mobile Services" was awarded the "Thomaidis" award for the best diploma thesis in NTUA for the year 2007. In 2010, he acquired an MSc in "Techno-Economic Systems" from the National Technical University of Athens and the University of Piraeus, ranking 1st in his class. In 2011, he received his PhD from the School of Electrical and Computer Engineering of NTUA in the area of computer vision and machine learning focusing on behaviour recognition from video. He has been and is currently involved in National and European research projects, being an Activity or Workshop leader, such as SCOVIS, My-e-Director 2012, VISION Cloud, and EXPERIMEDIA. He has published more than 40 papers in international journals, conferences and workshops. His main research interests include computer vision, machine learning, as well as ubiquitous and cloud computing.

Harry Wechsler received his PhD in Computer Science from University of California, Irvine, in 1975, and serves now as Professor of Computer Science at George Mason University (GMU) in Fairfax, VA. His current research is on adversarial learning and coping with incomplete, uncertain, and unstructured information, active authentication, biometrics for uncontrolled settings, change and anomaly / outlier detection, Contents-Based Image Retrieval (CBIR), cyber security and privacy, face recognition, identity management, interoperability, performance evaluation, re-identification, transfer learning and domain adaptation, and video processing for biometrics in the wild. He organized and directed the NATO Advanced Study Institute (ASI) on "Face Recognition: From Theory to Applications," held in Stirling, UK, in 1997 and was the principal co-editor for its seminal proceedings published by Springer. His book on *Reliable Face Recognition Methods*, which breaks new ground in applied modern pattern recognition and biometrics, was published by Springer in 2007. Dr. Wechsler directed at GMU the design and development of FERET, which has been the major database used for benchmark studies in face recognition. He is the author of 3 books, published over 300 scientific papers, and has 7 patents (together with his doctoral students). He is Fellow of IEEE and Fellow of IAPR (Int. Assoc. for Pattern Recognition).

Stefanos Zafeiriou is a Lecturer in Pattern Recognition/Statistical Machine Learning for Computer Vision in the Department of Computing, Imperial College London. He has been awarded one of the prestigious Junior Research Fellowships (JRF) from Imperial College London in 2011 to start his own independent research group. Dr. Zafeiriou currently serves as an Associate Editor in *IEEE Transactions on Cybernetics and Image and Vision Computing* journal. He has been guest editor in more than four journal special issues and co-organized more than five workshops/ special sessions in top venues such as CVPR/FG/ICCV/ECCV. He has co-authored more than 31 journal papers mainly on novel statistical machine learning methodologies applied to computer vision problems such as 2D/3D face and facial expression recognition, deformable object tracking, human behaviour analysis etc published in the most prestigious journals in his field of research (such as IEEE T-PAMI, IJCV, IEEE T-IP, IEEE T-NNLS, IEEE T-VCG, IEEE T-IFS, etc.). His students are frequent recipients of very prestigious and highly competitive fellowships such as Google Fellowship, Intel Fellowship and the Qualcomm fellowship. He has more than 1000 citations to his work (h-index=17).

Xuan Zou received BEng and MEng from Huazhong University of Science and Technology, Wuhan, China, in 1998 and 2001 respectively. In 2007, he received PhD in Electronics Engineering from University of Surrey, UK. He is currently with Dept of Multimedia, QualComm, and his main interest is on Realtime Computer Vision on mobile platform.

Index